T0178441

Lecture Notes in Computer Science　　　　14260

Founding Editors

Gerhard Goos
Juris Hartmanis

Editorial Board Members

Elisa Bertino, *Purdue University, West Lafayette, IN, USA*
Wen Gao, *Peking University, Beijing, China*
Bernhard Steffen , *TU Dortmund University, Dortmund, Germany*
Moti Yung , *Columbia University, New York, NY, USA*

The series Lecture Notes in Computer Science (LNCS), including its subseries Lecture Notes in Artificial Intelligence (LNAI) and Lecture Notes in Bioinformatics (LNBI), has established itself as a medium for the publication of new developments in computer science and information technology research, teaching, and education.

LNCS enjoys close cooperation with the computer science R & D community, the series counts many renowned academics among its volume editors and paper authors, and collaborates with prestigious societies. Its mission is to serve this international community by providing an invaluable service, mainly focused on the publication of conference and workshop proceedings and postproceedings. LNCS commenced publication in 1973.

Lazaros Iliadis · Antonios Papaleonidas ·
Plamen Angelov · Chrisina Jayne
Editors

Artificial Neural Networks and Machine Learning – ICANN 2023

32nd International Conference on Artificial Neural Networks
Heraklion, Crete, Greece, September 26–29, 2023
Proceedings, Part VII

 Springer

Editors
Lazaros Iliadis (ID)
Democritus University of Thrace
Xanthi, Greece

Antonios Papaleonidas (ID)
Democritus University of Thrace
Xanthi, Greece

Plamen Angelov (ID)
Lancaster University
Lancaster, UK

Chrisina Jayne (ID)
Teesside University
Middlesbrough, UK

ISSN 0302-9743   ISSN 1611-3349 (electronic)
Lecture Notes in Computer Science
ISBN 978-3-031-44194-3   ISBN 978-3-031-44195-0 (eBook)
https://doi.org/10.1007/978-3-031-44195-0

This Springer imprint is published by the registered company Springer Nature Switzerland AG
The registered company address is: Gewerbestrasse 11, 6330 Cham, Switzerland

Paper in this product is recyclable.

Preface

The European Neural Network Society (ENNS) is an association of scientists, engineers and students, conducting research on the modelling of behavioral and brain processes, and on the development of neural algorithms. The core of these efforts is the application of neural modelling to several diverse domains. According to its mission statement ENNS is the European non-profit federation of professionals that aims at achieving a worldwide professional and socially responsible development and application of artificial neural technologies.

The flagship event of ENNS is ICANN (the International Conference on Artificial Neural Networks) at which contributed research papers are presented after passing through a rigorous review process. ICANN is a dual-track conference, featuring tracks in brain-inspired computing on the one hand, and machine learning on the other, with strong crossdisciplinary interactions and applications.

The response of the international scientific community to the ICANN 2023 call for papers was more than satisfactory. In total, 947 research papers on the aforementioned research areas were submitted and 426 (45%) of them were finally accepted as full papers after a peer review process. Additionally, 19 extended abstracts were submitted and 9 of them were selected to be included in the front matter of ICANN 2023 proceedings. Due to their high academic and scientific importance, 22 short papers were also accepted.

All papers were peer reviewed by at least two independent academic referees. Where needed, a third or a fourth referee was consulted to resolve any potential conflicts. Three workshops focusing on specific research areas, namely Advances in Spiking Neural Networks (ASNN), Neurorobotics (NRR), and the challenge of Errors, Stability, Robustness, and Accuracy in Deep Neural Networks (ESRA in DNN), were organized.

The 10-volume set of LNCS 14254, 14255, 14256, 14257, 14258, 14259, 14260, 14261, 14262 and 14263 constitutes the proceedings of the 32nd International Conference on Artificial Neural Networks, ICANN 2023, held in Heraklion city, Crete, Greece, on September 26–29, 2023.

The accepted papers are related to the following topics:

Machine Learning: Deep Learning; Neural Network Theory; Neural Network Models; Graphical Models; Bayesian Networks; Kernel Methods; Generative Models; Information Theoretic Learning; Reinforcement Learning; Relational Learning; Dynamical Models; Recurrent Networks; and Ethics of AI.

Brain-Inspired Computing: Cognitive Models; Computational Neuroscience; Self-Organization; Neural Control and Planning; Hybrid Neural-Symbolic Architectures; Neural Dynamics; Cognitive Neuroscience; Brain Informatics; Perception and Action; and Spiking Neural Networks.

Neural applications in Bioinformatics; Biomedicine; Intelligent Robotics; Neuro-robotics; Language Processing; Speech Processing; Image Processing; Sensor Fusion; Pattern Recognition; Data Mining; Neural Agents; Brain-Computer Interaction; Neuro-morphic Computing and Edge AI; and Evolutionary Neural Networks.

September 2023

Lazaros Iliadis
Antonios Papaleonidas
Plamen Angelov
Chrisina Jayne

Organization

General Chairs

Iliadis Lazaros	Democritus University of Thrace, Greece
Plamen Angelov	Lancaster University, UK

Program Chairs

Antonios Papaleonidas	Democritus University of Thrace, Greece
Elias Pimenidis	UWE Bristol, UK
Chrisina Jayne	Teesside University, UK

Honorary Chairs

Stefan Wermter	University of Hamburg, Germany
Vera Kurkova	Czech Academy of Sciences, Czech Republic
Nikola Kasabov	Auckland University of Technology, New Zealand

Organizing Chairs

Antonios Papaleonidas	Democritus University of Thrace, Greece
Anastasios Panagiotis Psathas	Democritus University of Thrace, Greece
George Magoulas	University of London, Birkbeck College, UK
Haralambos Mouratidis	University of Essex, UK

Award Chairs

Stefan Wermter	University of Hamburg, Germany
Chukiong Loo	University of Malaysia, Malaysia

Communication Chairs

Sebastian Otte   University of Tübingen, Germany
Anastasios Panagiotis Psathas   Democritus University of Thrace, Greece

Steering Committee

Stefan Wermter   University of Hamburg, Germany
Angelo Cangelosi   University of Manchester, UK
Igor Farkaš   Comenius University in Bratislava, Slovakia
Chrisina Jayne   Teesside University, UK
Matthias Kerzel   University of Hamburg, Germany
Alessandra Lintas   University of Lausanne, Switzerland
Kristína Malinovská (Rebrová)   Comenius University in Bratislava, Slovakia
Alessio Micheli   University of Pisa, Italy
Jaakko Peltonen   Tampere University, Finland
Brigitte Quenet   ESPCI Paris, France
Ausra Saudargiene   Lithuanian University of Health Sciences,
                                            Lithuania
Roseli Wedemann   Rio de Janeiro State University, Brazil

Local Organizing/Hybrid Facilitation Committee

Aggeliki Tsouka   Democritus University of Thrace, Greece
Anastasios Panagiotis Psathas   Democritus University of Thrace, Greece
Anna Karagianni   Democritus University of Thrace, Greece
Christina Gkizioti   Democritus University of Thrace, Greece
Ioanna-Maria Erentzi   Democritus University of Thrace, Greece
Ioannis Skopelitis   Democritus University of Thrace, Greece
Lambros Kazelis   Democritus University of Thrace, Greece
Leandros Tsatsaronis   Democritus University of Thrace, Greece
Nikiforos Mpotzoris   Democritus University of Thrace, Greece
Nikos Zervis   Democritus University of Thrace, Greece
Panagiotis Restos   Democritus University of Thrace, Greece
Tassos Giannakopoulos   Democritus University of Thrace, Greece

Program Committee

Abraham Yosipof	CLB, Israel
Adane Tarekegn	NTNU, Norway
Aditya Gilra	Centrum Wiskunde & Informatica, Netherlands
Adrien Durand-Petiteville	Federal University of Pernambuco, Brazil
Adrien Fois	LORIA, France
Alaa Marouf	Hosei University, Japan
Alessandra Sciutti	Istituto Italiano di Tecnologia, Italy
Alessandro Sperduti	University of Padua, Italy
Alessio Micheli	University of Pisa, Italy
Alex Shenfield	Sheffield Hallam University, UK
Alexander Kovalenko	Czech Technical University in Prague, Czech Republic
Alexander Krawczyk	Fulda University of Applied Sciences, Germany
Ali Minai	University of Cincinnati, USA
Aluizio Araujo	Universidade Federal de Pernambuco, Brazil
Amarda Shehu	George Mason University, USA
Amit Kumar Kundu	University of Maryland, USA
Anand Rangarajan	University of Florida, USA
Anastasios Panagiotis Psathas	Democritus University of Thrace, Greece
Andre de Carvalho	Universidade de São Paulo, Brazil
Andrej Lucny	Comenius University, Slovakia
Angel Villar-Corrales	University of Bonn, Germany
Angelo Cangelosi	University of Manchester, UK
Anna Jenul	Norwegian University of Life Sciences, Norway
Antonios Papaleonidas	Democritus University of Thrace, Greece
Arnaud Lewandowski	LISIC, ULCO, France
Arul Selvam Periyasamy	Universität Bonn, Germany
Asma Mekki	University of Sfax, Tunisia
Banafsheh Rekabdar	Portland State University, USA
Barbara Hammer	Universität Bielefeld, Germany
Baris Serhan	University of Manchester, UK
Benedikt Bagus	University of Applied Sciences Fulda, Germany
Benjamin Paaßen	Bielefeld University, Germany
Bernhard Pfahringer	University of Waikato, New Zealand
Bharath Sudharsan	NUI Galway, Ireland
Binyi Wu	Dresden University of Technology, Germany
Binyu Zhao	Harbin Institute of Technology, China
Björn Plüster	University of Hamburg, Germany
Bo Mei	Texas Christian University, USA

Brian Moser	Deutsches Forschungszentrum für künstliche Intelligenz, Germany
Carlo Mazzola	Istituto Italiano di Tecnologia, Italy
Carlos Moreno-Garcia	Robert Gordon University, UK
Chandresh Pravin	Reading University, UK
Chao Ma	Wuhan University, China
Chathura Wanigasekara	German Aerospace Centre, Germany
Cheng Shang	Shanghai Jiaotong University, China
Chengqiang Huang	Huawei Technologies, China
Chenhan Zhang	University of Technology, Sydney, Australia
Chenyang Lyu	Dublin City University, Ireland
Chihuang Liu	Meta, USA
Chrisina Jayne	Teesside University, UK
Christian Balkenius	Lund University, Sweden
Chrysoula Kosma	Ecole Polytechnique, Greece
Claudio Bellei	Elliptic, UK
Claudio Gallicchio	University of Pisa, Italy
Claudio Giorgio Giancaterino	Intesa SanPaolo Vita, Italy
Constantine Dovrolis	Cyprus Institute, USA
Coşku Horuz	University of Tübingen, Germany
Cunjian Chen	Monash, Australia
Cunyi Yin	Fuzhou University, Singapore
Damien Lolive	Université Rennes, CNRS, IRISA, France
Daniel Stamate	Goldsmiths, University of London, UK
Daniel Vašata	Czech Technical University in Prague, Czech Republic
Dario Pasquali	Istituto Italiano di Tecnologia, Italy
David Dembinsky	German Research Center for Artificial Intelligence, Germany
David Rotermund	University of Bremen, Germany
Davide Liberato Manna	University of Strathclyde, UK
Dehao Yuan	University of Maryland, USA
Denise Gorse	University College London, UK
Dennis Wong	Macao Polytechnic University, China
Des Higham	University of Edinburgh, UK
Devesh Jawla	TU Dublin, Ireland
Dimitrios Michail	Harokopio University of Athens, Greece
Dino Ienco	INRAE, France
Diptangshu Pandit	Teesside University, UK
Diyuan Lu	Helmholtz Center Munich, Germany
Domenico Tortorella	University of Pisa, Italy
Dominik Geissler	American Family Insurance, USA

DongNyeong Heo	Handong Global University, South Korea
Dongyang Zhang	University of Electronic Science and Technology of China, China
Doreen Jirak	Istituto Italiano di Tecnologia, Italy
Douglas McLelland	BrainChip, France
Douglas Nyabuga	Mount Kenya University, Rwanda
Dulani Meedeniya	University of Moratuwa, Sri Lanka
Dumitru-Clementin Cercel	University Politehnica of Bucharest, Romania
Dylan Muir	SynSense, Switzerland
Efe Bozkir	Uni Tübingen, Germany
Eleftherios Kouloumpris	Aristotle University of Thessaloniki, Greece
Elias Pimenidis	University of the West of England, UK
Eliska Kloberdanz	Iowa State University, USA
Emre Neftci	Foschungszentrum Juelich, Germany
Enzo Tartaglione	Telecom Paris, France
Erwin Lopez	University of Manchester, UK
Evgeny Mirkes	University of Leicester, UK
F. Boray Tek	Istanbul Technical University, Turkey
Federico Corradi	Eindhoven University of Technology, Netherlands
Federico Errica	NEC Labs Europe, Germany
Federico Manzi	Università Cattolica del Sacro Cuore, Italy
Federico Vozzi	CNR, Italy
Fedor Scholz	University of Tuebingen, Germany
Feifei Dai	Chinese Academy of Sciences, China
Feifei Xu	Shanghai University of Electric Power, China
Feixiang Zhou	University of Leicester, UK
Felipe Moreno	FGV, Peru
Feng Wei	York University, Canada
Fengying Li	Guilin University of Electronic Technology, China
Flora Ferreira	University of Minho, Portugal
Florian Mirus	Intel Labs, Germany
Francesco Semeraro	University of Manchester, UK
Franco Scarselli	University of Siena, Italy
François Blayo	IPSEITE, Switzerland
Frank Röder	Hamburg University of Technology, Germany
Frederic Alexandre	Inria, France
Fuchang Han	Central South University, China
Fuli Wang	University of Essex, UK
Gabriela Sejnova	Czech Technical University in Prague, Czech Republic
Gaetano Di Caterina	University of Strathclyde, UK
George Bebis	University of Nevada, USA

Gerrit Ecke	Mercedes-Benz, Germany
Giannis Nikolentzos	Ecole Polytechnique, France
Gilles Marcou	University of Strasbourg, France
Giorgio Gnecco	IMT School for Advanced Studies, Italy
Glauco Amigo	Baylor University, USA
Greg Lee	Acadia University, Canada
Grégory Bourguin	LISIC/ULCO, France
Guillermo Martín-Sánchez	Champalimaud Foundation, Portugal
Gulustan Dogan	UNCW, USA
Habib Khan	Islamia College University Peshawar, Pakistan
Haizhou Du	Shanghai University of Electric Power, China
Hanli Wang	Tongji University, China
Hanno Gottschalk	TU Berlin, Germany
Hao Tong	University of Birmingham, UK
Haobo Jiang	NJUST, China
Haopeng Chen	Shanghai Jiao Tong University, China
Hazrat Ali	Hamad Bin Khalifa University, Qatar
Hina Afridi	NTNU, Gjøvik, Norway
Hiroaki Aizawa	Hiroshima University, Japan
Hiromichi Suetani	Oita University, Japan
Hiroshi Kawaguchi	Kobe University, Japan
Hiroyasu Ando	Tohoku University, Japan
Hiroyoshi Ito	University of Tsukuba, Japan
Honggang Zhang	University of Massachusetts, Boston, USA
Hongqing Yu	Open University, UK
Hongye Cao	Northwestern Polytechnical University, China
Hugo Carneiro	University of Hamburg, Germany
Hugo Eduardo Camacho Cruz	Universidad Autónoma de Tamaulipas, Mexico
Huifang Ma	Northwest Normal University, China
Hyeyoung Park	Kyungpook National University, South Korea
Ian Nabney	University of Bristol, UK
Igor Farkas	Comenius University Bratislava, Slovakia
Ikuko Nishikawa	Ritsumeikan University, Japan
Ioannis Pierros	Aristotle University of Thessaloniki, Greece
Iraklis Varlamis	Harokopio University of Athens, Greece
Ivan Tyukin	King's College London, UK
Iveta Bečková	Comenius University in Bratislava, Slovakia
Jae Hee Lee	University of Hamburg, Germany
James Yu	Southern University of Science and Technology, China
Jan Faigl	Czech Technical University in Prague, Czech Republic

Jan Feber   Czech Technical University in Prague,
                                     Czech Republic
Jan-Gerrit Habekost   University of Hamburg, Germany
Jannik Thuemmel   University of Tübingen, Germany
Jeremie Cabessa   University Paris 2, France
Jérémie Sublime   ISEP, France
Jia Cai   Guangdong University of Finance & Economics,
                                     China
Jiaan Wang   Soochow University, China
Jialiang Tang   Nanjing University of Science and Technology,
                                     China
Jian Hu   YiduCloud, Cyprus
Jianhua Xu   Nanjing Normal University, China
Jianyong Chen   Shenzhen University, China
Jichao Bi   Zhejiang Institute of Industry and Information
                                     Technology, China
Jie Shao   University of Electronic Science and Technology
                                     of China, China
Jim Smith   University of the West of England, UK
Jing Yang   Hefei University of Technology, China
Jingyi Yuan   Arizona State University, USA
Jingyun Jia   Baidu, USA
Jinling Wang   Ulster University, UK
Jiri Sima   Czech Academy of Sciences, Czech Republic
Jitesh Dundas   Independent Researcher, USA
Joost Vennekens   KU Leuven, Belgium
Jordi Cosp   Universitat Politècnica de Catalunya, Spain
Josua Spisak   University of Hamburg, Germany
Jozef Kubík   Comenius University, Slovakia
Junpei Zhong   Hong Kong Polytechnic University, China
Jurgita Kapočiūtė-Dzikienė   Vytautas Magnus University, Lithuania
K. L. Eddie Law   Macao Polytechnic University, China
Kai Tang   Independent Researcher, China
Kamil Dedecius   Czech Academy of Sciences, Czech Republic
Kang Zhang   Kyushu University, Japan
Kantaro Fujiwara   University of Tokyo, Japan
Karlis Freivalds   Institute of Electronics and Computer Science,
                                     Latvia
Khoa Phung   University of the West of England, UK
Kiran Lekkala   University of Southern California, USA
Kleanthis Malialis   University of Cyprus, Cyprus
Kohulan Rajan   Friedrich Schiller University, Germany

Koichiro Yamauchi	Chubu University, Japan
Koloud Alkhamaiseh	Western Michigan University, USA
Konstantinos Demertzis	Democritus University of Thrace, Greece
Kostadin Cvejoski	Fraunhofer IAIS, Germany
Kristína Malinovská	Comenius University in Bratislava, Slovakia
Kun Zhang	Inria and École Polytechnique, France
Laurent Mertens	KU Leuven, Belgium
Laurent Perrinet	AMU CNRS, France
Lazaros Iliadis	Democritus University of Thrace, Greece
Leandro dos Santos Coelho	Pontifical Catholic University of Parana, Brazil
Leiping Jie	Hong Kong Baptist University, China
Lenka Tětková	Technical University of Denmark, Denmark
Lia Morra	Politecnico di Torino, Italy
Liang Ge	Chongqing University, China
Liang Zhao	Dalian University of Technology, China
Limengzi Yuan	Shihezi University, China
Ling Guo	Northwest University, China
Linlin Shen	Shenzhen University, China
Lixin Zou	Wuhan University, China
Lorenzo Vorabbi	University of Bologna, Italy
Lu Wang	Macao Polytechnic University, China
Luca Pasa	University of Padova, Italy
Ľudovít Malinovský	Independent Researcher, Slovakia
Luis Alexandre	Universidade da Beira Interior, Portugal
Luis Lago	Universidad Autonoma de Madrid, Spain
Lukáš Gajdošech Gajdošech	Comenius University Bratislava, Slovakia
Lyra Puspa	Vanaya NeuroLab, Indonesia
Madalina Erascu	West University of Timisoara, Romania
Magda Friedjungová	Czech Technical University in Prague, Czech Republic
Manuel Traub	University of Tübingen, Germany
Marcello Trovati	Edge Hill University, UK
Marcin Pietron	AGH-UST, Poland
Marco Bertolini	Pfizer, Germany
Marco Podda	University of Pisa, Italy
Markus Bayer	Technical University of Darmstadt, Germany
Markus Eisenbach	Ilmenau University of Technology, Germany
Martin Ferianc	University College London, Slovakia
Martin Holena	Czech Technical University, Czech Republic
Masanari Kimura	ZOZO Research, Japan
Masato Uchida	Waseda University, Japan
Masoud Daneshtalab	Mälardalen University, Sweden

Mats Leon Richter	University of Montreal, Germany
Matthew Evanusa	University of Maryland, USA
Matthias Karlbauer	University of Tübingen, Germany
Matthias Kerzel	University of Hamburg, Germany
Matthias Möller	Örebro University, Sweden
Matthias Müller-Brockhausen	Leiden University, Netherlands
Matus Tomko	Comenius University in Bratislava, Slovakia
Mayukh Maitra	Walmart, India
Md. Delwar Hossain	Nara Institute of Science and Technology, Japan
Mehmet Aydin	University of the West of England, UK
Michail Chatzianastasis	École Polytechnique, Greece
Michail-Antisthenis Tsompanas	University of the West of England, UK
Michel Salomon	Université de Franche-Comté, France
Miguel Matey-Sanz	Universitat Jaume I, Spain
Mikołaj Morzy	Poznan University of Technology, Poland
Minal Suresh Patil	Umea universitet, Sweden
Minh Tri Lê	Inria, France
Mircea Nicolescu	University of Nevada, Reno, USA
Mohamed Elleuch	ENSI, Tunisia
Mohammed Elmahdi Khennour	Kasdi Merbah University Ouargla, Algeria
Mohib Ullah	NTNU, Norway
Monika Schak	Fulda University of Applied Sciences, Germany
Moritz Wolter	University of Bonn, Germany
Mostafa Kotb	Hamburg University, Germany
Muhammad Burhan Hafez	University of Hamburg, Germany
Nabeel Khalid	German Research Centre for Artificial Intelligence, Germany
Nabil El Malki	IRIT, France
Narendhar Gugulothu	TCS Research, India
Naresh Balaji Ravichandran	KTH Stockholm, Sweden
Natalie Kiesler	DIPF Leibniz Institute for Research and Information in Education, Germany
Nathan Duran	UWE, UK
Nermeen Abou Baker	Ruhr West University of Applied Sciences, Germany
Nick Jhones	Dundee University, UK
Nicolangelo Iannella	University of Oslo, Norway
Nicolas Couellan	ENAC, France
Nicolas Rougier	University of Bordeaux, France
Nikolaos Ioannis Bountos	National Observatory of Athens, Greece
Nikolaos Polatidis	University of Brighton, UK
Norimichi Ukita	TTI-J, Japan

Oleg Bakhteev	EPFL, Switzerland
Olga Grebenkova	Moscow Institute of Physics and Technology, Russia
Oliver Sutton	King's College London, UK
Olivier Teste	Université de Toulouse, France
Or Elroy	CLB, Israel
Oscar Fontenla-Romero	University of A Coruña, Spain
Ozan Özdenizci	Graz University of Technology, Austria
Pablo Lanillos	Spanish National Research Council, Spain
Pascal Rost	Universität Hamburg, Germany
Paul Kainen	Georgetown, USA
Paulo Cortez	University of Minho, Portugal
Pavel Petrovic	Comenius University, Slovakia
Peipei Liu	School of Cyber Security, University of Chinese Academy of Sciences, China
Peng Qiao	NUDT, China
Peter Andras	Edinburgh Napier University, UK
Peter Steiner	Technische Universität Dresden, Germany
Peter Sutor	University of Maryland, USA
Petia Georgieva	University of Aveiro/IEETA, Portugal
Petia Koprinkova-Hristova	Bulgarian Academy of Sciences, Bulgaria
Petra Vidnerová	Czech Academy of Sciences, Czech Republic
Philipp Allgeuer	University of Hamburg, Germany
Pragathi Priyadharsini Balasubramani	Indian Institute of Technology Kanpur, India
Qian Wang	Durham University, UK
Qinghua Zhou	King's College London, UK
Qingquan Zhang	Southern University of Science and Technology, China
Quentin Jodelet	Tokyo Institute of Technology, Japan
Radoslav Škoviera	Czech Technical University in Prague, Czech Republic
Raoul Heese	Fraunhofer ITWM, Germany
Ricardo Marcacini	University of São Paulo, Brazil
Riccardo Renzulli	University of Turin, Italy
Richard Duro	Universidade da Coruña, Spain
Robert Legenstein	Graz University of Technology, Austria
Rodrigo Clemente Thom de Souza	Federal University of Parana, Brazil
Rohit Dwivedula	Independent Researcher, India
Romain Ferrand	IGI TU Graz, Austria
Roman Mouček	University of West Bohemia, Czech Republic
Roseli Wedemann	Universidade do Estado do Rio de Janeiro, Brazil

Rufin VanRullen	CNRS, France
Ruijun Feng	China Telecom Beijing Research Institute, China
Ruxandra Stoean	University of Craiova, Romania
Sanchit Hira	JHU, USA
Sander Bohte	CWI, Netherlands
Sandrine Mouysset	University of Toulouse/IRIT, France
Sanka Rasnayaka	National University of Singapore, Singapore
Sašo Karakatič	University of Maribor, Slovenia
Sebastian Nowak	University Bonn, Germany
Seiya Satoh	Tokyo Denki University, Japan
Senwei Liang	LBNL, USA
Shaolin Zhu	Tianjin University, China
Shayan Gharib	University of Helsinki, Finland
Sherif Eissa	Eindhoven University of Technology, Afghanistan
Shiyong Lan	Independent Researcher, China
Shoumeng Qiu	Fudan, China
Shu Eguchi	Aomori University, Japan
Shubai Chen	Southwest University, China
Shweta Singh	International Institute of Information Technology, Hyderabad, India
Simon Hakenes	Ruhr University Bochum, Germany
Simona Doboli	Hofstra University, USA
Song Guo	Xi'an University of Architecture and Technology, China
Stanislav Frolov	Deutsches Forschungszentrum für künstliche Intelligenz (DFKI), Germany
Štefan Pócoš	Comenius University in Bratislava, Slovakia
Steven (Zvi) Lapp	Bar Ilan University, Israel
Sujala Shetty	BITS Pilani Dubai Campus, United Arab Emirates
Sumio Watanabe	Tokyo Institute of Technology, Japan
Surabhi Sinha	Adobe, USA
Takafumi Amaba	Fukuoka University, Japan
Takaharu Yaguchi	Kobe University, Japan
Takeshi Abe	Yamaguchi University, Japan
Takuya Kitamura	National Institute of Technology, Toyama College, Japan
Tatiana Tyukina	University of Leicester, UK
Teng-Sheng Moh	San Jose State University, USA
Tetsuya Hoya	Independent Researcher, Japan
Thierry Viéville	Domicile, France
Thomas Nowotny	University of Sussex, UK
Tianlin Zhang	University of Manchester, UK

Tianyi Wang	University of Hong Kong, China
Tieke He	Nanjing University, China
Tiyu Fang	Shandong University, China
Tobias Uelwer	Technical University Dortmund, Germany
Tomasz Kapuscinski	Rzeszow University of Technology, Poland
Tomasz Szandala	Wroclaw University of Technology, Poland
Toshiharu Sugawara	Waseda University, Japan
Trond Arild Tjostheim	Lund University, Sweden
Umer Mushtaq	Université Paris-Panthéon-Assas, France
Uwe Handmann	Ruhr West University, Germany
V. Ramasubramanian	International Institute of Information Technology, Bangalore, India
Valeri Mladenov	Technical University of Sofia, Bulgaria
Valerie Vaquet	Bielefeld University, Germany
Vandana Ladwani	International Institute of Information Technology, Bangalore, India
Vangelis Metsis	Texas State University, USA
Vera Kurkova	Czech Academy of Sciences, Czech Republic
Verner Ferreira	Universidade do Estado da Bahia, Brazil
Viktor Kocur	Comenius University, Slovakia
Ville Tanskanen	University of Helsinki, Finland
Viviana Cocco Mariani	PUCPR, Brazil
Vladimír Boža	Comenius University, Slovakia
Vojtech Mrazek	Brno University of Technology, Czech Republic
Weifeng Liu	China University of Petroleum (East China), China
Wenxin Yu	Southwest University of Science and Technology, China
Wenxuan Liu	Wuhan University of Technology, China
Wu Ancheng	Pingan, China
Wuliang Huang	ICT, China
Xi Cheng	NUPT, Hong Kong, China
Xia Feng	Civil Aviation University of China, China
Xian Zhong	Wuhan University of Technology, China
Xiang Zhang	National University of Defense Technology, China
Xiaochen Yuan	Macao Polytechnic University, China
Xiaodong Gu	Fudan University, China
Xiaoqing Liu	Kyushu University, Japan
Xiaowei Zhou	Macquarie University, Australia
Xiaozhuang Song	Chinese University of Hong Kong, Shenzhen, China

Xingpeng Zhang	Southwest Petroleum University, China
Xuemei Jia	Wuhan University, China
Xuewen Wang	China University of Geosciences, China
Yahong Lian	Nankai University, China
Yan Zheng	China University of Political Science and Law, China
Yang Liu	Fudan University, China
Yang Shao	Hitachi, Japan
Yangguang Cui	East China Normal University, China
Yansong Chua	China Nanhu Academy of Electronics and Information Technology, Singapore
Yapeng Gao	Taiyuan University of Technology, China
Yasufumi Sakai	Fujitsu, Japan
Ye Wang	National University of Defense Technology, China
Yeh-Ching Chung	Chinese University of Hong Kong, Shenzhen, China
Yihao Luo	Yichang Testing Technique R&D Institute, China
Yikemaiti Sataer	Southeast University, China
Yipeng Yu	Tencent, China
Yongchao Ye	Southern University of Science and Technology, China
Yoshihiko Horio	Tohoku University, Japan
Youcef Djenouri	NORCE, Norway
Yuan Li	Military Academy of Sciences, China
Yuan Panli	Shihezi University, China
Yuan Yao	Tsinghua University, China
Yuanlun Xie	University of Electronic Science and Technology of China, China
Yuanshao Zhu	Southern University of Science and Technology, China
Yucan Zhou	Institute of Information Engineering, Chinese Academy of Sciences, China
Yuchen Zheng	Shihezi University, China
Yuchun Fang	Shanghai University, China
Yue Zhao	Minzu University of China, China
Yuesong Nan	National University of Singapore, Singapore
Zaneta Swiderska-Chadaj	Warsaw University of Technology, Poland
Zdenek Straka	Czech Technical University in Prague, Czech Republic
Zhao Yang	Leiden University, Netherlands
Zhaoyun Ding	NUDT, China
Zhengwei Yang	Wuhan University, China

Invited Talks

Developmental Robotics for Language Learning, Trust and Theory of Mind

Angelo Cangelosi

University of Manchester and Alan Turing Institute, UK

Growing theoretical and experimental research on action and language processing and on number learning and gestures clearly demonstrates the role of embodiment in cognition and language processing. In psychology and neuroscience, this evidence constitutes the basis of embodied cognition, also known as grounded cognition (Pezzulo et al. 2012). In robotics and AI, these studies have important implications for the design of linguistic capabilities in cognitive agents and robots for human-robot collaboration, and have led to the new interdisciplinary approach of Developmental Robotics, as part of the wider Cognitive Robotics field (Cangelosi and Schlesinger 2015; Cangelosi and Asada 2022). During the talk we presented examples of developmental robotics models and experimental results from iCub experiments on the embodiment biases in early word acquisition and grammar learning (Morse et al. 2015; Morse and Cangelosi 2017) and experiments on pointing gestures and finger counting for number learning (De La Cruz et al. 2014). We then presented a novel developmental robotics model, and experiments, on Theory of Mind and its use for autonomous trust behavior in robots (Vinanzi et al. 2019, 2021). The implications for the use of such embodied approaches for embodied cognition in AI and cognitive sciences, and for robot companion applications, was also discussed.

Challenges of Incremental Learning

Barbara Hammer

CITEC Centre of Excellence, Bielefeld University, Germany

Smart products and AI components are increasingly available in industrial applications and everyday life. This offers great opportunities for cognitive automation and intelligent human-machine cooperation; yet it also poses significant challenges since a fundamental assumption of classical machine learning, an underlying stationary data distribution, might be easily violated. Unexpected events or outliers, sensor drift, or individual user behavior might cause changes of an underlying data distribution, typically referred to as concept drift or covariate shift. Concept drift requires a continuous adaptation of the underlying model and efficient incremental learning strategies. Within the presentation, I looked at recent developments in the context of incremental learning schemes for streaming data, putting a particular focus on the challenge of learning with drift and detecting and disentangling drift in possibly unsupervised setups and for unknown type and strength of drift. More precisely, I dealt with the following aspects: learning schemes for incremental model adaptation from streaming data in the presence of concept drift; various mathematical formalizations of concept drift and detection/quantification of drift based thereon; and decomposition and explanation of drift. I presented a couple of experimental results using benchmarks from the literature, and I offered a glimpse into mathematical guarantees which can be provided for some of the algorithms.

Reliable AI: From Mathematical Foundations to Quantum Computing

Gitta Kutyniok[1,2]

[1]Bavarian AI Chair for Mathematical Foundations of Artificial Intelligence, LMU Munich, Germany
[2]Adjunct Professor for Machine Learning, University of Tromsø, Norway

Artificial intelligence is currently leading to one breakthrough after the other, both in public life with, for instance, autonomous driving and speech recognition, and in the sciences in areas such as medical diagnostics or molecular dynamics. However, one current major drawback is the lack of reliability of such methodologies.

In this lecture we took a mathematical viewpoint towards this problem, showing the power of such approaches to reliability. We first provided an introduction into this vibrant research area, focussing specifically on deep neural networks. We then surveyed recent advances, in particular concerning generalization guarantees and explainability methods. Finally, we discussed fundamental limitations of deep neural networks and related approaches in terms of computability, which seriously affects their reliability, and we revealed a connection with quantum computing.

Intelligent Pervasive Applications for Holistic Health Management

Ilias Maglogiannis

University of Piraeus, Greece

The advancements in telemonitoring platforms, biosensors, and medical devices have paved the way for pervasive health management, allowing patients to be monitored remotely in real-time. The visual domain has become increasingly important for patient monitoring, with activity recognition and fall detection being key components. Computer vision techniques, such as deep learning, have been used to develop robust activity recognition and fall detection algorithms. These algorithms can analyze video streams from cameras, detecting and classifying various activities, and detecting falls in real time. Furthermore, wearable devices, such as smartwatches and fitness trackers, can also monitor a patient's daily activities, providing insights into their overall health and wellness, allowing for a comprehensive analysis of a patient's health. In this talk we discussed the state of the art in pervasive health management and biomedical data analytics and we presented the work done in the Computational Biomedicine Laboratory of the University of Piraeus in this domain. The talk also included Future Trends and Challenges.

Contents – Part VII

A Shallow Information Enhanced Efficient Small Object Detector Based on YOLOv5

Minhu Yang(ID) and Hexiang Bai(✉)(ID)

Key Laboratory of Computational Intelligence and Chinese Information Processing
Ministry of Education, School of Computer and Information Technology,
Shanxi University, Taiyuan 030006, China
`bai_research@163.com`

Abstract. Shallow information is crucial in small object detection. Based on YOLOv5, an efficient small object detection algorithm (ES-YOLO) is proposed to improve identification accuracy using novel shallow feature extraction strategies. First of all, a detection head corresponding to shallow features is used to replace the original detection head corresponding to the deepest features in YOLOv5. Secondly, an attention module is directly added to the output layers of the backbone to filter redundant information and select representative original shallow features. Next, half of the inputs to the SPPF module are processed by the cross-stage partial connection method to reduce model parameters. Finally, the SIoU (SCYLLA-IoU) loss is used during the training stage to ensure fast convergence. Ablation studies are performed on two publicly available small object datasets. Results show that all the proposed models increase the model detection accuracy. Compared with the YOLOv5, the proposed model increases the identification accuracy by 2.4% and 3.5% on the BDD100K and VisDrone datasets, respectively. In addition, compared with the other 8 commonly used or up-to-date one-stage models, the proposed model achieves the best performance in identification accuracy. Source code is released in https://gitee.com/bai-hexiang/es-yolo.

Keywords: Small object detection · Shallow information · YOLOv5

1 Introduction

In image processing, it is inevitable to identify objects represented by a few pixels which are generally referred to as small objects. The detection of small objects is crucial in many real-life applications. For example, finding early-stage small fire sources from aerial views is useful to prevent serious forest fires [26], and positioning key targets from drone-captured images is important in emergency rescue in disasters [3]. As a result, the correct and fast detection of small objects has drawn extensive attention and becomes a hot topic in object detection.

Currently, the most recent and effective small object detection methods are descendants of deep learning-based object detectors. As small object detection is closely related to shallow features, many small object detectors attempt to

L. Iliadis et al. (Eds.): ICANN 2023, LNCS 14260, pp. 1–13, 2023.
https://doi.org/10.1007/978-3-031-44195-0_1

extract more informative shallow features from the image [15]. One effective approach is increasing the number of detection heads/scales as it reduces partial loss of information during the downsampling stage [24]. Another commonly adopted strategy is highlighting hidden shallow features ignored by traditional detectors using attention modules in the neck part [9] when fusing information from different backbone output layers.

However, the extraction of shallow features is never an easy task. For example, adding one detection head into models with three heads may introduce about 20% more parameters compared with the original model. This in turn requires more computational resources during both the training and detection stages. This is also observed in adding attention models in the neck part, too many attention modules also add unnecessary parameters and may lead to overfitting.

In small object detectors, shallow feature detection heads are more effective than those for deep features. Therefore, the model complexity remains unchanged and more shallow features can be extracted, if adding additional shallow feature detection heads and dropping some deep feature detection heads at the same time. In addition, as the original features from the backbone (the foundational component responsible for extracting low-level features in deep learning models) are concatenated in the neck part (intermediate component connecting backbone and head, integrating features for high-level predictions), the number of parameters in the neck part is much larger than that in the backbone [28]. Moving the attention module from the neck part to the backbone can reduce the number of parameters. And attention module next to each backbone output layer can directly filter unnecessary information and highlight shallow features closely related to small objects before merging multi-scale features which mixes up all information together in the neck part.

Based on the above ideas, an efficient shallow feature enhanced YOLO (ES-YOLO) small object detector is proposed in this paper based on YOLOv5 [10]. The main contributions of this paper are as follows:

1) To efficiently extract more shallow features, the Path Aggregation Network (PANet) [13] in the neck part is upgraded to the small object-oriented PANet (SPAN).
2) To directly select representative original shallow features and reduce redundant model parameters, the attention module [23] is directly used next to the backbone output layer.
3) To alleviate the computation burden of ES-YOLO, the cross-stage partial connection (CSPC) [22], an effective parameter compression strategy, is integrated with the SPPF module.

2   Related Works

Currently, deep learning-based small object detectors can be divided into two categories: region proposal-based two-stage detectors and regression-based one-stage detectors [15]. Two-stage detectors first generate region proposals and then re-check each proposal to find targets [8]. The region proposals are generally generated using Selective Search [20] or Region Proposal Network [19]. Each proposal is then processed through a convolution neural network to further identify whether it is a small object [7]. Although these methods have been proven effective in identifying small objects, they are generally computationally expensive and cannot match the requirements of real-time detection.

One-stage detectors are more efficient than two-stage ones because they simplify the small object detection as an end-to-end regression problem, i.e., image features are directly extracted from images and then applied in positioning and classifying small objects [16]. In this way, the detection speed is increased to more than 30 fps with comparative identification accuracy. Most of these methods are SSD-based or YOLO-based. Compared with early-stage YOLO-based detectors [17], the SSD-based detectors further use multiple layers to better capture multi-scale features of small objects [14]. Currently, many YOLO-based methods also borrowed this strategy from SSD. For example, YOLOv3 [18] adopts the multi-scale framework and feature pyramid to detect objects in three different scales, and improves speed and accuracy on small object detection.

No matter the one-stage or the two-stage detectors are used, the successful detection of small objects heavily depends on sufficient shallow features. As a result, how to extract representative shallow features is the main concern of almost all up-to-date small object detectors. Multi-scale information fusion and attention mechanism are two popular methods for addressing this issue [15].

The fusion of multi-scale features is an effective approach for capturing shallow features closely related to small objects. Rather than directly using multiple-scale outputs from the backbone [14], Feature Pyramid Networks (FPN) [12] and PANet [13] have been widely used in recent years to reduce shallow information loss. As more and more effective shallow features are extracted, three detection heads are not sufficient for the accurate detection of small objects. Adding more detection heads has become a popular method for addressing this issue [24]. However, the detection speed drops sharply as more parameters are needed in such situations.

The attention mechanism is another important tool in the effective use of shallow features. Rather than extracting more features from images, it selects and regroups shallow features to reduce distractions from redundant information. In small object detection, the attention module is generally used in the neck part [9]. However, the backbone output layers may also contain redundant spatial or semantic information, and attention modules in the neck part are not sufficient to reduce such redundancy as they process merged features rather than the original features [28].

3   Method

The ES-YOLO model is based on the YOLOv5 model [10], which has been a popular baseline for many up-to-date detectors [24,28]. Its network structure is shown in Fig. 1. Similarly to YOLOv5, it includes three sequential parts: backbone, neck part and detection heads. The backbone is responsible for extracting general features from the original image; the neck part is responsible for fusing features from different scales; and each detection head locates and classifies small objects at different scales. The ES-YOLO updates YOLOv5 in the following four aspects: (1) the large-scale detection head is replaced with a small-scale detection head; (2) the attention module is next to each backbone output layer rather than in the neck part; (3) the SPPF module is upgraded to the spatial pyramid pooling fast with cross-stage partial connection (SPPFCSPC); and (4) the SIoU loss [6] is adopted in updating the network.

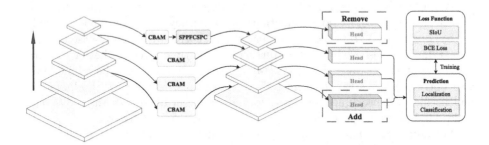

Fig. 1. The network structure of ES-YOLO.

3.1 SPAN

As deep feature maps with large receptive fields have limited discriminating power for small objects, the largest scale detection head in the PANet can hardly locate small objects. Adding more small-scale detection heads is more effective than preserving this detection head in extracting more shallow features closely related to small objects. Based on this idea, we upgrade the PANet to SPAN. SPAN drops the largest scale detection head in the PANet and adds one small-scale detection head at the same time in ES-YOLO, which effectively extracts richer shallow information from images and reduces parameters added by the additional detection head compared with four head-based detectors.

The details of SPAN are shown in Fig. 2. First of all, refined features by the attention module from output layers two to five in the backbone are passed into the SPAN feature pyramid. Next, in this feature pyramid, large-scale features are up-sampled using transposed convolution [4] and concatenated (Concat) with small-scale features next to it. And then small-scale features are down-sampled using group shuffle convolution (GSConv) [11] and concatenated (Concat) with large-scale features next to it. Finally, the outputs of concatenated features in the downsampling process are passed to three detection heads. During this process, the upsampling process gradually fuses semantic information to shallow features, and downsampling is then used to integrate shallow features into deep features. This is instructive in reducing computational costs and preventing overfitting.

The removed deep feature detection head in YOLOv5 uses a priori box with 20×20 pixels. Some small objects can hardly be located at this scale. As the newly added shallow feature detection head in ES-YOLO uses a priori box with 160×160 pixels, small objects missed by the large-scale detection heads can be successfully detected again. In addition, the removal of one deep detection head also reduces the number of parameters needed as much as possible. Therefore, ES-YOLO successfully balances between correctly identifying small object shallow features and the computational resources needed compared with four-head detectors.

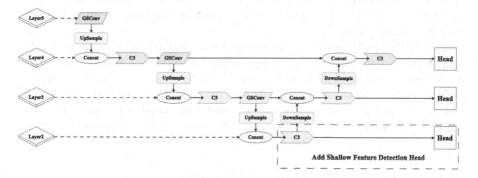

Fig. 2. The overall structure of SPAN.

3.2   Convolutional Block Attention Module (CBAM)

CBAM [23] is a simple but effective attention module. It is a lightweight module that can be integrated with the convolution modules in different networks to highlight the hidden features of small objects. For a feature map, CBAM sequentially first infers the attention map along the channel and spatial dimensions respectively, and then multiplies the attention map with the input feature map to perform adaptive feature refinement [28]. CBAM has been widely used by small object detectors in the neck part to extract representative features.

Different from other existing detectors, the CBAM attention module is directly added next to each backbone output layer in ES-YOLO rather than to the neck part. Each output layer of the backbone contains scale-specific features rather than mixed features from different scales. Therefore, representative shallow features are directly extracted from original small-scale outputs from the backbone. This can filter unnecessary information and highlight small object spatial information before merging multi-scale features in the neck part. Additionally, CBAM next to the backbone rather than in the neck part can further reduce model parameters because merged features in the neck part contain more elements than the original output from the backbone.

3.3 SPPFCSPC

The SPPF module in YOLOv5 is effective in perceiving objects of different sizes as it extracts multiple-scale information from the feature map. With the help of three pooling operations, SPPF gains large receptive fields in capturing contextual information. However, this detection of multi-scale information is at the price of additional pooling and concatenating operations. Fortunately, this limitation can be addressed by borrowing ideas from the CSPC [22].

The CSPC divides the input feature map into two parts. One part is processed following the original connection in the network, while another part skips the original connections and is directly passed to the next module. Inspired by the CSPC, we alleviate the computation burden by dividing the original SPPF module into two parts.

The SPPFCSPC module is shown in Fig. 3 and proceeds as follows. The input feature map is divided into two parts, the first part is processed using the original SPPF module to extract more hidden features at multiple scales, while the second part is processed using a CBS module. In the end, the outputs from these two parts are concatenated together and passed to the neck part. The SPPFCSPC module effectively alleviates the computation burden of the SPPF.

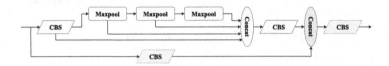

Fig. 3. The overall structure of SPPFCSPC.

3.4 Loss Function

The loss function of ES-YOLO has three parts. The first part is the regression loss L_{SIoU}, which is calculated using the SIoU loss function [6] rather than the commonly used CIoU loss function. SIoU loss considers angle loss and can add more penalties on predicted bounding boxes that are distant from the ground truth. The second part of the loss function is the classification loss L_{cls}, which refers to the classification error of small objects. Small L_{cls} indicates high agreements between the predicted and true labels of objects. Finally, the confidence loss L_{obj} is used to rule out empty predicted boxes. The overall loss function is a linear weighted combination of these three losses:

$$L = W_{SIoU}L_{SIoU} + W_{cls}L_{cls} + W_{obj}L_{obj} \tag{1}$$

where W_{SIoU}, W_{cls}, W_{obj} are regression, classification and confidence loss weights, respectively.

4 Experiments

4.1 Dataset

Two publicly available datasets, BDD100K [25] and VisDrone [27], are used to evaluate the effectiveness of ES-YOLO. Generally, objects which account for smaller than 0.3% of the entire image are recognized as small objects [24]. BDD100K consists of 80,000 labeled road target images with 75% small objects in all labeled objects. As one of the largest and most diverse driving datasets, it covers almost all typical cases of small objects in driving. 87.5% of images in this dataset are used as training data and the remaining images are used as test data. The drone vision dataset, VisDrone, contains 10209 images with 90% small objects in all labeled objects. Multiple scenes, such as urban, rural and seaside, covering various weather conditions and environmental backgrounds, are recorded in the dataset. 80% of images in this dataset are used as training data and the remaining images are used as test data. Some well-known datasets, such as PASCAL VOC and MS COCO, are not used in the experiment as there are not enough small objects to serve the comparison between small object detectors.

4.2 Evaluation Metrics

In the experiments, the mean Average Precision (mAP) is used to evaluate the performance of small object detectors. The mAP is based on two commonly used accuracy measures: Precision (P) and Recall (R). It uses the area under the curve of Precision and Recall to evaluate the accuracy of results, and is generally approximated as follows:

$$mAP = \frac{1}{k} \sum_{n=1}^{N} P(n) \cdot \Delta r(n) \tag{2}$$

where k represents the number of classes, N is the number of test images, $P(n)$ represents the precision of the first n images, and $\Delta r(n) = R(n) - R(n-1)$, $R(n)$ represents the recall of the first n images. mAP@0.5 represents the average accuracy of the model when the threshold is 0.5, and mAP@0.5:0.95 is the average mAP over thresholds from 0.5 to 0.95 with step 0.05.

4.3 Implementation Details

The proposed model is implemented based on Pytorch-1.14.0 and CUDA-11.7, and trained on an NVIDIA RTX3090 GPU. In the experiment, all images are scaled to 640 × 640 pixels. In the training phase, a pre-trained ResNet model on the COCO dataset is used as the backbone[1]. Each experiment is trained for 200 epochs with a batch size of 16. The SGD optimizer is adopted in the training phase. The initial learning rate and the weight decay are set to 0.01 and 0.0005, respectively. The warm-up step spends three epochs. The decay of the learning rate is implemented using the cosine annealing algorithm. The final learning rate is set to 0.001.

---

[1] https://github.com/ultralytics/yolov5/releases/download/v6.1/yolov5l.pt.

4.4   Ablation Studies

To demonstrate the effectiveness of the four modules added, SPAN, CBAM, SPPFCSPC and SIoU, for accurate detection of small objects, ablation experiments on both BDD100K and VisDrone datasets are performed for each module. mAP@0.5 and mAP@0.5:0.95 are used to compare the identification accuracy. The experiment results are summarized in Table 1.

Table 1. Ablation studies on two small object datasets (%).

Methods	BDD100K		VisDrone	
	mAP@0.5	mAP@0.5:0.95	mAP@0.5	mAP@0.5:0.95
YOLOv5l	58.1	33.9	36.4	21.4
+SPAN	59.9	34.4	39.5	22.9
+CBAM	58.6	34.0	36.5	21.4
+SPPFCSPC	58.3	33.9	36.5	21.4
+SIoU	58.5	34.0	36.9	21.5
+All	**60.5**	**35.1**	**39.9**	**23.2**

Effectiveness of SPAN. The new three-head detection with more consideration on shallow features increases mAP@0.5 and mAP@0.5:0.95 for both datasets. In BDD100K, the mAP@0.5 and mAP@0.5:0.95 increase by 1.8% and 0.5%, respectively. In VisDrone, the mAP@0.5 and mAP@0.5:0.95 increase by 3.1% and 1.5%, respectively. Furthermore, we also conduct a comparison study between SPAN and traditional four detection heads module (4heads) on the VisDrone dataset. Not only the FPS (Frames Per Second) during detection increases from 38 to 57, but also the identification accuracy increases slightly. The results demonstrate the superiority of SPAN, which is lightweight but performs better.

Effectiveness of CBAM. By integrating the CBAM attention module next to each backbone output layer, the mAP@0.5 and mAP@0.5:0.95 increase by 0.5% and 0.1% for the BDD100K dataset, respectively. And in VisDrone, the mAP@0.5 increases by 0.1%. The results show that filtering redundant information in the backbone output layer using the CBAM is instructive in improving identification accuracy.

Effectiveness of SPPFCSPC. By replacing the SPPF with the SPPFCSPC module, 261,376 model parameters are saved while the identification accuracy is not decreased but slightly increased on both datasets. This indicates SPPFCSPC module is effective in alleviating the computation burden while preserving accuracy.

Effectiveness of SIoU. By replacing the CIoU with SIoU loss in the training phase, the mAP@0.5 and mAP@0.5:0.95 increase by 0.4% and 0.1% for the BDD100K dataset, respectively. And in VisDrone, the mAP@0.5 and mAP@0.5:0.95 increase by 0.5% and 0.1%, respectively. It demonstrates that SIoU loss can make bounding boxes regress better and obtain higher-quality anchors.

4.5   Comparison with Other Models

In addition to the ablation studies, ES-YOLO is compared with other commonly used one-stage object detection algorithms on the BDD100K and VisDrone datasets, respectively. These algorithms include SSD [14], YOLOv3 [18], YOLOv4 [1], YOLOv5l [10], YOLOX-L [5], YOLOv7 [21], MCS-YOLO [2] and KPE-YOLOv5s [24]. mAP@0.5 are used to evaluate the identification accuracy.

In the left part of Table 2 shows the comparison results on the BDD100K dataset. Besides ES-YOLO, YOLOv5l achieves the best performance. But ES-YOLO increases the accuracy by 2.4% compared with YOLOv5l. Additionally, compared with the latest four detection heads model, MCS-YOLO, ES-YOLO gains an additional 6.9% increment in accuracy. This supports that replacing deep heads with shallow heads is more effective than directly using four heads in detecting small objects.

Table 2. Comparison of one-stage object detectors on two datasets (%).

BDD100K		VisDrone	
Methods	mAP@0.5	Methods	mAP@0.5
YOLOv3	40.1	SSD	23.9
YOLOv4	45.2	YOLOv5l	36.4
YOLOv5l	58.1	YOLOX-L	37.1
YOLOv7	48.7	YOLOv7	34.5
MCS-YOLO	53.6	KPE-YOLOv5s	39.2
ES-YOLO(ours)	**60.5**	ES-YOLO(ours)	**39.9**

The comparison results on the VisDrone dataset are shown in the right part of Table 2. It is clear that ES-YOLO achieves the best performance in mAP@0.5. Compared with the baseline model, the identification accuracy increases by 3.5%. Compared with SSD, the accuracy of ES-YOLO increases by 16%. With respect to the latest YOLO series, YOLOX-L and YOLOv7, the identification accuracy increases by 2.8% and 5.4%, respectively. Although the up-to-date four detection heads model, KPE-YOLOv5s, has an identification accuracy of 39.2%, ES-YOLO also increases additional 0.7% identification accuracy compared with it.

We have selected some representative images to visually inspect the advantage of ES-YOLO in Fig. 4. The first and second columns in Fig. 4 show the identification results from YOLOv5l and ES-YOLO, respectively. Taken the first line in Fig. 4 as an example. Only several cars in the long car lines in the middle left of the image are successfully identified by YOLOv5l, while ES-YOLO successfully labeled almost all of these cars using orange rectangles. Additionally, in the second line in Fig. 4, not only cars gradually disappeared and were missed by YOLOv5l at the end of the road are successfully identified using ES-YOLO, but also some objects wrongly labeled as 'car' by YOLOv5l are corrected by ES-YOLO. For example, the object next to the blue roof of buildings on the top right of the image is wrongly labeled as 'car' by YOLOv5l. This wrong identification is removed in the result from ES-YOLO.

Fig. 4. Comparison visualization results between YOLOv5l and ES-YOLO. (Color figure online)

5   Conclusion

Based on YOLOv5, an ES-YOLO model for small object detection is proposed in this paper. It replaces the feature detection head which concerns the deepest information with a shallow feature detection head, and directly adds the attention module in the backbone. Additionally, the SPPFCSPC module and SIoU loss are used to alleviate the computation burden in the training stage. The abolition and comparison experiments with other small object detectors show that the ES-YOLO increases the identification accuracy. The parameters used by ES-YOLO decrease by 25% compared with the baseline model as well. These experiments also support that shallow information plays an important role in detecting small objects. In the future, effective and efficient shallow feature representation and extraction methods are still worthy of further investigation. And the ES-YOLO will be tested on more object detection datasets and compared with two-stage object detection models, for example, Faster R-CNN [19], to further validate its effectiveness.

Acknowledgement. The work is supported by the National Natural Science Foundation of China (No. 41871286) and the 1331 Engineering Project of Shanxi Province, China.

References

1. Bochkovskiy, A., Wang, C.Y., Liao, H.Y.M.: YOLOv4: optimal speed and accuracy of object detection. arXiv preprint arXiv:2004.10934 (2020). https://doi.org/10.48550/arXiv.2004.10934
2. Cao, Y., Li, C., Peng, Y., Ru, H.: MCS-YOLO: a multiscale object detection method for autonomous driving road environment recognition. IEEE Access (2023). https://doi.org/10.1109/ACCESS.2023.3252021
3. Caputo, S., Castellano, G., Greco, F., Mencar, C., Petti, N., Vessio, G.: Human detection in drone images using YOLO for search-and-rescue operations. In: Bandini, S., Gasparini, F., Mascardi, V., Palmonari, M., Vizzari, G. (eds.) AIxIA 2021-Advances in Artificial Intelligence: 20th International Conference of the Italian Association for Artificial Intelligence, Virtual Event, 1–3 December 2021, Revised Selected Papers, vol. 13196, pp. 326–337. Springer, Cham (2022). https://doi.org/10.1007/978-3-031-08421-8_22
4. Dumoulin, V., Visin, F.: A guide to convolution arithmetic for deep learning. arXiv preprint arXiv:1603.07285 (2016). https://doi.org/10.48550/arXiv.1603.07285
5. Ge, Z., Liu, S., Wang, F., Li, Z., Sun, J.: YOLOX: exceeding YOLO series in 2021. arXiv preprint arXiv:2107.08430 (2021). https://doi.org/10.48550/arXiv.2107.08430
6. Gevorgyan, Z.: SIoU loss: more powerful learning for bounding box regression. arXiv preprint arXiv:2205.12740 (2022). https://doi.org/10.48550/arXiv.2205.12740
7. Girshick, R.: Fast R-CNN. In: Proceedings of the IEEE International Conference on Computer Vision, pp. 1440–1448 (2015). https://doi.org/10.1109/ICCV.2015.169
8. Girshick, R., Donahue, J., Darrell, T., Malik, J.: Rich feature hierarchies for accurate object detection and semantic segmentation. In: Proceedings of the IEEE Conference on Computer Vision and Pattern Recognition, pp. 580–587 (2014). https://doi.org/10.1109/CVPR.2014.81
9. Ji, S.J., Ling, Q.H., Han, F.: An improved algorithm for small object detection based on YOLO v4 and multi-scale contextual information. Comput. Electr. Eng. **105**, 108490 (2023). https://doi.org/10.1016/j.compeleceng.2022.108490
10. Jocher, G.: YOLOv5. In: GitHub https://github.com/ultralytics/yolov5
11. Li, H., Li, J., Wei, H., Liu, Z., Zhan, Z., Ren, Q.: Slim-neck by GSConv: a better design paradigm of detector architectures for autonomous vehicles. arXiv preprint arXiv:2206.02424 (2022). https://doi.org/10.48550/arXiv.2206.02424
12. Lin, T.Y., Dollár, P., Girshick, R., He, K., Hariharan, B., Belongie, S.: Feature pyramid networks for object detection. In: Proceedings of the IEEE Conference on Computer Vision and Pattern Recognition, pp. 2117–2125 (2017). https://doi.org/10.1109/CVPR.2017.106

13. Liu, S., Qi, L., Qin, H., Shi, J., Jia, J.: Path aggregation network for instance segmentation. In: Proceedings of the IEEE Conference on Computer Vision and Pattern Recognition, pp. 8759–8768 (2018). https://doi.org/10.1109/CVPR.2018.00913

14. Liu, W., et al.: SSD: single shot multibox detector. In: Leibe, B., Matas, J., Sebe, N., Welling, M. (eds.) ECCV 2016, Part I. LNCS, vol. 9905, pp. 21–37. Springer, Cham (2016). https://doi.org/10.1007/978-3-319-46448-0_2

15. Liu, Y., Sun, P., Wergeles, N., Shang, Y.: A survey and performance evaluation of deep learning methods for small object detection. Expert Syst. Appl. **172**, 114602 (2021). https://doi.org/10.1016/j.eswa.2021.114602

16. Redmon, J., Divvala, S., Girshick, R., Farhadi, A.: You only look once: unified, real-time object detection. In: Proceedings of the IEEE Conference on Computer Vision and Pattern Recognition, pp. 779–788 (2016). https://doi.org/10.1109/CVPR.2016.91

17. Redmon, J., Farhadi, A.: YOLO9000: better, faster, stronger. In: Proceedings of the IEEE Conference on Computer Vision and Pattern Recognition, pp. 7263–7271 (2017). https://doi.org/10.1109/CVPR.2017.690

18. Redmon, J., Farhadi, A.: YOLOV3: an incremental improvement. arXiv preprint arXiv:1804.02767 (2018). https://doi.org/10.48550/arXiv.1804.02767

19. Ren, S., He, K., Girshick, R., Sun, J.: Faster R-CNN: towards real-time object detection with region proposal networks. In: Advances in Neural Information Processing Systems, vol. 28 (2015). https://doi.org/10.1109/TPAMI.2016.2577031

20. Uijlings, J.R., Van De Sande, K.E., Gevers, T., Smeulders, A.W.: Selective search for object recognition. Int. J. Comput. Vision **104**, 154–171 (2013). https://doi.org/10.1007/s11263-013-0620-5

21. Wang, C.Y., Bochkovskiy, A., Liao, H.Y.M.: YOLOV7: trainable bag-of-freebies sets new state-of-the-art for real-time object detectors. arXiv preprint arXiv:2207.02696 (2022). https://doi.org/10.48550/arXiv.2207.02696

22. Wang, C.Y., Liao, H.Y.M., Wu, Y.H., Chen, P.Y., Hsieh, J.W., Yeh, I.H.: CSPNet: a new backbone that can enhance learning capability of CNN. In: Proceedings of the IEEE/CVF Conference on Computer Vision and Pattern Recognition Workshops, pp. 390–391 (2020). https://doi.org/10.1109/CVPRW50498.2020.00203

23. Woo, S., Park, J., Lee, J.-Y., Kweon, I.S.: CBAM: convolutional block attention module. In: Ferrari, V., Hebert, M., Sminchisescu, C., Weiss, Y. (eds.) ECCV 2018. LNCS, vol. 11211, pp. 3–19. Springer, Cham (2018). https://doi.org/10.1007/978-3-030-01234-2_1

24. Yang, R., Li, W., Shang, X., Zhu, D., Man, X.: KPE-YOLOv5: an improved small target detection algorithm based on YOLOv5. Electronics **12**(4), 817 (2023). https://doi.org/10.3390/electronics12040817

25. Yu, F., et al.: BDD100K: a diverse driving dataset for heterogeneous multitask learning. In: Proceedings of the IEEE/CVF Conference on Computer Vision and Pattern Recognition, pp. 2636–2645 (2020). https://doi.org/10.1109/CVPR42600.2020.00271

26. Zhou, M., Li, J., Liu, S.: Fire detection based on improved-YOLOV5s. In: Pimenidis, E., Angelov, P., Jayne, C., Papaleonidas, A., Aydin, M. (eds.) Artificial Neural Networks and Machine Learning-ICANN 2022: 31st International Conference on Artificial Neural Networks, Bristol, UK, 6–9 September 2022, Proceedings; Part IV, pp. 88–100. Springer, Cham (2022). https://doi.org/10.1007/978-3-031-15937-4_8

27. Zhu, P., Wen, L., Du, D., Bian, X., Fan, H., Hu, Q., Ling, H.: Detection and tracking meet drones challenge. IEEE Trans. Pattern Anal. Mach. Intell. **44**(11), 7380–7399 (2021). https://doi.org/10.1109/TPAMI.2021.3119563
28. Zhu, X., Lyu, S., Wang, X., Zhao, Q.: Tph-yolov5: Improved yolov5 based on transformer prediction head for object detection on drone-captured scenarios. In: Proceedings of the IEEE/CVF international conference on computer vision. pp. 2778–2788 (2021). https://doi.org/10.1109/ICCVW54120.2021.00312

Adaptive Dehazing YOLO for Object Detection

Kaiwen Zhang[1], Xuefeng Yan[1,2](✉), Yongzhen Wang[1],
and Junchen Qi[3]

[1] Nanjing University of Aeronautics and Astronautics, Nanjing, China
{kaiwenzhang,yxf}@nuaa.edu.cn
[2] Collaborative Innovation Center of Novel Software Technology and
Industrialization, Nanjing, China
[3] North China Electric Power University, Baoding, China

Abstract. While CNN-based object detection methods operate smoothly in normal images, they produce poor detection results under adverse weather conditions due to image degradation. To address this issue, we propose a novel Adaptive Dehazing YOLO (DH-YOLO) framework to reduce the impact of weather information on the detection tasks. DH-YOLO is a multi-task learning paradigm that jointly optimizes object detection and image restoration tasks in an end-to-end fashion. In the image restoration module, the feature extraction network serves as an encoder, and a Feature Filtering Module (FFM) is used to remove redundant features. The FFM contains an Adaptive Dehazing Module for image recovery, whose parameters are quickly calculated using a lightweight Cascaded Partial Decoder. This allows the framework to make use of weather-invariant information in hazy images to extract haze-free features. By sharing three feature layers at different scales between the two subtasks, the performance of the object detection network is improved by the use of clear features. DH-YOLO is based on YOLOv4 and forms a unified, end-to-end model with the above modules. Experimental results show that our method outperforms many advanced detection methods on real-world foggy datasets, demonstrating its effectiveness in object detection under adverse weather conditions.

Keywords: Object detection · Image restoration · Adverse weather

1 Introduction

In the past decade, the field of intelligent vehicles (IVs) has become a major research topic in intelligent transportation systems as traffic accidents have become common worldwide. Intelligent vehicles possess autonomous driving capabilities that rely on fast and accurate visual perception, such as target tracking [21], object detection [23], and lane detection [12].

Supported by organization the Basic Research for National Defense under Grant Nos. JCKY2020605C003.

L. Iliadis et al. (Eds.): ICANN 2023, LNCS 14260, pp. 14–27, 2023.
https://doi.org/10.1007/978-3-031-44195-0_2

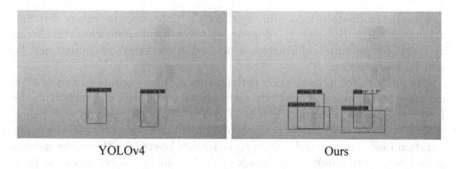

YOLOv4   Ours

Fig. 1. It is worth noting that even the human eye finds it difficult to detect the objects in the image under such adverse weather conditions. However, DH-YOLO demonstrates excellent detection accuracy and reduces the number of missed instances in real foggy weather.

In recent years, many detection models based on convolutional neural network have been introduced [1,25,26], which perform well on benchmark datasets. As the most critical part of IVs, object detection should detect object quickly and accurately in all-weather conditions. However, these general detection models are not satisfactory when they are generalized to adverse weather conditions. Images of adverse weather conditions typically include rain, snow, and fog, which inevitably leads to models learning these unnecessary features. The image quality degradation in adverse weather is mainly caused by the interaction between weather-specific information and objects, which leads to poor detection performance.

Previous studies have typically used the following approaches to improve detection accuracy in foggy conditions (Fig. 1).

A direct method is to pre-process hazed images by using the dehazing algorithm [8,13,15,22] and then send them to the detection network. However, the images processed with dehazing algorithms are better in visual quality but not necessarily beneficial for high-level computer vision tasks. On the one hand, some existing research [14,17] also recognises that there is no association between object detection accuracy and the visual quality of the dehazed image. On the other hand, the separation of the dehazing network and the object detection network inevitably reduces the inference speed of model. Besides, adjusting image quality adaptively, such as specific adjustments to image saturation, contrast, and gamma values will improve the detection accuracy. Because the adjustment of these metrics will make the object less similar to the background and more clearly outlined, but these operations will result in a significant domain shift [6,16] between the processed image and the original image. Therefore, it is difficult to reasonably adjust these parameters to enhance the image and allow the model to extract features from it that are beneficial for detection accuracy. For this reason, Liu et al. [20] introduced a small CNN-based parameter predictor to tune these parameters. This approach, however, will still lose some potential information in the original image due to the domain shift. Another approach combines object detection with an adversarial training strategy-based domain adaptation method [9], using clean images as the source domain and hazed images as the target domain to reduce the differences in feature distribution between them. However, the domain adaptive-based approaches still cannot fully utilize the potential information contained in the hazed image that may be beneficial for detection.

To improve the object detection performance in foggy conditions and to overcome the shortcomings of previous methods, a novel object detection model named the adaptive dehazing YOLO (DH-YOLO) is proposed in this paper. Specifically, our method jointly optimize the object detection task and the image restoration task. The two tasks share three feature layers, and the image restoration task is used to obtain clear features that benefit the object detection task, reduce the interference of weather information, and eliminate redundant fog features. We employ an excellent object detector (i.e., YOLOv4 [1]) for the detection task and use the autoencoder structure for image restoration. In the image restoration task, we use the backbone as the encoder, and the features are quickly integrated by a lightweight multi-scale feature cascaded partial decoder (CPD) and fed to the adaptive dehazing module (ADM) for fog removal to obtain a clear image. These two modules are the main components of the feature filtering module (FF). We use the MSE loss function (mean-square error) to measure the difference between the output and the ground truth and the network can also recover potential information in the image that is beneficial to improve the detection accuracy. As shown in Fig. 2, the above modules whole with the network and the parameters are shared within the network. Experiments show that our DH-YOLO method can adaptively reduce the fog information in the feature maps and improve the accuracy of object detection tasks in adverse weather. Our contributions are summarized as follows:

1. The proposed DH-YOLO improves the detection accuracy of the baseline by reducing the redundant weather information in the features, without adding additional inference time.
2. Our framework introduces low-level computer vision tasks to optimize high-level computer vision tasks, and the proposed feature filtering module provides haze-free features for the object detection task.
3. Compared to previous methods, our approach demonstrates superior performance on real-world foggy datasets.

2   Related Work

Object Detection is one of the hot spots of research in the field of computer vision. Detection methods based on deep convolutional neural networks can be divided into two major categories. The first one is two-stage region proposal-based approaches, such as R-CNN [5], Fast-RCNN [4], Faster-RCNN [27], etc. The second is the one-stage methods represented by YOLO series [1,3,24–26] and SSD [19], which treat object classification and localization as regression problems. In this paper, the classical one-stage method YOLOv4 is selected as the baseline and its detection performance in adverse weather conditions is improved.

Object detection in adverse conditions is a challenging task that has received less attention than normal object detection. In previous research, the most common approach was to use image dehazing algorithms as a pre-processing step to improve the visual quality of the input images before feeding them into a detection model. The effects of low-level image dehazing on high-level vision tasks were first studied by Li et al. [13]. However, it has been found that there is a weak correlation between the quality of the dehazed image and the precision of the object detection [14,17]. To address this issue, several approaches have been proposed. Huang et al. [10] proposed the use of a Selective Feature Absorption Network (SFA-Net) to improve object detection performance in rainy conditions by selecting beneficial features during training. Liu et al. [20] proposed a differentiable image processing module to enhance the images to be detected and a small neural network to predict the parameters of the image processing to improve detection accuracy in low light and adverse weather conditions. Another approach to addressing this problem is through the use of domain adaptation, which has been explored in several studies [2,28,29]. Hnewa et al. [9] proposed a multi-scale image-level adaptation YOLO model for addressing the problem of domain shifts between normal and severe weather conditions. Overall, these approaches show promise in improving object detection in adverse conditions.

3   Proposed Method

In this section, we first present an overview of DH-YOLO, a proposed redundant feature (fog) elimination network based on YOLOv4 that can effectively reduce the interference of weather information without increasing the inference speed of the baseline model and substantially improve the accuracy of object detection in severe weather conditions. Then we describe how we transform the features extracted from hazy images into clear images and combine this task with the object detection task to achieve joint optimization. Next, we provide a detailed description of the workflow of the feature filtering module (FFM) and the implementation details of its main components, the lightweight cascaded partial decoder (CPD), and the adaptive dehazing module (ADM).

3.1   Overview of DH-YOLO

We start from three aspects to improve the object detection accuracy in inclement weather: an encoder-decoder architecture, a feature filtering local work pipeline, and joint optimization of high-level and low-level tasks. The encoder-decoder architecture is used to fix hazy images and reduce the interference of weather information on the network. The feature filtering pipeline filters redundant weather information to improve the detection accuracy of the model. Finally, the high-level and low-level tasks are jointly optimized by sharing feature layers of different scales, improving the overall performance of the DH-YOLO framework. It is noteworthy that in our approach, the image restoration sub-task aims to provide clear features for object detection rather than detecting objects directly on the dehazed images.

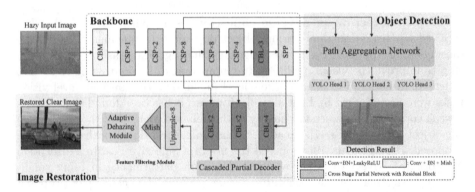

Fig. 2. Overview of our DH-YOLO. It comprises the backbone network (represented by the red dashed box) as the image restoration encoder, the YOLOv4 neck and head (depicted in blue) for object detection, and the image restoration network (shown in green) with the Feature Filtering Module (FFM). The FFM, consisting of the Cascaded Feature Decoder (CPD) and the Adaptive Dehazing Module (ADM), enhances detection accuracy by reducing redundant weather information in the features. (Color figure online)

3.2 Object Detection Network

Many CNN-based object detection models have been proposed, but the YOLOv4 is a classic single-stage detector that achieves a balance of speed and accuracy. YOLOv4 optimizes data processing and feature extraction using CSPDarknet53 as the backbone, SPP to expand the receptive field, and PANet with a shortcut to reconstruct clear images. Therefore, we use YOLOv4 as the basic detector in our proposed framework. The object detection network operates by passing the 416×416 input image through CSPDarknet53 and generating feature maps of three scales (52×52, 26×26, and 13×13) that are fused in the neck and used for prediction and localization by the head after nonmaximum suppression.

3.3 Obtain Haze-Free Features by Autoencoder Based Image Restoration Task

In the image restoration task, the encoder-decoder architecture is applied to accomplish this task. CSPDarknet53 is used as the encoder. We selected the same three feature layers as in the object detection task to recover the image. It is worth noting that the feature maps of these three scales are also used as the input for the neck of YOLOv4 at the same time. Previous research [30] has established that the features gradually change from low-level representation to high-level representation as the depth of the network deepens. The features extracted by the encoder are more concerned with the semantic information of the image but not with the pixel-level information. On the one hand, PANet in YOLOv4 is already an excellent feature fusion module, which aggregates the features between different network layers and ensures the integrity and diversity of features. On the other hand, we restore the clear image using the Cascaded

Partial Decoder (CPD) [30] as well as an Adaptive Dehazing Module (ADM). Because CPD can quickly integrate multi-level features. The above two processes enhance the expressiveness of features at each scale, taking into account both the image's high-level semantic information and pixel-level information.

After acquiring the three scales of features from the feature extraction network, the parameters required in the ADM are calculated by the CPD.

The integrated features F_a can be calculated by the following equation.

$$F_a = CPD\left[CBL(f_1), CBL(f_2), CBL(f_3)\right] \tag{1}$$

where CBL is a set of operation sequences including 1×1 convolution, batch normalization, and LeakyReLU activation functions. f_1, f_2, and f_3 are the feature layers extracted by CSPDarknet53, and they are send to the CPD to complete the feature cascade after unifying the number of channels to 64 after $CBL.gy$. With the 416×416 size image, the size of feature map F_a is 52×52 and the number of channels is 3.

Cascaded Partial Decoder. Generally, given features $\{f_i^c, i \in [n, ..., N]\}$ from backbone network, we generate new features $\{f_i^{c1}\}$ using the context module. Element-wise multiplication is adopted to decrease the gap between multi-level features. Especially, for the top-most feature $(i = N)$, we set $f_N^{c2} = F_N^{c1}$. For feature $\{f_i^{c1}, i < N\}$, we update it to f_i^{c2} via element-wise multiplying itself with all features of deeper layers. This operation is defined as follows:

$$f_i^{c2} = f_i^{c1} \odot \prod_{j=k+1}^{N} CBL\left(Up\left(f_j^{c1}\right)\right) \tag{2}$$

where $k \in [n, ..., N-1]$. $Up(\cdot)$ is an up-sampling operation and its ratio sets as 2^{j-k}. Finally, these discriminative features is combined via a concatenation operation (Fig. 3).

Adaptive Dehazing Module. Inspired by AOD-Net [13], the adaptive dehazing module is designed. It works in concert with the decoder (CPD) to accomplish the task of recovering clear images from features. Since the detection network and these modules share the features f_1, f_2, and f_3, the network will pay more attention to the information of the object to be detected in the image and reduce the interference of fog in the image to improve the accuracy of the object detection in adverse weather.

The relationship between blurred and clear images can be represented by the classical atmospheric scattering model as follows:

$$I(x) = J(x)t(x) + A(1 - t(x)) \tag{3}$$

where $I(x)$ is the hazy image and $J(x)$ is the clear image we need to restore. A is the global atmospheric light. $t(x)$ is the medium transmission map. Where $d(x)$ is the scene depth and β is the scattering coefficient of the atmosphere. We note that a clean image $J(x)$ can be obtained only by calculating the global

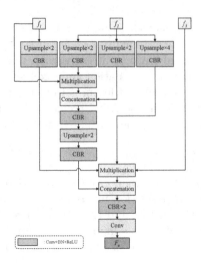

Fig. 3. The architecture of the Cascaded Partial Decode.

atmospheric light and the medium transmission map. If we estimate one of the parameters separately it will lead to an accumulation of errors and the increase of model complexity, which leads to sub-optimal results. So we unify the two parameters A and $t(x)$ into one formulation:

$$E(x) = \frac{\frac{1}{t(x)}(I(x) - A) + (A - b)}{I(x) - 1} \tag{4}$$

Finally, the clear image can be obtained from the following formulation:

$$J(x) = E(x)I(x) - E(x) + b \tag{5}$$

where b is the bias constant, which we set to 0.95.

In the image restoration task, the size of output clear image from ADM is equal to the input image. According to the above, the multi-layer features will be decoded by CPD to obtain a feature map F_a of size 52×52 and number of channels 3. To match the size of the output image, a bilinear interpolation is used to enlarge the size of F_a to 416×416. The final $E(x)$ required in ADM is obtained. Besides, we use the simple Mean Square Error (MSE) loss function to train the sub-network. Previous studies [18, 22] have found that using an $L1$ loss function can lead to improved performance in image restoration tasks, as measured by PSNR and SSIM. However, in our framework for object detection, we have observed that using an $L1$ loss function for dehazing can lead to stronger model dehazing performance, but at the cost of decreased gradient information for semantics, which is important for object detection.

4   Experiment

In this section, we will discuss the experimental results of DH-YOLO, as well as other object detection methods for adverse weather and generic object detection methods. Four object detection methods were selected for comparison with DH-YOLO, including IA-YOLO [20] for image adaptive method, MS-DAYOLO [9] with YOLOv4 as the baseline for domain adaptive method, DSNet [11] for multi-task learning algorithm, and *dehazing + detect* methods using four dehazing algorithms (DCP [7], AOD-Net [13], Semi-dehazing [15], and FFA-Net [22]) to pre-process images in the VOC-FOG dataset, and then feeding them into YOLOv4 for detection. The mean average precision (mAP) was used as the evaluation criterion with a threshold of 0.5.

4.1 Datasets

Train Set. To overcome the lack of object detection datasets for adverse weather and the requirement of having both clear and hazed images for our method, we created a foggy detection dataset called VOC-FOG based on the widely-used atmospheric scattering model. This model is also the basis for the imaging and dehazing models in the field of image dehazing, and datasets such as NYU2 and SOTS have been synthesized using this model. In VOC-FOG, we use Eq. 3 to deduce a hazed image $I(x)$ from a known clear image $J(x)$, where $d(x)$ in $t(x)$ is defined as follows:

$$d(x) = -0.04 * \rho + \sqrt{max(w, h)} \tag{6}$$

where ρ is the Euclidean distance from each pixel point in the image to the central pixel, and w, h is the scale information of the image. We set the global atmospheric light parameter in Eq. 3 to 0.05 and the fog concentration is determined by the parameter β in the medium transmission map. We set β randomly between 0.07 and 0.12 to obtain the VOC-FOG-train dataset. To ensure that the training and test sets have the same object classes, we selected the common annotated object classes of the three datasets used in this paper.

Table 1. Details of the training and testing datasets.

Dataset	Type	Nums	Train/Test	Per	Bus	Car	Mot	Bic
VOC-FOG	Synthetic	9578	Train	13,519	684	2453	801	836
RTTS	Real	4332	Test	7950	1838	18,413	862	534
Foggy Driving	Real	101	Test	269	17	425	9	17

Test Set. To test the detection performance of DH-YOLO and other methods in adverse weather condition and the ability to generalize from synthetic data to the real world, we selected two real-world foggy sets. The statistics of the dataset are demonstrated in Table 1.

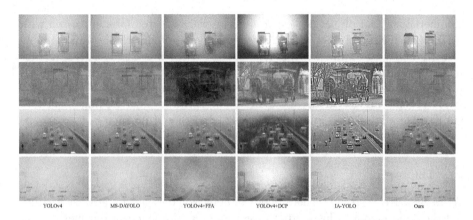

Fig. 4. Detection results by different methods on both synthetic and real-world foggy datasets with a confidence threshold of 0.5. (Color figure online)

4.2   Qualitative and Quantitative Results

To confirm the efficiency of DH-YOLO, we compared it with nine object detection algorithms on three test sets. To train each method, we used a pre-trained model on the VOC dataset and fine-tuned it on the VOC-FOG dataset according to the settings mentioned above. The 'Haze' in the third column refers to the corresponding method trained using the VOC-FOG dataset, and the 'Clear' refers to the training using the VOC dataset. Notes that the images in the VOC dataset are clear images from the VOC-FOG dataset. † is used to distinguish between two same models that use different training data. Red and blue colors are used to indicate the 1st and 2nd metrics, respectively. Where 'Per', 'Mot' and 'Bic' refer to Person, Motorbike and Bicycle (Fig. 4).

Table 2. Object detection results on RTTS dataset.

Method	Publication	Clear/Haze	Per	Car	Bic	Bus	Mot	mAP
YOLOv4 [1]	arXiv'20	Haze	76.59	61.57	29.97	27.02	31.41	45.29
YOLOv4† [1]	arXiv'20	Clear	79.78	63.48	30.30	21.34	17.61	42.45
YOLOv4+DCP [7]	TPAMI'11	Clear	78.76	63.76	28.50	22.29	16.66	41.99
YOLOv4+AOD [13]	ICCV'17	Clear	79.86	64.18	31.12	21.56	15.29	42.40
YOLOv4+Semi [15]	TIP'20	Clear	77.79	61.36	29.82	21.47	17.08	41.51
YOLOv4+FFA [22]	AAAI'20	Clear	79.11	63.61	30.51	21.03	17.48	42.35
MS-DAYOLO [9]	ICIP'21	Haze	71.89	70.16	44.11	34.49	38.06	51.74
DS-Net [11]	TPAMI'21	Haze	76.64	63.30	32.81	28.75	34.71	47.24
IA-YOLO [13]	AAAI'22	Haze	68.94	42.07	33.71	14.28	21.46	36.10
DH-YOLO	ours	Haze	78.09	71.63	47.94	33.31	32.34	52.66

Table 3 and Table 2 exhibit the mAP metric of each compared method on two real-world datasets. It is clear that the detection performance improvement of some image dehazing-based methods remains small or even decreases. Hazed images do improve the visual quality after being pre-processed by the dehazing algorithm, but object detection as a high-level computer vision tasks does not have a specific cause-and-effect relationship between the visual quality of image and final detection accuracy.

Table 3. Object detection results on Foggy Driving dataset.

Method	Per	Car	Bic	Bus	Mot	mAP
YOLOv4	22.47	57.42	31.57	41.24	6.08	31.75
YOLOv4†	18.99	56.99	24.18	40.13	2.13	28.48
YOLOv4+DCP	18.45	55.90	23.53	53.17	6.93	31.59
YOLOv4+AOD	20.88	57.63	31.65	40.76	4.21	31.02
YOLOv4+Semi	19.85	55.54	22.35	46.75	4.19	29.73
YOLOv4+FFA	18.01	52.56	20.10	54.89	3.57	29.82
MS-DAYOLO	21.18	56.82	34.79	46.89	8.08	33.56
DS-Net	23.91	58.15	31.94	42.63	6.55	32.64
IA-YOLO	15.57	41.66	12.01	17.57	4.43	18.24
DH-YOLO	27.77	59.65	37.31	42.72	7.87	35.06

The poor detection accuracy of the image dehazing-based method on the real-world dataset may be related to the following reasons: first, the pre-processed images lose some potential information that is beneficial for the detection accuracy improvement. Second, there are some low-light images in the real-world dataset, and these images become darker after dehazing, which makes it difficult for the network to detect. Overall, these results indicate that our DH-YOLO outperforms all competing methods on all three test datasets.

4.3   Ablation Study

In the previous section, our proposed method exhibited better detection performance than other state-of-art methods. To further evaluate the effectiveness of our designed framework, in this section, we use different frame structures and perform ablation experiments on the RTTS dataset and compare the detection accuracy with the original DH-YOLO. The experiments include the use of ADM, the selection of feature layer for image restoration and the use of CPD.

As shown in Fig. 2, the object detection task and the image restoration task share three feature layers, and when the size of the network input image is 416×416, the size of the feature maps outputted after these three feature layers are 52×52, 26×26, and 13×13, respectively. To explore the effects of multi-layer features and single features on the joint optimization of the whole network in the image restoration task, we used each of the above three scales of features with ADM to design three structures. Note that the feature maps output from the above three structures are sent to the ADM for image restoration.

Table 4. Ablation analysis on the different layers and feature scales in the image restoration task.

Structure	Baseline	S1	S2	S3	CPD
mAP	45.29	45.88	46.01	49.05	52.66

Table 4 shows the impact of the four features used for the image restoration task on the final detection results. $S1$ uses shallow, large-resolution features and achieves only a 0.59 improvement over baseline. $S3$ uses deep, low-resolution features and achieves a performance improvement of 3.76. CPD integrates multiple layers of features to achieve the best performance. The shallow features are rich in pixel information and are good for reconstructing spatial details, but both image restoration and object detection need to be jointly optimized in our framework, so the network learns best by integrating multi-layer multi-scale features.

We also explored the effect of the adaptive dehazing module on the proposed model. $M1$, $M2$, and $M3$ represent the baseline, the model without ADM, and the full model, respectively. Removing the ADM in M2 enables the use of CPD-processed features to generate clean images directly, resulting in a 4.2% improvement in mAP compared to M1. Joint optimization of image restoration and object detection tasks contributes to this improvement, while ADM minimizes reconstruction errors and allows for the extraction of more haze-free features.

4.4   Limitation and Discussion

One limitation of the DH-YOLO framework is its focus on improving object detection performance specifically in foggy weather conditions. It may face challenges when applied to other adverse weather conditions, such as heavy rain or snowstorms, which require further investigation and adaptation.

Future work can explore several directions to enhance the framework's capabilities. Firstly, integrating additional weather-specific modules or preprocessing techniques tailored to different adverse weather conditions can improve object detection accuracy across diverse scenarios. This could involve incorporating rain or snow removal algorithms or developing specialized models for specific weather phenomena.

By addressing these limitations and pursuing future work in these directions, the DH-YOLO framework can be enhanced to handle a broader range of adverse weather conditions, advancing the field of object detection in challenging environmental settings.

5   Conclusion

In this paper, we have presented the Adaptive Dehazing YOLO (DH-YOLO) framework, which significantly enhances object detection performance in adverse weather conditions, particularly fog. DH-YOLO is a multi-task learning framework that effectively combines object detection and image restoration tasks by leveraging shared feature layers at different scales within the backbone architecture. To further augment DH-YOLO's performance, we have introduced the Feature Filtering Module (FFM), comprising the Adaptive Dehazing Module (ADM) and the Cascaded Feature Decoder (CPD). The ADM effectively utilizes CPD-integrated features to restore clear images, thereby mitigating the impact of weather interference on the detection task. Furthermore, the clear features extracted from the FFM significantly contribute to improving the performance of the object detection network. By enabling DH-YOLO to exploit pixel-level and semantic information from various feature layers while filtering out redundant features, the FFM enhances both the efficiency and effectiveness of the model. Our experimental results showed that DH-YOLO outperformed many advanced detection methods on real-world foggy datasets, demonstrating the effectiveness of our approach in object detection under adverse weather conditions.

References

1. Bochkovskiy, A., Wang, C.Y., Liao, H.Y.M.: YOLOv4: optimal speed and accuracy of object detection. arXiv preprint arXiv:2004.10934 (2020)
2. Chen, Y., Li, W., Sakaridis, C., Dai, D., Van Gool, L.: Domain adaptive faster R-CNN for object detection in the wild. In: Proceedings of the IEEE Conference on Computer Vision and Pattern Recognition, pp. 3339–3348 (2018)
3. Ge, Z., Liu, S., Wang, F., Li, Z., Sun, J.: YOLOx: exceeding YOLO series in 2021. arXiv preprint arXiv:2107.08430 (2021)
4. Girshick, R.: Fast R-CNN. In: Proceedings of the IEEE International Conference on Computer Vision, pp. 1440–1448 (2015)
5. Girshick, R., Donahue, J., Darrell, T., Malik, J.: Rich feature hierarchies for accurate object detection and semantic segmentation. In: Proceedings of the IEEE Conference on Computer Vision and Pattern Recognition, pp. 580–587 (2014)
6. Gopalan, R., Li, R., Chellappa, R.: Domain adaptation for object recognition: an unsupervised approach. In: 2011 International Conference on Computer Vision, pp. 999–1006. IEEE (2011)
7. He, K., Sun, J., Tang, X.: Single image haze removal using dark channel prior. IEEE Trans. Pattern Anal. Mach. Intell. **33**(12), 2341–2353 (2011)
8. He, K., Zhang, X., Ren, S., Sun, J.: Deep residual learning for image recognition. In: Proceedings of the IEEE Conference on Computer Vision and Pattern Recognition, pp. 770–778 (2016)
9. Hnewa, M., Radha, H.: Multiscale domain adaptive YOLO for cross-domain object detection. In: Proceedings of the IEEE International Conference on Image Processing (ICIP), pp. 3323–3327. IEEE (2021)
10. Huang, S.C., Hoang, Q.V., Le, T.H.: SFA-Net: a selective features absorption network for object detection in rainy weather conditions. IEEE Trans. Neural Netw. Learn. Syst. **34**(8), 5122–5132 (2022)

11. Huang, S.C., Le, T.H., Jaw, D.W.: DSNet: joint semantic learning for object detection in inclement weather conditions. IEEE Trans. Pattern Anal. Mach. Intell. **43**(8), 2623–2633 (2020)
12. Ko, Y., Lee, Y., Azam, S., Munir, F., Jeon, M., Pedrycz, W.: Key points estimation and point instance segmentation approach for lane detection (2020)
13. Li, B., Peng, X., Wang, Z., Xu, J., Feng, D.: AOD-Net: all-in-one dehazing network. In: Proceedings of the IEEE International Conference on Computer Vision (ICCV), pp. 4770–4778 (2017)
14. Li, B., et al.: Benchmarking single-image dehazing and beyond. IEEE Trans. Image Process. **28**(1), 492–505 (2018)
15. Li, L., et al.: Semi-supervised image dehazing. IEEE Trans. Image Process. **29**, 2766–2779 (2020)
16. Li, W., Li, F., Luo, Y., Wang, P., et al.: Deep domain adaptive object detection: a survey. In: 2020 IEEE Symposium Series on Computational Intelligence (SSCI), pp. 1808–1813. IEEE (2020)
17. Li, Y., Liu, Y., Yan, Q., Zhang, K.: Deep dehazing network with latent ensembling architecture and adversarial learning. IEEE Trans. Image Process. **30**, 1354–1368 (2020)
18. Lim, B., Son, S., Kim, H., Nah, S., Mu Lee, K.: Enhanced deep residual networks for single image super-resolution. In: Proceedings of the IEEE Conference on Computer Vision and Pattern Recognition Workshops, pp. 136–144 (2017)
19. Liu, W., et al.: SSD: single shot multibox detector. In: Leibe, B., Matas, J., Sebe, N., Welling, M. (eds.) ECCV 2016. LNCS, vol. 9905, pp. 21–37. Springer, Cham (2016). https://doi.org/10.1007/978-3-319-46448-0_2
20. Liu, W., Ren, G., Yu, R., Guo, S., Zhu, J., Zhang, L.: Image-adaptive YOLO for object detection in adverse weather conditions. arXiv preprint arXiv:2112.08088 (2021)
21. Manjunath, A., Liu, Y., Henriques, B., Engstle, A.: Radar based object detection and tracking for autonomous driving, pp. 1–4 (2018)
22. Qin, X., Wang, Z., Bai, Y., Xie, X., Jia, H.: FFA-Net: feature fusion attention network for single image dehazing. In: Proceedings of the AAAI Conference on Artificial Intelligence, vol. 34, pp. 11908–11915 (2020)
23. Rakesh, N., Rajaram, E., Ohn-Bar, M., Manubhai, T.: RefineNet: refining object detectors for autonomous driving. IEEE Trans. Intell. Veh. **1**(4), 358–368 (2016)
24. Redmon, J., Divvala, S., Girshick, R., Farhadi, A.: You Only Look Once: unified, real-time object detection. In: Proceedings of the IEEE Conference on Computer Vision and Pattern Recognition, pp. 779–788 (2016)
25. Redmon, J., Farhadi, A.: YOLO9000: better, faster, stronger. In: Proceedings of the IEEE Conference on Computer Vision and Pattern Recognition, pp. 7263–7271 (2017)
26. Redmon, J., Farhadi, A.: YOLOv3: an incremental improvement. arXiv preprint arXiv:1804.02767 (2018)
27. Ren, S., He, K., Girshick, R., Sun, J.: Faster R-CNN: towards real-time object detection with region proposal networks. In: Advances in Neural Information Processing Systems, vol. 28 (2015)
28. Saito, K., Ushiku, Y., Harada, T., Saenko, K.: Strong-weak distribution alignment for adaptive object detection. In: Proceedings of the IEEE/CVF Conference on Computer Vision and Pattern Recognition (CVPR), pp. 6956–6965 (2019)

29. Sindagi, V.A., Oza, P., Yasarla, R., Patel, V.M.: Prior-based domain adaptive object detection for hazy and rainy conditions. In: Vedaldi, A., Bischof, H., Brox, T., Frahm, J.-M. (eds.) ECCV 2020. LNCS, vol. 12359, pp. 763–780. Springer, Cham (2020). https://doi.org/10.1007/978-3-030-58568-6_45
30. Wu, Z., Su, L., Huang, Q.: Cascaded partial decoder for fast and accurate salient object detection. In: Proceedings of the IEEE/CVF Conference on Computer Vision and Pattern Recognition, pp. 3907–3916 (2019)

Adaptive Training Strategies for Small Object Detection Using Anchor-Based Detectors

Shenmeng Zhang[1], Yongqing Sun[2], Jia Su[1(✉)], Guoxi Gan[1], and Zonghui Wen[1]

[1] Information Engineering College, Capital Normal University, Beijing 100048, China
`{2211002002,6561,2211002037,2211002094}@cnu.edu.cn`
[2] Nihon University, Tokyo, Japan
`nakahara.eisei@nihon-u.ac.jp`

Abstract. Small object detection is a crucial task in computer vision due to its wide range of real-world applications. Detecting small objects accurately and efficiently remains a challenging task due to the reduced size of the objects, low contrast to their surroundings, and potential occlusions. To tackle this issue, we proposed a method for detecting small objects in object detection tasks, including a new strategy for balancing positive and negative samples, a loss function that adapts the weight of detection losses according to object size, and an anchor mechanism that accommodates objects with diverse sizes and aspect ratios. The experimental data substantiates that our method has achieved a 12.9% increase in average accuracy for small objects on the COCO dataset, compared to the baseline.

Keywords: Anchor-based · Region Proposal Network · Small Object · Dynamic Training

1 Introduction

The RPN (Region Proposal Network) [1] is a key component in current object detection systems, providing high-quality proposals for object classification and bounding box regression. Its superior performance across various detection models is attributed to its accurate identification of candidate object regions. Nevertheless, some limitations still require attention. Detecting small objects is challenging in object detection due to their low resolution and difficulty in distinguishing them from the background. In Fig. 1, the ground truth box is shown as a red box, and several RPN-provided anchors are represented by yellow boxes. The intersection over union (IoU) value between the anchor of a small object and the ground truth box of "soccer" is often low, resulting in a low number of positive samples for small objects when using RPN's IoU threshold to filter samples. This could lead to small objects being incorrectly categorized as background during segmentation, due to their relatively small appearance. To address this, we propose an adaptive scheme that adjusts the number of positive and negative samples based on object size and IoU values. Specifically, our

---

S. Zhang and Y. Sun—Contributed equally to this work.

L. Iliadis et al. (Eds.): ICANN 2023, LNCS 14260, pp. 28–39, 2023.
https://doi.org/10.1007/978-3-031-44195-0_3

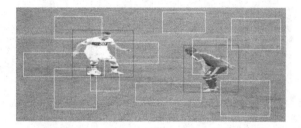

Fig. 1. Proposals provided by the RPN (Color figure online)

proposed approach can adjust the threshold used for small objects based on IoU distribution, effectively increasing the number of positive samples and improving detection accuracy while reducing computational costs. Details will be provided in Sect. 3.

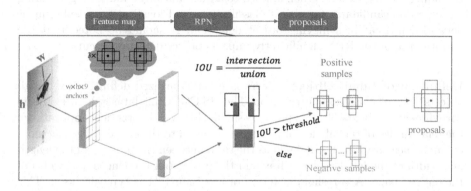

Fig. 2. Positive and negative samples screening process from Faster RCNN

Our approach can enhance the detection efficiency and accuracy of small objects in most feature pyramid-based object detection architectures. In summary, our work contributes the following:

- A sample balancing strategy to improve the detection of small objects
- An anchor mechanism for improved matching of objects with various sizes and aspect ratios
- A dynamically adjusted prediction loss function for faster convergence.

2 Related Works

Figure 2 demonstrates the process of filtering positive and negative samples in the RPN of Faster RCNN [1], which generates various anchors with different sizes

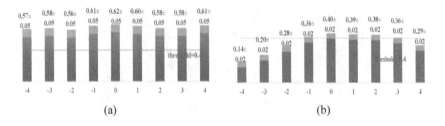

Fig. 3. Using a fixed IoU threshold to filter anchors near the center of objects with different sizes.

and aspect ratios on the feature map, usually generating nine anchors for each pixel. The IoU between the object and the anchor is calculated to distinguish positive and negative samples. If the IoU exceeds a predetermined threshold, the anchor is classified as a positive sample; otherwise, it is a negative sample. Bounding box regression is then applied to adjust anchor boundaries, generating more precise candidates for object classification and localization in subsequent networks, ultimately achieving object detection. It should be noted that the performance of the RPN significantly impacts object detection accuracy.

Definition of Small Object. There is no standardized definition for "small objects" in the field of computer vision. The MS COCO [2] dataset defines objects with dimensions below 32 × 32 pixels as small. However, in practical applications, the relative size of the labeled object box compared to the entire image is a more common measure, which is defined as the ratio between the product of the length and width of the labeled object box and the product of the length and width of the entire image. A threshold criterion of less than 12% is typically used. This method offers greater adaptability to varying image sizes and object dimensions and is more adjustable, so we adopt this definition in our study.

Anchor-Based Detector. Figure 3 shows how anchor points are selected near the centers of both large and small objects using the same IoU threshold. In particular, Fig. 3a and Fig. 3b display the IoU distribution near the center of the large and small objects, respectively. The horizontal axis represents the distance from the object center. When an IoU threshold of 0.4 is utilized for screening, all points of the large object surpass the threshold in the sampled points, indicating they are classified as positive samples. Current anchor-based object detection methods [3–6] have employed various techniques such as feature augmentation and data augmentation to enhance the detection performance. However, for the small object, only a few IoU values near the center position exceed the threshold and are labeled as positive samples, while the remaining points below the threshold are negative samples.

Recent object detection methods [7–10] have employed various techniques to enhance the detection performance of small objects. While methods like

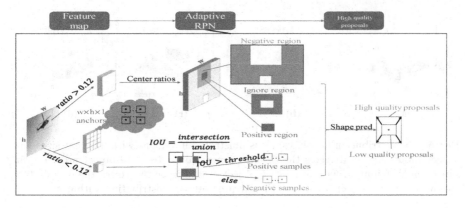

Fig. 4. Adaptive RPN with flexible sample selection strategy based on object size.

ATSS [11] and PAA [12] have proposed adaptive training sample selection or probabilistic anchor assignment, they still rely on IoU-based assignments and have yet to resolve the identified imbalance issue. GA-RPN [13] proposed a region filtering method that restricts calculations to the ground truth box's region, significantly reducing unnecessary computations. However, it may produce a minimal number of positive samples (sometimes even just a few pixels) for objects that occupy limited areas. This limitation can diminish small object detection performance. This paper mainly focuses on enhancing training strategies for small objects by addressing the issue of class imbalance between positive and negative samples and minimizing computations in non-object regions.

3 Proposed Work

3.1 Adaptive Sample Screening

Figure 4 demonstrates the flexible sample selection strategy employed by Adaptive RPN. During training, the RPN analyzes feature maps of images and employs ground truth boxes to first identify and describe objects by position and size. Objects larger than 12% of the original image are classified as general objects and then filtered into positive, negative, or ignore regions using a preset ratio parameter and region division approach. This reduces computational cost while maintaining detection accuracy. For small objects under 12%, fixed aspect ratio anchors are deployed at each point within the small object region, and the IoU between each anchor and the corresponding ground truth box is calculated to filter positive samples. The IoU distribution is approximated as a Gaussian distribution, and we set the filtering threshold to the quadratic standard deviation.

Figure 5 displays the distribution of IoU within small object regions of varying sizes and aspect ratios using the same anchor size of 8×8 to calculate IoU. Mean and standard deviation matrices are computed for each region, from which

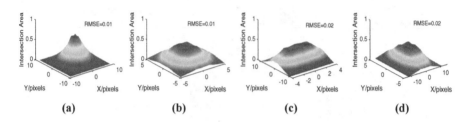

Fig. 5. The distribution of IoU values is illustrated in regions with different sizes and aspect ratios: Fig. 5a displays the distribution within a 10 × 10 object area, Fig. 5b shows the distribution within a 5 × 5 object area, Fig. 5c illustrates the distribution within a 4 × 12 object area, and Fig. 5d presents the distribution within a 15 × 5 object area.

the two standard deviations are derived. To evaluate model performance, we employ the *root mean square error* (RMSE) to measure the predicted values' discrepancy. The numerical values for each figure are presented in the upper right corner of the corresponding image. It is generally acknowledged that a value less than 0.1 indicates a satisfactory level of fitting performance. Obviously, the two-dimensional Gaussian function is more effective in fitting IoU distribution for small objects. The specific implementation process is outlined as follows: For the label of each point, we define it as:

$$\sum_{i \in GT_\alpha} label_i = \begin{cases} 1, \text{IoU}\{A_i, GT_\alpha\} < T_\alpha \\ 0, \qquad \text{else} \end{cases} \tag{1}$$

Here, $GT\alpha$ represents the α-th ground truth box in the image, i denotes the set of points lying around $GT\alpha$, and A_i represents the anchor box generated at the i-th point. With the introduction of a size prediction layer for anchors, we can reduce the size of candidate anchors after screening positive and negative samples. Consequently, generating anchors of the same size at each point is adequate. The IoU function represents the intersection over union between the anchor box generated at the i-th point and the ground truth box that contains the point. T_α represents the filter threshold that sets apart the α-th ground truth box in the image and is defined as follows:

$$T_\alpha = mean_\alpha + 2 \times \sqrt{var_\alpha}, \tag{2}$$

Here, $mean_\alpha$ represents the mathematical expectation of the IoU between all anchor boxes and the ground truth box within the region α. Similarly, var_α denotes the statistical variance of IoU distribution in the same region.

In Fig. 6, we conducted an empirical study by comparing the average number of positively labeled samples obtained from 100 small object proposals using different methods. The left panel displays the count of positive samples obtained using our suggested adaptive threshold processing, whereas the right panel depicts the count of positive samples obtained using conventional center

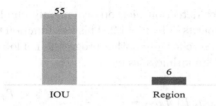

Fig. 6. Mathematical expectations for a positive sample screened out by 100 small proposals using different methods.

ratio partitioning techniques like GA-RPN. As indicated by the results, there was a notable increase in positively labeled samples for small objects. Specifically, our proposed method generated about ten times more positive samples than the conventional approach.

3.2 Candidate Box Size Prediction

The approach described in Sect. 3.1 can generate more positive samples for small objects, as shown in Fig. 4, but it uses fixed-size and fixed aspect ratio anchors, which has limitations. Using uniform-shaped anchors for small or large objects with varying aspect ratios results in lower coverage and incorrect matchings, leading to false positives or false negatives that reduce detection accuracy. To address this problem, we implemented a subnetwork that predicts anchor widths and heights to enable adaptive scaling and produce anchors matched to ground truth boxes. The subnetwork was added to the RPN and included a 1×1 convolution layer that provided two mapping channels for predicting width and height, allowing the subnetwork to learn the optimal shape for each location during training.

3.3 Loss Function Design

The proposed framework is optimized end-to-end by utilizing a multi-task loss. Apart from the traditional losses for classification L_{cls} and regression L_{reg}, we introduced an additional loss for anchor shape prediction, referred to as L_{shape}. These losses are jointly optimized to derive the total loss function presented below:

$$L = \lambda\, L_{shape} + L_{reg} + L_{cls}, \tag{3}$$

The modified version of the bounded IoU loss is used for optimizing the anchor's shape prediction. This version eliminates the need for explicit target computation. The loss is defined in Eq. 4. (ω, h) represents the predicted anchor shape, while (ω_g, h_g) represents the shape of the corresponding ground-truth bounding box. L_1 represents the smooth L1 loss.

$$L_{shape} = L_1\left(1 - min\left(\frac{\omega}{\omega_g}, \frac{\omega_g}{\omega}\right)\right) + L_1\left(1 - min\left(\frac{h}{h_g}, \frac{h_g}{h}\right)\right), \tag{4}$$

The prevalent object detection methods commonly employ the Smooth L1 loss, which merges the merits of L1 and L2. This loss function utilizes the squared function in proximity to zero for a smoother progression of loss derivative towards zero, resolving the non-smoothness issue.

$$Smooth\ L1\ Loss = \begin{cases} \frac{loss^2}{2T_\beta}, & x < T_\beta \\ loss - 0.5T_\beta, & xelse \end{cases} \qquad (5)$$

The parameter T_β is typically assigned a value of 1 and is used as the threshold for gradient changes in the loss function. As the model's training progresses, and the difference between the predicted anchor shape and ground-truth bounding box shape decreases, the gradient changes in the loss function become less pronounced. Consequently, the effects of the fixed T_β parameter gradually diminish, resulting in slower model fitting. To address this issue, we suggest dynamically adjusting the loss function gradient cutoff value by having T_β change adaptively during training based on input data distribution. We calculate the errors of the width and height predictions, sort them in ascending order, and use the geometric mean of the K-th smallest error, where K equals $P \times Length(Error)$ and the P-percentile position's value to identify the new cutoff value. This approach can effectively enhance training fitting efficacy.

$$T_\beta = \sqrt{Error_P \times Error_K}, \qquad (6)$$

Clearly, alternative methods for selecting the cutoff value include employing the minimum, maximum, median, or arithmetic mean of $Error_K$ and $Error_P$. Following a comprehensive evaluation, we selected the geometric mean as the optimal choice for the cutoff value.

4   Experiment

4.1   Experimental Setting

- We conducted experiments on the challenging MS COCO 2017 benchmark [2], which includes 118K training, 5K validation, and 20K test-dev images. The *train* split was used for training, and the performance was reported on the *val* split. Detection results were reported on the *test-dev* split.
- We utilized ResNet-50 with FPN as our backbone network, unless stated otherwise. Our method employed multi-scale training (resizing input such that the shorter side ranged from 480 to 800 and the longer side at most 1333), AdamW optimizer (initial learning rate of 0.0001, weight decay of 0.05, batch size of 16), and 1x schedule (12 epochs). In the multi-task loss function, we assign $\lambda = 0.1$ to balance the shape prediction branch. Runtime is measured on an A5000 GPU.

Table 1. Comparisons with different object detectors on COCO 2017 test-dev set.

Method	AP	AP_{50}	AP_{75}	AP_S	AP_M	AP_L	runtime(s/img)
RetinaNet	36.4	56.2	39.2	21.2	40.3	48.3	0.10
FCOS	41.6	60.9	45.8	23.6	45.1	53.5	0.12
Faster RCNN	38.2	59.5	41.9	30.2	41.6	50.0	0.09
GA-RPN	39.9	59.8	42.6	31.4	45.9	54.2	0.13
Sparse RCNN	40.8	60.2	44.4	31.4	44.4	55.7	0.23
ATSS	45.2	63.2	51.5	31.9	48.8	58.0	0.32
Adaptive RPN(OURS)	**46.2**	**64.1**	**52.6**	**34.1**	**50.4**	**58.2**	0.15

– The MS COCO dataset contains many objects with varying sizes and complex backgrounds. Performance was evaluated using average precision (AP) metrics, including AP with IoU threshold set at 0.5 (AP_{50}), AP with IoU threshold set at 0.75 (AP_{75}), as well as separate normalized AP metrics for object size: AP for small(AP_S), medium(AP_M), and large(AP_L) objects.

4.2 Results

Table 1 compares our proposed Adaptive RPN with state-of-the-art (SOTA) object detection methods on the COCO dataset, all trained using the same method. As demonstrated by Table 1, one-stage solutions encounter difficulties in achieving satisfactory results for small object detection. For example, RetinaNet and FCOS, representative one-stage object detection methods, deliver significantly lower performance than their two-stage counterparts. RetinaNet achieves an AP_S of 21.2, FCOS obtains 23.6, while other methods perform above 30. One-stage methods typically construct feature pyramids beginning from the C3 level. However, low-level features are critical for small objects, rendering the poor outcomes even when RetinaNet and FCOS start constructing the pyramid from the C2 level. This is mainly because one-stage methods lack feature alignment, hindering effective feature representations for small objects.

Faster RCNN continues to be a prominent two-stage object detection algorithm. Our evaluation of the COCO dataset indicates that Faster RCNN achieved an AP score of 38.2, while our proposed Adaptive RPN approach attained an AP score of 46.2. Accordingly, we observed an 8.0% performance improvement compared to Faster RCNN and a 1.0% improvement compared to ATSS, the current SOTA two-stage model. These outcomes underscore the effectiveness of our Adaptive RPN approach for object detection tasks. Notably, our approach led to improvements in both AP_S and AP_M by 2.2% and 1.6%, respectively. Such gains may be attributed to our relative size-based definition for small objects, which allows our program to optimize performance further by reclassifying some medium-sized objects as small. These findings attest to the efficiency of our optimized small object detection algorithm.

Table 2. The effect of each module in our design. A.T., S.P. and L.D. denote adaptive threshold, shape prediction and loss function design, respectively.

A.T.	S.P.	L.D.	AR_{100}	AR_{300}	AR_{1000}	AR_S	AR_M	AR_L	Training time
			46.1	53.4	58.0	30.4	53.9	63.1	24 h
✓			52.6	58.8	62.4	39.4	63.4	65.0	42 h
	✓		52.4	58.6	62.2	35.1	61.7	70.2	30 h
		✓	46.6	53.5	58.1	33.4	54.4	63.3	26 h
✓		✓	53.7	59.2	62.6	39.9	53.6	65.4	38 h
	✓	✓	53.4	59.0	62.3	35.2	61.8	70.2	28 h
✓	✓		57.8	63.9	67.1	42.6	68.1	77.5	45 h
✓	✓	✓	**59.0**	**65.0**	**67.6**	**45.9**	**69.6**	77.5	39 h

4.3   Ablation Study

To study the effectiveness and interrelationships of different components, we omitted various design elements, such as Adaptive Threshold, Shape Prediction, and Loss Function Design. We evaluated the performance using average recall rates (AR) at IoU thresholds ranging from 0.5 to 0.95 and reported AR_{100}, AR_{300}, and AR_{1000} or 100, 300, and 1000 proposals per image, respectively. The AR for small, medium, and large objects (AR_S, AR_M, AR_L) was calculated with 100 proposals. To evaluate the detection results, we used the standard COCO metric, measuring the mAP over IoUs ranging from 0.5 to 0.95. Table 2 shows the results, with both Adaptive Threshold and Shape Prediction improving overall performance by 4.4% and 4.2%, respectively. Loss Function Design was also utilized to accelerate convergence, resulting in significant improvements in training efficiency and shorter training times when used.

When examining the interrelationships between components, Adaptive Threshold and Shape Prediction yielded a 11.7% gain, while adding the proposed AR_S approach achieved a 15.5% improvement over individual modules. The Adaptive Threshold module adjusts object positive sample counts by manipulating thresholds, increases small object samples appropriately, leading to an overall enhancement of detection performance. Conversely, the Shape Prediction module resizes object positive samples for more accurate shape matching, leading to higher-quality proposal generation and higher detection accuracy. Essentially, the Adaptive Threshold module increases small object samples, while Shape Prediction improves their quality; these two modules work together to significantly improve small object detection performance.

Adaptive Threshold. In Sect. 3.1, we elaborated on our Adaptive Threshold module and discussed our threshold selection process. To ensure the scientific rigor and reliability of our approach, we conducted ablation experiments using different threshold selection methods. Table 3 presents the results obtained from various threshold selection techniques, including mathematical expectation,

Table 3. The ablation studies for using mean, median, mean-plus-variance, one standard deviation, two standard deviations, three standard deviations and nothing as the IoU threshold strategies.

Threshold method	AR_{100}	AR_{300}	AR_{1000}	AR_S
–	46.1	53.4	58.0	30.4
Mean	46.8	53.6	58.4	30.7
Median	46.9	53.5	58.2	30.5
Mean+$\sqrt{var}$	51.0	56.8	60.1	37.8
Mean+var	52.4	58.5	62.2	39.0
Mean+$3\sqrt{var}$	50.7	57.5	60.9	38.2
all	40.6	49.2	55.4	30.2
Mean+$2\sqrt{var}$	52.6	58.8	62.4	39.4

median, mathematical expectation plus variance, one standard deviation, two standard deviations, three standard deviations, and no thresholding for sample filtering. Our statistical approach demonstrated that all methods enhanced the recall rate for small objects. As we selected more positive samples, from mean and median to one standard deviation, then to variance and ultimately to two standard deviations, the recall rate for small objects increased gradually. However, a linear relationship between the recall rate and positive samples count was not indicated. Using three standard deviations to identify additional positive samples decreased the recall rate for small objects. When we did not employ a threshold for filtering out small object samples and treated all non-zero IoUs as positive samples, excessive high numbers of positive samples skewed the balance between positive and negative samples, erroneously labeled easy negative samples as positive, providing invalid information rendering the training process ineffective. A large number of falsely identified cases as positive also increased the false alarm rate and decreased the recall rate. Thus, selecting an appropriate positive sample selection method is critical. After careful consideration, we chose two standard deviations as our threshold selection method.

Loss Function Design. In Sect. 3.3, we presented a variant of smooth L1 loss to dynamically adjust gradient thresholds based on the distribution of training output losses, thereby hastening convergence speed. We evaluated the efficacy of using minimum, maximum, median, arithmetic mean, and geometric mean to adjust the threshold of the loss function gradient, as shown in Table 4. Among the proposed methods, those utilizing minimum, median, and mean adjustments outperformed the baseline method in terms of average precision. The highest improvement came from the geometric mean and arithmetic mean methods. The median adjustment method exhibited slightly less progress than the mean method. The smallest gain was achieved by the minimum adjustment method. For some performance measurements, such as the average precision of medium

Table 4. The Ablation studies for using geometric average, arithmetic average, maximum, minimum or median strategies to adjust the loss hyper-parameter.

Method	AP	$AP_{0.5}$	$AP_{0.75}$	AP_S	AP_M	AP_L
-	35.7	59.5	41.9	30.2	41.6	50.0
Min	38.3	59.3	42.3	30.6	41.5	49.7
Max	37.4	59.1	40.1	29.4	41.1	48.4
Median	39.0	59.2	43.7	31.9	43.1	50.0
Arithmetic	39.1	59.4	43.6	32.0	42.8	50.2
Geometric	39.2	59.4	43.5	32.1	42.9	50.2

objects, even the median adjustment method showed more improvement than the arithmetic mean method. It was found that different adjustment methods have varying effects on the accuracy of objects of various sizes. The median adjustment method and the mean adjustment method were deemed robust. The experimental findings for the maximum adjustment method were generally poor, even lower than the baseline method. This suggests that a larger threshold would reduce the quantity and quality of positive samples, ultimately decreasing the accuracy in detecting targets of various image sizes. After comprehensive consideration, we chose the geometric mean adjustment method for its superior precision in accelerating model convergence.

5   Conclusion

This paper proposes an anchor-based adaptive training method that improves object detection accuracy by adjusting the positive sample selection strategy to fit objects of different sizes. For small objects, specific sample selection and loss function strategies are defined to enhance the model's focus on detecting small objects. Anchor shape prediction and regression techniques are employed to optimize the anchor size and improve the candidate anchors' fit to the object size, resulting in higher quality detection results. The proposed method is applied to train Faster R-CNN on the MS COCO dataset, significantly improving the ability to detect small objects and demonstrating strong robustness towards objects with extreme aspect ratios.

Acknowledgement. This work was supported by "Youth Innovative Research Team of Capital Normal University", Project of High-level Teachers in Beijing Municipal Universities in the Period of 13th Five-year Plan CIT&TCD201804075 and STCSM 18DZ2270700.

References

1. Ren, S., He, K., Girshick, R., Sun, J.: Faster R-CNN: towards real-time object detection with region proposal networks. Cornell University - arXiv (2015)
2. Lin, T.-Y., et al.: Microsoft COCO: common objects in context. In: Fleet, D., Pajdla, T., Schiele, B., Tuytelaars, T. (eds.) Computer Vision – ECCV 2014. ECCV 2014. LNCS, vol. 8693, pp. 740–755. Springer, Cham (2014). https://doi.org/10.1007/978-3-319-10602-1_48, https://www.microsoft.com/en-us/research/publication/microsoft-coco-common-objects-in-context/
3. Wang, Y., Zhang, X., Yang, T., Sun, J.: Anchor DETR: query design for transformer-based detector. In: Proceedings of the AAAI Conference on Artificial Intelligence (2021)
4. Huang, T., et al.: DyRep: bootstrapping training with dynamic re-parameterization. In: 2022 IEEE/CVF Conference on Computer Vision and Pattern Recognition (CVPR), pp. 578–587 (2022). https://doi.org/10.1109/CVPR52688.2022.00067
5. Liu, S., et al.: DAB-DETR: dynamic anchor boxes are better queries for DETR (2022). https://arxiv.org/abs/2201.12329
6. Kaul, P., Xie, W., Zisserman, A.: Label, verify, correct: a simple few shot object detection method. In: 2022 IEEE/CVF Conference on Computer Vision and Pattern Recognition (CVPR), pp. 14217–14227 (2022). https://doi.org/10.1109/CVPR52688.2022.01384
7. Lim, J.-S., Astrid, M., Yoon, H.-J., Lee, S.-I.: Small object detection using context and attention. arXiv: Computer Vision and Pattern Recognition (2019)
8. Wang, C., Wang, H., Pan, P.: Local contrast and global contextual information make infrared small object salient again (2023)
9. Xiangsuo, F., Wenlin, Q., Juliu, L., Qingnan, H., Fan, Z.: Dim and small target detection based on spatio-temporal filtering and high-order energy estimation. IEEE Photonics J. **15**(2), 1–20 (2023). https://doi.org/10.1109/JPHOT.2023.3242991
10. Park, C.-W., Seo, Y., Sun, T.-J., Lee, G.-W., Huh, E.-N.: Small object detection technology using multi-modal data based on deep learning. In: 2023 International Conference on Information Networking (ICOIN), pp. 420–422 (2023). https://doi.org/10.1109/ICOIN56518.2023.10049014
11. Zhang, S., Chi, C., Yao, Y., Lei, Z., Li, S.Z.: Bridging the gap between anchor-based and anchor-free detection via adaptive training sample selection. In: 2020 IEEE/CVF Conference on Computer Vision and Pattern Recognition (CVPR), pp. 9756–9765 (2020). https://doi.org/10.1109/CVPR42600.2020.00978
12. Kim, K., Lee, H.S.: Probabilistic anchor assignment with IoU prediction for object detection (2020). https://arxiv.org/abs/2007.08103
13. Wang, J., Chen, K., Yang, S., Loy, C.C., Lin, D.: Region proposal by guided anchoring. In: 2019 IEEE/CVF Conference on Computer Vision and Pattern Recognition (CVPR), pp. 2960–2969 (2019). https://doi.org/10.1109/CVPR.2019.00308

Automatic Driving Scenarios: A Cross-Domain Approach for Object Detection

Shengheng Liu[1,2]([envelope]) [ID], Jiacheng Chen[2], Lei Li[3], Yahui Ma[4], and Yongming Huang[1] [ID]

[1] School of Information Science and Engineering, Southeast University,
Nanjing 210096, China
s.liu@seu.edu.cn
[2] Southeast University-Monash University Joint Graduate School,
Suzhou 215123, China
[3] Hella Shanghai Electronics Co., Ltd., Shanghai 201201, China
[4] China Academy of Electronics and Information Technology, Beijing 100041, China

Abstract. As autonomous driving technology advances, the need for accurate and robust object detection in various driving environments has become more urgent. However, domain adaptation presents a significant challenge due to the impact of weather, lighting, and scene context on object detection models. To address this issue, we propose a new method that utilizes pseudo-labels. Our approach involves two modules: the Category-Adversarial-Adaptive (CAA) and the Regression-Adversarial-Adaptive (RAA), which generate pseudo-labels. The detector is then trained on both source domain data and the target domain with pseudo-labels, resulting in improved cross-domain performance. The CAA and RAA modules operate independently and complement each other, allowing them to adapt to their respective detection tasks without interference. Furthermore, we demonstrate the effectiveness of loss smoothing in enhancing the model's generalization performance. Our experimental results indicate that our model outperforms classic models, achieving improvements of 0.9%, 2%, and 1.4% in the cross-domain challenges of SIM10K to Cityscape, KITTI to Cityscape, and Cityscape to foggyCityscape, respectively.

Keywords: Domain Adaptation · Pseudo-Label · Loss Smoothing · Automatic Driving · Object Detection

1 Introduction

Object detection is a fundamental task in autonomous driving scenarios to ensure the safety of passengers, pedestrians, and cars. In the past few years, the rapid development of the deep learning field has greatly enhanced the performance of the target detector [1–4] and achieved excellent performance on the benchmark dataset [5–7].

This work was supported in part by the National Natural Science Foundation of China under Grant Nos. 62001103 and U1936201.

Fig. 1. Images captured in various driving scenarios. Examples from KITTI [8], Foggy Cityscapes [9], SIM10K [10], Cityscapes [11] and real photos of China's traffic show visual dissimilarities, making cross-domain object detection challenging.

However, most of the existing object detection models are designed to work in a specific domain. There are still many challenges to be addressed in cross-domain object detection, which refers to detecting objects in a new domain that is significantly different from the source domain used for training. In autonomous driving scenarios, cross-domain object detection is particularly important since it is difficult to collect training data that cover all possible scenarios, and the appearance and texture of objects may vary significantly across different domains. Figure 1 shows several data sets related to automatic driving scenarios, where we can observe considerable changes in the field.

Current cross-domain object detection models [12–15] employ adaptive modules to reduce distribution disparities between source and target domains by aligning features at varying levels. However, instance-level adaptation may cause confusion between foreground and background features, leading to loss of actual objects and generation of false object proposals. Image-level adaptation can also merge features of different objects in a detected input image. The placement of these modules within the detection architecture influences the model's performance. Moreover, previous adaptive algorithms primarily addressed changes in object categories, overlooking regression prediction issues, necessitating further exploration.

To overcome these problems, we establish two crucial components after the detector, namely the Category-Adversarial-Adaptive (CAA) module and the Regression-Adversarial-Adaptive (RAA) module, which are designed to be independent of the detector to prevent the potential harm to its distinguishability caused by countermeasure alignment. To address the challenges of multitask, it is essential to recognize that different components of a system may need to adapt independently of one another. Therefore, the parameters of the regression-adversarial adaptive-module is independent of the Category-Adversarial-Adaptive module. Further, We explore how to enhance the generalization of cross-domain object detection models through smoothing the loss of two adversarial adaptive modules.

The contributions of this work are summarized as three-fold:

- We build a Category-Adversarial-Adaptive module and a Regression-Adversarial-Adaptive module for cross-domain object detection tasks, which are designed to be detector-independent and adapt to the respective tasks independently.
- We discuss how to optimize two Adversarial-Adaptive modules to further enhance the generalization of the cross-domain object detection model.
- We conducted experiments for autonomous driving scenarios show that compared with other classical models, our model has achieved 0.9%, 2% and 1.4% improvements in the three cross-domain challenges of SIM10K to Cityscape, KITTI to Cityscape and Cityscape to foggyCityscape, respectively.

2   Related Work

Object detection: Object detection is a crucial task in various applications, and CNN-based methods are widely adopted to improve detection performance. These methods can be categorized into one-stage and two-stage detectors. Two-stage detectors, including R-CNN [16], Fast R-CNN [17], and Faster R-CNN [18], have been proven to achieve high accuracy. Recently, Swin transformer [1] has emerged as a promising backbone network for two-stage detectors, achieving state-of-the-art performance. Meanwhile, one-stage detectors, such as SSD [19], YOLO-series detectors [3, 20–22], and Retina Net [23], directly predict bounding box and category confidence. However, improving domain adaptation for specific scenarios may not be sufficient for real-world applications with diverse target domains. Our paper aims to address this challenge by improving the generalization of object detectors to new target domains.

Domain adaptation for object detection: The pioneering work in transferring object detectors across domains is DA-Faster [12], which proposes aligning the backbone and ROI features. This approach inspires numerous subsequent studies to enhance detector transferability through improved feature alignment schemes [15, 24–26]. SWDA [15] prioritizes local over global feature alignment. Selective-DA [24] aligns discriminative regions to enhance object detection, and GPA [25] refines instance features with graph-based propagation for category alignment. MAF [26] employs hierarchical alignment and scale reduction modules to strengthen adversarial domain adaptation. Besides the DA-Faster [12] based variants, Petru [27] leverages pseudo-labels generated from target domain samples for cross-domain performance. RPNPA [28] improved Cross-domain detection by aligning RPN features, learnable prototypes, and improving proposal generation. KTNet [29] improves cross-domain object detection with shared classifier and knowledge constraints. Hsu [30] method employs foreground pixel-focused center-aware alignment for cross-domain adaptation, and CRDA [31] uses multi-label classification as an auxiliary task for feature regularization. Although the auxiliary task of creating domain-invariant features to deceive a domain discriminator can enhance transferability in most aforementioned methods, it may also negatively affect the detector's discriminability. In contrast,

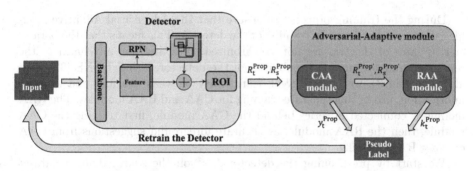

Fig. 2. Model network overview: Input processed by Detector to generate proposals, which train CAA and RAA modules. Trained modules generate pseudo-labels to retrain Detector.

our approach separates the adversarial adaptation module and detector into two distinct modules, focusing on domain transfer and performance improvement, respectively, which results in superior cross-domain outcomes.

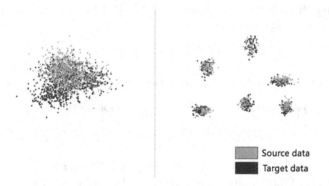

Fig. 3. The left image shows T-SNE visualizations of detector features, while the right image depicts those from the CAA module. Analysis reveals weaker regularity in features containing both classification and positioning information compared to classification-only features.

3 Proposed Method

3.1 Overall Process

For cross-domain target detection, we start with a labeled source dataset S of n items $R_s = \left\{ P_s^i, G_s^i, C_s^i \right\}_{i=1}^n$, where P_s^i denotes an image, G_s^i denotes the ground truth box, and C_s^i denotes the box category. We also have an unlabeled target dataset T of n items $R_t = \left\{ P_t^i \right\}_{i=1}^n$. Our goal is to train a detector D^{det} to achieve high performance on the target domain. The overall model schematic diagram is shown in Fig. 2.

During the training process, we ensure that the Adversarial-Adaptive modules are decoupled from the training of the detector. This means that the parameter updates of the two are not synchronized, thus avoiding any harm to the resolution and positioning capabilities of the detector. Using T-SNE [32] visualization (Fig. 3), we observe weak learnability between category and location information, prompting separate training for CAA and RAA modules. The RAA module is connected in series behind the CAA module, first training the CAA module, then the RAA module, as accurate foreground suggestions from CAA enhance RAA training.

We start by pre-training the detector D^{det} on the source domain dataset and use it to separate proposal distributions R_s^{Prop} and R_t^{Prop} from the source and target domains. The proposal distribution R^{Prop} is represented as $R^{Prop} = \{p^i, k^i, y^i, c^i\}_{i=1}^{n}$, with p as the proposed image region, k the predicted bounding boxes, y the predicted categories, and c the category confidence. We train the CAA module using these distributions, then use the trained CAA module to generate accurate foreground proposals for the Regression-Adversarial-Adaptive module training. Finally, we employ both trained adversarial-adaptive modules to obtain target domain category pseudo-label y_t^{cls} and regression pseudo-label k_t^{reg}, which are used to retrain the detector.

Regarding the detector, the Faster R-CNN [18] loss function is utilized for the first source domain training:

$$L_s^{det} = L_s^{rpn} + L_s^{roi} \tag{1}$$

The loss function used for retraining the Detector on the target domain is:

$$
\begin{aligned}
L_t^{det} = L_{cls}^{rpn}(y_t^{Prop}, y_t^{cls}) + \mathbb{J}(y_t^{cls})L_{reg}^{rpn}(k_t^{Prop}, k_t^{reg}) \\
+ L_{cls}^{roi}(y_t^{Prop}, y_t^{cls}) + \mathbb{J}(y_t^{cls})L_{reg}^{roi}(k_t^{Prop}, k_t^{reg})
\end{aligned}
\tag{2}
$$

where y_t^{Prop} and k_t^{Prop} are pertain to the proposal distribution R_t^{Prop}. The foreground indicator function $\mathbb{J}(y_t^{cls})$ is utilized to determine whether the predicted frame is classified as foreground, and the loss function is exclusively calculated in the case of a foreground classification.

3.2   Category-Adversarial-Adaptive (CAA) Module

This section covers the Category-Adversarial-Adaptive module, central to our approach. Understanding its mechanisms is key. The module aims to minimize L_{CAA} while maximizing adversarial loss L_{ad}^{cls} via the gradient reversal layer.

The construction of the Category-Adversarial-Adaptive module refers to the feature extractor and discriminator of the traditional DANN model and Fig. 4 displays the structural diagram. We denote the feature extractor as $f^{cls} = F^{cls}(x)$, the class predictor as $h^{cls} = H^{cls}(x)$, the discriminator as D^{cls} and the whole loss L_{CAA} can be defined as:

$$L_{CAA} = L_{CE}(H^{cls}(f_s^{cls}), y_s^{gt})_{R_s^{Prop}} + \lambda L_{ad}^{cls} \tag{3}$$

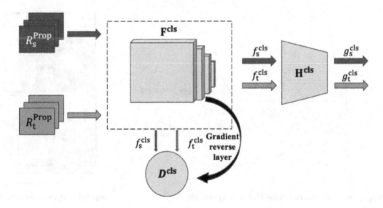

Fig. 4. Category-Adversarial-Adaptive (CAA) module: R_s^{Prop} and R_t^{Prop} feature extracted by F^{cls} module, and fed to D^{cls} discriminator and H^{cls} classifier. H^{cls} used for source domain classification loss, D^{cls} used for adversarial loss.

where L_{CE} is the cross-entropy loss, $f_s^{cls} = F^{cls}(p_s)$, L_{ad}^{cls} is the adversarial loss function explained in detail next, the trade-off between source risk and domain adversarial loss is represented by the symbol λ.

To improve training effectiveness, we adopt Jiang's [33] idea of discretizing input space and simplifying classification optimization. We use the confidence of each proposal to discretize input space. High-confidence proposals, either foreground or background, have a higher weight $\omega(c)$ in adaptation, and vice versa. This reduces the participation of proposals that are neither foreground nor background, and probabilistically improves input space discreteness. Thus, L_{ad}^{cls} is defined as:

$$L_{ad}^{cls} = \omega(c_s) \log D^{cls}(f_s^{cls}) + \omega(c_t) log[1 - D^{cls}(f_t^{cls})] \qquad (4)$$
$$f_s^{cls}, f_t^{cls} = F^{cls}(p_s), F^{cls}(p_t)$$

3.3 Regression-Adversarial-Adaptive (RAA) Module

In object detection regression, we only consider foreground boxes for regression prediction. Using the CAA module's predicted values y_t^{cls} and ground truth y_s^{gt}, we filter out irrelevant data from R_s^{Prop} and R_t^{Prop} to obtain $R_s^{Prop'}$ and $R_t^{Prop'}$ that only contain foreground bboxes. The RAA module has two key loss functions: regression loss L_{org}^{reg} and adversarial loss L_{ad}^{reg}. The RAA module's objective is to minimize the module loss L_{RAA} and maximizes adversarial loss L_{ad}^{reg}. This is accomplished through the utilization of gradient inversion layers. Figure 5 shows the diagram of the RAA module. The whole module loss L_{RAA} is defined as:

$$L_{RAA} = L_{org}^{reg} + \beta L_{ad}^{reg} \qquad (5)$$

where β is the trade-off between source risk and adversarial loss.

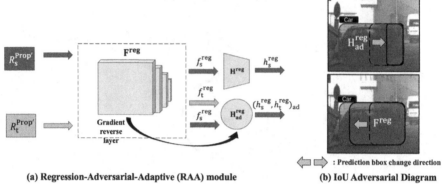

(a) Regression-Adversarial-Adaptive (RAA) module   **(b) IoU Adversarial Diagram**

Fig. 5. Regression-Adversarial-Adaptive (RAA) module:F^{reg} extracts $R_s^{Prop'}$ and $R_t^{Prop'}$, resulting in f_s^{reg} and f_t^{reg}. H^{reg} employs f_s^{reg} to generate h_s^{reg} for regression loss, while H_{ad}^{reg} uses both f_s^{reg} and f_t^{reg} for adversarial regression loss. F^{reg} minimizes the distance between H^{reg} and H_{ad}^{reg}'s predicted bounding boxes, while H_{ad}^{reg} maximizes their distance.

Our regression module uses smooth L1 loss to predict the bounding box offset for the object category. The ground-truth regression target for a class is denoted as $v = (v_x, v_y, v_w, v_h)$, and the predicted tuple as $t = (t_x, t_y, t_w, t_h)$. The feature extractor and class predictor are represented by $f^{reg} = F^{reg}(x)$ and $h^{reg} = H^{reg}(x)$, respectively. We use the following formula with the loss function L_{org}^{reg}:

$$L_{org}^{reg} = \sum_{i \in x,y,w,h} [Smooth_{L_1}(t_i^u)^m - v_i)]_{Rs Prop'} \tag{6}$$

$$t = H^{reg}(F^{reg}(p'_s))$$

We implement an IoU adversarial training strategy for regression adversarial loss based on [34]. As shown in Fig. 5(b), an adversarial component h_{ad}^{reg} is added to the prediction framework to keep it away from h^{reg} prediction while f^{reg} aligns their predictions. The resulting close prediction box encourages consistency between h_{ad}^{reg} and h^{reg} in the source domain, minimizing separation in the target domain. This technique effectively reduces the gap between h_{ad}^{reg} and h^{reg}, allowing f^{reg} to learn accurate source domain features and feature invariance across domains via IoU confrontation. The regression adversarial loss, L_{ad}^{reg}, is formulated as:

$$L_{ad}^{reg} = Smooth_{L_1}(H_{ad}^{reg}(F^{reg}(p'_t)), H^{reg}(F^{reg}(p'_t))) \\ - Smooth_{L_1}(H_{ad}^{reg}(F^{reg}(p'_s)), Hreg(Freg(p'_s))) \tag{7}$$

where $p'_t \in R_t^{Prop'}, p'_s \in R_s^{Prop'}$.

3.4   Smoothing Loss

Within this section, we aim to apply the concept of Sharpness-Aware Minimization (SAM) [35] to enhance the smoothness of our adversarial-adaptive module. The fundamental principle of SAM is to identify a smoother minimum (i.e., low loss within an ϵ neighborhood of θ) by optimizing the following objective function, which is formally expressed as:

$$\min_{\theta} \max_{\|\epsilon\|<\rho} L_{obj}(\theta + \epsilon) \tag{8}$$

where the objective of SAM is to minimize the objective function, L_{obj}, with a hyperparameter, $\rho \geq 0$, which defines the maximum norm for ϵ. For more information about SAM, please refer to the paper [35]. In a similar fashion, we can utilize the concept of SAM to identify the smooth minimum of the cross-entropy loss, L_{CE}, within the Category-Adversarial-Adaptive (CAA) module:

$$L_{CAA}^{Smooth} = L_{CE}(H^{cls}(\theta + \epsilon(\theta)), y_s^{gt})_{R_s^{Prop}} + \lambda L_{ad}^{cls} \tag{9}$$

where θ represents the model update weight.

We avoid adding a smoothness loss to the adversarial loss, as its main goal is to maximize the adversarial task. Using SAM in this loss would decrease the adversarial loss, hindering the model's cross-domain learning ability. Similarly, we don't use SAM in the regression module loss, as it measures frame offset using four predicted values. Introducing SAM would overcomplicate the loss function, impeding model convergence. We conducted experiments to confirm our theoretical analysis, with results in Table 3, supporting our argument.

4   Experiments

4.1   Settings

In our experiments, we use Faster R-CNN [18] with ResNet-101 [36] backbone as our object detector, trained and evaluated on two Nvidia RTX 3090 GPUs using PyTorch. We apply standard data augmentation techniques such as random flipping, scaling, and cropping.

To adapt to a new domain, we pre-train on the source domain for 12k iterations with a 0.005 learning rate, and then train the Adversarial-Adaptive module using ResNet-101. The Category-Adversarial-Adaptive (CAA) module uses SAM and SGD optimizers with a 0.01 learning rate, 0.9 momentum, and a batch size of 32 per domain. We set λ to 1 and $w(c)$ to 1 when $c > 0.5$, and 0 otherwise. The Regression-Adversarial-Adaptive module uses the same hyperparameters as the CAA module, with a training loss value of β set to 0.1. We double the Bounding Box Adapter's input size and train both modules for 10k iterations. Finally, we retrain the detector with pseudo-labels for 4k iterations, using an initial learning rate of 2.5 × 10-4, reduced to 2.5 × 10-5.

Table 1. Cityscape to Foggy Cityscape.

Method	Person	Rider	Car	Truck	Bus	Train	Motorcycle	Bicycle	mAP@0.5
Faster-rcnn (source)	33.8	34.8	39.6	18.6	27.9	6.3	18.2	25.5	25.6
DA-Faster [12]	23.0	31.0	40.5	22.1	35.3	20.2	20.0	27.1	27.7
BDC-Faster [15]	26.4	37.2	42.4	21.2	29.2	12.3	22.6	28.9	27.5
MAF [26]	28.2	39.5	43.9	23.8	39.9	33.3	29.2	33.9	34.0
Selective-DA [24]	33.5	38.0	48.5	26.5	39.0	23.3	28.0	33.6	33.8
CRDA [31]	32.9	43.8	49.2	27.2	**45.1**	36.4	30.3	34.6	37.4
CADA [30]	41.5	43.6	57.1	29.4	44.9	39.7	29.0	36.1	40.2
RPNPA [28]	45.5	36.8	49.6	**35.7**	33.6	**43.8**	**46.0**	32.5	40.5
KTNet [29]	**46.4**	43.2	60.6	25.8	41.2	40.4	30.7	38.8	40.9
Our model	42.5	**50.2**	**60.9**	30.5	43.1	37.5	35.4	**41.4**	**42.3**
Faster-rcnn (target)	44.7	43.9	64.7	31.5	48.8	44.0	31.0	36.7	43.2

Table 2. Experiments on two cross-domain challenges in SIM10K to Cityscape and KITTI to Cityscape

SIM10K to Cityscapes		KITTI to Cityscape	
Method	mAP@0.5 Car	Method	mAP@0.5 Car
Faster-rcnn (source)	34.6	Faster-rcnn (source)	35.7
DA-Faster [12]	38.9	DA-Faster [12]	38.5
BDC-Faster [15]	31.8	Selective DA [24]	42.5
MAF [26]	41.1	MAF [26]	41.0
MeGA-CDA [37]	44.8	MeGA-CDA [37]	43.0
CFFA [38]	43.8	CSL [27]	43.8
CADA [30]	49.0	CADA [30]	43.2
Our model	**49.9**	Our model	**45.8**
Faster-rcnn (target)	69.7	Faster-rcnn (target)	69.7

We evaluate our method using mAP@0.5 on target domain test sets and compare it with domain adaptation and non-adaptive object detection methods to prove its effectiveness. Our domain-adaptive model is tested on four datasets: KITTI, SIM10K, Cityscape, and Foggy Cityscape, across three adaptation scenarios: SIM10K to Cityscape, KITTI to Cityscape, and Cityscape to Foggy Cityscape.

4.2   Experiment Result

Table 1 presents a comparison between our proposed model and other existing models. The comparison reveals that our model outperforms others in the cross-domain challenges of Cityscape to Foggy Cityscape. Specifically, our model shows a remarkable improvement of 1.4 under the mAP 50.

Fig. 6. Visualization results: Faster-RCNN (source) on the left, DA-Faster in the middle, and our model on the right.

Table 2 presents the performance of our model when applied from challenges of SIM10K to Cityscape and KITTI to Cityscape. It should be noted that the backbones of the models in Table 2 are not consistent, however, we have taken the model with the best backbone performance for comparison purposes (Fig. 6).

4.3 Ablation Studies

This section investigates the impact of loss smoothing on adversarial-adaptive modules using ablation experiments. We compare performance with and without smoothing, using mAP $0.5(mAP@0.5)$ as the evaluation metric. Two domain shifts, SIM10K to KITTI and Cityscapes to KITTI, are assessed. Results:

Table 3. Ablation experiments based on two cross-domain challenges. Without smoothing: no smoothing measure, C: cls: SAM smoothing in the CAA classification loss, C: cls+adv: SAM smoothing in CAA classification and adversarial losses, R:cls: SAM smoothing in RAA classification loss, C+R: SAM smoothing in both CAA and RAA classification losses.

SIM10K to Cityscapes		KITTI to Cityscapes	
Method	$mAP@0.5\ Car$	Method	$mAP@0.5\ Car$
Our model (without smoothing)	46.67	Our model (without smoothing)	41.26
Our model (C:cls)	**49.95**	Our model (C:cls)	**45.79**
Our model (C:cls + adv)	48.06	Our model (C:cls+adv)	43.40
Our model (R:cls)	45.34	Our model (R:cls)	39.72
Our model (C+R)	46.53	Our model (C+R)	41.14

The experimental results in the Table 3 support our claim from Sect. 3.4 that smoothing adversarial loss and the RAA module significantly impacts model accuracy. However, it is crucial not to apply smoothing indiscriminately, as excessive smoothing can negatively affect model performance. Generally, the proposed loss function smoothing approach is effective for simple task loss functions, like classification loss functions. For more complex loss functions, like regression or adversarial loss, it's important to consider the potential impact of smoothing and make an informed decision based on the specific task and model architecture.

5   Conclusion

Our study proposes a novel approach for object detection domain adaptation in autonomous driving scenes. By incorporating adversarial-adaptive modules and loss smoothness, we have achieved significant improvements on the benchmark dataset for this domain, thereby validating the effectiveness of our proposed method. In practical applications, even more robust performance can be achieved by replacing the detector with a more powerful model. Additionally, we intend to explore the design of new adversarial-adaptive modules that can be extended to other vision tasks, beyond the scope of object detection.

References

1. Liu, Z., et al.: Swin transformer: hierarchical vision transformer using shifted windows. In: Proceedings of the IEEE/CVF International Conference on Computer Vision (2021)
2. Liu, Z., et al.: Swin Transformer V2: scaling up capacity and resolution. In: Proceedings of the IEEE/CVF Conference on Computer Vision and Pattern Recognition (2022)
3. Wang, C., Bochkovskiy, A., Liao, H.: YOLOv7: trainable bag-of-freebies sets new state-of-the-art for real-time object detectors. arXiv preprint arXiv:2207.02696 (2022)
4. Chen, Q., et al.: Group DETR v2: strong object detector with encoder-decoder pretraining. arXiv preprint arXiv:2211.03594 (2022)
5. Lin, T.-Y., et al.: Microsoft COCO: common objects in context. In: Fleet, D., Pajdla, T., Schiele, B., Tuytelaars, T. (eds.) ECCV 2014, Part V. LNCS, vol. 8693, pp. 740–755. Springer, Cham (2014). https://doi.org/10.1007/978-3-319-10602-1_48
6. Everingham, M., Van Gool, L., Williams, C.K.I., Winn, J., Zisserman, A.: The PASCAL visual object classes (VOC) challenge. Int. J. Comput. Vision 88, 303–338 (2010)
7. Sun, P., et al.: Scalability in perception for autonomous driving: Waymo open dataset. In: Proceedings of the IEEE/CVF Conference on Computer Vision and Pattern Recognition, pp. 2446–2454 (2020)
8. Geiger, A., Lenz, P., Stiller, C., Urtasun, R.: Vision meets robotics: the KITTI dataset. Int. J. Robot. Res. 32(11), 1231–1237 (2013)
9. Sakaridis, C., Dai, D., Van Gool, L.: Semantic foggy scene understanding with synthetic data. Int. J. Comput. Vision 126, 973–992 (2018)

10. Johnson-Roberson, M., Barto, C., Mehta, R., Sridhar, S.N., Rosaen, K., Vasudevan, R.: Driving in the matrix: can virtual worlds replace human-generated annotations for real world tasks? arXiv preprint arXiv:1610.01983 (2016)
11. Cordts, M., et al.: The cityscapes dataset for semantic urban scene understanding. In: Proceedings of the IEEE Conference on Computer Vision and Pattern Recognition, pp. 3213–3223 (2016)
12. Chen, Y., Li, W., Sakaridis, C., Dai, D., Van Gool, L.: Domain adaptive faster R-CNN for object detection in the wild. In: Proceedings of the IEEE Conference on Computer Vision and Pattern Recognition, pp. 3339–3348 (2018)
13. Xie, R., Yu, F., Wang, J., Wang, Y., Zhang, L.: Multi-level domain adaptive learning for cross-domain detection. In: Proceedings of the IEEE/CVF International Conference on Computer Vision Workshops. pp. 3213–3219 (2019)
14. Yang, X., Wan, S., Jin, P.: Domain-invariant region proposal network for cross-domain detection. In: 2020 IEEE International Conference on Multimedia and Expo (ICME), pp. 1–6. IEEE (2020)
15. Saito, K., Ushiku, Y., Harada, T., Saenko, K.: Strong-weak distribution alignment for adaptive object detection. In: Proceedings of the IEEE/CVF Conference on Computer Vision and Pattern Recognition, pp. 6956–6965 (2019)
16. Girshick, R., Donahue, J., Darrell, T., Malik, J.: Rich feature hierarchies for accurate object detection and semantic segmentation. In: Proceedings of the IEEE Conference on Computer Vision and Pattern Recognition, pp. 580–587 (2014)
17. Girshick, R.: Fast R-CNN. In: Proceedings of the IEEE International Conference on Computer Vision, pp. 1440–1448 (2015)
18. Ren, S., He, K., Girshick, R., Sun, J.: Faster R-CNN: towards real-time object detection with region proposal networks. In: Advances in Neural Information Processing Systems, vol. 28 (2015)
19. Liu, W., et al.: SSD: single shot multibox detector. In: Leibe, B., Matas, J., Sebe, N., Welling, M. (eds.) Computer Vision-ECCV 2016: 14th European Conference, Amsterdam, The Netherlands, 11–14 October 2016, Proceedings, Part I 14, pp. 21–37. Springer, Cham (2016). https://doi.org/10.1007/978-3-319-46448-0_2
20. Redmon, J., Divvala, S., Girshick, R., Farhadi, A.: You Only Look Once: unified, real-time object detection. In: Proceedings of the IEEE Conference on Computer Vision and Pattern Recognition, pp. 779–788 (2016)
21. Redmon, J., Farhadi, A.: YOLO9000: better, faster, stronger. In: Proceedings of the IEEE Conference on Computer Vision and Pattern Recognition, pp. 7263–7271 (2017)
22. Redmon, J., Farhadi, A.: YOLOv3: an incremental improvement. arXiv preprint arXiv:1804.02767 (2018)
23. Lin, T.Y., Goyal, P., Girshick, R., He, K., Dollár, P.: Focal loss for dense object detection. In: Proceedings of the IEEE International Conference on Computer Vision, pp. 2980–2988 (2017)
24. Zhu, X., Pang, J., Yang, C., Shi, J., Lin, D.: Adapting object detectors via selective cross-domain alignment. In: Proceedings of the IEEE/CVF Conference on Computer Vision and Pattern Recognition, pp. 687–696 (2019)
25. Xu, M., Wang, H., Ni, B., Tian, Q., Zhang, W.: Cross-domain detection via graph-induced prototype alignment. In: Proceedings of the IEEE/CVF Conference on Computer Vision and Pattern Recognition, pp. 12355–12364 (2020)
26. He, Z., Zhang, L.: Multi-adversarial faster-RCNN for unrestricted object detection. In: Proceedings of the IEEE/CVF International Conference on Computer Vision, pp. 6668–6677 (2019)

27. Soviany, P., Ionescu, R.T., Rota, P., Sebe, N.: Curriculum self-paced learning for cross-domain object detection. Comput. Vis. Image Underst. **204**, 103166 (2021)
28. Zhang, Y., Wang, Z., Mao, Y.: RPN prototype alignment for domain adaptive object detector. In: Proceedings of the IEEE/CVF Conference on Computer Vision and Pattern Recognition, pp. 12425–12434 (2021)
29. Tian, K., Zhang, C., Wang, Y., Xiang, S., Pan, C.: Knowledge mining and transferring for domain adaptive object detection. In: Proceedings of the IEEE/CVF International Conference on Computer Vision, pp. 9133–9142 (2021)
30. Hsu, C.C., Tsai, Y.H., Lin, Y.Y., Yang, M.H.: Every pixel matters: center-aware feature alignment for domain adaptive object detector. In: Vedaldi, A., Bischof, H., Brox, T., Frahm, J.M. (eds.) Computer Vision-ECCV 2020: 16th European Conference, Glasgow, UK, 23–28 August 2020, Proceedings, Part IX 16, vol. 12354, pp. 733–748. Springer, Cham (2020). https://doi.org/10.1007/978-3-030-58545-7_42
31. Xu, C.D., Zhao, X.R., Jin, X., Wei, X.S.: Exploring categorical regularization for domain adaptive object detection. In: Proceedings of the IEEE/CVF Conference on Computer Vision and Pattern Recognition, pp. 11724–11733 (2020)
32. Van der Maaten, L., Hinton, G.: Visualizing data using t-SNE. J. Mach. Learn. Res. **9**(11), 2579–2605 (2008)
33. Jiang, J., Chen, B., Wang, J., Long, M.: Decoupled adaptation for cross-domain object detection. arXiv preprint arXiv:2110.02578 (2021)
34. Zhang, Y., Liu, T., Long, M., Jordan, M.: Bridging theory and algorithm for domain adaptation. In: International Conference on Machine Learning. PMLR (2019)
35. Foret, P., Kleiner, A., Mobahi, H., Neyshabur, B.: Sharpness-aware minimization for efficiently improving generalization. arXiv preprint arXiv:2010.01412 (2020)
36. He, K., Zhang, X., Ren, S., Sun, J.: Deep residual learning for image recognition. In: Proceedings of the IEEE Conference on Computer Vision and Pattern Recognition, pp. 770–778 (2016)
37. Vs, V., Gupta, V., Oza, P., Sindagi, V.A., Patel, V.M.: Mega-CDA: memory guided attention for category-aware unsupervised domain adaptive object detection. In: Proceedings of the IEEE/CVF Conference on Computer Vision and Pattern Recognition, pp. 4516–4526 (2021)
38. Zheng, Y., Huang, D., Liu, S., Wang, Y.: Cross-domain object detection through coarse-to-fine feature adaptation. In: Proceedings of the IEEE/CVF Conference on Computer Vision and Pattern Recognition, pp. 13766–13775 (2020)

Dual Attention Feature Fusion
for Visible-Infrared Object Detection

Yuxuan Hu[1,2], Limin Shi[3], Libo Yao[4], and Lubin Weng[3(✉)]

[1] State Key Laboratory of Multimodal Artificial Intelligence Systems, Institute of Automation, Chinese Academy of Sciences, Beijing, China
[2] School of Artificial Intelligence, University of Chinese Academy of Sciences, Beijing, China
[3] Research Center of Aerospace Information, Institute of Automation, Chinese Academy of Sciences, Beijing, China
lubin.weng@ia.ac.cn
[4] Institute of Information Fusion, Naval Aviation University, Yantai, China

Abstract. Feature fusion is an essential component of multimodal object detection to exploit the complementary information and common information between multi-source images. When it comes to visible-infrared image pairs, however, the visible images are prone to illumination and visibility and there may be a lot of interference information and little useful information. We suggest performing common feature enhancement and spatial cross attention sequentially to solve this problem. For this purpose, a novel Dual Attention Transformer Feature Fusion (DATFF) module which is designed for feature fusion of intermediate feature maps is proposed. We integrate it into two-stream object detectors and achieve state-of-the-art performance on DroneVehicle and FLIR visible-infrared object detection datasets. Our code is available at https://github.com/a21401624/DATFF.

Keywords: Feature fusion · Visible-infrared · Object detection

1 Introduction

Multimodal image data, such as visible-infrared image pairs, have been widely used in image analysis such as object detection. Visible (RGB) images are rich in texture feature but are vulnerable to changes in illumination and visibility; infrared images mainly contains coarse contour information but are robust to such changes. Visible-infrared object detectors exploit complementary and common information of visible-infrared image pairs and are more robust. They are especially useful in autonomous vehicles, security monitoring and aerial remote sensing.

This research was supported by the National Key Research and Development Program of China under Grant No. 2018AAA0100400, and the National Natural Science Foundation of China under Grants 91538201, and 62076242.

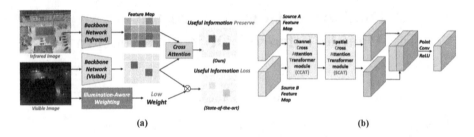

Fig. 1. (a) Holistic assessment of illumination may cause information loss. Our proposed method uses spatial cross attention to remedy this. (b) The components of our proposed DATFF module.

Pedestrian detection using visible-infrared image pairs is a representative application of multimodal object detection. Visible-infrared remote sensing data are also used for vehicle detection. Most existing works use two-stream object detectors with neural networks for feature fusion of intermediate feature maps of visible and infrared images. Various types of feature fusion modules using attention mechanisms have significantly improved the performance.

Despite the above mentioned progress, some issues still need to be considered. As visible images are prone to illumination and visibility, visible images taken at dark nights or on foggy days may only contain little useful information. This phenomenon is more common in remote sensing scenarios. Take the image pair in Fig. 1(a) as an example, only the areas lit by streetlamps contain useful information. Some state-of-the-arts [6, 25] calculate weights for feature maps or detection heads by holistic illumination assessment. The visible feature maps are assigned lower weights when the illumination conditions are poor. Such a mechanism suppresses interference information but also causes the loss of useful information as shown in Fig. 1(a).

To achieve the goal of utilizing useful information and getting rid of interference information, we propose to leverage spatial cross attention from infrared to visible feature maps. The useful information in the visible feature map will be retrieved by semantically similar parts of the infrared feature map while the interference information will have no effect. In essence, this is the process of extracting complementary information and the process should be bidirectional, i.e., from visible to infrared and vice versa. As there are common features and unique features in each modality, the common features play more roles in cross attention. Therefore, we amplify the common features of each modality before performing feature complement.

According to the above analysis, we put forward a novel Dual Attention Transformer Feature Fusion (DATFF) module consisting of a Channel Cross Attention Transformer (CCAT) module and a Spatial Cross Attention Transformer (SCAT) module. The CCAT module is responsible for amplifying the channels of common features while the SCAT module is designed to perform spatial-wise feature complement. Finally, a much more powerful feature representation is generated.

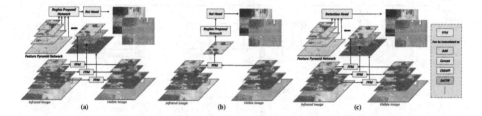

Fig. 2. Our two-stream object detectors used in this paper. FFM represents feature fusion module and can be instantiated into multiple modules. (a) depicts two-stage detectors w/ FPN. (b) depicts two-stage detectors w/o FPN. (c) depicts one-stage detectors w/ FPN.

Transformers [17] are adept at modeling long-range relationships in sequences and they are suitable for our purpose. Our DATFF design incorporates the advantages of prior works using transformers in computer vision [1,5] and multimodal feature fusion [11,24]. Our DATFF has good versatility as it can be used in different two-stream detectors. Experiment results on two visible-infrared object detection datasets demonstrate its effectiveness.

2   Related Work

2.1   Visible-Infrared Pedestrian Detection

Visible-infrared pedestrian detectors achieve around-the-clock monitoring. Recently, two-stream detectors based on common deep learning object detectors such as Faster R-CNN [14] and SSD [10] dominate the field. Generally, feature level fusion and decision level fusion are the two main streams of methodology. Simple concatenation [8] and addition operations represent early feature fusion solutions and various attention-based mechanisms have been proposed in recent years. Zhang *et al.* [23] used spatial attention in reweighting feature maps of two modalities to perform cross-modality feature interaction. Liu *et al.* [9] first divided the feature map of one modality into two parts to learn common features and unique features. Then the two parts of features were fused via channel attention. For decision level fusion, Li *et al.* [6] classified visible images into two types according to their illumination condition and generated fusion weights for two detection heads. Zhou *et al.* [25] further developed this approach and they used the weights on feature maps. Chen *et al.* [3] put forward a novel non-learned probabilistic ensembling method based on Bayes' rule and conditional independence assumption.

2.2   Visible-Infrared Remote Sensing Object Detection

Razakarivony *et al.* [13] proposed a small-scale visible-near infrared aerial vehicle detection dataset VEDAI. Sharma *et al.* [15] proposed YOLOrs which use simple concatenation for feature fusion. Fang *et al.* [12] designed two parallel modules

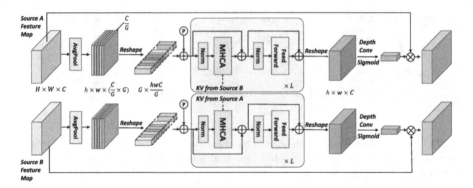

Fig. 3. The detailed structure of our proposed CCAT module.

utilizing channel attention. One module selects modality-shared features and the other enhances modality-specific features. Zhang *et al.* [22] introduced a super-resolution auxiliary task to help improve pixel-level fusion. Recently, Sun *et al.* [16] proposed the large-scale DroneVehicle visible-infrared vehicle detection dataset and the baseline method UA-CMDet which took the uncertainty of annotations into consideration. We use this dataset to verify the effectiveness of our method.

3   Methodology

Our proposed DATFF is a plug-and-play module for feature fusion of intermediate feature maps of visible-infrared image pairs. In Fig. 2, we depict the structure of the two-stream detectors we use in this paper. We adopt two-stage detectors w/ or w/o FPN [7] and one-stage detectors w/ FPN as usually FPN is used in one-stage detectors. As illustrated in Fig. 1(b), a DATFF consists of a CCAT module, a SCAT module and a convolution layer. The CCAT module can amplify the common features of two modalities while the SCAT module captures spatial-wise complementary information.

3.1   CCAT Module

There are common features between visible and infrared images and the CCAT module is designed to enhance such information. It is common knowledge that each channel in a feature map encodes a certain kind of information. Therefore, we can decompose the "abstract" common features into attention over some channels. If a channel of source A feature map contains the common feature, there are some channels containing the same feature in the source B feature map and the similarity score between this source A channel and those source B channels can be relatively high. We extract features to represent each channel and use cross attention to calculate the correlation between channels. Figure 3 illustrates the structure of the CCAT module.

We use adaptive average pooling to generate a feature vector of hw dims for each channel from the original $H \times W \times C$ feature map and flatten them into

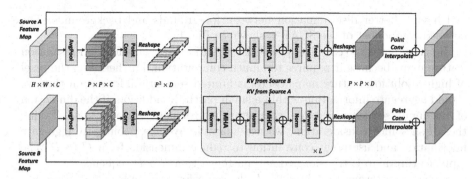

Fig. 4. The detailed structure of our proposed SCAT module.

a sequence. However, for high-dimensional feature maps (e.g., 2048 dims), the sequence is too long to compute the similarity matrix. We divide the C channels into G groups to reduce sequence length and every element of the sequence is of $\frac{hwC}{G}$ dims.

After adding the positional embedding vector, the two input sequences are fed into a cross transformer encoder with L blocks. The core component is the multi-head cross attention (MHCA) layer derived from multi-head attention (MHA) layer. MHA layer is a standard component of transformers which can be expressed as MHA($query$, key, $value$). Note that the $query$, key and $value$ are the same in MHA so we will denote it as MHA($\cdot$) below for brevity. For the MHCA layer, the $query$ and key are different while the key and $value$ remain the same. We will denote it as MHCA($query$, key, $value$). The computation process of the input sequence of source A can be formulated as follows:

$$S_i^{A'} = \text{MHCA}\left(\text{LN}(S_i^A), \text{LN}(S_1^B), \text{LN}(S_1^B)\right) + S_i^A \tag{1}$$

$$S_{i+1}^A = \text{FFN}\left(\text{LN}(S_i^{A'})\right) + S_i^{A'}, i = 1, ..., L \tag{2}$$

where S_i^A and S_i^B are input sequences of the ith transformer encoder from source A and B, LN($\cdot$) represents layer normalization and FFN($\cdot$) represents feed-forward network consists of two fully-connected layers and GeLU activation.

The output of the transformer encoder is reshaped to $h \times w \times C$ and processed by a depth convolution kernel with sigmoid activation to get a C-dimensional channel attention vector. Finally, the channels in the original feature map are reweighted by the vector.

3.2   SCAT Module

The SCAT module performs spatial cross attention. We use the transformer as the core of SCAT to perform global feature aggregation. This merit also contributes to better object detection for capturing relationships between objects and having better discrimination between foregrounds and backgrounds. The detailed component of the SCAT is shown in Fig. 4.

It is impractical to calculate pixel-wise attention especially for high-resolution feature maps because it requires too much computation. Furthermore, the pixel of high-resolution feature maps contains limited semantic information thus we should aggregate information within a small patch. In addition, if the dimension of the input sequence is large, computation problems will also arise. Taking these issues into consideration, we use adaptive average pooling to aggregate information and use point convolution to reduce dimension from C to D. The input feature map is transformed and flattened to a $P^2 \times D$ sequence.

Cross Transformer decoder with L blocks performs complementary information extraction and feature aggregation. There is an MHA layer and an MHCA layer in the decoder and the computation flow of the input sequence of source A can be formulated as follows:

$$S_i^{A'} = \text{MHA}\left(\text{LN}(S_i^A)\right) + S_i^A \tag{3}$$

$$S_i^{A''} = \text{MHCA}\left(\text{LN}(S_i^{A'}), \text{LN}(S_i^{B'}), \text{LN}(S_i^{B'})\right) + S_i^{A'} \tag{4}$$

$$S_{i+1}^A = \text{FFN}\left(\text{LN}(S_i^{A''})\right) + S_i^{A''}, i = 1, ..., L \tag{5}$$

where all the symbols have the same meaning as (1)-(2). The output sequences are rearranged and projected back to feature maps of C dims. Through bilinear interpolation, the feature maps are restored to the original resolution, and the final results are obtained by adding the original input feature maps.

4   Experiments

4.1   Data Description

We use two visible-infrared object detection datasets in our experiments. DroneVehicle [16] is a large-scale visible-infrared oriented aerial detection dataset with all images taken by a drone. There are 17990, 1469 and 8980 image pairs for training, validation, and testing. The images were taken in different illumination conditions and visibility. We use the annotations of infrared images as the ground truth. FLIR is a road scene dataset whose images were taken during daytime and nighttime. Zhang et al. [21] removed some unaligned image pairs and only kept the three most frequent classes. There are 4129 image pairs for training and 1013 pairs for testing. We use VOC2007 style AP50 as our evaluation metric for DroneVehicle and FLIR datasets.

4.2   Implementation Details

As we have mentioned in Sect. 3, we adopt two-stream detectors and the DATFF module is used to fuse intermediate feature maps of the same level. We use

Table 1. Comparisons on the DroneVehicle dataset. V denotes visible modality and I denotes infrared modality.

Methods	Modality	Car	Freight car	Truck	Bus	Van	mAP
UA-CMDet [16]	V+I	88.64	56.01	73.01	88.29	54.81	72.15
R^{3}Det [19]	I	90.07	46.76	58.12	87.45	40.36	64.55
R^{3}Det+CMAFF [12]	V+I	90.24	51.74	65.31	89.13	47.81	68.85
R^{3}Det+DATFF	V+I	90.31	55.20	68.41	89.33	51.85	71.02
Oriented R-CNN [18]	I	90.23	56.23	71.74	89.09	49.53	71.36
Oriented R-CNN+CMAFF [12]	V+I	90.36	58.49	76.73	89.66	56.81	74.41
Oriented R-CNN+DATFF	V+I	90.37	62.28	77.59	89.64	57.19	75.42
RoITransformer [4]	I	90.10	56.83	68.62	88.86	50.07	70.89
RoITransformer+CMAFF [12]	V+I	90.36	59.16	77.02	89.74	54.76	74.21
RoITransformer+DATFF	V+I	**90.39**	**63.56**	**78.08**	**89.89**	**58.10**	**76.00**

Table 2. Comparisons on the FLIR dataset.

Method	Modality	bicycle	person	car	mAP
Faster R-CNN [14]	Infrared	55.80	81.80	88.20	75.30
CFR[†] [21]	Visible+Infrared	57.77	74.49	84.91	72.39
GAFF[†] [20]	Visible+Infrared	59.40	76.60	85.50	73.80
CFT [11]	Visible+Infrared	61.73	**84.64**	**89.23**	78.53
UA-CMDet[†] [16]	Visible+Infrared	64.30	83.20	88.40	78.60
Faster R-CNN+CMAFF [12]	Visible+Infrared	65.83	82.78	88.95	79.19
Faster R-CNN+DATFF	Visible+Infrared	**68.87**	82.94	88.77	**80.19**

two two-stage oriented object detectors, Oriented R-CNN [18] and RoITransformer [4], an one-stage oriented object detector R^{3}Det [19] for the DroneVehicle dataset and a two-stage detector Faster R-CNN [14] for the FLIR dataset, with ImageNet-pretrained ResNet50 as the backbone. The FPN [7] in our detectors has four input stages. Our experiments are implemented on MMRotate [26] and MMDetection [2] toolbox using a TITAN RTX GPU. The training settings on DroneVehicle and FLIR datasets are identical to that in Sun et al.[16]. We experimented on Oriented R-CNN to determine the choices of hyperparameters of DATFF and keep them consistent on the other detectors. Specifically, we set the group number G and the reduced dimension D to 256. In the CCAT module, h and w are set to 16/8/8/4 for the four stages and P in SCAT is set to 10 for all stages. For the transformer blocks, the number of heads is set to 16 and the expand ratio of FFN is set to 4. We add sinusoidal positional embedding [17] in the CCAT module.

4.3   Comparison to State-of-the-Art

For the DroneVehicle dataset, we reimplement the state-of-the-art model UA-CMDet [16] thanks to the open-source code[1]. The dataset is newly-proposed and little work has used it, so we implement the CMAFF[12] module based on the original paper to increase competing methods. As shown in Table 1, when equipped with our proposed DATFF, the two-stream RoITransformer [4] achieves 76.00% mAP, which is 3.85% higher than the previous state-of-the-art. In addition, the three detectors integrated with DATFF consistently outperform their counterparts with the CMAFF module. R^3Det [19] is a one-stage detector while the rest two are two-stage detectors, illustrating the versatility of our DATFF module. For the FLIR dataset, our two-stage Faster R-CNN equipped with DATFF also surpasses the UA-CMDet model by a significant margin as shown in Table 2. Note that the results of methods marked with a dagger are copied from the paper of Sun *et al.*.

In Fig. 5, we visualize some detection results on the DroneVehicle and FLIR datasets in comparison to a state-of-the-art method, so readers can intuitively feel the superiority of our method.

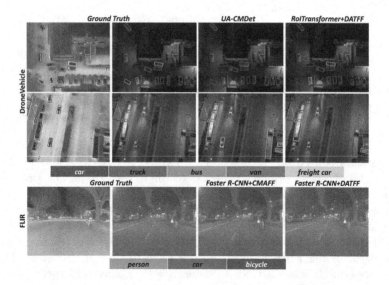

Fig. 5. Qualitative comparison of detection results on the two datasets. We visualize the results of our method, a state-of-the-art method and the ground truth annotations.

---

[1] https://github.com/SunYM2020/UA-CMDet.

Table 3. Ablation study on the DroneVehicle dataset. We use three different base detectors.

Component	Choice				
Add	✓				
Concat		✓	✓	✓	✓
CCAT			✓		✓
SCAT				✓	✓
R^3Det [19]	68.63	68.30	70.54	70.58	**71.02**
Oriented R-CNN [18]	73.62	73.6	74.78	74.86	**75.42**
RoITransformer [4]	72.93	72.71	74.71	75.02	**76.00**

4.4 Ablation Study

Table 3 shows the results of the ablation study on the structure of our DATFF module. As there is no official partition of validation set for the FLIR dataset, we use the DroneVehicle dataset in the ablation study. All three oriented object detectors are used for better persuasion. We can observe consistent improvements in mAP on the test set when using the SCAT module for feature fusion individually compared with simple addition or concatenation. Adding the CCAT module further improves the performance and they collaborate well to form the DATFF module. It is interesting to observe that using CCAT module alone is also effective in feature fusion.

Table 4. Effects of hyperparameters. We use Oriented R-CNN in this experiment.

(a) Effects of number of groups G.

G	64	128	256
mAP	74.94	75.09	**75.42**

(b) Effects of feature map size P.

P	8	10	12	14	16
mAP	75.26	**75.42**	75.24	75.15	74.99

4.5 Effects of Hyperparameters

The length of the input sequences to the transformer is an important hyperparameter. In our DATFF module, the number of groups G in the CCAT module and the square of the feature map size P in the SCAT module correspond to the sequence length. We change the two parameters separately and the results are shown in Table 4. Although the original scale of the four stages' feature maps is different, we keep G and P to be the same for convenience. According to Sect. 3.1, G is designed to be the same as the channel number of feature maps, and the highest mAP is achieved when $G=256$. As we changes P from 8 to 16, the highest mAP is achieved when $P=10$, which indicates the necessity of proper feature aggregation.

Table 5. Comparisons on the DroneVehicle dataset *dark* set.

Methods	mAP
UA-CMDet [16]	73.32
RoITransformer+CMAFF [12]	73.19
RoITransformer+DATFF	74.10
Oriented R-CNN+CMAFF [12]	74.09
Oriented R-CNN+DATFF	**74.92**

Table 6. Comparisons on the two datasets using detectors w/o FPN.

Methods	mAP
RoITransformer+CMAFF [12]	73.82
RoITransformer+DATFF	74.55
Oriented R-CNN+CMAFF [12]	73.51
Oriented R-CNN+DATFF	**74.64**
Faster R-CNN+CMAFF [12]	72.50
Faster R-CNN+DATFF	**72.99**

4.6   Other Experiments

As we have illustrated in Sect. 1, our DATFF module can improve the detection results when the visible images have bad illumination conditions. To verify this, we manually select a *dark* set from the DroneVehicle test set which consists of 1831 image pairs. We report the mAP of some detectors on this set in Table 5. When equipped with our DATFF module, the two-stream detectors have a better ability in utilizing the limited useful information of the visible images.

In Table 6, we report the mAP on the two datasets using two-stage detectors without FPN. The hyperparameters are the same with Sect. 4.2. The results indicate that our DATFF module is effective regardless of whether we use FPN.

5   Further Empirical Analysis

To better illustrate the principle of CCAT and SCAT, we use images from the DroneVehicle dataset and perform empirical analysis.

In Fig. 6, all the feature maps present are from the first stage of the ResNet50 backbone. According to Sect. 3.1, the final channel attention weights indicate common features. We randomly select four of the top ten channels with high channel attention weights from infrared and visible feature maps. These feature maps show a certain degree of similarity, which indicates that common features have been extracted. Each element in the attention matrix of the MHCA layer represents the similarity of two feature map channels from the two modalities. We select two channels from infrared and visible feature maps and show six feature map channels of the other modality with high or low similarity scores. The visualization conforms to the principle of the MHCA layer.

We explore the cross-modal spatial attention of the SCAT module in Fig. 7. Images in the third row are fourth-stage attention maps of MHCA illustrating the attention distribution between the queried patch of one modality and all image patches of the other modality. The areas with bright color have high similarity score with the queried patch. In Fig. 7(a) and (b), the queried car has blurred boundary and the clear boundary information in the infrared image is

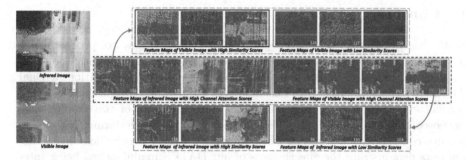

Fig. 6. Visualization of how CCAT works. All the feature maps present are from ResNet50's first stage. We randomly select and visualize four of the top ten channels with high channel attention weights from infrared and visible feature maps. For the 116th channel of the infrared feature map and the 163rd channel of the visible feature map, we randomly select and visualize three of the top ten and three of the bottom ten channels with high similarity scores from the feature map of the other modality. The white number in the bottom right corner of each feature map is the channel index. (Color figure online)

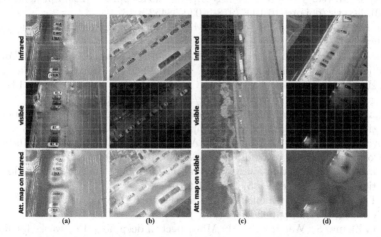

Fig. 7. Attention maps of the image patches marked by the red box in the SCAT module. Images in the first two rows are infrared and visible images. Images in the third row are fourth-stage attention maps of the other modality given the image patch marked by the red box as the query.

complementary. In Fig. 7(c), color information in the visible image complements the contour information in the infrared image for the queried vehicle. In Fig. 7(d), there are many cars in the image but only three cars are lit by the street light. The areas with high attention weights of the queried patch correspond with the bright areas, providing useful color information.

6 Conclusion

In the visible-infrared object detection task, visible images are prone to illumination and visibility that may contain a lot of interference information and little useful information. To make the most of the useful information, a Dual Attention Transformer Feature Fusion (DATFF) module is proposed to get better feature representation from intermediate feature maps of two sources. Our proposed DATFF module amplifies common features and performs spatial-wise feature complement sequentially. Experiments on the DroneVehicle and FLIR datasets demonstrate the effectiveness of our DATFF module when being integrated into two-stream object detectors. We will further implement our DATFF module on anchor-free and query-based detectors in the future.

References

1. Carion, N., Massa, F., Synnaeve, G., Usunier, N., Kirillov, A., Zagoruyko, S.: End-to-end object detection with transformers. In: Vedaldi, A., Bischof, H., Brox, T., Frahm, J.-M. (eds.) ECCV 2020. LNCS, vol. 12346, pp. 213–229. Springer, Cham (2020). https://doi.org/10.1007/978-3-030-58452-8_13
2. Chen, K., Wang, J., Pang, J., et al.: MMDetection: open mmlab detection toolbox and benchmark. arXiv preprint arXiv:1906.07155 (2019)
3. Chen, Y.-T., Shi, J., Ye, Z., Mertz, C., Ramanan, D., Kong, S.: Multimodal object detection via probabilistic ensembling. In: Avidan, S., Brostow, G., Cissé, M., Farinella, G.M., Hassner, T. (eds.) ECCV 2022. LNCS, vol. 13669, pp. 139–158. Springer, Cham (2022). https://doi.org/10.1007/978-3-031-20077-9_9
4. Ding, J., Xue, N., Long, Y., et al.: Learning RoI Transformer for oriented object detection in aerial images. In: CVPR, pp. 2844–2853 (2019)
5. Dosovitskiy, A., Beyer, L., Kolesnikov, A., et al.: An image is worth 16x16 words: transformers for image recognition at scale. In: ICLR (2021)
6. Li, C., et al.: Illumination-aware faster r-cnn for robust multispectral pedestrian detection. Pattern Recogn. **85**, 161–171 (2019)
7. Lin, T.Y., Dollár, P., Girshick, R., et al.: Feature pyramid networks for object detection. In: CVPR, pp. 936–944 (2017)
8. Liu, J., Zhang, S., Wang, S., et al.: Multispectral deep neural networks for pedestrian detection. In: BMVC, pp. 73.1-73.13 (2016)
9. Liu, T., Lam, K.M., Zhao, R., Qiu, G.: Deep cross-modal representation learning and distillation for illumination-invariant pedestrian detection. IEEE Trans. Circuits Syst. Video Technol. **32**(1), 315–329 (2022)
10. Liu, W., et al.: SSD: single shot multibox detector. In: Leibe, B., Matas, J., Sebe, N., Welling, M. (eds.) ECCV 2016. LNCS, vol. 9905, pp. 21–37. Springer, Cham (2016). https://doi.org/10.1007/978-3-319-46448-0_2
11. Qingyun, F., Dapeng, H., Zhaokui, W.: Cross-modality fusion transformer for multispectral object detection. arXiv preprint arXiv:2111.00273 (2021)
12. Qingyun, F., Zhaokui, W.: Cross-modality attentive feature fusion for object detection in multispectral remote sensing imagery. Pattern Recogn. **130**, 108786 (2022)
13. Razakarivony, S., Jurie, F.: Vehicle detection in aerial imagery: a small target detection benchmark. J. Vis. Commun. Image Represent. **34**, 187–203 (2016)
14. Ren, S., He, K., Girshick, R., Sun, J.: Faster R-CNN: towards real-time object detection with region proposal networks. In: NIPS, vol. 28, pp. 91–99 (2015)

15. Sharma, M., Dhanaraj, M., Karnam, S., et al.: YOLOrs: object detection in multimodal remote sensing imagery. IEEE J. Selected Topics Appli. Earth Observat. Remote Sensing **14**, 1497–1508 (2021)
16. Sun, Y., Cao, B., Zhu, P., et al.: Drone-based RGB-Infrared cross-modality vehicle detection via uncertainty-aware learning. IEEE Trans. Circuits Syst. Video Technol. **32**(10), 6700–6713 (2022)
17. Vaswani, A., Shazeer, N., Parmar, N., et al.: Attention is all you need. In: NIPS, vol. 30, pp. 5998–6008 (2017)
18. Xie, X., Cheng, G., Wang, J., Yao, X., Han, J.: Oriented R-CNN for object detection. In: ICCV, pp. 3500–3509 (2021)
19. Yang, X., Yan, J., Feng, Z., He, T.: R3det: refined single-stage detector with feature refinement for rotating object. In: AAAI, vol. 35(4), pp. 3163–3171 (2021)
20. Zhang, H., Fromont, E., Lefevre, S., et al.: Guided attentive feature fusion for multispectral pedestrian detection. In: WACV, pp. 72–80 (2021)
21. Zhang, H., Fromont, E., et al.: Multispectral fusion for object detection with cyclic fuse-and-refine blocks. In: ICIP, pp. 276–280 (2020)
22. Zhang, J., Lei, J., Xie, W., et al.: SuperYOLO: Super resolution assisted object detection in multimodal remote sensing imagery. IEEE Trans. Geosci. Remote Sens. **61**, 1–15 (2023)
23. Zhang, L., Liu, Z., Zhang, S., Yang, X., et al.: Cross-modality interactive attention network for multispectral pedestrian detection. Inform. Fusion **50**, 20–29 (2019)
24. Zhang, X., Jiang, H., Xu, N., et al.: MsIFT: multi-source image fusion transformer. Remote Sensing **14**(16) (2022)
25. Zhou, K., Chen, L., Cao, X.: Improving multispectral pedestrian detection by addressing modality imbalance problems. In: Vedaldi, A., Bischof, H., Brox, T., Frahm, J.-M. (eds.) ECCV 2020. LNCS, vol. 12363, pp. 787–803. Springer, Cham (2020). https://doi.org/10.1007/978-3-030-58523-5_46
26. Zhou, Y., Yang, X., Zhang, G., et al.: MMRotate: a rotated object detection benchmark using pytorch. arXiv preprint arXiv:2204.13317 (2022)

Feature Sniffer: A Stealthy Inference Attacks Framework on Split Learning

Sida Luo, Fangchao Yu, Lina Wang[(✉)], Bo Zeng, Zhi Pang, and Kai Zhao

Key Laboratory of Aerospace Information Security and Trusted Computing,
Ministry of Education, School of Cyber Science and Engineering,
Wuhan University,Wuhan, China
lnwang@whu.edu.cn

Abstract. Split learning, a novel privacy-preserving distributed machine learning framework, is proposed to overcome the resource limitations issue of devices in federated learning. Previous studies have explored the possibility of inference attacks on split learning. However, existing methods suffer from unrealistic threat models and poor robustness against defensive techniques. Remarkably, we propose a novel and general framework to perform inference attacks stealthily and reveal the privacy vulnerability of split learning at the convergence stage. In our framework, the malicious server distills knowledge on an auxiliary dataset and transfers the identity information of clients' data to the auxiliary feature space to sniff out the private data. The attack is behind the scenes and hard to detect. Empirically, we consider image classification as the desired task in split learning and evaluate the effectiveness of our method on common image classification datasets. Extensive experiments still obtain SOTA results in the face of strict differential privacy. The code is available at https://github.com/Rostar-github/FSA.

Keywords: Split learning · Neural network models · Transfer learning

1 Introduction

With the growing demand for data privacy protection, privacy-preserving distributed machine learning frameworks are becoming more noteworthy. Federated learning [4] is proposed to train models collaboratively without data leaving the device. Due to data preservation, federated learning is widely applied in finance and healthcare, and more organizations can join and benefit from collaborative learning. Nevertheless, federated learning suffers from the issue of resource limitations, wherein devices are unable to carry out local training tasks due to their limited computational resources, particularly in IoT scenarios [22]. To this end, another advanced distributed machine learning framework called split learning [13,24] is proposed, which splits the model into two parts located on the client and server. The client and the server execute both forward and backward computations, respectively, while the server only obtains the intermediate activation, also called *"smashed data"*, in the label-preservation mode[13].

L. Iliadis et al. (Eds.): ICANN 2023, LNCS 14260, pp. 66–77, 2023.
https://doi.org/10.1007/978-3-031-44195-0_6

Recently, it is remarkable that many studies have amalgamated the benefits of federated learning and split learning to considerably enhance the performance of split learning [7,21,23], which implies a broader spectrum of application scenarios. As the application of split learning is proposed, its security also needs to be re-examined. As it is known, federated learning is vulnerable to Deep Leakage from Gradients (DLG) [30], which raises the question of **whether a malicious server can launch attacks and reconstruct the inference data with *smashed data*** in split learning, rather than relying on the gradients. Although several attack schemes have been proposed for split learning, only a few have gained traction, the most viable of which is Model Inversion Attacks (MIA) [5,9,25,27]. It typically assumes that the malicious server has access to the client model in the *white-box* setting [14] and can query the client model but without knowledge of it in the *black-box* setting. Furthermore, the server needs an extra auxiliary dataset to perform the MIA [14,17]. However, there is no need for clients in split learning to share their models with the server. As a result, most of the current threat models are plagued by excessively stringent priors, rendering attacks impracticable.

We find that the last state *smashed data* in the training of split learning is the most vulnerable point. The distribution of the *smashed data* is always stable after the training convergence. The malicious server can map the distribution into a suitable and similar one with transfer learning to capture the significant features of the private data from the *smashed data*. This attack can be implemented offline to avoid interfering with the training of split learning. In this paper, we propose a novel and hard-to-detect attack approach called **Feature Sniffing Attack** (FSA). The scenario assumes a weak prior where the malicious server has no need to know or query the client's model. The malicious server can perform inference attacks stealthily without interfering with the desired task. The FSA constructs a suitable auxiliary feature space by distilling an auxiliary dataset, which is publicly available and distributed similarly to the client dataset. It surreptitiously builds a bridge between *smashed data* and the auxiliary feature space in the later training stage by utilizing cycle-consistent GAN [29]. In summary, the contributions of this paper can be listed as:

- We propose a novel and general attack framework, which can perform inference attacks without requiring access to the client's model.
- The client is hard to perceive and corrupt the attack in split learning.
- We show the robustness of the attack in the face of active defensive techniques and reveal the privacy vulnerability of split learning at the convergence stage.

2 Background and Related Work

2.1 Split Learning

Split learning as a distributed machine learning framework is widely used in IoT [3,10], healthcare, [19,24]and other fields for preserving users' private data. It divides the neural network into two parts, one on the client and the other on the server, to overcome the difficulty of training local models with limited local computing resources for federated learning. In the case of image classification, for example, the model on the client should have a few convolutional and pooling layers to adapt to the capabilities of the client. Instead, those computationally costly modules are located on the server, such as dense blocks. In the training, the client performs the forward computation and uploads the obtained *smashed data* to the server and the server performs the remaining forward computation before sending the gradients back to the client for the upgrade. The same process is repeated, and the parameters of models are delivered across clients for further training. Formally, all the clients collaboratively train a global model under the premise of data privacy.

2.2   Attacks on Split Learning

Deep learning models are often targeted by MIA, which exposes the models' privacy vulnerabilities [25]. There are two settings in MIA: the *white-box* and the *black-box*. In the *white-box* setting, the adversary has access to the target model, knowing the architecture and parameters. [9] first proposes and improves *white-box* based MIA, which maximizes the likelihood of observing the target model prediction according to the Maximum A Posterior (MAP) principle. [27] leverages GAN to distill the features of the public dataset to reduce the search space of optimization. [5] presents a novel inversion-specific GAN to improve knowledge distillation. In the *black-box* setting, the adversary is able to query the target model. [2] trains a surrogate model to approximate the decision and uses GAN to fit the distribution of the private dataset. With the help of a breached and independent dataset, [28] trains a surrogate model with explanation attention transfer to perform better MIA. To reduce the number of queries, [17] pretrains an inversion network to inverse high-level features of the auxiliary dataset and then transfers to the task of inverting the target network.

Especially, the model is split into two parts in split learning, which means that the implementation of MIA for the client model is possible if the adversary can query it. [14] first discusses MIA in split learning, considering both *white-box* and *black-box* settings. Despite the problem of over-reliance on the auxiliary dataset, they design a shadow model on the auxiliary dataset to solve the query-free problem. [18] proposes the feature-space hijacking attack to guide the client model to train in the desired direction so that the adversary can decode the *smashed data*. But it suffers from client-side differential privacy [1,11]. In order to reduce the constraints, [8] optimizes the input and the parameters of the model simultaneously without knowledge of the client model, but it seems to be less effective as the split depth grows.

3   Methodology

3.1   Threat Model

To better formalize our framework, we assume that the attack is performed on label-preservation split learning. In the rest of this paper, we consider split learning as label-preservation split learning. The adversary (the malicious server) has no access to the label. The malicious server follows the split learning protocol and trains the desired task normally. The adversary has no knowledge of the architecture and parameters of the client model. However, the adversary can acquire the dataset whose distribution is similar to the client's private dataset X_{pri} on the public internet as the auxiliary dataset X_{aux} [20,27]. It is a more realistic assumption than most previous works that the malicious server performs the attack only with the help of the auxiliary dataset and *smashed data*.

3.2 Feature Sniffing Attack

The feature sniffing attack aims to perform inference attacks in the inference phase of split learning without querying the client model and manipulating the gradients of that. The attack is an independent action of the adversary. The implementation pipeline of the feature sniffing attack can be divided into two phases, as demonstrated in Fig. 1. We focus on the data reconstruction task, which is a kind of challenging inference attack.

Auxiliary Knowledge Distillation. Given the black-box setting and limited priori capacities of the malicious server, the only available leverage for the attacker is the publicly accessible auxiliary dataset X_{aux}. In order to improve the fidelity of reconstructed images in the inference phase, the malicious server

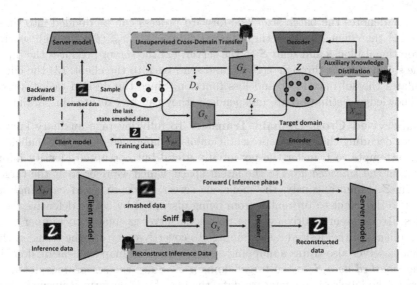

Fig. 1. The implementation pipeline of the feature sniffing attack. The malicious server trains an autoencoder on the auxiliary dataset to construct a suitable target domain. When the client model is close to convergence, the malicious server records the *smashed data* and trains the mapping network to perform unsupervised cross-domain transfer (above). In the inference phase, the malicious server sniffs the *smashed data* to reconstruct private data (below).

first utilizes an autoencoder network $(f(x; \theta_e), f(x; \theta_d))$ to distill the auxiliary dataset to acquire low-level feature prior knowledge. We denote θ_e and θ_d as the parameters of the encoder E and decoder D, respectively. Sample x_{aux} from the auxiliary dataset $\boldsymbol{X_{aux}}$ and minimize the loss function of the Mean Squared Error (MSE):

$$\mathcal{L}_{AE} = \arg \min_{\theta_e, \theta_d} MSE(f(f(x_{aux}; \theta_d); \theta_e)). \tag{1}$$

By training the autoencoder, the malicious server learns the high-level latent representation $\boldsymbol{Z} = f(x_{aux}; \theta_e)$ of the auxiliary dataset. With the latent representation $\boldsymbol{Z}$, the malicious server can pay more attention to the identity information of the image in inference rather than taking efforts to reconstruct the low-level pixel feature, which is common on $\boldsymbol{X_{pri}}$ and $\boldsymbol{X_{aux}}$. E.g. if we can learn a sufficiently dense latent distribution (e.g. ImageNet[6]), we can reconstruct the image by the potential identity information of *smashed data*.

As for the honest-but-curious server, it follows the split learning protocol and trains the desired task with clients. We use θ_c and θ_s to denote the client C and server S model parameters, respectively. For an image classification task, the client samples a batch of data (x^i_{pri}, y^i_{pri}) from $\boldsymbol{X_{pri}}$ and collaboratively minimizes the Cross-Entropy loss with the server:

$$\mathcal{L}_{CE} = \arg \min_{\theta_c, \theta_s} -\frac{1}{N} \sum_{i=1}^{N} y^i_{pri} \log(f(f(x^i_{pri}; \theta_c); \theta_s)), \tag{2}$$

where N denotes the batch size. The forward process can be divided into three steps: (1) the client produces the *smashed data* $\boldsymbol{S} = f(x_{pri}; \theta_c)$ through several convolutional blocks and send $\boldsymbol{S}$ to the server; (2) the server produces the input of the softmax layer through $f(\boldsymbol{S}; \theta_s)$ and send back to the client; (3) the client calculates the softmax layer and loss function. Since the desired task training and knowledge distillation are independent, they can be executed in parallel.

Unsupervised Cross-Domain Transfer. To fully leverage auxiliary knowledge for decoding the latent representation of the inference image, the malicious server attempts to transfer the potentially useful but corrupted identity information in the *smashed data* to the latent space, which we refer to as the target domain $\boldsymbol{Z}$. Simultaneously, the malicious server needs to avoid exposing the attack to the client to prevent it from being disrupted by active defensive techniques like differential privacy. The malicious server is unable to tamper with the gradients of the desired task training. To covertly carry out the transfer, the malicious server also trains a mapping network that can map the feature domain of the *smashed data* $\boldsymbol{S}$ to the target domain $\boldsymbol{Z}$. Since the server does not have access to the labels of the *smashed data*, the transfer is performed unsupervised in split learning.

We utilize GAN to implement the unsupervised cross-domain transfer. The distribution of *smashed data* is unstable during the desired task training. Therefore, the malicious server needs to intercept and retain a complete epoch of *smashed data* uploaded by the client when the training converges so as to obtain the final feature space that the client model maps. Sample x_s from the last state *smashed data* $\mathcal{S}$ as the input to the generator G_S, and sample x_z from the target domain $\mathcal{Z}$ as the input to the discriminator D_Z. The corresponding loss is

$$\mathcal{L}_{GAN}(G_S, D_Z, \mathcal{S}, \mathcal{Z}) = \mathbb{E}_{x_z \sim \mathcal{Z}}\left[\log D_Z(x_z)\right] + \mathbb{E}_{x_s \sim \mathcal{S}}\left[\log\left(1 - D_Z(G_S(x_s))\right)\right]. \tag{3}$$

The generator aims to generate data points in the target domain, while the adversarial discriminator attempts to distinguish them. To prevent the ineffective transfer of identity information in a high-dimensional feature space when the $\mathcal{S}$ and $\mathcal{Z}$ domain samples do not match, we train a reverse generator G to maintain consistent identity information. It minimizes the same loss $\mathcal{L}_{GAN}(G_Z, D_S, \mathcal{Z}, \mathcal{S})$ and maintains the cycle-consistency of samples by L1 penalty on the feature map reconstruction:

$$\mathcal{L}_{\text{cyc}}(G_S, G_Z) = \mathbb{E}_{x_s \sim \mathcal{S}}\left[\|G_Z(G_S(x_s)) - x_s\|_1\right] + \mathbb{E}_{x_z \sim \mathcal{Z}}\left[\|G_S(G_Z(x_z)) - x_z\|_1\right]. \tag{4}$$

The full loss function of the cross-domain transfer is:

$$\begin{aligned}\mathcal{L}(G_S, G_Z, D_S, D_Z) = &\mathcal{L}_{\text{GAN}}(G_S, D_Z, \mathcal{S}, \mathcal{Z}) + \mathcal{L}_{\text{GAN}}(G_Z, D_S, \mathcal{Z}, \mathcal{S}) \\ &+ \lambda\mathcal{L}_{\text{cyc}}(G_S, G_Z),\end{aligned} \tag{5}$$

where λ balances the relative importance of loss terms. After this step, the malicious server has constructed a mapping between the convergent *smashed data* distribution and the target distribution obtained by distilling on the auxiliary dataset. In other words, the malicious server indirectly builds a decoder that allows the malicious server to sniff out the significant information related to the inference data from the *smashed data*. Similar to model inversion attacks, the malicious server decodes the *smashed data* to reconstruct the inference data x_{pri} in the inference phase:

$$\hat{x}_{pri} = f(G_S(f(x_{pri}; \theta_c)); \theta_d) \tag{6}$$

The mapping construction can be completed offline during the feature sniffing attack. The only requirement for the malicious server is to capture the final state distribution that the client model maps. Moreover, the malevolent server enjoys significant flexibility in designing a suitable mapping network and autoencoder.

4   Experiment

4.1   Attack Implementations

We evaluate the feature sniffing attack on frequently used image classification datasets in this field: MNIST [16], Fashion-MNIST [26], and CIFAR10 [15]. In order to sample from different distributions, we consider the training sets as private datasets X_{pri} in split learning and the validation sets as the publicly available auxiliary datasets X_{aux}. We reshape the image of all these datasets to 32×32 to fit the same network architecture for comparison. In split learning,

Table 1. The split part of ResNet in the client. The higher the split level indicates the deeper the client's network.

Split level 1	Split level 2	Split level 3
$3 \times 3, 32$, s=1 BatchNorm Conv2d	$\begin{bmatrix} 3 \times 3, 32 \\ 3 \times 3, 32 \end{bmatrix} \times 2$ Resblocks	$\begin{bmatrix} 3 \times 3, 64 \\ 3 \times 3, 64 \end{bmatrix} \times 2$ Resblocks

we aim to achieve image classification as the desired task and train a residual network which is split into two parts positioned on the client and server, respectively. This split is conducted at three different levels. The split client model is illustrated in Table 1. For example, the client model consists of a convolutional layer and two residual blocks in level 2. In the auxiliary knowledge distillation, we define an encoder that contains downsampling layers without BN and a decoder that is symmetrical to the encoder. In the unsupervised cross-domain transfer, we stack convolutional blocks with the same kernel size and stride as the generator to transfer the potential identity information.

The autoencoder and the split network are trained in parallel. In the training of the generator, we assume that the client samples completely randomly from its dataset. The malicious server saves the *smashed data* from the last training epoch of the desired task to capture the last state distribution and follows the same batch size to sample from the target domain. We train the cycle-consistency GAN with the WGAN-GP [12] loss. The process is independent of the desired task.

We consider the training sets and validation sets as the private datasets and auxiliary datasets, respectively, for the distributional similarity condition. Without knowing the architecture of the client model, we adjust the depth of the autoencoder at different levels so that the target domain is as similar as possible to the smashed data. Empirically, we set up the autoencoder with increasing depth at different split levels. We perform the unsupervised cross-domain transfer and train the same network architecture over 200 epochs on the three datasets, as shown in Fig. 2, to obtain the generators and decoders that can be used to reconstruct the inference data. We attempt to adjust the GAN to achieve the close reconstruction loss at different split levels. At split level 3, the reconstructed inference image is shown in Fig. 3. With MNIST, Fashion-MNIST, CIFAR10 obtains the average MSE of 0.01270, 0.01472, and 0.00539. The results apparently indicate that the FSA is able to recover significant information from *smashed data* uploaded by clients. With high fidelity, the malicious server has almost completely reconstructed the inference data. This means that the malicious server has successfully extracted features that can be exploited in inference attacks. To increase the difference between X_{pri} and X_{aux}, we augment the validation set of CIFAR10, which is used as X_{aux} in the CIFAR10 experiment. We apply Gaussian blur and Gaussian noise simultaneously to X_{aux}. Finally, we

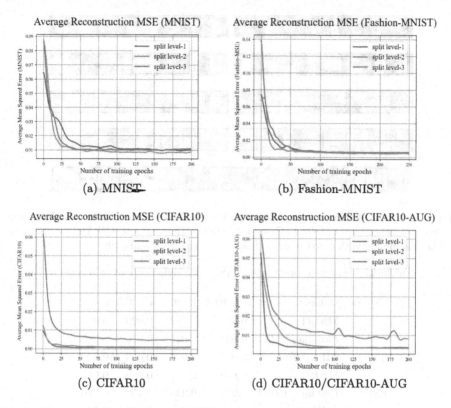

Fig. 2. The average reconstruction MSE with training epochs on different datasets. CIFAR10/CIFAR10-AUG means X_{pri} =CIFAR10, X_{aux} =CIFAR10-AUG.

still obtain an average MSE of 0.00832 on split level 3. The training curve is shown in Fig. 2 (d) and the visual result image is shown in Fig. 3.

4.2 Robustness Against Active Defense and Stealthiness

Differential Privacy (DP) [1] is an effective privacy-preservation technology popularly applied to privacy-preserving machine learning. DPSGD [1] is an optimization algorithm that applies DP. It makes the training dataset satisfy the DP of (ϵ, δ) by clipping the gradients over a preset threshold and adding noise, where ϵ denotes the privacy budget and δ denotes the loose boundary. The tighter the privacy budget, the better the privacy protection. The tighter privacy budget also means a smaller threshold and larger-scale noise. In split learning, DP can be actively implemented by the client. The client clips the backward gradient of the client model and adds noise. In order to evaluate the robustness of the FSA, we guarantee DP with the Pytorch differential privacy toolkit, **Opacus**, by adjusting the noise scale. As a comparison, we consider FSHA as the baseline for its effectiveness in label-preservation split learning. We set the maximum L2

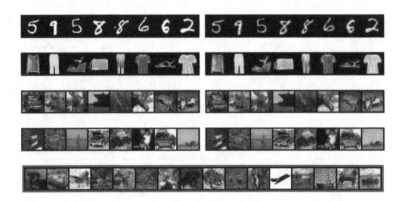

Fig. 3. Inference image and reconstructed inference image at split level 3. From top to bottom, the order is MNIST, Fashion-MNIST, CIFAR10, and CIFAR10/CIFAR10-AUG. The image with a red margin shows the augmentation result.

Table 2. Average reconstruction MSE with different ϵ at split level 3.

Method	Dataset	$\epsilon = 0.01$	$\epsilon = 0.1$	$\epsilon = 0.5$	$\epsilon = 1.0$
FSA	MNIST	0.019	0.017	0.020	0.019
	Fashion-MNIST	0.022	0.021	0.020	0.020
	CIFAR10	0.027	0.027	0.033	0.040
FSHA	MNIST	0.870	0.217	0.108	0.049
	Fashion-MNIST	0.978	0.248	0.155	0.116
	CIFAR10	0.507	0.465	0.104	0.762

of the gradient to 1.0 and create a tight privacy budget by varying the noise scale. As ϵ is the main factor impacting the noise scale[1], we set ϵ to 0.01, 0.1, 0.5, and 1.0, respectively, and keep the same $\delta = 0.00001$ in different groups, which means a large drop in classification accuracy (12% on CIFAR10).

The average reconstruction MSE obtained by training models over 50 epochs at split level 3 is shown in Table 2. It's obvious that the FSA is more robust against DP than the FSHA. Different sizes of privacy budgets have little effect on image reconstruction. The FSA overall has better reconstruction against DP. We argue that such discrepancies are caused by exposing the training of the generator to the client in the FSHA. The FSHA hijacks the client model as its generator in adversarial training, which allows the client to manipulate the attack through DP. In contrast, the FSA only employs the last state *smashed data*, and its training is independent of the client's. At the same time, it proves the vulnerability of split learning at the stage close to convergence. We show the results of inference data reconstruction in Fig. 4 when ϵ is equal to 0.1.

Furthermore, we add desired tasks to the FSHA and keep the server-side model the same as the FSA's to observe the impact of the two attacks on the accuracy of desired tasks within 100 training epochs. The results are shown in

Fig. 4. Reconstructed inference data of FSHA (left) and FSA (right).

Table 3. Due to the independence of the FSA, it hardly affects the accuracy of desired tasks. Nevertheless, the accuracy of desired tasks in the FSHA is contingent on both the efficacy of adversarial training and the similarity of distribution in auxiliary datasets. This implies that the client can readily identify a decrease in accuracy, which would reveal the vulnerability of the FSHA. Conversely, the FSA will not expose anything during regular training.

Table 3. Accuracy of desired tasks at different split levels for FSA, FSHA, and regular training.

Dataset	Level	FSA	FSHA	Regular
MNIST	1	98.8	98.9	98.9
	2	98.6	98.8	98.9
	3	98.6	98.4	99.0
Fashion-MNIST	1	91.9	90.7	92.4
	2	92.4	88.7	92.3
	3	92.1	81.5	91.9
CIFAR10	1	74.4	70.3	73.8
	2	74.5	61.2	74.4
	3	73.2	59.6	73.2
CIFAR10-AUG	1	74.2	67.5	73.8
	2	74.3	58.2	74.4
	3	72.8	54.8	73.2

5   Conclusion

In this work, we propose a stealthy inference attacks framework on split learning. In our framework, the malicious server builds an auxiliary feature space on a public dataset and then independently implements the unsupervised cross-domain transfer at the feature level to perform inference attacks, so that the client cannot be aware of the attack's presence. We consider image classification as the desired task in split learning and evaluate the performance. The extensive experiments reveal the privacy vulnerability of split learning at the convergence stage and show the effectiveness and robustness of the attack in the face of strict differential privacy. Actually, there remains a potential problem for the future work. The malicious server still needs a dataset similar to the client's. In the future, we will make efforts to mitigate the similarity dependency of datasets.

References

1. Abadi, M., et al.: Deep learning with differential privacy. In: Proceedings of the 2016 ACM SIGSAC Conference on Computer and Communications Security, pp. 308–318 (2016)
2. Aïvodji, U., Gambs, S., Ther, T.: Gamin: an adversarial approach to black-box model inversion. arXiv preprint arXiv:1909.11835 (2019)
3. Ayad, A., Renner, M., Schmeink, A.: Improving the communication and computation efficiency of split learning for iot applications. In: 2021 IEEE Global Communications Conference (GLOBECOM), pp. 01–06. IEEE (2021)
4. Bonawitz, K., et al.: Towards federated learning at scale: system design. Proc. Mach. Learn. Syst. **1**, 374–388 (2019)
5. Chen, S., Kahla, M., Jia, R., Qi, G.J.: Knowledge-enriched distributional model inversion attacks. In: Proceedings of the IEEE/CVF International Conference on Computer Vision, pp. 16178–16187 (2021)
6. Deng, J., Dong, W., Socher, R., Li, L.J., Li, K., Fei-Fei, L.: Imagenet: a large-scale hierarchical image database. In: 2009 IEEE Conference on Computer Vision and Pattern Recognition, pp. 248–255. Ieee (2009)
7. Duan, Q., Hu, S., Deng, R., Lu, Z.: Combined federated and split learning in edge computing for ubiquitous intelligence in internet of things: State-of-the-art and future directions. Sensors **22**(16), 5983 (2022)
8. Erdogan, E., Kupcu, A., Cicek, A.E.: Unsplit: data-oblivious model inversion, model stealing, and label inference attacks against split learning. arXiv preprint arXiv:2108.09033 (2021)
9. Fredrikson, M., Jha, S., Ristenpart, T.: Model inversion attacks that exploit confidence information and basic countermeasures. In: Proceedings of the 22nd ACM SIGSAC Conference on Computer and Communications Security, pp. 1322–1333 (2015)
10. Gao, Y., et al.: End-to-end evaluation of federated learning and split learning for internet of things. arXiv preprint arXiv:2003.13376 (2020)
11. Gawron, G., Stubbings, P.: Feature space hijacking attacks against differentially private split learning. arXiv preprint arXiv:2201.04018 (2022)
12. Gulrajani, I., Ahmed, F., Arjovsky, M., Dumoulin, V., Courville, A.C.: Improved training of wasserstein gans. In: Advances in Neural Information Processing Systems 30 (2017)
13. Gupta, O., Raskar, R.: Distributed learning of deep neural network over multiple agents. J. Netw. Comput. Appl. **116**, 1–8 (2018)
14. He, Z., Zhang, T., Lee, R.B.: Model inversion attacks against collaborative inference. In: Proceedings of the 35th Annual Computer Security Applications Conference, pp. 148–162 (2019)
15. Krizhevsky, A., Hinton, G., et al.: Learning multiple layers of features from tiny images (2009)

16. LeCun, Y., Bottou, L., Bengio, Y., Haffner, P.: Gradient-based learning applied to document recognition. Proc. IEEE **86**(11), 2278–2324 (1998)
17. Mo, K., Huang, T., Xiang, X.: Querying little is enough: model inversion attack via latent information. In: Chen, X., Yan, H., Yan, Q., Zhang, X. (eds.) ML4CS 2020. LNCS, vol. 12487, pp. 583–591. Springer, Cham (2020). https://doi.org/10.1007/978-3-030-62460-6_52
18. Pasquini, D., Ateniese, G., Bernaschi, M.: Unleashing the tiger: inference attacks on split learning. In: Proceedings of the 2021 ACM SIGSAC Conference on Computer and Communications Security, pp. 2113–2129 (2021)
19. Poirot, M.G., Vepakomma, P., Chang, K., Kalpathy-Cramer, J., Gupta, R., Raskar, R.: Split learning for collaborative deep learning in healthcare (2019). arXiv preprint arXiv:1912.12115 (2019)
20. Shokri, R., Stronati, M., Song, C., Shmatikov, V.: Membership inference attacks against machine learning models. In: 2017 IEEE Symposium on Security and Privacy (SP), pp. 3–18. IEEE (2017)
21. Thapa, C., Arachchige, P.C.M., Camtepe, S., Sun, L.: Splitfed: when federated learning meets split learning. In: Proceedings of the AAAI Conference on Artificial Intelligence, vol. 36, pp. 8485–8493 (2022)
22. Thapa, C., Chamikara, M.A.P., Camtepe, S.A.: Advancements of federated learning towards privacy preservation: from federated learning to split learning. In: Rehman, M.H., Gaber, M.M. (eds.) Federated Learning Systems. SCI, vol. 965, pp. 79–109. Springer, Cham (2021). https://doi.org/10.1007/978-3-030-70604-3_4
23. Turina, V., Zhang, Z., Esposito, F., Matta, I.: Combining split and federated architectures for efficiency and privacy in deep learning. In: Proceedings of the 16th International Conference on emerging Networking EXperiments and Technologies, pp. 562–563 (2020)
24. Vepakomma, P., Gupta, O., Swedish, T., Raskar, R.: Split learning for health: distributed deep learning without sharing raw patient data. arXiv preprint arXiv:1812.00564 (2018)
25. Wu, X., Fredrikson, M., Jha, S., Naughton, J.F.: A methodology for formalizing model-inversion attacks. In: 2016 IEEE 29th Computer Security Foundations Symposium (CSF), pp. 355–370. IEEE (2016)
26. Xiao, H., Rasul, K., Vollgraf, R.: Fashion-mnist: a novel image dataset for benchmarking machine learning algorithms. arXiv preprint arXiv:1708.07747 (2017)
27. Zhang, Y., Jia, R., Pei, H., Wang, W., Li, B., Song, D.: The secret revealer: generative model-inversion attacks against deep neural networks. In: Proceedings of the IEEE/CVF Conference on Computer Vision and Pattern Recognition, pp. 253–261 (2020)
28. Zhao, X., Zhang, W., Xiao, X., Lim, B.: Exploiting explanations for model inversion attacks. In: Proceedings of the IEEE/CVF International Conference on Computer Vision, pp. 682–692 (2021)
29. Zhu, J.Y., Park, T., Isola, P., Efros, A.A.: Unpaired image-to-image translation using cycle-consistent adversarial networks. In: Proceedings of the IEEE International Conference on Computer Vision, pp. 2223–2232 (2017)
30. Zhu, L., Liu, Z., Han, S.: Deep leakage from gradients. In: Advances in Neural Information Processing Systems 32 (2019)

Few-Shot Object Detection via Transfer Learning and Contrastive Reweighting

Zhen Wu, Haowei Li, and Dongyu Zhang$^{(\boxtimes)}$

Sun Yat-sen University,Guangzhou, China
`zhangdy27@mail.sysu.edu.cn`

Abstract. In recent years, there has been increasing interest in few-shot object detection (FSOD), which involves detecting novel objects from just a few annotated examples. Transfer learning has been identified as an effective method for solving this task, as it allows the model to learn better feature embedding. In this paper, we utilize the Faster R-CNN framework and its potential to address FSOD tasks. We optimize the fine-tuning process of the detector based on the characteristics of the data distribution in the few-shot scenario. Additionally, we propose a contrastive reweighting module that enhances the classification of detected objects by making the embedding space more discriminative. Our extensive experiments on PASCAL VOC and MS COCO benchmarks demonstrate that our proposed method outperforms existing works and achieves state-of-the-art results.

Keywords: few-shot learning · object detection · transfer learning · contrastive learning

1 Introduction

During the past ten years, object detection [3] has made enormous advancements because of the development of deep learning. Yet, the majority of the currently used algorithms are built on enough labeled training data. Anytime we want the model to recognize a new class, we have manually label the data for that class, which is time-consuming, expensive, and in certain rare situations even impossible. Because of its importance and utility, the challenge of few-shot object detection has increasingly caught researchers' attention in recent years.

Most few-shot object detection algorithms [1], which were influenced by few-shot picture classification, conduct feature aggregation for a class-specific prediction using meta-learning strategies [8,9,13,14]. In addition, several studies use the transfer learning paradigm [10–12,16] to improve the process of fine-tuning new courses. Early transfer learning-based methodologies had low success, while more recent investigations have suggested easy-to-use strategies, e.g. TFA [11].

In this paper, we follow the transfer learning [2] paradigm, employ Faster R-CNN [7] as the basic framework, and explore its ability to tackle the FSOD task. Aimed at poor performance problems when directly leveraging Faster R-CNN

L. Iliadis et al. (Eds.): ICANN 2023, LNCS 14260, pp. 78–87, 2023.
https://doi.org/10.1007/978-3-031-44195-0_7

into a few-shot object detection task, we improve and optimize the fine-tuning process. We adjust the NMS parameters of RPN to obtain more region proposals extracted by RPN. To resolve the inconsistency between RPN and RoI head, we adjust the gradient to control their influence on the backbone. Furthermore, we alleviate the foreground-background imbalance in the RoI head and adopt a fixed class-agnostic regressor during fine-tuning. To solve the problem that the model has poor discrimination in novel classes, we devise a module based on contrastive learning and background re-weighting to assist in fine-tuning the model, further refining the classification results. Extensive experiments show that our method achieves state-of-the-art results on PASCAL VOC and MS COCO benchmarks. The detection accuracy of the proposed algorithm is improved by 9% in AP_{50} on the 1-shot task of the PASCAL VOC dataset and 27% and 10% respectively in mAP on the 1-shot and 10-shot task of MS COCO dataset compared with the existing methods, which demonstrates the effectiveness of the proposed algorithm.

2   Related Work

2.1   Few-Shot Learning

With a large amount of base data and a small number of novel data, few-shot learning attempts to identify novel classes. Current techniques may be broadly classified into two categories: (a) The model may incorporate past information and a few innovative semantics using optimization-based methodologies, allowing for quick adaptation to novel classes. Without adding extra parameters, MAML suggests model-independent meta-learning that may be used immediately for any model that can be optimized by gradient descent. (b) The goal of metric learning-based techniques is to learn a suitable feature space, decrease intra-class distance, and increase inter-class distance. In order to predict, ProtoNet [5] suggests creating a prototype for each class and measuring the distance between the prototypes and the query embedding. Instead of utilizing cosine similarity or Euclidean distance, RelationNet [6] uses a deep neural network to learn metrics measurement.

RPN can filter out background and foreground that don't fall under the same category as the support set thanks to A-RPN [15]. Moreover, they develop three feature aggregation branches in the RoI head. By using context-aware feature aggregation, DCNet [8] uses the attention mechanism in feature aggregation to emphasize pixel-level information and solve the scale variation problem.

3   Method

This section explains the fundamentals of few-shot object detection before going into more detail about our few-shot detector using transfer learning and contrastive reweighting.

3.1 Problem Definition

Following the existing setting, we are given a dataset which will be divided into $\mathcal{D}_{base}$ and $\mathcal{D}_{novel}$. The base classes $\mathcal{C}_{base}$ in $\mathcal{D}_{base}$ and the novel classes $\mathcal{C}_{novel}$ in $\mathcal{D}_{novel}$ are disjoint, i.e., $\mathcal{C}_{base} \cap \mathcal{C}_{novel} = \varnothing$. $\mathcal{C}_{base}$ contains abundant annotated data while $\mathcal{C}_{novel}$ contains few annotated data ($\mathcal{D}_{novel}$ aka the support set). K-shot means that each novel class contains K annotated instances instead of images. We aim to train a robust detector based on $\mathcal{D}_{base}$ and $\mathcal{D}_{novel}$, then classify and localize objects of $\mathcal{C}_{novel}$.

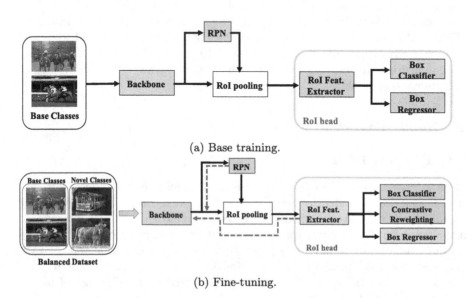

(a) Base training.

(b) Fine-tuning.

Fig. 1: Illustration of the architecture of our method. The parameters of the RoI feature extractor and box regressor will be fixed during fine-tuning. The dotted line indicates that the gradient returned by the module will be adjusted.

3.2 Few-Shot Object Detection via Transfer Learning

Figure 1 depicts the conceptual structure of our suggested approach. We build our model using TFA [11] and use the popular Faster R-CNN [7] as our basic detector. Base training and fine-tuning are the two phases of the training process. Without changing the Faster R-CNN [7], we try to enhance the fine-tuning process to increase detection performance.

After base training, the RPN in Faster R-CNN [7], which is typically thought of as class-agnostic, is biased in favor of base classes. The RPN is frozen and only the last layer of the Faster R-CNN [7] is fine-tuned by TFA [11]. As a result, the RPN may disregard numerous novel categories of objects. We underline that

RPN must be educated during fine-tuning in light of this observation. While perfecting RPN, there are two contradictions: 1) Base training ignores the associated annotations even when there are novel items in the training photos. These are taken into account by RPN as background information during base training but must be treated as foreground information during fine-tuning, which introduces inconsistency and leads to fewer suggestions for novel classes. 2) The parameter updating of the backbone can be impacted by the gradient of the RPN and RoI heads. The Region Proposal Network (RPN) and Region of Interest (RoI) head are two modules commonly used in object detection models. However, they have different objectives: while RPN extracts foreground regions independent of their class, the RoI head focuses on classifying these regions into specific categories. To address these inconsistencies, we propose two refinements. Firstly, we fine-tune the NMS parameters of RPN and reduce the number of proposals filtered out by NMS. This allows us to extract more foreground proposals with RPN. Secondly, we follow the approach proposed by DeFRCN and apply a gradient multiplier of 0 and 0.01 to the gradients from RPN and RoI head, respectively. This effectively truncates the gradient of RPN and controls the impact of the RoI head on the backbone.

In Faster R-CNN, it's crucial to address the class imbalance between foreground and background during training. To compute the loss in the Region of Interest (RoI) head, Faster R-CNN samples foreground and background proposals, with a maximum fraction of positives set to 0.25. However, in few-shot object detection, the foreground-background imbalance is even more severe because the Region Proposal Network (RPN) cannot provide enough foreground proposals. In fact, we observed that the number of background proposals is more than 10 times that of the foreground during fine-tuning. To tackle this problem, we reduce the number of sampled proposals used for loss computation in the RoI head to one-quarter of the original. This approach increases the proportion of positive samples, which is necessary because negative samples are the majority.

In the original Faster R-CNN, the regressor for each category is specific, which means that when fine-tuning for novel classes, the regression parameters need to be randomly initialized. This process can increase the burden of fine-tuning. To address this issue, we have implemented a class-agnostic regressor and have frozen its parameters during fine-tuning. By doing so, we can focus solely on the classification ability during fine-tuning and indirectly decouple the classification and regression processes. This approach has resulted in improved detection accuracy.

3.3 Contrastive Reweighting Module

Following TFA [11], we adopt a cosine similarity-based classifier in RoI head, the similarity $s_{i,j}$ between the i-th RoI feature and the feature embedding of j-th class can be calculated by:

$$s_{i,j} = \frac{\alpha F(x)_i^T w_j}{\|F(x)_i\| \|w_j\|}, \tag{1}$$

where $F(x)_i$ represents the instance feature and w_j represents the class weight, α is the scaling factor.

In order to improve the performance of our distance classifier, we utilize contrastive learning to extract more discriminative features from the RoI feature space. By reducing the intra-class distance and increasing the inter-class distance, we aim to enhance the accuracy of our model. To accomplish this, we employ a 2-layer multi-layer perception to further encode the feature embedding of each RoI feature. Then, we identify proposals of the same category as positive samples and proposals of different categories as negative samples. For each RoI feature, we calculate a contrastive loss using its corresponding positive and negative samples. This approach enables us to effectively learn and extract features that can better distinguish between different object categories, leading to improved classification performance. In the beginning, the contrastive loss is defined as follows:

$$\mathcal{L}_{contra} = -\frac{1}{N} \sum_{i=1}^{N} \mathcal{L}_i, \tag{2}$$

$$\mathcal{L}_i = \frac{1}{|C_i|} \sum_{j=1, C_j = C_i}^{N} \log \frac{\exp\left(sim\left(i, j\right)/\tau\right)}{\sum_{k=1}^{N} \exp\left(sim\left(i, k\right)/\tau\right)}, \tag{3}$$

where N indicates the total number of proposals, i indicates the i-th proposal, C_i is the category of i-th proposal, $sim(i, j)$ is the cosine similarity between i-th proposal and j-th proposal, τ is the temperature similar as in InfoNCE [17] loss. To ensure the quality of the proposals used for calculating the contrastive loss, only foreground proposals with IoU $>= 0.8$ will be used.

However, we find that using only the contrastive loss mentioned above can not improve the detection performance on the COCO dataset. We think this is due to the foreground-background class imbalance. As a result, in the denominator of Equation (3), the sum of similarity between i-th proposal and the background proposals is far more than the sum of similarity between i-th proposal and other foreground proposals. Therefore, we adopt parameters sigmoid function to reweight $sim(i, back)$, the denominator is devised as follows:

$$\sum_{j \in \{fore\}} \exp\left(sim\left(i, j\right)/\tau\right) + \sum_{j \in \{back\}} \frac{\gamma \exp\left(sim\left(i, j\right)/\tau\right)}{\alpha + \exp\left(-\beta sim\left(i, j\right)/\tau\right)}, \tag{4}$$

where *fore* represents the foreground proposals and *back* represents the background proposals, α, β, γ are all hyper-parameters with $\alpha = 1.5, \beta = 1.0, \gamma = 0.25$.

Finally, in fine-tuning stage, we use the weighted contrastive loss to train the detector together with the cross-entropy loss for classification and the smooth L1 loss for regression.

4   Experiments

In this section, we will begin by describing the experimental settings we used. Following this, we will compare our method with previous works on the PASCAL VOC and COCO benchmarks, highlighting the strengths and weaknesses of our approach. To provide a more comprehensive understanding of our methodology, we will conclude this section with a series of ablation studies.

4.1   Experimental Setting

PASCAL VOC. For the PASCAL VOC dataset, we follow the previous work and train our method on the VOC2007 trainval and VOC2012 trainval sets and test our method on the VOC2007 test set. The overall 20 categories are divided into 15 base categories and 5 novel categories. Each novel category has K-shot instances which are randomly sampled and K=1,2,3,5,10. We use two random partitions of base and novel categories referred to as split1 and split2, where novel categories are {"bird", "bus", "cow", "motorbike", "sofa"} and {"aeroplane", "bottle", "cow", "horse", "sofa"}, respectively.

COCO. As for the COCO dataset, 20 categories in common with the PASCAL VOC dataset are denoted as novel categories while the remaining 60 categories are denoted as base categories. We utilize 5k images from the validation set for evaluation, which is noted as minival. The process of constructing a few-shot dataset is similar to the PASCAL VOC dataset and we report the K=1,2,3,5,10 shots detection performance.

Implementation Details. Our method adopts Faster R-CNN with ResNet-101 and Feature Pyramid Network(FPN) as the base framework. The backbone is pre-trained on ImageNet. We adopt SGD to optimize our network end-to-end with a mini-batch size of 16, a momentum of 0.9, and a weight decay of $5e^{-4}$. As for the PASCAL VOC dataset, the learning rate is set to 0.02, and the model is trained for 18k iterations during base training, the learning rate is reduced to $2e^{-3}$ and $2e^{-4}$ at 12k and 16k iterations, respectively. The learning rate is set to 0.01 during fine-tuning and we scale the training steps with the number of shots. As for the COCO dataset, the learning rate is set to 0.02 while the model is trained for 110k iterations during base training, the learning rate is reduced to $2e^{-3}$ and $2e^{-4}$ at 85k, and 110k iterations, respectively. During fine-tuning, we will train the model for 6k iterations for the K=10 shot. All experiments are run on 4 Titan Xp GPUs.

4.2   Comparisons with State-of-the-Art Methods

PASCAL VOC Results. Results for all two novel splits from PASCAL VOC dataset are shown in Table 1. Our method outperforms all existing works in almost all shots and all splits, except for 3-shot in split2. In split1, our method is superior to MPSR [12] by a large margin, especially in 1-shot and 5-shot(up

Table 1: Experimental results on PASCAL VOC dataset. We report the mAP with IoU threshold 0.5 (AP50) under two different splits for novel categories.

Method/shot	split1					split2				
	1	2	3	5	10	1	2	3	5	10
FRCN+ft-full [14]	13.8	19.6	32.8	41.5	45.6	7.9	15.3	26.2	31.6	39.1
FSRW [9]	14.8	15.5	26.7	33.9	47.2	15.7	15.3	22.7	30.1	40.5
Meta R-CNN [14]	19.9	25.5	35.0	45.7	51.5	10.4	19.4	29.6	34.8	45.4
TFA [11]	39.8	36.1	44.7	55.7	56.0	23.5	26.9	34.1	35.1	39.1
FSDetView [13]	24.2	35.3	42.2	49.1	57.4	21.6	24.6	31.9	37.0	45.7
DCNet [8]	33.9	37.4	43.7	51.1	59.6	23.2	24.8	30.6	36.7	46.6
MPSR [12]	41.7	–	51.4	55.2	61.8	24.4	–	**39.2**	39.9	47.8
Ours	**45.5**	**47.7**	**51.9**	**59.0**	**61.9**	**26.3**	**30.0**	38.3	**40.8**	**49.6**

to 3.8 AP50). When the number of shots increases, the detection accuracy of our method also increases accordingly, which verifies its consistency.

COCO Results. Table 2 shows all evaluation results on the COCO dataset in different shots. Our approach outperforms previous SOTAs in all setups, we achieved 7% improvements compared with current SOTA DCNet [8]. Furthermore, our method gained +2.7mAP compared to FSDetview [13] in 3-shot and has reached the performance of TFA in 10-shot (10.0), which demonstrates the strong effectiveness of our method.

Table 2: Experimental results on COCO dataset in different shots. * indicates that the results are reproduced by us, using the official code.

Method/shot	1	2	3	5	10
FSRW [9]	–	–	–	–	5.6
Meta R-CNN [14]	–	–	–	–	8.7
MPSR [12]	–	–	–	–	9.8
TFA [11]	3.6*	4.9*	6.9*	8.6*	10.0
FSCE [10]	2.6*	4.5*	6.5*	8.8*	11.9
A-RPN [15]	–	4.8*	5.9*	8.1*	12.0
FSDetView [13]	4.5	6.6	7.2	10.7	12.5
DCNet [8]	–	–	–	–	12.8
Ours	**5.7**	**8.0**	**9.9**	**11.2**	**13.7**

In Table 3, we compare our method with the previous state-of-the-art results specifically under the 10-shot setting. Our method is remarkably superior to other existing works on almost all metrics. We outperform the latest method [8] by about 7% on the mAP metric. AP_S, AP_M and AP_L are commonly used to evaluate the performance of the detector for objects with different scales, where AP_S indicates the average accuracy for small objects. We achieves non-negligible performance gains over DCNet [8] on AP_S metric, i.e., 5.6 AP_S vs. 4.3 AP_S. We also achieve both high precision and high recall, the AR_{10} and AR_{100} of our method is 23% and 34% higher than DCNet [8] and FSDetView [13], respectively. The excellent performance on the AR metric shows that our algorithm will have less missed detection than other methods.

Table 3: Experimental results on COCO dataset in 10 shot. We report the mean Average Precision and mean Average Recall. * indicates that the results are reproduced by us, using the official code.

Method	mAP	AP_{50}	AP_{75}	AP_S	AP_M	AP_L	AR_1	AR_{10}	AR_{100}
FSRW [9]	5.6	12.3	4.6	0.9	3.5	10.5	10.1	14.3	14.4
Meta R-CNN [14]	8.7	19.1	6.6	2.3	7.7	14.0	12.6	17.8	17.9
MPSR [12]	9.8	17.9	9.7	3.3	9.2	16.1	15.7	21.2	21.2
TFA [11]	10.0	19.3*	10.0*	5.1*	10.1*	16.3*	15.5*	23.9*	24.2*
FSCE [10]	11.9	24.6*	10.5*	4.3*	11.8*	19.2*	16.0*	24.7*	24.9*
A-RPN [15]	12.0	22.4	11.8	2.9	12.2	20.7	18.8	26.4	26.4
FSDetView [13]	12.5	**27.3**	9.8	2.5	13.8	19.9	**20.0**	25.5	25.7
DCNet [8]	12.8	23.4	11.2	4.3	13.8	21.0	18.1	26.7	25.6
Ours	**13.7**	25.4	**13.6**	**5.6**	**13.9**	**21.3**	**20.0**	**32.8**	**34.5**

4.3 Ablation Study

Table 4 shows the ablation study of 4 optimization strategies during the fine-tuning process and contrastive reweighting (CR) module. All ablation studies are conducted on the COCO dataset with K=10. The first line shows our baseline, which is re-implemented from TFA [11] and adopts none of the 4 strategies. As we can see, gradient adjustment (GA) achieves performance improvements of 2.0 mAP, NMS adjustment (NMS-A) and RoI refinement (RoI-R) gains +0.5 mAP and +0.3 mAP, respectively. Class-agnostic regressor (CAR) can further improve 0.4 mAP and the CR module provides more performance gains.

Table 4: Ablation study of different components proposed in our method.

GA	NMS-A	RoI-R	CAR	CR	mAP
					10.0
✔					12.0(+2.0)
✔	✔				12.5(+0.5)
✔	✔	✔			12.8(+0.3)
✔	✔	✔	✔		13.2(+0.4)
✔	✔	✔	✔	✔	**13.7(+0.5)**

5 Conclusion

In this study, we provide a novel few-shot object detection technique based on transfer learning. In the most recent benchmarks, our technique performs noticeably better than the existing works. We make Faster R-CNN capable of successfully completing FSOD tasks by incorporating 4 techniques during the fine-tuning procedure. A contrastive reweighting module may be readily integrated into other existing detectors and enhances the detector's classification capabilities. We wish to encourage other academics to concentrate on few-shot object detection through our work.

Acknowledgements. This work was supported by the National Natural Science Foundation of China (NSFC) under Grant No. 61876224.

References

1. Li, B., Liu, C., Shi, M., Chen, X., Ji, X., Ye, Q.: Proposal Distribution Calibration for Few-Shot Object Detection
2. Iofinova, E., Peste, A., Kurtz, M., Alistarh, D.: How well do sparse imagenet models transfer?. In: Proceedings of the IEEE conference on computer vision and pattern recognition (CVPR) (Apr 2022)
3. Gupta, A., Narayan, S., Joseph, K.J., Khan, S., Khan, F.S., Shah, M.: OW-DETR: open-world detection transformer. In: Proceedings of the IEEE Conference on Computer Vision and Pattern Recognition (CVPR) (Apr 2022)
4. Finn, C., Abbeel, P., Levine, S.: Model-agnostic meta-learning for fast adaptation of deep networks. In: International Conference on Machine Learning, pp. 1126–1135. PMLR (2017)
5. Snell, J., Swersky, K., Zemel, R.: Prototypical networks for few-shot learning. In: Advances in Neural Information Processing Systems, pp. 4077–4087 (2017)
6. Sung, F., Yang, Y., Zhang, L., Xiang, T., Torr, P.H.S., Hospedales, T.M.: Learning to compare: relation network for few-shot learning. In: Proceedings of the IEEE Conference on Computer Vision and Pattern Recognition, pp. 1199–1208 (2018)
7. Ren, S., He, K., Girshick, R., Sun, J.: Faster r-cnn: towards real-time object detection with region proposal networks. In: Advances in Neural Information Processing Systems, pp. 91–99 (2015)
8. Hu, H., Bai, S., Li, A., Cui, J., Wang, L.: Dense relation distillation with context-aware aggregation for few-shot object detection. In: Proceedings of the IEEE Conference on Computer Vision and Pattern Recognition, page TBD (2021)
9. Kang, B., Liu, Z., Wang, X., Yu, F., Feng, J., Darrell, T.: Few-shot object detection via feature reweighting. In: Proceedings of the IEEE/CVF International Conference on Computer Vision, pp. 8420–8429 (2019)
10. Sun, B., Li, B., Cai, S., Yuan, Y., Zhang, C.: Fsce: few-shot object detection via contrastive proposal encoding. In: Proceedings of the IEEE Conference on Computer Vision and Pattern Recognition (CVPR) TBD (June 2021)
11. Wang, X., Huang, T., Gonzalez, J., Darrell, T., Yu, F.: Frustratingly simple few-shot object detection. In: International Conference on Machine Learning, pp. 9919–9928. PMLR (2020)

12. Wu, J., Liu, S., Huang, D., Wang, Y.: Multi-scale positive sample refinement for few-shot object detection. In: Vedaldi, A., Bischof, H., Brox, T., Frahm, J.-M. (eds.) ECCV 2020. LNCS, vol. 12361, pp. 456–472. Springer, Cham (2020). https://doi.org/10.1007/978-3-030-58517-4_27

13. Xiao, Y., Marlet, R.: Few-shot object detection and viewpoint estimation for objects in the wild. In: Vedaldi, A., Bischof, H., Brox, T., Frahm, J.-M. (eds.) ECCV 2020. LNCS, vol. 12362, pp. 192–210. Springer, Cham (2020). https://doi.org/10.1007/978-3-030-58520-4_12

14. Yan, X., Chen, Z., Xu, A., Wang, X., Liang, X., Lin, L.: Meta r-cnn: towards general solver for instance-level low-shot learning. In: Proceedings of the IEEE/CVF International Conference on Computer Vision, pp. 9577–9586 (2019)

15. Fan, Q., Zhuo, W., Tang, C.-K., Tai, Y.-W.: Few-shot object detection with attention-rpn and multi-relation detector. In: Proceedings of the IEEE/CVF Conference on Computer Vision and Pattern Recognition, pp. 4013–4022 (2020)

16. Limeng, Q., Yuxuan, Z., Zhiyuan, L., Xi, Q., Jianan, W., Chi, Z.: Defrcn: decoupled faster r-cnn for few-shot object detection. In: Proceedings of the IEEE/CVF International Conference on Computer Vision, pp. 8681–8690 (2021)

17. van den Oord, A., Li, Y., Vinyals, O.: Representation learning with contrastive predictive coding, pp. 1807 (2018), arXiv e-prints

GaitFusion: Exploring the Fusion of Silhouettes and Optical Flow for Gait Recognition

Yuxiang Feng[(✉)] [iD], Jiabin Yuan, and Lili Fan

College of Computer Science and Technology, Nanjing University of Aeronautics
and Astronautics, Nanjing 211106, China
Endeavor666@nuaa.edu.cn

Abstract. Gait recognition is a promising biometric technology with great potential for security applications. Many gait recognition methods introduce multiple modalities to extract more discriminative gait features. However, some of these methods fail to fully exploit the potential of multimodal data and neglect to account for possible noise and redundancies. In this paper, we propose a novel multimodal gait recognition framework called GaitFusion, combining silhouettes and optical flow. Firstly, to take full advantage of multimodal data, we propose the Bottleneck Fusion Feature Extractor (BFFE) based on Transformer, which can extract underlying commonalities and correlated attributes from both modalities. Secondly, the Motion Feature Enhancer (MFE) is introduced to enhance motion features and alleviate redundancies by leveraging channel attention. Lastly, experimental results demonstrate that our method outperforms other state-of-the-art gait recognition methods. It achieves an average Rank-1 accuracy of 83.1% on the GREW dataset and 93.9% on the CASIA-B dataset.

Keywords: Gait recognition · Multimodal fusion · Transformer

1 Introduction

Gait recognition is one of the most promising biometric technologies for recognizing individuals based on their walking patterns. Unlike other biometrics such as face, fingerprint, and iris, gait is difficult to disguise and can be captured at a long distance without the cooperation of subjects. In light of the COVID-19 pandemic, traditional biometric systems may encounter failures [9], making gait recognition a superior option for security applications such as identity verification and crime investigation.

Due to low computational cost and high efficiency, most existing gait recognition methods [3,6,7,15] utilize human silhouettes as input data. Although silhouettes retain rich appearance information, internal body structure information is partially lost [19]. For this reason, features extracted from silhouettes are vulnerable to view changes, outfits changes and other exterior factors in the

ⓒ The Author(s), under exclusive license to Springer Nature Switzerland AG 2023
L. Iliadis et al. (Eds.): ICANN 2023, LNCS 14260, pp. 88–99, 2023.
https://doi.org/10.1007/978-3-031-44195-0_8

real world. Therefore, extracting accurate and robust gait features in real-world situations remains a longstanding challenge.

To overcome this challenge, we propose to leverage human silhouettes and optical flow for gait recognition. Optical flow can capture micro-motion information between two frames, which is not affected by the change of view or outfits. Furthermore, several successful works [20,23] in the action recognition field have proved the effectiveness of optical flow. By combining both modalities, we aim to obtain more complete gait representations. However, due to the modality gap between silhouettes and optical flow data representations, it is challenging to fuse two modalities reasonably to represent gait characteristics. Previous feature-fusion approaches [1,13] in gait recognition fail to fully exploit the potential of multimodal data and neglect to account for possible noise and redundancies.

To this end, we propose a novel multimodal gait recognition framework called GaitFusion, which consists of two novel modules, the Bottleneck Fusion Feature Extractor (BFFE) and the Motion Feature Enhancer (MFE). We assume that each modality has unique feature subspace, but when two modalities fuse, underlying commonalities and correlated attributes will be induced, which we call fusion features. These fusion features belong to a newly-formed feature subspace. The Transformed-based BFFE is developed to extract and map these fusion features into the new subspace, effectively distinguishing them from the original features and fusing valuable information between inter-modality and intra-modality.

Additionally, given that silhouettes and optical flow are both extracted from RGB frames, and hence belong to the homogeneous multimodal category. Their feature subspaces may overlap partially. To address this issue, we develop the MFE, which enhances the motion features and alleviate redundancies. By applying GaitFusion, we can map the multimodal data (silhouettes and optical flow) into three distinct feature subspaces (see Fig. 1), including the original feature subspace for each modality, and the newly-formed feature subspace for the fusion features.

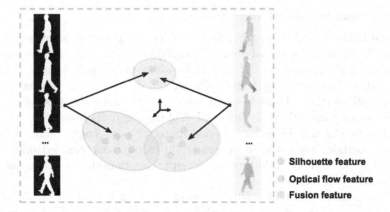

Silhouette feature
Optical flow feature
Fusion feature

Fig. 1. Learning multimodal data representations in three different feature subspaces.

Concretely, our major contributions are summarized as follows:

1. We propose a novel multimodal gait recognition framework GaitFusion. Gait-Fusion learns multimodal data representations in three different feature subspaces, to obtain more accurate and robust gait features.
2. We explore the fusion of silhouettes and optical flow. With the proposed BFFE and MFE, we take the potential information and redundancies into account, to give a comprehensive and efficient way to process multimodal data.
3. We evaluate the proposed method on two popular datasets: CASIA-B and GREW. The results of our experiments demonstrate that our method outperforms the current state-of-the-art methods.

2   Related Work

2.1   Singlemodal Gait Recognition

Existing mainstream singlemodal gait recognition methods can be divided into silhouettes-based [3,6,7,15] and pose-based [14,21] methods. Human silhouettes are obtained by background subtraction or segmentation methods based on deep learning. While silhouettes can effectively provide rich appearance information during the gait period, they are sensitive to variations in clothing and camera views. Due to this, some methods [14,21] attempt to extract 2D pose or 3D pose from the human body which should be more robust to view and clothing variations. However, when the resolution is not high enough, these methods are more prone to failure, which lacks practicality. Researchers have also explored other modalities such as optical flow [2], 3D point clouds [18], and depth images [17].

In recent years, there has been significant progress in optical flow extraction algorithms, such as FlowNet 2.0 [12]. Benefiting from it, we introduce optical flow for gait recognition which can provide micro-motion information between two frames that lacks in silhouettes. This subtle movement captured by optical flow is also helpful for gait recognition.

2.2   Multimodal Gait Recognition

Faced with the natural challenging factors in practical environment, more and more methods [1,13,25] choose multiple modalities to remedy the defects of a single modality. Castro et al. [1] explored various fusion techniques for multi-modal feature fusion with gray, optical flow, and depth images. Guo et al. [13] combined silhouettes and pose heatmaps to reduce the influence caused by clothing and carrying conditions. Zheng et al. [25] leveraged 3D human meshes and silhouettes to generate dense 3D representations for gait recognition in the wild. However, methods presented in papers [1,13] merely concatenated data from two modalities, without exploiting the potential relationships or accounting for possible noise and redundancies.

In this paper, we combine silhouettes and optical flow, which respectively represent appearance and motion features. To maximize the valuable information and minimize the redundancies brought by multimodal data, we propose a novel multimodal gait recognition framework called GaitFusion.

2.3   Transformer

Transformer [22] was initially introduced for natural language processing (NLP) tasks, which employed a powerful multi-head attention mechanism to capture long-range dependencies with different patterns in the input sequences. Its success in NLP tasks sparked interest in its applicability to computer vision. One notable approach was the Vision Transformer (ViT) [5], which converted the input image into a sequence of flattened patches and then fed them into Transformer to achieve tasks such as image classification and detection. In gait recognition, Guo et al. [13] used a Transformer-based STM to learn the temporal relativity of gait sequences. In this paper, the Transformer-based BFFE is proposed to extract fusion features.

3   Proposed Method

To learn multimodal data representations in three feature subspaces, we modify the GaitBase [6] feature extraction network into a two-stream backbone and incorporate two novel modules (BFFE and MFE). Our updated framework (see Fig. 2), which consists of appearance, motion and fusion branch, is now known as GaitFusion.

3.1   Pipeline

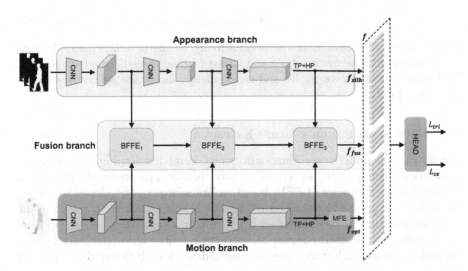

Fig. 2. The overall framework of GaitFusion. TP represents Temporal Pooling. HP represents Horizontal Pooling. BFFE represents Bottleneck Fusion Feature Extractor and MFE represents Motion Feature Enhancer. In particular, HEAD includes several separate FC layers and BNNeck.

As shown in Fig. 2, the silhouettes and optical flow are fed into GaitFusion frame by frame. Then we extract the spatial features $F_{S_i}^k$ $(F_{O_i}^k)$ for each frame S_i (O_i) by ResNet9 [6], as follows:

$$F_{S_i}^k = \text{ResNet9}\,(S_i)\,,\, F_{O_i}^k = \text{ResNet9}\,(O_i) \tag{1}$$

where $i \in 1, 2, 3, \ldots, t$ denotes the index of frame in gait sequence and $k \in 1, 2, 3$ denotes the spatial features extracted from which stage.

Then, in the appearance branch and motion branch, the TP module will work along the temporal dimension to obtain discriminative temporal features by maximum operation. Next, the wildly used HP module [3,8] horizontally splits the feature into n parts ($n = 16$) $p_j \in \mathbb{R}^{C \times W}$ and compresses the information into a column vector $p_j' \in \mathbb{R}^{C \times 1}$ for each part by global average pooling and global max pooling, as follows:

$$p_j' = \text{Avgpooling}(p_j) + \text{Maxpooling}(p_j) \tag{2}$$

where $j \in 1, 2, 3, \ldots, n$, C and W denotes the number of channels and the width of feature maps.

In the fusion branch, we will collect relevant information in each modality and condense them into a small number of bottleneck units by the Bottleneck Fusion Feature Extractor (BFFE) at different stages. Additionally, we introduce the Motion Feature Enhancer (MFE) at the end of motion branch, which can enhance the motion features and alleviate redundancies. Then, the elements from three branches will be merged, as follows:

$$f = \text{Cat}\,[f_{\text{silh}}, f_{\text{fus}}, f_{\text{opt}}] \tag{3}$$

where Cat means concatenate operation. Finally, we use several separate FC layers to map f into the metric space and adjust feature space by the BNNeck [16]. Meanwhile, the separate triplet and cross-entropy losses are generated to train the model jointly.

3.2 Bottleneck Fusion Feature Extractor

Considering the underlying commonalities and correlated attributes between two modalities which we call fusion features have their own subspace, the Bottleneck Fusion Feature Extractor (BFFE) based on Transformer is developed to extract them. We rely on the global receptive field of Transformer [22] to transmit and share information between inter-modality and intra-modality and finally condense them into a small number of bottleneck units, which not only induces valuable information but also prevents redundancies with the original modality features.

As shown in Fig. 3, we first concatenate the feature maps of each modality and add a learnable positional embedding, which is a trainable parameter, to get the input tokens of the BFFE. Note that the elements fed into the BFFE have passed through TP and HP module. Then, a multi-head attention mechanism

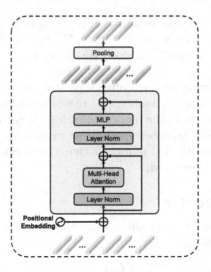

Fig. 3. The structure of Bottleneck Fusion Feature Extractor

(MHA) transmits and shares the information between two modalities. Specifically, by allowing tokens interact with each other, potential information such as underlying commonalities and correlated attributes from two modalities will be induced. After the nonlinear projection mapping worked by MLP block, we use the pooling operation to restrict and condense the necessary information into bottleneck units. The BFFE is formulated as follows:

$$z = \mathrm{Cat}[F_S, F_O] + pos \tag{4}$$
$$z' = \mathrm{MHA}(\mathrm{LN}(z)) + z \tag{5}$$
$$z'' = \mathrm{MLP}(\mathrm{LN}(z')) + z' = \mathrm{FC}_2(\mathrm{GELU}(\mathrm{FC}_1(z'))) + z' \tag{6}$$
$$z''' = \mathrm{Maxpooling}\,(z'') + \mathrm{Avgpooling}\,(z'') \tag{7}$$

where Cat denotes concatenate operation, pos represents positional embedding, MLP is a feed-forward network with two fully-connected layers and a GELU activation, and LN denotes Layer Normalization.

Different layers of a convolutional network have different receptive fields [3]. Hence, we apply the BFFE at different stages to collate multi-scale information. Multi-scale features are aggregated at last and the final f_{fus} is generated. It can be formalized as

$$f_{fus} = \sum_{k=1}^{3} z_k''' \tag{8}$$

3.3 Motion Feature Enhancer

Since silhouettes and optical flow belong to homogeneous multimodal category, both extracted from RGB frames, their feature subspaces may overlap partially. For instance, with the powerful optical flow extraction algorithm [12], the human body boundary can be shown clearly in optical flow, representing the similar semantic information with silhouettes. We believe that such information is redundant and unnecessary. To address this issue, we propose Motion Feature Enhancer (MFE).

In vision tasks, different channels often represent different objects [4]. Hence, in MFE, we leverage channel attention [11] to adaptively recalibrate the weight of each channel, which allows the motion branch to focus on extracting motion features. With two main branches specializing in learning and extracting uni-modal patterns (appearance and motion patterns), the complementarity of two modalities can be fully leveraged.

3.4   Training and Testing

Training Loss. During the training phase, the overall loss used to train the model can be formulated as:

$$L = L_{tri} + L_{ce} \tag{9}$$

The separate batch all (BA+) triplet loss [10] is generated from the corresponding column feature vectors among different samples. And the cross-entropy loss is generated from the features adjusted by the BNNeck [16]. Following batch all sampling strategy [10], the batch size is set to (p, k) where p denotes the number of persons and k denotes the number of training samples each person has in the batch.

Testing. During the test phase, the test set is divided into gallery and probe. The samples in the gallery are labeled, while the samples in the probe are used for prediction. We use the average Euclidean distance of the corresponding feature vectors to measure the similarities between gallery and probe.

4   Experiments

4.1   Datasets

Two datasets are applied to evaluate the GaitFusion, one is the in-the-lab dataset CASIA-B and the other is the in-the-wild dataset GREW.

CASIA-B. CASIA-B dataset [24] is the most widely used gait dataset composed of 124 subjects with 11 different viewing angles and 3 walking conditions. 11 different viewing angles range from 0∘ to 180∘ with 18∘ increments. And 3 walking conditions contain normal walking(NM), walking with a bag(BG), and walking with a coat(CL), respectively with 6, 2, and 2 gait sequences per person per view. Regarding protocol, the first 74 subjects are used for training, and the remaining 50 subjects are reserved for testing. In the testing stage, the first four sequences of NM (NM#1-4) are stored in the gallery, and the rest six sequences are conditionally divided into three probe subsets(NM#5-6, BG#1-2 and CL#1-2) to calculate Rank-1 accuracy.

GREW. GREW dataset [26] is the first large-scale dataset for gait recognition in the wild, which contains 26,345 subjects and 128,671 sequences from 882 cameras. Besides, GREW provides various input data types including silhouettes, Gait Energy Images (GEIs), 2D/3D pose and optical flow. Diverse and practical view variations, as well as more natural factors make it a more challenging dataset for gait recognition. Therefore, GREW is selected to verify the effectiveness of our method for practical gait recognition.

4.2 Implementation Details

As shown in Table 1, we list some hyper-parameters of our experiments for different datasets. All the source codes are based on OpenGait [6]. The optical flow is generated by FlowNet 2.0 [12]. The input resolution of silhouettes and optical flow is set to 64×44. We set the triplet loss margin as 0.2, the initial learning rate and the weight decay of SGD optimizer as 0.1 and 0.0005. We randomly select fixed 30 frames on CASIA-B and unfixed 20–40 frames on GREW for training input length. The data augmentation strategy is as same as in GaitBase [6].

Table 1. Implementation details.

Dataset	Batch Size	MultiStep Scheduler	Steps
CASIA-B	(8,16)	(20k,40k,50k)	60k
GREW	(32,4)	(80k,120k,150k)	180k

4.3 Comparison with State-of-the-Art Methods

We evaluate the performance of our proposed method, GaitFusion, against other state-of-the-art methods on two datasets, CASIA-B and GREW. The comparison includes four singlemodal (silhouettes) methods, i.e., GaitSet [3], GaitPart [7], GaitGL [15], and GaitBase [6], and one multimodal (silhouettes and pose heatmaps) method, TransGait [13].

As presented in Table 2 and Table 3, the results indicate that GaitFusion outperforms all the compared methods on both datasets. From the perspective of the number of methods selected in each category, multimodal gait recognition approaches are not currently mainstream. However, it is encouraging to note that multimodal methods achieve promising performance. Particularly, our method has achieved a significant improvement in performance on the in-the-wild dataset GREW, with an increase of 23% in Rank-1 accuracy than the best among compared methods. This finding highlights the necessity of a multimodal method for practical gait recognition.

Furthermore, we observe that while GaitBase's accuracy is less competitive on CASIA-B, it performs remarkably well on GREW. This observation suggests that research begins to promote gait recognition methods from in-the-lab settings to in-the-wild scenarios. Similarly, our approach aims to improve gait recognition performance in real-world situations.

Table 2. Rank-1 accuracy (%) on CASIA-B under all view angles and different conditions, excluding identical-view cases.

Gallery		0°–180°											Mean
	Probe	0°	18°	36°	54°	72°	90°	108°	126°	144°	162°	180°	
NM	GaitSet [3]	90.8	97.9	99.4	96.9	93.6	91.7	95.0	97.8	98.9	96.8	85.8	95.0
	GaitPart [7]	94.1	98.6	99.3	98.5	94.0	92.3	95.9	98.4	99.2	97.8	90.4	96.2
	GaitGL [15]	96.0	98.3	99.0	97.9	96.9	95.4	97.0	98.9	99.3	98.8	94.0	97.4
	TransGait [13]	**97.3**	99.6	99.7	99.0	97.1	95.4	97.4	99.1	99.6	98.9	**95.8**	98.1
	GaitBase [6]	-	-	-	-	-	-	-	-	-	-	-	97.6
	GaitFusion	97.2	**99.8**	**99.9**	**99.7**	**99.4**	**98.0**	**98.9**	**99.7**	**99.7**	**99.5**	94.4	**98.7**
BG	GaitSet[3]	83.8	91.2	91.8	88.8	83.3	81.0	84.1	90.0	92.2	94.4	79.0	87.2
	GaitPart [7]	89.1	94.8	96.7	95.1	88.3	84.9	89.0	93.5	96.1	93.8	85.8	91.5
	GaitGL [15]	92.6	96.6	96.8	95.5	93.5	89.3	92.2	96.5	98.2	96.9	91.5	94.5
	TransGait [13]	94.0	97.1	96.5	96.0	93.5	91.5	93.6	95.9	97.2	97.1	91.6	94.9
	GaitBase [6]	-	-	-	-	-	-	-	-	-	-	-	94.0
	GaitFusion	**96.7**	**98.9**	**98.4**	**97.7**	**96.6**	**96.3**	**96.9**	**98.0**	**99.5**	**98.8**	**92.1**	**97.3**
CL	GaitSet [3]	61.4	75.4	80.7	77.3	72.1	70.1	71.5	73.5	73.5	68.4	50.0	70.4
	GaitPart [7]	70.7	85.5	86.9	83.3	77.1	72.5	76.9	82.2	83.8	80.2	66.5	78.7
	GaitGL [15]	76.6	90.0	90.3	87.1	84.5	79.0	84.1	87.0	87.3	84.4	69.5	83.6
	TransGait [13]	**80.1**	89.3	91.0	89.1	84.7	83.3	85.6	**87.5**	**88.2**	**88.8**	**76.6**	**85.8**
	GaitBase [6]	-	-	-	-	-	-	-	-	-	-	-	77.4
	GaitFusion	78.5	**90.8**	**91.7**	**90.3**	**87.0**	**85.1**	**86.4**	85.8	87.2	86.0	74.7	**85.8**

Table 3. Rank-1 accuracy (%), Rank-5 accuracy (%), Rank-10 accuracy (%), and Rank-20 accuracy (%) on GREW.

Methods	Publication	Rank-1	Rank-5	Rank-10	Rank-20
GaitSet [3]	AAAI 2019	46.3	63.6	70.3	76.8
GaitPart [7]	CVPR 2020	44.0	60.7	67.3	73.5
GaitGL [15]	ICCV 2021	51.7	–	–	–
TransGait [13]	Appl. Intell. 2022	56.3	72.7	78.1	82.5
GaitBase [6]	CVPR 2023	60.1	75.5	80.4	84.2
GaitFusion		**83.1**	**91.3**	**93.6**	**95.2**

4.4   Ablation Study

We conduct several ablation studies on CASIA-B in the following parts to verify the effectiveness of each component in GaitFusion.

Analysis of Multimodal Approach. In this paper, we propose to leverage silhouettes and optical flow for gait recognition. By comparing three experiments (Group A,B, and C), as presented in Table 4, we demonstrate that the multi-modal fusion of silhouettes and optical flow yields superior performance com-

Table 4. Ablation experiments conducted on CASIA-B.

Group	Silhouettes	Optical Flow	BFFE	MFE	NM	BG	CL
A	✓	✗	✗	✗	97.6	94.0	77.4
B	✗	✓	✗	✗	93.5	90.1	75.1
C	✓	✓	✗	✗	98.3	96.1	83.9
D	✓	✓	✓	✗	98.4	96.8	85.6
E	✓	✓	✗	✓	98.5	96.5	84.9
F	✓	✓	✓	✓	**98.7**	**97.3**	**85.8**

pared to singlemodal approaches, validating the effectiveness of the multimodal approach. The micro-motion information captured by optical flow enriches gait representations significantly.

Analysis of BFFE and MFE. In order to validate the effectiveness of BFFE, we compare Group C (without BFFE) and Group D (with BFFE). As shown in Table 4, BFFE significantly improves the accuracy of gait recognition, providing evidence that it can extract valuable fusion features. Equally, we compare Group C (without MFE) and Group E (with MFE) to validate the effectiveness of MFE. As indicated by the increased results shown in Table 4, MFE can enhance motion features and alleviate redundancies. Although the effect of MFE is not significant compared to BFFE, it aligns with expectations as silhouettes and optical flow only share a small overlap in semantic information. Hence, we decide to utilize two modules together, and Group F demonstrates the best performance on CASIA-B, especially for BG (+1.2%) and CL (+1.9%) condition.

Analysis of the Number of Units for BFFE. To explore the optimal number of units for BFFE, we conduct four experiments, the results of which are presented in Table 5. It shows that the highest mean accuracy 93.9% is achieved when $N = 4$. Furthermore, compared to $N = 0$ (without BFFE), $N = 2$ shows limited improvement while $N = 8$ results in a drop in performance, which suggests that too many units will create excessive learning pressure on the network, leading to redundancies. Conversely, too few units may not adequately represent the fusion information. When $N = 4$, the number of units is small but still provides a tight representation of fusion features, which can preserve necessary information and prevent redundancies with the original modality features.

Table 5. Rank-1 accuracy (%) of different unit numbers (N) for BFFE.

N	NM	BG	CL	Mean
0	98.5	96.5	84.9	93.3
2	**98.7**	96.9	84.8	93.5
4	**98.7**	**97.3**	**85.8**	**93.9**
8	98.1	95.8	85.2	93.0

5   Conclusion

In this paper, we explore the fusion of silhouettes and optical flow for gait recognition and take the potential information and redundancies brought by multimodal data into account. Thus, GaitFusion is proposed, which consists of Bottleneck Fusion Feature Extractor and Motion Feature Enhancer. The core goal of two novel modules is to extract the potential valuable information when fusing two modalities and alleviate redundancies. Finally, the experimental results on CASIA-B and GREW demonstrate that the proposed method achieves the outperforming accuracy over the state-of-the-art methods.

References

1. Castro, F.M., Marin-Jimenez, M.J., Guil, N., Pérez de la Blanca, N.: Multimodal feature fusion for cnn-based gait recognition: an empirical comparison. Neural Comput. Appli. **32**, 14173–14193 (2020)
2. Castro, F.M., Marín-Jiménez, M.J., Guil, N., López-Tapia, S., de la Blanca, N.P.: Evaluation of cnn architectures for gait recognition based on optical flow maps. In: 2017 International Conference of the Biometrics Special Interest Group (BIOSIG), pp. 1–5. IEEE (2017)
3. Chao, H., He, Y., Zhang, J., Feng, J.: Gaitset: regarding gait as a set for cross-view gait recognition. In: Proceedings of the AAAI Conference on Artificial Intelligence, vol. 33, pp. 8126–8133 (2019)
4. Chen, L., et al.: Sca-cnn: spatial and channel-wise attention in convolutional networks for image captioning. In: Proceedings of the IEEE Conference on Computer Vision and Pattern Recognition, pp. 5659–5667 (2017)
5. Dosovitskiy, A., et al.: An image is worth 16x16 words: transformers for image recognition at scale. arXiv preprint arXiv:2010.11929 (2020)
6. Fan, C., Liang, J., Shen, C., Hou, S., Huang, Y., Yu, S.: Opengait: revisiting gait recognition towards better practicality. In: Proceedings of the IEEE/CVF Conference on Computer Vision and Pattern Recognition, pp. 9707–9716 (2023)
7. Fan, C., et al.: Gaitpart: temporal part-based model for gait recognition. In: Proceedings of the IEEE/CVF Conference on Computer Vision and Pattern Recognition, pp. 14225–14233 (2020)
8. Fu, Y., et al.: Horizontal pyramid matching for person re-identification. In: Proceedings of the AAAI Conference on Artificial Intelligence, vol. 33, pp. 8295–8302 (2019)

9. Guo, Y.: Impact on biometric identification systems of Covid-19. Sci. Program. **2021**, 1–7 (2021)
10. Hermans, A., Beyer, L., Leibe, B.: In defense of the triplet loss for person re-identification. arXiv preprint arXiv:1703.07737 (2017)
11. Hu, J., Shen, L., Sun, G.: Squeeze-and-excitation networks. In: Proceedings of the IEEE Conference on Computer Vision and Pattern Recognition, pp. 7132–7141 (2018)
12. Ilg, E., Mayer, N., Saikia, T., Keuper, M., Dosovitskiy, A., Brox, T.: Flownet 2.0: evolution of optical flow estimation with deep networks. In: Proceedings of the IEEE Conference on Computer Vision and Pattern Recognition, pp. 2462–2470 (2017)
13. Li, G., Guo, L., Zhang, R., Qian, J., Gao, S.: Transgait: multimodal-based gait recognition with set transformer. Appl. Intell. **53**(2), 1535–1547 (2023)
14. Liao, R., Yu, S., An, W., Huang, Y.: A model-based gait recognition method with body pose and human prior knowledge. Pattern Recogn. **98**, 107069 (2020)
15. Lin, B., Zhang, S., Yu, X.: Gait recognition via effective global-local feature representation and local temporal aggregation. In: Proceedings of the IEEE/CVF International Conference on Computer Vision, pp. 14648–14656 (2021)
16. Luo, H., Gu, Y., Liao, X., Lai, S., Jiang, W.: Bag of tricks and a strong baseline for deep person re-identification. In: Proceedings of the IEEE/CVF Conference on Computer Vision and Pattern Recognition Workshops (2019)
17. Nunes, J.F., Moreira, P.M., Tavares, J.M.R.S.: Benchmark RGB-D gait datasets: a systematic review. In: Tavares, J.M.R.S., Natal Jorge, R.M. (eds.) VipIMAGE 2019. LNCVB, vol. 34, pp. 366–372. Springer, Cham (2019). https://doi.org/10.1007/978-3-030-32040-9_38
18. Shen, C., Fan, C., Wu, W., Wang, R., Huang, G.Q., Yu, S.: Lidargait: benchmarking 3d gait recognition with point clouds. In: Proceedings of the IEEE/CVF Conference on Computer Vision and Pattern Recognition, pp. 1054–1063 (2023)
19. Shen, C., Yu, S., Wang, J., Huang, G.Q., Wang, L.: A comprehensive survey on deep gait recognition: algorithms, datasets and challenges. arXiv preprint arXiv:2206.13732 (2022)
20. Simonyan, K., Zisserman, A.: Two-stream convolutional networks for action recognition in videos. In: Advances in Neural Information Processing Systems 27 (2014)
21. Teepe, T., Khan, A., Gilg, J., Herzog, F., Hörmann, S., Rigoll, G.: Gaitgraph: graph convolutional network for skeleton-based gait recognition. In: 2021 IEEE International Conference on Image Processing (ICIP), pp. 2314–2318. IEEE (2021)
22. Vaswani, A., et al.: Attention is all you need. In: Advances in Neural Information Processing Systems 30 (2017)
23. Wang, L., et al.: Temporal segment networks: towards good practices for deep action recognition. In: Leibe, B., Matas, J., Sebe, N., Welling, M. (eds.) ECCV 2016. LNCS, vol. 9912, pp. 20–36. Springer, Cham (2016). https://doi.org/10.1007/978-3-319-46484-8_2
24. Yu, S., Tan, D., Tan, T.: A framework for evaluating the effect of view angle, clothing and carrying condition on gait recognition. In: 18th International Conference on Pattern Recognition (ICPR 2006), vol. 4, pp. 441–444. IEEE (2006)
25. Zheng, J., Liu, X., Liu, W., He, L., Yan, C., Mei, T.: Gait recognition in the wild with dense 3d representations and a benchmark. In: Proceedings of the IEEE/CVF Conference on Computer Vision and Pattern Recognition, pp. 20228–20237 (2022)
26. Zhu, Z., et al.: Gait recognition in the wild: a benchmark. In: Proceedings of the IEEE/CVF International Conference on Computer Vision, pp. 14789–14799 (2021)

Gradient Adjusted and Weight Rectified Mean Teacher for Source-Free Object Detection

Jiawen Peng[1], Jiaxin Chen[1], Yanxu Hu[1], Rong Pan[1], and Andy J. Ma[1,2,3](✉)

[1] School of Computer Science and Engineering, Sun Yat-sen University,
Guangzhou, China
{pengjw23,chenjx529,huyx69}@mail2.sysu.edu.cn,
{panr,majh8}@mail.sysu.edu.cn
[2] Guangdong Province Key Laboratory of Information Security Technology,
Guangzhou, China
[3] Key Laboratory of Machine Intelligence and Advanced Computing,
Ministry of Education, Guangzhou, China

Abstract. Source-free object detection (SFOD) aims at adapting object detectors to the unlabeled target domain without access to the labeled source domain. Recent SFOD methods are developed based on the Mean Teacher framework, which consists of a student and a teacher model for self-training. Despite the great success, existing methods suffer from the challenges of missing detections and fitting to incorrect pseudo labels. To overcome these challenges, we propose a Gradient Adjusted and Weight Rectified Mean Teacher framework with two novel training strategies for SFOD, i.e., Negative Gradient Adjustment (NGA) and Source Weight Rectification (SWR). The proposed Negative Gradient Adjustment suppresses the negative gradients caused by missing detections, while the Source Weight Rectification enhances the robustness by rectifying errors of pseudo labels. Additionally, weak-strong consistency data augmentation is introduced for stronger detector performance. Extensive experiments on four benchmarks demonstrate that our proposed method outperforms the existing works for SFOD.

Keywords: Source-free Object Detection · Negative Gradient Adjustment · Source Weight Rectification

1 Introduction

Convolutional neural networks have achieved satisfying results in object detection, but still suffer from the problem of significant performance degradation caused by domain shift. To address this issue, Cross-Domain Object Detection

This work was supported partially by the National Natural Science Foundation of China (No. 62276281) and the Special Funds for Central Government Guiding Development of Local Science & Technology (No. 2020B151531001).

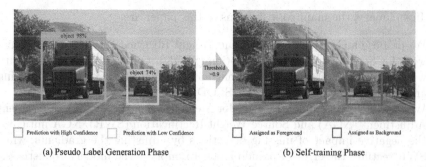

(a) Pseudo Label Generation Phase   (b) Self-training Phase

Fig. 1. Problems of missing detections in self-training. (a) In the pseudo label generation phase, only high-confidence pseudo-labels (green) can be preserved under a high threshold. (b) In the self-training phase, foreground regions with low prediction confidence (red) are assigned as background. (Color figure online)

(CDOD) [1, 2, 4, 7, 16, 25] is proposed to enhance the performance of object detectors by leveraging both labeled source domain and unlabeled target domain. However, CDOD presupposes the availability of labeled data from the source domain, which is not always practical. To ease the dependence on the source domain, Source-free Object Detection (SFOD) has been proposed recently. SFOD employs an object detector pre-trained on the source domain for model adaptation to the target domain. Among various recent SFOD methods, the Mean Teacher framework [5, 13, 24] extended from semi-supervised learning [23] to perform self-training have received a lot of attention due to its effectiveness.

Despite making significant strides, two challenges remain in recent SFOD research based on the self-training of Mean Teacher [5, 13, 24]. First, when high-quality pseudo labels used in the self-training phase are generated through a high threshold, the issue of missing detections may become severe. As illustrated in Fig. 1, low-confidence (yellow box in Fig. 1(a)) pseudo labels are filtered out by a high threshold, such that regions containing foreground objects are wrongly regarded as background during self-training (red box in Fig. 1(b)). Second, although with high confidence, some of the pseudo labels in the target domain are not correct. As analyzed in [17], it tends to fit the inaccurate pseudo labels in the later training iterations, leading to a performance drop in object detection.

In this paper, we propose a Gradient Adjusted and Weight Rectified Mean Teacher framework to address these two issues. To address the problem of missing detections, we propose Negative Gradient Adjustment (NGA). The NGA introduces an adjustment factor to adaptively adjust the massive negative gradients generated by missing detections. In addition, the Source Weight Rectification (SWR) is designed to regularize the student model by encouraging it to be similar to the pre-trained source model. The SWR can reduce the impact of inaccurate pseudo labels and improve robustness. Moreover, as data augmentation is beneficial in improving the model's performance in the target domain [2, 16], we employ the weak-strong consistency approach following the FixMatch [21]. With all these techniques, our method achieves substantial accuracy gains across all the SFOD experiments.

In summary, the main contributions of this paper are:

1. We propose a Gradient Adjusted and Weight Rectified Mean Teacher framework for Source-Free Object Detection (SFOD). Our method equipped with weak-strong consistency training enhances the effectiveness of self-training and improves the performance for SFOD.
2. We design two training strategies for Mean Teacher, i.e., Negative Gradient Adjustment (NGA) and Source Weight Rectification (SWR). NGA mitigates the negative impact of missing detections by adjusting the gradients, while SWR rectifies the error of pseudo labels to improve the model's robustness.
3. Extensive experiments on four different adaptation scenarios demonstrate the superiority of the proposed method for SFOD. For all cases, our proposed method achieves state-of-the-art performance.

2   Related Work

2.1   Cross-Domain Object Detection

Previous works on Cross-Domain Object Detection (CDOD) can be mainly categorized into adversarial training and self-training approaches. Adversarial training-based methods [4,7,11,16,19,25] perform cross-domain feature alignment for object detector with the help of a domain discriminator and a gradient reversal layer (GRL). Instead of directly minimizing the domain gap, methods based on self-training [1,2,7,14,16] utilize a student model and a teacher model for consistency regularization with pseudo labels. Though the self-training-based methods can achieve convincing performance, they rely on high-confidence pseudo labels, which exacerbates the issue of missing detections. Moreover, all these methods mentioned above are developed based on the availability of the source domain data, which may not be applicable in many practical scenarios.

2.2   Source-Free Object Detection

Compared to CDOD, Source-free Object Detection (SFOD) [5,9,13,15,24] is a more challenging but practical scenario as it does not require to access to the source domain. Most existing SFOD methods focus on Mean Teacher and pseudo labels. SED [15], an early work in SFOD, proposes self-entropy descent for the adaptive selection of high-quality pseudo-labels. HCL [9] proposes historical contrastive learning, which introduces historical contrastive instance discrimination and category discrimination. Recent SFOD methods [5,13,24] are developed based on Mean Teacher framework and achieve state-of-the-art performance. Both SOAP [24] and LODS [13] aim to reduce the domain gap through style transfer between images in the target domain. SOAP perturbs the target images with estimated domain-specific perturbation, while LODS enhances the domain style by reconstruction network and overlooks domain style by two graph alignments. A^{2}SFOD [5] designs a detection variance-based criterion to divide the target domain into source-similar and source-dissimilar parts and aligns them in

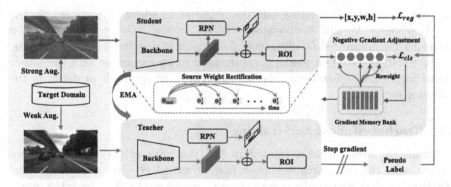

Fig. 2. Overview of our proposed Gradient Adjusted and Weight Regularized Mean Teacher. Our method consists of two modules: 1) Teacher model takes weakly-augmented images as the input and generates pseudo labels for the student model. 2) Student model takes strongly-augmented images as the input and trains with the pseudo labels from the teacher model. The student model updates the teacher model with Exponential Moving Average (EMA). Negative Gradient Adjustment (NGA) and Source Weight Rectification (SWR) are employed to mitigate the issue of missing detection and improve the robustness of the student model, respectively.

the feature space by adversarial learning. However, these methods are likely to suffer from the problem of missing detections and inaccurate pseudo labels. Similar to the previous self-training-based methods, the Mean Teacher framework is considered as the baseline in our method.

3 Proposed Method

3.1 Problem Formulation and Overview

In this section, we first review the problem formulation in Source-free Object Detection (SFOD). The labeled source domain is denoted as $\mathcal{D}_s = \{X_s, B_s, Y_s\}$, in which B_s denotes the bounding box annotations and Y_s denotes the corresponding class labels for the source images X_s. The unlabeled target domain is denoted as $\mathcal{D}_t = \{X_t\}$, where X_t denotes the target images. The pseudo labels of the target domain (i.e. $\hat{B}_t$ and $\hat{Y}_t$) are generated by the teacher model for self-training. The pre-trained detector Θ_{init} is obtained through standard supervised learning on the source domain $\mathcal{D}_s$. The objective of SFOD is to train a target domain detector by leveraging $\mathcal{D}_t$ and Θ_{init}.

The overview of our proposed Gradient Adjusted and Weight Regularized Mean Teacher framework is presented in Fig. 2. Our framework consists of two branches, i.e., the teacher model and the student model. The weakly-augmented images and strongly-augmented images are fed into the teacher model and the student model, respectively. The teacher generates pseudo labels to train the student while the student updates the learned knowledge back to the teacher via Exponential Moving Average (EMA). We propose two training strategies to improve the student model namely the Negative Gradient Adjustment (NGA) and the Source Weight Rectification (SWR). In the NGA, missing detection problems are suppressed by mitigating the impact of massive negative gradients. In the SWR, the student model is constrained to be consistent with the source model for better self-training. We will describe our approach in detail in the following sections.

3.2   Teacher-Student Self-training

Following the Mean Teacher framework [23], our approach is composed of two models with the same architecture: a teacher model Θ_T and a student model Θ_S. Both models are initialized with the pre-trained model Θ_{init} from the source domain. To facilitate self-training, we employ weak-strong consistency training. The student model is learned through the pseudo labels generated by the teacher model and the teacher model is updated with the Exponential Moving Average (EMA) of the weights from the student model.

Weak-Strong Consistency Training. The weak-strong consistency training strategy includes the weak augmentation $\mathcal{A}_W$ and strong augmentation $\mathcal{A}_S$. In all of our experiments, weak augmentation is RandomHorizontalFlip. For the strong augmentation, we employ manually designed data augmentations in SimCLR [3]. The strong data augmentation acts as a simple yet powerful domain perturbation. During training, the teacher model utilizes weakly-augmented images to generate reliable pseudo labels, and the student model uses strongly-augmented images for consistency training, as illustrated in Fig. 2.

Optimizing Student with Pseudo Labels. Without access to the annotations, We adopt a large threshold to produce pseudo labels with high confidence on the target domain. The pseudo labels are computed as $\{\hat{B}_t, \hat{Y}_t\} = \delta(f(\Theta_T, \mathcal{A}_W(X_t)))$, where δ is a high confidence threshold filter. The overall loss function is given by:

$$\mathcal{L}_{det} = \mathcal{L}_{reg}(f(\Theta_S, \mathcal{A}_S(x)), \hat{B}_t) + \mathcal{L}_{cls}(f(\Theta_S, \mathcal{A}_S(x)), \hat{Y}_t), \tag{1}$$

where $\mathcal{L}_{reg}$ and $\mathcal{L}_{cls}$ represent the Smooth L1 loss function and the cross entropy loss function of the RPN and the ROI head in Faster R-CNN [18], respectively. It is worth noting that we use an adjustment factor S_j in the $\mathcal{L}_{cls}$ for the ROI head, which will be introduced in Sect. 3.3.

Optimizing Teacher from Student Model. The teacher model is updated by the exponential moving average (EMA) of the student model,

$$\Theta_T = \alpha \Theta_T + (1 - \alpha)\Theta_S. \tag{2}$$

The EMA update strategy enables the teacher model to generate more stable pseudo labels than the student model, so as to help the student model learn the target domain features under strong augmentation.

3.3 Negative Gradient Adjustment

Due to the lack of annotations in the target domain, the teacher and student models may be biased by the missing detection problems. To address this issue, we propose Negative Gradient Adjustment (NGA), which reweights the logits of softmax cross-entropy and suppresses gradients caused by misclassified foreground boxes. We introduce an adjustment factor S_j for each class j and further elaborate on the details of NGA below.

We consider a batch of prediction boxes $\mathcal{M}$ generated by the student model, which are assigned with a one-hot label $\hat{y}_i = [\hat{y}_i^1, ..., \hat{y}_i^{|C|}]$ based on the pseudo boxes $\{\hat{B}_t, \hat{Y}_t\}$ generated by the teacher model. These prediction boxes may belong to either the foreground or background class in the object detection task. The proposed loss function $\mathcal{L}_{cls}$ with adjustment factor S_j is formulated as

$$\mathcal{L}_{cls} = -\sum_{i \in \mathcal{M}} \sum_{j \in \mathcal{C}} \hat{y}_i^j \log(\hat{p}_i^j),$$

$$\text{with } \hat{p}_i^j = \frac{e^{z_i^j}}{\sum_{k \in \mathcal{C} \setminus \{j\}} S_k e^{z_i^k} + e^{z_i^j}}. \tag{3}$$

Here, z_i^j is the output logit of the box classifier. In addition, the gradient computed by the positive class of the one-hot label $\hat{y}_i$ is denoted as the positive gradient. The gradients calculated by the other $|C| - 1$ negative classes are denoted as the negative gradients. The positive gradient ∇_{pos}^j and negative gradient ∇_{neg}^j with respect to the loss $\mathcal{L}_{cls}$ and foreground class j are formulated as

$$\nabla_{pos}^j(\mathcal{L}_{cls}) = \sum_{i \in \mathcal{M}} \hat{y}_i^j(\hat{p}_i^j - 1),$$

$$\nabla_{neg}^j(\mathcal{L}_{cls}) = S_j \sum_{i \in \mathcal{M}} (1 - \hat{y}_i^j) \frac{e^{z_i^j}}{e^{z_i^{\hat{y}_i}}} \hat{p}_i^{\hat{y}_i}. \tag{4}$$

To simplify the notation, we denote $z_i^{\hat{y}_i}$ and $p_i^{\hat{y}_i}$ as the output logit and probability for the class assigned to the one-hot label $\hat{y}_i$ in Eq. (3), respectively.

As numerous foreground boxes are wrongly classified as background, incorrect gradients contribute significantly to the negative gradients ∇_{neg}^j of foreground boxes. To address this issue, we can decrease the value of S_j to suppress the excessive negative gradients caused by missing detections. Instead of manually adjusting S_j, we employ the positive-negative gradient ratio r^j to adaptively adjust S_j, inspired by the research for long-tailed recognition in [22]. Specifically, we set S_j to $\min(r^j, 1)$. The positive-negative gradient ratio r^j is computed by

$$r^j = \frac{\sum_{\mathcal{B}} |\nabla_{pos}^j(\mathcal{L}_{cls})|}{\sum_{\mathcal{B}} |\nabla_{neg}^j(\mathcal{L}_{cls})|}, \tag{5}$$

where $\mathcal{B}$ is a gradient memory bank that stores the value of the positive and negative gradients from the historical batches. If the missing detections cause the negative gradients to be significantly larger than positive gradients, then reducing S_j can effectively suppress the negative effect of missing detections.

3.4 Source Weight Rectification

To prevent the model from overfitting to the inaccurate pseudo labels, we propose the second training strategy namely Source Weight Rectification (SWR). In the SWR, the pre-trained source model Θ_{init} are used to rectify the student model Θ_S after being optimized by $\mathcal{L}_{det}$ in Eq. (1), i.e.,

$$\Theta_S = (1 - \lambda)\Theta_S + \lambda\Theta_{init}, \tag{6}$$

where $\lambda \in [0, 1]$ is a hyperparameter in the SWR. This operation is equivalent to the implicit L2 regularization [12], which can be described as minimizing $\mathcal{L} = \lambda\|\Theta_S - \Theta_{init}\|^2$. By adjusting the value of λ, we can balance the influence between the pre-trained source model and target domain to achieve better robustness.

4 Experiments

4.1 Experiment Setup

Datasets and Evaluation. Following [15], we evaluate the performance of our proposed method for SFOD with four publicly available adaptation scenarios corresponding to five datasets: Cityscapes [6], Foggy Cityscapes [20], Sim10 k [10], KITTI [8], and BDD100k daytime [26]. We will provide a detailed introduction to the four adaptation scenarios in Sect. 4.2. The mean average precision (mAP) at an intersection over union (IOU) threshold of 0.5 is used as the evaluation metric. All results we report below are from the teacher model for better performance and robustness.

Implementation Details. We adopt the standard Faster RCNN [18] with ROI Align as the base object detector for a fair comparison. We employ VGG16 as the backbone pre-trained on ImageNet following previous works [15]. The input images are resized to have a shorter side length of 600 while maintaining their aspect ratios. The hyperparameter including $\alpha = 0.9995$ (Eq. (2)) and $\lambda = 0.001$ (Eq. (6)) are set as default for all experiments. We apply the Stochastic Gradient Descent (SGD) optimizer with a learning rate of 0.01 and weight decay of 0.0001 for the student model. We utilize a strong augmentation strategy from SimCLR [3], while weak augmentation only uses RandomHorizontalFlip. Each experiment is conducted on a single GPU with a batch size of 8.

4.2 Comparison with the State-of-the-Arts

In this section, we present a comprehensive evaluation of our proposed method in comparison to current methods of Cross-Domain Object Detection (CDOD) and Source-free Object Detection (SFOD). "Source Only" denotes the performance of the pre-trained source detector on the target domain. "SF" denotes whether methods follow the Source-free Object Detection setting or not. We strive to include results from existing literature.

Table 1. Detection results on Cityscapes → Foggy-Cityscapes.

Methods	SF	pson	rder	car	tuck	bus	tain	mcle	bcle	mAP
Source Only		25.8	33.3	35.2	13.0	26.4	9.1	19.0	32.3	24.3
DA-Faster [4]		25.0	31.0	40.5	22.1	35.3	20.2	20.0	27.1	27.6
MTOR [1]		30.6	41.4	44	21.9	38.6	40.6	28.3	35.6	35.1
ICR-CCR [25]		32.9	43.8	49.2	27.2	45.1	36.4	30.3	34.6	37.4
SAPNet [11]		40.8	46.7	59.8	24.3	46.8	37.5	30.4	40.7	40.9
SED [15]	✓	21.7	44.0	40.4	32.6	11.8	25.3	34.5	34.3	30.6
SED(M) [15]	✓	25.5	44.5	40.7	33.2	22.2	28.4	34.1	39.0	33.5
SOAP [24]	✓	35.9	45.0	48.4	23.9	37.2	24.3	31.8	37.9	35.5
A^{2}SFOD [5]	✓	28.1	44.6	44.1	32.3	29.0	31.8	**38.9**	34.3	35.4
HCL [9]	✓	38.7	46.0	47.9	**33.0**	**45.7**	**38.9**	32.8	34.9	39.7
LODS [13]	✓	34.0	45.7	48.8	27.3	39.7	19.6	33.2	37.8	35.8
Ours	✓	**45.5**	**50.9**	**62.0**	28.6	43.3	16.0	37.7	**47.4**	**41.4**

Table 2. Detection results on Cityscapes → BDD100k daytime.

Method	SF	pson	rider	car	tuck	bus	mcle	bcle	mAP
Source Only		14.0	40.7	24.4	22.4	14.5	20.5	16.1	21.8
DA-Faster [4]		29.4	26.5	44.6	14.3	16.8	15.8	20.6	24
SW-Faster [19]		30.2	29.5	45.7	15.2	18.4	17.1	21.2	25.3
ICR-CCR [25]		31.4	31.3	46.3	19.5	18.9	17.3	23.8	26.9
SED [15]	✓	31.0	32.4	48.8	20.4	21.3	15.0	24.3	27.6
SED(M) [15]	✓	32.4	32.6	50.4	20.6	23.4	18.9	25.0	29.0
HCL [9]	✓	32.7	33.2	52	21.3	**25.6**	21.5	26.0	30.3
A^{2}SFOD[5]	✓	26.6	**50.2**	36.3	**33.2**	22.5	**28.2**	24.4	31.6
Ours	✓	**41.7**	37.5	**59.8**	20.1	16.2	22.0	**29.3**	**32.4**

Adverse Weather Adaptation. The Cityscapes dataset comprises 2,975 training images and 500 validation images of outdoor street scenes, whereas the Foggy Cityscapes dataset simulates foggy weather conditions based on Cityscapes images. As given that weather variations can significantly reduce the effectiveness of object detectors, we evaluate our proposed method on Foggy Cityscapes and report its performance in Table 1. Our proposed method outperforms the state-of-the-art methods on Foggy Cityscapes, e.g., our performance is higher than current state-of-the-art HCL [9] by 1.7 mAP. Notably, our approach performs better than many CDOD methods, such as MTOR [1] and SAPNet [11]. However, we do not have access to any labeled data from the source domain.

Small to Large-Scale Dataset Adaptation. The BDD100k daytime dataset is designed for autonomous driving. It includes 36,728 training images and 5,258 validation images is significantly larger than Cityscapes dataset. We focus on

Table 3. Detection results on car category for KITTI → Cityscapes and Sim10k → Cityscapes.

Methods	SF	KITTI → Cityscapes	Sim10K → Cityscapes
Source Only		36.4	33.7
SED [15]	✓	43.6	42.3
SED(M) [15]	✓	44.6	42.9
SOAP [24]	✓	42.7	–
A²SFOD [5]	✓	44.9	44.0
LODS [13]	✓	43.9	–
Ours	✓	**46.4**	**53.6**

Table 4. Ablation studies on our proposed method. "MT*.", "NGA", "SWR" denote Mean Teacher framework with weak-strong consistency, Negative Gradient Adjustment, Source Weight Regularization, respectively.

MT*	NGA	SWR	KITTI → Cityscapes	Cityscapes → BDD100K
✓			44.6	27.7
✓	✓		45.2	31.3
✓		✓	46.0	31.6
✓	✓	✓	46.4	32.4

Table 5. Ablation studies on strong augmentation. "RF", "CJ", "RG", "GB", "RC" denote RandomHorizontalFlip, ColorJitter, RandomGrayscale, GaussianBlur and RandCrop, respectively.

RF	CJ	RG	GB	RC	mAP
✓					47.5
✓	✓				50.2
✓	✓	✓			50.6
✓	✓	✓	✓		52.8
✓	✓	✓	✓	✓	53.6

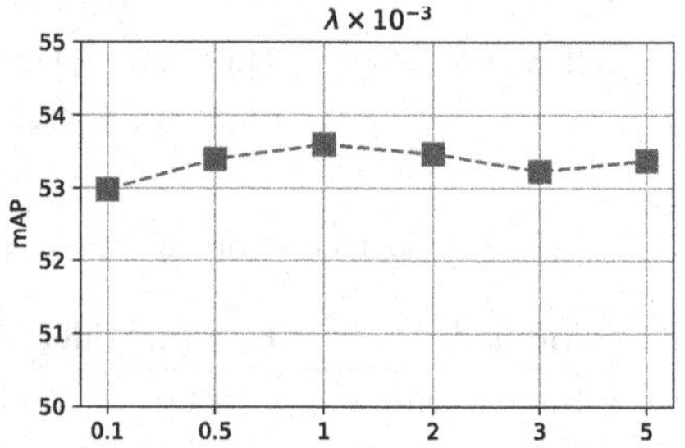

Fig. 3. Sensitivity analysis on Source Weight Rectification coefficient λ. All experiments are conducted on Sim10K → Cityscapes.

seven object categories following the SED [15], and the results are summarized in Table 2. Our proposed method achieves the best performance on all settings, e.g., our performance is 0.8 mAP and 5.5 mAP higher than the current method on SFOD and CDOD.

Synthetic to Real Adaptation and Cross-Camera Adaptation. To evaluate the adaptation performance of synthetic to real domain gap and cross-camera domain gap, we conduct experiments on Sim10k → Cityscapes and KITTI → Cityscapes, respectively. Sim10k is a synthetic dataset collected from Grand Theft Auto V, KITTI is collected from vehicle-mounted cameras, and Cityscapes is a real-world dataset collected from onboard cameras. There is a synthetic to real domain gap between Sim10K and Cityscapes, and a cross-camera domain gap between KITTI and Cityscapes. As shown in Table 3, our approach leads to the best result for the target domain on both settings (e.g. with 9.6 mAP and 1.5 mAP improvement on synthetic to real adaptation and cross-camera adaptation).

4.3   Further Analysis

Ablation Studies. Ablation results for the proposed modules including MT*, NGA, and SWR on KITTI → Cityscapes and Cityscapes → BDD100K are provided in Table 4. MT* denotes the Mean Teacher framework with weak-strong consistency and we set MT* as the default architecture. According to the ablation results, the NGA and SWR improve the performance by 0.6 mAP and 1.4 mAP on KITTI → Cityscapes, 3.6 mAP and 3.9 mAP on Cityscapes → BDD100K. By combining NGA and SWR onto MT*, the highest mAP performance is obtained. The experimental analysis above can fully verify the effectiveness of our proposed method.

Comparison of Different Augmentations. We use weak-strong data augmentation as the input in our method for better self-training. To analyze the effectiveness of the weak-strong mechanism, we compare the mAP results of different augmentation combinations in Table 5. We can see that the combination of RandomHorizontalFlip, ColorJitter, RandomGrayscale, GaussianBlur, and RandCrop operations is beneficial for SFOD. The results demonstrate that a more robust model can be learned by applying stronger data augmentation.

Hyper-parameters Sensitivity. For the hyperparameter of Source Weight Rectification coefficient λ (Eq. (6)), we conduct experiments with λ in the range of 0.0001 to 0.005 on Sim10K → Cityscapes. Based on the results shown in Fig. 3, we can observe that the model's performance is not sensitive to the hyperparameter λ. According to the sensitivity analysis, the Weight Decay coefficient λ is set as 0.001 as default for all experiments.

(a) Source Only   (b) Mean Teacher   (c) Ours

**Fig. 4. Qualitative results on Cityscapes→ BDD100k (top) and Sim10k →
Cityscapes (bottom).** True positives, false positives and false negatives are marked as green, gold and red boxes respectively. (Better viewed in color) (Color figure online)

4.4 Visualization

To verify the effect of our method, the visualization of qualitative results on Cityscapes→ BDD100k and Sim10k → Cityscapes is shown in Fig. 4. Without loss of generality, we display the plots with bounding boxes with scores greater than 0.5 including the Source Only model, Mean Teacher Baseline model, and our proposed method. From this figure, we can see that: *i.* The Source Only model shows a notable decline in performance due to the significant domain shift. *ii.* The Baseline model applies the Mean Teacher framework and performs slightly better than The Source Only model. *iii.* Our proposed method effectively reduces the incidence of false positives and false negatives compared to both the Baseline model and the Source Only model.

5 Conclusion

In this paper, we propose a novel Gradient Adjusted and Weight Rectified Mean Teacher framework for source-free object detection. The proposed method incorporates weak-strong consistency training to enhance the effectiveness of self-training, in which strong augmentation is one of the key factors in improving the performance of detectors. We design two training strategies for SFOD to address the issues of missing detections and inaccurate pseudo labels. The proposed Negative Gradient Adjustment suppresses the excessive negative gradients caused by missing detections. The Source Weight Rectification improves the model robustness by using the pre-trained source detector so as to reduce the negative impact of inaccurate pseudo labels. Comparative and ablation experiments demonstrate the effectiveness of our proposed method for SFOD.

References

1. Cai, Q., Pan, Y., Ngo, C.W., Tian, X., Duan, L., Yao, T.: Exploring object relation in mean teacher for cross-domain detection. In: CVPR, pp. 11457–11466 (2019)
2. Chen, M., et al.: Learning domain adaptive object detection with probabilistic teacher. In: ICML, vol. 162, pp. 3040–3055 (17–23 Jul 2022)
3. Chen, T., Kornblith, S., Norouzi, M., Hinton, G.: A simple framework for contrastive learning of visual representations. In: ICML, pp. 1597–1607. PMLR (2020)
4. Chen, Y., Li, W., Sakaridis, C., Dai, D., Van Gool, L.: Domain adaptive faster r-cnn for object detection in the wild. In: CVPR (June 2018)
5. Chu, Q., Li, S., Chen, G., Li, K., Li, X.: Adversarial alignment for source free object detection. arXiv preprint arXiv:2301.04265 (2023). https://arxiv.org/abs/2301.04265
6. Cordts, M., et alThe cityscapes dataset for semantic urban scene understanding. In: CVPR (June 2016)
7. Deng, J., Li, W., Chen, Y., Duan, L.: Unbiased mean teacher for cross-domain object detection. In: CVPR, pp. 4091–4101 (June 2021)
8. Geiger, A., Lenz, P., Stiller, C., Urtasun, R.: Vision meets robotics: the kitti dataset. Inter. J. Robotics Res. **32**(11), 1231–1237 (2013)

9. Huang, J., Guan, D., Xiao, A., Lu, S.: Model adaptation: historical contrastive learning for unsupervised domain adaptation without source data. In: NeurIPS, vol. 34, pp. 3635–3649 (2021)
10. Johnson-Roberson, M., Barto, C., Mehta, R., Sridhar, S.N., Rosaen, K., Vasudevan, R.: Driving in the matrix: can virtual worlds replace human-generated annotations for real world tasks? In: ICRA, pp. 746–753 (2017)
11. Li, C., et al.: Spatial attention pyramid network for unsupervised domain adaptation. In: Vedaldi, A., Bischof, H., Brox, T., Frahm, J.-M. (eds.) ECCV 2020. LNCS, vol. 12358, pp. 481–497. Springer, Cham (2020). https://doi.org/10.1007/978-3-030-58601-0_29
12. Li, R., Jiao, Q., Cao, W., Wong, H.S., Wu, S.: Model adaptation: unsupervised domain adaptation without source data. In: CVPR (June 2020)
13. Li, S., Ye, M., Zhu, X., Zhou, L., Xiong, L.: Source-free object detection by learning to overlook domain style. In: CVPR, pp. 8014–8023 (June 2022)
14. Li, W., Liu, X., Yuan, Y.: Sigma: semantic-complete graph matching for domain adaptive object detection. In: CVPR, pp. 5291–5300 (June 2022)
15. Li, X., et al.: A free lunch for unsupervised domain adaptive object detection without source data. AAAI **35**(10), 8474–8481 (2021)
16. Li, Y.J., et al.: Cross-domain adaptive teacher for object detection. In: CVPR, pp. 7581–7590 (June 2022)
17. Liu, S., Niles-Weed, J., Razavian, N., Fernandez-Granda, C.: Early-learning regularization prevents memorization of noisy labels. In: NeurIPS, vol. 33, pp. 20331–20342 (2020)
18. Ren, S., He, K., Girshick, R., Sun, J.: Faster r-cnn: towards real-time object detection with region proposal networks. In: NeurIPS 28 (2015)
19. Saito, K., Ushiku, Y., Harada, T., Saenko, K.: Strong-weak distribution alignment for adaptive object detection. In: CVPR (June 2019)
20. Sakaridis, C., Dai, D., Van Gool, L.: Semantic foggy scene understanding with synthetic data. Int. J. Comput. Vision **126**, 973–992 (2018)
21. Sohn, K., et al.: Fixmatch: simplifying semi-supervised learning with consistency and confidence. In: NeurIPS, vol. 33, pp. 596–608 (2020)
22. Tan, J., Lu, X., Zhang, G., Yin, C., Li, Q.: Equalization loss v2: a new gradient balance approach for long-tailed object detection. In: CVPR, pp. 1685–1694 (June 2021)
23. Tarvainen, A., Valpola, H.: Mean teachers are better role models: weight-averaged consistency targets improve semi-supervised deep learning results. In: NeurIPS, vol. 30 (2017)
24. Xiong, L., Ye, M., Zhang, D., Gan, Y., Li, X., Zhu, Y.: Source data-free domain adaptation of object detector through domain-specific perturbation. Int. J. Intell. Syst. **36**(8), 3746–3766 (2021)
25. Xu, C.D., Zhao, X.R., Jin, X., Wei, X.S.: Exploring categorical regularization for domain adaptive object detection. In: CVPR (June 2020)
26. Yu, F., et al.: Bdd100k: a diverse driving dataset for heterogeneous multitask learning. In: CVPR (June 2020)

IMAM: Incorporating Multiple Attention Mechanisms for 3D Object Detection from Point Cloud

Jing Zhou[✉] and Han Wu

School of Artificial Intelligence, Jianghan University, Wuhan 430056, China
zhj131@jhun.edu.cn

Abstract. Nowadays, 3D object detection technology from point clouds develops rapidly. However, lots of small objects emerge in real point cloud scenes, which are hard to be detected due to few points, hindering overall detection accuracy. To address this issue, we propose a novel two-stage 3D object detection method, which introduces an attention strategy to enhance key structure information of objects, so as to promote overall detection accuracy, especially for small objects. Specifically, in the first stage, we employ the convolutional block attention module on the 3D sparse convolution layer to extract voxel features and further apply the Swin Transformer to enhance Bird's Eye View (BEV) feature for generating high-quality proposals. Then, in the second stage, we apply a Voxel Set Abstraction (VSA) module to fuse voxel features and BEV features into keypoint features, followed by a Region of Interest (RoI) pooling module to obtain grid features for confidence prediction and box regression. Experiment results on the KITTI dataset prove that our method IMAM achieves excellent detection performance, especially for pedestrians and cyclists with small sizes.

Keywords: 3D point cloud · Object detection · Attention mechanism

1 Introduction

In recent years, autonomous driving technology has developed rapidly. To perceive the environment in autonomous driving, it is necessary to accurately detect objects in the scenes. Hence, the 3D object detection method plays a vital role in automatic driving technology.

The 3D object detection approaches are classified into single-stage detection methods and two-stage detectors. The single detection algorithms [1–5] convert point clouds into the regular data such as the voxel or the BEV view, and then adopts the Convolutional Neural Network (CNN) with fully convolution to predict the bounding box. In this way, the single-stage detector achieves efficient performance with simple architecture. However, the spatial feature is lost due to the conversion of the point cloud feature into BEV views, which damages the detection accuracy. Compared with the single-stage detector, the two-stage

L. Iliadis et al. (Eds.): ICANN 2023, LNCS 14260, pp. 112–123, 2023.
https://doi.org/10.1007/978-3-031-44195-0_10

detection methods [6–10] utilizes more accurate spatial information in stage two, which focuses on the region of interest predicted from stage one, thus generating more accurate bounding boxes. For example, PointRCNN [6] segments point clouds to extract foreground points for generating proposals in stage one, and then pool the region feature of interest based on proposals for box refinement in stage two. The advanced two-stage method PV-RCNN [7] adopts 3D sparse convolution to extract voxel features and uses 2D CNN to enrich BEV features for proposal generation in stage 1, then it adopts VSA operation and RoI pooling module to aggregate the voxel features and BEV features into grid feature for box refinement in the stage 2.

Nevertheless,in real point cloud scenes, many small objects are difficult to be perceived due to too few points with insufficient spatial information, which makes it hard for the above methods to accurately detect these small objects, and thus achieving limited detection accuracy. To address this problem, we establish a novel two-stage detection network based on the attention strategy [11] to highlight the crucial structural cues, thus boosting the detection accuracy of the object, especially for small objects such as pedestrians and cyclists. Specifically, in the first stage, we combine the 3D sparse convolution and Convolutional Block Attention Module (CBAM) [12] to construct a 3D backbone for extracting elaborative voxel features, which are then projected into BEV features, followed by a Swin Transformer [13] to enhance BEV features for predicting premium proposals. Subsequently, in the second stage, we first employ a voxel-to-keypoint module with VSA operation to encode the voxel features into keypoint features and then utilize the keypoint-to-grid module to integrate the keypoint features into grid features for box refinement. Attributed to the above attention-based modules, our method IMMA can focus on the key spatial information of objects, and localize the objects accurately, thus improving the overall detection accuracy.

The main contributions of this work are summarized as follows:

1) We append the convolution block attention module on the 3D sparse convolution layer to construct an attention-based 3D backbone network to capture the grain-fined voxel features with enhanced key spatial knowledge.
2) Considering that the downsampling operation of CNN drops the low-level structural information of objects, we apply the Swin Transformer that is adept at exploring global spatial correlation to substitute 2D CNN, thus highlighting the BEV feature to generate high-quality proposals.
3) Our proposed IMAM achieves satisfactory detection results on KITTI benchmark dataset, especially for pedestrians and cyclists with small sizes.

2   Related Work

2.1   Single-Stage Detection Method

Single-stage detection methods usually convert the sparse point cloud into regular data such as 2D views or 3D voxels, and then use the CNN to extract feature. Some approaches adopt 2D CNN to extract features from BEV and front views or use 3D CNN to process 3D voxels. For instance, The early method [1] divides point clouds into voxels and then adopts a multi-layer voxel feature encoding architecture to extract features of each point in the voxel. A major breakthrough is that the sparse convolution operations [2] and pillar structures [3] are established to greatly boost computational efficiency. The representative method [4] proposes a feature-based centroid sampling approach to sample more foreground points, thus improving the distance-based sampling strategy in PointNet++. And the literature [5] presents an auxiliary network to enhance the representation of sparse convolutional features with point-wise supervision.

2.2 Two-Stage Detection Methods

The two-stage detection approach uses a refinement subnetwork of stage two to fine-tune the proposals generated in the first stage for accurate detection. The classical detector PointRCNN [6] segments the point cloud of the whole scene into foreground and background points in the first stage, thus generating high-quality 3D proposals directly from the point cloud. The advanced two-stage method PVRCNN [7] first leverages 3D sparse convolution to capture voxel features in stage one, and then aggregates voxel features to grid features for proposal refinement in stage two. The literature [8] generates proposals by constructing a new spherical anchor for each point in stage 1, and then designs a 3D loU prediction branch for box prediction in stage 2 to improve the detection accuracy. The two-stage detection method achieves better proposals and higher detection accuracy than single-stage method. Hence, we adopt generic two-stage architecture to design our detector in this work.

2.3 Attention Mechanism

The attention mechanism focus on features in terms of the information importance implied in channel or spatial domains to efficiently enhance the attention of the critical information. The typical hybrid attention mechanism CBAM stacks attention maps of spatial and channel to enhance informative channels along with vital regions. To capture the global semantic correlation of the object, the Transformer architecture based on the self-attention mechanism is constructed, which is beneficial for the complex computer vision task. DETR [14] adopts a Transformer architecture to calculate the self-attention matrix of the output feature extracted by the backbone network, so as to directly predict the detection box, thus implementing end-to-end object detection. ViT [15] divides the image into multiple blocks and applies Transformer encoder to compute the global dependency among blocks, thus obtaining the global feature of the image. To improve the computation efficiency of the above traditional global attention strategy, the Swin Transformer based on shifted-window attention mechanism is proposed. It divides the input feature map into multiple patches and then uses a hierarchical structure to merge patches to obtain the global attention of the input feature map. In this way, the Swin Transformer has linear computational complexity and can be used as a generic backbone for computer vision.

3   Method

3.1   The Whole Architecture of IMAM

The IMAM first adopts voxelization operation to divide the raw point clouds into regular voxels, and then it integrates attention strategy into a 3D sparse convolution layer, thus forming a 3D backbone to extract the voxel feature with enriched key spatial cues. The voxel features are further projected to BEV features, followed by a Swin Transformer as the 2D backbone network to augment BEV features for proposal generation. Then, in stage two, a refinement sub-network consisting of voxel-to-keypoint module and keypoint-to-grid module is established to aggregate the voxel and BEV features into grid features, which are fed into the detection head for confidence prediction and box regression. The detailed structure of IMAM is shown in Fig. 1.

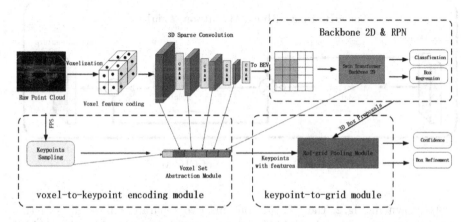

Fig. 1. The overall architecture of our two-stage detection network(IMAM) incorporating the attention mechanism.

3.2   Attention-Based 3D Backbone

For the input raw point cloud, we use a cube with the same depth, height and width (D, H, W) of the input point cloud to represent the entire input point cloud space, and then adopt sub-cubes with same sizes to divide this cube, where each sub-cube is called a voxel and the depth, height and width of each voxel are denoted as (Ud, Uh, Uw), thus, the number of voxel grids generated by coordinates of the whole point cloud space is illustrated as Eq. (1).

$$\left(\frac{D}{uD}, \frac{D}{uH}, \frac{D}{uW} \right) \tag{1}$$

We compute the mean of coordinates of all points in each voxel as the initial voxel feature, and then we design an attention-based 3D backbone network to encode the voxel feature. Each layer of the backbone consists of the 3D sparse convolution module and the CBAM module. The 3D sparse convolution module composes of a 3×3×3 sparse convolution, submanifold convolution, a ReLu layer, and a BatchNorm layer. And the CBAM module composes of a channel attention model and a spatial attention model. The four-layer 3D sparse convolution downsamples the spatial resolution of initial voxel feature to achieving the multi-scale feature.

Since the downsampling process inevitably loses key spatial cues of raw point clouds, we introduce the attention-based module CBAM to further learn the feature extracted by the 3D sparse convolution, thus strengthening the vital structural feature of the object. The CBAM module performs attention computation in both channel and spatial dimensions.

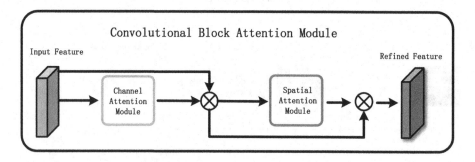

Fig. 2. The overview of CBAM.

As shown in Fig. 2, the CBAM contains two separate sub-modules of the Channel Attention Module (CAM) and the Spatial Attention Module (SAM). The input feature $F \in R^{C \times H \times W}$ is first sent to the channel attention module for 1D convolution calculation to achieve the feature $M_c \in R^{C \times 1 \times 1}$, which is then multiplied by the input feature to achieve the CAM output feature, followed by a SAM module for 2D convolution computation to obtain the feature $M_s \in R^{1 \times H \times W}$. At last, the feature $M_s \in R^{1 \times H \times W}$ is multiplied by the CAM output feature for feature reweighting, and the calculation process is illustrated as Eq. (2).

$$
\begin{aligned}
F' &= M_c(F) \otimes F, \\
F'' &= M_s(F') \otimes F'
\end{aligned}
\tag{2}
$$

In the channel attention module, we first apply the global max pooling and global average pooling operations to compress the spatial dimension of the features to obtain two pooled features. They are concatenated on the channel dimension, followed by a two-layer Multi-Layer Perceptual(MLP) network to learn the correlations among channels of the pooled features. Then we employ a sigmoid function to obtain the channel attention map, which is multiplied with the input feature to obtain the re-weighted channel feature. The calculation process is demonstrated as Eq. (3).

$$M_C(F) = \sigma(MLP(AvgPool(F) + MaxPool(F)))$$
$$= \sigma\left(W_1\left(W_0\left(F_{avg}^c\right) + W_0\left(F_{max}^c\right)\right)\right) \tag{3}$$

In the spatial attention module, we take the feature map output from the CAM as the input feature. We first employ the global max pooling and global average pooling operations to condense the channel dimensions of the input feature, thus achieving two H×W×1 feature maps. Then we perform the channel splicing operation to concatenate the two feature maps at the channel dimension, followed by a sigmoid function to generate a spatial attention feature map. And it is multipied by the input feature to get the reweighted feature, as shown in Eq. (4).

$$M_s(F) = \sigma\left(f([AvgPool(F); MaxPool(F)])\right)$$
$$= \sigma\left(f\left(\left[F_{avg}^s; F_{max}^s\right]\right)\right) \tag{4}$$

Attributed to the above CBAM module, the vital spatial and channel information of the voxel features extracted by the 3D sparse convolution is enhanced, which makes the detection network focus on the crucial structural feature of the objects.

3.3   The 2D Backbone Based on the Swin Transformer

For the above 3D voxel feature extracted from the 3D backbone, we stack it along the Z axis to obtain the BEV feature, followed by a 2D backbone to generate high-quality proposals. Since the downsampling operation of CNN drops the low-level structural information, we apply the Swin Transformer to substitute 2D CNN for constructing the 2D backbone, thus exploring the global spatial correlation to augment the BEV feature for proposal generation.

As shown in Fig. 3, the Swin Transformer first divides the input feature map into multiple patches, and then uses a hierarchical structure to calculate the local attention of each patch in each layer, and merges the patches layer by layer to obtain the global attention of the feature map with the original spatial resolution. In this way, the computation efficiency of the Swin Transformer is significantly higher than the traditional Transformer.

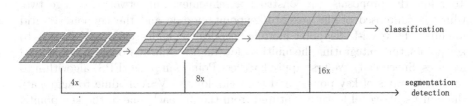

Fig. 3. Swing Transformer extracts visual features at different levels by means of a hierarchical structure.

The detailed architecture of four-layer Swin Transformer is shown in Fig. 4. In the first layer, the input feature map with size H×W×256 is segmented into 4×4 patches to get a feature map with size H/4×W/4×4096, which is then converted to a H/4×W/4×C map by linear embedding operation, and then a Swin Transformer block is adopted to further update the feature map. Then, the updated feature map is fed into the next layer, in which a patch merging operation is performed to merge the four neighboring patches for getting H/8×W/8 patches, followed by a Swin Transformer block to achieve a H/8×W/8×2C feature map. Next, two layers with similar architecture are stacked to further merge patches and update the feature maps, finally obtaining global attention feature with size H/32×W/32×8C for the input feature map.

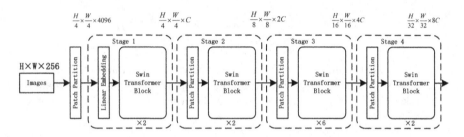

Fig. 4. The overview of Swin Transformer.

Notably, the Swin Transformer block constructs a novel shifted-window-based module to substitute the traditional multi-head self-attention model. Concretely, the Swin Transformer block adopts the shifted-window self-attention mechanism to calculate the local attention feature of each patch, followed by a linear norm model and a two-layer MLP module to further the attention feature.

Owing to the 2D backbone based on the Swin Transformer, the global spatial correlation implied in the BEV feature is efficiently explored to enhance the 2D feature representation of the object, and then the enhanced 2D BEV feature is sent to the detection head for generating high-quality proposals.

3.4   Refinement Subnetwork

To refine the proposals, we construct a refinement subnetwork in stage two, which is composed of the voxel-to-keypoint module and the keypoint-to-grid module. The voxel-to-keypoint module encodes the multi-scale voxel feature to key points, thus integrating the multi-scale semantic information with raw spatial features. Specifically, we first apply Farthest Point Sampling (FPS) algorithm to capture a series of key points, and then employ the VSA module to aggregate the multi-scale voxel feature captured from the 3D backbone to the key points. Subsequently, the keypoint features are sent to the keypoint-to-grid module to aggerate the keypoint features on the center point of the grid for proposal refinement.

Voxel-to-Keypoint Encoding Module. To reduce the memory consumption caused by encoding the scene represented by voxels, we adopt the FPS method to select N points and then employ VSA operation to aggregate the voxel-wise features on these points.

Specifically, for the k-th layer of 3D backbone that has N_k non-empty voxels, we select M_k neighboring voxels $V^{(lk)} = \left\{ v_1^{(lk)}, \cdots, v_{Mk}^{(lk)} \right\}$ in the scope of radius r_k for the keypoint p_i to obtain M_k corresponding voxel features $F^{(lk)} = \left\{ f_1^{(lk)}, \cdots, f_{Mk}^{(lk)} \right\}$. Then we adopt the set abstraction operation of Point-Net++ to gather M_k neighboring voxel features $F^{(lk)} = \left\{ f_1^{(lk)}, \cdots, f_{Mk}^{(lk)} \right\}$ to key point p_i, as shown in Eq. (5).

$$S_i^{(lk)} = \left\{ \left[f_j^{(l_k)} ; v_j^{(l_k)} - p_i \right]^T \middle| \begin{matrix} \|v_j^{(l_k)} - p_i\|^2 < r_k, \\ \forall v_j^{(l_k)} \in v^{(l_k)}, \\ \forall f_j^{(l_k)} \in F^{(l_k)} \end{matrix} \right\} \tag{5}$$

where $v_j^{(l_k)} - p_i$ denotes the relative position information between the key point p_i and the corresponding voxel $v_j^{(l_k)}$ within radius r_k.

Subsequently, we perform the multi-layered perceptron network $MLP(\cdot)$ and maxpooling operation $maxpool(\cdot)$ on $S_i^{l_k}$ to achieve the aggregated feature $f_i^{(pv_k)}$ of the k-th layer, as denoted in Eq. (6).

$$f_i^{(pv_k)} = \max \left\{ MLP \left(S_i^{l_k} \right) \right\} \tag{6}$$

After performing similar aggregation operation denoted as Eq. (5) and Eq. (6) for each layer, we obtain four aggregated features $\left[f_i^{(pv_1)}, f_i^{(pv_2)}, f_i^{(pv_3)}, f_i^{(pv_4)} \right]$, and then we concatenate them to achieve the final keypoint $feature f_i^{(pv)}$, as shown in Eq. (7).

$$f_i^{(pv)} = \left[f_i^{(pv_1)}, f_i^{(pv_2)}, f_i^{(pv_3)}, f_i^{(pv_4)} \right] \tag{7}$$

Keypoint-to-Grid Module. To further refine proposals, it is necessary to integrate keypoint features into the region of proposals. Hence, we establish keypoint-to-grid module based on RoI-grid pooling operation to aggregate the keypoint features on the grid of the proposal region. Specifically, we first divide each proposal into 6×6×6 grid points, then we determine the neighboring j-th keypoint p_j within radius r for i-th grid point g_i to obtain its keypoint feature $\tilde{f}_j^{(p)}$, as illustrated in Eq. (8).

$$\tilde{\Psi} = \left\{ \left[\tilde{f}_j^{(p)} ; p_j - g_i \right]^T \middle| \begin{matrix} \|p_j - g_i\|^2 < \tilde{r}, \\ \forall p_j \in K, \forall \tilde{f}_j^{(p)} \in \tilde{F} \end{matrix} \right\} \tag{8}$$

Then we employ a PointNet-like network to aggregate the key point features to produce the grid feature, as demonstrated in Eq. (9).

$$\tilde{f}_i^{(g)} = \max\{G(M(\tilde{\Psi}))\} \tag{9}$$

where $M(\cdot)$ represents a random sampling operation to select the keypoint features within a fixed radius, $G(\cdot)$ represents a MLP network. $max(\cdot)$ denotes the maxpooling operation.

For all the key points located within the radius $\tilde{r}$, we perform the same operation as shown in Eq. (8) and Eq. (9) to aggregate these key points on grid g_i, thus obtaining the final grid features for boxrefinement.

4   Experiments

4.1   Experimental Details

Dataset. IMAM is evaluated on a popular 3D object detection dataset KITTI, which provides 7481 training samples and 7518 test samples. The training samples are further divided into 3712 samples for training (train split), and 3769 samples for validation (val split). Meanwhile, we adopt the Average Precision (AP) as theevaluation metric. And the samples are classified into three classes of car, pedestrian, and cyclist, where each class is divided into three difficulty levels of easy, moderate, and hard.

Experimental Details. Our proposed IMAM is trained on the GeForce RTX3090 GPU for 80 epochs with batchsize of 6. We adopt ADAM optimizer and set initial learning rate to 0.01. In the training phase, the Non-Maximum Suppression (NMS) method is adopted with a threshold of 0.8 to select 512 initial proposals, then the IOU threshold was defined as 0.55 to collect 128 final proposals. In the testing phase, 100 proposals are selected under the NMS threshold of 0.85, and the redundant proposals are removed.

4.2   Evaluation of IMAM

In this section, we first report the comparison results between IMAM and the state-of-the-art 3D detectors on the KITTI test set, and then we further evaluate IMAM on the KITTI val split. All results are evaluated by the AP value with an IOU threshold 0.7 for cars and 0.5 for pedestrians and cyclists, and the AP value is calculated with 40 recall positions on the test split and 11 recall positions on the val split.

Evaluation on Test Set. We compare our IMAM with other methods on KITTI test set, as shown in Table 1. It is noted that our method attains highest accuracy for the 3D detection of cyclist and pedestrian. Meanwhile, our method outperforms all one-stage detectors displayed in Table 1 at three difficulty levels. And compared with the recent two-stage methods such as PointRCNN, Part-A2, and PV-RCNN, our IMAM achieves the highest moderate AP and hard AP on car class.

Table 1. Comparison with the state-of-the-art methods on KITTI test set. The results are evaluated by the Average Precision with IoU threshold 0.7 for car and 0.5 for pedestrian/cyclist.

Method	Reference	Stage	Car-3D Detection			Cyclist-3D Detection			Ped-3D Detection		
			Easy	Mod	Hard	Easy	Mod	Hard	Easy	Mod	Hard
VoxelNet [1]	CVPR 2018	One-Stage	77.47	65.11	57.73	61.22	48.36	44.37	39.48	33.69	31.51
SECOND [2]	Sensors 2018	One-Stage	83.13	73.66	66.20	70.51	53.85	46.90	51.07	42.56	37.29
PointPillars [3]	CVPR 2019	One-Stage	79.05	74.99	68.30	75.78	59.07	52.92	52.08	43.53	41.49
3DSSD [4]	CVPR 2020	One-Stage	88.36	79.57	74.55	82.48	64.10	56.90	54.64	44.27	40.23
SA-SSD [5]	CVPR 2020	One-Stage	88.75	79.79	74.16	–	–	–	–	–	–
PointRCNN [6]	CVPR 2019	Two-Stage	85.94	75.76	68.32	73.93	59.60	53.59	49.43	41.78	38.63
Fast PointRCNN [10]	ICCV 2019	Two-Stage	84.28	75.73	67.39	–	–	–	–	–	–
STD [8]	ICCV 2019	Two-Stage	86.61	77.63	76.06	78.89	62.53	55.77	53.08	44.24	41.97
Part-A2 [9]	TPAMI 2020	Two-Stage	85.94	77.86	72.00	78.58	62.73	57.74	–	–	–
PV-RCNN [7]	CVPR 2020	Two-Stage	**90.25**	81.43	76.82	78.60	63.71	57.65	52.17	43.29	40.29
IMAM(Ours)		Two-Stage	90.21	**81.59**	**76.95**	**82.56**	**67.25**	**61.35**	**54.83**	**45.67**	**42.65**

Evaluation on Val Split. To further verify the effectiveness of our method, we conduct a fair comparison between our method and other detectors on KITTI val split, as delivered in Table 2. It can be seen from Table 2 that our IMAM outperforms all previous methods on KITTI val split. And compared with the recent state-of-the-art detectors of Part-A2, 3DSSD, SASSD, and PV-RCNN, our method leads them with AP gains from 0.22% to 4.67% at moderate level.

Table 2. Comparison with the state-of-the-art methods on KITTI val split, where the moderate AP for car class is calculated with 11 recall positions.

Method	Reference	Stage	3D AP
VoxelNet [1]	CVPR 2018	One-Stage	76.23
SECOND [2]	Sensors 2018	One-Stage	76.48
PointPillars [3]	CVPR 2019	One-Stage	77.43
3DSSD [4]	CVPR 2020	One-Stage	79.45
SA-SSD [5]	CVPR 2020	One-Stage	79.91
PointRCNN [6]	CVPR 2019	Two-Stage	78.63
Fast PointRCNN [10]	ICCV 2019	Two-Stage	79.00
STD [8]	ICCV 2019	Two-Stage	79.8
Part-A2 [9]	TPAMI 2020	Two-Stage	79.47
PV-RCNN [7]	CVPR 2020	Two-Stage	83.90
IMAM(Ours)	-	Two-Stage	**84.12**

4.3 Ablation Studies

To further discuss the contribution of our designed components for IMAM, we conduct a series of ablation studies on KITTI val split with 11 recall positions for car class.

Concretely, we explore the effect of each module for IMAM in Table 3. We first report the detection accuracy of baseline PVRCNN in the first row, and then we append the CBAM module on the baseline in the second row, which bring up slight AP gains. Subsequently, we add Swin Transformer on the baseline PVRCNN in the third row, leading to AP improvements of 0.33%, 0.41%, and 0.31% at three difficulties. At last, we integrate CBAM and Swing Transformer to the baseline to enhance the feature representation of the object, as shown in the last row. And we observe that the highest detection accuracy is achieved by using the two attention modules simultaneously. This proves that the CBAM module can strengthen the vital voxel feature and Swin Transformer highlights the BEV features, thus enhancing the feature representation of the object for improving detection accuracy.

Table 3. The ablation studies on the CBAM model and Swin Transformer module.

PVRCNN Baseline	CBAM	Swin Transformer	3D AP		
			Easy	Mod	Hard
✓	✗	✗	92.12	85.67	83.86
✓	✓	✗	92.39	85.83	83.92
✓	✗	✓	92.45	86.08	84.17
✓	✓	✓	**92.52**	**86.23**	**84.26**

5 Conclusion

We propose a novel attention-based two-stage 3D object detection method to enhance the feature representation of the object, thus promoting overall detection accuracy, especially for the objects with small sizes. Specifically, in stage one, we first embed the CBAM module on the 3D sparse convolution layer to enhance key spatial information of voxel features, and then we adopt the Swin Transformer to strengthen the spatial correlation of BEV feature for generating high-quality proposals. Then, in stage two, we employ a voxel-to-keypoint module to aggregate voxel features into keypoint features, followed by a Region of Interest (RoI) pooling operation to obtain grid features for confidence prediction and box regression. Extensive experiments on the KITTI dataset show that our detector IMAM achieves satisfactory detection accuracy.

Acknowledgment. This work is supported by National Natural Science Foundation of China (No. 62106086) and the Natural Science Foundation of Hubei Province (No. 2021CFB564).

References

1. Zhou, Y., Tuzel, O.: Voxelnet: End-to-end learning for point cloud based 3d object detection. In: Proceedings of the IEEE Conference on Computer Vision and Pattern Recognition, pp. 4490–4499 (2018). https://doi.org/10.1109/CVPR.2018.00472
2. Yan, Y., Mao, Y., Li, B.: Second: sparsely embedded convolutional detection. Sensors 18(10), 3337 (2018)
3. Lang, A.H., Vora, S., Caesar, H., Zhou, L., Yang, J., Beijbom, O.: Pointpillars: fast encoders for object detection from point clouds. In: Proceedings of the IEEE/CVF Conference on Computer Vision and Pattern Recognition, pp. 12697–12705 (2019). https://doi.org/10.1109/CVPR.2019.01298
4. Yang, Z., Sun, Y., Liu, S., Jia, J.: 3dssd: point-based 3d single stage object detector. In: Proceedings of the IEEE/CVF Conference on Computer Vision and Pattern Recognition, pp. 11040–11048 (2020). https://doi.org/10.1109/CVPR42600.2020.01105
5. He, C., Zeng, H., Huang, J., Hua, X.S., Zhang, L.: Structure aware single-stage 3d object detection from point cloud. In: Proceedings of the IEEE/CVF Conference on Computer Vision and Pattern Recognition, pp. 11873–11882 (2020). https://doi.org/10.1109/CVPR42600.2020.01189
6. Shi, S., Wang, X., Li, H.: Pointrcnn: 3d object proposal generation and detection from point cloud. In: Proceedings of the IEEE/CVF Conference on Computer Vision and Pattern Recognition, pp. 770–779 (2019)
7. Shi, S., et al.: Pv-rcnn: point-voxel feature set abstraction for 3d object detection. In: Proceedings of the IEEE/CVF Conference on Computer Vision and Pattern Recognition, pp. 10529–10538 (2020). https://doi.org/10.1109/CVPR42600.2020.01054
8. Yang, Z., Sun, Y., Liu, S., Shen, X., Jia, J.: Std: sparse-to-dense 3d object detector for point cloud. In: Proceedings of the IEEE/CVF International Conference on Computer Vision, pp. 1951–1960 (2019). https://doi.org/10.1109/ICCV.2019.00204
9. Shi, S., Wang, Z., Wang, X., Li, H.: Part-A2 net: 3d part-aware and aggregation neural network for object detection from point cloud, vol. 2(3), pp. 1–10. arXiv preprint arXiv:1907.03670 (2019). https://doi.org/10.1109/TPAMI.2020.2977026
10. Chen, Y., Liu, S., Shen, X., Jia, J.: Fast point r-cnn. In: Proceedings of the IEEE/CVF International Conference on Computer Vision, pp. 9775–9784 (2019)
11. Vaswani, A., et al.: Attention is all you need. Adv. Neural. Inf. Process. Syst. 30, 1–15 (2017)
12. Woo, S., Park, J., Lee, J.-Y., Kweon, I.S.: CBAM: convolutional block attention module. In: Ferrari, V., Hebert, M., Sminchisescu, C., Weiss, Y. (eds.) ECCV 2018. LNCS, vol. 11211, pp. 3–19. Springer, Cham (2018). https://doi.org/10.1007/978-3-030-01234-2_1
13. Liu, Z., et al.: Swin transformer: hierarchical vision transformer using shifted windows. In: Proceedings of the IEEE/CVF International Conference on Computer Vision, pp. 10012–10022 (2021). https://doi.org/10.1109/ICCV48922.2021.00986
14. Carion, N., Massa, F., Synnaeve, G., Usunier, N., Kirillov, A., Zagoruyko, S.: End-to-end object detection with transformers. In: Vedaldi, A., Bischof, H., Brox, T., Frahm, J.-M. (eds.) ECCV 2020. LNCS, vol. 12346, pp. 213–229. Springer, Cham (2020). https://doi.org/10.1007/978-3-030-58452-8_13
15. Dosovitskiy, A., et al.: An image is worth 16x16 words: transformers for image recognition at scale, pp. 1–22. arXiv preprint arXiv:2010.11929 (2020)

LGF²: Local and Global Feature Fusion for Text-Guided Object Detection

Shuyu Miao[1(✉)], Hexiang Zheng[2], Lin Zheng[1], and Hong Jin[1]

[1] Tiansuan Lab, Ant Group, Hangzhou, China
miaoshuyu.msy@antgroup.com
[2] Business School, University of Shanghai for Science and Technology, Shanghai, China

Abstract. A baby can successfully learn to identify objects in an image with the corresponding text description provided by their parents. This learning process leverages the multimodal information of both the image and text. However, classical object detection approaches only utilize the image modality to distinguish objects, neglecting the text modality. While many Vision-Language Models have been explored in the object detection task, they often require large amounts of pre-training data and can only specify a particular model structure. In this paper, we propose a lightweight and generic Local and Global Feature Fusion (LGF²) framework for text-guided object detection to enhance the performance of image modality detection models. Our adaptive text-image fusion module is designed to learn optimal fusion rules between image and text features. Additionally, we introduce a word-level contrastive loss to guide the local-focused fusion of multimodal features and a sentence-level alignment loss to drive the global consistent fusion of multimodal features. Our paradigm is highly adaptable and can be easily embedded into existing image-based object detection models without any extra modification. We conduct extensive experiments on two multimodal detection datasets, and the results demonstrate that our LGF² significantly improves their performance.

Keywords: Local and Global Feature Fusion · Text-guided object detection · Text-Image Fusion

1 Introduction

During infancy, humans learn to recognize objects through a process in which parents point to an object in an image and verbally identify it. With the rapid development of artificial intelligence and neural networks, object detection technology has been proposed for automating object recognition. Object detection aims to identify the categories and locations of objects in an image, as shown in Fig. 1. This technology has played a crucial role in many areas of human society, such as intelligent transportation [6,25], intelligent medicine [13,20,26], and autonomous driving [1,8,18].

S. Miao and H. Zheng—contribute equally.

Fig. 1. The presented visualization exemplifies the effectiveness of text-guided object detection. The original image can result in the misclassification of the two cats as a single entity, given their proximity. However, with the aid of text as a guide, the two cats can be accurately identified as separate entities with ease. This demonstrates the utility of text guidance in addressing the challenging task of object detection in images.

In recent years, much of the literature on object detection has focused on improving performance by modeling image modalities effectively. One-stage models, such as those proposed in [27,31,37], treat the detection problem as a regression task with end-to-end training. By contrast, two-stage models, such as those put forth in [10,32], first generate region proposals and then refine the results through regression. To enhance feature representation, multi-layer semantic fusion has been employed [9,21], with corresponding optimization strategies designed to address multi-scale issues [19,33]. Additionally, object relationships have been modeled to encourage feature interaction [3,12,16,28,29]. Recent research on object detection has primarily focused on improving performance through single-image modality feature representation.

However, evidence from human development suggests that multimodal information, such as the combination of image and text, plays a crucial role in identifying objects. As shown in Fig. 1, non-maximum suppression-like post-processing can result in misdetection when overlapping objects are present. This issue can be addressed through the use of text information 'two cats are sleeping together', which provides additional guidance to the model. Therefore, under the guidance of text, the model can obtain more precise object detection results. While the text-guided approach has been explored to enhance object detection performance in some Vision-Language Models (VLM) [7,11,17], these methods often require the construction of large-scale graphical datasets for pre-training, and are limited to specific network structures. This results in a significant consumption of computing resources and training costs. Unfortunately, lightweight text-guided image object detection has been underexplored. A challenging problem in the multimodal object detection task is to establish a local association between text words and image local areas. This is because objects occur in specific regions within an image, each of which corresponds to specific words in the text description.

Based on the above discussions, we propose a new Local and Global Feature Fusion paradigm for text-guided object detection, named LGF^2, which utilizes both text and image modality information to improve detection performance. To achieve this, LGF^2 divides the mission into two subtasks: feature fusion and feature guidance. An adaptive Text-Image Fusion Module (TIFM) is presented to learn the optimal feature interaction rules between image and text information in the same feature space. TIFM supplements the insufficient image features with newly introduced text information. Additionally, we introduce Word-level Contrastive Loss (WCloss) and Sentence-level Alignment Loss (SAloss) to guide multimodal feature fusion at the local and global level. WCloss promotes more fine-grained word-level feature details via contrastive learning, while SAloss maintains the consistency of fusion features by mapping global features of text and images into the same semantic space. LGF^2 is highly versatile and can be easily integrated into existing detection models without modification. Experimental results show that LGF^2 improves existing image-based detection methods' performance by a significant margin of 6%.

The main contributions of our proposed LGF^2 are as follows:

- We introduce text modality information to object detection in a multimodal manner, which is a novel approach that significantly improves the performance of existing image-based detection models.
- We present an adaptive Text-Image Fusion Module that learns optimal feature fusion rules and prioritizes the most related text entities and image regions.
- We introduce Word-level Contrastive loss and Sentence-level Alignment loss to guide modality features at the local and global levels, respectively.
- Our proposed paradigm is trained in an end-to-end manner, which achieves a significant performance improvement in extensive experiments.

2   Related Work

2.1   Object Detection

Object detection is a fundamental and widely used vision task. It aims to identify and detect the objects contained in the image. In recent years, the research community has shown increasing interest in object detection, resulting in various methods, including one and two-stage detection models mentioned above, or anchor-based [10,22,24,32] and anchor-free detection models [5,14,15,34,40,41]. Anchor-based models use a fixed set of pre-determined anchors to perform an offset size regression to learn the final detection box [10,22,24,32]. This method effectively uses prior knowledge of the dataset to guide model learning, resulting in high efficiency. On the other hand, anchor-free models do not rely on predefined anchors. Instead, they directly regress the center position and object size of detection objects using a density score [14,34,41]. Other models [5,15,40] use keypoint detection to determine the position and category of the object, such as top-left and bottom-right corners. However, these methods rely solely on image modality for object detection. In contrast, our work focuses on exploring a lightweight text-guided detection framework. By incorporating text modality information, we aim to improve the performance of existing object detection models.

2.2 Vision-Language Model

As the recent emergence of large Vision-Language Models (VLM) continues to gain momentum, numerous studies have examined the use of textual guidance to promote learning of visual tasks based on a vast amount of image-test pair data. One of the most notable examples is CLIP [30], which demonstrates that predicting the appropriate caption for a given image is a highly efficient and scalable pre-training task that can yield state-of-the-art (SOTA) image representations from scratch, utilizing a dataset of 400 million (image, text) pairs collected from the internet. CoOp [38] proposes a simple yet effective approach called Context Optimization that adapts CLIP-like vision-language models for downstream image recognition. However, these models are primarily utilized for whole-image recognition or feature extraction. ViLD [11] distills knowledge from a pre-trained open-vocabulary image classification model (teacher) into a two-stage detector using category texts and image regions of object proposals as encoded by the teacher. Moreover, GLIP [17] unites object detection and phrase grounding for pre-training, enabling the acquisition of object-level, language-aware, and semantic-rich visual representations. Promptdet [7] establishes a scalable pipeline for expanding an object detector to novel or unseen categories without manual annotations. Although these VLMs possess potent feature representation at the object level, they rely heavily on specific model architecture and large amounts of image-text data (such as O365, GoldG, and ExtraData) for pre-training. In this article, we seek to explore a lightweight text-guided object detection algorithm framework that does not necessitate pre-training.

3 Our Method

3.1 Overview of the New Paradigm

In this section, we present the Local and Global Feature Fusion (LGF^2) paradigm for text-guided object detection, as depicted in Fig. 2(a). Unlike current single-modality image-based object detection models, LGF^2 aims to incorporate text modality information to address the lack of image features. This is achieved through the application of the Text-Image Fusion Module, detailed in Sect. 3.2, Word-level Contrastive loss, elaborated in Sect. 3.3, and Sentence-level Alignment loss, discussed in Sect. 3.4.

We define the inputs of our model as an image I and its corresponding text description T. We utilize existing detection models to process the image I and generate the embedded image feature. The feature produced between

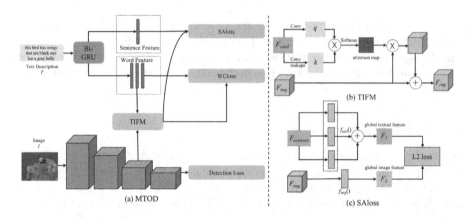

Fig. 2. The architecture of a proposed Text-guided Object Detection (LGF^2) , which takes both images and corresponding textual information as inputs. The LGF^2 framework is composed of three key components: an adaptive Text-Image Fusion Module, a Word-level Contrastive Loss, and a Sentence-level Alignment Loss.

the backbone model and the detection head is utilized as the overall visual feature $F_{img} \in \mathbb{R}^{C \times H \times W}$, which is crucial for the alignment and representation of fused feature semantics. To encode the text description T, we feed it into a Bidirectional Gated Recurrent Unit (Bi-GRU). The output of the Bi-GRU is then adopted as the word embedding feature $F_{word} \in \mathbb{R}^{C \times D}$. The sentence feature $F_{sentence} \in \mathbb{R}^C$ is obtained by considering the last hidden state of the Bi-GRU, which encapsulates the complete global text representation information.

3.2   Text-Image Fusion Module

Text features and image features are stored in different feature spaces, making it challenging to effectively fuse them. Moreover, for a given text description, only a few words carry guiding significance to identify the object in the corresponding image. For instance, in the sentence *'It is a cat with white hair'*, the words *'cat white hair'* signify the class of the object and its properties, and their high-level semantics play a crucial role in cat identification. To overcome these challenges, we propose the Text-Image Fusion Module (TIFM), as depicted in Fig. 2(b), which can adaptively explore the most appropriate rule of fusion.

The Text-Image Fusion Module (TIFM) takes the image feature vector F_{img} and the word feature vector F_{word} as inputs. Initially, we pass F_{word} through two 1×1 convolutional layers to obtain the query feature block $q \in \mathbb{R}^{C \times D}$ and the key feature block $k \in \mathbb{R}^{C \times D}$. To concentrate on the word feature semantics that are most relevant, we reshape the k tensor, perform matrix multiplication with q, and subsequently apply a softmax operation to obtain a word semantic self-attention matrix $a \in \mathbb{R}^{C \times C}$. Additionally, we map the attention matrix a to the image feature semantic to enhance the most appropriate local feature of the image using matrix product. To prevent model degradation due to noisy text information, we introduce a shortcut connection. To fuse multimodal features in the same feature space, we convert the text features to an attention map, which enhances the image features and produces the initial weighted image feature. The formal representation of this process is as follows:

$$F_{img} = F_{img} + softmax(conv(F_{word})) \times conv(F_{word})^t) \circ F_{img} \qquad (1)$$

where $softmax(\cdot)$ represents the softmax function, $conv(\cdot)$ denotes the convolution operation, t represents matrix transformation, and $\circ$ denotes the matrix product.

3.3 Word-Level Contrastive Loss

In the context of an image and its corresponding text description, it is important to identify specific regions in the image and words in the text that warrant attention. This necessitates a focused approach to fuse the features of these distinct regions and words. To this end, we propose word-level contrastive loss (WCloss) to guide the local fusion of multimodal features. We calculate the similarity $S_{(img,text)}$ of the text entities and image regions as presented in [36].

Assuming that the training data contains $\{(i_1, t_1), (i_1, t_2), \cdots, (i_m, t_n)\}$ image-text pairs in one batch, where i_m denotes the mth image and t_n denotes the word embedding of nth text description. Inspired by contrastive learning, we calculate the similarity $S_{(i_m, t_n)}$ of any image-text pair (i_m, t_n). When $m = n$, the pair is regarded as positive sample, e.g., $p(i_m, t_n) = 1$; when $m \neq n$, the pair is denoted as negative sample, e.g., $p(i_m, t_n) = 0$. Accordingly, we perform WCloss based on cross-entropy loss using the following equation:

$$\mathcal{L}_{wc} = -\sum_{m,n} p(i_m, t_n) log(S(i_m, t_n)) \qquad (2)$$

This procedure treats the image and text components as sub-elements, enabling the model to focus more on local text and image information.

3.4 Sentence-Level Alignment Loss

Maintaining consistency in the joint space of visual representation and textual semantics is essential in efficiently fusing multimodal features. In this regard, we undertake global alignment of image features and text features. As a means to achieve global consistent fusion, we propose the sentence-level alignment loss, as depicted in Fig. 2(c).

In order to embed the global feature, we encode the visual feature F_{img} and textual feature $F_{sentence}$. Specifically, F_{img} is first processed by an embedding convolution layer using 1×1 convolution to model the high-level semantics, followed by a soft convolution layer to make the feature softer using 1×1 convolution, and finally an adaptive average pooling layer to obtain the global-level visual feature, denoted as $f_{img}(\cdot)$. On the other hand, $F_{sentence}$ is processed by three parallel embedding layers with a 1-d convolution and an adaptive average pooling layer to capture cross-semantic global textual features. The outputs of the three parallel layers are then concatenated and passed through a fully linear connection layer to ensure that the textual and visual features are in the same dimension, which is denoted as $f_{text}(\cdot)$. Finally, to guide the global fusion of multimodal features, we adopt the following loss function:

$$\mathcal{L}_{sa} = ||f_{img}(F_{img}), f_{text}(F_{sentence})||^2 \qquad (3)$$

This aligns the global features of image and text to guide the feature fusion at the global level in the same feature space.

3.5   Loss Functions

The training process takes image and text description inputs. The original detection loss is denoted as $\mathcal{L}_{det}$, and the total loss of the LGF^2 can be expressed as:

$$\mathcal{L}_{total} = \lambda_{det}\mathcal{L}_{det} + \lambda_{wc}\mathcal{L}_{wc} + \lambda_{sa}\mathcal{L}_{sa} \qquad (4)$$

where λ_{det}, λ_{wc}, and λ_{sa} are weights used to balance the different losses. The model is trained in an end-to-end manner and utilizes multimodal features.

4   Experiments

4.1   Experimental Setup

Datasets. In order to validate the effectiveness of the proposed method, we conducted experiments on multimodal object detection datasets. Specifically, we performed all experiments on the CUB200 [35] and MS-COCO [23] datasets, which contain both image and text information. The Caltech-UCSD-Birds-200-2011 (CUB200) dataset consists of 200 categories of unique birds with 11,788 samples that include bounding boxes and corresponding text descriptions. We followed the official setting, using 5,994 samples for training and 5,794 for testing. To generate the text descriptions for our method, we collected image descriptions from the MS-COCO dataset [23]. These descriptions were used as the text descriptions for our proposed method.

Metrics. In this study, we employed widely-adopted evaluation metrics in object detection tasks. Specifically, we used the Average Precision (AP) to assess the performance of the model under various IoU threshold settings between the predicted and bounding boxes. Our evaluation results are presented as AP, AP_{50}, and AP_{75}. API[1].

---

[1] https://github.com/cocodataset/cocoapi.

Table 1. Experiments of our LGF^2 on MS-COCO dataset.

Method	Backbone	AP	AP$_{50}$	AP$_{75}$
STDN [39]	DenseNet169	31.8	51.0	33.6
CCAGNet [27]	VGG16	35.6	55.0	36.9
FPN [21]	ResNet101	36.2	59.1	39.0
R-FCN [4]	ResNet101	29.9	51.9	–
SSD [22]	ResNet101	31.2	50.4	33.3
SSD + LGF^2	ResNet101	**34.4**(+3.2)	**53.7**(+3.3)	**35.8**(+2.5)
Faster R-CNN [32]	ResNet101	36.2	59.1	39.0
Faster R-CNN + LGF^2	ResNet101	**38.9**(+2.7)	**62.0**(+2.9)	**42.1**(+3.1)
RetinaNet [22]	ResNet101	39.1	59.1	42.3
RetinaNet + LGF^2	ResNet101	**41.5**(+2.4)	**61.4**(+2.3)	**44.9**(+2.6)

Table 2. Experiments of our LGF^2 on CUB200 dataset.

Method	Backbone	AP	AP$_{50}$	AP$_{75}$
FCOS [34]	ResNet50	22.1	27.3	25.6
FCOS + LGF^2	ResNet50	**28.6**(+6.5)	**35.1**(+7.8)	**31.8**(+6.2)
FCOS [34]	ResNet101	25.5	31.0	29.4
FCOS + LGF^2	ResNet101	**30.6**(+5.1)	**36.4**(+5.4)	**34.3**(+4.9)
ATSS [37]	ResNet50	34.8	42.4	40.1
ATSS + LGF^2	ResNet50	**38.3**(+3.5)	**45.4**(+3.0)	**43.8** (+3.7)
ATSS [37]	ResNet101	37.0	43.3	41.4
ATSS + LGF^2	ResNet101	**40.3**(+3.3)	**47.2**(+3.9)	**44.4** (+3.0)

Experimental Details. We implement the experimental source code with the Pytorch framework based on MMdetection [2]. Our proposed LGF^2 can be easily embedded in the existing detection methods, making them suitable for multi-modal object detection pipelines. To demonstrate the effectiveness of LGF^2, we perform extensive experiments on popular detection models as the baselines, e.g., RetinaNet [22], Faster R-CNN [32], FCOS [34], and ATSS [37]. To be fair, we adopt the same strategies, like data augmentation, preprocess pipeline, input scale, backbone models, non-maximum suppression step, and other basic settings.

4.2   Overall Performance

We evaluated the performance of our proposed LGF^2 model on two datasets. Our evaluation methodology was consistent with the baselines used in these datasets.

Table 3. Experiments on each module of LGF^2.

Method	Backbone	AP	AP$_{50}$	AP$_{75}$
FCOS [34]	ResNet50	22.1	27.3	25.6
FCOS + TIFM	ResNet50	23.2	28.7	26.8
FCOS + TIFM + WCloss	ResNet50	25.3	31.4	29.3
FCOS + TIFM + SAloss	ReNset50	24.2	29.8	27.9
FCOS + LGF^2	ResNet50	**28.6**	**35.1**	**31.8**

Table 4. Ablation experiments of the loss weight in Eq. (4).

λ_{det}	λ_{wc}	λ_{sa}	Backbone	AP	AP$_{50}$	AP$_{75}$
Baseline [34]			ResNet50	0.221	0.273	0.256
1.0	1.0	1.0	ResNet50	0.264	0.325	0.305
1.0	1.0	0.1	ResNet50	0.275	0.340	0.319
1.0	0.1	1.0	ResNet50	0.269	0.332	0.311
1.0	0.1	0.1	ResNet50	0.286	0.351	0.318

Results on MS-COCO. Table 1 presents the summary statistics for the performance of our proposed LGF^2 model on the MS-COCO dataset. In our evaluation, we conducted tests on three popular models, namely, SSD [24], RetinaNet [22], and Faster R-CNN [32]. Our results show that LGF^2 significantly improves the Average Precision AP, AP_{50}, and AP_{75} metrics for these models, with improvements of 3.2%, 3.3%, and 2.5%, 2.7%, 2.9%, and 3.1%, and 2.4%, 2.3%, and 1.6% respectively. These findings indicate that LGF^2 consistently enhances performance across different models.

Results on CUB200. Table 2 reports the summary statistics for the performance of our proposed LGF^2 model on the CUB200 dataset. In our experiments, we used FCOS [34] and ATSS [37] as the baselines and integrated LGF^2 with them to demonstrate the superior performance of multimodal-based object detection. Our results indicate that LGF^2 substantially enhances the performance of all the baselines. For FCOS with ResNet50 as the backbone, we observed improvements of 6.5%, 7.8%, and 6.2% in AP, AP_{50}, and AP_{75} metrics, respectively. Similarly, for FCOS with ResNet101 as the backbone, we observed improvements of 5.1%, 5.4%, and 4.9% in AP, AP_{50}, and AP_{75} metrics, respectively. Regarding ATSS based on ResNet50, we observed improvements of 3.5%, 3.0%, and 3.7% in AP, AP_{50}, and AP_{75} metrics, respectively. For ATSS with ResNet101, we observed improvements of 3.3%, 3.9%, and 3.0% in AP, AP_{50}, and AP_{75} metrics, respectively. Moreover, for ATSS based on both ResNet50 and ResNet101, we observed a substantial improvement in all the metrics.

4.3   Ablation Study

Experiments on each module of LGF^2. Table 3 highlights that the evaluation metrics show a substantial decline when our model is based on non-full proposed modules, emphasizing the significance and rationality of each module. This observation suggests that all modules play an essential role in our proposed model, and their collective performance is critical for achieving sota results. Our experimental results provide strong evidence supporting the importance of each module and demonstrate the effectiveness of our proposed approach.

Experiments on Loss Weights. The Eq. (4) presents three super parameters: λ_{det}, λ_{wc}, and λ_{sa}, which are responsible for managing different losses in the proposed model. To explore the optimal parameter settings, we tested various parameter combinations, and the results are presented in Table 4. The table demonstrates that different parameter values lead to varied loss proportions and affect the learning focus of the model. Notably, the best performance is achieved when λ_{det}, λ_{wc}, and λ_{sa} are set as 1.0, 0.1, and 0.1, respectively. Moreover, it is important to emphasize that λ_{det} has the most significant weight as it is the primary objective of the model to achieve object detection. Furthermore, λ_{wc} and λ_{sa} have equal weights, indicating the critical role of guiding both local and global fusion of image and text information for optimal performance.

5   Conclusion

This paper proposes a new multimodal text-guided object detection paradigm to enhance the feature guidance in existing detection models, which are solely based on image modality information. Our proposed framework consists of a text-image fusion module, word-level contrastive loss, and sentence-level alignment loss, which promote multimodal feature fusion both locally and globally. Importantly, our approach can be easily integrated into existing detection models to facilitate multimodal learning. The extensive experiments conducted in this study demonstrate the superior performance of our proposed model.

References

1. Cai, Y., et al.: Yolov4-5d: an effective and efficient object detector for autonomous driving. IEEE Trans. Instrum. Meas. **70**, 1–13 (2021)
2. Chen, K., et al.: Mmdetection: Open mmlab detection toolbox and benchmark. arXiv (2019)
3. Chen, S., Li, Z., Tang, Z.: Relation R-CNN: a graph based relation-aware network for object detection. IEEE Signal Process. Lett. **27**, 1680–1684 (2020)
4. Dai, J., et al.: Deformable convolutional networks. In: Proceedings of the IEEE International Conference on Computer Vision, pp. 764–773 (2017)
5. Duan, K., Bai, S., Xie, L., Qi, H., Huang, Q., Tian, Q.: Centernet: keypoint triplets for object detection. In: Proceedings of the IEEE/CVF International Conference On Computer Vision, pp. 6569–6578 (2019)

6. Fabbri, M., et al.: Motsynth: How can synthetic data help pedestrian detection and tracking? In: Proceedings of the IEEE/CVF International Conference on Computer Vision (ICCV), pp. 10849–10859 (2021)

7. Feng, C., et al.: Promptdet: Towards open-vocabulary detection using uncurated images. In: Computer Vision-ECCV 2022: 17th European Conference, Tel Aviv, Israel, October 23–27, 2022, Proceedings, Part IX. pp. 701–717. Springer (2022). https://doi.org/10.1007/978-3-031-20077-9_41

8. Feng, D., et al.: Deep multi-modal object detection and semantic segmentation for autonomous driving: datasets, methods, and challenges. IEEE Trans. Intell. Transp. Syst. **22**(3), 1341–1360 (2020)

9. Ghiasi, G., Lin, T.Y., Le, Q.V.: Nas-fpn: Learning scalable feature pyramid architecture for object detection. In: CVPR, pp. 7036–7045 (2019)

10. Girshick, R., Donahue, J., Darrell, T., Malik, J.: Rich feature hierarchies for accurate object detection and semantic segmentation. In: CVPR, pp. 580–587 (2014)

11. Gu, X., Lin, T.Y., Kuo, W., Cui, Y.: Open-vocabulary object detection via vision and language knowledge distillation. arXiv preprint arXiv:2104.13921 (2021)

12. Hu, H., Gu, J., Zhang, Z., Dai, J., Wei, Y.: Relation networks for object detection. In: CVPR, pp. 3588–3597 (2018)

13. Jaeger, P.F., et al.: Retina u-net: Embarrassingly simple exploitation of segmentation supervision for medical object detection. In: Machine Learning for Health Workshop, pp. 171–183. PMLR (2020)

14. Kong, T., Sun, F., Liu, H., Jiang, Y., Li, L., Shi, J.: Foveabox: beyound anchorbased object detection. IEEE Trans. Image Process. **29**, 7389–7398 (2020)

15. Law, H., Deng, J.: Cornernet: Detecting objects as paired keypoints. In: Proceedings of the European Conference on Computer Vision (ECCV), pp. 734–750 (2018)

16. Li, H., Miao, S., Feng, R.: Dg-fpn: Learning dynamic feature fusion based on graph convolution network for object detection. In: ICME, pp. 1–6 (2020)

17. Li, L.H., et al.: Grounded language-image pre-training. In: Proceedings of the IEEE/CVF Conference on Computer Vision and Pattern Recognition, pp. 10965–10975 (2022)

18. Li, Y., et al.: A deep learning-based hybrid framework for object detection and recognition in autonomous driving. IEEE Access **8**, 194228–194239 (2020)

19. Li, Y., Chen, Y., Wang, N., Zhang, Z.: Scale-aware trident networks for object detection. In: ICCV, pp. 6054–6063 (2019)

20. Li, Z., Dong, M., Wen, S., Hu, X., Zhou, P., Zeng, Z.: Clu-CNNs: object detection for medical images. Neurocomputing **350**, 53–59 (2019)

21. Lin, T.Y., Dollár, P., Girshick, R., He, K., Hariharan, B., Belongie, S.: Feature pyramid networks for object detection. In: CVPR, pp. 2117–2125 (2017)

22. Lin, T.Y., Goyal, P., Girshick, R., He, K., Dollár, P.: Focal loss for dense object detection. In: ICCV, pp. 2980–2988 (2017)

23. Lin, T.-Y., Maire, M., Belongie, S., Hays, J., Perona, P., Ramanan, D., Dollár, P., Zitnick, C.L.: Microsoft COCO: common objects in context. In: Fleet, D., Pajdla, T., Schiele, B., Tuytelaars, T. (eds.) ECCV 2014. LNCS, vol. 8693, pp. 740–755. Springer, Cham (2014). https://doi.org/10.1007/978-3-319-10602-1_48

24. Liu, W., et al.: SSD: D. In: Leibe, B., Matas, J., Sebe, N., Welling, M. (eds.) ECCV 2016. LNCS, vol. 9905, pp. 21–37. Springer, Cham (2016). https://doi.org/10.1007/978-3-319-46448-0_2

25. Liu, W., Liao, S., Ren, W., Hu, W., Yu, Y.: High-level semantic feature detection: a new perspective for pedestrian detection. In: CVPR, pp. 5187–5196 (2019)

26. Loey, M., Manogaran, G., Taha, M.H.N., Khalifa, N.E.M.: Fighting against Covid-19: a novel deep learning model based on yolo-v2 with Resnet-50 for medical face mask detection. Sustain. Urban Areas **65**, 102600 (2021)

27. Miao, S., et al.: Balanced single-shot object detection using cross-context attention-guided network. Pattern Recogn. **122**, 108258 (2022)

28. Miao, S., Feng, R., Zhang, Y., Fan, W.: Learning class-based graph representation for object detection. In: AAAI, pp. 2752–2759 (2020)

29. Miao, S., Zheng, L., Jin, H., Feng, R.: Dynamically connected graph representation for object detection. In: International Conference on Neural Information Processing, pp. 347–358. Springer (2022). https://doi.org/10.1007/978-3-031-30111-7_30

30. Radford, A., et al.: Learning transferable visual models from natural language supervision. In: International Conference on Machine Learning, pp. 8748–8763. PMLR (2021)

31. Redmon, J., Divvala, S., Girshick, R., Farhadi, A.: You only look once: Unified, real-time object detection. In: CVPR (2016)

32. Ren, S., He, K., Girshick, R., Sun, J.: Faster R-CNN: Towards real-time object detection with region proposal networks. Arxiv (2015)

33. Singh, B., Davis, L.S.: An analysis of scale invariance in object detection snip. In: CVPR, pp. 3578–3587 (2018)

34. Tian, Z., Shen, C., Chen, H., He, T.: Fcos: Fully convolutional one-stage object detection. In: Proceedings of the IEEE/CVF International Conference on Computer Vision, pp. 9627–9636 (2019)

35. Wah, C., Branson, S., Welinder, P., Perona, P., Belongie, S.: The caltech-ucsd birds-200-2011 dataset (2011)

36. Xu, T., et al.: Attngan: Fine-grained text to image generation with attentional generative adversarial networks. In: CVPR (2018)

37. Zhang, S., Chi, C., Yao, Y., Lei, Z., Li, S.Z.: Bridging the gap between anchor-based and anchor-free detection via adaptive training sample selection. In: CVPR (2020)

38. Zhou, K., Yang, J., Loy, C.C., Liu, Z.: Learning to prompt for vision-language models. Int. J. Comput. Vision **130**(9), 2337–2348 (2022)

39. Zhou, P., Ni, B., Geng, C., Hu, J., Xu, Y.: Scale-transferrable object detection. In: proceedings of the IEEE Conference on Computer Vision and Pattern Recognition, pp. 528–537 (2018)

40. Zhou, X., Zhuo, J., Krahenbuhl, P.: Bottom-up object detection by grouping extreme and center points. In: Proceedings of the IEEE/CVF Conference on Computer Vision and Pattern Recognition, pp. 850–859 (2019)

41. Zhu, C., He, Y., Savvides, M.: Feature selective anchor-free module for single-shot object detection. In: Proceedings of the IEEE/CVF Conference On Computer Vision and Pattern Recognition, pp. 840–849 (2019)

MLF-DET: Multi-Level Fusion for Cross-Modal 3D Object Detection

Zewei Lin, Yanqing Shen, Sanping Zhou$^{(\boxtimes)}$, Shitao Chen, and Nanning Zheng

National Key Laboratory of Human-Machine Hybrid Augmented Intelligence,
National Engineering Research Center for Visual Information and Applications, and
Institute of Artificial Intelligence and Robotics, Xi'an Jiaotong University,
Xi'an, China
{xianjiaoda2017zw,qing1159364090}@stu.xjtu.edu.cn,
{spzhou,chenshitao,nnzheng}@mail.xjtu.edu.cn

Abstract. In this paper, we propose a novel and effective Multi-Level Fusion network, named as MLF-DET, for high-performance cross-modal 3D object DETection, which integrates both the feature-level fusion and decision-level fusion to fully utilize the information in the image. For the feature-level fusion, we present the Multi-scale Voxel Image fusion (MVI) module, which densely aligns multi-scale voxel features with image features. For the decision-level fusion, we propose the lightweight Feature-cued Confidence Rectification (FCR) module which further exploits image semantics to rectify the confidence of detection candidates. Besides, we design an effective data augmentation strategy termed Occlusion-aware GT Sampling (OGS) to reserve more sampled objects in the training scenes, so as to reduce overfitting. Extensive experiments on the KITTI dataset demonstrate the effectiveness of our method. Notably, on the extremely competitive KITTI car 3D object detection benchmark, our method reaches 82.89% moderate AP and achieves state-of-the-art performance without bells and whistles.

Keywords: Multi-level fusion · 3D object detection · Cross modality · Autonomous driving

1 Introduction

3D object detection aims to get the object's location, size, and direction in 3D space, which are indispensable information for path planning and motion control in autonomous driving. The most frequently used sensors in 3D detection are LiDAR and camera. LiDAR point clouds can capture the structural and depth information, with low resolution and lack of semantic information. Instead, camera images provide rich semantic information, such as color and texture, while suffering from an inherent 3D information ambiguity. Considering the complementarity of point clouds and images, many works attempt to fuse the two sensor modalities to improve detection accuracy [7,16,25,27,31,33]. Nevertheless, how to overcome the modality gap and make good use of the two sensor data remains a tremendous challenge.

L. Iliadis et al. (Eds.): ICANN 2023, LNCS 14260, pp. 136–149, 2023.
https://doi.org/10.1007/978-3-031-44195-0_12

Currently, cross-modal 3D detection methods can be mainly divided into two lines, *i.e.*, feature-level fusion ones and decision-level fusion ones. Feature-level fusion methods [1,7,25,29,33] use different backbone networks to extract the features of different modalities and merge the cross-modal features into a unified representation, which would be used for detection. Decision-level fusion methods [16,17] use different detectors to process different modalities and ensemble the output boxes of the detectors to get the final results. Generally, the feature-level fusion methods can leverage the rich semantic features of images, but the complex fusion network is prone to overfitting and the image features may not be used properly. The decision-level fusion methods can use accurate 2D detection boxes to boost 3D detection performance but are short of fine-grained information interaction between two modalities.

In this paper, we present a novel 3D detection framework termed MLF-DET, which incorporates the advantages of feature-level fusion and decision-level fusion to fully exploit image information and achieve better performance. Specifically, instead of projecting LiDAR points onto the image plane and building sparse connections between point features and image features [7,14,25], the designed Multi-scale Voxel Image fusion (MVI) module projects multi-scale voxel centers at non-empty locations onto the image plane. In this way, a dense connection between voxel features and image features would be built. That's because the regular sparse convolution network [5] dilates the sparse voxel features and produces new occupied voxels. To further squeeze the juice of the image, the Feature-cued Confidence Rectification (FCR) module treats the projected 3D RoIs as 2D RoIs and refines them to produce confidence scores, respectively. Afterwards, the confidence scores of 3D RoIs and 2D RoIs along with their features are fed into a lightweight MLP to produce the rectified scores. It is worth noting that this module does not introduce much complexity to the network due to the shared RoIs between the two modalities.

In addition, we also investigate cross-modal data augmentation to further improve detection performance. Data augmentation is essential for cross-modal networks for they contain more parameters and suffer from overfitting. The previous work [26] extends the commonly used GT Sampling data augmentation [28] from LiDAR-only methods to cross-modal methods. However, the severe occlusion on the image plane is ignored. Since the space on the image plane is quite limited, most sampled objects would be removed for they are heavily occluded with other objects, making GT Sampling less effective. Therefore, we propose Occlusion-aware GT Sampling (OGS) to carefully deal with the occlusion of objects. By removing the most severely occluded sampled objects in order, we reserve more sampled image patches and alleviate overfitting in training.

Our main contributions can be summarized in three-fold. (1) We propose a novel multi-level fusion framework to fuse point clouds and images in the feature level and decision level to make full use of semantic information of images. (2) We present a novel occlusion-aware GT Sampling strategy to augment the data which can preserve more sampled objects and diversify the training scenes. (3) We experimentally validate the superiority of our method on the KITTI dataset [4]. Without exploiting test time augmentation or model ensemble or extra data, we surpass state-of-the-art cross-modal methods with remarkable margins.

2   Related Work

Camera-Only 3D Detection. Camera-only methods are rewarding because the cost of a camera is much lower than a LiDAR sensor. RTM3D [9] predicts the nine perspective key points of a 3D bounding box in image space, and then utilizes the geometric constraints of perspective projection to estimate a stable 3D box. SMOKE [13] regresses 3D boxes directly with a single keypoint estimation and proposes a multi-step disentangling strategy to improve accuracy. MonoFlex [32] optimizes the detection performance of truncated objects by decoupling the edge of the feature map and predicts the depth by uncertainty-guided ensemble. Because of the inherent depth ambiguity of images, these methods suffer from low precision.

LiDAR-Only 3D Detection. According to point cloud representations, LiDAR-only 3D detectors can be classified into point-based ones and grid-based ones. The point-based detectors extract representative features directly from raw points with PointNet [19] or its variant [20]. PointRCNN [23] produces RoIs from foreground points in a bottom-up manner, which is followed by a refinement network. VoteNet [18] learns to predict the instance centroids by introducing a novel deep Hough voting. IA-SSD [30] argues that points are not equally important and presents two sampling strategies to preserve more foreground points. Grid-based detectors divide unstructured points into regular grids and extract features with Convolutional Neural Network (CNN). SECOND [28] makes use of sparse convolutions to speed up the feature extraction of voxels. PointPillars [8] converts point clouds organized in pillars into pseudo images, so as to cut off the inefficient 3D convolutions. Voxel R-CNN [3] argues the precise positions of points are not needed and devises a voxel RoI pooling to extract RoI features. Since point clouds are very sparse, especially in the long range, the performance of LiDAR-only detectors is limited.

Cross-Modal 3D Detection. To take advantage of both LiDAR and camera, many cross-modal methods are proposed. PointPainting [25] decorates each raw point with class scores from an image-based semantic segmentation network. EPNet [7] builds a LI-Fusion module to fuse point features with image features adaptively. EPNet++ [14] improves EPNet by introducing the CB-Fusion module and MC loss. A drawback of these approaches is the sparse correspondences between LiDAR points and image pixels, which leads to severe information loss of images. DVF [15] builds a dense voxel fusion pipeline by weighting each voxel feature with the foreground mask constructed from a 2D detector. However, the foreground mask of the image is highly abstract and still causes information

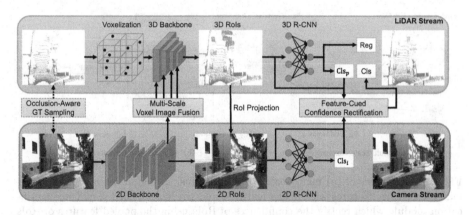

Fig. 1. Overview of MLF-DET. First, the Camera stream extracts the image features with ResNet and FPN. Second, the LiDAR stream voxelizes the point cloud and extracts voxel features with sparse convolutions. Simultaneously, the MVI module enhances the voxel features with image features. Then, the 3D RoIs generated from 3D RPN are shared with camera stream via projecting. Subsequently, the 3D and 2D RoIs are refined, respectively. Finally, the FCR module is applied to rectify the confidence of detection candidates. The OGS module shown in dashed lines is used to preserve more sampled objects in training and would be turned off in inference.

loss. SFD [27] generates pseudo point clouds from images with depth completion and fuses them with original point clouds in 3D space. CLOCs [16] fuses the candidates of a 3D detector and a 2D detector before NMS in the decision level. Fast-CLOCs [17] reduces the memory usage and computational complexity of CLOCs by the 3D-Q-2D image detector, which shares 3D candidates with the image branch. Nevertheless, the process of constructing the sparse tensor is still cumbersome and time-consuming.

3   MLF-DET

In this section, we show the detailed design of MLF-DET. As illustrated in Fig. 1, MLF-DET is composed of a LiDAR stream, a camera stream, and three modality interaction modules. MVI aims to utilize image semantic features to enhance voxel features and FCR plays a role in rectifying the confidence of detection candidates. As for OGS, it is used to reserve more sampled objects in training scenes.

3.1   Multi-scale Voxel Image Fusion

In order to build a dense connection between point cloud and image and fully utilize image features to enrich voxel features, we devise the MVI module, as depicted in Fig. 2 (a). Specifically, we use ResNet50 [6] to extract image features and further use FPN [12] to build the feature pyramid $\{I_0, I_1, I_2, I_3, I_4\}$, where I_0

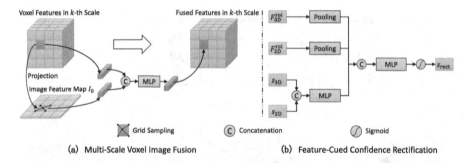

(a) Multi-Scale Voxel Image Fusion   (b) Feature-Cued Confidence Rectification

Fig. 2. Illustrations of (a) multi-scale voxel image fusion module which densely fuses multi-scale voxel features with image features, and (b) feature-cued confidence rectification module which rectify the confidences of RoIs using the pooled features of RoIs as cues.

is the feature map with the finest level. Meanwhile, several 3D sparse convolution blocks are selected to extract multi-scale voxel features for voxelized point clouds. The features of occupied voxels in the k-th scale ($k \in \{0, 1, 2, 3\}$) can be denoted by $V^k \in \mathbf{R}^{N_k \times C_k}$, where N_k is the number of occupied voxels, C_k is the number of feature channels. The centers of these voxels are denoted by $P^k \in \mathbf{R}^{N_k \times 3}$. For a particular voxel with features v^k and center p^k, the corresponding position p_{img}^k on the image plane can be calculated as follows

$$p_{\text{img}}^k = T_{\text{img} \leftarrow \text{cam}} T_{\text{cam} \leftarrow \text{lidar}} p^k, \tag{1}$$

where $T_{\text{cam} \leftarrow \text{lidar}}$ and $T_{\text{img} \leftarrow \text{cam}}$ are transformation matrixes from the coordinate of LiDAR to camera and the coordinate of camera to image, respectively. Instead of sampling image features v_{img}^k in the feature map with corresponding scale, we sample them in the finest feature map I_0 for it contains rich semantics with high resolution, which is important to detect distant objects. It is written as

$$v_{\text{img}}^k = G \left(I_0, p_{\text{img}}^k \right), \tag{2}$$

where $G(\cdot, \cdot)$ denotes the grid sampler that samples features of a position on a feature map with bilinear interpolation. Finally, we concatenate v^k and v_{img}^k and employ an MLP to aggregate these features, which is formulated as

$$v_{\text{fuse}}^k = \text{MLP} \left(\text{CONCAT} \left(v^k, v_{\text{img}}^k \right) \right), \tag{3}$$

where v_{fuse}^k denotes the fused features which share the same channels with v^k. Although there are other fusion manners, e.g., simple attention [7] or cross attention [29], we select concatenation for efficiency. Since the regular sparse convolution would dilate the features of occupied voxels to their neighbors, P^k changes along with k. It means that voxels in different scales may fetch different image features, and thus much more image features would be sampled in total.

3.2 Featured-Cued Confidence Rectification

We introduce the FCR module to further reduce the information loss of images, as depicted in Fig. 2 (b). Considering images provide rich textural and semantic information which makes them superior in classification, FCR aims to correct the confidence of detection candidates with the help of images. However, generating 3D and 2D detection candidates separately from two branches is computation-intensive. Inspired by [17], we project 3D RoIs onto the image plane to get 2D RoIs and refine them respectively to obtain 3D and 2D detection candidates. Note that the 2D Region-based Convolutional Neural Network (R-CNN) only needs to classify these 2D RoIs, instead of both classifying and regressing them. The confidence scores of a 3D detection candidate and the corresponding 2D candidate, denoted by s_{3D} and s_{2D} respectively, represent the probabilities LiDAR stream and camera stream predict that there is a foreground object. What we want to do is to fuse the two scores in a learnable way. Nevertheless, it is difficult for a network to learn a more accurate score with only two scores. Therefore, we feed the features of RoIs into the network as cues to rectify the confidence scores. In more detail, denote the features of a 3D RoI and a 2D RoI by F_{3D}^{roi} and F_{3D}^{roi}, we combine them as

$$F_{fuse}^{roi} = \text{CONCAT}\left(\text{AvgPool}\left(F_{3D}^{roi}\right), \text{AvgPool}\left(F_{2D}^{roi}\right)\right), \qquad (4)$$

where $\text{AvgPool}(\cdot)$ is the average pooling operation used to reduce the feature channels. To avoid the confidence rectification being dominated by the RoI features, we concatenate s_{3D} and s_{2D}, and map them to a higher dimension

$$F_{fuse}^{score} = \text{MLP}\left(\text{CONCAT}\left(s_{3D}, s_{2D}\right)\right). \qquad (5)$$

Finally, we employ an MLP with a sigmoid activation function σ to predict the rectified confidence score

$$s_{rect} = \sigma\left(\text{MLP}\left(\text{CONCAT}\left(F_{fuse}^{roi}, F_{fuse}^{score}\right)\right)\right), \qquad (6)$$

Given that the spatial localization ability of point clouds is much better than images, we do not exploit images to rectify the regression.

3.3 Occlusion-Aware GT Sampling

Data augmentation is essential to reduce the overfitting of the network. For LiDAR-based 3D object detection, GT Sampling is a frequently used data augmentation. It randomly samples several objects from the database and pastes them into the current training scene. A collision test should be performed to remove sampled objects which are heavily occluded with other objects.

As for cross-modal 3D object detection, it is necessary but hard to main consistency between point clouds and images during data augmentation. PointAugmenting [26] pastes point cloud-image patch pairs into the training scene and performs the collision test on both the bird's eye view (BEV) and the image plane.

Algorithm 1: Occlusion-Aware GT Sampling

Input: Ground Truth Boxes $\mathbf{G} = \{\mathbf{g_1}, \mathbf{g_2}, ..., \mathbf{g_N}\}$, Sampled Boxes
$\quad$ $\mathbf{S} = \{\mathbf{s_1}, \mathbf{s_2}, ..., \mathbf{s_M}\}$, Occlusion Threshold on BEV Plane τ_1, Occlusion
$\quad$ Threshold on Image Plane τ_2.

1: $\mathbf{I_1} \leftarrow$ CalculateBEVIoU($\mathbf{S}, \mathbf{S} \bigcup \mathbf{G}$)
2: $\mathbf{I_2} \leftarrow$ CalculateImageIoU($\mathbf{S}, \mathbf{S} \bigcup \mathbf{G}$)
3: $\mathbf{O} \leftarrow$ CalculateOcclusionNum($\mathbf{I_1}, \mathbf{I_2}, \tau_1, \tau_2$)
4: **while** O $\neq$ empty **do**
5: $\quad$ // find and delete the most heavily occluded sampled object
6: $\quad$ i $\leftarrow$ Argmax O
7: $\quad$ $\mathbf{S} \leftarrow \mathbf{S} - \{\mathbf{s_i}\}$
8: $\quad$ // remove the items related to the i-th sampled object in the IoU tables
9: $\quad$ $\mathbf{I_1} \leftarrow$ Remove($\mathbf{I_1}, i$)
10: $\quad$ $\mathbf{I_2} \leftarrow$ Remove($\mathbf{I_2}, i$)
11: $\quad$ $\mathbf{O} \leftarrow$ CalculateOcclusionNum($\mathbf{I_1}, \mathbf{I_2}, \tau_1, \tau_2$)
12: **end while**
Output: S

Although the consistency problem is solved, most of the sampled objects would be removed for severe occlusion on the image plane, which weakens the effect of GT Sampling. To solve this problem, we devise the OGS module. Because a sampled object may be severely occluded with many other objects, if we only remove the most severely occluded sampled object, other sampled objects occluded with this object could be retained. Therefore, we calculate how many other objects each sampled object is occluded with and remove the most severely occluded sampled object one by one. We find that this simple strategy is useful to reserve more sampled objects in training scenes, especially when we train multiple categories together. The detailed implementation is shown in Algorithm 1.

4   Experiments

4.1   Dataset and Evaluation Metrics

We evaluate our method in the KITTI 3D object detection dataset [4]. It contains 7,481 training frames and 7,518 testing frames. Following the data split routine, the training frames are further divided into a *train* set with 3,712 frames and a *val* set with 3,769 frames. According to the size, occlusion, and truncation, objects are grouped into three difficulty levels, *i.e.*, easy, moderate and hard. We evaluate the results by the mAP. Following [22], the mAP is calculated with 11 recall positions on the *val* set and with 40 recall positions on the *test* set.

4.2   Implementation Details

We select Voxel R-CNN [3] as the default baseline. MLF-DET is trained in three stages. First, we leverage 2D labels of KITTI dataset to train the Faster R-CNN [21] with batch size 40, learning rate 0.02 for 12 epochs. Then we load the

Table 1. Performance comparison for three classes with state-of-the-art 3D detectors on the KITTI *test* set. L and I in the Modality column refer to LiDAR and image, respectively. DM, RI, SS and IS in the Extra Data column refer to depth map, right image and semantic segmentation label and instance segmentation label, respectively. The best results without using extra data are highlighted in bold and the best results using extra data are underlined.

Method	Reference	Modality	Extra Data	Car (IoU=0.7)			Pedetrian (IoU=0.5)			Cyclist (IoU=0.5)			mAP
				Easy	Mod.	Hard	Easy	Mod.	Hard	Easy	Mod.	Hard	
SECOND [28]	Sensors 2018	L	-	84.65	75.96	68.71	45.31	35.52	33.14	75.83	60.82	53.67	59.29
PointRCNN [23]	CVPR 2019	L	-	86.96	75.64	70.70	47.98	39.37	36.01	74.96	58.82	52.53	60.33
PointPillars [8]	CVPR 2019	L	-	82.58	74.31	68.99	51.45	41.92	38.89	77.10	58.65	51.92	60.65
Part-A^2 [24]	TPAMI 2020	L	-	87.81	78.49	73.51	53.10	43.35	40.06	79.17	63.52	56.93	63.99
PV-RCNN [22]	CVPR 2020	L	-	90.25	81.43	76.82	52.17	43.29	40.29	78.60	63.71	57.65	64.91
Voxel R-CNN [3]	AAAI 2021	L	-	90.90	81.62	77.06	-	-	-	-	-	-	-
IA-SSD [30]	CVPR 2022	L	-	88.87	80.32	75.10	49.01	41.20	38.03	80.78	66.01	58.12	64.16
FocalsConv [2]	CVPR 2022	L	-	90.20	82.12	77.50	-	-	-	-	-	-	-
EPNet [7]	ECCV 2020	L+I	-	89.81	79.28	74.59	-	-	-	-	-	-	-
CLOCs-PVCas [16]	IROS 2020	L+I	-	88.94	80.67	77.15	-	-	-	-	-	-	-
Fast-CLOCs-PV [17]	WACV 2022	L+I	-	89.11	80.34	76.98	52.10	42.72	39.08	82.83	65.31	57.43	65.10
FocalsConv-F [2]	CVPR 2022	L+I	-	90.55	82.28	77.59	-	-	-	-	-	-	-
VFF [11]	CVPR 2022	L+I	-	89.50	82.09	79.29	-	-	-	-	-	-	-
CAT-DET [29]	CVPR 2022	L+I	-	89.87	81.32	76.68	**54.26**	**45.44**	41.94	83.68	68.81	61.45	67.05
HMFI [10]	ECCV 2022	L+I	-	88.90	81.93	77.30	50.88	42.65	39.78	**84.02**	70.37	62.57	66.49
DVF-PV [15]	WACV 2023	L+I	-	90.99	82.40	77.37	-	-	-	-	-	-	-
PointPainting [25]	CVPR 2020	L+I	SS	82.11	71.70	67.08	50.32	40.97	37.84	77.63	63.78	55.89	60.81
EPNet++ [14]	TPAMI 2022	L+I	IS	91.37	81.96	76.71	52.79	44.38	41.29	76.15	59.71	53.67	64.23
VPFNet [33]	TMM 2022	L+I	RI+IS	91.02	83.21	78.20	-	-	-	-	-	-	-
SFD [27]	CVPR 2022	L+I	DM	91.73	84.76	77.92	-	-	-	-	-	-	-
BiProDet [31]	ICLR 2023	L+I	IS	89.13	82.97	80.05	55.59	48.77	46.12	86.74	74.32	67.45	70.13
MLF-DET (ours)	-	L+I	-	**91.18**	**82.89**	**77.89**	50.86	45.29	**42.05**	83.31	**70.71**	**63.71**	**67.54**

pre-trained weights of ResNet and FPN in Faster R-CNN and train the LiDAR stream and the MVI module with batch size 16, learning rate 0.01 for 80 epochs. OGS and other widely adopted data augmentations, *i.e.*, random flipping, global scaling, and global rotation, are used in this stage. Finally, we train the FCR module with batch size 48, learning rate 0.01 for 10 epochs. The Adam optimizer with cosine annealing learning rate strategy is adopted in the second and third stages. All the experiments are done with 4 RTX 2080TI GPUs. Note that we do not use any extra data for training or testing.

4.3 Comparison with State-of-the-Arts

We compare our MLF-DET with other LiDAR-only and cross-modal state-of-the-art methods on both the *test* and *val* sets. We show the input modality and the extra data used in the tables for each method for a fair comparison. It is worth noting that many previous approaches train different models for different categories to get better performance, which we argue is meaningless for practical application. Instead, we train our network for the three classes and report the results on a single model. Besides, we do not employ any test time augmentation or model ensemble, so as to provide the actual performance of our method.

Table 2. Performance comparison with state-of-the-art 3D detectors on the KITTI *val* set. MLF-DET-PV and MLF-DET-V denote MLF-DET based on PV-RCNN and Voxel R-CNN, respectively.

Method	Reference	Modality	Extra Data	Car (IoU=0.7)			Pedetrian (IoU=0.5)			Cyclist (IoU=0.5)			mAP
				Easy	Mod.	Hard	Easy	Mod.	Hard	Easy	Mod.	Hard	
SECOND [28]	Sensors 2018	L	-	88.61	78.62	77.22	56.55	52.98	47.73	80.58	67.15	63.10	68.06
PointRCNN [23]	CVPR 2019	L	-	88.72	78.61	77.82	62.72	53.85	50.24	86.84	71.62	65.59	70.67
Part-A^2 [24]	TPAMI 2020	L	-	89.55	79.40	78.84	65.68	60.05	55.44	85.50	69.90	65.48	72.20
PV-RCNN [22]	CVPR 2020	L	-	89.03	83.24	78.59	63.71	57.37	52.84	86.06	69.48	64.50	71.65
Voxel R-CNN [3]	AAAI 2021	L	-	89.41	84.52	78.93	-	-	-	-	-	-	-
FocalsConv [2]	CVPR 2022	L	-	89.52	84.93	79.18	-	-	-	-	-	-	-
EPNet [7]	ECCV 2020	L+I	-	88.76	78.65	78.32	66.74	59.29	54.82	83.88	65.50	62.70	70.96
CLOCs-PVCas [16]	IROS 2020	L+I	-	89.49	79.31	77.36	62.88	56.20	50.10	87.57	67.92	63.67	70.50
FocalsConv-F [2]	CVPR 2022	L+I	-	89.82	85.22	85.19	-	-	-	-	-	-	-
VFF [11]	CVPR 2022	L+I	-	89.51	84.76	79.21	-	-	-	-	-	-	-
CAT-DET [29]	CVPR 2022	L+I	-	90.12	81.46	79.15	74.08	66.35	58.92	87.64	72.82	68.20	75.42
HMFI [10]	ECCV 2022	L+I	-	-	85.14	-	-	62.41	-	-	74.11	-	-
SFD [27]	CVPR 2022	L+I	DM	89.74	87.12	85.20	-	-	-	-	-	-	-
BiProDet [31]	ICLR 2023	L+I	IS	89.73	86.40	79.31	71.77	68.49	62.52	89.24	76.91	75.18	77.73
MLF-DET-PV (ours)	-	L+I	-	89.48	86.71	79.33	68.99	61.94	59.55	87.16	72.53	66.02	74.63
MLF-DET-V (ours)	-	L+I	-	89.70	**87.31**	**79.34**	71.15	**68.50**	61.72	86.05	72.14	65.42	**75.70**

Comparison on KITTI *test* set. As represented in Table 1, MLF-DET achieves competitive or superior performance over recently published state-of-the-art methods and obtains the highest mAP among the methods that do not use extra data. Compared with our LiDAR-only baseline Voxel R-CNN, we achieve up to 1.27% and 0.83% gains in $AP_{Mod.}$ and AP_{Hard} of the car class, respectively, indicating the effectiveness of our fusion scheme. Although some methods perform better than ours, they need extra sensor data or annotations, which limits their real-world deployment. By contrast, our approach only needs the LiDAR point clouds and monocular images as input and adopts the 3D and 2D bounding box annotations as training labels.

Comparison on KITTI *val* set. As shown in Table 2, MLF-DET also achieves the best mAP compared with the methods not using extra data in the *val* set. Remarkably, MLF-DET-V gets 87.31% and 68.50% $AP_{Mod.}$ for car and pedestrian, which even outperform methods using extra data. To show the generalization capability of our fusion scheme, we also select PV-RCNN [22] as the baseline. MLF-DET-PV surpasses PV-RCNN consistently in different categories and different difficulty levels and gives a 2.98% mAP gain. In addition, we provide the qualitative results of our method in Fig. 4. It is shown that MLF-DET can accurately detect objects of different classes, despite some of them being severely occluded or far away from the ego-vehicle. In the first column of Fig. 4, we surprisingly find that MLF-DET can even detect a pedestrian with few LiDAR points that is ignored by human annotators.

4.4 Ablation Study

To analyze the effectiveness of the individual components of our method, we conduct an ablation study on the KITTI *val* set. Since the proportion of the pedestrian and cyclist classes is much smaller than that of the car class and their performance is unstable, we only report the recall of RoIs and AP on the car class. As shown in Table 3, our MLF-DET can bring a 2.57% gain in recall with IoU 0.7 and a 3.09% gain in $AP_{Mod.}$.

Table 3. Effects of three proposed modules for car class on the KITTI *val* set. τ denotes the 3D IoU threshold of ground truth boxes and predicted boxes. [†] means the re-implemented results with the official code on our device.

Method	MVI	OGS	FCR	Recall		Average Precision			
				τ=0.5	τ=0.7	Easy	Mod.	Hard	mAP
Baseline[†] [3]	-	-	-	97.14	86.01	89.47	84.22	78.77	84.15
Ours	-	-	√	97.14	86.01	89.49	86.25	78.98	84.91
	√	-	-	97.18	87.66	89.65	86.42	79.13	85.07
	√	√	-	97.44	88.58	89.69	86.57	79.23	85.16
	√	√	√	97.44	88.58	89.70	87.31	79.34	85.45
Improvements				+0.30	+2.57	+0.23	+3.09	+0.57	+1.30

Table 4. Inference speed comparison with other cross-modal 3D detectors.

PointPainting [25]	VPFNet [33]	SFD [27]	CAT-DET [29]	BiProDet [31]	HMFI [10]	MLF-DET
2.5 FPS	5.9 FPS	15.0 FPS	10.2 FPS	3.3 FPS	9.5 FPS	10.8 FPS

Effect of Multi-scale Voxel Image Fusion. When MVI module is applied to the baseline, the recall with IoU 0.7 is improved by 1.65% and $AP_{Mod.}$ is enhanced by 2.20%. We attribute the improvements to the dense feature-level fusion scheme that fetches rich semantic features from the high-resolution image feature map. With these features, the network is able to detect some distant objects with few LiDAR points, but it is hard for the LiDAR-only baseline.

Effect of Feature-Cued Confidence Rectification. FCR module leads to 2.03% and 0.74% performance boost for the baseline and the baseline with MVI and OGS modules in $AP_{Mod.}$. The latter boost demonstrates the significance of combining feature- and decision-level fusion. The feature-level fusion enables our baseline detector to generate high-quality RoIs, but some of these RoIs could not be correctly classified. By rectifying the scores of RoIs, the FCR module reduces false positives and false negatives, thus enhancing the AP. Since the FCR module only operates on the scores of RoIs, there are no gains in the recall.

Effect of Occlusion-Aware GT Sampling.
Although OGS module does not bring many
improvements in the AP, it effectively increases
the recall by 0.92%. The reason is that OGS
provides more sampled objects in training, forcing the network to find more objects. To further
understand the effect of OGS, we calculate the
average number of reserved objects of three GT
Sampling methods on the *train* set with a fixed
random seed, as shown in Fig. 3. This shows that
OGS could preserve more sampled objects than
vanilla cross-modal GT Sampling, especially in the car class.

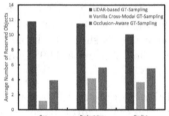

Fig. 3. Comparison in the average number of reserved objects
among different GT Sampling
methods.

Inference Speed. Since MLF-DET integrates feature- and decision-level fusion
into a single framework, an intuitive concern is that the inference speed of MLF-
DET would be slow. To investigate it, we run our model on an NVIDIA RTX
2080TI GPU and measure the FPS with the full GPU memory utilization. As
shown in Table 4, MLF-DET is not very slow compared with other cross-modal
methods. The reason lies in two aspects. First, the LiDAR branch of MLF-
DET is lightweight and fast. Second, MLF-DET does not apply the attention
mechanism to fuse cross-modal features and the RoIs are shared between LiDAR
and image branches. Therefore, the RPN in the 2D detector can be removed.

Fig. 4. Qualitative results on KITTI *val* set. Green, cyan and yellow boxes indicate
predicted objects of car, pedestrian and cyclist classes, respectively. Red boxes indicate
ground truth objects. Best viewed in color. (Color figure online)

5   Conclusion

In this paper, we propose a multi-level fusion network termed MLF-DET for
cross-modal 3D detection. To fully utilize images, we design the MVI module
to densely combine the features of images and point clouds, and the FCR module to rectify the scores of RoIs by fusing the scores and features of RoIs from

LiDAR branch and camera branch. Additionally, we propose the OGS module to preserve more sampled objects in training. Experiments on the KITTI dataset demonstrate the accuracy of our detector and the effectiveness of these modules. In future work, we would like to explore a more reasonable architecture or training strategy to optimize the feature-level and decision-level fusion modules in an end-to-end manner.

Acknowledgements. This work was supported by the National Natural Science Foundation of China under Grant No.62088102.

References

1. Bai, X., et al.: Transfusion: Robust lidar-camera fusion for 3D object detection with transformers. In: Proceedings of the IEEE/CVF Conference on Computer Vision and Pattern Recognition, pp. 1090–1099 (2022)
2. Chen, Y., Li, Y., Zhang, X., Sun, J., Jia, J.: Focal sparse convolutional networks for 3D object detection. In: Proceedings of the IEEE/CVF Conference on Computer Vision and Pattern Recognition, pp. 5428–5437 (2022)
3. Deng, J., Shi, S., Li, P., Zhou, W., Zhang, Y., Li, H.: Voxel R-CNN: Towards high performance voxel-based 3d object detection. In: Proceedings of the AAAI Conference on Artificial Intelligence, vol. 35, pp. 1201–1209 (2021)
4. Geiger, A., Lenz, P., Urtasun, R.: Are we ready for autonomous driving? the kitti vision benchmark suite. In: 2012 IEEE Conference on Computer Vision and Pattern Recognition, pp. 3354–3361. IEEE (2012)
5. Graham, B., Engelcke, M., Van Der Maaten, L.: 3D semantic segmentation with submanifold sparse convolutional networks. In: Proceedings of the IEEE Conference on Computer Vision and Pattern Recognition, pp. 9224–9232 (2018)
6. He, K., Zhang, X., Ren, S., Sun, J.: Deep residual learning for image recognition. In: Proceedings of the IEEE Conference on Computer Vision and Pattern Recognition, pp. 770–778 (2016)
7. Huang, T., Liu, Z., Chen, X., Bai, X.: EPNet: enhancing point features with image semantics for 3D object detection. In: Vedaldi, A., Bischof, H., Brox, T., Frahm, J.-M. (eds.) ECCV 2020. LNCS, vol. 12360, pp. 35–52. Springer, Cham (2020). https://doi.org/10.1007/978-3-030-58555-6_3
8. Lang, A.H., Vora, S., Caesar, H., Zhou, L., Yang, J., Beijbom, O.: Pointpillars: fast encoders for object detection from point clouds. In: Proceedings of the IEEE/CVF Conference on Computer Vision and Pattern Recognition, pp. 12697–12705 (2019)
9. Li, P., Zhao, H., Liu, P., Cao, F.: RTM3D: real-time monocular 3d detection from object keypoints for autonomous driving. In: Vedaldi, A., Bischof, H., Brox, T., Frahm, J.-M. (eds.) ECCV 2020. LNCS, vol. 12348, pp. 644–660. Springer, Cham (2020). https://doi.org/10.1007/978-3-030-58580-8_38
10. Li, X., et al.: Homogeneous multi-modal feature fusion and interaction for 3D object detection. In: Computer Vision-ECCV 2022: 17th European Conference, Tel Aviv, Israel, October 23–27, 2022, Proceedings, Part XXXVIII, pp. 691–707. Springer (2022). https://doi.org/10.1007/978-3-031-19839-7_40
11. Li, Y., et al.: Voxel field fusion for 3d object detection. In: Proceedings of the IEEE/CVF Conference on Computer Vision and Pattern Recognition, pp. 1120–1129 (2022)

12. Lin, T.Y., Dollár, P., Girshick, R., He, K., Hariharan, B., Belongie, S.: Feature pyramid networks for object detection. In: Proceedings of the IEEE Conference on Computer Vision and Pattern Recognition, pp. 2117–2125 (2017)

13. Liu, Z., Wu, Z., Tóth, R.: Smoke: Single-stage monocular 3D object detection via keypoint estimation. In: Proceedings of the IEEE/CVF Conference on Computer Vision and Pattern Recognition Workshops, pp. 996–997 (2020)

14. Liu, Z., Huang, T., Li, B., Chen, X., Wang, X., Bai, X.: Epnet++: Cascade bi-directional fusion for multi-modal 3D object detection. IEEE Transactions on Pattern Analysis and Machine Intelligence (2022)

15. Mahmoud, A., Hu, J.S., Waslander, S.L.: Dense voxel fusion for 3D object detection. In: Proceedings of the IEEE/CVF Winter Conference on Applications of Computer Vision, pp. 663–672 (2023)

16. Pang, S., Morris, D., Radha, H.: Clocs: Camera-lidar object candidates fusion for 3D object detection. In: 2020 IEEE/RSJ International Conference on Intelligent Robots and Systems (IROS), pp. 10386–10393. IEEE (2020)

17. Pang, S., Morris, D., Radha, H.: Fast-clocs: fast camera-lidar object candidates fusion for 3d object detection. In: Proceedings of the IEEE/CVF Winter Conference on Applications of Computer Vision, pp. 187–196 (2022)

18. Qi, C.R., Litany, O., He, K., Guibas, L.J.: Deep hough voting for 3D object detection in point clouds. In: Proceedings of the IEEE/CVF International Conference on Computer Vision, pp. 9277–9286 (2019)

19. Qi, C.R., Su, H., Mo, K., Guibas, L.J.: Pointnet: deep learning on point sets for 3D classification and segmentation. In: Proceedings of the IEEE Conference on Computer Vision and Pattern Recognition. pp. 652–660 (2017)

20. Qi, C.R., Yi, L., Su, H., Guibas, L.J.: Pointnet++: deep hierarchical feature learning on point sets in a metric space. Adv. Neural Inform. Process. Syst. **30** (2017)

21. Ren, S., He, K., Girshick, R., Sun, J.: Faster R-CNN: towards real-time object detection with region proposal networks. Adv. Neural Inform. Process. Syst. **28** (2015)

22. Shi, S., et al.: PV-RCNN: Point-voxel feature set abstraction for 3D object detection. In: Proceedings of the IEEE/CVF Conference on Computer Vision and Pattern Recognition, pp. 10529–10538 (2020)

23. Shi, S., Wang, X., Li, H.: Pointrcnn: 3D object proposal generation and detection from point cloud. In: Proceedings of the IEEE/CVF Conference on Computer Vision and Pattern Recognition, pp. 770–779 (2019)

24. Shi, S., Wang, Z., Shi, J., Wang, X., Li, H.: From points to parts: 3D object detection from point cloud with part-aware and part-aggregation network. IEEE Trans. Pattern Anal. Mach. Intell. **43**(8), 2647–2664 (2020)

25. Vora, S., Lang, A.H., Helou, B., Beijbom, O.: Pointpainting: sequential fusion for 3d object detection. In: Proceedings of the IEEE/CVF Conference on Computer Vision and Pattern Recognition, pp. 4604–4612 (2020)

26. Wang, C., Ma, C., Zhu, M., Yang, X.: Pointaugmenting: cross-modal augmentation for 3D object detection. In: Proceedings of the IEEE/CVF Conference on Computer Vision and Pattern Recognition, pp. 11794–11803 (2021)

27. Wu, X., et al.: Sparse fuse dense: Towards high quality 3D detection with depth completion. In: Proceedings of the IEEE/CVF Conference on Computer Vision and Pattern Recognition, pp. 5418–5427 (2022)

28. Yan, Y., Mao, Y., Li, B.: Second: sparsely embedded convolutional detection. Sensors **18**(10), 3337 (2018)

29. Zhang, Y., Chen, J., Huang, D.: Cat-det: Contrastively augmented transformer for multi-modal 3d object detection. In: Proceedings of the IEEE/CVF Conference on Computer Vision and Pattern Recognition, pp. 908–917 (2022)
30. Zhang, Y., Hu, Q., Xu, G., Ma, Y., Wan, J., Guo, Y.: Not all points are equal: Learning highly efficient point-based detectors for 3D lidar point clouds. In: Proceedings of the IEEE/CVF Conference on Computer Vision and Pattern Recognition, pp. 18953–18962 (2022)
31. Zhang, Y., Zhang, Q., Hou, J., Yuan, Y., Xing, G.: Bidirectional propagation for cross-modal 3d object detection. arXiv preprint arXiv:2301.09077 (2023)
32. Zhang, Y., Lu, J., Zhou, J.: Objects are different: flexible monocular 3D object detection. In: Proceedings of the IEEE/CVF Conference on Computer Vision and Pattern Recognition, pp. 3289–3298 (2021)
33. Zhu, H., et al.: Vpfnet: Improving 3d object detection with virtual point based lidar and stereo data fusion. IEEE Transactions on Multimedia (2022)

Object Detection in Foggy Images with Transmission Map Guidance

Zhihao Luo[1]⬤, Jin Xie[1,2(✉)]⬤, and Jing Nie[1]⬤

[1] Chongqing University, 400044 Chongqing, China
{20204107,xiejin,jingnie}@cqu.edu.cn
[2] Shanghai Artificial Intelligence Laboratory, 200232 Shanghai, China

Abstract. The performance of object detection methods is adversely affected by the low-quality images caused by fog. The main reasons are as follows: (i) object detection methods are difficult to recognize and locate the objects due to weak discriminative features extracted from low-quality images; (ii) existing methods are hard to adapt to variable fog densities. The transmission map, one important component from the atmospheric scattering model, containing depth and fog density information, is the key to addressing the above two problems. In this paper, we propose a novel network using the transmission map guidance, termed TGNet, which mines depth information to infer the existence and locations of objects and mines fog density information to help adapt to various fog densities. Experiments conducted on the two real-world object detection datasets in foggy conditions (*i.e.*, RTTS and FoggyDriving) demonstrate that our TGNet outperforms the state-of-the-art methods. Additionally, our TGNet provides consistent improvements on various detection paradigms and backbones.

Keywords: Object detection · foggy scenes · neural networks

1 Introduction

Object detection is a hot issue in computer vision with plenty of real-world applications, *e.g.*, autonomous driving, intelligent video surveillance, and so on. With the development of deep learning, object detection methods [1,21,22,25] based on deep learning have achieved great success. However, existing works mostly focus on object detection in clear scenes. Object detection in foggy images is rarely considered, which results in detection performance being significantly below that required for real-world applications. Therefore, it is of great significance to study how to improve the detection performance in foggy images.

This work is supported in part by the National Key Research and Development Program of China (Grant No. 2022ZD0160404), in part by the National Natural Science Foundation of China (Grant No. 62206031), and in part by China Postdoctoral Science Foundation (Grant No. 2021M700613 and 2022M720581).

Modern object detection methods in foggy images could be classified into two categories. The first one is predicting clear images by image dehazing models such as GridDehazeNet [17], FFANet [20], PFFNet [18], and Dehamar [5] at first and then using object detection methods to conduct object detection on the dehazed images. These methods improve the detection accuracy in the fog. However, they still have some disadvantages: (1) the dehazed images are clearer but tend to lose a lot of details, resulting in limited detection accuracy improvement; (2) image dehazing models increase a lot of computational burdens. The other kind of method is the joint learning method. Li *et al.* [10] proposed to combine the dehazing network with Faster R-CNN [22] to realize end-to-end training. Huang *et al.* [8] proposed to jointly perform image enhancement and object detection by utilizing two sub-networks. The two sub-networks can optimize shared features jointly, which is useful to attenuate the impact of image degradation. Son *et al.* [24] proposed a recognition-friendly image enhancement network, termed URIE, to improve recognition performance. These joint learning methods improve the detection performance, but the difficulty in balancing the importance of image dehazing and object detection limits improving the detection accuracy.

Different from the above methods, we hope to mine valuable information during the image dehazing process for improving detection performance in foggy images. We first revise the atmospheric scattering model, which is utilized in state-of-art model-based image dehazing methods, to find which part is the key. The atmospheric scattering model can be written as:

$$I(x,y) = J(x,y)t(x,y) + A(1 - t(x,y)) \tag{1}$$

where $I(x,y)$ and $J(x,y)$ are the foggy image and the corresponding clear image, respectively. A and $t(x,y)$ are the atmospheric light and the transmission map, respectively, in which (x,y) represents the position of the image. $t(x,y) = e^{-\beta d(x,y)}$, where β is a parameter describing the fog density and d is the scene depth. It can be found that the transmission map contains scene depth and fog density information. For the object detection task, the scene depth information can help determine the existence and locations of objects, and the fog density information can help the network adapt to different fog densities. Therefore, we propose a novel network, termed TGNet, which consists of two key components: one is a transmission map prediction module (TPM), which predicts transmission map under supervision to improve the detection accuracy by multi-task training; the other one is a guided attention module (GAM), which is proposed to enhance the feature representation by exploring scene depth and fog density information from the transmission maps.

The main contributions of our method are as follows: We propose a novel network with transmission map guidance, termed TGNet, to enhance feature discriminability and robustness. Two modules, the transmission map prediction module (TPM) and guided attention module (GAM), are designed in our TGNet to predict transmission map and enrich features, respectively. The TPM can collect information on scene depth and fog density, which can boost detection performance due solely to the benefits of multi-task training. The GAM can enhance the features for objection detection by making use of the information on scene depth and fog density from the predicted transmission map. As a result, our TGNet is capable of achieving fast and accurate object detection in real-world foggy images with state-of-the-art performance on the FoggyDriving dataset and RTTS dataset. In addition, our TGNet is generic and leads to consistently improved detection performance while being integrated into diverse detectors (including anchor-based and anchor-free detectors), and various backbones (including CNN and Transformer).

2   Related Work

2.1   Object Detection

With the development of deep learning, object detection has made significant progress. Object detection methods based on deep learning can be roughly divided into two categories: anchor-based methods [3,12–14,22,27] and anchor-free methods [9,25,29,31,32]. Anchor is a set of pre-defined bounding boxes. Anchor-based methods usually predict the detection results by classifying the anchor boxes and regressing the offsets to refine the anchor boxes. Different from anchor-based methods, anchor-free methods predict the classifications, scales, and locations of objects. RetinaNet [14] is one of the popular anchor-based detection methods, which introduces a novel loss function to alleviate the problem of the unbalance between positive samples and negative samples during training. Reppoints [29] is a classical anchor-free detection method, which employs a set of points to locate and classify objects. Both anchor-based and anchor-free methods aim at improving the way of prediction but ignore the factors of adverse weather. Therefore, their performance in foggy scenes is limited. It is noted that our proposed method can be combined with both anchor-based and anchor-free methods to improve detection accuracy in foggy scenes.

2.2   Object Detection in Foggy Scenes

Although object detection has become the research hotspot, there are few pieces of research on object detection in foggy scenes. Existing object detection methods in foggy scenes can be roughly divided into three categories. (i) The methods conduct image dehazing and object detection in sequential ways [11,28]. In detail, the image dehazing methods are utilized to pre-process the foggy images, and the processed images then go through the object detection network to obtain the detection results. (ii) Multi-task learning-based methods [8,10,24]. These methods use multi-task learning to train image dehazing and object detection to improve the detection accuracy in foggy scenes. AOD-Net [10] is the first work to attempt to train the image dehazing and object detection by jointly optimizing. In the DS-Net [8], image dehazing and object detection share the feature extraction layers to improve the robustness of features extracted from foggy images. (iii) Domain adaption-based methods [7,30]. In the absence of labels in foggy conditions, these methods use the label in good weather conditions to detect objects in foggy conditions through domain adaption. Despite making progress, these approaches still have some drawbacks. Specifically, the methods performing image dehazing and object detection in sequential ways suffer from artifacts and color distortion introduced by image dehazing methods. The multi-task learning-based methods are difficult to balance the weight of image dehazing and object detection. Contrary to the multi-task learning methods, image dehazing is not utilized in our method. We propose to mine detection-friendly information from the transmission map (the most important component in the image dehazing process) to enhance the discriminability and robustness of features extracted from foggy images.

3   Method

3.1   Overall Architecture

The overall architecture of our proposed TGNet is shown in Fig. 1. The TGNet comprises a detection branch and a transmission map guidance (TG) branch. In the next sections, we would detail these two branches.

3.1.1   Detection Branch

The detection branch consists of a backbone network, a feature pyramid network (FPN), and a detection head network. The backbone network (*e.g.*, ResNet50 [6], PVT [26]) first extracts multi-scale features $\{C_2, C_3, C_4, C_5\}$ with the strides of $\{4, 8, 16, 32\}$ from the input image. Then the feature pyramid network is utilized to fuse features from the backbone to obtain the features $\{P_2, P_3, P_4, P_5, P_6\}$. In the original methods, the enhanced features P_i are fed into the detector to predict the classification scores and bounding box locations.

Limitations: Despite achieving promising results in clear scenes, the above pipeline still struggles in the foggy scenes. The main reason is likely that the features extracted from foggy images are weakly discriminative, which brings great difficulty in recognizing and locating the objects. In addition, variable fog densities result in poor robustness of the pipeline. To address the above issues, in this paper, we propose an attention network with transmission map guidance, which mines fog density information and scene depth information from transmission maps to enhance the feature discriminability and robustness.

3.1.2   Transmission Map Guidance Branch

The transmission map guidance (TG) branch first employs a transmission map prediction module (TPM) to predict transmission maps, and then the predicted transmission maps go through a guided attention module (GAM) to enhance the features by exploring depth and fog density information.

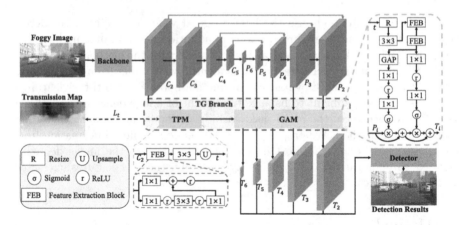

Fig. 1. The overall network architecture of our TGNet. It comprises a detection branch (shown in blue) and our proposed novel transmission map guidance (TG) branch (enclosed in the purple dashed box). The TG branch consists of a transmission map prediction module (TPM) and a guided attention module (GAM). (Color figure online)

Transmission map Prediction Module (TPM): The inputs of the TPM are the features C_2 which are extracted from the backbone network. Firstly, one feature extraction block (FEB) is employed to extract features, after that the obtained features go through one 3×3 convolutional layer and an up-sampling layer to predict the transmission map. In detail, the feature extraction block (FEB) consists of two branches. One branch first employs one 1×1 convolutional layer followed by Rectified Linear Unit (ReLU) to reduce the number of channels, then one 3×3 convolutional layer followed by RELU is utilized to extract features, and finally one 1×1 convolutional layer is utilized to increase the number of channels. The other branch employs one 1×1 convolutional layer to adjust the number of channels. The outputs of these two branches are added together and then go through ReLU to obtain the outputs of FEB.

Guided Attention Module (GAM): The transmission map predicted by the TPM could be taken as the guidance to learn two types of attention weights to enhance the features $\{P_2, P_3, P_4, P_5, P_6\}$ from the FPN for improving detection accuracy in foggy scenes.

We denote the predicted transmission map as t. Firstly, a resize operation based on nearest neighbor sampling is employed to resize the transmission map to the same resolution of the features from FPN (*i.e.*, P_i), and then the resized transmission map goes through one 3×3 convolutional layer and two feature extraction blocks to learn transmission features F_i. For an image, the scene depth is diverse in different places, and the fog density is constant. To mine the information on scene depth and fog density, the transmission features F_i are utilized to learn channel-wise attention weights and position-aware attention weights, respectively.

We first employ a global average pooling operation. And then two 1×1 convolutional layers followed by a sigmoid operation are utilized to generate the attention weights by exploiting the inter-channel relationship. At last, the attention weights are multiplied by the transmission features. The computation process can be written as follows:

$$\tilde{T}_i = P_i + P_i \odot a_c$$
$$a_c = \sigma(\textbf{Conv}_{1 \times 1}(\textbf{Conv}_{1 \times 1}(\textbf{GAP}(F_i)))), \tag{2}$$

where $\tilde{T}_i$ and a_c are the modulated output features and channel-wise attention weights, $\textbf{GAP}$ and $\textbf{Conv}_{1 \times 1}$ are the global average pooling layer and 1×1 convolutional layer, respectively. $\odot$ is the element-wise product. During multiplication, the attention value a_c are broadcaster along the spatial dimension. Due that the fog density is variable, the global average pooling and convolutional layers could capture global information and help the model adapt to the variable fog density.

We employ two 1×1 convolutional layers and a sigmoid operation to learn position-aware attention weights from the transmission features. The position-aware attention weights are multiplied by the features $\tilde{T}_i$ to enhance them with depth information. The computational process can be written as:

$$T_i = \tilde{T}_i + \tilde{T}_i \odot a_p$$
$$a_p = \sigma(\textbf{Conv}_{1 \times 1}(\textbf{Conv}_{1 \times 1}(F_i))), \tag{3}$$

where a_p is the position-aware attention weight and T_i is the enriched features. During multiplication, the attention value a_p are broadcaster along the channel dimension. Due to the scene depth being diverse in different places of an image, position-wise attention weights would help the model infer the existence and locations of objects by making use of the scene depth prior.

Finally, we feed enriched features T_i, instead of the features from FPN P_i, to the following detection head network to obtain the detection results.

3.2   Loss Function

The loss function L of our network is expressed as follows:

$$L = L_d + \omega L_t, \tag{4}$$

where ω is the balanced weight. We set $\omega = 1.0$ by default. L_d denotes the loss function of the detection branch. L_t is the loss function for training the transmission map, which can be formulated as:

$$L_t = \frac{1}{HW} \sum_{x}^{W} \sum_{y}^{H} \|t(x,y) - \hat{t}(x,y)\|_2^2, \tag{5}$$

where $t(x,y)$ is the transmission map predicted by our proposed TPM, and $\hat{t}(x,y)$ is the corresponding ground truth. W and H are the width and height of the transmission map.

4   Experimental Results

4.1   Dataset and Evaluation Metric

As it is difficult to obtain the transmission maps for real-world foggy images, we adopt the Foggy Cityscapes dataset [23] and Foggy VOC dataset [16], two synthetic foggy datasets, as the training sets. To evaluate the effectiveness of our proposed method in real foggy scenes, we utilize the two real-world foggy datasets including FoggyDriving [23] dataset and RTTS [11] dataset as the test sets. Specifically, the model trained on the Foggy Cityscapes dataset is tested on the FoggyDriving dataset. And the model trained on the Foggy VOC dataset is tested on the RTTS dataset. It is noted that both the Foggy Cityscapes dataset and Foggy VOC dataset provide the ground-truth transmission map because both datasets are synthesized based on the atmosphere scattering model. In the next, we would present the details of these datasets.

Foggy Cityscapes Dataset: Sakaridis *et al.* [23] synthesized a Foggy Cityscapes dataset based on the atmosphere scattering model. They adjusted the values of the atmospheric light A and the scattering coefficient β to produce foggy images. The value of β is randomly chosen from 0.005, 0.01, and 0.02. The corresponding ground truth transmission maps could be generated via $t = e^{-\beta d}$. The Foggy Cityscapes dataset includes eight categories (*i.e.*, person, rider, car, truck, bus, train, motorcycle, and bicycle).

Foggy VOC Dataset: Liu *et al.* [4] utilize the atmosphere scattering model to synthesize the Foggy VOC dataset based on the popular object detection dataset Pascal VOC dataset. There are five categories in the Foggy VOC dataset (*i.e.*, person, bicycle, car, bus, and motorbike).

FoggyDriving Dataset: FoggyDriving dataset [23] is a real-world foggy object detection dataset with 101 images, in which 51 images are captured by a cell phone camera in foggy conditions in Zurich and the rest 50 images are collected from the Internet. The dataset is annotated by 8 categories, which is the same as the Foggy Cityscapes dataset.

RTTS Dataset: RTTS is a real-world object detection benchmark in foggy conditions with 4322 images. And the categories are the same as the Foggy VOC dataset.

Evaluation Metric: The mean Average Precision (mAP) defined by the Pascal VOC dataset [4] is chosen as the evaluation metric.

4.2   Implementation Details

The Foggy Cityscapes dataset and Foggy VOC dataset are used to train our TGNet. We first detail the common settings. We implement our TGNet by utilizing a PyTorch [19]-based object detection toolbox MMDetection [2]. Our TGNet is trained on two NVIDIA GeForce GTX 3090 and a mini-batch comprises 2 images. Stochastic Gradient Descent (SGD) is chosen as the optimizer, where momentum and weight-decay are set as 0.9 and 0.0001, respectively. And then we detail the settings specific to the two datasets.

Table 1. Comparison (in mean average precision(%)) of our TGNet with the baseline (RetinaNet [14] with ResNet50 [6]). For a fair comparison, all the methods are trained on the same dataset. We observe a consistent improvement in detection accuracy due to progressively integrating TPM and GAM. In addition, the effect of L_T (*i.e.*, using transmission map guidance or self-learning) is verified.

	$mAP(\%)$
Baseline	42.8
Baseline + TPM	43.9
Our TGNet: Baseline + TPM + GAM	45.6
Baseline + TPM(w/o L_t) + GAM	44.4

Foggy Cityscapes dataset (Train) and Foggy Driving dataset (Test): The backbone network and detection head network are pre-trained on the COCO dataset [15]. The network is trained for 8 epochs. We set the learning rate as 2.5×10^{-3} initially for 6 epochs and then decay it to 2.5×10^{-4} and perform 2 epochs. Data augmentation methods are employed in the training stage, *i.e.*, randomly horizontal flip and scale jitter, where the image size is randomly sampled from 800×1600 to 1024×2048. In the test stage, the shorter side is set to be 1024.

Foggy VOC Dataset (Train) and RTTS Dataset (Test): The backbone network is pre-trained on the ImageNet dataset. The network is trained for 12 epochs in total. The initial learning rate is set as 2.5×10^{-3}, and decay the learning rate by a factor of 10 at the 8th and 11th epochs. Data augmentation methods are employed in the training stage, *i.e.*, randomly horizontal flip. we resize the input images to make their shorter edge 600 pixels and their long edge less than 1000 pixels. In the test stage, the shorter side is set to be 600 pixels.

4.3   Experiments on FoggyDriving Dataset

4.3.1   Ablation Study
To demonstrate the effectiveness of each module in TGNet, we perform the ablation studies on the FoggyDriving dataset. Table 1 gives the impacts of integrating our TPM and GAM into the baseline. We choose Faster RCNN [22] with

ResNet50 [6] as the baseline. For a fair comparison, the experimental settings are kept the same for all experiments in Table 1. The baseline obtains 42.8% mAP. When we introduce the TPM to predict transmission maps, the detection accuracy improves by 1.1%. It demonstrates that the transmission map prediction would attenuate the negative effects of fog. Our final TGNet, utilizing the predicted transmission maps from TPM as the input of the GA module to enhance the features by exploring the information of depth and fog density, obtains 45.6% in mAP. In addition, we also report the performance of our TGNet without L_T, the detection accuracy decreases from 45.6% to 44.4%. It demonstrates the effectiveness of transmission map guidance.

Robustness on Different Detectors: We integrate our TGNet into different popular detectors: RetinaNet [14], and RepPoints [29]. For a fair comparison, except for the detectors, all the methods utilize the same experimental settings. The results are given in Table 2. Integrating our TGNet into RetinaNet and Reppoints obtains 2.8% and 1.7% mAP improvements, respectively. The results in Table 2 demonstrate the effectiveness and the generality of our TGNet.

Robustness on Different Backbones: We evaluate the effects of different backbones on our TGNet in terms of mAP on the FoggyDriving dataset. We conduct experiments on two different backbone networks: ResNet50 [6] and PVT-v2-

Table 2. Comparison (in mean average precision (%)) of integrating our TGNet into both of anchor-based and anchor-free detection methods on the FoggyDriving dataset. For a fair comparison, all the methods use the same backbone (ResNet50), training data, input scale, and experimental settings.

Detectors	Type	Methods	mAP(%) ↑
RetinaNet	Anchor-based	Baseline	42.8
		TGNet	**45.6(↑2.8)**
Reppoints	Anchor-free	Baseline	44.4
		TGNet	**46.1(↑1.7)**

Table 3. Comparison (in mean average precision (%)) of integrating our TGNet into both CNN-based and Transformer-based backbones on the FoggyDriving dataset. For a fair comparison, we choose the same detector (RetinaNet). All the methods use the same training data, input scale, and experimental settings.

Backbones	Type	Methods	mAP(%) ↑
ResNet50	CNN	Baseline	42.8
		TGNet	**45.6(↑2.8)**
PVT-V2-B1	Transformer	Baseline	48.0
		TGNet	**49.5(↑1.5)**

B1 [26]. Table 3 reports the results. The results in Table 3 demonstrate that our TGNet is robust on *various* backbones including CNN-based and Transformer-based networks.

4.3.2   State-of-the-Art Comparisons

We compare the detection accuracy of our TGNet with the following methods: RetinaNet trained on the Foggy Cityscapes training set, FFA [20], Dehamer [5], AOD-Net [10], URIE [24], DSNet [8], and IANet [16]. Table 4 gives the results on the FoggyDriving dataset. Note that FFA and Dehamer are two image dehazing methods, these two methods pre-process the foggy images, and then the dehazed images go through a RetinaNet trained on the clean Cityscapes training detest to obtain the final results. It can be found that concatenating different dehazing methods (*i.e.*, FFA, Dehamer) with the detection methods (*i.e.*, RetinaNet) improves detection accuracy. However, the image dehazing methods increase the running time. Compared with Retinanet (baseline), the joint learning methods (*i.e.*, AOD-Net, URIE, and DSNet) can improve the detection accuracy. But the improvements are limited, the main reason is the difficulty in balancing the importance of image dehazing and object detection. The URIE [24] provides the best results among the existing methods with the mean average precision of 44.3%, respectively. Our TGNet outperforms URIE with an absolute gain of 1.3%. Additionally, the running speed of our TGNet is faster than URIE.

Table 4. Comparison (in mean average precision (%) and running speed (FPS)) with the different methods on the FoggyDriving dataset. For a fair comparison, the speed of all the methods is tested on a single NVIDIA GeForce RTX 3090 GPU. Our TGNet outperforms all existing methods. The best results are boldfaced.

Methods	$mAP(\%)$	Speed (FPS)
RetinaNet (Baseline)	42.8	23
FFANet [20]	42.8	1
Dehamer [5]	43.3	2
AOD-Net [10]	43.1	21
URIE [24]	44.3	13
DSNet [8]	43.6	23
IANet [16]	44.1	17
TGNet(Ours)	**45.6**	20

4.4   Experiments on RTTS Dataset

We conduct experiments on the popular foggy object detection dataset RTTS. We compare the detection accuracy of our TGNet with the following methods: RetinaNet trained on the Foggy VOC dataset, FFA [20], AOD-Net [10],

Table 5. Comparison (in mean average precision (%)) with the different methods on the RTTS [10] dataset. Best results are boldfaced.

Methods	$mAP(\%)$
RetinaNet(Baseline)	54.7
FFA-Net [20]	51.6
AOD-Net [10]	55.6
URIE [24]	55.7
DSNet [8]	55.0
TGNet(Ours)	**56.7**

URIE [24], DSNet [8], and IANet [16]. The results are given in Table 5. Among existing methods, URIE provides the best results with a mAP of 55.7%. Our TGNet achieves superior results with a mAP of 56.7%. In addition, we find that utilizing image dehazing methods (FFA) as the pre-processing step to perform image dehazing would decrease the detection accuracy. It demonstrates that the image dehazing method might not be beneficial for object detection which is claimed in the above section. Experimental results on the RTTS dataset demonstrate the effectiveness and the generality of our TGNet.

5   Conclusion

In this paper, we have proposed a network with transmission map guidance, termed TGNet, for object detection in foggy scenes. Our TGNet first learns transmission maps with rich information on scene depth and fog density by multi-task training. To improve the detection accuracy, we employ an attention mechanism with transmission map guidance to enhance the feature discriminability and robustness by exploring the information of scene depth and fog density. Experiments on two real-world datasets demonstrate the effectiveness and generality of our approach.

References

1. Cai, Z., Vasconcelos, N.: Cascade R-CNN: delving into high quality object detection. In: IEEE Conference on Computer Vision and Pattern Recognition, pp. 6154–6162 (2018)
2. Chen, K., et al.: MMDetection: Open mmlab detection toolbox and benchmark. arXiv:1906.07155 (2019)
3. Dai, J., Li, Y., He, K., Sun, J.: R-FCN: object detection via region-based fully convolutional networks. arxiv:1605.06409 (2016)
4. Everingham, M., Van Gool, L., Williams, C.K., Winn, J., Zisserman, A.: The pascal visual object classes (voc) challenge. Int. J. Comput. Vision **88**(2), 303–338 (2010)
5. Guo, C., Yan, Q., Anwar, S., Cong, R., Ren, W., Li, C.: Image dehazing transformer with transmission-aware 3D position embedding. In: IEEE Conference on Computer Vision and Pattern Recognition (2022)

6. He, K., Zhang, X., Ren, S., Sun, J.: Deep residual learning for image recognition. In: IEEE Conference on Computer Vision and Pattern Recognition (2016)
7. Hnewa, M., Radha, H.: Multiscale domain adaptive YOLO for cross-domain object detection. arXiv:2106.01483 (2021)
8. Huang, S.C., Le, T.H., Jaw, D.W.: Dsnet: joint semantic learning for object detection in inclement weather conditions. IEEE Trans. Pattern Anal. Mach. Intell. **43**(8), 2623–2633 (2021)
9. Law, H., Deng, J.: Cornernet: detecting objects as paired keypoints. In: European Conference on Computer Vision (2018)
10. Li, B., Peng, X., Wang, Z., Xu, J., Dan, F.: Aod-net: All-in-one dehazing network. In: IEEE International Conference on Computer Vision (2017)
11. Li, B., et al.: Benchmarking single-image dehazing and beyond. IEEE Trans. Image Process. **28**(1), 492–505 (2019)
12. Li, Y., Chen, Y., Wang, N., Zhang, Z.: Scale-aware trident networks for object detection. arXiv:1901.01892 (2019)
13. Li, Z., Peng, C., Yu, G., Zhang, X., Deng, Y., Sun, J.: Light-head R-CNN: in defense of two-stage object detector. arXiv:1711.07264 (2017)
14. Lin, T.Y., Goyal, P., Girshick, R., He, K., Dollár, P.: Focal loss for dense object detection. IEEE Trans. Pattern Anal. Mach. Intell. **PP**(99), 2999–3007 (2017)
15. Lin, T., et al.: Microsoft COCO: common objects in context. arXiv:1405.0312 (2014)
16. Liu, W., Ren, G., Yu, R., Guo, S., Zhu, J., Zhang, L.: Image-adaptive yolo for object detection in adverse weather conditions. arXiv:2112.08088 (2022)
17. Liu, X., Ma, Y., Shi, Z., Chen, J.: Griddehazenet: Attention-based multi-scale network for image dehazing. In: IEEE International Conference on Computer Vision (2019)
18. Mei, K., Jiang, A., Li, J., Wang, M.: Progressive feature fusion network for realistic image dehazing. arXiv:1810.02283 (2018)
19. Paszke, A., et al.: Automatic differentiation in pytorch. In: NIPS-W (2017)
20. Qin, X., Wang, Z., Bai, Y., Xie, X., Jia, H.: Ffa-net: Feature fusion attention network for single image dehazing. In: AAAI Conference on Artificial Intelligence (2020)
21. Redmon, J., Farhadi, A.: Yolov3: An incremental improvement. arXiv:1804.02767 (2018)
22. Ren, S., He, K., Girshick, R., Sun, J.: Faster R-CNN: towards real-time object detection with region proposal networks. IEEE Trans. Pattern Anal. Mach. Intell. **39**(6), 1137–1149 (2017)
23. Sakaridis, C., Dai, D., Van Gool, L.: Semantic foggy scene understanding with synthetic data. Int. J. Comput. Vision **126**(9), 973–992 (2018)
24. Son, T., Kang, J., Kim, N., Cho, S., Kwak, S.: URIE: universal image enhancement for visual recognition in the wild. In: European Conference on Computer Vision (2020)
25. Tian, Z., Shen, C., Chen, H., He, T.: FCOS: fully convolutional one-stage object detection. arXiv:1904.01355 (2019)
26. Wang, W., et al.: Pvtv 2: improved baselines with pyramid vision transformer. Comput. Visual Media **8**(3), 1–10 (2022)
27. Wei, L., et al.: SSD: Single shot multibox detector. In: European Conference on Computer Vision (2016)
28. Yang, W., et al.: Advancing image understanding in poor visibility environments: a collective benchmark study. IEEE Trans. Image Process. **29**, 5737–5752 (2020)

29. Yang, Z., Liu, S., Hu, H., Wang, L., Lin, S.: Reppoints: Point set representation for object detection. In: IEEE International Conference on Computer Vision. IEEE (2019)

30. Zhang, S., Tuo, H., Hu, J., Jing, Z.: Domain adaptive yolo for one-stage cross-domain detection. In: Proceedings of Asian Conference on Machine Learning. vol. 157, pp. 785–797 (2021)

31. Zhang, X., Wan, F., Liu, C., Ji, R., Ye, Q.: FreeAnchor: learning to match anchors for visual object detection. Adv. Neural Inform. Process. Syst. (2019)

32. Zhou, X., Wang, D., Krähenbühl, P.: Objects as points. arXiv preprint arXiv:1904.07850 (2019)

PE-YOLO: Pyramid Enhancement Network for Dark Object Detection

Xiangchen Yin[1,2(✉)], Zhenda Yu[2,3], Zetao Fei[4], Wenjun Lv[1], and Xin Gao[5]

[1] University of Science and Technology of China, Hefei, China
yinxiangchen@mail.ustc.edu.cn, wlv@ustc.edu.cn
[2] Institute of Artificial Intelligence, Hefei Comprehensive National Science Center,
Hefei, China
wa22201140@stu.ahu.edu.cn
[3] Anhui University, Hefei, China
[4] Qufu Normal University, Qufu, China
[5] China University of Mining and Technology, Beijing, China
bqt2000405024@student.cumtb.edu.cn

Abstract. Current object detection models have achieved good results on many benchmark datasets, detecting objects in dark conditions remains a large challenge. To address this issue, we propose a pyramid enhanced network (PENet) and joint it with YOLOv3 to build a dark object detection framework named PE-YOLO. Firstly, PENet decomposes the image into four components of different resolutions using the Laplacian pyramid. Specifically we propose a detail processing module (DPM) to enhance the detail of images, which consists of context branch and edge branch. In addition, we propose a low-frequency enhancement filter (LEF) to capture low-frequency semantics and prevent high-frequency noise. PE-YOLO adopts an end-to-end joint training approach and only uses normal detection loss to simplify the training process. We conduct experiments on the low-light object detection dataset ExDark to demonstrate the effectiveness of ours. The results indicate that compared with other dark detectors and low-light enhancement models, PE-YOLO achieves the advanced results, achieving 78.0% in mAP and 53.6 in FPS, respectively, which can adapt to object detection under different low-light conditions. The code is available at https://github.com/XiangchenYin/PE-YOLO.

Keywords: Object detection · Low-light perception · Pyramid enhancement

1 Introduction

In recent years, the emergence of convolutional neural networks (CNNs) has promoted the development of object detection. A large number of detectors have been proposed, and the performance of the benchmark datasets is getting enjoyable results [1,8,14,19]. However, most of the existing detectors are studied

L. Iliadis et al. (Eds.): ICANN 2023, LNCS 14260, pp. 163–174, 2023.
https://doi.org/10.1007/978-3-031-44195-0_14

in high-quality images under normal conditions. In the real environment, there are often many bad lighting conditions such as night, dark light, and exposure, so that the quality of the image decreases affects the performance of the detector. The visual perception model enables the automatic system to understand the environment and lay the foundation for subsequent tasks such as trajectory planning, which requires a robust object detection or semantic segmentation model. Figure 1 is an example of dark object detection. It can be found that if the image is appropriately enhanced and restores more potential information of the original fuzzy object according to environmental conditions, the object detection model is adapted to different low-light conditions, which is also a great challenge in the practical application of the model.

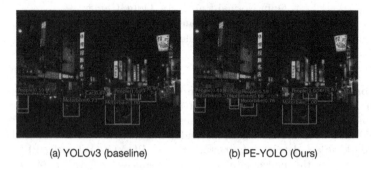

(a) YOLOv3 (baseline)   (b) PE-YOLO (Ours)

Fig. 1. Example of dark object detection. In dark conditions PE-YOLO can recover more potential information of object to get better detection results.

Currently, many methods have been proposed to solve the robustness problem in the dark scenes. Many low-light enhancement models [7,10,24,26] have been proposed to restore image details and reduce the impact of poor lighting conditions. However, the structure of the low light enhancement model is complex, which is not conducive to the real-time performance of the detector after image enhancement. Most of these methods cannot be end-to-end trained with the detector, and supervised learning is required for paired low-light images and normal images. Object detection under low-light conditions can also be seen as a domain adaptation problem. Some researchers [4,13,21] have used adversarial learning to transfer the model from normal light to dark light. But they focus on matching data distribution and overlook the potential information contained in low-light images. In the past few years, some researchers [11,15] have proposed the method of using differentiable image processing (DIP) modules to enhance images and train detectors on in an end-to-end manner. However, DIP are traditional methods such as white balance, which have limited enhancement effects on images.

To address the above issues, we propose a pyramid enhancement network (PENet) that enhance low-light images and capture potential information about objects. We have joint PENet with YOLOv3 to construct an end-to-end dark object detection framework called PE-YOLO. In PENet, we first decompose the image into multiple components of different resolutions using the Laplacian pyramid. In each scale of the pyramid, we propose detail processing module (DPM) and low-frequency enhancement filter (LEF) to enhance the components. DPM consists of context branch and edge branch, which context branch globally enhance components by capturing long-range dependencies and edge branch enhance the texture of components. LEF uses a dynamic low-pass filter to obtain low-frequency semantics and prevent high-frequency noise to enrich feature information. We only use normal detection loss during model training to simplify the training process, without the need for clear ground truth of the image. We validated the effectiveness of our method in the low-light object detection dataset ExDark [16], the results show that compared with other dark detectors and low-light enhancement models, PE-YOLO achieved the advanced results, reaching 78.0% in mAP and 53.6 in FPS respectively, which can adapt to object detection in dark conditions.

Our contribution could be summarised as follow:

- We build a pyramid enhancement network (PENet) to enhance different low-light images. We propose a detail processing module (DPM) and a low-frequency enhancement filter (LEF) to enhance the components.
- By jointing PENet with YOLOv3, we propose an end-to-end trained dark object detection framework PE-YOLO to adapt the dark conditions. During training, we only use normal detection loss.
- Compared with other dark detectors and low light enhancement models, our PE-YOLO achieved advanced results in ExDark dataset, achieving enjoyable accuracy and speed.

2   Related Work

2.1   Object Detection

Object detection models are divided into three categories: one-stage models, two-stage models, and anchor-free-based models. Faster RCNN [20] does not obtain region recommendations through selective search, but rather through a region proposal network (RPN). It enables candidate region proposals, feature extraction, classification, and regression to be trained end-to-end within the same network. Cai et al. propose Cascade RCNN [2], which cascades multiple detection heads, and the current level will refine the regression and classification results of the previous level. YOLOv3 [19] proposed the new feature extraction network DarkNet-53. Inspiring from the feature pyramid nework (FPN), YOLOv3 adopts multi-scale feature fusion. In addition, recently anchor-free-based detectors [12, 23] have appeared, they abandoned anchor and changed it to key point-based detection.

2.2   Low-Light Enhancement

The goal of low-light enhancement tasks is to improve human visual perception by restoring image details and correcting color distortion and to provide high-quality images for high-level visual tasks such as object detection. Zhang et al. [26] propose Kind, it can be trained through paired images with different levels of illumination, without the need for ground truth. Guo et al. [9] propose Zero DCE, which transforms low-light enhancement tasks into image-specific curve estimation problems. Lv et al. [17] propose a multi-branch low light enhancement network (MBLLEN), which extracts features at different levels and generates output images through multi branch fusion. Cui et al. [5] propose an Illumination Adaptive Transformer (IAT), through dynamic query learning to construct an end-to-end Transformer. After the low-light enhancement model restores the details of the image, the effect of the detector is improved. However, most low-light enhancement models are complex and have a great impact on the real-time performance of the detector.

2.3   Object Detection in Adverse Condition

Object detection under adverse conditions is crucial for the robust perception of robots, and robust object detection models have emerged for some adverse conditions. Some people transfer detectors from the source domain to the target domain through unsupervised domain adaptation [4,13,21], adapting the model to harsh environments. Liu et al. [15]propose IA-YOLO, which adaptively enhances each image to improve detection performance. They propose a differentiable image processing (DIP) module for harsh weather and used a small convolutional neural network (CNN-PP) to adjust the parameters of DIP. On the basis of IA-YOLO, Kalwar et al. [11] propose GDIP-YOLO. GDIP proposes a gating mechanism that allows multiple DIPs to operate in parallel. Qin et al. [18] propose detection-driven enhancement network (DENet) is used for object detection in adverse weather condition. Cui et al. [6] propose a multi-task automatic encoding transform (MAET) for dark object detection, exploring the potential space behind lighting conversion.

3   Method

Dark images have poor visibility due to low-light interference, which affects the performance of the detector. To address this issue, we propose a pyramid enhanced network (PENet) and joint YOLOv3 to construct a dark object detection framework PE-YOLO. The overview of the framework of PE-YOLO is shown in Fig. 2.

3.1   Overview of PE-YOLO

PENet decomposes the image into components of different resolutions through the Laplacian pyramid. In PENet, we enhance the components of each scale through proposed detail processing module (DPM) and low-frequency enhancement filter (LEF).

Define the image $I \in R^{h \times w \times 3}$ as input, we obtain sub images of different resolutions using a Gaussian pyramid.

$$G(x) = Down(Gaussian(x)) \qquad (1)$$

where **Down** represents downsampling, **Gaussian** represents Gaussian filter, and the size of Gaussian kernel is 5×5. After each Gaussian pyramid operation, the width and height of the image are halved, which means the resolution is the original $\frac{1}{4}$. Obviously, the downsampling operation of the Gaussian pyramid is irreversible. In order to recover the original high-resolution image after upsampling, the lost information is required, and the lost information constitutes the components of the Laplacian pyramid. The definition of the Laplacian pyramid is

$$L_i = G_i - Up(G_{i+1}) \qquad (2)$$

among which L_i is the ith layer of the Laplacian pyramid, G_i represents the ith layer of the Laplacian pyramid, and **Up** represents bilinear upsampling operation. When reconstructing the image, we only need to perform the reverse operation of (2) to restore the high-resolution image.

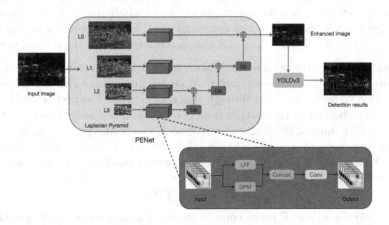

Fig. 2. Overview of PE-YOLO. We use detail processing module (DPM) and low-frequency enhancement filter (LEF) to enhance the images.

We obtained four components of different scales through the Laplace pyramid, as shown in Fig. 3. We found that the Laplacian pyramid pays more attention to global information from bottom to top, while on the contrary it pays more attention to local details. They are all information lost during the image downsampling process, which is also the object of our PENet enhancement. We enhance the components through detail processing module (DPM) and low-frequency enhancement filter (LEF), and the operations of DPM and LEF are parallel. We will provide introduction to DPM and LEF later in next section. By decomposing and reconstructing the Laplacian pyramid, PENet can be made lightweight and effective, which helps to improve the performance of PE-YOLO.

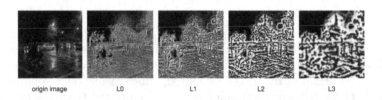

Fig. 3. Visualization of each layer in the Laplacian pyramid. The second to fourth column is the component of the Laplacian pyramid, and the resolution is reduced from left to right.

3.2   Detail Enhancement

We propose a detail processing module (DPM) to enhance the components in the Laplacian pyramid, which is divided into contextual branch and edge branch. The details of DPM are shown in Fig. 4. Context branch obtains contextual information by capturing remote dependencies, and globally enhances components. The edge branch uses two Sobel operators in different directions to calculate image gradients to obtain edges and enhance the texture of the components.

Context Branch. We use a residual block to process features in before and after obtaining remote dependencies, and residual learning allows rich low-frequency information to be transmitted through skip connections. The first residual block changes the channel of the feature from 3 to 32, and the second residual block changes the channel of the feature from 32 to 3. Capturing global information in the scene has been proven to be beneficial for low-level visual tasks such as low-light enhancement. The structure of the context branch is described in Fig. 4, which is defined as

$$CB(x) = x + \gamma(F_1(\hat{x})) \tag{3}$$

where $\hat{x} = \sigma(F_2(x)) \cdot x$, F is the convolutional layer with kernel 3×3, γ is Leaky ReLU, and σ is the Softmax function.

Edge Branch. Sobel operator is a discrete operator that uses both Gaussian filter and differential derivation. It can find edges by calculating gradient approximation. We use Sobel operators in both the horizontal and vertical directions to re-extract edge information through convolutional filters and use residuals to enhance the flow of information. This process is represented as

$$EB(x) = F_3(Sobel_h(x) + Sobel_w(x)) + x \tag{4}$$

where $Sobel_h$ and $Sobel_w$ represents Sobel operations in the vertical and horizontal directions, respectively.

3.3 Low-Frequency Enhancement Filter

In each scale component, the low-frequency component has most of the semantic information in the image, and they are the key information for the detector prediction. To enrich the semantics of the reconstructed image, we propose low-frequency enhancement filter (LEF) to capture low-frequency information in the components. The details of LEF are shown in Fig. 5. Assuming the component $f \in R^{h \times w \times 3}$, we first transform it into $f \in R^{h \times w \times 32}$ through a convolutional layer. We use a dynamic low-pass filter to capture low-frequency information, and we use average pooling for feature filtering, which only allows information below the cutoff frequency to pass through. The low-frequency thresholds for different semantics are different. Considering the multi-scale structure of Inception [22], we used adaptive average pooling with sizes of 1×1, 2×2, 3×3, 6×6, and used upsampling at the end of each scale to restore the original size of the features. A low-pass filter is formed under average pooling of different kernel sizes. We divide f into four parts through channel separation, namely $\{f_1, f_2, f_3, f_4\}$. Each part is processed using different sizes of pooling, which is described as

$$Filter(f_i) = Up(\beta_s(f_i)) \tag{5}$$

where f_i is part of f divided on the channel, **Up** is bilinear interpolation sampling, β_s is an adaptive average pooling of different sizes of $s \times s$. Finally, after tensor splicing each $\{f_i, i = 1, 2, 3, 4\}$, we restore them to $f \in R^{h \times w \times 3}$.

4 Experiments

4.1 Dataset and Implementation Details

Dataset: We use the ExDark dataset to validate the effectiveness of our PE-YOLO. ExDark is a low-light object detection dataset used for research on object detection and image enhancement. It collected a total of 7363 images under 10 different lighting conditions, from extremely low light to dusk, with 12 bounding box annotations of objects in the images. We divided ExDark into 80% for training and 20% for testing, and the specific division is consistent with IAT [5] and MAET [6].

Details: All trained and tested images are resized to 608×608, and data augmentation methods such as random cropping, flipping, and multi-scale resizing are used during training. Batch-size is set to 8, the optimizer uses SGD, the initial learning rate is set to 0.001, and the weight decay is set to 0.0005. Train PE-YOLO for 30 epochs and run our model on a single RTX 3090 GPU. The deep learning framework is Pytorch, and we use mmdetection [3] to achieve our model.

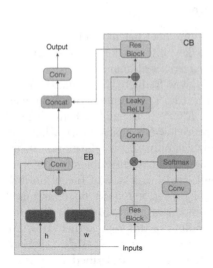

Fig. 4. Detail of DPM, contains context branch (CB) and edge branch (EB).

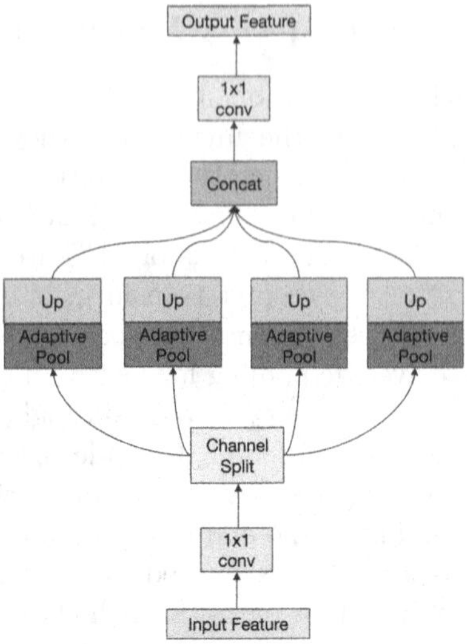

Fig. 5. Details of low-frequency enhancement filter (LEF). LEF is composed of adaptive averge pooling in different sizes to intercept low-frequency components.

Evaluation: We use mAP and FPS to validate the effectiveness of our model. mAP is the average AP of all categories in the detection model, and a larger value indicates a higher accuracy of the model. It is represented as

$$mAP = \frac{\sum_{i=1}^{C} AP_i}{C} \tag{6}$$

where C is the number of categories, and AP is the Averge Precision for each category, calculated by the area of the Precision Recall curve. FPS is the number of image frames detected by the model per second, and a larger FPS indicates a faster model detection speed.

4.2 Experimental Results

To verify the effectiveness of PE-YOLO, we conducted many experiments on the ExDark dataset. Firstly, we compare PE-YOLO with other low-light enhancement models. Due to the lack of detection capability of the low light enhancement model, we will use the same detector as PE-YOLO to experiment on all enhanced images. We set the IoU threshold of mAP to 0.5, and the performance comparison is shown in Table 1. We found that directly using low-light enhanced models before YOLOv3 did not significantly improve detection performance. Our PE-YOLO is 1.2% and 1.1% higher on mAP than MBLLEN and Zero-DCE, respectively, achieving the best results.

Table 1. Performance comparisons between PE-YOLO and low-light enhancement models. It shows mAP and AP in each class. The bold number has the highest score in each column.

Model	Venue	Bicycle	Boat	Bottle	Bus	Car	Cat	Chair	Cup	Dog	Motorbike	People	Table	mAP
YOLOv3 [19]	arXiv	79.8	75.3	78.1	92.3	83.0	68.0	69.0	79.0	78.0	77.3	81.5	55.5	76.4
KIND [26]	MM2019	80.1	77.7	77.2	**93.8**	83.9	66.9	68.7	77.4	79.3	75.3	80.9	53.8	76.3
MBLLEN [17]	BMVC 2018	82.0	77.3	76.5	91.3	**84.0**	67.6	69.1	77.6	**80.4**	75.6	**81.9**	**58.6**	76.8
Zero-DCE [9]	CVPR 2020	84.1	77.6	78.3	93.1	83.7	70.3	69.8	77.6	77.4	76.3	81.0	53.6	76.9
PE-YOLOv3 (Ours)	-	**84.7**	**79.2**	**79.3**	92.5	83.9	**71.5**	**71.7**	**79.7**	79.7	**77.3**	81.8	55.3	**78.0**

We visualized the detection results of different low light enhancement models, as shown in Fig. 6. We found that although MBLLEN and Zero DCE can significantly improve the brightness of the image, they also enlarge the noise in the image. PE-YOLO mainly captures the potential information of objects in low-light images, while suppressing noise in high-frequency components, thus PE-YOLO has better detection performance.

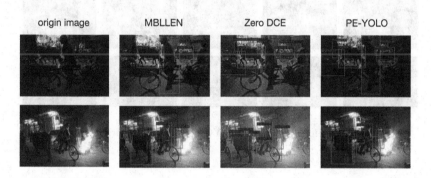

Fig. 6. Detection Results in PE-YOLO and other low-light enhancement models.

We compared the performance of PE-YOLO with other dark detectors, as shown in Table 2. In addition, we visualized the detection results of the dark detector and PE-YOLO, as shown in Fig. 7, which clearly showed that PE-YOLO was more accurate in object detection. PE-YOLO is 0.7% and 0.2% higher in mAP compared to DENet and IAT-YOLO pre-trained with the LOL dataset, and our PE-YOLO is also almost the highest on FPS. The above data indicate that PE-YOLO is more suitable for detecting objects in dark conditions.

4.3 Ablation Study

To analyze the effectiveness of each component in PE-YOLO, we conducted ablation studies, and the results are shown in Table 3. After adopting context branching, PE-YOLO increased from 76.4% to 77.0% in mAP, indicating that capturing remote dependencies is effective for enhancement. After adopting edge

Table 2. Performance comparisons between PE-YOLO and dark detectors. The bold number has the highest score in each column.

Model	Venue	Bicycle	Boat	Bottle	Bus	Car	Cat	Chair	Cup	Dog	Motorbike	People	Table	mAP	FPS
YOLOv3 [19]	arXiv	79.8	75.3	78.1	92.3	83.0	68.0	69.0	79.0	78.0	77.3	81.5	55.5	76.4	54.0
MAET [6]	ICCV 2021	83.1	78.5	75.6	**92.9**	83.1	73.4	71.3	79.0	**79.8**	77.2	81.1	57.0	77.7	-
IAT-YOLOV3 (LOL pretrain) [5]	BMVC2022	79.8	76.9	78.6	92.5	83.8	**73.6**	**72.4**	78.6	79.0	**79.0**	81.1	**57.7**	77.8	52.6
DENet [18]	ACCV2022	80.4	**79.7**	77.9	91.2	82.7	72.8	69.9	**80.1**	77.2	76.7	**82.0**	57.2	77.3	**54.8**
PE-YOLOv3 (Ours)	-	**84.7**	79.2	**79.3**	92.5	**83.9**	71.5	71.7	79.7	79.7	77.3	81.8	55.3	**78.0**	53.6

branch, the mAP increased from 77.0% to 77.6%, indicating that edge branch can enhance the texture of components and enhance the details of the enhanced image. After adopting LEF, the mAP increased from 77.6% to 78.0%, indicating that capturing low-frequency components is beneficial for obtaining potential information in the image. In the end, our model improved from 76.4% to 78.0% on mAP and only decreased by 0.4 on FPS.

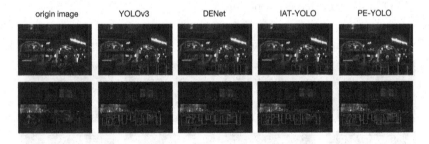

Fig. 7. Detection Results in PE-YOLO and other dark detectors.

Table 3. Ablation study on PE-YOLO. "CB" represents context branch, "EB" represents edge branch, and LEF represents low-frequency enhancement filter.

DPM		LEF	mAP	FPS
CB	EB			
			76.4	54.0
✓			77.0	53.9
✓	✓		77.6	53.8
✓	✓	✓	78.0	53.6

5   Conclusion

To achieve more robust dark object detection, we propose a pyramid enhancement network (PENet) that performs detail restoration and captures potential information. By combining PENet and YOLOv3, we build a dark object detection framework named PE-YOLO. We first use the Laplacian pyramid to decompose the image into four components with different resolutions, and propose a detail processing module (DPM) and a low-frequency enhancement filter (LEF) for component enhancement. In addition, PE-YOLO trains in an end-to-end way, without additional loss function. We conducted experiments in the ExDark dataset, and the experimental results show that compared with the low-light enhancement models and the dark detectors, PE-YOLO achieves the best results and can effectively detect objects in dark conditions. However, our model should be studied on more detectors and further improve performance while maintaining lightweight.

References

1. Bochkovskiy, A., Wang, C.Y., Liao, H.Y.M.: Yolov4: optimal speed and accuracy of object detection. arXiv preprint arXiv:2004.10934 (2020)
2. Cai, Z., Vasconcelos, N.: Cascade R-CNN: delving into high quality object detection. In: Proceedings of the IEEE Conference on Computer Vision and Pattern Recognition, pp. 6154–6162 (2018)
3. Chen, K., et al.: MMdetection: open MMlab detection toolbox and benchmark. arXiv preprint arXiv:1906.07155 (2019)
4. Chen, Y., Li, W., Sakaridis, C., Dai, D., Van Gool, L.: Domain adaptive faster R-CNN for object detection in the wild. In: Proceedings of the IEEE Conference on Computer Vision and Pattern Recognition, pp. 3339–3348 (2018)
5. Cui, Z., et al.: You only need 90k parameters to adapt light: a light weight transformer for image enhancement and exposure correction. In: 33rd British Machine Vision Conference 2022, BMVC 2022, London, UK, November 21–24, 2022. BMVA Press (2022). https://bmvc2022.mpi-inf.mpg.de/0238.pdf
6. Cui, Z., Qi, G.J., Gu, L., You, S., Zhang, Z., Harada, T.: Multitask AET with orthogonal tangent regularity for dark object detection. In: Proceedings of the IEEE/CVF International Conference on Computer Vision, pp. 2553–2562 (2021)
7. Dudhane, A., Zamir, S.W., Khan, S., Khan, F.S., Yang, M.H.: Burst image restoration and enhancement. In: Proceedings of the IEEE/CVF Conference on Computer Vision and Pattern Recognition, pp. 5759–5768 (2022)
8. Everingham, M., Van Gool, L., Williams, C.K., Winn, J., Zisserman, A.: The pascal visual object classes (VOC) challenge. Int. J. Comput. Vision **88**, 303–338 (2010)
9. Guo, C., et al.: Zero-reference deep curve estimation for low-light image enhancement. In: Proceedings of the IEEE/CVF Conference on Computer Vision and Pattern Recognition, pp. 1780–1789 (2020)
10. Guo, X., Li, Y., Ling, H.: Lime: Low-light image enhancement via illumination map estimation. IEEE Trans. Image Process. **26**(2), 982–993 (2016)
11. Kalwar, S., Patel, D., Aanegola, A., Konda, K.R., Garg, S., Krishna, K.M.: GDIP: gated differentiable image processing for object-detection in adverse conditions. arXiv preprint arXiv:2209.14922 (2022)
12. Law, H., Deng, J.: CornerNet: detecting objects as paired keypoints. In: Proceedings of the European Conference on Computer Vision (ECCV), pp. 734–750 (2018)
13. Li, C., et al.: Spatial attention pyramid network for unsupervised domain adaptation. In: Vedaldi, A., Bischof, H., Brox, T., Frahm, J.-M. (eds.) ECCV 2020. LNCS, vol. 12358, pp. 481–497. Springer, Cham (2020). https://doi.org/10.1007/978-3-030-58601-0_29

14. Lin, T.-Y., et al.: Microsoft COCO: common objects in context. In: Fleet, D., Pajdla, T., Schiele, B., Tuytelaars, T. (eds.) ECCV 2014. LNCS, vol. 8693, pp. 740–755. Springer, Cham (2014). https://doi.org/10.1007/978-3-319-10602-1_48
15. Liu, W., Ren, G., Yu, R., Guo, S., Zhu, J., Zhang, L.: Image-adaptive yolo for object detection in adverse weather conditions. In: Proceedings of the AAAI Conference on Artificial Intelligence, vol. 36, pp. 1792–1800 (2022)
16. Loh, Y.P., Chan, C.S.: Getting to know low-light images with the exclusively dark dataset. Comput. Vis. Image Underst. **178**, 30–42 (2019)
17. Lv, F., Lu, F., Wu, J., Lim, C.: MBLLEN: low-light image/video enhancement using CNNs. In: BMVC, vol. 220, p. 4 (2018)
18. Qin, Q., Chang, K., Huang, M., Li, G.: DENet: detection-driven enhancement network for object detection under adverse weather conditions. In: Proceedings of the Asian Conference on Computer Vision, pp. 2813–2829 (2022)
19. Redmon, J., Farhadi, A.: Yolov3: an incremental improvement. arXiv preprint arXiv:1804.02767 (2018)
20. Ren, S., He, K., Girshick, R., Sun, J.: Faster R-CNN: towards real-time object detection with region proposal networks. In: Advances in Neural Information Processing Systems, vol. 28 (2015)
21. Sasagawa, Y., Nagahara, H.: YOLO in the dark - domain adaptation method for merging multiple models. In: Vedaldi, A., Bischof, H., Brox, T., Frahm, J.-M. (eds.) ECCV 2020. LNCS, vol. 12366, pp. 345–359. Springer, Cham (2020). https://doi.org/10.1007/978-3-030-58589-1_21
22. Szegedy, C., et al.: Going deeper with convolutions. In: Proceedings of the IEEE Conference on Computer Vision and Pattern Recognition, pp. 1–9 (2015)
23. Tian, Z., Shen, C., Chen, H., He, T.: FCOS: fully convolutional one-stage object detection. In: Proceedings of the IEEE/CVF International Conference on Computer Vision, pp. 9627–9636 (2019)
24. Wei, C., Wang, W., Yang, W., Liu, J.: Deep retinex decomposition for low-light enhancement. arXiv preprint arXiv:1808.04560 (2018)
25. Wu, A., Han, Y., Zhu, L., Yang, Y.: Instance-invariant domain adaptive object detection via progressive disentanglement. IEEE Trans. Pattern Anal. Mach. Intell. **44**(8), 4178–4193 (2021)
26. Zhang, Y., Zhang, J., Guo, X.: Kindling the darkness: a practical low-light image enhancer. In: Proceedings of the 27th ACM International Conference on Multimedia, pp. 1632–1640 (2019)

Region Feature Disentanglement
for Domain Adaptive Object Detection

Rui Wang[1,2], Shouhong Wan[1,2(✉)], and Peiquan Jin[1,2]

[1] University of Science and Technology of China, Hefei, China
wr666@mail.ustc.edu.cn, {wansh,jpq}@ustc.edu.cn
[2] Key Laboratory of Electromagnetic Space Information, CAS, Hefei, China

Abstract. In recent years, deep learning based object detection has shown impressive results. However, applying an object detector learned from one data domain to another one often faces performance degradation due to the domain shift problem. To improve the generalization ability of object detectors, the majority of existing domain adaptation methods alleviate the domain bias either on the feature encoder or instance classifier by adversarial learning. Differently, we try to alleviate domain discrepancy in the region proposal network (RPN) by performing feature disentanglement. To this end, an extractor is devised to extract domain-specific foreground representations from both the source and target features, respectively. Then, domain-invariant representations are decomposed from the domain-specific features by the disentanglement module. Through the decoupling operation, the gap between the domain-specific and domain-invariant features is enlarged, which promotes RPN feature to contain more domain-invariant information. Furthermore, we propose dynamic weighted adversarial training to alleviate the unstable training caused by adversarial learning. We conduct extensive experiments on multiple domain adaptation scenarios, and our experiment results demonstrate the effectiveness of our proposed approach.

Keywords: Domain adaptation · Object detection · Feature disentanglement

1 Introduction

Object detection is one of the fundamental computer vision tasks which aims to assign a bounding box and category prediction for each foreground instance. In the past decade, owing to the emergence of deep learning, object detection has achieved many advances [11,18]. However, the detection model learned from the data in a domain (i.e., source domain) would suffer significant performance degradation caused by domain discrepancy when tested in scenarios with domain gaps (i.e., target domain). For example, model trained with normal weather images is unable to effectively detect objects in foggy weather. On the other hand, accurately annotating all new samples for each new domain is impractical in real applications, because usually it is costly and time-consuming.

© The Author(s), under exclusive license to Springer Nature Switzerland AG 2023
L. Iliadis et al. (Eds.): ICANN 2023, LNCS 14260, pp. 175–186, 2023.
https://doi.org/10.1007/978-3-031-44195-0_15

To tackle this problem, unsupervised domain adaptation (UDA) [16] is developed to empower the learned model to be transferred from the annotated source to the target domain, i.e., enabling the model work well in target domain by utilizing unlabeled target samples in training phase. Researchers have proposed various approaches, such as domain discriminator, to address the task of domain adaptive object detection [3,4,7,19,28]. Region proposal network (RPN) is used to generate foreground proposals. Actually, an RPN feature contains the foreground and background information, and has a high impact on the overall performance of a detector. However, the above works mainly eliminate the domain discrepancy in the feature extractor network and region-based classification network, and ignore the domain shift in RPN.

Motivated by the aforementioned observations, we propose a component, named region feature disentanglement module (RFDM), to alleviate domain discrepancy in the RPN by employing disentangled representation learning [15]. As a method of feature decomposition, disentangled representation learning can eliminate domain-specific factors existing in the aligned features. Concretely, given a feature map extracted by a backbone, two extractors are devised for the source and target domain to extract domain-specific representations from the feature map. Then, to make the feature extracted by RPN contain more domain-invariant information, we conduct metric learning to enlarge the gap between domain-specific and domain-invariant representations. Meanwhile, a domain discriminator is used to help the domain-specific feature contain much more domain-specific information. With this mechanism, domain-invariant RPN feature is decomposed from the domain-specific features. Considering that domain discriminator is challenging for getting stable results during adversarial learning [17], we propose dynamic weighted adversarial training (DWAT) to dynamically weight the loss of adversarial learning. We experimentally demonstrate that our method delivers higher quality bounding boxes and reduces the time required for training.

The main contributions of this work are summarized as follows:

- We design a region feature disentanglement module (RFDM) to solve the domain shift problem in RPN, which can enhance the cross-domain performance of the region proposal network and generate more accurate and effective proposals for target domain.
- We propose dynamic weighted adversarial training (DWAT) to make the adversarial learning converge more stably and more rapidly.
- We conduct extensive experiments on multiple cross-domain scenarios to validate the effectiveness of our proposed approach, and the results demonstrate the superior performance of our method.

2   Related Work

2.1   Domain Adaptive Object Detection

Domain Adaptive Object Detection (DAOD) aims to solve the performance drop caused by domain distribution mismatch problem without the need for annotations on the target domain. Since the introduction of generative adversarial networks (GAN) [10], a lot of domain adaptive methods based on adversarial learning spring up [22,28]. Chen et al. [4] proposed to align both image-level and instance-level features distributions to reduce the domain gap. Saito et al. [19] proposed to align the local and global feature distributions to alleviate the domain-shift impact. HTCN [3] harmonizes transferability and discriminability in the context of adversarial adaptation for adapting object detectors by exploring the transferability of different local-regions, images, and instances. MeGA-CDA [22] employs category-wise discriminators to ensure category-aware feature alignment for learning domain-invariant discriminative features. TIA [28] alleviates the domain shift in classification and localization task spaces separately.

To obtain the domain-invariant RPN for more accurate proposals, some other methods have been proposed. DI FR [26] uses an RPN domain classifier to classify the examples into target/source domains. RPA [27] constructs foreground and background prototpyes, and then enforces the RPN features to align with the prototypes for both the source and target domains. Despite the accuracy gain, these methods neglect the impact of the domain-specific factors existing in the aligned features, which may affect the adaptation performance. Different from these methods, we utilize feature disentanglement to eliminate domain-specific factors in RPN.

2.2 Feature Disentanglement

As an effective way to extract invariant features, recently, feature disentanglement [2,14] has been demonstrated to be effective in many tasks, including domain adaptive object detection [24]. A related work is DSN [1] which proposed to explicitly separate representations private to each domain and shared between source and target domains in object classification task. There are some differences between DSN and our method. DSN uses a shared decoder to reconstruct the input sample, while we do not use it. DSN directly optimizes the Euclidean distance between domain invariant and domain specific features. We use adversarial learning to optimize encoders because RPN characteristics are significantly different between the source and target domains in a mini-batch which are different from global image features. Another related work is DDF [13] which utilized feature disentanglement to decompose the shared and private features. Although DDF performs feature disentanglement to align features, it is essentially different from our proposed approach. First, they have different features to align. DDF adopts feature disentanglement to align image-level features. Our method adopts feature disentanglement to align RPN features. Second, they adopt different encoders. DDF use a part of backbone network to extract domain-specific features from both source and target domain. Considering that foreground and background features of different domains vary greatly, it is improper to extract domain-specific RPN features for both domains with one encoder. We plug two domain-aware encoders after region proposal network to address this issue. In addition, we propose dynamic weighted adversarial training to help the encoders extract domain-specific features more stably and more rapidly.

3 The Proposed Approach

3.1 Network Overview

In this subsection, we overview the architecture of our proposed method. Figure 1 shows the framework of our proposed domain adaptation model. We apply multi-level image and instance feature alignment in the network masked by yellow and green respectively. To perform region feature disentanglement (orange dashed box), we particularly propose domain-specific feature extractors to get domain-specific representations for both the source and target domain, and metric learning among the domain-invariant and domain-specific features to enlarge the discrepancy. In the following, we will first introduce the image- and instance-level feature alignment in the network, which servers as our baseline model. Then we deeply discuss the proposed region feature disentanglement module and dynamic weighted adversarial training.

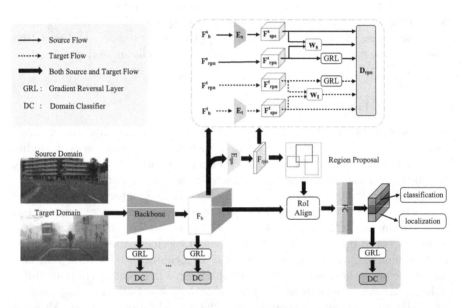

Fig. 1. The overview architecture of our proposed method. E_s and E_t separately indicate domain-specific encoder for the source and target domain. E_{rpn} denotes the convolutional neural layer of RPN. F_{rpn} denotes the global RPN features. 'GRL' indicates Gradient Reversal Layer. 'DC' denotes domain classifier. D_{rpn} denotes the domain classifier for RPN features.

3.2 Baseline Model

Following previous works [4,19], we use Faster RCNN with the VGG16 [21] backbone as our basic object detector. We take the multi-level feature alignment method [25] as our baseline, which actually conducts multiple domain classifiers to align the distributions of image-level features and instance-level features simultaneously. In particularly, multiple domain classifiers are used to reduce the image-stage shift in middle-layer and high-layer features. The loss of image-stage adaptation can be written as:

$$\mathcal{L}_{img} = -\sum_{i,k,u,v} [d_i \log f_k(\Phi_{i,k}^{u,v}) + (1 - d_i) \log(1 - f_k(\Phi_{i,k}^{u,v}))], \tag{1}$$

where d_i denotes the domain label of the i-th image, which is set to 0 for the source domain and 1 for the target domain. And $\Phi_{i,k}^{u,v}$ denotes the activation located at (u, v) of the feature map of the i-th image after the k-th layers, and f_k is its corresponding domain classifier.

To align instance-level features, a domain classifier is employed to supervise the feature alignments in the instance features. The instance-stage adaptation loss is defined as:

$$\mathcal{L}_{ins} = -\sum_{i,j} [d_i \log p_{i,j} + (1 - d_i) \log(1 - \log p_{i,j})], \tag{2}$$

where $p_{i,j}$ represents the probability that the j-th region proposal in the i-th image is from target domain.

In order to ensure that all the domain classifiers are consistent, consistency regularization is used to alleviate the domain shift in layers between different domain classifiers [4]. The consistency regularization loss can be presented as follows:

$$\mathcal{L}_{cst} = \sum_{i,j} \|\frac{1}{|I|} \sum_{u,v} f(\Phi_i^{u,v}) - p_{i,j}\|_2, \tag{3}$$

where $|I|$ indicates the total number of pixels in the i-th image and $\|\cdot\|_2$ denotes the Euclidean norm.

The overall adaptation loss of the baseline model is the summation of image-stage adaptation loss, instance-stage adaptation loss and consistency regularization loss:

$$\mathcal{L}_{adv} = \mathcal{L}_{img} + \mathcal{L}_{ins} + \mathcal{L}_{cst}. \tag{4}$$

3.3 Region Feature Disentanglement Module

In this subsection we describe how we construct feature disentanglement in RPN. Concretely, given a source image x_s and a target image x_t, we first obtain feature maps F_b^s and F_b^t that are the output of the backbone. Then RPN takes F_b into a convolutional layer E_{rpn} to produce the global RPN features. Next, to facilitate the region feature disentanglement, we define two identical domain-specific extractors E_s and E_t consisting of multiple convolutional layers to decompose domain-specific foreground features from F_b respectively. As shown in Fig. 1 and (5), F_{spe}^t and F_{spe}^s indicate the domain-specific RPN features, and F_{rpn}^t and F_{rpn}^s represent the domain-invariant RPN features:

$$F_{spe}^t = E_t(F_b^t), F_{spe}^s = E_s(F_b^s), F_{rpn}^t = E_{rpn}(F_b^t), F_{rpn}^s = E_{rpn}(F_b^s). \tag{5}$$

In order to obtain the domain-specific RPN features for feature decomposition, we utilize the adversarial training mechanism [8] and design a domain discriminator network D_{rpn} to perform domain classification,

$$\mathcal{L}_{spe} = -\sum_{u,v}[\log(1 - \log D_{rpn}(F_{spe}^s)^{u,v}) + \log D_{rpn}(F_{spe}^t)^{u,v}]. \quad (6)$$

To promote domain-invariant features to contain more domain-irrelevant information, we also adopt the domain classifier D_{rpn} to align the RPN features. The loss of the RPN domain classifier is shown as follows:

$$\mathcal{L}_{rpn} = -\sum_{u,v}[\log(1 - \log D_{rpn}(F_{rpn}^s)^{u,v}) + \log D_{rpn}(F_{rpn}^t)^{u,v}]. \quad (7)$$

To enlarge the discrepancy between the domain-invariant and domain-specific features within each domain, and meanwhile to align the domain-invariant features across the domains, following [13], we utilize metric learning on F_{spe}^t, F_{spe}^s, F_{rpn}^t and F_{rpn}^s, in which the triplet loss is adopted to measure the discrepancy between features. Specifically, the triplet loss $\mathcal{L}_{dis}$ is defined as:

$$\begin{aligned}
\mathcal{L}_{dis} = \frac{1}{2}(&\max(\|\hat{F}_{rpn}^s - \hat{F}_{rpn}^t\| - \|\hat{F}_{rpn}^t - \hat{F}_{spe}^t\| + \alpha, 0) \\
&+ \max(\|\hat{F}_{rpn}^s - \hat{F}_{rpn}^t\| - \|\hat{F}_{rpn}^s - \hat{F}_{spe}^s\| + \alpha, 0)),
\end{aligned} \quad (8)$$

where $\hat{F}_{rpn}^s = softmax(F_{rpn}^s)$, and $\|\cdot\|$ indicates the square Euclidean distance, α denotes the triplet loss margin.

3.4   Dynamic Weighted Adversarial Training

When the similarity between domain-invariant features and domain-specific features is small, the encoders have a large learning space, and we increase the weight of adversarial loss to accelerate convergence. Considering that adversarial learning is unstable during the training process, we alleviate the instability of adversarial learning by reducing the weight of adversarial loss when the features are well decoupled. Specifically, we use cosine similarity to measure the similarity between extracted features. That is, the weight is generated by

$$\begin{aligned}
w_s = 1 + cos(m(F_{rpn}^s), m(F_{spe}^s)), \\
w_t = 1 + cos(m(F_{rpn}^t), m(F_{spe}^t)).
\end{aligned} \quad (9)$$

where $cos(x_1, x_2) = \frac{x_1^T \cdot x_2}{\|x_1\|\|x_2\|}$ is the cosine similarity, $m(F) = \frac{1}{HW}\sum_{h,w} F(h, w)$. Then we weight the adversarial loss by the similarity dynamically. The weighted adversarial loss is defined by:

$$\begin{aligned}
\mathcal{L}_{rpn} = -\sum_{u,v}[w_s \log(1 - \log D_{rpn}(F_{rpn}^s)^{u,v}) + w_t \log D_{rpn}(F_{rpn}^t)^{u,v}], \\
\mathcal{L}_{spe} = -\sum_{u,v}[w_s \log(1 - \log D_{rpn}(F_{spe}^s)^{u,v}) + w_t \log D_{rpn}(F_{spe}^t)^{u,v}].
\end{aligned} \quad (10)$$

3.5   Overall Loss

Combined with the baseline model, the overall loss is the summation of detection loss and adaptation loss:

$$\mathcal{L} = \mathcal{L}_{det} + \lambda(\mathcal{L}_{adv} + \mathcal{L}_{spe} + \mathcal{L}_{rpn} + \mathcal{L}_{dis}), \tag{11}$$

where $\mathcal{L}_{det}$ is the detection loss of Faster RCNN, λ is a coefficient to balance detection loss and adaptation loss.

4   Performance Evaluation

4.1   Datasets and Scenarios

Following [4,23,28], we evaluate our method under the three adaptation scenarios.

Normal-to-Foggy. Cityscapes [5] is a large-scale city street scene dataset collected from different cities in the clear weather. Foggy Cityscapes [20] is synthesized from Cityscapes for the foggy weather. In this scenario, we use Cityscapes and Foggy Cityscapes as the source and target domains, respectively. Results are reported in the validation set of Foggy Cityscapes.

Synthetic-to-Real. SIM10k [12] consisting of 10,000 images is rendered by the game Grand Theft Auto (GTA-V). In synthetic data adaptation, we utilize the SIM10k dataset as the source domain and the Cityscapes as the target domain. Since only Car is annotated in both domains, we report the performance of Car on the validation set of Cityscapes.

Cross-Camera. KITTI [9] is also a city street scene dataset that is different from Cityscapes on camera setup. To simulate the cross-camera adaptation, we adopt both KITTI and Cityscapes as the source and target domains and transfer them in both adaptation directions. In line with the protocol of [4], we only evaluate detection performance on their common category, Car.

4.2   Implementation Details

Here we adopt the Faster R-CNN with VGG16 as the backbone that is pre-trained on ImageNet [6]. We resize the shorter sides of all images to 600 pixels. The batch size is set to 2, i.e., one image per domain. During the training phase, only the source domain provides annotations. The detector is trained with SGD for six epoches with the learning rate of 2e−3, and it is then dropped to 2e-4 for another four epoches. We set the weight decay and momentum of SGD as 5e-4 and 0.9, respectively. Besides, the factor $\lambda = 0.1$ is set. The triplet loss margin α is set to 0.8. We report mAP with an IoU threshold of 0.5 for evaluation.

Table 1. Detection performance (%) on Normal-to-Foggy cross-domain adaptation task, Cityscapes → Foggy Cityscapes.

Method	Bus	Bicycle	Car	Motor	Person	Rider	Train	Truck	mAP
No DA	26.7	25.8	27.2	16.8	25.6	30.1	4.7	11.5	21.0
DAF [4]	35.3	27.1	40.5	20.0	25.0	31.0	20.2	22.1	27.6
SWDA [19]	36.2	35.3	43.5	30.0	29.9	42.3	32.6	24.5	34.3
DI-FR [26]	44.6	38.9	49.4	35.1	36.9	45.8	34.9	28.2	39.2
HTCN [3]	47.4	37.1	47.9	32.3	33.2	47.5	40.9	31.6	39.8
RPA [27]	43.6	36.8	50.5	29.7	33.3	45.6	42.0	30.4	39.0
VDD [24]	52.0	36.8	51.7	34.2	33.4	44.0	34.7	33.9	40.0
UMT [7]	56.5	37.3	48.6	30.4	33.0	46.7	46.8	34.1	41.7
MeGA-CDA [22]	49.2	39.0	52.4	34.5	37.7	49.0	46.9	25.4	41.8
DDF [13]	43.9	40.8	51.9	33.5	37.2	46.3	34.2	24.7	39.1
TIA [28]	52.1	38.1	49.7	37.7	34.8	46.3	48.6	31.1	42.3
Ours	50.5	42.5	57.6	37.1	39.9	50.0	39.8	29.1	43.3

4.3 Comparison Experiments

Here we compare our proposed method with published state-of-the-art methods, including DAF [4], SWDA [19], DI-FR [26], HTCN [3], RPA [27], VDD [24], UMT [7], MeGA-CDA [22], DDF [13], TIA [28]. 'No DA' denotes the Faster R-CNN without domain adaptation. Table 1 shows the results of different methods for Normal-to-Foggy scenario, and we have the following observations. Our method greatly outperforms the RPA [27] which also performs the RPN feature alignment across domains (43.3% vs. 39.0%). Besides, our method obtains 1.0% performance gain compared with the state-of-the-art model TIA [28]. Table 2 reports the results on the car category in Synthetic-to-Real scenario and Cross-Camera scenario. Compared with the similar method RPA [27], our method has an mAP gain of 1.8% and 1.5%. We can see that that our model boosts the performance compared with the state-of-the-art model TIA [28] in both adaptations, which verifies the effectiveness of our model.

4.4 Ablation Studies

We make an ablation analysis on the Normal-to-Foggy cross-domain adaptation task. Table 3 shows the results. Here, we use mAP as the metric. 'RFDM*' indicates the Region Feature Disentanglement Module with one encoder, and 'RFDM' indicates the Region Feature Disentanglement Module with domain-aware encoders. 'DWAT' denotes the Dynamic Weighted Adversarial Training. Compared with the Baseline, 'RFDM' can boost the performance by 6.2%, which shows the features disentanglement in RPN is indeed helpful for domain adaptation. Besides, we can also see that domain-aware encoders could improve the performance than one encoder. This shows our domain-aware extractors promote to extract more domain-specific representations, which improves the disentangled

Table 2. Detection performance (%) on Synthetic-to-Real and Cross-Camera adaptation tasks, SIM10k → Cityscapes and Cityscapes ↔ KITTI.

Method	SIM10k → Cityscapes	KITTI → Cityscapes	Cityscapes → KITTI
No DA	34.6	30.2	53.5
DAF [4]	39.0	38.5	64.1
SWDA [19]	42.3	37.9	71.0
DI-FR [26]	45.5	-	75.4
HTCN [3]	42.5	42.1	73.2
RPA [27]	45.7	-	75.1
UMT [7]	43.1	-	-
MeGA-CDA [22]	44.8	43.0	75.5
DDF [13]	44.3	46.0	75.0
TIA [28]	-	44.0	75.9
Ours	47.5	44.2	76.6

ability. Moreover, by employing DWAT, our model only requires 50k iterations (5k iterations per epoch) to train, while other methods are trained with 70k iterations.

Table 3. Ablation study on Normal-to-Foggy cross-domain adaptation task, Cityscapes → Foggy Cityscapes.

Method	$\mathcal{L}_{det}$	$\mathcal{L}_{adv}$	RFDM*	RFDM	DWAT	**mAP**
No DA	✓					21.0
Baseline	✓	✓				35.9
Ours	✓	✓	✓			42.1
	✓	✓		✓		42.7
	✓	✓		✓	✓	43.3

4.5 Further Analyses

Error Analysis of Proposals. To further clarify the effectiveness of the proposed region feature disentanglement module, in line with [28], we categorize the proposals into 3 types: Correct with IoU greater than 0.5, Mis-localized with IoU between 0.3 and 0.5, Background with IoU smaller than 0.3. Take the Normal-to-Foggy cross-domain adaptation task as an example, comparing the candidate proposals generated by TIA [28] and our method, as shown in the Fig. 2, our components improves the rate of Correct proposals, from 45.1% to 46.4%. Furthermore, our method obtains 1.8% improvements compared with the Baseline. The contrast clearly demonstrates that our method effectively enhances the transferability of RPN features.

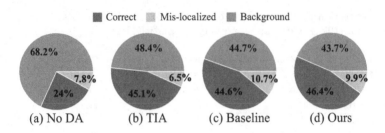

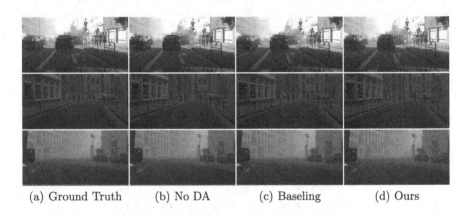

Fig. 2. Error analysis of the proposals in different models on Normal-to-Foggy cross-domain adaptation task, Cityscapes → Foggy Cityscapes.

Visualization. Figure 3 shows the detection results and visualized features on the Normal-to-Foggy cross-domain adaptation task. Compared with vanilla detector and Baseline, ours identifies more foreground objects, as well as focuses on foreground instances.

Fig. 3. Examples of detection results from Cityscapes → Foggy Cityscapes.

5 Conclusion

In this paper, we present a novel domain-aware region feature disentanglement method for domain adaptive object detection, which eliminates the severe domain discrepancy in region proposal network. In particular, we design two simple yet effective domain-specific encoders to extract the domain-specific features. Furthermore, to decompose domain-invariant RPN features from domain-specific features, we employ the metric learning on the domain-specific and domain-invariant features. By doing so, we are able to eliminate the domain-specific factors in RPN features, thereby resulting in better overall alignment. Furthermore, we propose dynamic weighted adversarial learning to make the encoders converge more stably and more rapidly. Extensive experimental results, as well as ablation studies, validate the effectiveness of the proposed method.

Acknowledgements. This work is supported by Natural Science Foundation of Anhui Province (Grant No. 2208085MF157).

References

1. Bousmalis, K., Trigeorgis, G., Silberman, N., Krishnan, D., Erhan, D.: Domain separation networks. In: Proceedings of the 30th International Conference on Neural Information Processing Systems, pp. 343–351. NIPS 2016 (2016)
2. Cai, R., Li, Z., Wei, P., Qiao, J., Zhang, K., Hao, Z.: Learning disentangled semantic representation for domain adaptation. In: Proceedings of the 28th International Joint Conference on Artificial Intelligence, pp. 2060–2066. IJCAI 2019 (2019)
3. Chen, C., Zheng, Z., Ding, X., Huang, Y., Dou, Q.: Harmonizing transferability and discriminability for adapting object detectors. In: 2020 IEEE/CVF Conference on Computer Vision and Pattern Recognition (CVPR), pp. 8866–8875 (2020)
4. Chen, Y., Li, W., Sakaridis, C., Dai, D., Van Gool, L.: Domain adaptive faster R-CNN for object detection in the wild. In: Proceedings of the IEEE Conference on Computer Vision and Pattern Recognition, pp. 3339–3348 (2018)
5. Cordts, M., et al.: The cityscapes dataset for semantic urban scene understanding. In: Proceedings of the IEEE Conference on Computer Vision and Pattern Recognition, pp. 3213–3223 (2016)
6. Deng, J., Dong, W., Socher, R., Li, L.J., Li, K., Fei-Fei, L.: ImageNet: a large-scale hierarchical image database. In: 2009 IEEE Conference on Computer Vision and Pattern Recognition, pp. 248–255 (2009)
7. Deng, J., Li, W., Chen, Y., Duan, L.: Unbiased mean teacher for cross-domain object detection. In: 2021 IEEE/CVF Conference on Computer Vision and Pattern Recognition (CVPR), pp. 4089–4099 (2021)
8. Ganin, Y., Lempitsky, V.: Unsupervised domain adaptation by backpropagation. In: Proceedings of the International Conference on Machine Learning, pp. 1180–1189 (2015)
9. Geiger, A., Lenz, P., Stiller, C., Urtasun, R.: Vision meets robotics: the KITTI dataset. Int. J. Robot. Res. **32**(11), 1231–1237 (2013)
10. Goodfellow, I.J., et al.: Generative adversarial nets. In: Proceedings of the 27th International Conference on Neural Information Processing Systems, vol. 2, pp. 2672–2680 (2014)
11. He, K., Gkioxari, G., Dollár, P., Girshick, R.: Mask R-CNN. In: 2017 IEEE International Conference on Computer Vision (ICCV), pp. 2980–2988 (2017)
12. Johnson-Roberson, M., Barto, C., Mehta, R., Sridhar, S.N., Rosaen, K., Vasudevan, R.: Driving in the matrix: can virtual worlds replace human-generated annotations for real world tasks? arXiv preprint arXiv:1610.01983 (2016)
13. Liu, D., Zhang, C., Song, Y., Huang, H., Wang, C., Barnett, M., Cai, W.: Decompose to adapt: cross-domain object detection via feature disentanglement. IEEE Trans. Multimedia **25**, 1333–1344 (2022)
14. Liu, Y.C., Yeh, Y.Y., Fu, T.C., Wang, S.D., Chiu, W.C., Wang, Y.C.F.: Detach and adapt: Learning cross-domain disentangled deep representation. In: 2018 IEEE/CVF Conference on Computer Vision and Pattern Recognition, pp. 8867–8876 (2018)

15. Locatello, F., et al.: Challenging common assumptions in the unsupervised learning of disentangled representations. In: Proceedings of the 36th International Conference on Machine Learning, ICML 2019, 9–15 June 2019, Long Beach, California, USA, vol. 97, pp. 4114–4124 (2019)
16. Pan, S.J., Yang, Q.: A survey on transfer learning. IEEE Trans. Knowl. Data Eng. **22**(10), 1345–1359 (2010)
17. Radford, A., Metz, L., Chintala, S.: Unsupervised representation learning with deep convolutional generative adversarial networks. In: 4th International Conference on Learning Representations, ICLR 2016, Conference Track Proceedings (2016)
18. Ren, S., He, K., Girshick, R., Sun, J.: Faster R-CNN: towards real-time object detection with region proposal networks. IEEE Trans. Pattern Anal. Mach. Intell. **39**(6), 1137–1149 (2017)
19. Saito, K., Ushiku, Y., Harada, T., Saenko, K.: Strong-weak distribution alignment for adaptive object detection. In: Proceedings of the IEEE Conference on Computer Vision and Pattern Recognition, pp. 6956–6965 (2019)
20. Sakaridis, C., Dai, D., Van Gool, L.: Semantic foggy scene understanding with synthetic data. Int. J. Comput. Vision **126**(9), 973–992 (2018)
21. Simonyan, K., Zisserman, A.: Very deep convolutional networks for large-scale image recognition. In: 3rd International Conference on Learning Representations, ICLR 2015, San Diego, CA, USA, May 7–9, 2015, Conference Track Proceedings (2015)
22. VS, V., Gupta, V., Oza, P., Sindagi, V.A., Patel, V.M.: MeGA-CDA: memory guided attention for category-aware unsupervised domain adaptive object detection. In: 2021 IEEE/CVF Conference on Computer Vision and Pattern Recognition (CVPR), pp. 4514–4524 (2021)
23. Wang, Y., Zhang, R., Zhang, S., Li, M., Xia, Y., Zhang, X., Liu, S.: Domain-specific suppression for adaptive object detection. In: 2021 IEEE/CVF Conference on Computer Vision and Pattern Recognition (CVPR), pp. 9598–9607 (2021)
24. Wu, A., Liu, R., Han, Y., Zhu, L., Yang, Y.: Vector-decomposed disentanglement for domain-invariant object detection. In: 2021 IEEE/CVF International Conference on Computer Vision (ICCV), pp. 9322–9331 (2021)
25. Xie, R., Yu, F., Wang, J., Wang, Y., Zhang, L.: Multi-level domain adaptive learning for cross-domain detection. In: 2019 IEEE/CVF International Conference on Computer Vision Workshop (ICCVW), pp. 3213–3219 (2019)
26. Yang, X., Wan, S., Jin, P.: Domain-invariant region proposal network for cross-domain detection. In: 2020 IEEE International Conference on Multimedia and Expo (ICME), pp. 1–6 (2020)
27. Zhang, Y., Wang, Z., Mao, Y.: RPN prototype alignment for domain adaptive object detector. In: 2021 IEEE/CVF Conference on Computer Vision and Pattern Recognition (CVPR), pp. 12420–12429 (2021)
28. Zhao, L., Wang, L.: Task-specific inconsistency alignment for domain adaptive object detection. In: 2022 IEEE/CVF Conference on Computer Vision and Pattern Recognition (CVPR), pp. 14197–14206 (2022)

ROFusion: Efficient Object Detection Using Hybrid Point-Wise Radar-Optical Fusion

Liu Liu, Shuaifeng Zhi$^{(\boxtimes)}$, Zhenhua Du, Li Liu, Xinyu Zhang, Kai Huo, and Weidong Jiang

College of Electronic Science, National University of Defense Technology, Changsha, China
{liuliucn,zhishuaifeng}@outlook.com

Abstract. Radars, due to their robustness to adverse weather conditions and ability to measure object motions, have served in autonomous driving and intelligent agents for years. However, Radar-based perception suffers from its unintuitive sensing data, which lack of semantic and structural information of scenes. To tackle this problem, camera and Radar sensor fusion has been investigated as a trending strategy with low cost, high reliability and strong maintenance. While most recent works explore how to explore Radar point clouds and images, rich contextual information within Radar observation are discarded. In this paper, we propose a hybrid point-wise Radar-Optical fusion approach for object detection in autonomous driving scenarios. The framework benefits from dense contextual information from both the range-doppler spectrum and images which are integrated to learn a multi-modal feature representation. Furthermore, we propose a novel local coordinate formulation, tackling the object detection task in an object-centric coordinate. Extensive results show that with the information gained from optical images, we could achieve leading performance in object detection (97.69% recall) compared to recent state-of-the-art methods FFT-RadNet [17] (82.86% recall). Ablation studies verify the key design choices and practicability of our approach given machine generated imperfect detections. The code will be available at https://github.com/LiuLiu-55/ROFusion.

Keywords: Radar-Optical Fusion · Object Detection · Deep Learning

1 Introduction

Autonomous driving and Advanced Driver Assistance Systems (ADAS) often rely on different types of sensors to acquire a reliable perception. Mainstream sensors equipped in automotive vehicles are camera, Lidar and Radar, which are fused together thanks to their unique working mechanism and specialties. Existing mainstream multi-sensor fusion strategy uses camera and Lidar sensors for 3D object detection [2,21]. Mainly because Lidar owns a high angular resolution and range detection accuracy in a way of dense point clouds, and is complementary to camera images which are rich in contextual and semantic information of

© The Author(s), under exclusive license to Springer Nature Switzerland AG 2023
L. Iliadis et al. (Eds.): ICANN 2023, LNCS 14260, pp. 187–198, 2023.
https://doi.org/10.1007/978-3-031-44195-0_16

scenes. However, both camera and Lidar suffer from huge performance degradation in adverse weather conditions, which is a crucial requirement for long-term stable autonomous driving.

Radars are active sensors that measure the environment from reflected electromagnetic waves. Compared to Lidar, Radar has a robust capacity in severe weather conditions and can detect objects and obstacles within 250m with their distances and velocities. Furthermore, its low deployment cost makes Radar a requisite sensor in assistance systems. Radar data have developed different types of representations, including Radar occupancy grid maps, micro-Doppler signature, dense Range-Doppler-Azimuth (RAD) tensors and point clouds, with various processing costs and representational capacity.

Despite Radar's advantages in stable and long-term scene perception, there have been few investigations on fusing Radar with other sensors in this task. This is partly caused by its entirely different imaging mechanism in contrast to cameras and Lidars, leading to extremely sparse point clouds or intuitive dense RAD spectrum, and relatively low elevation angular resolution as well. Fortunately, this problem has been partly solved with the development of the 4D imaging Radar, with a high angular resolution of about 1° in both azimuth and elevation. Some recent works also tried to conduct image-Radar fusion to alleviate the high sparsity of Radar point clouds [9,10,14].

Motivated by the above-mentioned challenges, we propose ROFusion, a hybrid point-wise approach to fuse Radar and camera data. Different from previous work in Radar-optical fusion, we seek to fuse dense contextual features from both modalities. We first acquire Radar and camera features respectively from single-modality extractors [8,17], and then use image-Radar association and hybrid point-based fusion strategy to merge cross-modality features at multiple hierarchies. Finally, a local coordinate formulation is proposed to decompose our tasks into classification and regression in an object-centric manner. Our method achieves a new state-of-the-art performance in both easy and hard cases of public RADIal dataset [17].

To summarize, our contributions are as follows:

- We propose a hybrid point-wise fusion strategy to effectively associate dense Radar and image features.
- We propose a local coordinate formulation that simplifies object detection by classification and regression sub-tasks in an object-centric manner.
- We conduct extensive experiments on the RADIal [17] benchmark and achieve a new state-of-the-art detection performance, with a significant boost over Radar-based baseline.

2   Related Work

2.1   Point-Based Methods

PointNet [15] designs a novel type of neural network that directly consumes the point cloud, which makes point-based detection methods process. For Radar point clouds, sparse structures take a challenge to object detection. One strategy

[3] is to accumulate radar points into a dense occupancy grid mapping (OGM). For lightweight demand, [19] utilize novel point structure [16]. With the sparsity issue, [13] observes that a global message could enhance perception performance.

2.2   Camera-Radar Fusion Methods

Complementary information gives the opportunity for sensor fusion between the camera and Radar. Radar extracts the distance and velocity of objects, while semantic information is captured by cameras. There are normally three fusion levels between Radar and camera: early level, feature level, and late level. Radars are often used to generate the region of interest (ROI) for early-level fusion. Then, the predicted region is processed as an auxiliary refining optical task [4,7], which is computationally expensive. The decision level contrary utilizes two sources independently detect, proposing a strategy [1,24] defining whether one of the sensors failed. With different probability spaces, late-level fusion could not efficiently exert the capability of two sensors.

A naive approach is fusing Radar and camera in a latent feature space where the key point is Radar-camera association. CramNet [9] applies a dynamic vox-elization fusing Radar and camera features, projecting each camera pixel with a 3D ray to rectify its location, which makes a robust performance for sensor failure. In [14], authors propose a frustum association that fully exploits Radar vertical information. CRAFT [10] also associates Radar and image, but implements them in a polar coordinate to handle the discrepancy between the coordinate system and spatial properties. The feature maps are then fused by a consecutive cross-attention strategy.

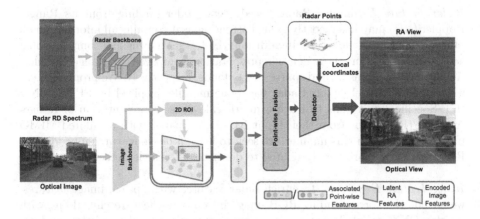

Fig. 1. ROFusion network architecture. Latent RA feature maps and camera-encoded semantics are first obtained by Radar and image backbone. The image 2D bounding boxes are used to associate the image and Radar feature maps via point cloud candidates. The point-wise module is next used for feature-level fusion, proposing a hybrid point feature to produce final Radar detection formulated in object-centric local coordinates.

3   Method

In this section, we present architectural details of our method ROFusion as well as key design choices enabling accurate object detection with a hybrid point-wise optical-Radar fusion. An overall architecture is provided in Fig. 1. We first take Radar RD spectrums with corresponding images as our network inputs and extract their dense features. Radar points filtered by prior information such as image detection bounding boxes are then adopted as anchors to associate Radar and image features. Furthermore, a hybrid point-wise fusion complements the surrounding semantics of targets to produce new point features. A detection header finally predicts object locations in per-object local coordinates.

To summarize, our pipeline consists of three main modules including: (1) a dense feature extraction module from both RGB images and corresponding high-definition RD tensors to acquire contextual information of scenes (Sect. 3.1); (2) a hybrid point-based fusion module to associate dense Radar embedding of scattering points with image features (Sect. 3.2); (3) a local coordinate module formulating object detection task in an object-centric manner (Sect. 3.3). We finally show the training configurations of our method in Sect. 3.4.

3.1   Dense Feature Extraction

In order to acquire rich contextual information about objects within 3D scenes, we leverage dense convolutional neural networks (CNNs) to extract dense feature embedding of both Range-Doppler (RD) Radar maps and camera image observations.

Radar Feature Extractor. Radar-based scene understanding from its Range-Doppler (RD) map has recently gained attention as it contains all information on range, azimuth and elevation. In addition, the RD map owns less computational acquisition costs and is a dense representation compared to Range-Doppler-Azimuth (RAD) tensors and sparse point clouds, respectively. We propose to use a dense CNN model as our Radar backbone module, inspired by FFT-RadNet [17]. Specifically, it aims to learn a multi-scale dense representation of Range-Azimuth (RA) maps from their input RD counterparts, with a tailored MIMO pre-encoder [17]. In this manner, we seek to learn a dense feature embedding of RA maps as they are closely related to downstream vehicle detection tasks.

Image Feature Extractor. To enrich radar features with optical image features, we encode the corresponding RGB image into a dense feature embedding with a vision CNN model. To reduce computational overhead, we simply use an ImageNet [18] pre-trained ResNet-18 model [8] and keep the weights intact during training. Please note that our image backbone module could be replaced by stronger vision models such as ResNet-152 [8] and vision Transformers [20], depending on the computation budgets.

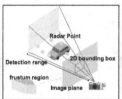

Fig. 2. Image-Radar Association. 2D Detector using image features provides the azimuth of interest (left), which leads to a frustum region to select candidate object-related point clouds (middle). We filter noise and background points depending on whether their relative radial or angular distance to the object center is beyond a certain threshold or not, as discussed in Sect. 3.3 (right).

3.2 Point Fusion

Image-Radar-Association. In this section, we explain how to establish a cross-modality association of target objects with provided sensor calibration information and prior optical detection results.

As dense features of RA maps and images are difficult to conduct dense alignment due to their different imaging mechanism, we rely on Radar point clouds to bridge them at point-level. Specifically, we represent each Radar point as a 3D point $p = (r, a, d, u, v, x, y, z)$, where (r, a, d) and (x, y, z) are its locations within RAD tensors and real word coordinates, respectively. With the intrinsic and extrinsic of the camera model, we transform Radar points into image coordinates as follows:

$$u = f_x \frac{x'}{z'} - p_x, \qquad v = f_y \frac{y'}{z'} - p_y, \tag{1}$$

where (f_x, f_y, p_x, p_y) are camera intrinsic parameters, (x', y', z') is 3D position within camera coordinate transformed by camera extrinsic $[R|t]$ and (x, y, z).

2D object bounding boxes within images are treated as Region of Interest (ROI) filters separating the region of interests out of background and noises, as explained in Fig. 2. The 2D bounding boxes provide strong prior angular information of objects, eliminating the uncertainty caused by Radar sidelobe jamming. At this stage, we treat all points within these 2D ROIs as candidate points for the next fusion stage. However, these boxes within images cannot cope with range estimation, as points within 3D space in the cone area (middle of Fig. 2) all project within the 2D ROIs. To address the range inaccuracy, we consider a local coordinate strategy as detailed in Sect. 3.3.

Hybrid Point Fusion. We propose a point-based method that generates per Radar point fused feature from pixel-level RA and image features. Inspired by DenseFusion [22], we implement a variant architecture that fuses semantics and velocity.

Assume there are k 3D Radar points from the previous association stage, we collect pixel-wise features from encoded RA features F_R and semantic image features F_I, respectively. Concretely, with a set of k point clouds $P = \{p_1, p_1, ..., p_k\}$,

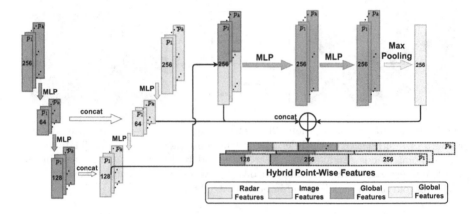

Fig. 3. Hybrid point fusion architecture. Extracted dense Radar and image features are processed by a series of MLPs and fused at multiple scales. With a per-object global feature from max-pooling across points, we reach a hybrid multi-modal feature with spatial and semantic information by concatenating all fused features of various scales.

we extract corresponding per-pixel features $F_R = \{F_r^{p_1}, F_r^{p_2}, ..., F_r^{p_k}\}$ and RA features $F_I = \{F_i^{p_1}, F_i^{p_2}, ..., F_i^{p_k}\}$, where $F_r^{p_k}$ and $F_i^{p_k}$ are pixel-level features from RA and image of point p_k. As shown in Fig. 3, considering the difference within local distribution and semantics of these two feature spaces, the obtained point-wise features are combined in a hierarchical manner. As low-level and high-level fusions are both efficiently discriminative point-level features, we fuse them at different scales via concatenation after being sequentially processed by a set of shared MLPs. Another key point here is to obtain a per-object global contextual feature which, in principle, reveals the attributes of the same target which shares across domains. The global point-level feature is obtained via a max-pooling operation of fused features across all candidate points of the same object. We obtain a set of hybrid point-wise features by concatenating all above mentioned fused features at various scales. These features are fed into a detector that predicts per-point object center locations (see Sect. 3.4).

3.3 Object-Centric Local Coordinates

We have experimentally found that directly regressing object locations is not only challenging to achieve purely from extremely sparse point clouds, but also involved with the absolute scale of sensing environments, imaging resolutions and object locations. To tackle this problem, we propose to decompose object detection task into a combination of classification and regression sub-tasks at an object-centric local coordinate.

As shown in Fig. 4, we establish a new coordinate whose origin is at object center, and x, y axes are parallel to range and azimuth axes of RA. For Radar points within 2D bounding boxes, we encode their relative distance to the center position of targets at both axes based on a set of discrete bins at a certain reso-

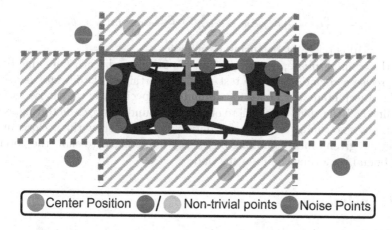

Center Position ● / ● Non-trivial points ● Noise Points

Fig. 4. Illustration of the local coordinates originated at object center position. Non-trivial points lying within or around the object are kept during training, while noise points are discarded.

lution. We further predict a residual offset via regression on top of classification results to reach the final localization prediction. The motivation comes from the fact that we only focus on the features around the target and this formulation decouples the network prediction from the above-mentioned imaging conditions. In this paper, the relative distance between center labels and Radar points is modeled by discretizing object dimension into 5 bins and 11 bins for azimuth and range, respectively.

It is also worth noting that although Radar points around objects are considered candidates, points which also lie within bounding boxes but are reflected by context near objects also have valuable information. We term such points 'non-trivial' points if their relative distance at *any* axes satisfies our above-mentioned discretization. For example, points reflected by non-object regions within boxes may have a large variation w.r.t. range dimension, but share a large correlation to object at angle dimension. In such cases, we may still include these points as training data and only penalize our network prediction by the deviation at the angle-axis prediction. This investigation also filters radar foreground and background points, eliminating range uncertainty as explained in Sect. 3.2.

In the training loop, we use non-trivial points as a data augmentation, which could partly relieve the spatial sparsity of object Radar points. All other points are regarded as background points or noises and are not involved during network training and inference.

3.4 Object Detection and Training Configurations

As described in Sect. 3.3, the detection task is divided into two parts, a RA map coarse classification and a refined regression. The two-part predictions are trained with a combined loss composed of a Cross-Entropy loss and a Smooth-L1 loss [6]. Denote the network prediction of classification and regression as $\hat{y}_{cls}^{B \times N \times 16}$ and $\hat{y}_{reg}^{B \times N \times 2}$, the training loss is:

$$\mathcal{L} = \mathcal{L}_{CrossEntropy}(y_{cls}, \hat{y}_{cls}) + \alpha \mathcal{L}_{Smooth-L1}(y_{reg}, \hat{y}_{reg}), \qquad (2)$$

where $\alpha = 10$ is a weight balancing parameter.

In the training phase, we use the object's 2D ground truth bounding box to get a precise association. In the test phase, a pertained 2D detector is used to provide object bounding boxes for evaluation. Specifically, we choose to use a pre-trained off-the-shelf YoloX [5] to obtain 2D bounding boxes on testing images without any fine-tuning on the target datasets. We also show the performance of our method given oracle bounding boxes as a limited case to show the potential upper bound performance of our method.

4 Experiments

4.1 Dataset and Metrics

Dataset. We evaluate our model on the RADIal dataset [17] consisting of RD spectrums and Radar points of a high-definition Radar with corresponding camera observations. Its 91 sequences are divided into hard and easy cases depending on the intensity of Radar perturbation. We strictly follow the official splits into training, validation, and test division at a portion of 70%, 15%, 15%. Since our proposed point-based architecture requires there are Radar reflection peaks from objects, we remove training candidates where no Radar points are included within object bounding boxes.

Metric. The evaluation metrics for object detection are Average Precision (AP) and Average Recall (AR), given a validated positive prediction whose Intersection-over-Union (IoU) to the ground truth is greater than 50% [17]. We also present the absolute Range and Angle error to analyze the prediction accuracy.

4.2 Baseline

Implement Details. We implement our image backbone with a pre-trained ResNet-18 [8] model. The color image is of size 960×540 and we use the semantic features of the last layer as dense image features. The Radar backbone adopts the design of FFT-RadNet [17] while we further simplify the FPN [12] model to reduce computational complexity. Due to the high definition nature of used Radar sensor, $\frac{1}{4}$ of native resolution is taken and has been proven to be enough for near-by object discrimination [17]. We train our ROFusion model for 40 epochs with a batch size of 8 and 1×10^{-4} learning rate with Adam optimizer [11] on a single NVIDIA Tesla V100 GPU. During inference, the bottom Radar points inside objects' 2D bounding boxes are considered as sensor-facing endpoints and are used to generate the heuristic object-centric local coordinates (hLC).

Results. In Table 1 we report object detection results of our method compared to leading state-of-the-art methods FFT-RadNet [17] and baseline method Pixor [23]. Ground truth bounding boxes and object positions are used to demonstrate the effectiveness of ROFusion. We also evaluate the performance of our method

ROFusion	FFT-RadNet	ROFusion	FFT-RadNet

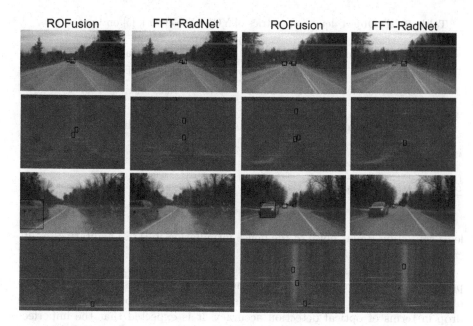

Fig. 5. Qualitative results for object detection from Camera (row 1 & 3) and RA (row 2 & 4) view. In the RA plots, the detection boxes are presented corresponding to RA dense maps in Euclidean space.

Table 1. Object detection performance on RADIal dataset [17]. AR (%) is computed with an IoU threshold of 50%. R(m) and A($°$) indicate the mean Range and Angle error. PC, RA, RD and IM mean point clouds, range-azimuth maps, range-doppler maps and images, respectively.

Method	Input	Overall			Easy			Hard		
		AR(%) ↑	R(m) ↓	A($°$) ↓	AR(%) ↑	R(m) ↓	A($°$) ↓	AR(%) ↑	R(m) ↑	A($°$) ↓
Pixor [23]	PC	32.32	0.17	0.25	28.83	0.15	0.19	38.69	0.19	0.33
Pixor [23]	RA	81.68	**0.10**	0.20	88.02	**0.09**	0.16	70.10	0.12	0.27
FFT-RadNet [17]	RD	82.18	0.11	0.17	91.69	0.10	0.13	64.82	0.13	0.26
FFT-RadNet* [17]	RD	82.86	0.12	**0.11**	93.12	0.11	**0.10**	64.13	0.15	**0.13**
Ours	IM+RD+PC	**97.69**	0.12	0.21	**97.79**	0.11	0.19	**97.52**	**0.12**	0.22
Ours-hLC	IM+RD+PC	93.64	0.12	0.23	95.21	0.12	0.22	91.22	0.13	0.25

• We denote that FFT-RadNet* [17] as detector with 0.5 discrimination threshold for a fair comparison, using authors' provided weights.

with proposed heuristic local coordinates estimation for practical purposes. Although the radar sparsity causes the worse Angle error, we have observed a clear performance boost despite using sparse point-level features thanks to the optical information and our local coordinate formulation. Our method outperforms [17] at overall recall rate with a gap of +14.83%. It is worth to highlight that our hybrid point-wise fusion scheme achieves a promising +27.65% recall boost and a 0.12m Range error in the hard cases, overcoming interference prob-

Table 2. 2D Object detection metrics of YOLOX Network [5] on the test set.

Method	Input	Overall		Easy		Hard	
		AP(%)	AR(%)	AP(%)	AR(%)	AP(%)	AR(%)
YOLOX [5]	IM	90.48	91.03	89.79	91.86	91.77	89.54

Table 3. Detection performance on RADIal [17] given predicted 2D boxes.

Method	Overall				Easy				Hard			
	AP(%) ↓	AR(%) ↑	R(m) ↓	A(°) ↓	AP(%) ↓	AR(%) ↑	R(m) ↓	A(°) ↓	AP(%) ↓	AR(%) ↑	R(m) ↑	A(°) ↓
FFT-RadNet* [17]	**97.39**	82.86	**0.12**	**0.11**	**98.96**	93.12	**0.11**	**0.10**	**93.46**	64.13	0.15	**0.13**
Ours(YOLOX)-hLC	91.58	**95.15**	0.13	0.21	91.03	**96.07**	0.13	0.20	92.63	**93.47**	**0.13**	0.23

lems caused by Radar noise to the dense formulation in [17]. Qualitative results can be found in Fig. 5.

To further demonstrate the practicability of our method, we use network predicted detection results to conduct the evaluation. We first reveal the quality of the adopted YOLOX [5] 2D detector in Table 2, with a moderate performance drop in terms of optical detection accuracy, it is expected that the imperfect 2D detection results would affect the filtering process of our pipeline. Table 3 compares the *AP* and *AR* metrics with machine-generated bounding boxes in both easy and hard cases as well. While the AP metric lack behind baseline model due to the quality of network inferred 2D bounding boxes, our method with YOLOX [5] 2D detector still achieves a higher AR metric for both overall and especially difficult cases. The AR performance gain comes from the 2D bounding boxes association and heuristic local coordinates. The Range error of our method also outperforms FFT-RadNet∗ [17] in difficult cases. These results show that our local coordinates successfully extract the range information for sparse Radar points even though the prior 2D detection is less accurate.

4.3 Ablation

In this section, we conduct ablative experiments to validate the key components of our method: local coordinate (LC) formulation and image fusion module (IM).

As shown in Table 4, we have shown two variants of ROFusion: Ours (w/o LC) is the variant where we remove the local coordinate formulation in the training stage, but conduct the two classification and regression sub-tasks in the original RA maps; we also remove the image level feature fusion module out of training process. From the statistics, we conclude that the local coordinate formulation is significant in enabling accurate learning from spare Radar point clouds. The integration of image features gives further performance boost upon competing performance. It is also worth noting that in addition to the image feature, the prominent prior information introduced by optical detection is another key factor supporting the overall learning process from sparse Radar point clouds.

Table 4. Ablation study on the key components of ROFusion.

Method	Input	Overall			Easy			Hard		
		AR(%) ↑	R(m) ↓	A(°) ↓	AR(%) ↑	R(m) ↓	A(°) ↓	AR(%) ↑	R(m) ↓	A(°) ↓
Ours (w/o LC)	RD+PC	27.4	0.22	0.46	32.94	0.24	0.40	15.78	0.20	0.57
Ours	RD+PC	96.58	**0.09**	0.22	96.31	**0.08**	0.22	96.85	**0.09**	0.24
Ours	IM+RD+PC	**97.69**	0.12	**0.21**	**97.79**	0.11	**0.19**	**97.52**	0.12	**0.22**

5 Conclusion

In this paper, we present ROFusion, a novel point-wise Radar-Optical fusion network for object detection. We have demonstrated that our method could effectively exploit camera semantics to enhance Radar detection. With hybrid point fusion and local coordinate formulation, ROFusion achieves state-of-the-art performance on the public RADIal dataset [17], showing the potential capability for multi-sensor fusion. However, our method still relied on the quality of 2D object detection as prior information to filter potential object Radar points. In addition, considering the difference in imaging mechanism, more in-depth analysis of camera-Radar fusion stratify at the feature level is worth investigating, possibly aided by a powerful Transformer backbone using attention mechanism. This can be an exciting venue for our future work.

Acknowledgements. This work was partially supported by the National Key Research and Development Program of China (Grant No. 2021YFB3100800), the National Natural Science Foundation of China (Grant No. 61921001, 62201603) and Research Program of National University of Defense Technology (Grant No. ZK22-04).

References

1. Ćesić, J., Marković, I., Cvišić, I., Petrović, I.: Radar and stereo vision fusion for multitarget tracking on the special euclidean group. Robot. Auton. Syst. **83**, 338–348 (2016)
2. Chen, X., Ma, H., Wan, J., Li, B., Xia, T.: Multi-view 3d object detection network for autonomous driving. In: Proceedings of the IEEE Conference on Computer Vision and Pattern Recognition (CVPR), pp. 1907–1915 (2017)
3. Dreher, M., Erçelik, E., Bänziger, T., Knol, A.: Radar-based 2d car detection using deep neural networks. In: Proceedings of the International IEEE Conference on Intelligent Transportation Systems (ITSC), pp. 1–8 (2020)
4. Gaisser, F., Jonker, P.P.: Road user detection with convolutional neural networks: An application to the autonomous shuttle wepod. In Journal of Machine Vision and Applications, pp. 101–104. IEEE (2017)
5. Ge, Z., Liu, S., Wang, F., Li, Z., Sun, J.: Yolox: exceeding yolo series in 2021. arXiv preprint arXiv:2107.08430 (2021)
6. Girshick, R.: Fast R-CNN. In: Proceedings of the International Conference on Computer Vision (ICCV), pp. 1440–1448 (2015)
7. Guo, X., Du, J., Gao, J., Wang, W.: Pedestrian detection based on fusion of millimeter wave radar and vision. In: International Conference on Artificial Intelligence and Pattern Recognition, pp. 38–42 (2018)

8. He, K., Zhang, X., Ren, S., Sun, J.: Deep residual learning for image recognition. In: Proceedings of the IEEE Conference on Computer Vision and Pattern Recognition (CVPR), pp. 770–778 (2016)
9. Hwang, J.-J., et al.: Cramnet: camera-radar fusion with ray-constrained cross-attention for robust 3d object detection. In: Proceedings of the European Conference on Computer Vision (ECCV), pp. 388–405. Springer (2022)
10. Kim, Y., Kim, S., Choi, J.W., Kum, D.: Craft: camera-radar 3d object detection with spatio-contextual fusion transformer. arXiv preprint arXiv:2209.06535 (2022)
11. Kingma, D.P., Ba, J.: Adam: a method for stochastic optimization. arXiv preprint arXiv:1412.6980 (2014)
12. Lin, T.-Y., Dollár, P., Girshick, R., He, K., Hariharan, B., Belongie, S.: Feature pyramid networks for object detection. In: Proceedings of the IEEE Conference on Computer Vision and Pattern Recognition (CVPR), pp. 2117–2125 (2017)
13. Liu, J., Xiong, W., Bai, L., Xia, Y., Huang, T., Ouyang, W., Zhu, B.: Deep instance segmentation with automotive radar detection points. IEEE Trans. Intell. Vehicles (2022)
14. Nabati, R., Qi, H.: Centerfusion: center-based radar and camera fusion for 3d object detection. In: Proceedings of the IEEE Workshop on Applications of Computer Vision (WACV), pp. 1527–1536 (2021)
15. Qi, C.R., Su, H., Mo, K., Guibas, L.J.: Pointnet: deep learning on point sets for 3d classification and segmentation. In: Proceedings of the IEEE Conference on Computer Vision and Pattern Recognition (CVPR), pp. 652–660 (2017)
16. Qi, C.R., Yi, L., Su, H., Guibas, L.J.: Pointnet++: deep hierarchical feature learning on point sets in a metric space. In: Neural Information Processing Systems (NIPS), 30 (2017)
17. Rebut, J., Ouaknine, A., Malik, W., Pérez, P.: Raw high-definition radar for multi-task learning. In: Proceedings of the IEEE/CVF Conference on Computer Vision and Pattern Recognition, pp. 17021–17030 (2022)
18. Russakovsky, O., et al.: Imagenet large scale visual recognition challenge. Int. J. Comput. Vis. (IJCV) **115**, 211–252 (2015)
19. Scheiner, N., Kraus, F., Appenrodt, N., Dickmann, J., Sick, B.: Object detection for automotive radar point clouds-a comparison. AI Perspect. **3**(1), 1–23 (2021)
20. Vaswani, A., et al.: Attention is all you need. In: Advances in Neural Information Processing Systems, 30 (2017)
21. Vora, S., Lang, A.H., Helou, B., Beijbom, O.: Pointpainting: sequential fusion for 3d object detection. In: Proceedings of the IEEE Conference on Computer Vision and Pattern Recognition (CVPR), pp. 4604–4612 (2020)
22. Chen Wang, A., et al.: Densefusion: 6d object pose estimation by iterative dense fusion. In: Proceedings of the IEEE/CVF Conference on Computer Vision and Pattern Recognition, pp. 3343–3352 (2019)
23. Yang, B., Luo, W., Urtasun, R.: Pixor: real-time 3d object detection from point clouds. In: Proceedings of the IEEE Conference on Computer Vision and Pattern Recognition (CVPR), pp. 7652–7660 (2018)
24. Zhong, Z., Liu, S., Mathew, M., Dubey, A.: Camera radar fusion for increased reliability in adas applications. Electron. Imaging **2018**(17), 258-1 (2018)

SDGC-YOLOv5: A More Accurate Model for Small Object Detection

Zhiming Lu, Ying Chen📵, Shaojie Li📵, and Ming Ma$^{(\boxtimes)}$📵

Inner Mongolia University, Hohhot 010000, China
csmaming@imu.edu.cn

Abstract. Small objects often suffer from size and resolution limitations, resulting in poor detection performance when employing traditional object detection models. To address these challenges, we propose SDGC-YOLOv5, a novel model based on YOLOv5. Our contributions are as follows: a) Replacement of the original convolution layer with spatial depth convolution (SD) to enable dense feature extraction and improve the detection of small objects. b) Utilization of a lightweight global context network (GC) to enhance small object recognition capabilities. c) Incorporation of the shifted window scheme to enhance the extraction of small target features at the bottom of the pyramid in the YOLOv5 architecture. Experimental results demonstrate the superiority of SDGC-YOLOv5 over existing YOLO algorithms on multiple publicly available datasets, including MS-COCO, Pascal-VOC2012, and DOTA, achieving performance improvements of 3%, 4.4%, and 0.6%, respectively. Moreover, an unprecedented mAP accuracy of 91% is achieved on the self-built dataset PhotovoltaicPanels. In summary, SDGC-YOLOv5 effectively addresses the limitations of traditional YOLO-based object detection methods and exhibits remarkable performance in detecting small objects with low resolution and small size.

Keywords: small object detection · spatial depth convolution · global dependencies

1 Introduction

Raja Sunkara and Tie Luo [12] argue that when objects are small, the structure of the convolution and ensemble suffers from fine-grained information, making it more difficult to learn small objects with limited features. To overcome this problem, The spd-based convolution used in SDGC-YOLOv5 modifies the original convolution, which is designed to handle the challenges of detecting small objects with limited features. The model can downsample the feature map while preserving all channel information, avoiding data loss. Additionally, non-layered convolution operations can be added after each SPD layer to adjust the number of channels in the convolution layer.

Y. Chen—These authors contributed equally to this work.

L. Iliadis et al. (Eds.): ICANN 2023, LNCS 14260, pp. 199–209, 2023.
https://doi.org/10.1007/978-3-031-44195-0_17

It is interesting to note that the attention graphs of several query points were found to be identical in the object detection task. This discovery prompted Yue Cao and Jiarui Xu et al. to present GCNet [1], it is a lightweight module that models global dependencies using a self-attentive mechanism, which is similar to the non-local (NL)) [15] block. Meantime, GCNet combines the benefits of the NL [15] and squeeze-excitation (SE) [5] modules, resulting in higher accuracy with lower computational effort, and improve the ability of the model to capture global dependencies.

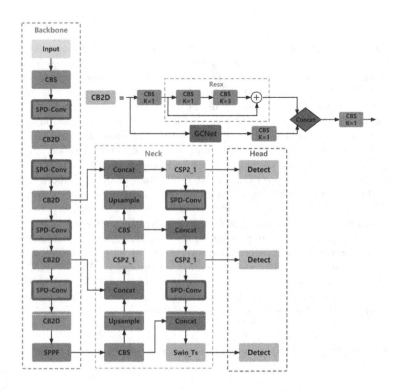

Fig. 1. Model structure for SDGC-YOLOv5

Transformer pertain three benefits in field of vision: Global features, multi-modal fusion and multiple-tasking capabilities. The Transformer-based model has limitations when it comes to applying it to images of various sizes, due to it use the fixed-sized tokens. Swin-transformer [9] build a hierarchical representation via shifting windows to solution this problem. This approach enables it to process images of different sizes and scales efficiently. It divides the input image into non-overlapping local windows, and then applies self-attention calculations to each window. By limiting the attention calculations to these local windows, the computational complexity is greatly reduced compared to the square of the image size. Furthermore, cross-window connections are enabled, allowing the model to learn global features from the input image. And it also has multiple tasking capabilities, enabling it to perform various downstream vision tasks such as object detection. Overall, Swin-transformer [9] is a promising approach for vision tasks, providing both efficiency and high accuracy.

2 Related Work

2.1 Overview of YOLOv5

At present, deep learning-based object detection methods can be classified into 2 types, two-stage approach such as Faster R-CNN [11] as well as one-stage method include YOLO [10], SSD [8] etc.

YOLO (You Only Look Once) [10] is a popular object detection algorithm that can detect objects in images and videos with high accuracy and speed. One of the key improvements in YOLOv5, which is the fifth iteration of this algorithm, is the replacement of the BottleneckCSP module with the C3 module. The C3 module is designed to improve feature extraction and reduce computation, resulting in faster and more accurate object detection. In addition to the C3 module, YOLOv5 also uses other advanced techniques, such as the SPPF (Spatial Pyramid Pooling Fusion) layer and PANet (Path Aggregation Network) to improve performance.

2.2 Small-Object Detection

Small objects can be challenging to detect accurately in images, They often have low resolution and blurry features. This can limit the number of features that the extraction process can use to detect small objects, leading to lower accuracy. To address this issue, various techniques have been proposed, such as multiscale feature extraction, feature fusion, and context aggregation, to improve the detection performance of small objects.

2.3 Based on Multi-scale Prediction Method in Object Detection

Existing deep learning-based small object detection techniques outperform common object detection models in terms of effectiveness. Model enhancement is affected differently by different improvement ideas. Some common methodologies used for small object detection include multi-scale prediction, incorporating contextual data, utilizing data augmentation methods, and employing different training approaches. These approaches aim to improve the accuracy and robustness of small object detection algorithms.

Object Detection at Various Scales Based on Image Pyramids. Image pyramids are the most commonly used method for building multi-scale features in the stage of machine learning-based object detection. This approach first scales the image to various resolutions and creates a multi-scale representation by isolating features on the images of various resolutions, and it then carries out object identification on each resolution image individually using a shift window-based approach to find small objects at the base of the pyramid.

The Feature Pyramid Networks Algorithm (FPN). Similar to the idea of the DSSD [3], an FPN-based strategy is suggested in the literature [6] to improve the semantic information of the underlying features in the object detection algorithm. The FPN fully integrates high-level and underlying characteristics, so that each layer of detection features is rich in semantic information, facilitating the detection of small objects. FPNs is an end-to-end trainable structure and it can be seamlessly incorporated into existing models to increase object detection algorithms' performance.

3   SDGC-YOLOv5

3.1   Overview of YOLOv5

The one-stage object identification method YOLOv5 has four different models: YOLOv5s, YOLOv5m, YOLOv5l, and YOLOv5x. YOLOv5 is the fifth iteration of this algorithm. The upgraded version 6.2, released on August 17, 2022, is more streamlined and offers improved speed and inference performance. In yolov5, the BottleneckCSP module is replaced with the C3 module using the CSPDarknet53 backbone architecture. This replacement reduces the computational parameters while maintaining accuracy. The SPPF layer serves as the backbone of the left rear layer, the PANet acts as the neck, and the YOLO detection head forms the head of the model. These components work together to perform object detection efficiently.

Based on the evaluation on the PhotovoltaicPanels and DOTA small object datasets, it was observed that YOLOv5s outperformed YOLOv5m, YOLOv5l, and YOLOv5x by more than 1.5% in terms of Average Precision (AP) values, as shown in the Table 1. YOLOv5s also has the fewest parameters among these models, leading to faster convergence speed. As a result, YOLOv5s was chosen as the baseline in order to optimize the feature fusion for small objects and achieve the best detection performance.

Additionally, comparing the PV dataset on YOLOv5, YOLOv6s, YOLOv7s [14], YOLOv8, and YOLOXs [4], it was found that YOLOv5s still achieved the highest detection accuracy.

3.2   SDGC-YOLOv5

Figure 1 depicts the SDGC-YOLOv5 framework. The original YOLOv5s is modified in this study to make it more suitable for the detection of microscopic objects, specifically for the PhotovoltaicPanels dataset.

Prediction Framework for Small Objects. After the CB2D convolution, an SPD layer is introduced in the prediction framework to enhance the extraction of features for small objects. As shown in Fig. 2, the SPD layer downsamples the

Table 1. The training results of photovoltaic panel data set in each version of YOLO s-scale.

PhotovoltaicPanels Dataset		
Method	mAP50 (%)	mAP50-95 (%)
YOLOv5s	78.2	33
YOLOv6s	70	31
YOLOv7s	73.6	32.9
YOLOv8s	73.8	34.3
YOLOXs	77.5	38.1

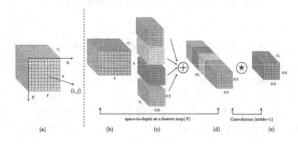

Fig. 2. Illustration of SPD convolution with stride = 2.

feature map and maps all information of size $S \times S \times C1$ in the channel dimension. While divides it into four sub-features by extracting information from adjacent pixels in a step-wise manner. This process is performed separately for even and odd rows/columns in both the spatial and channel dimensions. The resulting sub-feature mappings are then concatenated along the channel dimension to obtain a feature mapping X'. The spatial dimension of X' is reduced by a step size of 2, while the channel dimension is increased by a step size of 2. After adding the SPD feature transformation layer, we further transform $x' \left(\frac{S}{scale}, \frac{S}{scale}, \frac{scale^2}{C1} \right)$ to $x'' \left(\frac{S}{scale}, \frac{S}{scale}, C2 \right)$ ensure that all discriminative feature information is retained where feasible. This approach helps in transforming the feature representation for better analysis and detection of small objects.

GCNet: Non-local And Squeeze-Excitation Networks. As shown in Fig. 3, GCNet is similar to a residual structure, where the input feature map X is first modeled by the global context, then the features are transformed by the Transform module and finally fused with the original input features. The input feature map X has dimensions of $C \times H \times W$ (number of channels × height × width). It is divided into two branches: the left branch expands the input feature map to $C \times H \times W$, while the right branch applies a 1×1 convolution to convert the feature map to $1 \times H \times W$, which is then expanded to $H \times W \times 1 \times 1$. The output features from the convolution are multiplied by the softmax function to

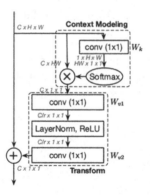

Fig. 3. Global Context Module GCNet.

create a global attention weight. 1×1 convolution is then applied to change the dimension of the attention weight from C to C/r, where r is the sample rate used to reduce the processing burden of the network.

The modeled features are fused with the original features, incorporating global information into each of the original features. The fused features remain C×H×W in dimension, resulting in more accurate feature extraction for small objects.

The non-local network's [15] self-attention method [13], which simulates global dependencies using one layer of convolution and combine aggregated features with features from each object pixel, it can address direct superposition of convolution layers global dependencies issue. Thus, we replaced original C3 module with the GC module of the non-local squeeze-excitation network. Below is a display of the equations of GC module:

$$z_i = x_i + W_{v2}ReLU(LN(W_{v1}\sum_{j=1}^{N_p}\frac{e^{W_k x_j}}{sum_{m=1}^{N_p}e^{W_k x_m}x_j})) \tag{1}$$

Prediction Head for Small Objects. The network structure of the Neck in YOLOv5-6.2 follows the structure of FPN+PAN, where the FPN and PAN execute multi-scale feature fusion on the feature images. The higher layer has greater object semantic information due to the deep layer of the network, and the lower layer has less object location information due to the less convolution layer. The FPN structure upsamples from the top down so that the bottom feature map has greater object semantic information; the PAN structure downsamples from the bottom up so that the top feature contains object location information. Finally, the two features are fused so that the feature maps of different sizes contain both object semantic information and feature information. The precision of feature-length films of various sizes is guaranteed.

However, small objects require more fine convolution and low-level feature extraction connections. Therefore, the convolution layer is adjusted to a step

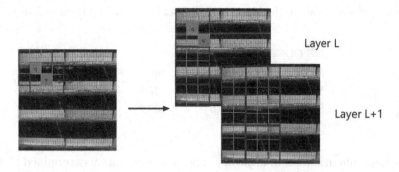

Fig. 4. The traditional sliding-window approach (left), which is less friendly to store access and slower in practice because different queries use different sets of keywords. The shifted non-overlapping window approach (right) is faster in practice and thus more practical as the different queries share keyword.

Table 2. Enhancements to the DOTA dataset based on YOLOv5s improvements.

DOTA Small Object Dataset		
Method	mAP50 (%)	mAP50-95 (%)
YOLOv5s	82.5	57.8
SDGC-YOLOv5	84.3	58.9

size of 1 when extracting the lowest feature. In addition, the SPD module is introduced to enhance the learning of small object features.

For feature extraction of small objects, the traditional convolution method is not sufficient to learn all the information, as shown in Fig. 4 (left), the shift window uses different neighborhood windows to calculate the interrelationship of different points, which is not hardware friendly. We therefore introduced the Swin Transformer, shown in Fig. 4 (right), which s used non-overlapping windows in which points within the same window are set to the same neighborhood for calculation, which is much more speed friendly. According to practical tests, the non-overlapping window method is almost twice as fast as the sliding window method [9]. In addition, the shift operation ensures information sharing between non-overlapping windows. In this paper, we show that adding Swin before Detect can significantly improve the accuracy of finding small objects.

4   Experiments

4.1   Datasets for Detection

Multiple datasets have been made available to the public to address the challenges of object detection. The PASCAL VOC [2] and MS COCO [7] datasets are commonly used for general object detection tasks, while the DOTA [16] small object dataset contains aerial photos of objects with arbitrary shapes, but it is

Table 3. Enhancements to the MS COCO dataset based on YOLOv5s improvements.

MS COCO Dataset		
Method	mAP50 (%)	mAP50-95 (%)
YOLOv5s	56.8	37.4
SDGC-YOLOv5	59.9	40.2

marked as a quadrilateral of arbitrary shape and orientation determined by four points (rather than a typical pair-parallel bbox), which makes this dataset more difficult and more challenging.

Small-scale Object Detection Dataset. The PhotovoltaicPanels dataset is a self-built micro-object dataset, consisting of 4144 infrared photos with two categories: defect and hot spot, and a total of 8176 cases. The objects in this dataset are tiny, with sizes smaller than 10×10 pixels, making the task of object detection even more demanding and challenging. The fine granularity of the objects makes it more difficult to extract features and identify the objects accurately.

The use of multiple datasets is essential for the development and testing of new object detection algorithms and models. By training and evaluating these models on different datasets, researchers and developers can create more robust and accurate object detection systems and applied in a variety of real-world scenario.

4.2 Implementation Details

On Pytorch 1.8.1, we implement SDGC-YOLOv5. All models in this study were trained and evaluated on a dual card server equipped with a V100 GPU with 16 GB RAM. The models in this research were trained using the SGD optimizer, with 0.01 as the initial training value and 0.01 as the starting learning rate for the cosine.

Evaluation Indicators: In this paper, we use the commonly used evaluation criteria for object detection: Average-Precision (AP), mean Average Precision (mAP) and Intersection over Union (IOU). AP and mAP are metrics that are widely used for various object detection tasks and reflect the accuracy and completeness of the detection results. Generally, the threshold values for IOU are set at 0.5 and 0.5–0.95. In this paper, we are more concerned with finding objects than with positional accuracy; therefore we choose IOU set at 0.5 as the primary threshold for evaluation, so that the model identifies as many faults as possible.

4.3 Experimental Results on Small Object Data Sets

After experimental comparison as shown on Table 1, we decided to use the most effective YOLOv5 as the base model. We examined how each proposed innovation

Table 4. Enhancements to the PhotovoltaicPanels dataset based on YOLOv5s improvements.

PhotovoltaicPanels Dataset						
Method	(mAP50) (%)	(mAP50 -95) (%)	$(mAP50)^{obj1}$(%)	$(mAP50)^{obj2}$(%)	$(mAP50-95)^{obj1}$(%)	$(mAP50-95)^{obj2}$(%)
YOLOv5-S	78.20	33.00	89.40	67.00	42.50	23.50
SDGC-YOLOv5	85.25(7.05 ↑)	34.75	99.10	71.40	44.00	25.50

Table 5. Enhancements to the VOC2012 dataset based on YOLOv5s improvements.

VOC2012 Dataset		
Method	mAP50(%)	mAP50-95(%)
YOLOv5s	54.30	34.60
SDGC-YOLOv5	**58.70**	**38.10**

will affect the YOLOv5s in for photovoltaicPanels dataset, and the results are shown in Table 4. It is evident that our model's MAP improves overall by 7 % points and YOLOv5x by 6% points. Therefore, our model is quite efficient.

4.4 Enhancements on Publicly Available Data Sets

Similarly, we demonstrate the advantages of our model for other datasets. For the DOTA small object dataset, the MS COCO dataset and the VOC2012 dataset, SDGC-YOLOv5 increases the mAP by 0.6%, 3% and 4.4% respectively. The results of the experiment are shown in the Table 2, Table 3 and Table 5.

4.5 Ablation Studies

The Effects of the Spatial Depth Convolution for Small Objects. By converting the original convolution to a single-step convolution plus SPD layer and adding a non-convolutional step layer after the SPD, the model size of the original YOLOv5s increases from 14.06 M to 15.16 M and the GFLOPs increases from 15.8 to 16.1. The results of the experiment are shown in the Table 6. The computation effort is just slightly increased, but the mAP is much improved. As a result, the SPD enhancement for the backbone network is effective.

Introduce the Validity of the GCNet Module. After adding the GCNet module, the model size increased from 14.06 M to 14.77 M, while GFLOPs increased from 15.8 to 16.9, the computation speed decreased. The results of the experiment are shown in the Table 6. The reason is that adding GCNet just to reduce the problem of repeated convolution after adding SPD. However, before adding the SPD module, the number of repeated convolutions in the model was relatively small. This made the impact of adding the GCNet module less significant. However, the combined effect of GCNet and SPD was more favorable for improving the model's performance. Therefore, it is necessary to add the GCNet module to the model.

Table 6. Ablation experiments based on YOLOv5s improvements on the Photovoltaic-Panels dataset.

PhotovoltaicPanels Dataset				
Method	mAP50 (%)	mAP50-95 (%)	param	FLOPs
YOLOv5-S	78.20	33.00	14.06	15.8
YOLOv5-S+SPD	**79.30**(1.1 ↑)	**34.15**(1.15 ↑)	15.16	16.1
YOLOv5-S+GCNet	**78.75**(0.55 ↑)	**33.30**(0.3 ↑)	14.77	16.9
YOLOv5-S+Swin	**79.55**(1.25 ↑)	**33.75**(0.75 ↑)	12.54	25.1
SDGC-YOLOv5	**85.25**(7.05 ↑)	**34.75**(1.75 ↑)	26.15	46.8
YOLOv5-M	78.7	33.4	41.19	47.9

What Happens When We Add a Window Converter. In order to more fully extract the details of the small object in the probe head, the Swin transformer module is added to reduce the model size of the original YOLOv5s from 14.06 M to 12.54 M, and the GFLOPs are increased from 15.8 to 25.1. The results of the experiment are shown in the Table 6. Although more calculations are needed, the accuracy of the model and the significant improvement of mAP prove that the addition of the Swin transformer module is critical and effective.

5 Conclusion

The paper describes the integration of advanced technologies into the YOLOv5 model, resulting in a new detector called SDGC-YOLOv5. The new model has demonstrated improved performance in small object detection in UAV capture scenarios, achieving an unprecedented 7 percentage point improvement in mAP on the PhotovoltaicPanels dataset. The technologies integrated into the model include the Swin Transformer module, GCNet, and SPD layers. The Swin Transformer [9]module is an efficient transformer architecture that has been shown to improve performance in various computer vision tasks. GCNet [1] is a module that improves the modeling of global context information in deep neural networks, while SPD [12]layers introduce symmetric positive-definite matrices to enhance the representation of features. The model also demonstrates improved performance on other datasets, such as the DOTA small object dataset by 4.4 percent, MS COCO dataset by 3percent, and VOC2012 dataset by 0.6 percent, highlighting the effectiveness of the model for small object detection. Future work will involve extending the approach to smaller datasets and addressing other small object detection challenges, such as defect detection or remote sensing image object detection. Future work will involve extending the approach to smaller datasets and addressing other small object detection challenges, such as defect detection or remote sensing image object detection.

Acknowledgement. This work was supported by the Inner Mongolia Natural Science Foundation of China under Grant No. 2021MS06016 and No. 2023MS06020. This work was supported in part by the Inner Mongolia Science and Technology Plan Project (No. 2020GG0187).

References

1. Cao, Y., Xu, J., Lin, S., Wei, F., Hu, H.: Gcnet: non-local networks meet squeeze-excitation networks and beyond. In: Proceedings of the IEEE/CVF International Conference on Computer Vision Workshops (2019)
2. Everingham, M., Van Gool, L., Williams, C.K., Winn, J., Zisserman, A.: The pascal visual object classes (VOC) challenge. Int. J. Comput. Vision **88**, 303–308 (2009)
3. Fu, C., Liu, W., Ranga, A., Tyagi, A., Berg, A.C.: DSSD: deconvolutional single shot detector. CoRR **abs/1701.06659** (2017). http://arxiv.org/abs/1701.06659
4. Ge, Z., Liu, S., Wang, F., Li, Z., Sun, J.: Yolox: exceeding yolo series in 2021 (2021)
5. Hu, J., Shen, L., Sun, G.: Squeeze-and-excitation networks. In: Proceedings of the IEEE Conference on Computer Vision and Pattern Recognition, pp. 7132–7141 (2018)
6. Lin, T.Y., Dollár, P., Girshick, R., He, K., Hariharan, B., Belongie, S.: Feature pyramid networks for object detection (2017)
7. Lin, T.-Y., et al.: Microsoft COCO: common objects in context. In: Fleet, D., Pajdla, T., Schiele, B., Tuytelaars, T. (eds.) ECCV 2014. LNCS, vol. 8693, pp. 740–755. Springer, Cham (2014). https://doi.org/10.1007/978-3-319-10602-1_48
8. Liu, W., et al.: SSD: single shot MultiBox detector. In: Leibe, B., Matas, J., Sebe, N., Welling, M. (eds.) ECCV 2016. LNCS, vol. 9905, pp. 21–37. Springer, Cham (2016). https://doi.org/10.1007/978-3-319-46448-0_2
9. Liu, Z., et al.: Swin transformer: hierarchical vision transformer using shifted windows (2021)
10. Redmon, J., Divvala, S., Girshick, R., Farhadi, A.: You only look once: unified, real-time object detection. In: Proceedings of the IEEE Conference on Computer Vision and Pattern Recognition, pp. 779–788 (2016)
11. Ren, S., He, K., Girshick, R., Sun, J.: Faster R-CNN: towards real-time object detection with region proposal networks. In: Advances in Neural Information Processing Systems 28 (2015)
12. Sunkara, R., Luo, T.: No more strided convolutions or pooling: a new CNN building block for low-resolution images and small objects, pp. 443–459. Springer, Heidelberg (2023)
13. Vaswani, A., et al.: Attention is all you need. In: Advances in Neural Information Processing Systems 30 (2017)
14. Wang, C.Y., Bochkovskiy, A., Liao, H.Y.M.: Yolov7: trainable bag-of-freebies sets new state-of-the-art for real-time object detectors (2022)
15. Wang, X., Girshick, R., Gupta, A., He, K.: Non-local neural networks. In: Proceedings of the IEEE Conference on Computer Vision and Pattern Recognition, pp. 7794–7803 (2018)
16. Xia, G.S., et al.: Dota: a large-scale dataset for object detection in aerial images. In: Proceedings of the IEEE Conference on Computer Vision and Pattern Recognition, pp. 3974–3983 (2018)

The Statistical Characteristics of P3a and P3b Subcomponents in Electroencephalography Signals

Resfyanti Nur Azizah[1], Karine Ravienna[1]([⊠])[iD], Lyra Puspa[1],
Yudiansyah Akbar[1], Lula Kania Valenza[1], Galih Restu Fardian Suwandi[2][iD],
Siti Nurul Khotimah[2][iD], and Mohammad Haekal[1][iD]

[1] Vanaya NeuroLab Brain and Behavior Research Center, Jakarta 12450, Indonesia
neurolab@vanaya.co.id
[2] Nuclear Physics and Biophysics Research Group, Department of Physics,
Faculty of Mathematics and Natural Sciences, Institut Teknologi Bandung,
Bandung 40132, Indonesia

Abstract. The P300 waveform is a common event-related potential (ERP) component in electroencephalography (EEG) signals used in clinical neurophysiology, brain-computer interface (BCI), and cognitive neuroscience research. Comprehensive documentation of P300 is needed to support research growth in those areas, especially for P300 subcomponents, P3a and P3b, which commonly used to quantify EEG characteristic. Therefore, this study aims to explore the quantitative characteristics of P3a and P3b subcomponents during the flanker test and Stroop task experiment. ERP waveforms were obtained from 16 healthy subjects to analyze the statistical features of the P3a and P3b subcomponents. This study also used decision trees for measuring the importance index. The result indicates that P3a can be defined as a prominent peak in the time window of 250–350 ms at the frontal area. Positive peak amplitude, area amplitude, mean amplitude, and the prominence of the positive peak have different distributions between group with P3a subcomponent and group without. Whereas P3b is characterized as a positive sloping peak in 300–700 ms at the parietal area. All statistical features influence P3a and P3b identification. However, features related to statistical characteristics of positive peaks have a greater importance index compared with others.

Keywords: EEG Features · P3a · P3b

1 Introduction

The P300 waveform is an event-related potential (ERP) component elicited by auditory or visual stimuli in an electroencephalography (EEG) signal. The P300 is characterized as a positive deflection of 5 μV up to 40 μV at approximately 300 to 400 ms following stimulus onset [16]. The P300 peak and latencies change

L. Iliadis et al. (Eds.): ICANN 2023, LNCS 14260, pp. 210–220, 2023.
https://doi.org/10.1007/978-3-031-44195-0_18

over the scalp, becoming higher and faster from frontal to parietal [6]. Nevertheless, P300 characteristics may vary due to the influence of biological and environmental factors [12]. Those factors must be considered to obtain a more precise result in the interpretation process. In this study, we observed healthy subjects from the same population to diminish the effect of those factors.

Based on the activation area, P300 has two subcomponents which are commonly referred as the P3a and the P3b. The P3a subcomponent originates from stimulus-driven frontal attention during task processing [19]. Meanwhile, the P3b subcomponent originates from the temporal-parietal activity and is related to subsequent memory processing [19]. The differences in cognitive processes underlying P3a and P3b subcomponents may prove to be useful in different applications, such as clinical neurophysiology [13,15,16], brain-computer interfaces (BCI) [4], and cognitive neuroscience research [15,22]. Therefore, the quantitative characteristics of both subcomponents needed to be explored separately.

Previous studies mainly focused on the neurophysiological basis of the P3a and P3b subcomponents [9,19]. However, the quantitative characteristics of both subcomponents are yet to be well documented, especially those related to P3a and P3b subcomponents quantitative identification even though large-scale analysis of EEG, which use quantitative features of the EEG and its subcomponents, promises new insights into brain processes [1]. Therefore, this study aims to analyze and identify the quantitative characteristic of the P3a and P3b subcomponents by using feature importance index obtained from decision trees feature selection.

2 Methods

2.1 Data Acquisition

EEG data were collected from sixteen healthy participants who performed a letter version of the Eriksen flanker test [5] and Stroop task [21] experiment paradigms. These stimuli were presented in Pyschopy [17] stimuli presentation software. In the flanker task, the participants were instructed to respond to the middle letter of five letters on the screen, with the 'H' letter and 'K' letter requiring a left arrow key response, and 'S' letter and 'C' letter requiring a right arrow key response. The test consisted of 90 stimuli, with a ratio of congruent stimuli to incongruent stimuli of 4 : 5. Each stimulus was displayed for 450 ms followed by fixation for 2000 ms, as shown in Fig. 1.

During the Stroop task, on the other hand, the participants were asked to identify the color of the presented word by pressing the initial letter of the color's name. All stimuli were presented in the Indonesian language so, the participants need to press 'G' for green, 'R' for red, 'Y' for yellow, and 'B' for blue. The Stroop task has 135 stimuli with a pro-portion of congruent to incongruent stimuli of 5 : 4. Each stimulus was presented for a 200 ms followed by a 2000 ms response period. The experiment design of the Stroop task is presented in Fig. 2.

The EEG activities were recorded using an EMOTIV EPOC X (Emotiv Inc., San Francisco, California), which is an EEG headset with a sampling frequency

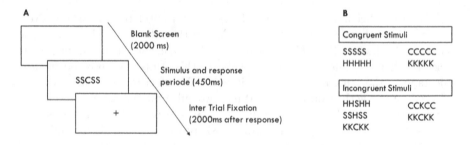

Fig. 1. Experiment design of flanker task (A). Stimulus items of flanker test (B).

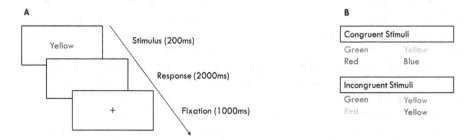

Fig. 2. Stroop task experiment design. (A) Experiment flow. (B) Stimulus.

of 256 Hz and a response frequency of 0.3–45 Hz. EMOTIV EPOC X headset is a proven consumer-grade EEG headset for ERP research [7] and has a reasonably precise event marking system [24]. This device follows a 10–20 system EEG placement with 14 electrodes: $AF3$, $F7$, $F3$, $FC5$, $T7$, $P7$, $O1$, $O2$, $P8$, $T8$, $FC6$, $F4$, $F8$, and $AF3$. This study uses serial communication to send event markers from Psychopy to Emotiv PRO software in order to obtain a precise ERP timing.

2.2 Data Processing

Figure 3 shows the EEG data processing overview used in this study. Before ERP extraction, pre-processing process was implemented to minimize artifacts and noise. Data with a sampling frequency greater than 128 Hz is re-sampled to 128 Hz to standardize the sampling frequency of all data. The process followed by applying a bandpass filter from 1 to 30 Hz and removing eyeblinks using *icaeyeblinkmetrics* extension in EEGLAB [20]. Then, epochs were extracted with a stimulus-locked duration of −100 to 1000 ms. Epochs were corrected using mean amplitudes within the baseline range (100 − 0 ms). Any epochs with an amplitude exceeding 75 μV were excluded from the analysis.

The epochs from each electrode were averaged to obtain ERP waveforms locked to stimulus onset. However, this study only used F3 and F4 for P3a analysis and P7 and P8 for P3b analysis, since the highest P3a was identified in the frontal area while the highest P3b was identified in the parietal area [9].

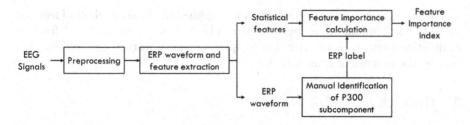

Fig. 3. EEG data processing overview.

Table 1. Statistical features of the P300 subcomponent. Features related with peak analysis were calculated by applying MATLAB *findpeaks*.

Feature	Equation	Feature	Equation
Area amplitude [11]	$\sum_{i=0}^{N} x_i$	Positive peak Z score (Z_{max}) [8]	$\dfrac{x_{max} - \mu}{\sigma}$
Mean amplitude (μ) [11]	$\dfrac{\sum_{i=0}^{N} x_i}{N}$	Positive peak latencies [11]	$t_{x,max}$
Standard deviation (σ) [23]	$\sqrt{\dfrac{\sum_{i=0}^{N}(x_i - \mu)^2}{N}}$	Negative peak (x_{min}) [11]	$\min(x_{i,...,N})$
Kurtosis [14]	$\dfrac{E(x - \mu)^4}{\sigma^4}$	The prominence of the negative peak $(Prom_{min})$ [18]	$x_{min} - x_{lmax}$
Skewness $(\tilde{\mu})$ [3]	$\dfrac{E(x - \mu)^3}{\sigma^3}$	Negative peak width at half maximum [2]	$W_{Prom,min=50\%}$
Positive peak $(x_{m}ax)$ [11]	$\max(x_{i,...,N})$	Negative peak-to-mean ratio	$\dfrac{x_{min}}{\mu}$
The prominence of the positive peak $(Prom_{max})$ [18]	$x_{max} - x_{lmin}$	Negative peak Z score (Z_{min}) [8]	$\dfrac{x_{min} - \mu}{\sigma}$
Positive peak width at half maximum [2]	$W_{Prom,max=50\%}$	Negative peak latencies [11]	$t_{x,min}$
Positive peak-to-mean Ratio	$\dfrac{x_{max}}{\mu}$	1st polynomial coefficient	p_1

Statistical features of P3a were extracted from the ERP amplitude x_i, where $i = 1, \ldots, M$ with x_i is the i−th amplitude in the M data point range within 250–350 ms. Meanwhile, statistical features of P3b were extracted from the ERP amplitude x_i, where $i = 1, \ldots, M$ with x_i is the i−th amplitude in the M data point range within 300–700 ms. The detailed formula of each feature is shown in Table 1. This study uses ERP waveform images in the manual identification of P3a and P3b subcomponents.

Decision trees [10] features selection was applied to obtain a subset of features that provide optimal model performance. The feature importance is defined as cumulative changes in the risk due to splits on every feature and dividing the sum by the number of branch nodes.

3 Results

3.1 The Statistical Characteristics of P3a

Subjects were divided into two groups based on visual evaluations of each ERP waveform at F3 and F4: those with a P3a subcomponent and those without. The ERP waveform with the P3a subcomponent was averaged to determine the P3a pattern between subjects. A positive amplitude higher than 5 μV or a prominent positive deflection from the surrounding amplitude in a time window of 250–350 ms is discovered as a P3a pattern. The comparison between P3a and non-P3a subcomponents is shown in Fig. 4.

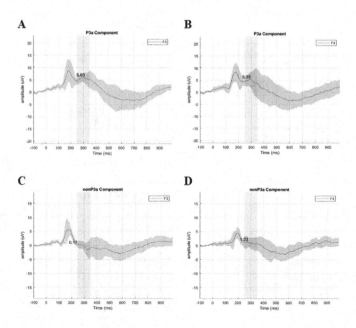

Fig. 4. ERP waveform with P3a subcomponent at F3 (A) and F4 (B). ERP waveform without P3a subcomponent at F3 (C) and F4 (D).

The statistical features of each ERP waveform group were extracted to summarize each group's characteristics. Figure 5 displays each feature distribution. Positive peak amplitude, area amplitude, mean amplitude, and the prominence of the positive peak have different distributions between groups compared to other features. Thus, those features may be used to distinguish the group with

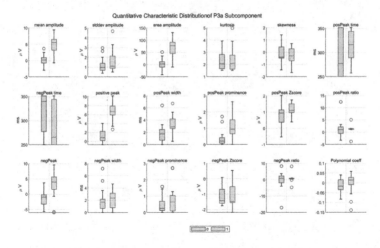

Fig. 5. The distribution of P3a subcomponent statistical features between subjects. The blue bar indicates the distribution of non-P3a subcomponents and the orange bar indicates the distribution of the P3a subcomponent. (Color figure online)

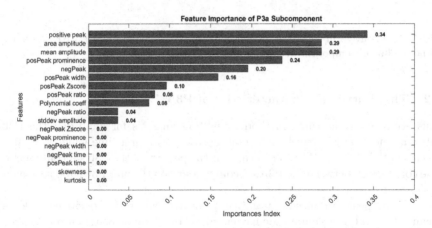

Fig. 6. Feature importance of P3a subcomponent.

P3a subcomponents from the group without P3a subcomponents. With peak latencies of 318.08 ms at F3 and 311.63 ms at F4, the P3a subcomponent shows a prominent positive peak (mean of positive peak = 6.60 µV at F3 and 6.65 µV at F4). The result aligns with the feature importance generated using the decision trees in Fig. 6. The method chooses positive peak amplitude, area amplitude, mean amplitude, and the prominence of the positive peak as the four most important features (mean of area amplitude = 74.38 µV at F3 and 64.33 µV at F4; mean of mean amplitude = 5.31 µV at F3 and 4.59 µV at F4; and mean of positive peak prominence = 1.23 µV at F3 and 1.04 µV at F4).

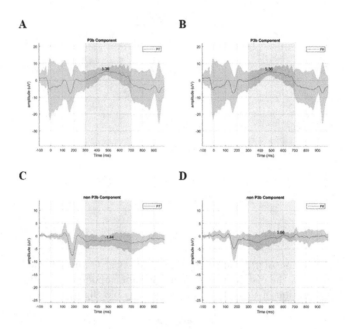

Fig. 7. ERP waveform with P3b subcomponent at P7 (A) and P8 (B). ERP waveform without P3b subcomponent at P7 (C) and P8 (D).

3.2   The Statistical Characteristics of P3b

This study used the same method as in P3a analysis for analyzing the P3b subcomponent. Qualitatively, a sloping positive peak in a time window of 300–700 ms both in P7 and P8 was identified as the pattern of the P3b subcomponent. The comparison between the P3b subcomponent and the non-P3b subcomponent is shown in Fig. 7.

Positive peak amplitude, negative peak-to-mean ratio, positive peak-to-mean ratio, and mean amplitude have minimal overlapping distribution between groups (mean of positive peak = 7.69 μV at P7 and 6.47 μV at P8; negative peak-to-mean ratio = −0.50 μV at P7 and −3.94 μV at P8; positive peak-to-mean ratio = 2.18 μV at P7 and 4.21 μV at P8). Those features also have a smaller standard deviation between subjects compared to other features (standard deviation of positive peak = 3.47 μV at P7 and 5.01 μV at P8; negative peak-to-mean ratio = 2.13 μV at P7 and 6.49 μV at P8; positive peak-to-mean ratio = 2.15 μV at P7 and 4.11 μV at P8). The P3b subcomponent has more features with a feature importance index of >0.20 compared to the P3a subcomponent. The distribution of P3b subcomponent statistical features between subjects is shown in Fig. 8. In addition, the feature importance index of the P3b subcomponent is shown in Fig. 9.

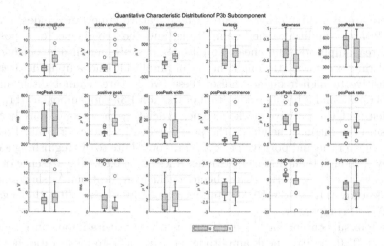

Fig. 8. The distribution of P3b subcomponent statistical features between subjects. The blue bar indicates the distribution of non-P3a subcomponents and the orange bar indicates the distribution of the P3a subcomponent. (Color figure online)

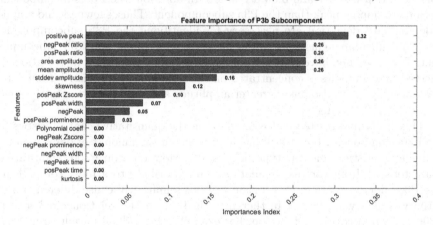

Fig. 9. Feature importance of P3b subcomponent.

4   Discussion

P300 manual identification usually relies on peak amplitude, mean amplitude, or area amplitude [11]. Positive peak becomes the best feature in identifying P3a and P3b subcomponents based on the feature's importance ranking. P3a has a positive peak standard deviation between subjects 1.54 μV at F3 and 2.27 μV at F4. Additionally, there is only one subject whose positive peak value was beyond the $\mu \pm 2\sigma$. These findings indicate that P3a positive peaks are consistent between subjects. Therefore, positive peak amplitude at around 6–7 μV may be used as a reference for identifying these subcomponents.

There are also three other features whose feature importance index is more than 0.2: area amplitude, mean amplitude, and the prominence of a positive peak. Area amplitude and mean amplitudes describe amplitude behavior in selected time windows. Although the mean amplitude and amplitude area are less sensitive to high-frequency noise, these two features cannot distinguish a clear P3a peak and a broader deflection of the non-P3a subcomponent [11]. The prominence of the positive peak becomes crucial in these conditions because it measure the intrinsic height of the peak to identify the clear peak. Positive peak-to-mean ratio and positive peak Z score contribute to distinguishing a clear peak, even though their importance index is less than 0.05. The presence of negative peaks also helps in the P3a subcomponent identification. As shown in the previous study [11,19], the P300 component usually appears after the negative peak (N200) component.

The P3b subcomponent has five features whose feature importance index is more than 0.20: positive peak amplitude, positive peak-to-mean ratio, negative peak-to-mean ratio, area amplitude, and mean amplitude. P3b has a higher positive peak amplitude standard deviation between subjects than the P3a subcomponent, 3.47 µV at P7 and 5.00 µV at P8. In addition, the P3b subcomponent has a more sloping peak than the P3a subcomponent. Thus, skewness and amplitude standard deviation are necessary for identifying the P3b subcomponent. The P3b subcomponent has more negative skewness than non P3b subcomponent. P3b does not have a stand-out peak, but the amplitude distribution in selected time windows is concentrated on the right side of the distribution. The P3b subcomponent also has a greater amplitude standard deviation in the time window of 300–700 ms.

This study had started collecting data on the quantitative characteristics of the P300 component, but it still has limitations in the amount of data, population characteristics, and the type of stimulus. More data on P300 quantitative characteristics from various populations will contribute to a more comprehensive P300 documentation. In addition, various stimuli will cause different brain activity, which will allow a further investigation on the relationship between P300 and brain cognitive function. For example, the oddball paradigm may be used for researching working memory [22] or the use of other stimulus with an adjustment in the research objective. Should future studies collect additional data consistently, it will prove to be invaluable for the growth of brain processes comprehension and its application.

5   Conclusion

This study analyzed the quantitative features of P3a and P3b by using the feature importance index obtained by decision trees feature selection. Positive peak feature has the highest feature importance index for both subcomponents P3a and P3b. P3a has three more features other than positive peak feature which possesses high feature importance index, however, only one can identify the peak of P3a: prominence of a positive peak. Meanwhile, P3b has four other features which possesses high feature importance index. Therefore, other features of P300 aside from peak amplitude, mean amplitude and area amplitude may be used to analyze P300 quantitative characteristics.

References

1. Bigdely-Shamlo, N., Makeig, S., Robbins, K.A.: Preparing laboratory and real-world EEG data for large-scale analysis: a containerized approach. Front. Neuroinform. **10**, 7 (2016)
2. Bruyns-Haylett, M., et al.: The neurogenesis of p1 and n1: a concurrent EEG/LFP study. Neuroimage **146**, 575–588 (2017)
3. Doane, D.P., Seward, L.E.: Measuring skewness: a forgotten statistic? J. Stat. Educ. **19**(2) (2011)
4. Elshout, J.: Review of brain-computer interfaces based on the P300 evoked potential. Master's thesis (2009)
5. Eriksen, B.A., Eriksen, C.W.: Effects of noise letters upon the identification of a target letter in a nonsearch task. Percept. Psychophys. **16**(1), 143–149 (1974)
6. Johnson, R., Jr.: On the neural generators of the p300 component of the event-related potential. Psychophysiology **30**(1), 90–97 (1993)
7. Kotowski, K., Stapor, K., Leski, J., Kotas, M.: Validation of emotiv EPOC+ for extracting ERP correlates of emotional face processing. Biocybernetics Biomed. Eng. **38**(4), 773–781 (2018)
8. Kreyszig, E., Kreyszing, H., Norminton, E.: Advanced engineering mathematics, 2011. BS Grewal, Higher Engineering Mathematics (2014)
9. Kujala, A., Näätänen, R.: Auditory environment and change detection as indexed by the mismatch negativity (mmn). Detection of change: event-related potential and fMRI findings, pp. 1–22 (2003)
10. Loh, W.Y.: Classification and regression trees. Wiley Interdisc. Rev. Data Mining Knowl. Discov. **1**(1), 14–23 (2011)
11. Luck, S.J.: An Introduction to the Event-Related Potential Technique. MIT Press (2014)
12. Luck, S.J., Kappenman, E.S.: The Oxford handbook of event-related potential components. Oxford University Press (2011)
13. Lukhanina, E., Mel'nik, N., Berezetskaya, N., Karaban', I.: Correlations between indices of p300 EEG potential, cognitive tests, and variational pulsometry in parkinsonian patients. Neurophysiology **40**, 39–47 (2008)
14. Moors, J.J.A.: The meaning of kurtosis: darlington reexamined. Am. Stat. **40**(4), 283–284 (1986)
15. Nieman, D.H., Koelman, J., Linszen, D., Bour, L., Dingemans, P., De Visser, B.O.: Clinical and neuropsychological correlates of the p300 in schizophrenia. Schizophr. Res. **55**(1–2), 105–113 (2002)
16. Patel, S.H., Azzam, P.N.: Characterization of n200 and p300: selected studies of the event-related potential. Int. J. Med. Sci. **2**(4), 147 (2005)
17. Peirce, J.W.: Psychopy-psychophysics software in python. J. Neurosci. Methods **162**(1–2), 8–13 (2007)
18. Phinyomark, A., Scheme, E.: An investigation of temporally inspired time domain features for electromyographic pattern recognition. In: 2018 40th Annual International Conference of the IEEE Engineering in Medicine and Biology Society (EMBC), pp. 5236–5240. IEEE (2018)

19. Polich, J.: Updating p300: an integrative theory of P3a and P3b. Clin. Neurophysiol. **118**(10), 2128–2148 (2007)
20. Pontifex, M.B., Miskovic, V., Laszlo, S.: Evaluating the efficacy of fully automated approaches for the selection of eyeblink ICA components. Psychophysiology **54**(5), 780–791 (2017)
21. Stroop, J.R.: Studies of interference in serial verbal reactions. J. Exp. Psychol. **18**(6), 643 (1935)
22. Themanson, J.R., Rosen, P.J.: Examining the relationships between self-efficacy, task-relevant attentional control, and task performance: Evidence from event-related brain potentials. Br. J. Psychol. **106**(2), 253–271 (2015)
23. Ventouras, E.M., Asvestas, P., Karanasiou, I., Matsopoulos, G.K.: Classification of error-related negativity (ERN) and positivity (pe) potentials using kNN and support vector machines. Comput. Biol. Med. **41**(2), 98–109 (2011)
24. Williams, N.S., McArthur, G.M., Badcock, N.A.: It's all about time: precision and accuracy of emotiv event-marking for ERP research. PeerJ **9**, e10700 (2021)

Transforming Limitations into Advantages: Improving Small Object Detection Accuracy with SC-AttentionIoU Loss Function

Mingle Zhou[1,2], Changle Yi[1,2], Min Li[1,2], Honglin Wan[3],
Gang Li[1,2(✉)], and Delong Han[1,2]

[1] Key Laboratory of Computing Power Network and Information Security,
Ministry of Education, Shandong Computer Science Center
(National Supercomputer Center in Jinan), Qilu University of Technology
(Shandong Academy of Sciences), Jinan, China
lig@qlu.edu.cn
[2] Shandong Provincial Key Laboratory of Computer Networks,
Shandong Fundamental Research Center for Computer Science, Jinan, China
[3] College of Physics and Electronic Science,
Shandong Normal University, Jinan, China

Abstract. Small object detection is widely used in industries, military, autonomous driving and other fields. However, the accuracy of existing detection models in small object detection needs to be improved. This paper proposes the SC-AttentionIoU loss function to stress the issue. Due to the less features of small objects, SC-AttentionIoU introduces attention within the true bounding box, allowing the existing detection models to focus on the critical features of small objects. Besides, considering attention perhaps ignore non-critical features, SC-AttentionIoU proposes an adjustment factor to balance the critical and non-critical feature areas. Using the YOLOv5s model as a baseline, compared with the widely used CIoU, SC-AttentionIoU achieved an average improvement of 1% in mAP@.5 on the SSDD dataset and an average improvement of 1.47% in mAP@.5 on the PCB dataset in this experiment.

Keywords: Object detection · Small objects · Loss function · Attention

1 Introduction

The object detection has been developed significantly with the emergence of a large number of models such as Swin-Transformer [8] and DAMO-YOLO [12]. Small object detection is important in many fields such as industry, military, and autonomous driving. However, small objects themselves have few features while detection scenes often require high accuracy and real-time performance. Therefore how to balance them is a challenge to researchers [4].

There are some models such as Next-ViT [7], PPYOLOE [11] and PP-PicoDet [14], have been proposed with high detection accuracy and lightweight weights. The existing improvement of loss functions has focused on more accurate calculation of the deviation between predicted and ground-truth bounding boxes. There is few work on improving loss functions based on the characteristics of detection targets. Existing loss functions include IoU [15], GIoU [10], DIoU [19], CIoU [19], EIoU [17], and Alpha-IoU [5]. Researchers have explored factors such as intersection over union, center point distance, aspect ratio, and orientation, to make the loss function more accurate. By providing more accurate guidance during training, the detection model can improve its performance.

In this paper, the novel attention-based loss function called SC-AttentionIoU is presented which guides the network to pay more attention to the key regions of the detection target. This loss function identifies the spatial region with significant features of the detection target and incorporates this prior knowledge. Loss function attention determines the weight of the internal ground-truth bounding box. High weight is assigned to the key feature regions of small targets, while low weight is assigned to irrelevant or defective regions. In summary, this paper presents the following innovations:

1. The attention-based loss function SC-AttentionIoU is proposed. It incorporates attention into the loss calculation and guides the model to focus on the key features of small objects to improve detection accuracy.
2. A novel weight generation strategy is proposed in SC-AttentionIoU. Different weight regions are generated within the predicted box based on the distribution characteristics of small objects, which calculates the loss value of the SC-AttentionIoU more accurately.
3. The factor is proposed to address the potential problems caused by introducing attention into the loss function. This factor allows the model to not only focus on key features but also consider other regions during training, resulting in more accurate prediction box locations.

This paper is organized as follows. Section 2 provides a brief review of related methods for loss functions. Section 3 describes the proposed methods. Section 4 presents experimental results, and Sect. 5 provides conclusions.

2   Related Work

2.1   Small Object Detection

Small object detection has always been a challenging problem. The definition of small objects usually refers to objects with a size in the image that is very small, even less than 10 pixels. In this case, small objects are often affected by various factors such as image blur, noise, and scale variation, making it difficult to accurately detect and recognize them. To address the problem of small object detection, Facebook AI proposed a Transformer-based small object detection method called DETR [2], which uses deformable convolution and feature pyramid techniques to effectively solve the problem of object size and scale variation in small object detection. Many researchers have also attempted to improve small object detection by improving network structures and feature extraction methods. Yang et al. combined spatial attention, channel attention, and self attention to improve the detection effect of small objects in intelligent transportation [13]. The model has faster convergence speed and higher accuracy. Zhao et al. proposed a detection model [18] based on feature fusion and anchor point improvement, which reduces the missed detection rate of small targets in complex backgrounds and has considerable detection speed.

2.2   Loss Funcation

The most important in the loss function for object detection is the bounding box regression which is used to calculate the offset from the detection box to the ground-truth box. IoU [15] was first proposed to calculate the intersection-over-union ratio between the detection box and the ground-truth box. GIoU [10] used the minimum enclosing rectangle to calculate the offset between the predicted box and the ground-truth box based on IoU. DIoU [19] replaced the minimum enclosing rectangle with the Euclidean distance between the center points, which more accurately calculates the distance between the predicted box and the ground-truth box. CIoU [19] adds an aspect ratio penalty to DIoU to solve the problem of IoU being insensitive to shape. EIoU [17] further improved the aspect ratio by using the ratio of the lengths of the width and height sides, resulting in more accurate results. SIoU discovered the influence of the direction between the detection box and the ground-truth box.

3   Method

The SC-AttentionIoU proposed in this paper is focused on the coarseness of object detection annotation and the lack of features in small objects. It is well known that in annotated images, the detected object does not always occupy the entire area of the bounding box [9]. There are often other unrelated regions such as other objects or backgrounds within the bounding box, as shown in Fig. 1. These unrelated regions interfere with the model training. Since small objects contain fewer features, it is feasible to improve detection accuracy by focusing on the key features of small objects. To reduce the impact of unrelated regions, this paper introduces attention within the bounding box to assign different regions within the bounding box with different weights. This allows the model to focus more on regions with higher weights during bounding box regression, and reduces the interference of unrelated regions on the model. However, if the model focuses too much on the key features, it may generate predicted boxes that are closer to the distribution of key features but do not match the ground truth boxes. To avoid this issue, this paper further improves AttentionIoU and proposes SC-AttentionIoU.

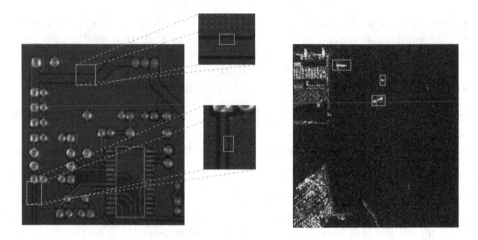

Fig. 1. PCB data set and SSDD data set small object data set picture.

3.1   AttentionIoU

In IoU calculations, the weights of the internal regions of the predicted and detected boxes were averaged. When the overlap area remains constant and the sizes of the detection box and true box are consistent, predicted boxes of varying shapes have an identical intersection over union ratio to the true box. This result is insensitive to shape variations. In the initial training stage, the averaging of the weights of the internal regions of the true box leads to equal attention being given by the model to both irrelevant regions and critical features within the true box, which is disadvantageous for model training.

When the target itself contains a large number of features, it is difficult to select the key features, as the importance of the detection target's features for model training cannot be determined based on prior knowledge. Conversely, small targets with fewer features can be more easily identified with key features, thus allowing the model to focus on critical features and improve detection accuracy. As shown in Fig. 1, it is evident that the key features are located at the center position of the true box.

When applying weights to the key features of detection targets, the attention-based network [3,6] is used to add pixel-level weight annotations to the object within the true box. However, the approaches greatly increases the annotation cost. Therefore, this paper combines the distribution of the key feature regions to adjust the true box and generate a novel weight box. The weight box is located inside the true box and is closer to the distribution of key feature regions. The weight box annotates the critical features of small targets to match high-weight areas. The region between the weight box and the true box is referred to as the low-weight area, primarily comprising irrelevant regions, as depicted in Fig. 2.

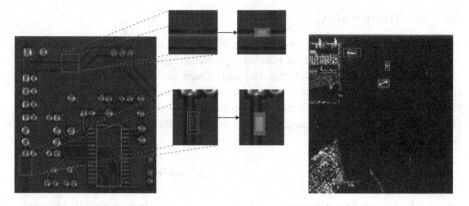

Fig. 2. The red box is the annotation box, and the yellow box is the weight box. (Color figure online)

The formula of AttentionIoU is

$$AttentionIoU = \frac{(\theta \cap \rho) + \varepsilon(\exists \cap \rho)}{(\theta + \rho + \varepsilon^* \exists) - (\theta \cap \varphi)} \tag{1}$$

where ρ denotes a prediction box, θ denotes a real box, $\exists$ denotes a weight box, and ε denotes the weight factor of the weight box that ε in [1,5]

The weight box is located inside the true box, and the intersection between the weight box and the predicted box is contained within the intersection between the true box and the predicted box. When calculating IoU, the intersection of the internal regions of the weight box is increased by a factor $1+\varepsilon$. This increases the weight of the weight box region. The formula to generate the coordinates of the weight box is

$$\exists_{xi} = x_i^{gt} + (-1)^{i+1} * \frac{w^{gt}}{\tau} \tag{2}$$

$$\exists_{yi} = y_i^{gt} + (-1)^{i+1} * \frac{h^{gt}}{\mu} \tag{3}$$

where τ is the generation factor for the x-coordinate of the weight box. μ is the generation factor for the y-coordinate of the weight box. Both generation factors are based on prior knowledge of the detection targets. $\exists_{xi}$ denotes the x-coordinates of the top-left and bottom-right corners of the weight box, $\exists_{yi}$ denotes the y-coordinates of the top-left and bottom-right corners of the weight box, (x_1, y_1) and (x_2, y_2) are the top-left and bottom-right coordinates of the true box, respectively, w^{gt} is the width of the true box, and h^{gt} is the height of the true box. x_i^{gt} denotes the x-coordinate of the true box. The variable y_i^{gt} represents the y-coordinate of the true box, where i lies within the range of [1, 2].

3.2 SC-AttentionIoU

Adding a weight box inside the real box allows the model to focus on the key features of the small object as much as possible. However, this will also make the detection box more closely related to the size and shape of the weight box. If the difference between the weight box and the real box is large, it will affect the detection accuracy. To solve this problem, this paper uses aspect ratio as the weight of AttentionIoU and proposes SC-AttentionIoU. The formula for SC-AttentionIoU is

$$SC - AttentionIoU = 1 - \partial * AttentionIoU + \frac{\rho^2(b, b^{gt})}{c^2} \qquad (4)$$

where ∂ is the weight calculated based on aspect ratio. After using AttentionIoU, the IOU value becomes sensitive to the shape of the predicted box. In exploring the aspect ratio of the predicted box, CIoU and EIoU respectively explored two ways of calculating the aspect ratio penalty term. However, since AttentionIoU itself is sensitive to shape, the previous approach of separating the IOU from the aspect ratio factor is no longer feasible. This paper proposes to use aspect ratio as the weight for IoU value, and combine it with AttentionIoU for calculation. The formula for ∂ is

$$\partial = 1 - \frac{\left(\frac{\rho^2(w, w^{gt}))}{(w^c)^2} + \frac{\rho^2(h, h^{gt}))}{(h^c)^2}\right)}{T} \qquad (5)$$

where ∂ cannot be 0. $T \geq 2$ is a regulation factor for the value range of ∂. In this paper, the value range of ∂ is set to $[(T-2)/T, 1]$. w^{gt} denotes the width of the annotated box, h^{gt} denotes the height of the annotated box. w^c is the width of the bounding rectangle between the real box and the predicted box. h^c is the height of the bounding rectangle between the real box and the predicted box.

SC-AttentionIoU already takes into account the effect of aspect ratio, so no aspect ratio penalty is added in SC-AttentionIoU. In CIoU when IoU is 0, the loss is guided by Euclidean distance instead of the aspect ratio. The proposal in loss function can speed up the convergence of the model training. The comparison of different loss functions and the proposed loss function on the PCB dataset are shown in Fig. 3. The results show that SC-AttentionIoU converges faster and has a lower loss convergence value.

4 Experiment

4.1 Experiment Setting

In this paper, the YOLOv5 was used as the baseline and compared with existing loss functions on two datasets: ship remote sensing dataset [16] released by the Department of Electronic and Information Engineering of the Naval Aeronautical and Astronautical University, and printed circuit board defect dataset (PCB dateset) released by the Intelligent Robot Open Laboratory of Peking University.

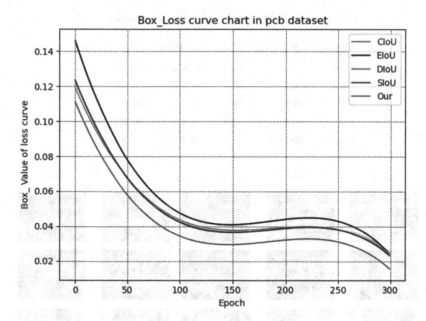

Fig. 3. Boundary box regression Loss function image.

The former dateset consists mostly of small targets. The latter dateset contains 1,386 images with six types of small defect targets.

In training, the image size is adjusted to 640×640, and data augmentation techniques such as mosaic [1], translation, and flipping are used. The optimizer used is SGD, and the learning rate follows a cosine annealing scheme with an initial value of 0.01. Results were obtained after running 300 epochs on a Tesla A100-SXM4 GPU.

4.2 Experimental Indicators

According to the needs of small target detection scenarios, this article selects precision, recall, and mAP as detection indicators. Precision mainly measures the accuracy of the model in identifying targets. The recall rate mainly measures the model's ability to identify all true targets. mAP reflects the comprehensive level of accuracy and recall rate. mAP@0.5 primarily focuses on the average precision of the model at relatively lenient thresholds, while mAP@0.5–0.95 specifically focuses on the average precision of the model at stricter thresholds.

4.3 Comparative and Ablation Experiments

Table 1 shows the experimental results of SC-AttentionIoU and other loss functions on the SSDD [16] dataset. This loss function is designed based on the characteristics of small objects. The SSDD dataset has a simple background,

Table 1. SSDD dataset loss function comparative test

Method	Precision	Recall	mAP@.5	mAP@.5-.95
DIoU	95.4%	90%	94.6%	59.4%
CIoU	96%	90%	94.1%	58.5%
EIoU	96%	90%	94%	59.4%
SIoU	93.6%	90.4%	94.8%	59.3%
Our	**95.5%**	**92%**	**95.3%**	**61.8%**

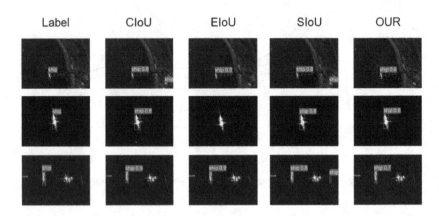

Fig. 4. Comparison of partial detection results with different loss functions.

few categories, and contains a small number of relatively large objects. The experiment results show that the mAP@.5 score of this loss function exceeds DIoU by 0.7%, CIoU by 1.2%, EIoU by 1.3%, and SIoU by 0.5%. It demonstrate that this loss function can maintain effectiveness in the presence of relatively large objects interference. The test results are shown in Fig. 4.

Table 2 shows the experiments of SC-AttentionIoU and other loss functions on the PCB defect dataset in this paper. The PCB defect dataset has more types of defects and various defect shapes compared to SSDD, which verifies the improvement effect of the proposed loss function in complex backgrounds. The experimental results show that the proposed loss function outperforms DIoU by 6.6%, CIoU by 4.5%, EIoU by 6.2%, and SIoU by 3.6% in terms of recall rate. This demonstrates that the proposed loss function can improve the detection ability of small targets in complex backgrounds. In terms of mAP@.5-.95, the proposed loss function is 1.85% higher than the average level of other loss functions. Therefore, the proposed loss function can effectively improve the detection ability of the model on small target datasets. The test results are shown in Fig. 5.

Table 3 shows the experiments of SC-AttentionIoU and other detection models on the PCB defect dataset in this paper. We compare the advanced models such as PPYOLOE, YOLOv6, PP-PicoDet, combined with SC-AttentionIoU

Table 2. PCB dataset loss function comparative test

Method	Precision	Recall	mAP@.5	mAP@.5-.95
DIoU	97.2%	83.4%	92%	49.4%
CIoU	88.1%	85.5%	90%	49.1%
EIoU	96.5%	83.8%	91.4%	49.5%
SIoU	93.1%	86.4%	89.9%	49.4%
Our	**91%**	**90%**	**92.3%**	**51.1%**

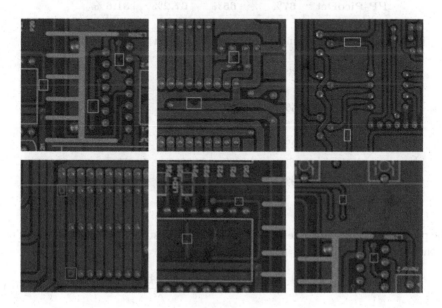

Fig. 5. PCB Dataset Detection Results.

proposed in this paper with the widely used CIoU to verify the robustness of SC-AttentionIoU in different detection models. * indicates the use of the proposed loss function in this paper. The experimental results show that after being combined with SC-AttentionIoU, the YOLOv6 model improves the mAP@.5-.95 score by 1.4%, the PPYOLOE-s model improves by 4.3%, and the PP-PicoDet model improves by 2.6%. Therefore, the proposed loss function has strong robustness on different detection models.

Table 4 shows the experiments of AttentionIoU and other Loss Funcation on the SSDD ship dataset in this paper. We combine the widely used CIoU, EIoU, SIoU, and attentionIoU and replace the IoU in the loss function with attentionIoU to validate the effectiveness and robustness of the proposed attentionIoU idea. * denotes the use of attentionIoU proposed in this paper. Experimental results show that when combined with attentionIoU, CIoU* improves MAP@.5-.95 by 2% compared to CIoU, EIoU* improves MAP@.5-.95 by 2% compared to EIoU, and SIoU* improves MAP@.5-.95 by 2% compared to SIoU. Therefore,

Table 3. Ablation experiments of SC-AttentionIoU on different detection models

Method	Precision	Recall	mAP@.5	mAP@.5-.95
YOLOv6	95.4%	83.6%	86.4%	45.4%
YOLOv6*	**90.7%**	**85.9%**	**86.9%**	**46.8%**
PPYOLOE	92.9%	76.2%	83.5%	37.5%
PPYOLOE*	**91.7%**	**80.2%**	**84.1%**	**41.8%**
PP-PicoDet	67.6%	64%	67.1%	29%
PP-PicoDet*	**67%**	**65%**	**67.2%**	**31.6%**

Table 4. Ablation Experiments of Attention IoU on Different Loss Functions

Method	Precision	Recall	mAP@.5	mAP@.5-.95
CIoU	96%	90%	94.1%	58.5%
CIoU*	**94.5%**	**90.7%**	**94.2%**	**59.8%**
EIoU	96%	90%	94%	59.4%
EIoU*	**93.2%**	**91.6%**	**94.7%**	**60.2%**
SIoU	93.6%	90.4%	94.8%	59.3%
SIoU*	**92.9%**	**91.1%**	**94.8%**	**60.5%**

the proposed attentionIoU demonstrates strong robustness and effectiveness. The formula for CIoU*, EIoU*, and siou* is shown below.

$$\text{CIoU}^* = 1 - AttentionIoU + \frac{\rho^2(\mathbf{b}, \mathbf{b}^{gt})}{c^2} + \alpha v \qquad (6)$$

$$\text{EIoU}^* = 1 - AttentionIoU + \frac{\rho^2(\mathbf{b}, \mathbf{b}^{gt})}{c^2} + \frac{\rho^2(\mathbf{w}, \mathbf{w}^{gt})}{C_w^2} + \frac{\rho^2(\mathbf{h}, \mathbf{h}^{gt})}{C_h^2} \qquad (7)$$

$$\text{SIoU}^* = 1 - AttentionIoU + \frac{\rho^2(\mathbf{b}, \mathbf{b}^{gt})}{c^2} + \frac{\Delta + \Omega}{2} \qquad (8)$$

α is a trade-off parameter, and v is a parameter used to measure the consistency of the aspect ratio. $\frac{\rho^2(\mathbf{w}, \mathbf{w}^{gt})}{C_w^2} + \frac{\rho^2(\mathbf{h}, \mathbf{h}^{gt})}{C_h^2}$ represents the width and height losses of the prediction frame and the real frame. Δ represents distance loss. Ω represents shape loss. The above variables are not discussed due to the limited length of the article.

In summary, SC-AttentionIoU has shown a certain improvement in small object detection datasets. This paper also points out the potential problems caused by changing the weights of the internal regions of the ground truth boxes and proposes corresponding solutions. This proves that exploring the weights of the internal regions of ground truth boxes is beneficial. Our work provides a new direction for exploring loss functions in small object detection and is beneficial for the development of future object detection technologies.

5   Conclusion

This paper proposed the AttentionIoU loss which extends the IoU loss in the bounding box regression to stress small object detection accuracy. Moreover, to address the issue that changing the internal weights of the predicted boxes affects the aspect ratio loss in AttentionIoU, the SC-AttentionIoU loss function is presented. Finally, the proposed loss function is validated on two small object datasets and compared with other existing loss functions, demonstrating its effectiveness in small object detection.

Acknowledgements. This work was supported by Key R&D Program of Shan dong Province, China (2022RZB02012), the Taishan Scholars Program (NO. tscy2 0221110).

References

1. Bochkovskiy, A., Wang, C.Y., Liao, H.Y.M.: YOLOv4: optimal speed and accuracy of object detection (2020)
2. Carion, N., Massa, F., Synnaeve, G., Usunier, N., Kirillov, A., Zagoruyko, S.: End-to-end object detection with transformers (2020)
3. Chu, X., et al.: Twins: revisiting the design of spatial attention in vision transformers (2021)
4. Ge, Z., Liu, S., Wang, F., Li, Z., Sun, J.: YOLOX: exceeding YOLO series in 2021 (2021)
5. He, J., Erfani, S., Ma, X., Bailey, J., Chi, Y., Hua, X.S.: Alpha-IoU: a family of power intersection over union losses for bounding box regression (2022)
6. Hou, Q., Zhou, D., Feng, J.: Coordinate attention for efficient mobile network design (2021)
7. Li, J., et al.: Next-ViT: next generation vision transformer for efficient deployment in realistic industrial scenarios (2022)
8. Liu, Z., et al.: Swin transformer: hierarchical vision transformer using shifted windows (2021)
9. Prathima, G., Lakshmi, A.Y.N., Kumar, C.V., Manikanta, A., Sandeep, B.J.: Defect detection in PCB using image processing. Int. J. Adv. Sci. Technol. **29**(4) (2020)
10. Rezatofighi, H., Tsoi, N., Gwak, J., Sadeghian, A., Reid, I., Savarese, S.: Generalized intersection over union: a metric and a loss for bounding box regression (2019)
11. Xu, S., et al.: PP-YOLOE: an evolved version of YOLO (2022)
12. Xu, X., Jiang, Y., Chen, W., Huang, Y., Zhang, Y., Sun, X.: DAMO-YOLO: a report on real-time object detection design (2023)
13. Yang, L., Zhong, J., Zhang, Y., Bai, S., Li, G., Yang, Y., Zhang, J.: An improving faster-RCNN with multi-attention ResNet for small target detection in intelligent autonomous transport with 6G. IEEE Trans. Intell. Transp. Syst., 1–9 (2022). https://doi.org/10.1109/TITS.2022.3193909
14. Yu, G., et al.: PP-PicoDet: a better real-time object detector on mobile devices (2021)
15. Yu, J., Jiang, Y., Wang, Z., Cao, Z., Huang, T.: UnitBox: an advanced object detection network. In: Proceedings of the 24th ACM International Conference on Multimedia, pp. 516–520 (2016). https://doi.org/10.1145/2964284.2967274

16. Zhang, T., et al.: SAR Ship Detection Dataset (SSDD): official release and comprehensive data analysis. Remote Sensing **13**(18), 3690 (2021). https://doi.org/10.3390/rs13183690
17. Zhang, Y.F., Ren, W., Zhang, Z., Jia, Z., Wang, L., Tan, T.: Focal and efficient IOU loss for accurate bounding box regression (2022)
18. Zhao, W., Kang, Y., Chen, H., Zhao, Z., Zhai, Y., Yang, P.: A target detection algorithm for remote sensing images based on a combination of feature fusion and improved anchor. IEEE Trans. Instrum. Meas. **71**, 1–8 (2022). https://doi.org/10.1109/TIM.2022.3181927
19. Zheng, Z., Wang, P., Liu, W., Li, J., Ye, R., Ren, D.: Distance-IoU loss: faster and better learning for bounding box regression. In: Proceedings of the AAAI Conference on Artificial Intelligence, vol. 34(07), pp. 12993–13000 (2020). https://doi.org/10.1609/aaai.v34i07.6999

Visual-Haptic-Kinesthetic Object Recognition with Multimodal Transformer

Xinyuan Zhou[1], Shiyong Lan[1(✉)], Wenwu Wang[2], Xinyang Li[1], Siyuan Zhou[1], and Hongyu Yang[1]

[1] College of Computer Science, Sichuan University, Chengdu 610065, China
`lanshiyong@scu.edu.cn`
[2] University of Surrey, Guildford GU2 7XH, UK

Abstract. Humans recognize objects by combining multi-sensory information in a coordinated fashion. However, visual-based and haptic-based object recognition remain two separate research directions in robotics. Visual images and haptic time series have different properties, which can be difficult for robots to fuse for object recognition as humans do. In this work, we propose an architecture to fuse visual, haptic and kinesthetic data for object recognition, based on the multimodal Convolutional Recurrent Neural Networks with Transformer. We use Convolutional Neural Networks (CNNs) to learn spatial representation, Recurrent Neural Networks (RNNs) to model temporal relationships, and Transformer's self-attention and cross-attention structures to focus on global and cross-modal information. We propose two fusion methods and conduct experiments on the multimodal AU dataset. The results show that our model offers higher accuracy than the latest multimodal object recognition methods. We conduct an ablation study on the individual components of the inputs to demonstrate the importance of multimodal information in object recognition. The codes will be available at https://github.com/SYLan2019/VHKOR.

Keywords: Object Recognition · Multimodal Deep Learning · Multimodal Fusion · Attention Mechanism

1 Introduction

In the real world, object recognition is fundamental to many of the cognitive and interactive capabilities of robots. With the development of sensor technology, machine vision performs well in terms of object appearance recognition [12] and object detection [29], as does machine haptics in texture recognition [5,19] and material classification [20]. These methods are often relying on only one type of sensory information. However, the information from a single modality may not be

---

This work was funded by 2035 Innovation Pilot Program of Sichuan University, China.

L. Iliadis et al. (Eds.): ICANN 2023, LNCS 14260, pp. 233–245, 2023.
https://doi.org/10.1007/978-3-031-44195-0_20

sufficiently reliable for object recognition. For example, the quality of the visual data can be affected by the quality of the camera, the presence of object occlusion and illumination, while the haptic data can be affected by the type of the haptic sensor used, the area of the sensor placed, and the background noise presented in the environment. Even with the best hardware and ideal scene conditions, there are other issues that can cause significant challenges for object recognition with a single modality, for example, when recognising the glass materials, or objects with the same appearance but different content. To address these limitations, we consider robotic object recognition by using multimodal information.

Recent studies have explored methods for fusing visual and haptic data [3, 6, 8, 9, 13, 18, 21, 24, 27, 28], but several challenges remain. Firstly, data in different modalities have different characteristics and representations. For example, image data is static, with a single image containing a wealth of visual information. Tactile data, on the other hand, is time-series and has a high sampling rate. Consequently, how to extract features from them effectively is still an important issue. Secondly, it is challenging to make accurate connections between data in more than two different modalities. Finally, multimodal fusion methods often require a large amount of computational resources and time, and how to improve computational efficiency with expected recognition accuracy is also a practical challenge. To address these issues, we design feature extraction networks for data in three different modalities: visual, haptic and kinesthetic, where the kinesthetic represents the kinematics information (more details can be seen in Sect. 4.1) of the robot's wrist, fingers and palm. Then, we propose two fusion methods based on Transformer's attention mechanisms and further improve the accuracy and efficiency of robotic object recognition with multimodal information.

In this paper, we design a Convolutional Recurrent Neural Network (CRNN) to extract features for data in three different modalities: visual, tactile and kinesthetic. We use Convolutional Neural Networks (CNNs) to extract the features of each modality, and use a Bi-directional Long Short Term Memory Network (Bi-LSTM) [15] to model the temporal relationships of the tactile sequences. Then, we use Transformer's attention mechanism to fuse unaligned signals, thus further improving the accuracy and efficiency of multimodal fused robotic object recognition. The proposed method has an advantage of using fewer Transformer encoders to achieve better performance than existing transformer based fusion methods. We conducted experiments on the latest AU dataset [4] and compared our method with popular methods in the field of robotic multimodal object recognition.

The main contributions of this paper are summarized as follows:

- We design two new multimodal object recognition methods based on visual, haptic, and kinesthetic signals. A holistic neural network structure is used for multi-input single-output classification with unaligned multimodal data. Ablation experiments are performed to demonstrate the importance of complementary multimodal signals for object recognition.
- We design different feature extraction networks based on the characteristics of each signal, and combine the transformer with CNN and RNN. We compare

the effects of different fusion methods and the attention mechanisms on multimodal classification networks. Our methods offer a higher accuracy than the mainstream methods in the field of robotic multimodal object recognition, and use fewer Transformer modules than the latest Transformer-based multimodal fusion methods, which result in a model of fewer parameters and higher training speed.

2 Related Work

The study of multimodal fusion methods for robotic object recognition, grasping, and other operations is an emerging field. Initially, vision and haptics were used jointly to generate descriptions of object surfaces [1], and later extended to object recognition tasks [2]. Early works explored different ways of representing and encoding visual images and haptic sequences, using Dynamic Time Warping (DTW), K Nearest Neighbor (K-NN), and the Extreme Learning Machine (ELM) for classification [18, 21, 27]. However, more complex, higher-dimensional real-world data cannot be described by fixed equations, and the computational cost of the model designed for each specific task is prohibitive.

Since 2010s, Deep Learning (DL) has made outstanding contributions to various tasks, thanks to its ability in learning abstract and high-level representations of the data with a layered structure of the network. In recent years, CNNs have been widely used for multimodal object recognition tasks. The vast majority of work chooses CNNs or RNNs to extract features for each modal information, and then fuse them in a connected layer [13, 28]. Some of these methods require a large amount of strictly aligned multimodal data to achieve good recognition results [23], while others may use a CNN-only or RNN-only network, which has disadvantages of a single network being difficult to effectively integrate different modal information characteristics [17]. As for CNN-only network, the performance of CNN is affected by the window size, where a small window may lead to loss of information over long distances, while a large window may lead to data sparsity problems and difficulties in training. As for RNN-only network, although LSTM as a typical RNN network is a natural choice for understanding haptic time series signals, it has been shown to be inferior to CNNs for haptic classification [13]. The DL methods do not explicitly translate from one modality to the other, as this is often very challenging.

Recent studies have demonstrated the effectiveness of attention mechanisms for sequential and spatially distributed inputs. Recently proposed Multimodal Transformer architecture (MulT [25]) in the field of Emotion Understanding uses Transformer based models for cross-modal representation of language, audio and visual modalities. Subsequently, some studies have extended attention mechanisms to visual-haptic setting, focusing on the ability to extract fused features of two modalities simultaneously. In [9], the self-attention mechanism is used, while ignoring the modality-to-modality connection. In [8], the integration of the self-attention mechanism and the cross-modal attention mechanism in a single Transformer encoder may result in a limited expressive capability of the model.

The recent work Visuo-Tactile Transformers (VTT) [6] is a variant of Vision Transformer (ViT) [11] where the inputs are sliced into many patches. It breaks the internal structure of each modal information and requires a large amount of training data and computational resources, which limits its practical applications. Although these studies explore the application of attention mechanisms to multimodal fusion, they only consider visual and haptic modalities and neglect other possible modalities. Arguably, little work has been done using the fusion structure of CNN, RNN with Transformer in the field of robotic multimodal object recognition.

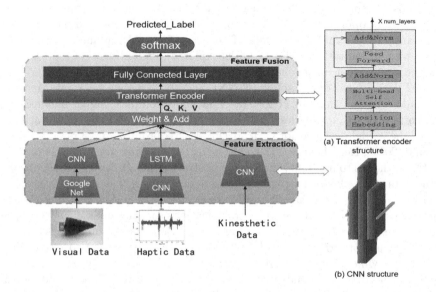

Fig. 1. CRNN-SA network structure

3   Model Architectures

In general, our Multimodal CRNN with Transformer structure includes four modules. (i) Tactile time series module: features are extracted using CNN and Bi-LSTM networks, which preserve the spatial information and temporal relationships of the time series. (ii) Visual image module: due to the small number of images, features are extracted using pre-trained GoogLeNet and CNNs. (iii) Kinesthetic sequence module: features are extracted using CNNs. All the above three modules are the same in the subsequent methods. (iv) Transformer encoder-based fusion module: for this we propose two different structures. The first method (CRNN-SA) fuses the features of all modalities by computing the weights and enhances the fusion by the self-attention mechanism (Fig. 1). The second method (CRNN-CA) obtains the cross-attention of each modality with the fused modality and then concatenates them (Fig. 2). Finally, the features are classified based on the fused features. These two methods explore the effect of different attention mechanisms and fusion methods on the object recognition. Our approach belongs to feature-level fusion among information fusion methods (the remaining two are data-level and decision-level fusion) and has been proven to be more effective than other types of fusion methods in similar tasks [3].

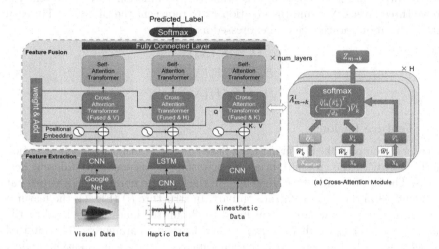

Fig. 2. CRNN-CA network structure

3.1   Feature Extraction

Kinesthetic CNN Model. The kinesthetic data collected in AU dataset [4] consist of readings from the robot's wrist and the infra-red proximity sensor, and the positions of each of the hand 's five fingers. It is formally represented as sequence data of short length and does not include temporal information. Therefore, a three-layer one-dimensional convolutional neural network is used to extract the features of the information. Each layer includes a batch normalization and a rectified linear unit (ReLU) function as the activation function. Finally, a global average pooling layer is added to replace the fully connected layer to retain the global information. The CNN of the same structure is used for each modality, as shown in Fig. 1.

Visual CNN Model. Due to the high cost of data collection in real-world tasks, visual data in practical applications usually consists of a limited number of images. As a result, the parameters of a large network may not be sufficiently optimized with limited data. We adopt the idea of migration learning, using the pre-trained Inception-v3 [22] model on the ImageNet [10] dataset as the basic model, and then add the same convolutional neural network and an average pooling layer as mentioned above to enhance feature extraction.

Haptic CRNN Model. The haptic data in the AU dataset [4] are time series collected by five microphones set on the robot's hands. Firstly, the spatial features of the haptic data are extracted using the same convolutional neural network. Then the temporal features are extracted with a bi-directional LSTM (Bi-LSTM) [14]. Similarly, a global average pooling layer is added at the end.

Let $\{X_k, X_v, X_h\}$ represent the kinesthetic, visual and haptic raw inputs. We use the function F_g to represent Inception-v3, the function F_c to represent the above three-layer CNN, and the function F_r to represent the Bi-LSTM. For each input, the above process can be expressed as follows:

$$D_k = F_c(X_k)$$
$$D_v = F_c(F_g(X_v))$$
$$D_h = F_r(F_c(X_h)) \tag{1}$$

3.2   Feature Fusion

In order to compare the fusion methods based on the Transformer's self-attention mechanism with the cross-attention mechanism, we designed two different networks. The two network structures differ in the fusion of multimodal features but are identical in the feature extraction part. In structure (i) (Fig. 1), the features of each modality are weighted and fused to obtain the kinesthetic-visual-tactile fusion vector D_{merger}, where w_k, w_v, w_h are learnable parameters. The internal connections of the fused features are then reinforced by the self-attention module of the Transformer encoder as

$$D_{merger} = [w_k \cdot D_k^T + w_v \cdot D_v^T + w_h \cdot D_h^T]^T \tag{2}$$

In structure (ii) (Fig. 2), we draw on the idea of MulT for modal fusion using the encoder module of the Transformer. The potential connections between different modalities are represented using cross-modal attention, followed by a sequence model using fused features for prediction. The difference is that we only use three cross-modal attention modules and three self-attention module (six in total), whereas MulT uses six cross-modal attention modules and three self-attention modules (nine in total). This is because we first fused the modal features initially by the way of Eq. (2), and then used the fusion vector D_{merger} as the common modality to perform cross-modal attention with each individual modal feature. This allows the potential representation of each modality for the common modality to be learned and reduces the number of parameters that need to be trained.

Before sending features to the transformer encoder to compute self or cross attention, positional embedding needs to be added to the inputs, otherwise the distance dependencies in the features would be lost. Let the input feature be D, let its max length be L, its dimension be d_k, and the position embedding vector of element $D_{i,j}$ be $PE_{i,j}$, given as

$$PE_{i,j} = \begin{cases} \sin(\frac{i}{10000^{j/d_k}}), & \text{if } j \text{ is even} \\ \cos(\frac{i}{10000^{(j-1)/d_k}}), & \text{if } j \text{ is odd} \end{cases} \tag{3}$$

Then, the final input to the encoder, X, is

$$X = D + PE \tag{4}$$

It is necessary to note that we do not perform word embedding on the input, as here each element of the sequence feature corresponds to its native meaning and has no higher dimensional meaning.

Multi-head Self-attention. We implement the self-attention mechanism by modifying the multi-head self-attention method in the Transformer architecture [26]. The multi-headed self-attention mechanism is used to extract the internal connections of the features of the fused modalities. Its structure is shown in Fig. 1. The Transformer encoder consists of N identical self-attention layers. Each self-attentive layer has two parts: (i) the Multi-Head Self-Attention and Normalisation, (ii) the Feed Forward network. The number of attention heads is H. Taking the n-th self-attention layer and the i-th attention head as an example, and let the output of the previous layer be Z_{n-1}. For $n = 1$, $Z_{n-1} = X$, where X is defined in Eq. (4). In this part, $Q, K, V \in \mathbb{R}^{m \times d_k}$ are the projected queries, keys, and values respectively, and $W_Q, W_K, W_V \in \mathbb{R}^{d_{model} \times d_k}$ are the learned weight matrices for the projection, where d_k is defined in the position embedding and m is the number of samples in the input data.

$$Q_n^i = Z_{n-1} W_Q^i, \quad K_n^i = Z_{n-1} W_K^i, \quad V_n^i = Z_{n-1} W_V^i \tag{5}$$

Then the scaled dot-product attention is computed for each set, where $A_n^i \in \mathbb{R}^{m \times d_k}$ is the output for the set, and $\sqrt{d_k}$ is a scaling factor to stabilize the gradients during training.

$$A_n^i = \text{softmax}\left(\frac{Q_n^i (K_n^i)^T}{\sqrt{d_k}}\right) V_n^i \tag{6}$$

Finally, the attention outputs corresponding to the H sets are concatenated and projected using another learned weight matrix, where $W_n^O \in \mathbb{R}^{Hd_k \times d_{model}}$ is the learned weight matrix for the final projection,

$$A_n = \text{concat}(A_n^1, A_n^2, ..., A_n^H) W_n^O \tag{7}$$

The layer also uses residual connectivity and layer normalization. After a feed-forward network, $Z_n \in \mathbb{R}^{m \times d_{model}}$ is the final output of the n-th multi-head self-attention encoder,

$$Z_n' = \text{LayerNorm}(Z_{n-1} + A_n)$$
$$Z_n = \text{FFN}(Z_n') = \text{LayerNorm}(Z_n' + f_n(Z_n'))$$
$$\text{where} \quad f(Z_n') = W_1 max(0, W_0 Z_n' + b_0) + b_1 \tag{8}$$

Multi-modal Cross-attention. We uses multi-headed cross-modal attention to obtain the potential adaptation of a single modality to a multimodal fused signal, with the structure shown in Fig. 2. For each modality, only one layer of cross-modal attention is used, which helps reduce over-parameterization of the model. The fused features D_{merger} are shown in Eq. (2). For clarity, we follow the deductive process in Multi-Head Self-Attention because the structure within the two is similar. The difference lies in the calculation of the Q, K, V. The multi-modal cross-attention of kinesthetic features $\hat{A}_k^i$ can be described as follows, and other modalities can be generalized in the same way.

$$\hat{Q}_m^i = X_{merger}\hat{W}_Q^i, \quad \hat{K}_k^i = X_k\hat{W}_K^i, \quad \hat{V}_k^i = X_k\hat{W}_V^i$$
$$\hat{A}_{m\to k}^i \sim \hat{Q}_m^i(\hat{K}_k^i)^T\hat{V}_k^i$$
$$\hat{A}_{m\to k} = \text{concat}(\hat{A}_{m\to k}^1, \hat{A}_{m\to k}^2, ..., \hat{A}_{m\to k}^H)W^O$$
$$Z'_{m\to k} = \text{LayerNorm}(X_k + \hat{A}_{m\to k})$$
$$Z_{m\to k} = \text{FFN}(Z'_{m\to k}) \tag{9}$$

The cross-modal attention of each modal feature is then fed into a Transformer encoder with the self-attention module, and the resulting three vectors are concatenated and passed through fully-connected layers for object class prediction.

$$Z_{merger} = [(Z_{m\to k}); (Z_{m\to v}); (Z_{m\to h})] \tag{10}$$

4   Experiments and Results

In this section, we compare the performance of the two methods in this paper with popular multimodal fusion techniques on the latest AU dataset used for multimodal object recognition. Next, we perform a set of ablation studies to evaluate the impact of multiple modal combinations on object recognition. Finally, we analyse the reasons for false object prediction results.

4.1   Data Description and Preprocessing

Publicly available datasets in multimodal object recognition field are still rare and of small size. We compared the PHAC-2 dataset (2015) [7], VHAC dataset (2022) [28], Toprak S' dataset (2018) [24] and the AU dataset (2021) [4]. Finally, we chose the AU dataset because it is open source, has the largest number of objects and contains three types of modal data. This dataset presents multimodal data for 63 objects with some visual and haptic ambiguity, which contains visual, kinesthetic and haptic (audio/vibrations) data. The data for each modal are not collected simultaneously and are therefore unaligned.

Visual Data. The visual data in AU dataset consist of four RGB images, a background image for each object and three images of different faces of the object. Because the amount of visual data in the AU dataset is small, we use image enhancement techniques to make the training samples richer and more diverse and to ensure there is no duplicated images in the training and test sets. The methods are as follows: (i) Adjust the brightness and contrast of the images to 0.7–1.3 times of their original values. (ii) Flip the image horizontally and vertically. (iii) Rotate the image by 180°. The final visual data of each object is expanded from 3 images to 50 images. During training and testing, each image used as input is resized to 256 × 256 pixels, normalized, and the object is segmented using background subtraction.

Kinesthetic Data. The kinesthetic data includes the current readings of the robot's wrist, the positions of the five fingers and the readings of the IR proximity sensor at the center of the palm for each exploration process ("unsupported holding", "enclosure", and "pressure-squeeze"). We did not perform complex preprocessing of the kinesthetic data, but simply concatenated them of each sample in the same dimension.

Haptic Data. The haptic data comprises vibration data collected by the five channels/microphones during each exploration ("feel" and "pressure-poke") with a sampling rate of 400 kHz. Firstly, to compensate for the noise generated by the robot actuators, cooling fans and other moving parts changes during data collection, we subtracted background noise from the raw haptic data. In addition, since the sampling rate of the haptic data is much higher than that of other modal data, we downsampled it to 2500 Hz to save the time and space cost of computing. Finally, we normalized the haptic data as follows,

$$\hat{S} = \frac{S - \bar{S}}{\sigma} \tag{11}$$

where $\bar{S}$ and σ are the mean and standard deviation of the data in each microphone channel, respectively.

4.2 Experimental Settings

Baseline Structures. To evaluate the performance of the two methods in this paper, we use two popular multimodal object recognition methods as baselines: the concatenation method similar to Zhang et al. (MMM) [28] and the method adapted from MulT [25]. For feature extraction, we compare the CNN-only method (CNN-T) and the RNN-only method (RNN-T) with the CRNN method in this paper. In fusion level, we compared data-level fusion (Early), decision-level fusion (Late) with the feature-level fusion of this paper.

Implementation Detail. Adam [16] is used as the optimizer of the model, and the learning rate lr is initially 0.0001. When the evaluation metric no longer improves after 10 epochs, the learning rate is reduced to $lr = lr * 0.5$. The size of batch is 8, and the number of training epochs is 200. To quantitatively evaluate our model, we use the classification accuracy and the weighted F1-score as our evaluation metrics. The experiments were deployed on a host computer configured with an NVIDIA GeForce RTX 3090 (24GB) GPU, and the GPU was used for training throughout.

Loss Function. We use the categorical crossentropy shown below as the loss function,

$$Loss = \sum_{i}^{\text{output size}} y_i \cdot \log \hat{y}_i \tag{12}$$

where y_i is the desired output and $\hat{y}_i$ is the actual output.

4.3   Experimental Results

Table 1 shows the results of our methods against other popular methods on AU dataset, where the red numbers are the best results and the blue numbers are the second best results.

Table 1. Comparison of the multimodal fusion methods on AU dataset.

Models	Feature Extraction	Fusion	Accuracy	F1_score	Parameters
MMM [28]	CNN+RNN	concatenation	0.8571	0.8317	1,060,482
MulT [25]	CNN+RNN	Transformer	0.8286	0.8026	1,110,842
CNN-T	CNN	Transformer	0.8632	0.8317	848,082
RNN-T	RNN	Transformer	0.8234	0.8101	715,474
Early	CNN	concatenation	0.7222	0.6866	273,855
Late	CNN+RNN	decision fusion	0.8535	0.8212	1,096,703
CRNN-SA(ours)	CNN+RNN	Transformer	0.9127	0.9061	1,070,128
CRNN-CA(ours)	CNN+RNN	Transformer	0.8746	0.8505	1,105,190

The results show that our method CRNN-SA has the best performance, followed by our method CRNN-CA. Both have less number of parameters than the MulT method. Based on the analysis of the results, we can draw the observations that (i) The complex modal fusion method does not improve the accuracy of classification. (ii) The higher the degree of retaining the original features of each modality, the more improvements it will lead to in terms of classification results. (iii) Enhancing the attention within the fused features can help improve classification performance.

Ablation Study. To further investigate the impact of individual modal data in a multimodal object recognition task, we conducted ablation studies on AU dataset and the results are shown in Table 2. Firstly, we compare the classification accuracy on our method (CRNN-SA) using only unimodal data (visual, haptic or kinesthetic) as input. Then, we compared the classification accuracy on our method (CRNN-SA) using a combination of two modal data as input.

Table 2. Comparison of the visual-haptic-kinesthetic inputs on AU dataset.

Inputs data	Accuracy	F1_score
visual	0.6195	0.6013
haptic	0.7635	0.7495
kinesthetic	0.5970	0.5903
visual+haptic	0.8889	0.8630
visual+kinesthetic	0.6540	0.6255
haptic+kinesthetic	0.8071	0.7781
visual+haptic+kinesthetic	0.9127	0.9061

Table 2 shows the comparison results on AU dataset using our method and different combinations of inputs, where the red numbers are the best results. Because this dataset contains objects that are visually or haptically ambiguous, the classification results for unimodal data are much lower than multimodal, which is consistent with our experience in life. And the results demonstrate the importance of the haptic data.

5   Conclusion

In this paper, we have presented two multimodal object recognition methods (CRNN-SA, CRNN-CA), where we have made improvements for existing methods in both the feature extraction and feature fusion steps. After extracting each modal feature using the CRNN method, we fuse the features with Transformer's self-attention mechanism and fully connected layers in CRNN-SA, and with the multi-modal cross-attention mechanism adapted from MulT in CRNN-CA. Both methods are applicable to unaligned multimodal data. Among them, the CRNN-SA method outperforms the most popular CNN-only with concatenation method in terms of classification accuracy, and the CRNN-CA method proposes a new cross-modal attention mechanism and uses fewer encoder modules than the MulT method. Future work aims to create a multimodal object recognition dataset, and explore the integration of deep learning with reinforcement learning, with a view to deploying the results in real-world applications.

References

1. Allen, P.K.: Surface descriptions from vision and touch. In: IEEE International Conference on Robotics & Automation, pp. 394–397 (1984)
2. Allen, P.K.: Integrating Vision and Touch for Object Recognition Tasks, pp. 407–440. Ablex Publishing Corp., USA (1995)
3. Bednarek, M., Kicki, P., Walas, K.: On robustness of multi-modal fusion-robotics perspective. Electronics 9, 1152 (2020)
4. Bonner, L.E.R., Buhl, D.D., Kristensen, K., Navarro-Guerrero, N.: Au dataset for visuo-haptic object recognition for robots (2021)
5. Cao, G., Zhou, Y., Bollegala, D., Luo, S.: Spatio-temporal attention model for tactile texture recognition. In: 2020 IEEE/RSJ International Conference on Intelligent Robots and Systems (IROS), pp. 9896–9902 (2020)
6. Chen, Y., Sipos, A., Van der Merwe, M., Fazeli, N.: Visuo-tactile transformers for manipulation. In: 2022 Conference on Robot Learning (CoRL). Proceedings of Machine Learning Research, vol. 205, pp. 2026–2040 (2022)
7. Chu, V., et al.: Robotic learning of haptic adjectives through physical interaction. Robot. Auton. Syst. 63, 279–292 (2015)
8. Cui, S., Wei, J., Li, X., Wang, R., Wang, S.: Generalized visual-tactile transformer network for slip detection. IFAC-PapersOnLine 53(2), 9529–9534 (2020)
9. Cui, S., Wang, R., Wei, J., Hu, J., Wang, S.: Self-attention based visual-tactile fusion learning for predicting grasp outcomes. IEEE Robot. Autom. Lett. 5(4), 5827–5834 (2020)
10. Deng, J., Dong, W., Socher, R., Li, L.J., Li, K., Fei-Fei, L.: Imagenet: a large-scale hierarchical image database. In: 2009 IEEE Conference on Computer Vision and Pattern Recognition, pp. 248–255 (2009)
11. Dosovitskiy, A., et al.: An image is worth 16x16 words: transformers for image recognition at scale (2020)
12. Fanello, S.R., Ciliberto, C., Noceti, N., Metta, G., Odone, F.: Visual recognition for humanoid robots. Robot. Auton. Syst. 91, 151–168 (2017)
13. Gao, Y., Hendricks, L.A., Kuchenbecker, K.J., Darrell, T.: Deep learning for tactile understanding from visual and haptic data (2015)
14. Graves, A., Schmidhuber, J.: Framewise phoneme classification with bidirectional LSTM and other neural network architectures. Neural Networks Official J. Int. Neural Network Soc. 18, 602–10 (2005)
15. Hochreiter, S., Schmidhuber, J.: Long short-term memory. Neural Comput. 9(8), 1735–1780 (1997)
16. Kingma, D., Ba, J.: Adam: a method for stochastic optimization. In: International Conference on Learning Representations, December 2014
17. Le, M., Rathour, V., Truong, Q., Mai, Q., Brijesh, P., Le, N.: Multi-module recurrent convolutional neural network with transformer encoder for ECG arrhythmia classification, pp. 1–5 (2021)
18. Liu, H., Yu, Y., Sun, F., Gu, J.: Visual-tactile fusion for object recognition. IEEE Trans. Autom. Sci. Eng. 14(2), 996–1008 (2017)
19. Luo, S., Yuan, W., Adelson, E., Cohn, A.G., Fuentes, R.: Vitac: feature sharing between vision and tactile sensing for cloth texture recognition. In: 2018 IEEE International Conference on Robotics and Automation (ICRA), pp. 2722–2727 (2018)
20. Strese, M., Brudermueller, L., Kirsch, J., Steinbach, E.: Haptic material analysis and classification inspired by human exploratory procedures. IEEE Trans. Haptics 13(2), 404–424 (2020)

21. Sun, F., Liu, C., Huang, W., Zhang, J.: Object classification and grasp planning using visual and tactile sensing. IEEE Trans. Syst. Man Cybern. Syst. **46**(7), 969–979 (2016)
22. Szegedy, C., Vanhoucke, V., Ioffe, S., Shlens, J., Wojna, Z.: Rethinking the inception architecture for computer vision. In: 2016 IEEE Conference on Computer Vision and Pattern Recognition (CVPR), pp. 2818–2826. Los Alamitos, CA, USA, June 2016
23. Tatiya, G., Sinapov, J.: Deep multi-sensory object category recognition using interactive behavioral exploration. In: 2019 International Conference on Robotics and Automation (ICRA), pp. 7872–7878 (2019)
24. Toprak, S., Navarro-Guerrero, N., Wermter, S.: Evaluating integration strategies for visuo-haptic object recognition. Cognitive Comput. **10**, 408–425 (2018)
25. Tsai, Y.H., Bai, S., Liang, P., Kolter, J., Morency, L.P., Salakhutdinov, R.: Multimodal transformer for unaligned multimodal language sequences, vol. 2019, pp. 6558–6569, July 2019
26. Vaswani, A., et al.: Attention is all you need. In: Proceedings of the 31st International Conference on Neural Information Processing Systems, NIPS 2017, pp. 6000–6010. Curran Associates Inc., Red Hook (2017)
27. Yang, J., Liu, H., Sun, F., Gao, M.: Object recognition using tactile and image information. In: 2015 IEEE International Conference on Robotics and Biomimetics (ROBIO), pp. 1746–1751 (2015)
28. Zhang, P., Zhou, M., Shan, D., Chen, Z., Wang, X.: Object description using visual and tactile data. IEEE Access **10**, 54525–54536 (2022)
29. Zhao, Z.Q., Zheng, P., Xu, S.T., Wu, X.: Object detection with deep learning: a review. IEEE Trans. Neural Networks Learn. Syst. **30**(11), 3212–3232 (2019)

X-shape Feature Expansion Network for Salient Object Detection in Optical Remote Sensing Images

Lisu Huang[1,2], Minghui Sun[1,2]([✉]), Yanhua Liang[1,2], and Guihe Qin[1,2]

[1] College of Computer Science and Technology, Jilin University, Changchun, China
smh@jlu.edu.cn
[2] Key Laboratory of Symbolic Computation and Knowledge Engineering of Ministry of Education, Jilin University, Changchun, China

Abstract. Salient object detection in optical remote sensing images (RSI-SOD) is a valuable and challenging task. Some factors in RSI, such as the extreme complexity of scale and topological structure as well as the uncertainty of location of the salient object, significantly reduce the accuracy and completeness of salient object prediction. To address these issues, we propose a novel X-shape Feature Expansion Network (XFNet). Specifically, XFNet consists of a traditional encoder-decoder network, complemented by a new component called the X-shape Feature Expansion Module (XFEM). In XFEM, from the perspective of receptive field and multi-scale information, we utilize two branches to enhance the model's receptive field and multi-scale information. Moreover, we design a core component in XFEM to facilitate the fusion of feature of each branch. Extensive experiments conducted on two commonly used datasets demonstrate that our approach outperforms 11 state-of-the-art methods, including NSI-SOD and RSI-SOD methods.

Keywords: Salient object detection · Optical remote sensing images · Feature expansion · Multiscale

1 Introduction

Salient object detection (SOD) simulates the human visual attention mechanism, with the main purpose of extracting the most prominent and attention-grabbing regions in an image. It has been widely used in many computer vision tasks, such as object segmentation [1] and quality assessment [2] etc. Unlike SOD in natural scene images (NSI-SOD), salient object detection in optical remote sensing images (RSI-SOD) aims to highlight objects in optical remote sensing images that attract human attention, such as airplanes, buildings, rivers, lakes, and so

Supported by National Natural Science Foundation of China (61872164), Program of Science and Technology Development Plan of Jilin Province of China (20220201147GX) and Fundamental Research Funds for the Central Universities (2022-JCXK-02).

L. Iliadis et al. (Eds.): ICANN 2023, LNCS 14260, pp. 246–258, 2023.
https://doi.org/10.1007/978-3-031-44195-0_21

on. RSI-SOD has high practical value, including change detection (CD) for high-resolution remote-sensing images [3], ship detection [4], and oil tank detection [5], etc.

With the development of convolutional neural networks, the research of NSI-SOD has made significant progress, and numerous outstanding works have emerged, including MINet [6], EGNet [7], BASNet [8], etc. In recent years, RSI-SOD has also received widespread attention. RSIs are different from NSIs in two main aspects: first, RSIs are acquired from a high-altitude view through remote sensing satellites, resulting in uncertainty in object position; Second, in optical RSIs, the scale and structure of salient objects are extremely complex and varied. Due to the issues mentioned above, NSI-SOD methods are difficult to directly apply to RSI-SOD.

In recent years, some excellent RSI-SOD methods have also been proposed. Specifically, LVnet [9] proposes a dual-stream pyramid module and handles the problem of object scale diversity by fusing multi-scale inputs in a nested linking way. DAFnet [11] establishes a Global Context-aware Attention (GCA) mechanism to address the problem of incomplete salient object prediction caused by limited convolutional receptive fields. In [16], the authors deploy three encoders with different resolutions to better extract multi-scale information, thereby dealing with the complex scales and shapes of salient objects in RSI. These methods solve the complexity of the scale and shape of salient objects in RSI from the perspective of multi-scale information extraction and receptive field enhancement.

Based on the above observations, we design a novel X-shape Feature Expansion Module (XFEM) to parallelly extract multiscale information and enhance the model's receptive field. Specifically, our XFEM consists of three parts, including left and right branches and a core component. The left branch extracts multiscale information through convolution combined with downsampling. The right branch deploys dilated convolutions with different dilation rates to address the limited receptive field of ordinary convolutions. The core component is designed to facilitate feature aggregation between the left and right branches. In addition, we implement XFEMs of different scales and fuse them into an encoder-decoder network to form a simple but effective X-shape Feature Expansion Network (XFNet).

Our main contributions are summarized as follows:

- We propose an end-to-end X-shape Feature Expansion Network with the aim of complex object scales, shapes, and uncertain positions in RSI.
- We propose an X-shape Feature Expansion Module that parallelizes multiscale feature extraction and receptive field enhancement, and achieves better feature aggregation between the two branches through a core component.
- We conduct comprehensive experiments on two RSI-SOD datasets. The experimental results show that XFNet outperforms 11 state-of-the-art methods and demonstrate the effectiveness of XFEM on various evaluation metrics.

2 Related Work

2.1 Salient Object Detection for NSIs

During the early stages, traditional salient object detection methods are based on handcrafted features. In [13], jiang et al. propose a method based on multi-scale local region contrast, which calculates saliency values across multiple segmentation for robustness purposes and combines these saliency values to get the final saliency map. In [14], liu et al. proposed the saliency tree framework based on saliency region merging and saliency node selection.

With the development of convolutional neural networks, the research of NSI-SOD has made significant progress. For instance, in [15], Zhang et al. fuse features of different scales to extract multi-scale information. While Pang et al [6]. integrate features of two adjacent layers and current layers to extract the relation information between current layers and adjacent layers while extracting multi-scale information. Qin et al. [8]combine SSIM loss, IoU loss, and BCE loss as their boundary-aware loss function to achieve better salient object detection.

2.2 Salient Object Detection for RSIs

Although many efforts have been devoted to salient object detection in nature scene images, the research on optical RSIs saliency models is insufficient. There are only a small number of prior works on salient object detectionin optical RSIs. In [9], Li et al. design a dual-stream pyramid structure called L-shape module to extract complementary information hierarchically and combine encoder detail features with decoder semantic features through nested connections to generate high-quality salient maps. While in [11], Zhang et al. construct an attention-flow module to propagate shallow features. In addition, they propose a cascaded attention pyramid structure to solve the scale variation in RSI. PDFNet [10] uses dense connections to integrate high-level and low-level information, enabling cross-information and multi-resolution characteristics to be fully utilized. Wang et al. [16]. utilize three encoders with different input scales to extract multi-scale features and introduce boundary constraints to sharpen the boundaries of salient maps.

Although these RSI-SOD methods have made impressive progress, their performance is unsatisfactory when faced with difficult samples in Fig. 3. Therefore, we design XFNet from the perspective of multiscale information and receptive field to enhance the features. This method enhances features through the left and right branches in XFEM, for the purpose of the extreme complexity of scale changes and salient objects in RSI.

3 Approach

3.1 Overall

The architecture of the proposed XFNet is shown in Fig. 1, which is a typical encoder-decoder structure, consisting of three essential components: backbone,

XFEM and decoder. To be specific, VGG-16 is used as the backbone network to extract a hierarchical set of feature maps. Note that the last pooling and fully connected layes of VGG-16 are removed. The feature maps are sent to XFEM for further processing. In XFEM, the input features are separately sent to the left and right branches for convolution, and information fusion is facilitated through the core component. Finally, the decoder containing five blocks infers the salient object based on the features generated by XFEM in a progressive resolution restoration manner. Following [12], we conduct the deep supervision strategy that attaches BCE, IoU, and F-measure losses to each decoder block during the network training.

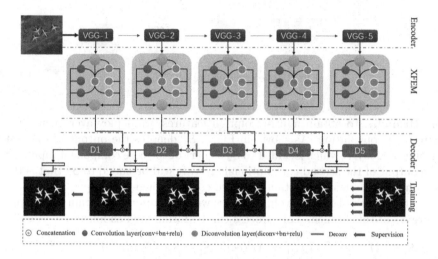

Fig. 1. The architecture of XFNet.

3.2   X-shape Feature Expansion Module

We illustrate the structure of XFEM in Fig. 2, which consists of regular convolution, dilated convolution, and downsampling. The module is divided into three parts: left and right feature expansion branches, and a feature aggregation core in the middle. The left branch incorporates downsampling during convolution to enrich multi-scale information, while the right branch employs dilated convolutions with different dilation rates and removes downsampling to further increase the receptive field. Additionally, the middle layer outputs of the left and right branches is fused with the processed original features as inputs to the core component. Then, the features are re-entered into the left and right branches, achieving the feature aggregation between the two branches. Note that the number of channels of input features will be reduced to one-fourth by the input layer.

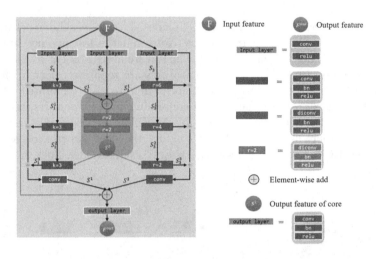

Fig. 2. The architecture of XFEM.

Left Branch. To obtain multi-resolution features, we deploy average pooling before each convolution. As shown in Fig. 2, S_1^1 denotes the output of the first convolutional layer, which is added to S_2 as part of the core component input. S_1^2 is the output of the second convolutional layer. It will be added to S^2 that is the core component output to obtain the third convolutional layer input. Finally, we add each output of three convolution layes with S_1, aiming to obtain the output feature S^1 of this branch. This process can be formulated as follows:

$$S_1^1 = AP(conv(S_1)); S_1^2 = AP(conv(S_1^1)); S_1^3 = AP(conv(S_1^2 \oplus S^2)) \quad (1)$$

$$S^1 = conv(S_1 \oplus S_1^1 \oplus S_1^2 \oplus S_1^3) \quad (2)$$

where AP means average pooling, $conv$ denote the 3×3 convolution layer, S^1 means the output of left branch, S_1^1, S_1^2, and S_1^3 represent the output features of the three convolutional layers respectively, $\oplus$ denotes element-wise add.

Right Branch. The processing flow of the right branch is similar to the left branch, except for the removal of downsampling and the utilization of dilated convolutions with different dilation rates. The specific formulaic process is as follows:

$$S_3^1 = DiConv(S_3); S_3^2 = DiConv(S_3^1); S_3^3 = DiConv(S_3^2 \oplus US(S^2)) \quad (3)$$

$$S^3 = conv(S_3 \oplus S_3^1 \oplus S_3^2 \oplus S_3^3) \quad (4)$$

where S_3^1, S_3^2 and S_3^3 mean the outputs of the dilated convolutional layers, S^3 denotes the output of the right branch, $DiConv$ denotes the dilated convolution (kernel size=3 dilation rates=2,4,6), and US means upsampling.

Core Component. The core component consists of two dilated convolutional layers with a dilation rate of 2. To ensure dimension alignment with the left branch, downsampling is deployed before the convolutional operation, which is formalized as follows:

$$S^2 = DiConv(AP(DiConv(AP(S_1^1 \oplus S_2 \oplus S_3^1)))) \tag{5}$$

where S^2 denotes the output of core component.

Finally, the features of the left and right branches will be fused with the original features and the channel count will be restored to that of the original features using the output layer, resulting in the output features. This can be formulated as:

$$F^{out} = conv_{out}(F \oplus S^1 \oplus S^3) \tag{6}$$

where F^{out} denotes the output feature and $conv_{out}$ means the output layer (kernel size = 3, stride = 1).

3.3 Hybrid Loss

We employ a hybrid loss function for our model, which consists of cross-entropy loss, F-value loss, and IoU loss. The binary cross-entropy (BCE) loss ensures local optimality and addresses the issue of incorrect predictions. Meanwhile, the F-value loss balances precision and recall, and the IoU loss guarantees the completeness of the predicted foreground regions and resolves the issue of insufficient predictions. The overall loss function can be formulated as follows:

$$Loss = \sum_{l=1}^{5} loss_{bce}(S, G_s) + loss_f(S, G_s) + loss_{IoU}(S, G_s) \tag{7}$$

where $loss_{bce}$, $loss_f$ and $loss_{IoU}$ denote BCE loss, F-measure loss and IoU loss, respectively. S and G_s denote the predicted image and corresponding ground truth, respectively.

4 Experiment

4.1 Experimental Protocol

Implementation Details. We train and evaluate our method and compare it to other methods on two publicly available RSI-SOD datasets, including EORSSD [11] and ORSSD [9]. Their training sets are augmented by flipping and rotating to reach 11,200 and 4,800 samples, respectively. We employ the proposed XFNet model and train it on Pytorch platform using an NVIDIA RTX 3090 GPU. During training, input images are resized to 256×256. The backbone of XFNet and other newly added convolutional layers are initialized with a pre-trained VGG-16 model and normal distribution, respectively. We conduct Adam optimizer for network optimization with a batch size of 8 and an initial learning rate of 1e−4, which is divided by 10 after 30 epochs.

Evaluation Metrics. We use four commonly used evaluation metrics to evaluate the performance of the proposed model: MAE denotes mean absolute error. F-measure [18] provides a combined evaluation of precision and recall. We set β^2 to 0.3 to emphasize the precision over recall and adopts its maximum, mean, and adaptive forms (i.e., F_β^{max}, F_β^{mean}, F_β^{adp}). E-measure [19] is an improved version of the F-measure and combines precision, recall, and the region similarity between the segmentation result and the GT. We report its maximum, mean and adaptive values (i.e., E_ξ^{max}, E_ξ^{mean}, E_ξ^{adp}). S-measure [17] ($S_\alpha, \alpha = 0.5$) is responsible for evaluating the structural similarity at object-aware and region-aware levels.

4.2   Comparison with State-of-the-Art

In order to demonstrate the effectiveness of the proposed method, we compare our network with 11 other SOTA methods, including six NSI-SOD methods (i.e., EGNet [7], MINet [6], U2Net [21], SUCA [22], PA-KRN [23]) and five excellent RSI-SOD methods (i.e., LVNet [9], DAFNet [11], EMFINet [16], MCCNet [12], AGNet [24]). All NSI-SOD methods are retrained and evaluated on the EORSSD and ORSSD datasets using the code open-sourced by the authors. For the RSI-SOD methods, we re-evaluate the saliency maps provided by the authors.

Quantitative Comparison. In Table 1, we report the quantitative comparison results of our method and all comparison methods in terms of MAE, F_β^{max}, F_β^{mean}, F_β^{adp}, E_ξ^{max}, E_ξ^{mean}, E_ξ^{adp} and S_α on EORSSD and ORSSD. The first evaluation metric is better when lower, while others are the opposite. Overall, our XFNet shows quite promising performance. Specifically, on the EORSSD dataset, XFNet has significant advantages over the second-ranked method in two metrics, namely F_β^{mean} and S_α, e.g., F_β^{mean}: 0.8718 (ours) vs. 0.8614 (MCCNet), and S_α: 0.9353 (ours) vs. 0.9290 (MCCNet). Although XFNet is noticeably weaker than DAFNet in the MAE metric, our method has significant advantages over DAFNet in the other metrics. While on the ORSSD dataset, XFNet ranks first in three metrics, namely F_β^{mean}, E_ξ^{mean}, S_α, and performs much better than DAFNet, e.g., S_α: 0.9472 (ours) vs. 0.9191 (DAFNet) and E_ξ^{mean}: 0.9766 (ours) vs. 0.9539 (DAFNet). Although our method falling slightly short on two metrics compare to MCCNet on the EORSSD dataset, our model also has a impressive advantage in terms of parameter count, e.g., 41.33M (ours) vs. 67.65M (MCCNet) and 41.33M (ours) vs. 107.26M (EMFINet). In addition, from Table 1, it can be seen that our method and most RSI-SOD methods are far ahead of all NSI methods, which proves the necessity of designing models for RSI-SOD.

Qualitative Comparison. In Fig. 3, we present several visual examples of optical RSI, including airplanes, rivers, islands, buildings, vehicles, and roads. The saliency maps in the third row illustrate the importance of incorporating multi-scale information. Our XFNet successfully detects all three vehicles, while

Table 1. Quantitative evaluation of EORSSD dataset and ORSSD dataset. The best three results are highlighted in red, blue and green.

method	EORSSD [11]								ORSSD [9]							
	MAE	F_β^{max}	F_β^{mean}	F_β^{adp}	E_ξ^{max}	E_ξ^{mean}	E_ξ^{adp}	S_α	MAE	F_β^{max}	F_β^{mean}	F_β^{adp}	E_ξ^{max}	E_ξ^{mean}	E_ξ^{adp}	S_α
R3Net [20]	.0171	.7488	.6302	.4176	.9483	.8294	.6460	.8184	.0399	.7556	.7383	.7369	.8923	.8681	.8897	.8141
EGNet [7]	.0110	.7885	.6967	.5398	.9590	.8775	.7599	.8601	.0216	.8342	.7500	.6498	.9781	.9013	.8289	.8721
MINet [6]	.0093	.8349	.8174	.7789	.9459	.9346	.9256	.9040	.0144	.8799	.8574	.8521	.9565	.9454	.9423	.9040
U2Net [21]	.0076	.8754	.8329	.7242	.9665	.9373	.8989	.9199	.0166	.8798	.8492	.8076	.9539	.9387	.9326	.9162
SUCA [22]	.0097	.8289	.7949	.7260	.9520	.9277	.9082	.8988	.0145	.8484	.8237	.7768	.9584	.9400	.9194	.8989
PA-KRN [23]	.0104	.8639	.8358	.7993	.9676	.9536	.9416	.9192	.0139	.8890	.8727	.8548	.9680	.9620	.9579	.9239
LVNet [9]	.0146	.7794	.7328	.6284	.9254	.8801	.8445	.8630	.0207	.8263	.7995	.7506	.9456	.9259	.9195	.8815
DAFNet [11]	.0060	.8614	.7845	.6427	.9861	.9291	.8446	.9166	.0113	.8928	.8511	.7876	.9771	.9539	.9360	.9191
EMFINet [16]	.0084	.8720	.8486	.7984	.9711	.9604	.9501	.9290	.0109	.9002	.8856	.8617	.9737	.9671	.9663	.9366
MCCNet [12]	.0066	.8904	.8604	.8137	.9755	.9685	.9538	.9327	.0087	.9155	.9054	.8957	.9800	.9758	.9735	.9437
AGNet* [24]	.0067	.8758	.8516	.8021	.9752	.9656	.9540	.9287	.0091	.9098	.8956	.8723	.9811	.9728	.9729	.9389
Ours	.0066	.8890	.8718	.8318	.9728	.9681	.9596	.9353	.0093	.9183	.9125	.8958	.9814	.9766	.9729	.9472

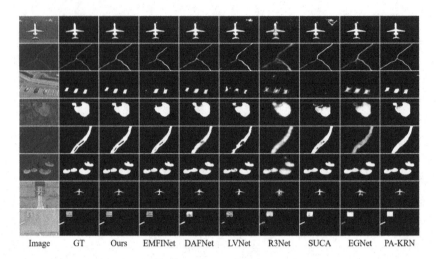

Image   GT   Ours   EMFINet   DAFNet   LVNet   R3Net   SUCA   EGNet   PA-KRN

Fig. 3. Visual comparison of different methods.

EMFINet fails to detect salient objects and LVNet, R3Net, and others have issues with incomplete and insufficient detection. The saliency maps in the second row demonstrate the significance of expanding the model's receptive field. With a larger receptive field, the model can observe a larger area, which greatly improves the detection accuracy of salient targets with larger spans. However, both EMFINet and LVNet have incomplete detection. Encoding local information can enhance the model's ability to perceive details, as demonstrated in the saliency maps in the fourth, fifth, and sixth rows, where XFNet outperforms the compared methods in detecting details. Specifically, in the saliency maps in the fifth and sixth rows, the black crannies are either completely undetected or detected with issues such as incomplete and blurry salient objects, except for XFNet, which is able to detect them accurately. The saliency map in the first row illustrates the importance of expanding the carried feature information to enhance the model's anti-interference ability, where only XFNet is not affected by the white car in the top right corner of the airplane's head.

4.3   Ablation Studies

In this section, we conducted comprehensive experiments to fully evaluate the effectiveness of XFEM on the EORSSD and ORSSD datasets. We trained a total of 6 variants by combining the two branches and core component of XFEM. The structures of each variant are shown in Fig. 4. For each XFEM variant, we rigorously retrain the variant with the same training settings as in Sect. 4.2. The quantitative and qualitative comparisons of the experiments are presented in Table 2 and Fig. 5, respectively.

According to the comparison results between the second, fourth, and fifth variants in Table 2 and the baseline, it can be seen that the left branch, core

Table 2. Quantitative evaluation of ablation studies on the EORSSD dataset and ORSSD dataset. Baseline is the basic encoder-decoder network. LB, CORE and RB denote Left Branch, Core Component and Right branch respectively. The best result is highlighted in red

No.	Baseline	LB	CORE	RB	EORSSD			ORSSD		
					F_β^{max}	E_ξ^{max}	S_α	F_β^{max}	E_ξ^{max}	S_α
1	√				.8601	.9571	.9168	.8803	.9526	.9239
2	√	√			.8746	.9609	.9289	.9109	.9722	.9379
3	√	√	√		.8807	.9715	.9341	.9062	.9758	.9373
4	√		√		.8679	.9587	.9211	.8933	.9648	.9295
5	√			√	.8747	.9610	.9279	.9119	.9734	.9379
6	√		√	√	.8812	.9689	.9302	.9116	.9750	.9388
7	√	√		√	.8869	.9735	.9342	.9131	.9754	.9391
8	√	√	√	√	.8890	.9741	.9353	.9183	.9814	.9472

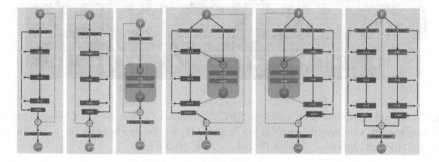

Fig. 4. Structures of six XFEM variants.

component, and right branch have all improved the performance of the model in terms of the F_β^{max}, E_ξ^{max}, and S_α metrics. For example, the left branch shows a 1.3% improvement in S_α. As shown in Fig. 5, the comparison between columns e and c in the first row indicates that variant 2 with the left branch added can detect a more complete fan-shaped region. The comparison between columns h and c also suggests that improving the receptive field has a positive effect on detecting large salient objects. Based on Table 2, it can be observed from the comparison results of variants 3, 6, 7, and 8 that abandoning any part of the XFEM would have a negative influence on its performance. This is also confirmed by the comparison of the saliency maps in the second row of Fig. 5 between columns f, h, i and column j.

Based on the comparison results between variant 2 and variant 5 with variant 7 in Table 2, it can be inferred that parallelizing multi-scale feature extraction and enhancing receptive fields can further improve the model's performance. After combining the left and right branches, variant 7 shows significant improvement in all metrics compared to other variants. For instance, on the EORSSD dataset, variant 7 achieves a 3.1% improvement in F_β^{max} compared to the baseline. Receptive field and multi-scale information enhancement are complementary, rather than isolated. In Fig. 5, the comparison of column E and column h with column g also shows that enhancing multiscale features and receptive fields simultaneously improves the model's sensitivity to scale changes and robustness to salient objects of different shapes. From the comparison results between variant 7 and the complete XFEM in Table 2, it can be observed that the core component can facilitate the aggregation of left and right branch features, thereby improving the model's performance.

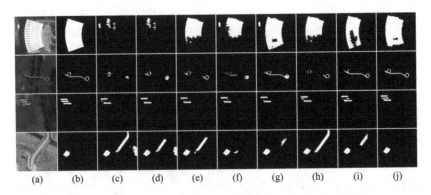

(a)   (b)   (c)   (d)   (e)   (f)   (g)   (h)   (i)   (j)

Fig. 5. Visual comparison of different XFEM variants. (a) Image; (b) Ground truth; (c) baseline; (d) core component; (e) left branch; (f) left branch + core; (g) left + right branch; (h) right branch; (i) right branch + core; (j) XFEM

5   Conclusion

In this paper, we propose a novel X-shape Feature Expansion Module to parallelize multi-scale feature extraction and receptive field enhancement, for the purpose of the uncertainty of object positions and the complexity of scale and shape in RSI-SOD. In XFEM, the multi-scale information and receptive field are enhanced by left and right branches, and each feature of the branches are fused by the core component. Furthermore, we equip XFEM into an encoder-decoder network and propose an X-shape Feature Expansion Network for RSI-SOD. We conduct extensive experiments on two public RSI-SOD datasets, and the results demonstrate that our method outperforms 11 state-of-the-art methods. XFNet and XFEM proposed in this paper can address the challenges of object scale, shape, and position mentioned above. In the future, we will attempt to integrate XFEM with attention mechanisms and effectively utilize boundary information to promote the practical application of RSI-SOD.

References

1. Li, G., Liu, Z., Shi, R., Wei, W.: Constrained fixation point based segmentation via deep neural network. Neurocomputing **368**, 180–187 (2019)
2. Ke, G., et al.: Saliency-guided quality assessment of screen content images. IEEE Trans. Multimedia **18**(6), 1098–1110 (2016)
3. Feng, W., Sui, H., Jihui, T., Huang, W., Sun, K.: A novel change detection approach based on visual saliency and random forest from multi-temporal high-resolution remote-sensing images. Int. J. Remote Sens. **39**(22), 7998–8021 (2018)
4. Dong, C., Liu, J., Fang, X.: Ship detection in optical remote sensing images based on saliency and a rotation-invariant descriptor. Remote Sens. **10**(3), 400 (2018)
5. Liu, Z., Zhao, D., Shi, Z., Jiang, Z.: Unsupervised saliency model with color Markov chain for oil tank detection. Remote Sens. **11**(9), 1089 (2019)
6. Pang, Y., Zhao, X., Zhang, L., Lu, H.: Multi-scale interactive network for salient object detection. In: Proceedings of the IEEE/CVF Conference on Computer Vision and Pattern Recognition, pp. 9413–9422 (2020)
7. Zhao, J.-X., Liu, J.-J., Fan, D.-P., Cao, Y., Yang, J., Cheng, M.-M.: Egnet: edge guidance network for salient object detection. In: Proceedings of the IEEE/CVF International Conference on Computer Vision, pp. 8779–8788 (2019)
8. Qin, X., Zhang, Z., Huang, C., Gao, C., Dehghan, M., Jagersand, M.: Basnet: boundary-aware salient object detection. In: Proceedings of the IEEE/CVF Conference on Computer Vision and Pattern Recognition, pp. 7479–7489 (2019)
9. Li, C., Cong, R., Hou, J., Zhang, S., Qian, Y., Kwong, S.: Nested network with two-stream pyramid for salient object detection in optical remote sensing images. IEEE Trans. Geosci. Remote Sens. **57**(11), 9156–9166 (2019)
10. Li, C., et al.: A parallel down-up fusion network for salient object detection in optical remote sensing images. Neurocomputing **415**, 411–420 (2020)
11. Zhang, Q., et al.: Dense attention fluid network for salient object detection in optical remote sensing images. IEEE Trans. Image Process. **30**, 1305–1317 (2020)
12. Li, G., Liu, Z., Lin, W., Ling, H.: Multi-content complementation network for salient object detection in optical remote sensing images. IEEE Trans. Geosci. Remote Sens. **60**, 1–13 (2021)
13. Jiang, H., Wang, J., Yuan, Z., Liu, T., Zheng, N., Li, S.: Automatic salient object segmentation based on context and shape prior. In: BMVC, vol. 6, p. 9 (2011)
14. Liu, Z., Zou, W., Le Meur, O.: Saliency tree: a novel saliency detection framework. IEEE Trans. Image Process. **23**(5), 1937–1952 (2014)
15. Zhang, P., Wang, D., Lu, H., Wang, H., Ruan, X.: Amulet: aggregating multi-level convolutional features for salient object detection. In: Proceedings of the IEEE International Conference on Computer Vision, pp. 202–211 (2017)
16. Zhou, X., Shen, K., Liu, Z., Gong, C., Zhang, J., Yan, C.C.: Edge-aware multiscale feature integration network for salient object detection in optical remote sensing images. IEEE Trans. Geosci. Remote Sens. **60**, 1–15 (2021)
17. Fan, D.-P., Cheng, M.-M., Liu, Y., Li, T., Borji, A.: Structure-measure: a new way to evaluate foreground maps. In: Proceedings of the IEEE International Conference on Computer Vision, pp. 4548–4557 (2017)
18. Achanta, R., Hemami, S., Estrada, F., Susstrunk, S.: Frequency-tuned salient region detection. In: 2009 IEEE Conference on Computer Vision and Pattern Recognition, pp. 1597–1604. IEEE (2009)
19. Fan, D.-P., Gong, C., Cao, Y., Ren, B., Cheng, M.-M., Borji, A.: Enhanced-alignment measure for binary foreground map evaluation. arXiv preprint arXiv:1805.10421 (2018)

20. Deng, Z., et al.: R3net: recurrent residual refinement network for saliency detection. In: Proceedings of the 27th International Joint Conference on Artificial Intelligence, pp. 684–690. AAAI Press Menlo Park, CA, USA (2018)
21. Qin, X., Zhang, Z., Huang, C., Dehghan, M., Zaiane, O.R., Jagersand, M.: U2-net: going deeper with nested u-structure for salient object detection. Pattern Recogn. **106**, 107404 (2020)
22. Li, J., Pan, Z., Liu, Q., Wang, Z.: Stacked u-shape network with channel-wise attention for salient object detection. IEEE Trans. Multimedia **23**, 1397–1409 (2020)
23. Binwei, X., Liang, H., Liang, R., Chen, P.: Locate globally, segment locally: a progressive architecture with knowledge review network for salient object detection. In: Proceedings of the AAAI Conference on Artificial Intelligence, vol. 35, pp. 3004–3012 (2021)
24. Lin, Y., Sun, H., Liu, N., Bian, Y., Cen, J., Zhou, H.: Attention guided network for salient object detection in optical remote sensing images. In: Pimenidis, E., Angelov, P., Jayne, C., Papaleonidas, A., Aydin, M. (eds.) ICANN 2022. LNCS, vol. 13529, pp. 25–36. Springer, Cham (2022). https://doi.org/10.1007/978-3-031-15919-0_3

Aggregate Distillation for Top-K Recommender System

Hao Shen, Tengfei Chu, Yulou Yang, and Ming Yang[(✉)]

Nanjing Normal University, Nangjing, China
{202202019,202202020,192202018,myang}@njnu.edu.cn

Abstract. As knowledge distillation techniques have gained prominence in recommender systems (RS), they have proven instrumental in maintaining exceptional recommendation performance while simultaneously reducing model size. Nonetheless, conventional single-teacher bidirectional distillation methods present two significant limitations. First, the restricted knowledge from a solitary teacher hinders comprehensive learning for student model. Second, both teacher and student models are susceptible to overfitting due to the traditional distillation loss function. In response to these challenges, we introduce an innovative Aggregated Distillation (AD) framework explicitly designed for RS. We propose an ensemble-based bidirectional knowledge distillation method, utilizing multiple teacher models to furnish a more diverse knowledge base and capitalizing on their synergistic effects to bolster the student model's performance. Moreover, we devise a novel regularization module that integrates a high-performance teacher model (supervisor) into the primary model. This module mitigates overfitting by directing the principal model towards the gradient direction of the incorporated high-performance teacher model, diminishing the risk of optimization towards an overfitting gradient direction. Rigorous experiments on two real-world datasets substantiate that our proposed framework outperforms its counterparts, with each component contributing significantly to the superior performance.

Keywords: Recommendation Algorithm · Knowledge Distillation · Deep Learning · Ensemble Learning

1 Introduction

Recommender systems pervade various aspects of daily life, significantly facilitating users' experiences on online shopping platforms [8], educational sites [4], news and information platforms [16,27], movie streaming applications, and music software. They tackle the challenge of extracting pertinent information from massive quantities of data [1] and contribute to enhancing individuals' experiences and overall satisfaction [30].

Collaborative filtering-based recommender systems exhibit laudable performance [23] but suffer from marked head effect and restricted generalization capabilities. To ameliorate sparse matrix handling, Koren et al. [10] proposed a matrix

© The Author(s), under exclusive license to Springer Nature Switzerland AG 2023
L. Iliadis et al. (Eds.): ICANN 2023, LNCS 14260, pp. 259–271, 2023.
https://doi.org/10.1007/978-3-031-44195-0_22

factorization algorithm. Subsequently, various combinations of logistic regression models, factorization machine models, and hybrid models were integrated. With the advent of deep learning, recommender systems have also ventured into this domain, resulting in an expanded scale of models.

Although larger models offer the prospect of superior performance, deploying them in resource-constrained and low-latency scenarios may not be suitable due to increased computational resource demands and extended computation time. Achieving a balance between reduced model complexity and high performance has been a consistently popular research focus.

Despite the Bidirectional Distillation (BD) model's [11] promising performance, it exhibits inherent limitations, such as reliance on knowledge transfer from a singular teacher model and susceptibility to overfitting. To overcome these challenges, we present an innovative Aggregated Distillation (AD) framework for recommender system. Our approach diverges from existing models by enabling the student model to acquire knowledge from multiple teacher models, fostering mutual knowledge transfer and improvement. Experimental results indicate significantly enhanced performance compared to the BD model with a single teacher model.

To counter the overfitting problem, we introduce an advanced regularization technique. This method ensures more comprehensive training for both the student and teacher models, ultimately culminating in superior performance. Specifically, we integrate a high-performance teacher model into the extant model, which serves as a regularizer when overfitting is detected, mitigating the risk of over-optimization towards overfitting gradients.

The primary contributions of this paper encompass:

(1) The proposition of an innovative AD framework for top-K recommender systems, enabling the student model to learn diverse knowledge from a teacher ensemble model and augment performance. Valuable insights from the student model can reciprocally assist the teacher ensemble model in refining its own performance.
(2) The introduction of a novel regularization model to address overfitting during model training, effectively alleviating overfitting in the model and enhancing performance.
(3) The validation of our proposed model's superiority through rigorous experiments on real-world datasets. In comparison with other knowledge distillation models, the AD model exhibits the most remarkable performance. Additionally, we provide qualitative and quantitative analyses to corroborate the effectiveness of each component.

2   Related Work

As recommender systems models evolve and their parameter volume increases, the models become larger and more complex, leading to reduced online inference response speed. To address this issue, model compression techniques have been proposed. This paper discusses two primary categories: **conventional model** compression methods and **knowledge distillation-based model compression methods**.

2.1 Conventional Model Compression Methods

Network pruning [15] diminishes the number of operations in the model by eliminating low-importance connections. Commonly employed information includes absolute values of connection parameters [13] and filter medians [6]. However, pruning may result in decreased accuracy. Structured matrices [18] reduce memory consumption and expedite inference and training but may suffer from accuracy loss due to imposed structural constraints.

2.2 Knowledge Distillation-Based Model Compression Methods

Knowledge distillation capitalizes on knowledge transfer for model compression [2]. The teacher-student paradigm is a quintessential application, wherein the high-performance teacher model is intricate, and the student model is more straightforward. The teacher model aids the student model during training and conveys "dark knowledge." In natural language processing, BERT [3] is challenging to utilize in real-time scenarios due to its large number of parameters. Existing distillation methods [9,17,20,24,25,29] yield lightweight student model. However, general knowledge distillation solely transfers knowledge from the Teacher Model to the student model, potentially constraining distillation effectiveness.

To circumvent the limitations of knowledge distillation, Kweon proposes a bidirectional knowledge distillation method [11], facilitating mutual knowledge exchange between teacher model and student model. This method bolsters the performance of the student model but retains drawbacks, such as insufficient knowledge diversity. We introduce an Aggregated Distillation (AD) framework that fosters reciprocal knowledge transfer between teacher ensemble model and student model. Simultaneously, we present a novel regularization method to alleviate mutual overfitting issues, enabling the model to continuously enhance performance.

3 Problem Definition and Formulation

In this section, we define the problem and formulate it in a mathematical framework. We use $\mathcal{U} = \{u_1, u_2, ..., u_n\}$ and $\mathcal{I} = \{i_1, i_2, ..., i_m\}$ as the sets of users and items, respectively, where n denotes the number of users, and m represents the number of items. Additionally, we have a user-item interaction matrix $R \in \{0, 1\}^{n \times m}$, where $r_{ui} = 1$ indicates that user u has interacted with item i, and $r_{ui} = 0$ otherwise.

For a user u, the data is divided into two parts: unobserved items $\mathcal{I}_u^- = \{i \in \mathcal{I} | r_{ui} = 0\}$ and interacted items $\mathcal{I}_u^+ = \{i \in \mathcal{I} | r_{ui} = 1\}$. The primary goal of a top-K recommender system is to identify the optimal recommendation list of unobserved items for each user. The system ranks the unobserved items based on the predicted score $\hat{r}_{ui} = p(r_{ui} = 1|u, i)$, which estimates the likelihood of interaction between the user u and item i.

Formally, a top-K recommender system seeks to learn a function $f : \mathcal{U} \times \mathcal{I} \rightarrow \mathbb{R}$ such that for a given user u, the system can generate a recommendation list $\mathcal{L}_u^k$ consisting of the top-K items from $\mathcal{I}_u^-$, ranked by the predicted scores:

$$\mathcal{L}_u^k = \text{Top-K} \left\{ (i, \hat{r}_{ui}) \, | \, i \in \mathcal{I}_u^- \right\}. \tag{1}$$

The objective of the Aggregated Distillation (AD) framework is to improve the performance of the top-K recommender system by enabling the student model to learn from multiple teacher models, allowing mutual knowledge transfer and improvement. Furthermore, the proposed regularization technique aims to mitigate overfitting during model training, leading to better performance.

4   Method

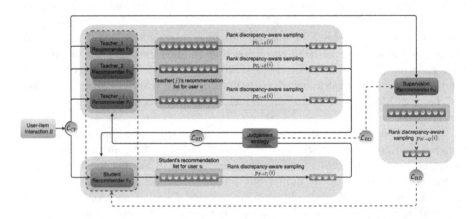

Fig. 1. Description of Aggregate Distillation (AD) for top-K recommender system.

4.1   Overview

Figure 1 presents an overview of our proposed model. In the AD framework, we adopt a teacher ensemble model consisting of multiple teacher models, a departure from traditional knowledge distillation-based recommender systems. Each teacher model generates a diverse set of recommendations for users. We employ the rank difference-aware sampling scheduler [11] to extract less noisy, beneficial knowledge for both teacher and student models.

During training, overfitting may arise, leading to a decline in model performance. To address this issue, we incorporate a high-performance teacher model as a regularization module. Although knowledge distillation provides some regularization, its impact is limited. Our AD framework introduces an innovative regularization module, activated under specific circumstances. This module not only enhances the regularization effect of knowledge distillation but also reduces computational overhead. Moreover, our proposed regularization method improves model efficacy when knowledge distillation regularization is insufficient.

In summary, the training process for non-overfitting modules proceeds as follows:

$$\mathcal{L}_{T_i}(\theta_T) = \mathcal{L}_{CF}(\theta_{T_i}) + \lambda_{S \to T_i} \cdot \mathcal{L}_{AD}(\theta_{T_i}; \theta_S) \tag{2}$$

$$\mathcal{L}_S(\theta_S) = \sum_{i=1}^{n} [\mathcal{L}_{CF}(\theta_S) + \lambda_{T_i \to S} \cdot \mathcal{L}_{AD}(\theta_S; \theta_{T_i})] \tag{3}$$

The training of each module when judged to be overfitting is as follows:

$$\mathcal{L}_{\mathcal{M}}(\theta_M) = \mathcal{L}_{CF}(\theta_M) + \sum_{i=1}^{n} [\lambda_{T_i \to M} \cdot \mathcal{L}_{AD}(\theta_M; \theta_{T_i})] + \lambda_{S \to M} \cdot \mathcal{L}_{AD}(\theta_M; \theta_S) \tag{4}$$

$$\mathcal{L}_Q(\theta_Q) = \sum_{i=1}^{n} [\mathcal{L}_{CF}(\theta_{T_i}) + \lambda_{M \to T_i} \cdot \mathcal{L}_{AD}(\theta_{T_i}; \theta_M)] \\ + \mathcal{L}_{CF}(\theta_S) + \lambda_{M \to S} \cdot \mathcal{L}_{AD}(\theta_S; \theta_M) \tag{5}$$

where T_i and S denote the i-th Teacher Model and the Student Model, respectively, M represents the high-performance teacher model, n indicates the number of Teacher Models, and $\theta(\cdot)$ denotes the model parameters. $\mathcal{L}_{CF}$ represents the collaborative filtering loss, which depends on the base model that can be any existing recommender, while $\mathcal{L}_{AD}$ denotes the aggregate distillation loss. For each distillation direction, $\lambda_{S \to T_i}$, $\lambda_{T_i \to S}$, $\lambda_{M \to S}$, $\lambda_{M \to T_i}$, $\lambda_{T_i \to M}$, and $\lambda_{S \to M}$ serve as hyperparameters that control the effects of the distillation loss.

4.2 Distillation Loss

We propose a generalized distillation loss function for facilitating knowledge transfer among various recommenders. For a user u, the distillation loss is defined as:

$$\mathcal{L}_{AD}(\theta_A; \theta_B) = \sum_{j \in \mathcal{RDS}_{A \to B}(I_u^-)} \mathcal{L}_{BCE}\left(\hat{r}_{uj}^A, \hat{r}_{uj}^B\right) \tag{6}$$

In this context, A and B represent different recommenders, such as the student model (S), the teacher ensemble model (T_i), or the high-performance teacher model (M). The binary cross-entropy loss is denoted by $\mathcal{L}_{BCE}(p, q)$, and is calculated as $\mathcal{L}_{BCE}(p, q) = q \log p + (1 - q) \log(1 - q)$. The prediction of a recommender is given by $r_{uj} = p(r_{uj} = 1 | u, j)$, and $\mathcal{RDS}_*(I_u^-)$ is a set of the unobserved items sampled by the rank discrepancy-aware sampling. The computation of r_{uj} involves $\delta(z_{uj}/T)$, where $\delta(\cdot)$ stands for the sigmoid function, z_{uj} represents the logit, and the temperature parameter T controls the smoothness. Finally, Q consists of the ensemble of teacher and student models.

By adjusting the values of A and B, this generalized distillation loss function can be applied to various scenarios, including student-teacher, student-high-performance teacher model, and teacher-high-performance teacher model interactions.

4.3   Knowledge Sampling

Experiments reveal that without regularization, the student model's performance declines in later training stages (Fig. 2). We introduce a high-performance teacher model, structurally similar to the teacher. When the student model enters an overfitting state, the teacher ensemble model and student model are treated as a learning unit Q, and the module intervenes to alleviate overfitting by guiding the learning of Q.

We employ Rank Discrepancy-aware Sampling [11] and bidirectional sampling between Q and the supervisor, enabling each module to select beneficial knowledge based on self-assessment. We provide a unified knowledge distillation formula:

$$p_{A \to B}(i) \propto g\left((\text{rank } B(i) - \text{rank } A(i)) \cdot \epsilon\right) \tag{7}$$

where A and B represent teacher, student, or supervisor; $g(\cdot)$ is an activation function, $\epsilon(> 0)$ is a hyperparameter controlling the smoothness of the probabilities. The general formula can be adjusted for different scenarios:

- **Teacher to Student (1)**: $A = T_j, B = S, g(x) = \tanh(\max(x, 0)), \epsilon = \epsilon_t$
- **Student to Teacher (2)**: $A = S, B = T_j, g(x) = \exp(x), \epsilon = \epsilon_e$
- **Q to Supervisor (3)**: $A = Q, B = M, g(x) = \exp(x), \epsilon = \epsilon_e$
- **Supervisor to Q (4)**: $A = M, B = Q, g(x) = \exp(x), \epsilon = \epsilon_e$

In these scenarios, tanh ensures even sampling of items with grade differences above a threshold, while exp emphasizes items with significant ranking differences, allowing models to persist in predictions only on items with high confidence and unstable ranking.

5   Experiments

5.1   Experimental Setup

Datasets. We use two real-world datasets: CiteULike [26] and MovieLens Latest(ML). We split the data following [11], and keep at least 5 users for interaction.

Evaluation Protocol and Metrics. We use leave-one-out evaluation protocol which is widely used. For data splitting, we select this user's last interaction as the test, and the penultimate interaction as the validation [5,11,12]. As for the data without timestamp, we add the timestamp of the last data to it.

We use Hit Ratio($H@K$) [14] which is a commonly used metric to measure recall and Normalized Discounted Cumulative Gain ($N@K$) [7]. $H@K$ measures whether the test item is present in the top-K list and $N@K$ assigns a higher score to the hits at higher rankings in the top-K list. $N@K$ is used for evaluating the accuracy of the result list.

We compute the average score of these two metrics for each user. Lastly, we report the average of six independent experiments.

Base Models. AD is a model-agnostic framework that can be used for any top-K RS. We use two base models with different model structures and learning strategies to validate the superiority of our AD framework, as follows:

- CDAE [28]: CDAE is an improved version of AutoRec [21] that uses implicit feedback data to model users' preferences.
- BPR [19]: BPR mainly uses implicit feedback from users (e.g. clicks, favourites, etc.) to rank items by the maximum posterior probability obtained from a Bayesian analysis of the problem, which in turn generates recommendations.

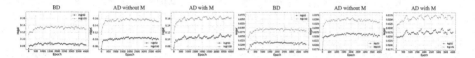

Fig. 2. Various framework student performance. The left three figures display student H@K performance in BD, AD without M, and AD frameworks, while the right three showcase student N@K performance in the same contexts.

Comparison of Methods. In this section we compare the proposed framework with the state-of-the-art KD framework for top-K RS.

- Bidirectional Distillation (BD) [11]: A state-of-the-art KD method for top-K RS. BD makes distillation not just about transferring knowledge from teacher to student, but also about enabling the teacher to draw on the student's helpful knowledge for it's own improvement.

5.2 Performance Comparison

We report the recommended performance of each knowledge distillation method on two real datasets and two different types of models in Table 1.

In our experiment, we utilized a teacher ensemble model consisting of three teachers with varying dimensions for a concise and clear illustration. Table 1 shows the pre-trained base model data for T, T2, T3, and S. AD-T, AD-T2, AD-T3, and AD represent the teacher ensemble model and student model trained with AD, while BD denotes the student model trained with BD. We analyzed the experimental results from various perspectives.

Table 1 reveals that, in the AD framework, the student imparts significant knowledge improvements to individual teachers on the H@50 indicator (23%, 17%, and 25%, respectively). This suggests that both the student and supervisor modules positively affect the teacher ensemble model.

For the CiteULike dataset, the BPR student model improved by 48.97%, with the AD-trained student model showing a 35.87% improvement compared to the BD-trained student model.

Table 1. Performance comparison. *Improv.∗* denotes the improvement of the respective model over its original version (teacher-*x*, BD framework, or student), with ∗ representing *Tx*, *BD*, or *S*.

Base Model	Method	CiteULike				ML			
		H@50	H@100	N@50	N@100	H@50	H@100	N@50	N@100
BPR	T	0.1224	0.1892	0.0328	0.0415	0.2039	0.3191	0.0552	0.0738
	T2	0.1424	0.205	0.0405	0.0506	0.2188	0.3174	0.0559	0.0741
	T3	0.1483	0.218	0.0454	0.0567	0.2237	0.3289	0.0564	0.0744
	AD-T	0.1502	0.2269	0.0408	0.0532	0.222	0.3454	0.0575	0.0761
	AD-T2	0.1663	0.2533	0.0458	0.0598	0.2237	0.3438	0.0564	0.0786
	AD-T3	0.1849	0.2614	0.0517	0.0641	0.2286	0.3322	0.0577	0.0771
	AD	0.1159	0.1661	0.0305	0.0385	0.2056	0.2993	0.056	0.0694
	BD	0.0853	0.1378	0.0213	0.0298	0.1809	0.2878	0.0499	0.0673
	S	0.0717	0.1217	0.0171	0.0251	0.1776	0.2681	0.0476	0.0623
	Improv.T	22.71%	19.93%	24.39%	28.19%	8.88%	8.24%	4.17%	3.12%
	Improv.T2	16.78%	23.56%	13.09%	18.18%	2.24%	8.32%	0.89%	6.07%
	Improv.T3	24.68%	19.91%	13.88%	13.05%	2.19%	1.00%	2.30%	3.63%
	Improv.BD	**35.87%**	**20.54%**	**43.19%**	**29.19%**	**13.65%**	**4.00%**	**12.22%**	**3.12%**
	Improv.S	61.65%	36.48%	78.36%	53.39%	15.77%	11.64%	17.65%	11.40%
CDAE	T	0.171	0.2445	0.0492	0.0611	0.1776	0.2878	0.0475	0.0652
	T2	0.191	0.2512	0.0601	0.0699	0.1875	0.2993	0.0489	0.067
	T3	0.1952	0.2476	0.0653	0.0738	0.1974	0.3224	0.0528	0.073
	AD-T	0.2043	0.2721	0.0624	0.0718	0.2056	0.3174	0.0554	0.0734
	AD-T2	0.2144	0.2633	0.0735	0.0814	0.2122	0.3207	0.0559	0.0735
	AD-T3	0.2311	0.2698	0.0812	0.0875	0.227	0.3388	0.0586	0.0768
	AD	0.1163	0.1736	0.0342	0.0434	0.2007	0.2993	0.0526	0.0684
	BD	0.0943	0.147	0.0269	0.0355	0.1826	0.2944	0.0479	0.0661
	S	0.0724	0.109	0.0198	0.0257	0.1661	0.2895	0.0396	0.0595
	Improv.T	19.47%	11.29%	26.83%	17.51%	15.77%	10.28%	16.63%	12.58%
	Improv.T2	12.25%	4.82%	22.30%	16.45%	13.17%	7.15%	14.31%	9.70%
	Improv.T3	18.39%	8.97%	24.35%	18.56%	14.99%	5.09%	10.98%	5.21%
	Improv.BD	**23.33%**	**18.10%**	**27.14%**	**22.25%**	**9.91%**	**1.66%**	**9.81%**	**3.48%**
	Improv.S	60.64%	59.27%	72.73%	68.87%	20.83%	3.39%	32.83%	14.96%

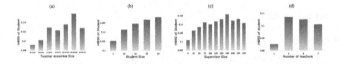

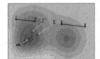

Fig. 3. Performance of student at different teacher ensemble model size, student size, supervisor size, and varying number of teachers, respectively.

Fig. 4. Diagram of Supervisor M's work.

The AD framework benefits from several factors:

- Employing a multi-teacher ensemble model allows the student to acquire more comprehensive and diverse knowledge than a single-teacher setup.
- The student model enhances its ability by fitting the knowledge transferred from the teachers. The improved student then conveys new knowledge to the teachers, creating a virtuous cycle. As the teachers' knowledge boosts the

student's performance, the rapidly advancing student passes useful knowledge to the teachers, consequently improving teachers performance.

- The supervisor module mitigates overfitting in the teacher ensemble model and student model, enabling consistent performance improvements without multiple enhancements. We further analyze the contribution of regularization in Sect. 5.3.

In Fig. 3, we observe the performance of the student model under various conditions. Figure 3 (a) illustrates the performance of the student model with different sizes of teacher ensemble model, where "25–50–75" represents an ensemble comprising three teacher models of sizes 25, 50, and 75, respectively. From the figure, it can be seen that the larger the size disparities and the overall scale among teacher models, the better the performance of the student model. Moreover, with similar model sizes, a greater difference in teacher model sizes leads to improved student performance. Figure 3 (b) demonstrates the relationship between the student model size and its performance, indicating that larger student model exhibit superior performance. However, as the model size continues to expand, the performance improvement advantage gradually diminishes. Figure 3 (c) showcases the impact of varying high-performance teacher model sizes on student model performance, with the student model exhibiting optimal performance when the size is 160. Figure 3 (d) displays the influence of the number of teacher models in the ensemble on student model performance, revealing that the student model achieves optimal performance when the ensemble contains three teacher models. Subsequently, as the number of teacher models increases, the student model performance declines. We postulate that when the number of teacher models is limited, it is easier to control overfitting phenomena. However, with an increasing number of teacher models, the student model may require more sophisticated strategies to integrate knowledge from multiple teacher models, potentially leading to an increased risk of overfitting.

5.3 High-Performance Teacher Module Regularization Analysis

Regularization, typically used to combat overfitting, achieves a balance between model complexity and performance. Common penalty terms for loss functions include L_1 and L_2 regularization, as well as weight decay, which resembles L_2 regularization. Regularization penalizes large parameters, potentially impacting model performance [22]. Nonetheless, non-knowledge distillation models can attain superior performance with L_1 or L_2 regularization. This is attributed to specific characteristics of knowledge distillation models, where teacher ensemble model outputs exhibit regularization effects, and accurate supervision from strong teacher ensemble model enables student model to adequately mimic data distribution. However, performance declines during late epochs of model training, as knowledge distillation's inherent regularization is insufficient. To address this, we introduce a novel regularization method: the supervisor mechanism.

Supervisor Mechanism. In the AD framework, we evaluate every p epochs, recording the highest value and corresponding epoch for each cycle. If no new highest value emerges within b cycles, we infer overfitting and activate the supervisor mechanism. First, we update the supervisor mechanism's parameters through pretraining to ensure recommendation list accuracy. Then, we consider the teacher ensemble model and student model as an integrated entity, Q. The supervisor mechanism M conveys sampled knowledge to Q, while Q transfers filtered knowledge to M. Unlike traditional regularization treating all parameters uniformly, our proposed supervisor mechanism guides appropriate parameter changes by transmitting useful knowledge. As depicted in Fig. 4 (b), the teacher and student occupy distinct locations after pretraining, then learn from one another. Initially, both levels improve, reaching locations T' and S'. Subsequent training brings them to T'' and S'', but overfitting slows progress. The supervisor mechanism propels them towards its direction, enhancing performance. Our experiments show that the AD framework excels as epoch numbers increase, with the best results attained under this mechanism.

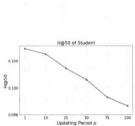

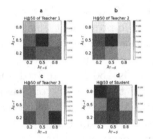

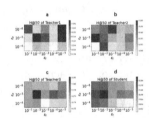

Fig. 5. Recommendation performance (H@50) with different updating periods p.

Fig. 6. Recommendation performance (H@50) of teachers and student with different $\lambda_{T \to S}$ and $\lambda_{S \to T}$.

Fig. 7. Recommendation performance (H@50) of teachers and student with different ϵ_e and ϵ_t.

5.4   Hyperparameter Analysis

In this section, we conduct a thorough experiment to analyze the effects of each hyperparameter in our experiments. We present the BPR results on the CiteU-Like dataset. To accelerate the training process, we set the model dimension sizes for the teacher size to 25, 50, and 75, the supervisor size to 100, and the student to 5. The experimental results for other datasets and models demonstrate similar behavior.

As depicted in Fig. 6, the influence of different values of $\lambda_{T \to S}$, $\lambda_{S \to T}$ on regulating the distillation losses is observed. With the sizes of Teacher 1, Teacher 2, and Teacher 3 set as 25, 50, and 75, respectively, we find that the student's H@50 (d) achieves satisfactory performance when $\lambda_{T \to S} = 0.2$, $\lambda_{S \to T} = 0.5$. The same applies for $\lambda_{M \to T}$, $\lambda_{M \to S}$, $\lambda_{S \to M}$, and $\lambda_{T \to M}$.

In the probability function, when ϵ_t is large and ϵ_e is small, the probability function becomes smoother. As shown in Fig. 7, the student's performance is optimal when $\epsilon_t = 10^{-2}$ and $\epsilon_e = 10^{-5}$.

To assess the impact of the update period p of the recommendation list on the student, we update the list every p epochs. Through our experiments, as depicted in Fig. 5, we discovered that updating the recommendation list every epoch can optimize the student's performance, but it consumes considerable time and computational resources. We set p to 10, which we believe strikes a better balance between reducing computational time and resources while maintaining minimal experimental bias.

6   Conclusion

In this study, we present a novel knowledge distillation technique for recommender systems, employing a teacher ensemble model and a singular student model. The ensemble harnesses multifaceted knowledge from various teachers, enhancing student performance. To address overfitting, we introduce a decision policy and an high-performance teacher model for regularization, which intervenes upon overfitting detection, steering the primary model towards an optimized gradient direction. Our experiments indicate significant performance improvements in both tasks.

References

1. Adomavicius, G., Tuzhilin, A.: Toward the next generation of recommender systems: a survey of the state-of-the-art and possible extensions. IEEE Trans. Knowl. Data Eng. **17**(6), 734–749 (2005)
2. Bucilă, C., Caruana, R., Niculescu-Mizil, A.: Model compression. In: Proceedings of the 12th ACM SIGKDD International Conference on Knowledge Discovery and Data Mining, pp. 535–541 (2006)
3. Devlin, J., Chang, M.W., Lee, K., Toutanova, K.: BERT: pre-training of deep bidirectional transformers for language understanding. arXiv preprint arXiv:1810.04805 (2018)
4. Gong, J., et al.: Attentional graph convolutional networks for knowledge concept recommendation in MOOCs in a heterogeneous view. In: Proceedings of the 43rd International ACM SIGIR Conference on Research and Development in Information Retrieval, pp. 79–88 (2020)
5. He, X., Liao, L., Zhang, H., Nie, L., Hu, X., Chua, T.S.: Neural collaborative filtering. In: Proceedings of the 26th International Conference on World Wide Web, pp. 173–182 (2017)
6. He, Y., Liu, P., Wang, Z., Hu, Z., Yang, Y.: Filter pruning via geometric median for deep convolutional neural networks acceleration. In: Proceedings of the IEEE/CVF Conference on Computer Vision and Pattern Recognition, pp. 4340–4349 (2019)
7. Järvelin, K., Kekäläinen, J.: Cumulated gain-based evaluation of IR techniques. ACM Trans. Inf. Syst. (TOIS) **20**(4), 422–446 (2002)
8. Ji, H., et al.: Large-scale comb-k recommendation. In: Proceedings of the Web Conference 2021, pp. 2512–2523 (2021)

9. Jiao, X., et al.: TinyBERT: distilling BERT for natural language understanding. arXiv preprint arXiv:1909.10351 (2019)

10. Koren, Y., Bell, R., Volinsky, C.: Matrix factorization techniques for recommender systems. Computer **42**(8), 30–37 (2009)

11. Kweon, W., Kang, S., Yu, H.: Bidirectional distillation for top-k recommender system. In: Proceedings of the Web Conference 2021, pp. 3861–3871 (2021)

12. Lee, J.W., Choi, M., Lee, J., Shim, H.: Collaborative distillation for top-n recommendation. In: 2019 IEEE International Conference on Data Mining (ICDM), pp. 369–378. IEEE (2019)

13. Li, H., Kadav, A., Durdanovic, I., Samet, H., Graf, H.P.: Pruning filters for efficient convnets. arXiv preprint arXiv:1608.08710 (2016)

14. Li, H., Hong, R., Lian, D., Wu, Z., Wang, M., Ge, Y.: A relaxed ranking-based factor model for recommender system from implicit feedback. In: IJCAI, pp. 1683–1689 (2016)

15. Li, H., Chan, T.N., Yiu, M.L., Mamoulis, N.: Fexipro: fast and exact inner product retrieval in recommender systems. In: Proceedings of the 2017 ACM International Conference on Management of Data, pp. 835–850 (2017)

16. Liu, P., Shivaram, K., Culotta, A., Shapiro, M.A., Bilgic, M.: The interaction between political typology and filter bubbles in news recommendation algorithms. In: Proceedings of the Web Conference 2021, pp. 3791–3801 (2021)

17. Mukherjee, S., Awadallah, A.H.: Distilling transformers into simple neural networks with unlabeled transfer data. arXiv preprint arXiv:1910.01769 1 (2019)

18. Pan, V.Y., Tsigaridas, E.P.: Nearly optimal computations with structured matrices. In: Proceedings of the 2014 Symposium on Symbolic-Numeric Computation, pp. 21–30 (2014)

19. Rendle, S., Freudenthaler, C., Gantner, Z., Schmidt-Thieme, L.: BPR: Bayesian personalized ranking from implicit feedback. arXiv preprint arXiv:1205.2618 (2012)

20. Sanh, V., Debut, L., Chaumond, J., Wolf, T.: DistilBERT, a distilled version of BERT: smaller, faster, cheaper and lighter. arXiv preprint arXiv:1910.01108 (2019)

21. Sedhain, S., Menon, A.K., Sanner, S., Xie, L.: AutoRec: autoencoders meet collaborative filtering. In: Proceedings of the 24th International Conference on World Wide Web, pp. 111–112 (2015)

22. Shen, Z., Savvides, M.: Meal v2: boosting vanilla resnet-50 to 80%+ top-1 accuracy on imagenet without tricks. arXiv preprint arXiv:2009.08453 (2020)

23. Su, X., Khoshgoftaar, T.M.: A survey of collaborative filtering techniques. In: Advances in Artificial Intelligence 2009 (2009)

24. Sun, S., Cheng, Y., Gan, Z., Liu, J.: Patient knowledge distillation for BERT model compression. arXiv preprint arXiv:1908.09355 (2019)

25. Sun, Z., Yu, H., Song, X., Liu, R., Yang, Y., Zhou, D.: MobileBERT: task-agnostic compression of BERT by progressive knowledge transfer (2019)

26. Wang, H., Chen, B., Li, W.J.: Collaborative topic regression with social regularization for tag recommendation. In: Twenty-Third International Joint Conference on Artificial Intelligence (2013)

27. Wang, X., Ounis, I., Macdonald, C.: Leveraging review properties for effective recommendation. In: Proceedings of the Web Conference 2021, pp. 2209–2219 (2021)

28. Wu, Y., DuBois, C., Zheng, A.X., Ester, M.: Collaborative denoising auto-encoders for top-n recommender systems. In: Proceedings of the Ninth ACM International Conference on Web Search and Data Mining, pp. 153–162 (2016)

29. Zhao, S., Gupta, R., Song, Y., Zhou, D.: Extreme language model compression with optimal subwords and shared projections (2019)
30. Zheng, Z., et al.: Drug package recommendation via interaction-aware graph induction. In: Proceedings of the Web Conference 2021, pp. 1284–1295 (2021)

Candidate-Aware Dynamic Representation for News Recommendation

Liancheng Xu, Xiaoxiang Wang, Lei Guo, Jinyu Zhang, Xiaoqi Wu, and Xinhua Wang[✉]

School of Information Science and Engineering, Shandong Normal University, Jinan 250358, China
{lcxu,guolei}@sdnu.edu.cn, {2021317083,2021021010}@stu.sdnu.edu.cn, w16678893038@163.com

Abstract. With the application of collaborative filtering and deep neural network in news recommendation, it becomes more feasible and easier to capture users' preferences of news browsing. However, different from traditional recommendation tasks, the collaborative filtering process of news recommendation requires additional consideration of news content. In addition, to capture users' real intentions from multi granularity interactive behavior information is still challenging. To address above challenges, we propose a hierarchical structure, namely Candidate-Aware Self-Attention enhanced convolution network (CASA). Specifically, we first devise a hierarchical self-attention networks to simultaneously extract the collaborative filtering signals between users and candidate news and their global correlations in multiple dimensions. Secondly, we employ a convolutional networks to map the keywords and important statements of the relevant news into the high dimensional feature space. By considering the additional content-level information, we can further reinforce the the collaborative filtering signals among news. Moreover, we also incorporate time and location relations during the news representation learning to better capture the user's contextual information. Extensive experiments on two real-world datasets demonstrates that CASA outperforms all the other state-of-the-art baselines on news recommendation task.

Keywords: News recommendation · Attention model · Dynamic model

1 Introduction

In the era of big data, recommendation systems are ubiquitous. Their main goal is to extract users' true intentions from multi-granularity interaction behavior information. Unlike traditional recommendation tasks, news has unique characteristics such as authenticity, accuracy, and timeliness. Newly released news

L. Iliadis et al. (Eds.): ICANN 2023, LNCS 14260, pp. 272–284, 2023.
https://doi.org/10.1007/978-3-031-44195-0_23

lacks historical interaction data, which leads to serious cold-start problems. Over-personalized news recommendations also face challenges in information privacy [1].

The success of news recommendation systems depends on their ability to accurately match user interests with relevant news content. Most models get the user's interest representation based on the news clicked by the user's history, and based on news content, make recommendations for the user on the news that the user is interested in, which is centered on learning the user and the news representation. When modeling news, it is common to learn from word entities and texts. One method proposed for achieving this is a knowledge-aware graph network, which helps to learn news embeddings from news headlines and entities [2]. User modeling is equally important in analyzing users' interest in news. Long-term and short-term user interests are modeled by GRU networks and user IDs [3]. CNN networks use a user's reading history and matched news texts to model the user's interest in news [4]. NAML [5] learns user embeddings through attention networks, and an attention memory network for learning user embeddings is proposed [6]. Candidate news is considered for inclusion in user modeling, and is used to match with specific users' interests [7]. User interests are accurately and efficiently modeled by fine-grained word-level interactions of clicked news [8]. These approaches are designed to learn accurate user representations to capture their interests, however, this also leads to users receiving news recommendation lists with similar content that only occur at different times, and appears echo chamber problem [9], where they do not receive the latest news or news with different perspectives in a timely manner, impairing the user experience.

The news recommendation problem is also closely related to time, both news and users' interests change over time and are uncertain [10], model needs to capture the latest news to constantly update user dynamics preferences. For user preferences, long-term and short-term user interests are modeled from news click behaviors with temporal factors, and newness and near-real-time clicks to time-aware news representations are added to recommend [11], and [12] adjusts the news weights by the time decay function, and multiplies the decay rate with the RNN layer output to obtain the final recommendation prediction results. These works demonstrate that models incorporating time achieve great results.

Motivated by the above observations, we propose a Candidate-Aware Self-Attention enhanced convolution network (CASA). On the one hand, we designed a hierarchical structure that utilizes multi-head self-attention mechanism and CNN to capture their global correlations across multiple dimensions while extracting collaborative filtering signals between users and candidate news. On the other hand, we incorporate temporal and positional relationships to better capture the context information of users. The main contributions of our work are as follows:

- We propose a hierarchical structure called the Candidate-Aware Self-Attention enhanced convolution network (CASA) to extract useful information from news at multiple granularities and enhance the collaborative filtering signals among news.

- By incorporating time and location relationships in news representation learning to better capture users' contextual information, we provide more accurate recommendations.
- Experiments on two real datasets show that the proposed CASA model significantly outperforms most approaches for the news recommendation task.

2   Related Work

2.1   Fine-Grained News Recommendation

Extracting valuable insights from news text is essential for enhancing user engagement. Therefore, many techniques summarize the content and themes of news by considering entities such as titles or keywords and utilize other information, such as news category and location [13], to analyze the news, beyond relying on the news text itself. News content information is essential, which includes both sentence and word entities, and captures details at a finer granularity by learning potential representations of a set of words or phrases through word embeddings [14]. [15] extracts keywords through annotations and text-specific keyword triggers, while annotations and text-specific keyword triggers can extract keywords, the availability of fine-grained data is uncertain, and this approach has limitations.

In contrast, our approach uses attention mechanisms to implicitly measure the importance of words and sentences, allowing us to extract the most significant information and capture fine-grained correlations between user behavior and news candidates. Additionally, we incorporate location and temporal embeddings to gain a more comprehensive and accurate understanding of user interest in specific news articles.

2.2   Dynamic News Recommendation

The primary goal of news recommendation is to evaluate the click-through rate of news articles by utilizing user preferences and news features, in order to recommend interesting stories that best match their reading interests. Existing news recommendations mainly rely on the interaction behavior and the processing on news content to establish the association between users and news, for example, the dichotomous graph shows the historical click behavior of users, and then uses graph attention network to combine neighboring information [16]. [17] are establishing high-order relationships between users and news by utilizing interaction graph, knowledge graph, and heterogeneous graph, and propagating and encoding these high-order information in the graph, however, these are static news processing, which statically represent general preferences and may have some problems if they want to accurately represent newly released news. Households are keen to watch/read recent news, but sometimes readers are interested in news related to the past, and due to the special properties of news, where updates of new items are numerous and rapid, the cold-start problem becomes very common, and news cannot be simply represented using IDs [18], and although researchers have used social network information to enhance user representation, these personalization methods tend to recommend similar items that users have already read, which makes it difficult for users to receive new news information and may decrease users' trust and satisfaction with the system [19]. Therefore, achieving a balance between real-time updates and personalized recommendations is crucial to ensure the quality of the recommendations.

Due to the instability of the news domain, such as the emergence of breaking news, users' reading interests also change short-term over time and have short-term dependencies [20]. Short-term interests are often associated with hot news and change frequently, and the next behavior may be associated with the most recent behavior [21]. Short-term interests are modeled using pages that users visit together over a short period of time, while long-term interests are modeled using the results of user interest clustering. Models short-term interest from the perspective of news trends [22], i.e., using public click patterns rather than just users' own feedback.

3   Methodology

3.1   Candidate-Aware Attention Networks

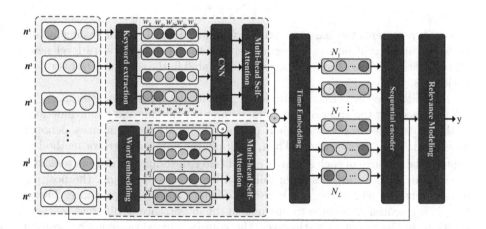

Fig. 1. The CASA model framework consists of three main modules: content extraction module, temporal embedding module, and sequence prediction module.

Fine-grained news modeling is a common approach in news processing. In the process of handling news, the focus is on "key events" information from different angles, rather than a large number of action verbs that represent action details in the story. Therefore, this paper proposes the idea of extracting key events from a single news text. The key entities (time, place, people, groups [16], other keywords) are extracted by natural language processing techniques such as entity recognition, time extraction, causality extraction, etc. Most of the news [23] is composed of these keywords. As the related entities of news topics, the corresponding keywords of each sentence are summed up correspondingly to obtain the overall dense low-dimensional embedding representation of time, place, people, groups, and other keywords [23], i.e.$\{w_{jt}, w_{jp}, w_{jm}, w_{jg}, w_{ja}\}$. These keywords in the news are stitched together into core sentences representing the whole news, represented by n_w^j. The body text in each news is long, but each sentence is relatively short, compressing the body text into a core sentence, so it is especially important to extract the keywords in it to represent different informativeness. In this paper, we consider the joint use of CNN and multi-head self-attention, which can capture global information and model local information, thereby modeling more fine-grained information. The multi-head self-attention mechanism uses scaled dot-product attention to interact and aggregate information. Combining historical click news and candidate news information, represented as n_w^j, and performing linear transformation to get Q_h^w, K_h^w and V_h^w, then calculating the importance and relevance of keywords among them to get keyword-based news representation n^w. The specific formula is as follows (Fig. 1):

$$\gamma_h^w = \text{soft max} \left(\frac{(K_h^w)^T Q_h^w}{\sqrt{D_K}} \right); \tag{1}$$

$$n^w = \|_h^H \gamma_h^w V_h^w, \tag{2}$$

where γ_h^w represents the learned attentive weights and $\sqrt{D_K}$ is the scaling factor. H is the number of heads. The word representation $n_w^{j^*}$ and word-level news representation n^{w*} of candidate news are calculated in the same way as historical click news.

In addition to keywords, we also learn the information of news utterances. To take into account the order of sentences, we first use the sine and cosine functions in the transformer to obtain implicit position information of sentences, denoted as P_{2l}^j and $P_{(2l+1)}^j$, respectively. Then, we apply the paragraph vector method to capture the features of each sentence and obtain embeddings. Since the semantic information in news articles often follows a hierarchical structure, the position of each sentence within the article carries different levels of importance. Therefore, it is essential to be able to distinguish the importance of different sentence positions in the target text. However, the approach based on sentence position may vary across domains. For instance, in some domains, the topic is introduced in the first sentence of the paragraph, while in others, it appears in the last sentence. In the news domain, sentences that contain high information content usually appear at the beginning of the article or the first few sentences of each paragraph, which are considered as dominant positions. The threshold value ω = 3 in Eq. (3):

$$\text{Score}_{loc}\left(s_l^j\right) = \begin{cases} 1, & l < \omega \text{ or} \\ & s_l^j \text{ is the first sentence} \\ & \text{of a paragraph;} \\ 1 - \log l / \log L, & others, \end{cases} \tag{3}$$

where $s_l^j \in R^d$ represents the l sentence vector in the j news item, L represents the number of sentences, i represents the i_{th} dimension of the sentence, d is the potential dimension, and the position code is expressed as $p_n = \left\{P_{2i}^j, P_{(2i+1)}^j\right\}$. The same operation is applied to the candidate news, where the positional encoding and the sentence embedding are added element by element to obtain the representation vector of the sentence.

$$s_l^j = \left(s_l^j \oplus p_n\right) \cdot \text{Score}_{loc}\left(s_l^j\right); \tag{4}$$

$$s_l^{j^*} = \left(s_l^{j^*} \oplus p_n^*\right) \cdot \text{Score}_{loc}\left(s_l^{j^*}\right); \tag{5}$$

$$a_{s_l^j, s_l^{j^*}} = \frac{\left[\left(\mathbf{u}_i \| s_l^j\right)\mathbf{W}_{s1}\right] \cdot \left[\mathbf{W}_{s2}\left(\mathbf{u}_i \| s_l^{j^*}\right)\right]^T}{\sqrt{D_K}}, \tag{6}$$

where $a_{s_l^j, s_l^{j^*}}$ is a contextual vector that measures the relevance of a clicked news sentence to a candidate news sentence and highlights the importance of that sentence in the overall document. $\mathbf{W}_{s1} \in R^{2d \times d}$, $\mathbf{W}_{s2} \in R^{2d \times d}$ is the training weight, α_{sj} is the weight derived by softmax. Finally, we obtain the final sentence-based representation of the news n^s, using an attention mechanism as follows:

$$n^s = \alpha_{sj} \cdot \left[\mathbf{u}_i \sum_{l=1}^L s_l^j\right]; \quad \alpha_{sj} = \frac{\exp\left(a_{s_l^j, s_l^{j^*}}\right)}{\sum_{j^*=1}^L \exp\left(a_{s_l^j, s_l^{j^*}}\right)}, \tag{7}$$

where L represents the number of sentences. Ultimately, the elements and sentence level representation are stitched to get the news representation $n = n^w + n^s$. The computation of candidate news is also the same, obtaining n^*.

3.2   Dynamic News Representation

To capture the impact of user clicks on news on candidate news in a time-aware scenario, a temporal context encoding scheme is used in order to incorporate changes in user click news dynamics into our user architecture. Specifically, inspired by the positional encoding in transformer, given the click behavior between user u and news c, we map their corresponding interaction timestamp t_j into the time slot as $\tau(t_j)$, and use the sine and cosine function generated by obtaining the embedding $T_{2i}^j, T_{(2i+1)}^j \in R^{2d}$ to:

$$T_{2i}^j = \sin\left(\frac{\tau(t_j)}{10000^{\frac{2i}{d}}}\right); \quad T_{(2i+1)}^j = \cos\left(\frac{\tau(t_j)}{10000^{\frac{2i+1}{d}}}\right), \tag{8}$$

where $2l$ and $2l + 1$ in the sine and cosine functions represent the odd and even position time indexes, respectively. The time of clicking on historical news and the time of candidate news are represented as T_{abs} and T_{abs}^* respectively and d is the potential dimension. The absolute time is added for each news representation as follows:

$$n_1 = T_{abs} \oplus n; \quad n_1^* = T_{abs}^* \oplus n^*, \tag{9}$$

where n_1 is the sum of the elements between the embedding term of the news, absolute time and news embedding have the same dimension. In fact, the absolute time reflects the sequential nature of the sequence to some extent. Modeling the time interval in the interaction sequence as a relationship between two items, i.e., the relative time interval T_{int}, using historical clicked news and candidate news to make a difference yields:

$$T_{int} = |T_{abs} - T_{abs}^*|; \quad n_2 = [n_1 T_{int}]. \tag{10}$$

The advantages of absolute time and relative time interval coding are combined for self-attention, and then the interaction properties between sequence learning items are considered and a novel interval-aware self-attention mechanism is designed, and then calculate the final news representation N and candidate news representation N^*:

$$N = n_1 \cdot n_2 \cdot n; \quad N^* = n^* \cdot n_1^*. \tag{11}$$

In order to take into account the impact of the order and consecutive clicks of news articles on a user's interests, we set the sequence length to S. Given a sequence of user u clicks, the transformer editor and the attention mechanism are used to distinguish the impact of the user's historical clicks.

3.3 Model Training

User interests are matched with candidate news to predict the probability of candidate news clicked by users. The clicked news features and the temporal information of the news sequence are first fully concatenated to obtain the user preferences of the end-user clicked news I. We compare the similarity between the final generated user interest I and the candidate news embedding I^*, and predict the probability $\tilde{y}$ of the user clicked on the candidate news by the cosine function. During the training process, we determine the positive and negative samples and label y based on whether the news has been clicked, and use binary cross-entropy loss function [24] to calculate the model's loss as follows:

$$L = -\sum_{n \in Z^+} \tilde{y} \log y - \sum_{n \in Z^-} (1 - \tilde{y}) \log(1 - y), \tag{12}$$

where Z^+, Z^- are positive and negative sample sets respectively. In addition, we also discarded and $l2$ regularized the weight parameters after using the attention.

4   Experiments

We evaluate our model on two real-world datasets and provide research answers to the following four questions:

- RQ1: How does our CASA model perform?
- RQ2: How does the effect of different fusion methods for information obtained by different modules change?
- RQ3: How do different hyperparameter Settings affect our model?

4.1   Experimental Settings

Datasets and Experimental Parameters. We employ two real-world datasets: Adressa and XHA to verify the validity of the proposed model (Table 1).

Table 1. Experimental data statistics

Datasets	Adressa	XHA
# Uers	66,649	2,210
# Items	11,660	5,265
# Interactions	1604,879	70,127

- **Adressa**[1]: This is a news reading dataset that includes the time users spend clicking on news articles.
- **XHA**: This dataset is from a Chinese news website, which contains 5,265 news articles, 2,210 users and 70,127 user interactions.

In the model experiments, the maximum length of all user history behaviors is 10, the grid search with the user inputs of [16, 32, 64, 128], and in training, we use Adam, the batch size is set to 1024. The same settings are shared by all models.

Baselines. To validate the model's effectiveness, we will compare it against the following baselines:

- **LSTUR** [3]: This approach models long-term and short-term user interests through GRU networks and user IDs.
- **BPR** [25]: This method makes recommendations based on explicit and implicit feedback data and optimizes the latent factor model.
- **DAN** [26]: Learning news and user representations using a two-layer neural network, learning news representations from words and entities in news headlines via a CNN network, and learning user interest representations via a focused LSTM network.

---

[1] http://reclab.Idi.ntnu.no/dataset.

- **GRU4Rec++** [27]: This method is a boosted version of GRU4Rec that takes the content information of news into further processing.
- **Caser** [28]: This method has multiple objectives, using CNNs to learn features of sequences and hidden factor models to learn user features
- **NRMS** [5]: This method is a deep neural network news recommendation model that uses the context of expression words using multi-headed self-attentive to get news representations and make news recommendations.

4.2   Recommendation Performance Comparison(RQ1)

We employ two frequently used metrics (i.e., HR and NDCG) [29] to evaluate each instance on the testing sets and report their values in the Table 2. The results showed that 1) CASA outperformed the traditional model BPR significantly. 2) Compared with the neural network-based methods (LSTUR, DAN, GRU4Rec++, Caser, and NRMS), the multi-granularity information extraction is critical for representing users' real intentions, and the integration of time and location relationships strengthens the contextual dependence, resulting in significant performance improvement.

Table 2. Experimental comparison results of message fusion methods

Methods	Adressa				XHA			
	HR@5	HR@10	NDCG@5	NDCG@10	HR@5	HR@10	NDCG@5	NDCG@10
LSTUR	0.861	0.9502	0.6736	0.7121	0.8211	0.8916	0.6729	0.6755
DAN	0.8577	0.9475	0.6696	0.6995	0.8036	0.8898	0.6695	0.6987
BPR	0.2586	0.4198	0.1689	0.2176	0.4451	0.5376	0.3497	0.3791
GRU4Rec++	0.7329	0.8688	0.5501	0.5940	0.5287	0.5658	0.4681	0.4776
Caser	0.7198	0.8679	0.5403	0.5862	0.5798	0.6292	0.5249	0.5398
NRMS	0.8591	0.9484	0.6723	0.7063	0.8187	0.8895	0.6712	0.6732
CASA	**0.9283**	**0.973**	**0.7952**	**0.809**	**0.9265**	**0.9533**	**0.8336**	**0.8478**

4.3   The Effect of Time and Location(RQ2)

Our model differs from others in that it includes both explicit and implicit location and time factors. Explicit location refers to the overall structure of the news content, while implicit location refers to the position encoded by the transformer model. CASA-S represents a method for removing the location factor, while CASA-T represents a method for removing the time factor. The results in Fig. 2(a) and (b) show that CASA outperforms CASA-T and CASA-S, demonstrating the importance of news time and location for capturing user context information.

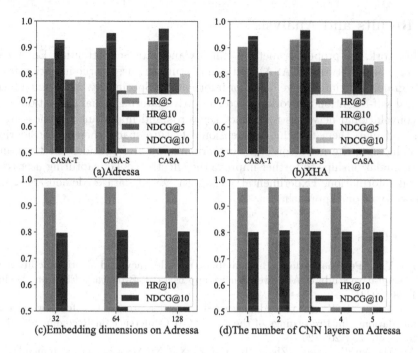

Fig. 2. The results of the ablation experiments and parameter analysis

4.4 Influence of Hyper-parameters(RQ3)

(1) Effect of different embedding dimensions: From the trend in Fig. 2(c), we notice that the experimental metric reaches its optimum performance when the embedding dimension is 64. A smaller embedding dimension may cause the model to be unable to capture subtle relationships between words, which could make it difficult for the model to identify important keywords. As the embedding dimension increases, the model's performance may decline. Increasing the dimension may also lead to overfitting, as the model may overfit to noise in the training data.

(2) Effect of the number of CCN layers: We conducted several experiments to investigate the impact of CNN layers, as shown in Fig. 2(d). When the number of layers was set to 2, our model achieved the best performance. This may be because GCN can effectively aggregate information through 2 layers, which is beneficial for representing user interests. Performance decreases when the number of layers is too large, possibly due to the problem of over-smoothing. Performance also decreases when the number of layers is too small, as useful information cannot be fully captured, making it difficult to learn accurate news representations.

5   Results and Analysis

In this work, we propose a method called Candidate Self-Attention Enhanced Convolutional Network (CASA) that can capture the user's true intention from multi-granularity interactive behavior information. Specifically, we design a hierarchical self-attention network and collaborative filtering signal extraction, and use convolutional networks to extract keywords and important sentences from news and map them to a high-dimensional feature space, thereby considering and enhancing the news content. Furthermore, we also consider the time and location relationships to further improve the effectiveness of capturing user contextual information. Experimental results on a real dataset demonstrate the superiority of our approach.

References

1. Du, Y.R.: Personalization, echo chambers, news literacy, and algorithmic literacy: a qualitative study of AI-powered news app users. J. Broadcast. Electron. Media, 1–28 (2023)
2. Liu, D., et al.: Kred: knowledge-aware document representation for news recommendations. In: Proceedings of the 14th ACM Conference on Recommender Systems, pp. 200–209 (2020)
3. An, M., Wu, F., Wu, C., Zhang, K., Liu, Z., Xie, X.: Neural news recommendation with long-and short-term user representations. In: Proceedings of the 57th Annual Meeting of the Association for Computational Linguistics, pp. 336–345 (2019)
4. Wang, H., Wu, F., Liu, Z., Xie, X.: Fine-grained interest matching for neural news recommendation. In: Proceedings of the 58th Annual Meeting of the Association for Computational Linguistics, pp. 836–845 (2020)
5. Wu, C., Wu, F., Ge, S., Qi, T., Huang, Y., Xie, X.: Neural news recommendation with multi-head self-attention. In: Proceedings of the 2019 Conference on Empirical Methods in Natural Language Processing and the 9th International Joint Conference on Natural Language Processing (EMNLP-IJCNLP), pp. 6389–6394 (2019)
6. Wang, H., Zhang, F., Xie, X., Guo, M.: DKN: deep knowledge-aware network for news recommendation. In: Proceedings of the 2018 World Wide Web Conference, pp. 1835–1844 (2018)
7. Qi, T., Wu, F., Wu, C., Huang, Y.: News recommendation with candidate-aware user modeling. In: Proceedings of the 45th International ACM SIGIR Conference on Research and Development in Information Retrieval, pp. 1917–1921 (2022)
8. Qi, T., Wu, F., Wu, C., Huang, Y.: FUM: fine-grained and fast user modeling for news recommendation. In: Proceedings of the 45th International ACM SIGIR Conference on Research and Development in Information Retrieval, pp. 1974–1978 (2022)
9. Fantl, J.: Fake news vs. echo chambers. Soc. Epistemol. **35**(6), 645–659 (2021)
10. Guo, L., Yin, H., Wang, Q., Chen, T., Zhou, A., Quoc Viet Hung, N.: Streaming session-based recommendation. In: Proceedings of the 25th ACM SIGKDD International Conference on Knowledge Discovery and Data Mining, pp. 1569–1577 (2019)
11. Qi, T., Wu, F., Wu, C., Huang, Y.: Pp-rec: News recommendation with personalized user interest and time-aware news popularity. arXiv preprint arXiv:2106.01300 (2021)

12. Zhang, L., Liu, P., Gulla, J.A.: A deep joint network for session-based news recommendations with contextual augmentation. In: Proceedings of the 29th on Hypertext and Social Media, pp. 201–209 (2018)
13. Son, J.W., Kim, A.Y., Park, S.B.: A location-based news article recommendation with explicit localized semantic analysis. In: Proceedings of the 36th International ACM SIGIR Conference on Research and Development in Information Retrieval, pp. 293–302 (2013)
14. Mehta, S., Islam, M.R., Rangwala, H., Ramakrishnan, N.: Event detection using hierarchical multi-aspect attention. In: The World Wide Web Conference, pp. 3079–3085 (2019)
15. Li, Q., Ji, H., Huang, L.: Joint event extraction via structured prediction with global features. In: Proceedings of the 51st Annual Meeting of the Association for Computational Linguistics (Volume 1: Long Papers), pp. 73–82 (2013)
16. Ge, S., Wu, C., Wu, F., Qi, T., Huang, Y.: Graph enhanced representation learning for news recommendation. In: Proceedings of The Web Conference 2020, pp. 2863–2869 (2020)
17. Hu, L., Li, C., Shi, C., Yang, C., Shao, C.: Graph neural news recommendation with long-term and short-term interest modeling. Inf. Process. Manag. **57**(2), 102142 (2020)
18. Domann, J., Lommatzsch, A.: A highly available real-time news recommender based on apache spark. In: Jones, G.J.F., et al. (eds.) CLEF 2017. LNCS, vol. 10456, pp. 161–172. Springer, Cham (2017). https://doi.org/10.1007/978-3-319-65813-1_17
19. Wu, Q., Liu, Y., Miao, C., Zhao, B., Zhao, Y., Guan, L.: PD-GAN: adversarial learning for personalized diversity-promoting recommendation. In: IJCAI, vol. 19, pp. 3870–3876 (2019)
20. Zhao, Q., Chen, X., Zhang, H., Ma, S.: D-han: dynamic news recommendation with hierarchical attention network. arXiv preprint arXiv:2112.10085 (2021)
21. Wu, C., Wu, F., Qi, T., Li, C., Huang, Y.: Is news recommendation a sequential recommendation task? In: Proceedings of the 45th International ACM SIGIR Conference on Research and Development in Information Retrieval, pp. 2382–2386 (2022)
22. Liu, J., Dolan, P., Pedersen, E.R.: Personalized news recommendation based on click behavior. In: Proceedings of the 15th International Conference on Intelligent User Interfaces, pp. 31–40 (2010)
23. Ao, X., Yu, X., Liu, D., Tian, H.: News keywords extraction algorithm based on textrank and classified tf-idf. In: 2020 International Wireless Communications and Mobile Computing (IWCMC), pp. 1364–1369. IEEE (2020)
24. Heaton, J., Goodfellow, I., Bengio, Y., Courville, A.: Deep Learning, 800 p. The MIT Press, Cambridge (2016). ISBN: 0262035618. Genet. Program. Evol. Mach. **19**(1-2), 305–307 (2018)
25. Rendle, S., Freudenthaler, C., Gantner, Z., Schmidt-Thieme, L.: BPR: Bayesian personalized ranking from implicit feedback. arXiv preprint arXiv:1205.2618 (2012)
26. Zhu, Q., Zhou, X., Song, Z., Tan, J., Guo, L.: DAN: deep attention neural network for news recommendation. In: Proceedings of the AAAI Conference on Artificial Intelligence, vol. 33, pp. 5973–5980 (2019)
27. Hidasi, B., Karatzoglou, A.: Recurrent neural networks with top-k gains for session-based recommendations. In: Proceedings of the 27th ACM International Conference on Information and Knowledge Management, pp. 843–852 (2018)

28. Tang, J., Wang, K.: Personalized top-n sequential recommendation via convolutional sequence embedding. In: Proceedings of the Eleventh ACM International Conference on Web Search and Data Mining, pp. 565–573 (2018)
29. Guo, L., Yin, H., Chen, T., Zhang, X., Zheng, K.: Hierarchical hyperedge embedding-based representation learning for group recommendation. ACM Trans. Inf. Syst. (TOIS) 40(1), 1–27 (2021)

Category Enhanced Dual View Contrastive Learning for Session-Based Recommendation

Xingfan Shi[1], Yuliang Shi[1,3]($\boxtimes$), Jihu Wang[1], Hongfeng Sun[2], Hui Liu[2], Xinjun Wang[1,3], and Zhiyong Chen[1]

[1] School of Software, Shandong University, Jinan, China
shiyuliang@sdu.edu.cn
[2] School of Data and Computer Science, Shandong Women's University, Jinan, China
[3] Dareway Software Co., Ltd., Jinan, China

Abstract. Session-based recommendation aims to predict the next item based on users' behavior sequence within a short time. Traditional session-based recommendation models usually assume that there exists only one type of interaction between users and items and fails to consider the impact of multiple types of behaviors. Although some recent studies have proposed to utilize different types of behaviors, they still have some challenges. First, they do not consider the impact of category information on user preferences. Secondly, they do not leverage the complementary information between multiple behaviors. To overcome the above challenges, we propose a novel Category Enhanced Dual View Contrastive Learning (**CaDVCL**) model, which explores the influence of item categories and multiple interaction behaviors on user interests. The model combines category sequence information and item sequence information to learn session representations through an attention mechanism and captures the correlation between different behaviors by maximizing the mutual information of session representations obtained from different behavioral views through contrastive learning. Extensive experiments on two public datasets show that CaDVCL can outperform the state-of-the-art models.

Keywords: Session-based recommendation · Multi-behavior modeling · Contrastive learning · Graph neural network

1 Introduction

Session-based recommendation provides users with recommendation services by mining the features of short-term behavior sequences of anonymous users, which meets the need for privacy protection and has attracted extensive attention [14].

Early works in this field introduce Markov Chains [3,12] to model user sequential behavior. Subsequently, recurrent neural networks (RNNs) have

© The Author(s), under exclusive license to Springer Nature Switzerland AG 2023
L. Iliadis et al. (Eds.): ICANN 2023, LNCS 14260, pp. 285–297, 2023.
https://doi.org/10.1007/978-3-031-44195-0_24

demonstrated a strong advantage in modeling sequential data, resulting in a large number of RNNs-based models [4,7,8]. Nowadays, since sequential session data can be modeled as graphs, graph neural networks (GNNs)-based models [16–18] have also emerged in large numbers. However, most existing session-based recommendation approaches [4,7,8,17] capture user preferences based on only a single type of user behavior, which overlooks the complementary impact of other kinds of behaviors on user's interests. Taking an e-commerce website as an example, users can perform multiple micro-behaviors such as click, add to cart, and purchase. Different behaviors can reflect user preferences from different intention dimensions and supplement each other to enhance user preference learning.

There are several studies [9,15] that exploit multiple micro-behaviors to improve the performance of session-based recommendation. Although the above methods have been proven to be effective, they still have some issues as follows: (1) They lack the individual analysis of each micro-behavior, thus failing to explicitly capture the user preferences embedded in each micro-behavior. (2) They don't take category information into account, resulting in an inability to obtain a comprehensive capture of the user's interest preferences. (3) The mutual complementary effects between different behaviors are not sufficiently utilized. Sequences of different types of behaviors are complementary and have complex dependencies, so it is important to make full use of the complementary information between multiple behaviors to improve the model effect.

In order to solve the above problems, we propose a novel Category Enhanced Dual View Contrastive Learning (**CaDVCL**) model. The model constructs an individual item graph for each micro-behavior sequence separately to perform subsequent item representation learning, which considers diverse user intents which motivate different types of behaviors. Besides, the model considers category information under different behavioral views and fuse category information and item information by using an attention mechanism. Finally, the model introduces contrastive learning to maximize the similarity between different micro-behavior sequences, which leverages the mutual complementary effects between different behaviors. We consider only the click and purchase behaviors in this paper and perform click-based recommendation and purchase-based recommendation tasks on two publicly available datasets, but our model is scalable and can be extended to three and more behaviors.

2 Related Work

2.1 Multi-behavior Recommendation

Multi-behavior session-based recommendation is based on multiplex behavior session sequences to predict the next item. MKM-SR [9] adopts GGNN to model the item sequence to learn the item embedding and GRU to model the corresponding operation sequence to learn the operation embedding. [15] build a Multi-Relational Item Graph based on all behavior sequences from all sessions, which can learn global item-to-item relations and further obtain user preferences.

MBGNN [11] constructs a multi-behavior session graph to capture the transition pattern of a global item, and adaptively fuse feature information according to the importance of different sequences to obtain a more refined local representation. However, they do not take category information into account, which may prevent recommendation performance from being optimal.

2.2   Self-supervised Learning

Self-supervised learning [1,2,5], as a novel machine learning paradigm, focuses on mining its own supervised information from large-scale unsupervised data. There are a few studies that combine self-supervised with recommender systems [13,18,19,21]. CL4SRec [19] puts the original sequences through three data augmentation operations (drop, mask, reorder) to get the transformed sequences from different perspectives, and uses the contrast learning framework to efficiently extract the self-supervised signals from the different sequences. These methods mentioned above are not suitable for session-based recommendation since most of them employ random discard or masking strategies, which makes the session data more sparse and prevents the use of self-supervised signals. The most relevant work to ours is S^2-DHCN [18] which constructs two types of hypergraphs to learn inter- and intra-session information and uses self-supervised learning to enhance session-based recommendation. However, their approach only targets one type of behavior, ignoring the interactions between multiple micro-behaviors and abandoning their cooperative effects.

3   The Proposed Method

In this section, we first formulate the research problem of session-based recommendation and then introduce the details of our model. The overall framework of the model is shown in Fig. 1.

3.1   Problem Definition

Let $V = \{v_1, v_2, v_3, \ldots, v_m\}$ denote a set of unique items among all sessions. Given a set of sessions, each session is described as a purchase behavior sequence $P = \{p_1, p_2, p_3, \ldots, p_k\}$ and a click behavior sequence $Q = \{q_1, q_2, q_3, \ldots, q_l\}$, where $p_i, q_i \in V$. The items in the sequence are ordered in the temporal order of user interactions. The purpose of session-based recommendation is to generate $\hat{y}$, where $\hat{y} = \{y_1, y_2, y_3, \ldots, y_m\}$ is the score of all items and y_i denotes the probability score of item v_i. The top-K items in $\hat{y}$ are the candidate items recommended to the user.

3.2   Graph Construction

Item Graph Construction. We construct the click-item graph $\mathcal{G} = (\mathcal{V}, \mathcal{E})$ based on items of user click behavior sequences from all sessions, where $\mathcal{V}$ is

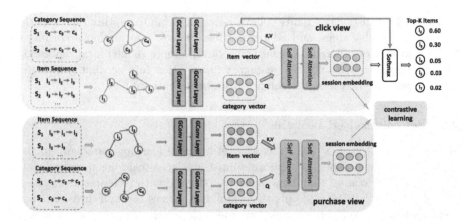

Fig. 1. The overview of the proposed CaDVCL model.

the set of nodes in the graph containing all available items and $\mathcal{E}$ is the edge sets. We construct an edge for each adjacent item in the same session and assign a normalized weight to each edge, which is calculated by dividing the number of occurrences of the edge by the outdegree of the starting node of the edge. The purchase-item graph based on items of user purchase behavior sequences is constructed in the same way.

Category Graph Construction. In addition to the item graph, we construct the category graph based on the sequence of categories corresponding to the sequence of items. For example, if a user clicks on item a in category c_1, followed by item b in category c_3, we construct an edge from c_1 to c_3 in the graph, and so on for the whole category graph.

3.3   Item Representation Learning

After getting the click-item graph, we adopt a simplified GCN [6] to capture the transition pattern of the global item. The representation of nodes is updated by aggregating the features of neighboring nodes, which can further capture user preferences. The item information propagation on the click-item graph follows,

$$\mathbf{X}_q^{(l+1)} = \hat{\mathbf{D}}_q^{-1}\hat{\mathbf{A}}_q\mathbf{X}_q^{(l)}\mathbf{W}_q^{(l)}, \tag{1}$$

where q is a subscript indicating that the click-item graph is used as input. The input to the lth layer network is $\mathbf{X}_q^{(l)} \in \mathbb{R}^{N \times D}$, where N is the number of nodes in the click-item graph, and each node is represented using a D-dimensional feature vector. $\hat{\mathbf{A}}_q = \mathbf{A}_q + \mathbf{I}$, $\mathbf{A}_q$ is the adjacency matrix, $\mathbf{I}$ is the identity matrix. $\hat{\mathbf{D}}_q$, $\mathbf{W}_q$ are the corresponding degree matrix and the parameter matrix.

We initialize the input vector $X_q^{(0)}$ to graph convolution layers through the embedding layer. After $X_q^{(0)}$ passes through L graph convolution layers, we average item representation from each layer to obtain the final item representation,

$$\mathbf{X}_q = \frac{1}{L+1} \sum_{l=0}^{L} \mathbf{X}_q^{(l)}. \tag{2}$$

Similarly, the item information propagation on the purchase-item graph follows,

$$\mathbf{X}_p^{(l+1)} = \hat{\mathbf{D}}_p^{-1} \hat{\mathbf{A}}_p \mathbf{X}_p^{(l)} \mathbf{W}_p^{(l)}, \mathbf{X}_p = \frac{1}{L+1} \sum_{l=0}^{L} \mathbf{X}_p^{(l)}. \tag{3}$$

3.4   Category Representation Learning

Besides, we introduce category sequence information across different micro-behavior views and model the category graph to capture transitions between categories. We implement the propagation of category information on a click-category graph through graph convolution networks,

$$\mathbf{C}_q^{(l+1)} = \hat{\mathbf{D}}_q^{-1} \hat{\mathbf{A}}_q \mathbf{C}_q^{(l)} \mathbf{W}_q^{(l)}, \mathbf{C}_q = \frac{1}{L+1} \sum_{l=0}^{L} \mathbf{C}_q^{(l)}. \tag{4}$$

where q is a subscript representing that the click-category graph is used as input. The input to the lth layer network is $\mathbf{C}_q^{(l)} \in \mathbb{R}^{N \times D}$, where N is the number of nodes in the click-category graph, and each node is represented using a D-dimensional feature vector.

Similarly, the category information propagation on the purchase-category graph is as follows,

$$\mathbf{C}_p^{(l+1)} = \hat{\mathbf{D}}_p^{-1} \hat{\mathbf{A}}_p \mathbf{C}_p^{(l)} \mathbf{W}_p^{(l)}, \mathbf{C}_p = \frac{1}{L+1} \sum_{l=0}^{L} \mathbf{C}_p^{(l)}. \tag{5}$$

3.5   Micro-behavior Sequence Representation

After learning item representation and category representation of different micro-behaviors, we need to further combine the two-part representation to learn the micro-behavior sequence representation.

Click-View Sequence Representation. For the click behavior sequence of the current session $Q = \{q_1, q_2, q_3, \ldots, q_k\}$, following [16], we add a learnable position matrix $\mathbf{M} = [\mathbf{m}_1, \mathbf{m}_2, \mathbf{m}_3, \ldots, \mathbf{m}_k]$ to the item representation, where k is the length of the click behavior sequence and $\mathbf{m}_i \in \mathbb{R}^d$ is the position vector for particular position i. The i-th item embedding is combined with the position information and represented as,

$$\mathbf{q}_i = \tanh\left(\mathbf{W}_1 \left[\mathbf{x}_{q_i} \oplus \mathbf{m}_{k-i+1}\right] + \mathbf{b}_1\right), \tag{6}$$

where $\mathbf{W}_1 \in \mathbb{R}^{d \times 2d}$ and $\mathbf{b}_1 \in \mathbb{R}^d$ are learnable parameters, $\mathbf{x}_{q_i}$ is the representation of the i-th item in the click sequence.

The session information from the click view is obtained by averaging the pooling of item representations from the click sequence,

$$\mathbf{s}^* = \frac{1}{k} \sum_{i=1}^{k} \mathbf{x}_{q_i},\tag{7}$$

Next, since different items in a session may have different priorities when learning session representation, we use a soft-attention mechanism to distinguish the importance of different items,

$$\alpha_i = \sigma\left(\mathbf{W}_2 s^* + \mathbf{W}_3 \mathbf{q}_i + \mathbf{b}_2\right),\tag{8}$$

where $\mathbf{W}_2, \mathbf{W}_3 \in \mathbb{R}^{d \times d}$ and $\mathbf{b}_2 \in \mathbb{R}^d$ are trainable parameters.

Finally, the session representation in click view can be obtained by linearly combining the item representations and the category representations,

$$\mathbf{S}_q = \sum_{i=1}^{k} \alpha_i \mathbf{q}_i \mathbf{c}_{q_i}.\tag{9}$$

where $\mathbf{c}_{q_i}$ is the category representation corresponding to the i-th item in the click sequence.

Purchase-View Sequence Representation. We combine item representation and category representation to obtain session representation in the purchase view,

$$\mathbf{p}_i = \tanh\left(\mathbf{W}_4 \left[\mathbf{x}_{p_i} \oplus \mathbf{m}_{l-i+1}\right] + \mathbf{b}_3\right),\tag{10}$$

$$\mathbf{s}^{'} = \frac{1}{l} \sum_{i=1}^{l} \mathbf{x}_{p_i},\tag{11}$$

$$\beta_i = \sigma\left(\mathbf{W}_5 s^{'} + \mathbf{W}_6 \mathbf{p}_i + \mathbf{b}_4\right),\tag{12}$$

$$\mathbf{S}_p = \sum_{i=1}^{l} \beta_i \mathbf{p}_i \mathbf{c}_{p_i}.\tag{13}$$

where $\mathbf{W}_4 \in \mathbb{R}^{d \times 2d}$, $\mathbf{W}_5, \mathbf{W}_6 \in \mathbb{R}^{d \times d}$ and $\mathbf{b}_3, \mathbf{b}_4 \in \mathbb{R}^d$ are trainable parameters, $\mathbf{x}_{p_i}$ is the representation of the i-th item and $\mathbf{c}_{p_i}$ is the category representation corresponding to the i-th item in the purchase sequence.

3.6   Dual-View Contrastive Learning

Each micro-behavior sequences in the session contain rich semantic information and exist complex dependencies among them. Following [10], we adopt InfoNCE to optimize the session representations learned from different behavioral views. For the mini-batch including n sessions $\{s_1, s_2, ..., s_n\}$, the session representations that are learned from the click view and the purchase view respectively are $\{S_q^1, S_q^2, ..., S_q^n\}$, $\{S_p^1, S_p^2, ..., S_p^n\}$. Taking the i-th session s_i in this batch as an example, we label $\left(S_q^i, S_p^i\right)$ as the positive pairs, otherwise $(S_p^i, S_p^1), ..., (S_q^i, S_p^{i-1}), ..., (S_q^i, S_p^n)$ as negative pairs. Our goal is to make the distance between positive examples as close as possible and the distance between negative examples as far as possible. The loss function is as follows,

$$l_i = -\log \frac{\exp\left(\text{sim}\left(\mathbf{S}_q^i, \mathbf{S}_p^i\right)/\tau\right)}{\sum_{k=1}^{n} [k \neq i] \exp\left(\text{sim}\left(\mathbf{S}_q^i, \mathbf{S}_p^k\right)/\tau\right)}, \mathcal{L}_{ssl} = \sum_{i=1}^{n} l_i. \qquad (14)$$

where $\text{sim}(\cdot, \cdot)$ is the discriminator function that takes two vectors as the input and then scores the agreement between them. We simply implement the discriminator as the dot product between two vectors. τ is the temperature coefficient that amplifies the contrast effect, we use 0.02 in our experiments.

3.7   Model Optimization

To validate the effectiveness of our model, we perform both click-based and purchase-based recommendation tasks. We first obtain the score of each candidate item $v_i \in V$ by doing the inner product between the current session representation o_s with the item representation x_i from the click view,

$$\hat{z}_i = o_s^\top x_i, \qquad (15)$$

where the current session representation is obtained based on the click behavior sequence, $o_s = S_q$. For the purchased-based recommendation task, $o_s = S_p$.

The softmax function is applied to normalize scores over all items to get the probability distribution $\hat{y}$:

$$\hat{y} = \text{softmax}(\hat{z}). \qquad (16)$$

Then, we adopt the cross-entropy loss as the optimization objective function,

$$\mathcal{L}_r = -\sum_{i=1}^{m} y_i \log(\hat{y}_i) + (1 - y_i) \log(1 - \hat{y}_i), \qquad (17)$$

where y denotes the one-hot representation of the ground-truth item.

Finally, we unify the main recommendation task with the auxiliary contrastive learning task. The total loss $\mathcal{L}$ is defined as:

$$\mathcal{L} = \mathcal{L}_r + \beta \mathcal{L}_{ssl}. \qquad (18)$$

where $\mathcal{L}_r, \mathcal{L}_{ssl}$ are the loss functions for the main recommendation task and the contrastive learning task, respectively. β is a hyper-parameter to control the scale of the contrastive learning and we jointly optimize the two tasks.

4   Experiment

4.1   Datasets

We evaluate our model on two publicly available realistic datasets, Cosmetics, and JData. Cosmetics[1] dataset is published on the Kaggle competition platform.

---
[1] https://www.kaggle.com/mkechinov/ecommerce-events-history-in-cosmetics-shop.

Table 1. Dataset statistics.

Data	Cosmetics	JData
sessions	826148	455481
items	28915	13650
categories	491	9
avg.length of click	5.42	5.95
avg.length of purchase	4.25	3.22

We use Oct month user behavior record of a medium cosmetics online store. JData[2] dataset is extracted from JD.com. It contains records of user actions performed on JD.com within one month (2016.2.1–2016.2.29). The dataset statistics are shown in Table 1. Specifically, we filter out all sessions whose length is 1 and items appearing less than 3 times. The dataset is divided according to the order of the session time, the first 80% is used as the training set, 10% is used as the validation set, and 10% is used as the test set.

4.2   Baselines

In order to evaluate the performance of CaDVCL, we compare it with the representative models. The baseline models are divided into four main groups:

(1) traditional method: FPMC [12]. It introduces Markov Chains to session-based recommendation to model the sequential behavior of users.
(2) RNN-based methods: GRU4Rec [4], NARM [7], STAMP [8]. They combine the attention mechanism with RNN while capturing the sequential behavior characteristics and the main purpose of users.
(3) GNN-based methods: SR-GNN [17], GCE-GNN [16], S²-DHCN [18]. They introduce graph models to the representation of session sequences and are able to efficiently consider the complex structure and transitions between items.
(4) multi-behavior methods: MGNN-SPred [15], MKM-SR [9], GNNH [20]. They construct multi-relational item graphs to capture item-to-item relations.

4.3   Experimental Setup

Evaluation Metrics. Following [8,17], we use P@K (Precision) and MRR@K (mean inverse rank) to evaluate the recommendation results. P@K denotes the proportion of correctly recommended items among the top-k items. MRR@K represents the average reciprocal ranks of the correctly-recommended items. In this paper, we select the cases K = 10, 20 for the experiments.

---

² https://jdata.jd.com/html/detail.html?id=8.

Parameter Setup. For all datasets, we set the item embedding dimension to 100, the batch size to 100, and the L2 penalty to 10^{-5}. All parameter matrices are initialized with a Gaussian distribution with a mean of 0 and a standard deviation of 0.1, and the parameter matrices are optimized using the Adam Optimization Method. For the baseline model, the optimal parameter settings reported in the original paper are referenced.

4.4   Performance Comparison

The experimental results for the overall performance are shown in Tables 2, 3. The best results in each column are boldfaced and the second best in each column is underlined. To validate the effectiveness of our model, we perform both click-based and purchase-based recommendation tasks. By analyzing the experimental results, we can draw the following observations.

Deep learning-based models (RNN-based, GNN-based) generally outperform the traditional model, which illustrates the significant role of deep learning techniques in session-based recommendation. Besides, GNN-based models are better than RNN-based methods, because these methods utilize graph neural networks to learn high-order transition information between items. Multi-behavior models outperform single-behavior models, which indicates that considering multi-behavior information can improve the performance of recommendations.

CaDVCL outperforms multi-behavior models, which indicates the performance can be further improved by leveraging the auxiliary effects between different behavioral sequences through contrastive learning.

Table 2. Results of all models on Cosmetics.

Method	click-based recommendation				purchase-based recommendation			
	P@10	P@20	MRR@10	MRR@20	P@10	P@20	MRR@10	MRR@20
FPMC	28.78	34.67	15.67	16.34	3.13	6.75	1.23	1.55
GRU4Rec	37.61	38.95	20.40	20.79	8.47	11.99	3.54	3.97
NARM	34.65	41.08	19.42	19.91	8.58	12.05	3.59	4.03
STAMP	36.78	41.90	20.05	20.98	6.82	10.07	2.73	3.47
SR-GNN	38.95	45.81	20.40	21.20	8.90	12.71	3.93	4.22
GCE-GNN	40.05	47.23	21.23	21.56	12.67	16.46	4.05	4.51
S2-DHCN	38.79	46.36	20.91	21.44	11.82	15.95	3.99	4.28
MGNN-SPred	40.14	47.23	21.45	21.76	13.60	18.21	4.35	5.13
MKM-SR	41.23	48.35	21.78	22.31	15.65	19.66	5.01	5.35
GNNH	_41.78_	_48.92_	_21.96_	_22.81_	_15.78_	_20.34_	_5.82_	_5.65_
CaDVCL	**42.49**	**49.63**	**22.35**	**22.90**	**16.50**	**22.34**	**6.05**	**6.40**

Table 3. Results of all models on JData.

Method	click-based recommendation				purchase-based recommendation			
	P@10	P@20	MRR@10	MRR@20	P@10	P@20	MRR@10	MRR@20
FPMC	14.47	17.53	8.13	8.63	1.21	1.36	0.13	0.20
GRU4Rec	29.45	35.34	13.04	13.95	3.22	3.30	1.18	1.95
NARM	28.78	36.86	15.98	16.82	3.27	3.33	2.15	2.82
STAMP	27.65	35.55	11.87	12.93	2.21	2.28	1.87	1.93
SR-GNN	32.74	40.58	14.64	15.96	4.41	6.29	2.64	2.96
GCE-GNN	33.12	41.34	15.81	16.12	4.54	6.50	3.81	4.12
S2-DHCN	32.85	40.97	14.54	15.87	4.43	6.30	3.54	3.87
MGNN-SPred	33.84	41.23	15.87	16.37	5.70	8.06	4.87	5.37
MKM-SR	34.98	42.56	16.48	17.35	6.06	8.67	5.48	6.35
GNNH	<u>35.01</u>	<u>42.89</u>	<u>16.90</u>	<u>17.68</u>	<u>6.49</u>	<u>8.91</u>	<u>5.87</u>	<u>6.70</u>
CaDVCL	**35.66**	**43.67**	**17.34**	**18.51**	**6.60**	**9.57**	**6.34**	**7.51**

4.5 Ablation Study

In order to validate the contribution of the key components designed for session-based recommendation, we further perform ablation studies on CaDVCL.

CaDVCL-cl represents removing the contrastive learning module and simply using the gated attention to perform the fusion of representations of different micro-behavior views. *CaDVCL-category* denotes removing the category information. *CaDVCL-base* represents only modeling the session data from a single behavior view. *base-NP* means that the position embedding is removed from *CaDVCL-base*. *base-NA* means that the soft-attention mechanism is removed from *CaDVCL-base* and replaced by an average item representation as a representation of each session.

According to the result in Figs. 2, 3, we derived the following results. The performance of *CaDVCL-cl* is worse than that of *CaDVCL*, which illustrates contrastive learning can promote the acquisition of user preferences by maximizing the similarity between different behavioral sequences. The performance of *CaDVCL-ca* indicates that fusing category information under different behavioral views can further provide some enhancement to session representation.

The result of *CaDVCL-base* shows when removing the data from other behavior views, a certain degree of decrease occurs on both metrics, which proves multi-behavior can provide additional auxiliary information for session recommendation. The results of *base-NA* demonstrate the importance score of distinguishing different items through an attention mechanism.

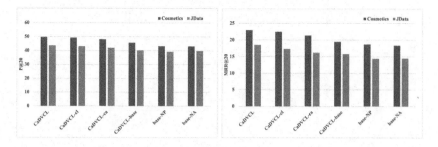

Fig. 2. Ablation results in the click-based recommendation.

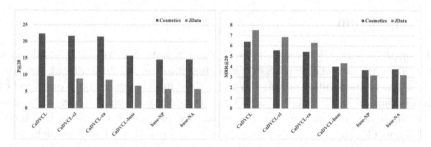

Fig. 3. Ablation results in the purchase-based recommendation.

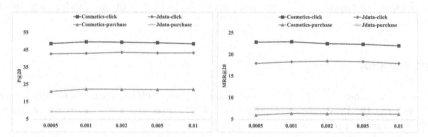

Fig. 4. The impact of the magnitude of contrastive learning.

4.6   The Impact of Hyperparameters

We introduce a hyper-parameter β into the model to control the magnitude of contrastive learning. According to the results in Fig. 4 for the Cosmetics dataset, the model obtained optimal results at $\beta = 0.001$. For the JData dataset, the model obtained optimal results at $\beta = 0.002$.

Besides, to investigate the impact of the number of layers in graph convolution network, we range the number of layers in $\{1, 2, 3, 4, 5\}$. The results in Fig. 5 show that for both datasets, the best performance is obtained at layer number 3. As the layer increases further, the performance of the model decreases due to the over-smoothing problem.

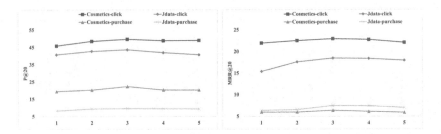

Fig. 5. The impact of the number of layers.

5 Conclusion

Existing session-based recommendation models have the following challenges: firstly, they do not utilize category sequence information to augment the representation of item information; secondly, they mostly utilize only one type of user interaction data, while ignoring the possibility of other types of behavior as auxiliary information. In this paper, we propose a Category Enhanced Dual View Contrastive Learning model to address these issues, which takes into account category information, and multi-behavior information, and also uses contrastive learning to maximize the mutual information between behaviors. Extensive experiments demonstrate the superiority of our model over other baseline models.

References

1. Beyer, L., Zhai, X., Oliver, A., Kolesnikov, A.: S4L: self-supervised semi-supervised learning. In: Proceedings of 2019 IEEE/CVF International Conference on Computer Vision, pp. 1476–1485 (2019)
2. Devlin, J., Chang, M., Lee, K., Toutanova, K.: BERT: pre-training of deep bidirectional transformers for language understanding. In: Proceedings of the 2019 Conference of the North American Chapter of the Association for Computational Linguistics, pp. 4171–4186 (2019)
3. He, R., McAuley, J.J.: Fusing similarity models with Markov chains for sparse sequential recommendation. In: ICDM 2016, pp. 191–200
4. Hidasi, B., Karatzoglou, A., Baltrunas, L., Tikk, D.: Session-based recommendations with recurrent neural networks. In: ICLR (2016)
5. Hjelm, R.D., et al.: Learning deep representations by mutual information estimation and maximization. In: 7th International Conference on Learning Representations (2019)
6. Kipf, T.N., Welling, M.: Semi-supervised classification with graph convolutional networks. In: 5th International Conference on Learning Representations (2017)
7. Li, J., Ren, P., Chen, Z., Ren, Z., Lian, T., Ma, J.: Neural attentive session-based recommendation. In: Proceedings of the 2017 ACM on Conference on Information and Knowledge Management, pp. 1419–1428 (2017)

8. Liu, Q., Zeng, Y., Mokhosi, R., Zhang, H.: STAMP: short-term attention/memory priority model for session-based recommendation. In: SIGKDD, pp. 1831–1839 (2018)

9. Meng, W., Yang, D., Xiao, Y.: Incorporating user micro-behaviors and item knowledge into multi-task learning for session-based recommendation. In: SIGIR, pp. 1091–1100 (2020)

10. van den Oord, A., Li, Y., Vinyals, O.: Representation learning with contrastive predictive coding. CoRR abs/1807.03748 (2018)

11. Pan, W., Yang, K.: Multi-behavior graph neural networks for session-based recommendation. In: MLBDBI, pp. 756–761 (2021)

12. Rendle, S., Freudenthaler, C., Schmidt-Thieme, L.: Factorizing personalized Markov chains for next-basket recommendation. In: WWW, pp. 811–820 (2010)

13. Sun, F., et al.: Bert4rec: sequential recommendation with bidirectional encoder representations from transformer. In: Proceedings of the 28th ACM International Conference on Information and Knowledge Management, pp. 1441–1450 (2019)

14. Wang, S., Cao, L., Wang, Y., Sheng, Q.Z., Orgun, M.A.: A survey on session-based recommender systems. ACM Comput. Surv. **54**(7), 154:1–154:38 (2022)

15. Wang, W., et al.: Beyond clicks: modeling multi-relational item graph for session-based target behavior prediction. In: Proceedings of The Web Conference 2020, pp. 3056–3062 (2020)

16. Wang, Z., Wei, W., Cong, G., Li, X., Mao, X.: Global context enhanced graph neural networks for session-based recommendation. In: SIGIR, pp. 169–178 (2020)

17. Wu, S., Tang, Y., Zhu, Y., Wang, L., Xie, X., Tan, T.: Session-based recommendation with graph neural networks. In: AAAI, pp. 346–353 (2019)

18. Xia, X., Yin, H., Yu, J., Wang, Q., Cui, L.: Self-supervised hypergraph convolutional networks for session-based recommendation. In: AAAI, pp. 4503–4511 (2021)

19. Xie, X., et al.: Contrastive learning for sequential recommendation (2021)

20. Yu, B., Zhang, R., Chen, W., Fang, J.: Graph neural network based model for multi-behavior session-based recommendation. GeoInformatica **26**(2), 429–447 (2022)

21. Zhou, K., et al.: S'3-rec: Self-supervised learning for sequential recommendation with mutual information maximization. CoRR (2020)

Electronic Medical Record Recommendation System Based on Deep Embedding Learning with Named Entity Recognition

Yuqian Zheng[1] , Xu Yan[2]([✉]) , Xin Cao[3], and Chunhui Ai[2]

[1] Basecare Medical Device Co., Ltd., Suzhou, China
[2] Soochow University, Suzhou, China
`yyxx20150909@163.com, 20215227120@stu.suda.edu.cn`
[3] Hefei University of Techology, Hefei, China
`caoxin@mail.hfut.edu.cn`

Abstract. Electronic medical records (EMR) provide valuable insights into patients' medical history, symptoms, and treatments. Similar EMRs can help clinicians make an accurate diagnosis and develop an appropriate treatment plan for their patients, which makes the EMR recommendation a hot topic. However, searching for similar cases in a database containing many EMRs would be labor-intensive, while a recommendation system can return results quickly. In order to improve the recommendation accuracy and reduce the time-consuming at the same time, a similar EMR recommendation framework is proposed, which consists of three parts: Data Preprocessing, Prefetching, and Similarity Assessment. In the preprocessing module, named entities are extracted by a Named Entity Recognition (NER) tool and sliced by a particular rule. In the prefetching module, a pretrained deep learning model is fine-tuned on a classification task and generates embeddings for EMRs to avoid redundant calculations and filter candidate samples by computing cosine similarity. Furthermore, Weight-DSC is proposed to assess the similarity of EMR pairs, which is calculated by entity frequency and outperforms other entity-based methods. Experiments on real data show that this framework demonstrates superior recommendation performance compared to previous approaches across all metrics and saves 2/3 of the query time, notably achieving a 2.89% increase in Mean Reciprocal Rank (MRR).

Keywords: Electronic Medical Records · Recommend Framework · Deep Learning

1 Introduction

It is common for clinicians to rely on their professional knowledge and experience when developing treatment plans. In addition, they can leverage electronic medical records (EMRs) to retrieve information about similar cases and identify patients with similar physical symptoms. By analyzing similar EMRs, clinicians

L. Iliadis et al. (Eds.): ICANN 2023, LNCS 14260, pp. 298–309, 2023.
https://doi.org/10.1007/978-3-031-44195-0_25

can gain insights into medication use and prognosis, facilitating comparative effectiveness studies and improving their understanding of their patients [9]. Identifying similar patients from large-scale medical databases can be challenging, particularly when working with unstructured texts like EMRs. Developing an accurate AI recommendation framework can help search medical records and evaluate the similarity quickly.

Medical records are not standardized due to differences in hospital systems and clinician writing habits. This lack of uniformity challenges extracting valuable information from medical records while excluding irrelevant information. Several similar EMR recommendation methods [1,9,14] aim to address this issue by focusing on entity features in the records. However, these methods often include irrelevant or noisy entities recognized by Named Entity Recognition (NER) tools. Additionally, some studies [1,7,14] assign the same weight to all entities, even though the importance of entities varies in medical records. To solve these problems, an EMR recommendation framework is proposed that uses a new entity weight allocation method and filters out invalid entities during data preprocessing. The proposed framework has achieved superior results in similar medical record recommendation tasks compared to previous methods. Additionally, it is important to note that when dealing with an extensive database in a recommendation system, calculating similarity must be done in pairs. This process can significantly increase computational overhead. Previous studies have failed to consider the time and memory consumption of the recommended model. A data prefetching method based on EMR embedding has been developed to address this issue and improve efficiency. This method allows for the extraction of a subset of EMRs from the entire database, reducing the time complexity of the model and improving recommendation efficiency.

Our framework has substantially enhanced the retrieval performance in the experiment compared to previous approaches, achieving a noteworthy increase of 2.89% in MRR. More impressively, the prefetching method has reduced the overall time consumption by two-thirds.

2   Related Work

The extraction of useful insights from vast medical records is a challenging task. Over the years, researchers have proposed similar EMR recommendation systems based on generating embeddings or extracting entities. One approach for learning patient embeddings involved utilizing the bag-of-words (BoW) technique [3]. Moreover, Convolutional Neural Networks (CNNs) and Recurrent Neural Networks (RNNs) have also been employed, as demonstrated in [4] and [12]. Another method called TAPER [2] calculated representations based on the Transformer [11] model, which considered patients' visit time. EMR embeddings can recommend similar patient records by measuring the spatial distance. Therefore, the embedding pair needs to reflect the relevance between EMR pairs, and the embedding generation model should be trained in a paired context. However, in some studies, each EMR was individually inputted during training [2,3,12], negatively impacting the embedding quality and the similarity measurement performance. In contrast, in our framework's training phase, a pair of EMRs is inputted simultaneously to address this limitation.

Some researchers [1,7,9,14] utilized keyword extraction, NER, and semantic similarity calculation techniques to extract relevant information and match user queries with clinical documents. DSC was used in [14] to recommend similar medical records according to the named entities contained, but all the entities had the same weight. In ISim [9], although TFIDF calculated the weight of entities, this method still had a drawback: it included all entities identified by the NER tool, and the calculation of weight took a lot of time, as the query needed to calculate the similarity with all the samples in the database. In the framework of this paper, some thresholds are used to eliminate redundant entities. Additionally, not all samples are included in the similarity comparison, significantly enhancing the time efficiency.

Previous studies utilizing unstructured text data have assessed similarity based on context or named entities [1,3,7,9,14]. The whole context corresponds to the information presented in the text, while the entity represents the critical keywords. We have improved recommendation performance by combining these two methods.

3   Methodology

This section proposes a new similar EMR recommendation framework to improve recommendations' accuracy and reduce time consumption. As shown in Fig. 1, the framework for similar EMR recommendations consists of 3 modules: Data Preprocessing, EMR Prefetching, and Similarity Assessment.

3.1   Data Preprocessing

Data preprocessing plays a crucial role in Natural Language Processing (NLP) tasks as it impacts the quality of the training data. Given the extensive length of the EMR context, preprocessing is employed to extract the salient points of the passage.

Named Entity Recognition Processing EMRs poses significant challenges due to the substantial amount of text they contain. Consequently, it is crucial to find critical information, such as disease names, symptoms, organs, treatments, and compounds, from these EMRs. One popular biomedical NER tool named Scispacy [8] is utilized to identify and extract these words. NER is a subtask of NLP that involves identifying and classifying named entities in text into predefined categories. The extracted named entities are used in the similarity assessment module of EMR recommendation.

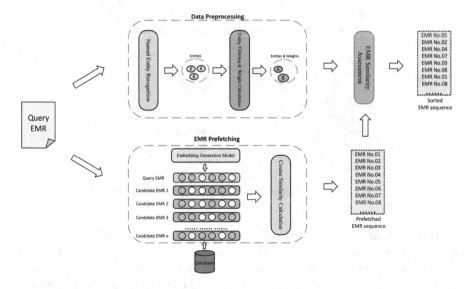

Fig. 1. Flowchart of similar EMRs recommendation for a query.

Entity Processing and Weight Calculation. Due to the large amount of terminology in the biomedical industry, most identified entities are composed of multiple words. During data preprocessing, all entities are cut by space and only contain individual word. Word-level entities can help discover more associations between similar EMRs in the following similarity assessment, as some entities with similar meanings contain the same word. The recommended performance using raw and processed entities is compared in the ablation experiment of Sect. 4.3. Moreover, it is important to ascertain the inherent value of diverse entities in EMRs. Entities with high frequency are considered more relevant to the theme of an EMR. To improve the performance of similarity calculation, reasonable weight allocation is required, and the Term Frequency-Inverse Document Frequency (TFIDF) [10] score is used as the standard (Fig. 2).

3.2 EMR Prefetching

Calculating similarities among all medical records in the database would be resource-intensive. However, not all pairs of medical records are valuable for similarity assessment. Prefetching a portion of the data to exclude irrelevant samples before performing similarity calculations can improve the efficiency of the recommendation. EMR embeddings are used in prefetching and generated by the Robustly Optimized BERT Pretraining Approach (RoBERTa) model [6], trained on a classification task, and stored in the database. The spatial distance between the embedding pairs is utilized to measure the degree of similarity of the EMRs. The matrix operation requires only a fraction of the time and can quickly filter out irrelevant samples to complete the prefetching process.

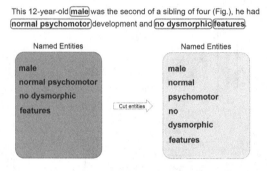

Fig. 2. An example of NER and entity processing.

EMR Embedding Cosine Similarity. To evaluate the similarity between two EMR embeddings E_a and E_b in vector space, we use Cosine Similarity, a widely adopted technique in the fields of NLP and information retrieval, where it plays a crucial role in determining the similarity between texts or documents.

$$CosineSimilarity_{a,b} = \frac{E_a \cdot E_b}{|E_a| \times |E_b|} \tag{1}$$

where $|E_a|$ represents the length of the embedding E_a. The closer the cosine similarity between two EMRs is to 1, the more similar they are. A threshold of 0 is utilized to distinguish whether a pair of EMRs is similar. EMRs with embedding cosine similarity greater than 0 to the query embedding are regarded as positive samples and are prefetched (Fig. 3).

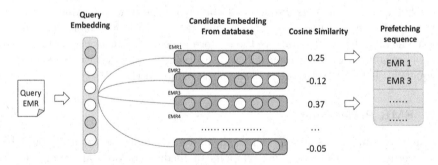

Fig. 3. The prefetching process by calculating the cosine similarity of EMR embeddings.

Generating EMR Embeddings. RoBERTa [6] is a transformer-based language model, and we use this model as the baseline for prefetching. When an EMR is an input to the RoBERTa model, the representation of the [CLS] token is utilized as the EMR embedding, containing the contextual information of the input text. We fine-tune the RoBERTa-base model using a binary classification task to generate EMR embeddings. The training process is illustrated in Fig. 4. The [CLS] representations in the last layer serve as temporary EMR embeddings, and their cosine similarity is computed to determine whether the input EMRs are relevant.

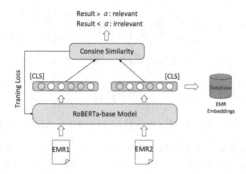

Fig. 4. The process of training prefetching model. The parameter α is the threshold to judge whether a pair of EMRs are relevant.

The training data for the model are EMR text pairs with a label of 1 or -1, representing whether the EMR pair is relevant or irrelevant. The final embedding is generated by inputting an EMR into the fine-tuned model, with the [CLS] token representing a unique EMR. These embeddings are fixed after generation and stored in the database to avoid duplication of operations during the prefetching process, thereby saving time. When recommending similar EMRs, the embedding for the query case is generated first, followed by calculating cosine similarity with all embeddings in the dataset. Only candidate EMRs with a similarity greater than 0 are prefetched for subsequent steps.

3.3 Similarity Assessment

Scoring similarity by comparing the number of entities intersecting in two articles is a common method for similar EMR recommendations, such as ISim [9] and DSC [14]. Different entities are given the same weight when calculating DSC, which is unreasonable because not all entities are highly relevant to the theme of the EMR. A new evaluation rule named Weight-DSC is proposed to improve the shortcomings of the original method based on DSC, and the TFIDF score is used as the weight allocation criteria.

Although ISim also applies the TFIDF scores of named entities to calculate similarity scores, it does not use this score to filter entities. Entities that appear only once in a specific EMR in the database could not establish relationships between EMR pairs, which will be excluded when using Weight-DSC. Entities with high frequency in an EMR are also limited. If a large weight is assigned to high-frequency entities, low-frequency entities become invalid in the calculation.

The performance of three methods is compared, and the results are detailed in Sect. 4.2, where they are defined as:

$$DSC = \frac{len(set(E_a) \cap set(E_b))}{len(set(E_a) + len(set(E_b))} \tag{2}$$

$$ISim = \frac{\sum_{i \in N} min(f_{a_i}, f_{b_i}) \times IDF_i}{avg(\sum_{i \in N}(f_{a_i} \times IDF_i), \sum_{i \in N}(f_{b_i} \times IDF_i))} \tag{3}$$

$$N = \{i | i \in E_a\} \cup \{i | i \in E_b\} \tag{4}$$

$$DSC_{Weight} = \frac{\sum_{i \in S}(min(f_{a_i}, f_{b_i}, T_1) \times IDF_i)}{avg(\sum_{i \in S}(f_{a_i} \times IDF_i), \sum_{i \in S}(f_{b_i} \times IDF_i))} \tag{5}$$

$$S = \{i | i \in E_a, IDF_i > T_2\} \cup \{i | i \in E_b, IDF_i > T_2\} \tag{6}$$

E_a and E_b correspond to two EMR entity sequences, which can contain duplicate entities, and i is a named entity in sequences. The $set(E_a)$ operation is defined to transform the sequence E_a into a set. T_1 and T_2 are the thresholds used to limit word frequency. T_1 limits the maximum number of occurrences of an entity in an EMR, and this threshold is set to 4 based on multiple experimental attempts on the training set. T_2 deletes entities that appear only once in the database by comparing the IDF scores.

The higher the similarity score, the greater the similarity between EMRs. The candidate EMRs are sorted in descending order by score and returned as a prediction sequence.

4 Experiment

In this section, we implemented the experiments using the method mentioned in Sect. 3. The dataset, parameter settings and results are discussed in detail.

4.1 Dataset and Data Preprocessing

The dataset used is PMC-Patients [14], which contains 167,034 electronic medical records, much larger than a well-known dataset MIMIC-III (46,146 records) [5]. EMRs are typically long texts, with 57.05% of the samples in the dataset containing more than 512 tokens. Therefore, it is necessary to extract important information from the entire text. Named entities extracted by the NER tool are divided into individual words by spaces. Before segmentation, the entities that only appear once in the entire database accounted for 71.26%, and after processing, dropped to 60.56%, which is very significant because entities with a frequency of one cannot participate in the matching of similar EMRs.

Figure 5 illustrates the impact of the preprocessing on the number of named entities contained in an EMR. For the raw data, the majority of EMRs contain

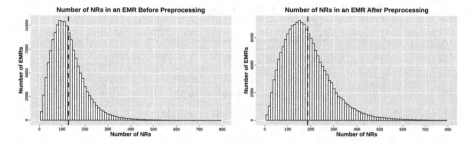

Fig. 5. The Frequency Distribution of Named Entities (NRs) Contained in an EMR After Preprocessing.

between 50 and 150 entities, with a mean value of 128. There are 10.56% of EMRs that only contain less than 50 entities, which had a greater impact on the performance of recommendations, as fewer candidate EMRs are explored based on entity occurrences. After data preprocessing, the mean value of entities in one EMR grew to 186, and 4.79% of EMRs contain less than 50 entities, which mitigated the data deficiency.

4.2 Experimental Setup and Evaluation

Similarity Assessment Experiment Settings. The samples used for similarity assessment provide information about similar EMRs, and the matching EMRs for each query are stored in the list. The EMRs associated with a query can be one or more, and their order in the list is independent of the similarity. DSC, ISim, and Weight-DSC can be used to evaluate the similarity between two EMRs, and their performances are compared in the experiment (Table 1).

Table 1. Statistics of Similarity Assessment Dataset

Split	Query	Document	Similarity Annotations
Train	94.6k	155.2k	257.4k
Dev	3.7k	161.1k	10.0k
Test	3.7k	161.1k	11.5k

Prefetching Experiment Settings. The input data for prefetching consists of pairs of EMR labeled with the *{0,1,2}*. The negative sample is labeled *0*, meaning that the input pair is irrelevant; Both *1* and *2* represent positive samples, but they are derived from different sources, they are combined into one category since distinguishing the source of the relevant EMR is not the purpose of training the model (Table 2).

Table 2. Statistics of Prefetching Assessment Dataset

Split	Instances	Positive	Negative
Train	257.4k	128.7k	128.7k
Dev	16.4k	8.2k	8.2k
Test	19.0k	9.5k	9.5k
Total	292.7k	146.4k	146.4k

The model used to generate the EMR embedding is a fine-tuned RoBERTa-base, trained on a Tesla V100 32G with the following hyperparameter settings: the learning rate is 2.5e−6, the epoch is 3, and the batch size is 16.

Evaluating Indicator. The recommended result is a list where the EMRs near the front of the list have higher similarity scores, and this result is compared with another list that holds true similar EMRs. Precision, Recall, and Mean Reciprocal Rank (MRR) [13] are selected as evaluating indicators. MRR is defined as:

$$MRR = \frac{1}{Q} \sum_{q=1}^{Q} MRR_q = \frac{1}{Q} \sum_{q=1}^{Q} \frac{1}{r_q} \tag{7}$$

where r_q is the index number (start from one) of the first true sample in the result list for a query q, and $MRR_q = 1/r_q$. When this list contains no true similar EMR, $MRR_q = 0$.

4.3   Experiment Results

The comparison of different similarity assessment methods, prefetching according to EMR embedding, and results of the ablation experiment will be presented and analyzed in detail in this section.

Comparing Three Similarity Assessment Methods. Table 3 compares the three evaluation methods regarding MRR, P@10, R@1k, and R@10k using the preprocessed test set. Weight-DSC has achieved the best scores on all metrics with MRR of 51.66, P@10 of 12.23, R@1k of 80.98, and R@10k of 94.01. The performance of DSC is the worst, and its score is far less than that of ISim and Weight-DSC on four indexes. The performance of ISim is slightly poorer than that of Weight-DSC, with its MRR being 0.34 and R@1K being 0.26 smaller. For P@10 and R@10k, scores of ISim are also lower than Weight-DSC, and the difference is about 0.1.

Exploring the Effect of Prefetching on Time Performance. The whole database contains 161,100 EMRs. Without prefetching, a query would calculate the similarity with all EMRs, resulting in significant time consumption. By

Table 3. Recommended Performance for DSC, ISim, and Weight-DSC with Preprocessed Data (in Percentages).

Method	MRR	P@10	R@1k	R@10k
DSC (Preprocessed)	48.06	10.88	71.97	89.53
ISim (Preprocessed)	51.32	12.11	80.72	93.90
Weight-DSC (Preprocessed)	<u>51.66</u>	<u>12.23</u>	<u>80.98</u>	<u>94.01</u>

reducing the number of candidate samples, prefetching saves time in the recommendation process. The RoBERTa model with 0.872 classification accuracy in the test set helps prefetch an average of 44,149 EMRs for a query. This technique is applied to three similarity assessment methods, with time performance shown in Table 4.

Table 4. The Time Performance of Prefetching on Different Assessment Methods (in Seconds).

Method	Prefetch	Average Time	Total Time
DSC	N	3.57	13231.12
DSC	Y	1.11	4108.43
ISim	N	26.57	98456.04
ISim	Y	7.88	29219.74
Weight-DSC	N	25.90	95984.41
Weight-DSC	Y	7.74	28674.03

DSC takes the shortest time, only 1.11 s, to complete a query when prefetching, which is about one-seventh of ISim (7.88 s) and Weight-DSC (7.74 s) as it involves only set operations and does not use the weights of entities. Compared to ISim, Weight-DSC is a bit faster because its entities are filtered, and the calculation involving entity weights is reduced. Prefetching performs well on all three similarity evaluation methods and about two-thirds decreases the average query time. The improvement in time performance through prefetching is of great significance to the recommendation, given that it determines the algorithm to be successfully applied in clinical scenarios.

Ablation Experiment. The ablation experiments verify that the following techniques have a positive impact on recommendation performance: Slicing entities in data preprocessing (Preprocess); Assigning weights to entities using TFIDF scores (Weight); Prefetching according to EMR embedding (Prefetch); Using a threshold to limit highest entity frequencies (T_1); Using a threshold to filter low-frequency entities (T_2).

Table 5. Results of Ablation Experiment (in Percentages).

Method	MRR	P@10	R@1k	R@10k
ISim	48.90	11.17	73.68	89.19
DSC (Baseline)	45.15	9.98	63.21	82.76
DSC+Preprocess	48.06	10.88	71.97	89.53
DSC+Weight	48.61	11.16	72.87	88.79
DSC+Prefetch	45.56	10.09	66.01	87.17
DSC+Weight+Preprocess	50.92	11.96	81.39	94.35
DSC+Weight+Preprocess+T_2	51.21	12.03	81.58	94.43
DSC+Weight+Preprocess+T_2+T_1	51.66	12.23	80.98	94.01
DSC+Weight+Preprocess+T_2+T_1+Prefetch	51.79	12.21	81.11	94.00

The experimental results are exhibited in Table 5. *DSC+Weight+Preprocess+T_2+T_1* is equivalent to Weight-DSC. According to the table, Weight-DSC outperforms DSC and Isim markedly. This represents the contribution of our paper to recommendation performance.

5   Conclusion

We proposed a similar EMR recommendation framework that utilizes deep learning algorithms to analyze and compare patient records to benefit clinical medicine significantly. This framework has greatly advanced performance with respect to the previous methods by improving data preprocessing and similarity evaluation rule. Furthermore, the incorporation of a prefetching module has resulted in reduced time consumption.

This framework also has some flaws, which are expected to be addressed in future work. Firstly, the experiments only use one dataset, and supplementing the results with multiple datasets could make the performance of the model more convincing. It is worth considering adding other well-known medical field datasets, such as MIMIC-III [5], even though it contains fewer data. In addition, the problem of truncating long text pairs has not been solved. In the prefetching model, the texts of two EMRs are fed into the RoBERTa model separately. Although this approach somewhat mitigates information loss, text truncation still exists, as over 50% of EMRs contain more than 512 tokens. Therefore, it is necessary to apply some long text processing methods, such as splitting and abbreviating text, to retain the full contextual information.

References

1. Bissoyi, S., Patra, M.R.: A similarity matrix based approach for building patient centric social networks. Int. J. Inf. Technol. **13**(4), 1449–1455 (2021). https://doi. org/10.1007/s41870-021-00692-0, https://link.springer.com/10.1007/s41870-021-00692-0
2. Darabi, S., Kachuee, M., Fazeli, S., Sarrafzadeh, M.: TAPER: time-aware patient EHR representation. IEEE J. Biomed. Health Inform. **24**(11), 3268–3275 (2020). https://doi.org/10.1109/JBHI.2020.2984931, https://ieeexplore.ieee. org/document/9056492/
3. Dhayne, H., Kilany, R., Haque, R., Taher, Y.: EMR2vec: bridging the gap between patient data and clinical trial. Comput. Ind. Eng. **156**, 107236 (2021). https://doi.org/10.1016/j.cie.2021.107236, https://linkinghub. elsevier.com/retrieve/pii/S0360835221001406
4. Gupta, V., Sachdeva, S., Bhalla, S.: A novel deep similarity learning approach to electronic health records data. IEEE Access **8**, 209278–209295 (2020). https://doi.org/10.1109/ACCESS.2020.3037710, https://ieeexplore.ieee. org/document/9257424/
5. Johnson, A.E., et al.: MIMIC-III, a freely accessible critical care database. Sci. Data **3**(1), 160035 (2016). https://doi.org/10.1038/sdata.2016.35, https://www. nature.com/articles/sdata201635
6. Liu, Y., et al.: RoBERTa: a robustly optimized BERT pretraining approach (2019). http://arxiv.org/abs/1907.11692, arXiv:1907.11692 [cs]
7. Memarzadeh, H., Ghadiri, N., Shahreza, M.L., Pokharel, S.: Heterogeneous electronic medical record representation for similarity computing. CoRR abs/2104.14229 (2021). https://arxiv.org/abs/2104.14229
8. Neumann, M., King, D., Beltagy, I., Ammar, W.: ScispaCy: fast and robust models for biomedical natural language processing. In: Proceedings of the 18th BioNLP Workshop and Shared Task, pp. 319–327 (2019). https://doi.org/10.18653/v1/ W19-5034, http://arxiv.org/abs/1902.07669, arXiv:1902.07669 [cs]
9. Pokharel, S., Li, X., Zhao, X., Adhikari, A., Li, Y.: Similarity computing on electronic health records. In: Hirano, M., Myers, M.D., Kijima, K., Tanabu, M., Senoo, D. (eds.) 22nd Pacific Asia Conference on Information Systems, PACIS 2018, Yokohama, Japan, 26–30 June 2018, p. 198 (2018). https://aisel.aisnet.org/pacis2018/ 198
10. Salton, G., Buckley, C.: Term-weighting approaches in automatic text retrieval. Inf. Process. Manag. **24**(5), 513–523 (1988). https://doi.org/10.1016/0306-4573(88)90021-0, https://linkinghub.elsevier.com/retrieve/pii/0306457388900210
11. Vaswani, A., et al.: Attention is all you need (2017). http://arxiv.org/abs/1706. 03762, number: arXiv:1706.03762 [cs]
12. Wang, Y., Chen, W., Li, B., Boots, R.: Learning fine-grained patient similarity with dynamic Bayesian network embedded RNNs. In: Li, G., Yang, J., Gama, J., Natwichai, J., Tong, Y. (eds.) DASFAA 2019. LNCS, vol. 11446, pp. 587–603. Springer, Cham (2019). https://doi.org/10.1007/978-3-030-18576-3_35
13. Wu, Y., Mukunoki, M., Funatomi, T., Minoh, M., Lao, S.: Optimizing mean reciprocal rank for person re-identification. In: 2011 8th IEEE International Conference on Advanced Video and Signal Based Surveillance (AVSS), pp. 408–413 (2011). https://doi.org/10.1109/AVSS.2011.6027363
14. Zhao, Z., Jin, Q., Chen, F., Peng, T., Yu, S.: PMC-patients: a large-scale dataset of patient summaries and relations for benchmarking retrieval-based clinical decision support systems. arXiv e-prints arXiv-2202 (2022)

Incremental Recommendation Algorithm Based on the Influence Propagation Model

Siqi Wu[1], Jianming Lv[1(✉)], Chen Liu[2], and Hongmin Cai[1(✉)]

[1] School of Computer Science and Engineering, South China University of Technology, Guangzhou 510006, People's Republic of China
{jmlv,hmcai}@scut.edu.cn
[2] School of Information, North China University of Technology, Beijing 100144, China

Abstract. Recently, Graph based recommendation algorithms have gained more and more attention due to their flexible and unified embedding representation of both users and items as well as the effective modeling of context information for efficient recommendation. However, most of the existing graph recommendation methods are designed upon the static interaction graph, while neglecting the dynamic evolution of the graph. This paper proposes a lightweight Influence Propagation Model, namely IPM, for efficient recommendation on the dynamic evolving graphs. Specifically, IPM models the accumulating and propagating procedure of influence on the user-item interaction graph to obtain the characteristics of users and items. For dynamic changed edges of the graph, the amount of information about the relevant users and items can be quickly updated by propagating the impact associated with the added interactions. Our model exhibits very efficient performance and comparable recommendation results with the same experimental setup compared to advanced graph recommendation algorithms and dynamic graph embedding algorithms.

Keywords: Recommendation Algorithm · Incremental Algorithm · Graph Machine Learning · Influence Propagation Procedure

1 Introduction

With the development of the Internet and the popularity of mobile devices, vast amounts of data are generated every second, which causes the "Information overload" problem. It is difficult for people to find the parts they are interested in from the massive data. As a result, the recommended system was created. As a hot research topic in recent years, graph machine learning has also received much attention from recommendation algorithm researchers. Much research has been devoted to integrating graph machine learning into the recommendation domain [12,19,20,25,27–29]. However, due to the dynamic nature of real-world

L. Iliadis et al. (Eds.): ICANN 2023, LNCS 14260, pp. 310–324, 2023.
https://doi.org/10.1007/978-3-031-44195-0_26

recommendation tasks and the large scale of the data used for recommendations, it is a challenging problem to handle the incremental data for recommendation tasks efficiently.

There are many recent studies related to dynamic graph embedding. However, there needs to be more research on dynamic graph embedding in the recommendation domain. For the scenario of using graphs to model user-item interactions, the dynamic changes of graphs are mainly reflected in the new interactions between users and items. Training with incremental data is a problem that must be addressed in realistic recommendations.

GloDyNE [15] is the advanced dynamic graph embedding algorithm. It designs a node selection strategy to choose the nodes to be updated and then uses a Skip-Gram-based embedding method to perform the update. FILDNE [2] integrates feature vectors of different time steps, obtained using static graph embedding methods, into a single representation using convex combinatorial functions and alignment mechanisms. It is a framework for incremental learning of dynamic graph embeddings. However, these algorithms are not designed for recommendation tasks. Direct application of these algorithms does not yield good performance, although good efficiency can be obtained.

PinSAGE [28] is an application of the classical algorithm of graph machine learning, GraphSAGE [11], in realistic recommendation scenarios. However, it trains a graph-based aggregator to extract features of nodes by aggregation, which is only applicable to systems where nodes have initial features. NGCF [25] first applies graph convolution to collaborative filtering, which can achieve good performance when nodes do not have meaningful initial features. LightGCN [12] analyzed that feature transformation and nonlinear transformation are redundant in recommendation scenarios without initial features. Their removal further improves recommendation performance and makes the model more lightweight. The above two methods are advanced applications of graph convolution networks in collaborative filtering. However, the recommendation is a dynamic incremental process, and a simple approach to handling the incremental process is to retrain with static methods. But retraining can be time-consuming and resource-intensive.

We designed an **I**nfluence **P**ropagation **M**odel based on incremental recommendation scenarios (IPM) to tackle the above challenge. Influence propagation procedures for social networks have been studied for a long time in social science and marketing [1,8]. Inspired by this, we first randomly initialize the amount of information of nodes on the user-item interaction graph, then define the strength of influence propagation, obtain the final features of users and items by propagating and accumulating their amount of information, and finally update the amount of information of triple based on the idea of **B**ayesian **P**ersonalized **R**anking (BPR). Specifically, the training set used by BPR is a triple $<v_u, v_i, v_j>$, and it is considered that item v_i, which has interacted with user v_u, is ranked higher than item v_j, which has not interacted with it. So we build such triples and update the amount of node information by propagating positive influence between v_u and v_i and negative influence between v_u and v_j.

Compared with current graph recommendation algorithms, our model does not have to pass through the forward propagation and gradient back-propagation mechanisms of neural networks, but directly updates the node vector representing the node features by computing the propagation influence through the graph. It is more efficient and can be directly extended to the incremental case. For the added user-item interactions, we similarly construct triples and then propagate the account of information through the graph to efficiently update the relative nodes. For incremental recommendation algorithms, we use a new evaluation method to evaluate the incremental application of each method.

In summary, the main contributions of this work are as follows:

- We propose a recommendation algorithm based on an influence propagation model. It obtains and updates node features by propagating and accumulating the amount of information on the user-item interaction graph to generate the user's recommendation list.
- We design an efficient node informativeness update method for incremental data of recommendations and apply a new evaluation method to evaluate the recommendation performance of incremental scenarios.
- We conducted experiments on four classical recommendation datasets to validate the effectiveness of our model. The experimental results show that the model can significantly improve the efficiency of incremental training and achieve advanced recommendation performance.

2   Related Work

In this section, we introduce two directions related to our work: graph recommendation systems and dynamic graph embeddings.

2.1   Graph Neural Networks for Recommendation Systems

According to the taxonomy of [6], recommendation systems can be classified according to stages. In industrial applications, recommendation systems are split into three stages: matching, ranking, and re-ranking. The characteristics of the data at each stage are different and the requirements for the model are different. The work of this paper mainly designs the recommendation model for the data characteristics of the matching stage. The matching stage needs to generate a candidate list from the vast item library for ranking in the subsequent stage, so the model complexity of this stage should be low, and the deep neural network cannot be used.

PinSAGE [28] is the first application of graph convolutional neural networks to a realistic industrial matching model, and its underlying algorithm is GrapSAGE [11]. Although the inductive setting of GrapSAGE allows it to handle incremental data, as the amount of data increases, parameters that are not continually trained may cause the model to fail to recognize data patterns. NGCF [25] implements collaborative filtering directly on the user-item interaction graph using graph convolutional networks. Inspired by the simplified graph convolutional network [26], He et al. [12] found that the feature transformation and nonlinear transformation modules have a negative impact on the scene where the nodes in the graph have no initial attributes, so they proposed a LightGCN model that removes these two parts. IMP-GCN [19] believes that an important factor of the over-smoothing problem in recommendation is that the aggregation may contain users who have no common interests, so an unsupervised subgraph generation module is designed to identify users with common interests, and perform deeper graph convolutions on the sub-graphs. SGL [27] designs a self-supervised method by masking nodes, masking edges, and performing special random walks to improve the robustness of graph convolution recommendations. HS-GCN [20] projects users and items into Hamming space for efficiency and performs graph convolution in Hamming space. LGCN [29] improves the current low-pass collaborative filtering network from the perspective of spectral graph convolution, defines the graph space directly on the bipartite graph, and designs experiments to search for the most suitable network structure to achieve better performance.

Despite the great efforts of these algorithms to improve recommendation performance using graph machine learning, there is relatively little research on incremental graph recommendation algorithms that meet the requirements of the matching stage. We are committed to developing incremental recommendation algorithms that are more efficient and better effective.

2.2 Dynamic Graph Embedding

The early dynamic graph embedding methods mainly design continued training strategies on some popular static graph embedding methods, such as DynGEM [7], Dynnode2vec [21], and DynLINE [5], which are dynamic versions of the static graph embedding methods SDNE [24], Node2vec [9], and LINE [23], respectively. Unlike the previous approaches, GloDyNE [15] considers that the incremental learning paradigm of updating the most affected nodes is not conducive to preserving the global topology of the graph and therefore devises a strategy to diversify the selection of representative nodes on the network. SG-EDNE [14] improves the robustness of embeddings by integrating embeddings learned by learners with different restart probabilities of random walks to capture different levels of local-global topology. FILDNE [2] wants to leverage the advanced algorithms of static graph embedding to dynamic graph embedding, so an incremental learning framework for dynamic graph embedding is created. The static graph embedding method is used to obtain the embedding of incremental data. Then the developed alignment mechanism and convex combination function are used to obtain the node's updated embedding.

These algorithms have done much research on balancing the efficiency and performance of incremental graph algorithms. However, due to the specificity of user-item interaction graphs in recommendation systems (the user-item interaction graph is bipartite), advanced performance cannot be achieved by using these algorithms directly.

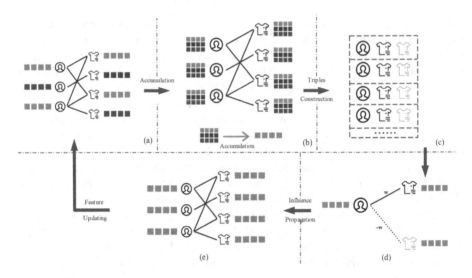

Fig. 1. The overall framework of the Influence Propagation Model.

3   The Proposed Model

Inspired by the influence propagation procedure of social networks, we propose a graph recommendation algorithm based on the influence propagation model as shown in Fig. 1, which can be divided into five main steps, namely Graph Construction, Propagation and Accumulation, Triple Construction, Propagation Influence, and Feature Updating. The first two steps can obtain the final features of nodes for the recommendation. The last three steps are to enhance the node's information, which can improve the performance of the recommendation. We describe each step in detail next.

3.1   Description of Information Propagation Model Steps

a) Graph Construction. We first construct the user-item interaction as a bipartite graph as in Fig. 1(a), where nodes represent users and items, and we use v_n to denote node n. The edges of the graph represent connected user-item interactions. $\mathcal{N}_n$ denotes the set of neighbors of a node v_n, and the degree of that node can be denoted by d_n, then $d_n = |\mathcal{N}_n|$. The degree is essential information to reflect the graph topology.

For users and items that only have IDs with no concrete semantics besides being an identifier, we randomly initialize a d-dimensional vector representing node information for each node. For node v_n, the initial node vector is denoted as $\mathbf{x_n} \in \mathbb{R}^d$.

b) Accumulation. In order to portray the propagation pattern of influence in the interaction graph, we first define the propagation coefficient of the amount of information on the interaction graph as

$$c_{n,i} = \frac{1}{\sqrt{d_n \times d_i}}, \tag{1}$$

where $c_{n,i}$ denotes the propagation coefficient of the edge connecting the nodes v_n and v_i. d_n and d_i are the degrees of nodes v_n and v_i, respectively. The coefficient embeds the topological information and takes the value in the range of $(0, 1]$, which does not cause the information explosion.

According to the defined propagation coefficient, we can propagate the information of the node on the interaction graph. The amount of information the node receives after each propagation is accumulated and used to propagate to the next hop's nodes. The following equation can express the amount of information a node receives after each dissemination.

$$\mathbf{x_n^{(l)}} = \sum_{i \in \mathcal{N}_n} c_{n,i} \cdot \mathbf{x_i^{(l-1)}}, \tag{2}$$

where $\mathbf{x_n^{(l)}}$ denotes the amount of information received by node v_n after l propagation, and we define the information of each node for the 0-th layer as its initial node vector, i.e., $\mathbf{x_n^{(0)}} = \mathbf{x_n}$.

After several propagations, we accumulate the amount of information received by the node and the initial node vector to obtain the final feature, i.e.

$$\mathbf{z_n} = \frac{1}{L+1} \sum_{l=0}^{L} \mathbf{x_n^{(l)}}. \tag{3}$$

The propagation number L is a parameter that can be adjusted and is generally set to 3.

Each node acquires the final feature by propagating and accumulating the amount of node information on the graph. The feature not only contains information about the node but also contains information about its neighborhood based on collaborative filtering. Each user node receives information about the item with which it directly interacts after disseminating information once on the interaction graph; after disseminating information twice on the interaction graph, each user node receives information about users with whom it has a common interest, i.e., who have interacted with the same item. Multiple disseminations of information can obtain higher-order synergistic information for the nodes. The same effect is achieved for item nodes. So the final feature has information on both user-based and item-based collaborative filtering.

We can directly use the final feature to generate a recommendation list for the user. The simplest way is to use the inner product of the user's features and the item's features as the recommendation preference score, and then recommend the top-ranked items to the user. The recommendation score $\hat{y}$ is calculated as

$$\hat{y} = \mathbf{z_u} \cdot \mathbf{z_i}, \tag{4}$$

where $\mathbf{z_u}$ and $\mathbf{z_i}$ denote the final features of user v_u and item v_i, respectively.

The recommendation effect of the final features at the current stage needs to be improved because the amount of information in each node is randomly initialized, and we need further updates to achieve better recommendation performance.

c) Triple Construction. The Bayesian personalized ranking is a commonly used recommendation algorithm, which believes that users have interacted with should receive a higher ranking than items that users have not interacted with. Based on this idea, we sample multiple triples on the interaction graph, defined as $<v_u, v_i, v_j>$, where item node v_i has interacted with user node v_u, obtained by random sampling among the neighbors $\mathcal{N}_u$ of the user node. v_j is an item node that has not interacted with user node v_u, obtained by random sampling among all items except those with whom the user has interacted.

d) Influence Propagation. The propagation performed in step **b)** is to enable each node to obtain information about its higher-order neighbors. The final features contain information about the initial features of the node and its neighbors. However, the initial features of the node still need to be updated. We update the nodes' initial features in this stage based on the Bayesian personalized ranking idea. For the triplet $<v_u, v_i, v_j>$, positive influence is propagated between v_u and v_i and negative influence is propagated between v_u and v_j. The parameters of the influence propagation are defined as follows:

$$\mathbf{w} = \alpha \cdot \sigma(\beta(\mathbf{z_u} \cdot \mathbf{z_j} - \mathbf{z_u} \cdot \mathbf{z_i})), \tag{5}$$

where α and β are hyper-parameters that control the strength of influence propagation, σ is the Sigmoid function, $\sigma = \frac{1}{1+exp(-x)}$, used to map the influence parameters to $(0, 1)$. The final features of the triple jointly determine the magnitude of the influence. According to the function property of Sigmoid, when $\mathbf{z_u} \cdot \mathbf{z_j} > \mathbf{z_u} \cdot \mathbf{z_i}$, the feature $\mathbf{z_j}$ of the un-interacted item is ranked more forward than the feature $\mathbf{z_i}$ of the interacted item, which is not what we want, so the influence should be greater. Vice versa, the influence should be smaller.

As shown in Fig. 1(d), we propagate influence between nodes v_u and v_i with influence parameter w, and negative influence between nodes v_u and v_j with influence parameter $-\mathbf{w}$. The influence is then spread and propagated in the interaction graph, as shown in Fig. 1(e).

e) Feature Updating. With step **d)**, we obtain the influence of Bayesian personalized ranking-based propagation. In this stage, we update the initial features of the nodes by superimposing this influence. Repeating the process of Fig. 1 until the influence propagation parameter tends to 0 to complete the training of the initial graph.

3.2 Incremental Data Processing

When a new interaction is generated, according to the influence propagation procedure, the associated nodes change from inactive to active and spread the influence in the network. Therefore, we construct the triple for each new interaction as in step **c)**, propagate the influence, and update the node features in the following steps.

It is important to note that we do not need to update the entire graph but only sample the sub-graph composed of nodes involved in the propagation range. This can significantly reduce the time and memory required for model updates. In addition, when a new node is added, we randomly initialize the information features of the new node. Its final features by propagation contain most of the features that were trained and stabilized at the last moment. So there is no destructive effect on the original information network, but it still tends to be stable after a small number of iterations.

The incremental processing makes users pay more attention to the most recent interactions. And recent interactions tend to be more important than earlier interactions [4, 16]. This is the reason why our model can achieve advanced recommendation performance.

4 Experiments

4.1 Experiment Settings

Datasets. We conduct experiments on four publicly available datasets, MovieLens-1M[1], MovieLens-10M (see footnote 1), LastFM [3] and Gowalla [18], We refer to the processing of [10, 13, 20] to convert the interaction to an implicit feedback form of 1 or 0 to indicate whether the user interacts with the item, and we show the information of the preprocessed datasets in Table 1.

Table 1. Statistics of the four datasets after pre-processing

Dataset	#Users	#Items	#Interactions	#Start_date	#End_date	#Split_point	#Split_interval
MovieLens-1M	6,040	3,706	1,000,209	2000/4/26	2003/3/1	2002/5/1	1 month
MovieLens-10M	69,804	10,656	10,000,054	1995/1/9	2009/1/5	2004/1/1	6 months
LastFM	983	35,432	18,138,847	2005/2/14	2009/6/19	2007/11/1	2 months
Gowalla	25,811	47,108	2,042,065	2009/2/4	2010/10/23	2010/1/1	1 month

Baseline Methods. We compare the proposed IPM method with the fully trained lightweight model LightGCN[2] [12] and the classical graph embedding

---

[1] http://files.grouplens.org/datasets/movielens/.

[2] https://github.com/gusye1234/LightGCN-PyTorch.

algorithm DeepWalk[3] [22], as well as the SOTA methods GloDyNE[3] [15] and FILDNE[4] [2] for dynamic graph embedding.

- **LightGCN:** LightGCN is a model that applies graph convolution to collaborative filtering by removing the feature transform and nonlinear transform modules.
- **DeepWalk:** This is the classical algorithm based on random wandering in static graph embedding and is also the base algorithm for the currently popular dynamic graph embedding.
- **GloDyNE:** GloDyNE is the best dynamic graph embedding method in recent years in terms of balancing efficiency and performance. It uses a new node selection strategy to select representative nodes for updating so that the global topology remains after incrementing the graph embedding.
- **FILDNE:** This is the latest incremental learning framework that can be based on any static graph embedding method. After training the incremental data with the base static method, FILDNE uses a combination of alignment mechanisms and convex functions for embedding. Here we use the LINE method, which works best, as the base method.

The data in the matching stage of the recommendation system is mass and limited by the memory of the machine and the time required. We chose LightGCN, which has implemented the lightest model in recent years and has open-source code, as one of our baselines and ignored graph recommendation methods with higher complexity, such as SGL [27]. In addition, IPM is a recommendation algorithm based on the user-item graph, and the obtained user and item embeddings contain higher-order synergistic information about interactions, which can be combined with other models that make use of side information.

Evaluation Protocol. To better simulate the arrival of data streams, we divide the dataset into two parts by temporal order with reference to [17,30]: (i) about the first 60% of the data is used to build the initial graph and train the original model; (ii) the remaining 40% of the data is called the candidate test set and is used to simulate the stream setup. We divide the candidate test set into 10 parts in temporal order, i.e., the number of days in each part is 4% of the total number of days, as shown in Fig. 2.

The first part of the candidate test set is used as the test set for the original model, i.e., 60%–64%. These data are then provided to the original model for incremental training, and then the next part, i.e., 64%–68%, is used as the test set. This process is repeated until 96%–100% are tested. The division of each dataset is shown in Table 1.

Evaluation Metrics. For each user in the test set, we consider all items that the user has not interacted with as a list of candidate items to be recalled, and then

---

[3] https://github.com/houchengbin/GloDyNE .
[4] https://gitlab.com/fildne.

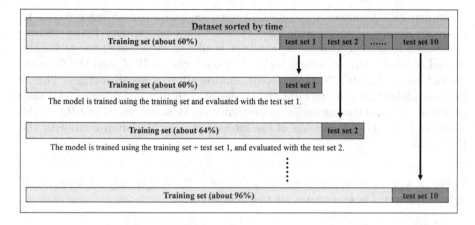

Fig. 2. Overview of the evaluation protocol.

output the user's preference scores with these items for each method. Typically, we recommend only the top-K items for the user. To evaluate the effectiveness of these preference score rankings, we use the same metrics as [12,25]: Precision@K, Recall@K, and NDCG@K. In our experiments, we fix K to be 20.

Implementation Details. The embedding size is set to 128 for all methods to ensure a fair comparison. For LightGCN, DeepWalk, and GloDyNE, we use the parameter settings recommended in the paper to train the models. For FILDNE, we use the hyperparameter search method provided in the open-source code to obtain the hyperparameters before training. For our IPM method, the number of sampling triples of the initial graph is set to 5 times the number of initial graph interactions, the propagation layer is set to 3 hops, α in the propagation parameter is set to 0.001, and β is set to 0.5. We perform trains and tests on a system with 20 Intel Xeon-Silver4114-2.2 GHz logical CPUs and 128 GB of memory, as well as a GeForce-GTX-1080Ti GPU with 12 GB of memory.

4.2 Experimental Results

In this section, we describe and analyze experiments on four datasets and demonstrate the effectiveness of our model IPM.

Performance Comparison with Baseline. Based on the settings of the evaluation protocol, we obtained the Precision, Recall, and NDCG recommended performance for each model in 10 incremental steps. We repeated running each experiment 5 times and obtained the mean and standard deviation for each incremental step, and then depicted the average results for all incremental steps in Table 2.

In general, the direct application of dynamic graph embedding methods to bipartite graphs of recommendation systems does not achieve better recommendation results. IPM achieves the best results in most cases, except for the MovieLens-10M dataset, where LightGCN outperforms IPM, and the Gowalla dataset where LightGCN slightly outperforms IPM in Recall metrics. This is because LightGCN fully retrains the model at each incremental step, and thus achieves advanced recommendation performance. However, retraining the model loses the temporal information of the interactions, so it is often inferior to the IPM model.

Table 2. Average recommended performance(all in %) of IPM and baseline methods in four datasets. The best results are shown in bold.

Dataset Methods	MovieLens-1M			MovieLens-10M		
	Precision	Recall	NDCG	Precision	Recall	NDCG
GloDyNE	0.841 ± 0.157	1.852 ± 0.64	1.511 ± 0.341	1.267 ± 0.055	0.745 ± 0.071	1.385 ± 0.069
FILDNE	0.149 ± 0.069	0.26 ± 0.27	0.236 ± 0.173	0.239 ± 0.122	0.267 ± 0.261	0.304 ± 0.169
DeepWalk	0.595 ± 0.104	1.34 ± 0.377	0.992 ± 0.227	2.755 ± 0.076	2.107 ± 0.107	3.239 ± 0.109
LightGCN	4.388 ± 0.11	7.972 ± 0.401	7.619 ± 0.179	$\mathbf{10.023 \pm 0.061}$	$\mathbf{5.371 \pm 0.063}$	$\mathbf{11.912 \pm 0.058}$
IPM (Ours)	$\mathbf{4.405 \pm 0.09}$	$\mathbf{8.063 \pm 0.4}$	$\mathbf{7.718 \pm 0.181}$	8.856 ± 0.056	4.229 ± 0.063	10.352 ± 0.067
Dataset Methods	LastFM			Gowalla		
	Precision	Recall	NDCG	Precision	Recall	NDCG
GloDyNE	0.7 ± 0.05	0.04 ± 0.021	0.737 ± 0.068	0.769 ± 0.012	1.648 ± 0.036	1.306 ± 0.021
FILDNE	0.075 ± 0.012	0.002 ± 0.001	0.081 ± 0.012	0.016 ± 0.003	0.032 ± 0.007	0.025 ± 0.005
DeepWalk	0.819 ± 0.043	0.052 ± 0.02	0.864 ± 0.055	0.815 ± 0.012	1.768 ± 0.029	1.425 ± 0.016
LightGCN	1.35 ± 0.483	0.099 ± 0.05	1.375 ± 0.466	1.778 ± 0.014	$\mathbf{3.809 \pm 0.052}$	3.276 ± 0.027
IPM (Ours)	$\mathbf{2.894 \pm 0.098}$	$\mathbf{0.158 \pm 0.025}$	$\mathbf{3.046 \pm 0.086}$	$\mathbf{1.796 \pm 0.018}$	3.728 ± 0.048	$\mathbf{3.364 \pm 0.047}$

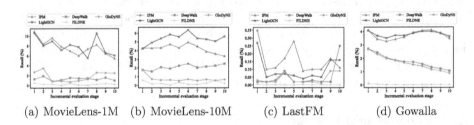

(a) MovieLens-1M   (b) MovieLens-10M   (c) LastFM   (d) Gowalla

Fig. 3. Recall on different datasets over all incremental steps.

Then, to better visualize the comparison among the methods, we show the Recall rate for each incremental step in the line chart (Fig. 3). Similar results are found for other metrics, and limited by space, we only show the results for Recall. From the line chart, we can observe more clearly that the Recall rate of IPM can achieve comparable results to LightGCN, the fully trained method, while being far better than other baseline methods. This proves the effectiveness of IPM in the incremental training of recommendation systems.

Training Time Comparison with Baseline. In this part, Table 3 reports the total time spent in the incremental training stage for all methods run on the same machine. It is clear that IPM is the most efficient method among all methods on all datasets. Compared to the second-least time-consuming method, IPM is ×20.5, ×9.6, ×3.3, and ×5.6 more efficient on the MovieLens-1M, MovieLens-10M, LastFM, and Gowalla datasets, respectively. LightGCN is efficient when the graph is small (MovieLens-1M) or sparse (Gowalla), but when the graph is dense (LastFM) or large (MovieLens-10M), the training efficiency of LightGCN is low and it takes up a lot of memory. In the last part, we noted that LightGCN can achieve better recommendation results, but considering the required training time, we found that the time efficiency of LightGCN makes it difficult to apply it in reality. GloDyNE can still maintain good efficiency when the graph is large or dense, but its recommendation performance needs to be improved. In summary, IPM is the best solution for incremental training of recommendation systems.

Table 3. Training time (in Seconds) over all incremental steps

Time (s)	MovieLens-1M	MovieLens-10M	LastFM	Gowalla
GloDyNE	379	8134	754	4829
FILDNE	325	10607	1073	17612
DeepWalk	1143	45276	6022	8245
LightGCN	308	13836	62243	732
IPM (Ours)	**15**	**846**	**230**	**131**

Parameter Sensitivity Analysis. In this part, we conduct experiments to evaluate the parameter sensitivity of the IPM model. In Fig. 4(a), the sensitivity results for the propagation range (layers) are given. The highest performance is achieved when the layer is 3. When the propagation range is too small, the influence cannot be fully propagated; while if the propagation range is too large it will make the node features over-smooth. The sensitivity results for embedding size are given in Fig. 4(b). As the embedding size increases, the accuracy rate is slowly decreasing, while the recall rate is slowly increasing. Considering the training difficulty of the model, we choose 128 dimensions as the parameters of the model. The sensitivity results of β in the influence parameter are given in Fig. 4(c). This parameter can control the strength of influence propagation. The experimental results prove that the model has good adaptivity and the influence propagation parameter has little effect on the model effect, and we choose the best effect of 0.5 as the model parameter.

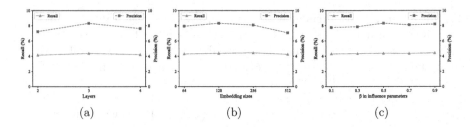

Fig. 4. Parameter sensitivity analysis. Results of different parameters.

5   Conclusion

In this paper, we propose an incremental recommendation algorithm based on the influence propagation model. We view user-item interactions as a process of information propagation over the interaction graph. Based on this idea, when a new interaction is generated, we can propagate the influence generated by the new interaction to its related neighbors for local node information updates. Experimental results on four widely used datasets demonstrate that our approach not only has advanced recommendation performance, but is also efficient. In the future, we will continue to explore if combining attribute information and temporal information when nodes have initial attributes can further improve recommendation performance while maintaining model efficiency.

Acknowledgements. This work was supported by the Science and Technology Program of Guangzhou, China (2023B03J1388) and the Key-Area Research and Development Program of Guangzhou City (202206030009).

References

1. Bass, F.M.: A new product growth for model consumer durables. Manage. Sci. **15**(5), 215–227 (1969)
2. Bielak, P., Tagowski, K., Falkiewicz, M., Kajdanowicz, T., Chawla, N.V.: FILDNE: a framework for incremental learning of dynamic networks embeddings. Knowl.-Based Syst. **236**, 107453 (2022)
3. Celma, O.: Music Recommendation and Discovery: The Long Tail, Long Fail, and Long Play in the Digital Music Space. Springer, Heidelberg (2010). https://doi.org/10.1007/978-3-642-13287-2
4. Dai, H., Wang, Y., Trivedi, R., Song, L.: Deep coevolutionary network: embedding user and item features for recommendation. arXiv preprint arXiv:1609.03675 (2016)
5. Du, L., Wang, Y., Song, G., Lu, Z., Wang, J.: Dynamic network embedding: an extended approach for skip-gram based network embedding. In: IJCAI, vol. 2018, pp. 2086–2092 (2018)
6. Gao, C., et al.: A survey of graph neural networks for recommender systems: challenges, methods, and directions. ACM Trans. Recommender Syst. **1**, 1–51 (2022)
7. Goyal, P., Kamra, N., He, X., Liu, Y.: DynGEM: deep embedding method for dynamic graphs. arXiv preprint arXiv:1805.11273 (2018)

8. Granovetter, M.: Threshold models of collective behavior. Am. J. Sociol. **83**(6), 1420–1443 (1978)
9. Grover, A., Leskovec, J.: node2vec: scalable feature learning for networks. In: Proceedings of the 22nd ACM SIGKDD International Conference on Knowledge Discovery and Data Mining, pp. 855–864 (2016)
10. Guo, L., Yin, H., Wang, Q., Chen, T., Zhou, A., Quoc Viet Hung, N.: Streaming session-based recommendation. In: Proceedings of the 25th ACM SIGKDD International Conference on Knowledge Discovery & Data Mining, pp. 1569–1577 (2019)
11. Hamilton, W., Ying, Z., Leskovec, J.: Inductive representation learning on large graphs. In: Advances in Neural Information Processing Systems, vol. 30 (2017)
12. He, X., Deng, K., Wang, X., Li, Y., Zhang, Y., Wang, M.: LightGCN: simplifying and powering graph convolution network for recommendation. In: Proceedings of the 43rd International ACM SIGIR Conference on Research and Development in Information Retrieval, pp. 639–648 (2020)
13. He, X., Zhang, H., Kan, M.Y., Chua, T.S.: Fast matrix factorization for online recommendation with implicit feedback. In: Proceedings of the 39th International ACM SIGIR Conference on Research and Development in Information Retrieval, pp. 549–558 (2016)
14. Hou, C., Fu, G., Yang, P., Hu, Z., He, S., Tang, K.: Robust dynamic network embedding via ensembles. arXiv preprint arXiv:2105.14557 (2021)
15. Hou, C., Zhang, H., He, S., Tang, K.: GloDyNE: global topology preserving dynamic network embedding. IEEE Trans. Knowl. Data Eng. **34**(10), 4826–4837 (2020)
16. Kumar, S., Zhang, X., Leskovec, J.: Predicting dynamic embedding trajectory in temporal interaction networks. In: Proceedings of the 25th ACM SIGKDD International Conference on Knowledge Discovery & Data Mining, pp. 1269–1278 (2019)
17. Latifi, S., Jannach, D.: Streaming session-based recommendation: when graph neural networks meet the neighborhood. In: Proceedings of the 16th ACM Conference on Recommender Systems, pp. 420–426 (2022)
18. Liang, D., Charlin, L., McInerney, J., Blei, D.M.: Modeling user exposure in recommendation. In: Proceedings of the 25th International Conference on World Wide Web, pp. 951–961 (2016)
19. Liu, F., Cheng, Z., Zhu, L., Gao, Z., Nie, L.: Interest-aware message-passing gcn for recommendation. In: Proceedings of the Web Conference 2021, pp. 1296–1305 (2021)
20. Liu, H., Wei, Y., Yin, J., Nie, L.: HS-GCN: hamming spatial graph convolutional networks for recommendation. IEEE Trans. Knowl. Data Eng. (2022)
21. Mahdavi, S., Khoshraftar, S., An, A.: dynnode2vec: scalable dynamic network embedding. In: 2018 IEEE International Conference on Big Data (Big Data), pp. 3762–3765. IEEE (2018)
22. Perozzi, B., Al-Rfou, R., Skiena, S.: DeepWalk: online learning of social representations. In: Proceedings of the 20th ACM SIGKDD International Conference on Knowledge Discovery and Data Mining, pp. 701–710 (2014)
23. Tang, J., Qu, M., Wang, M., Zhang, M., Yan, J., Mei, Q.: LINE: large-scale information network embedding. In: Proceedings of the 24th International Conference on World Wide Web, pp. 1067–1077 (2015)
24. Wang, D., Cui, P., Zhu, W.: Structural deep network embedding. In: Proceedings of the 22nd ACM SIGKDD International Conference on Knowledge Discovery and Data Mining, pp. 1225–1234 (2016)

25. Wang, X., He, X., Wang, M., Feng, F., Chua, T.S.: Neural graph collaborative filtering. In: Proceedings of the 42nd International ACM SIGIR Conference on Research and Development in Information Retrieval, pp. 165–174 (2019)
26. Wu, F., Souza, A., Zhang, T., Fifty, C., Yu, T., Weinberger, K.: Simplifying graph convolutional networks. In: International Conference on Machine Learning, pp. 6861–6871. PMLR (2019)
27. Wu, J., et al.: Self-supervised graph learning for recommendation. In: Proceedings of the 44th International ACM SIGIR Conference on Research and Development in Information Retrieval, pp. 726–735 (2021)
28. Ying, R., He, R., Chen, K., Eksombatchai, P., Hamilton, W.L., Leskovec, J.: Graph convolutional neural networks for web-scale recommender systems. In: Proceedings of the 24th ACM SIGKDD International Conference on Knowledge Discovery & Data Mining, pp. 974–983 (2018)
29. Yu, W., Zhang, Z., Qin, Z.: Low-pass graph convolutional network for recommendation. In: Proceedings of the AAAI Conference on Artificial Intelligence, vol. 36, pp. 8954–8961 (2022)
30. Zhang, Y., et al.: How to retrain recommender system? A sequential meta-learning method. In: Proceedings of the 43rd International ACM SIGIR Conference on Research and Development in Information Retrieval, pp. 1479–1488 (2020)

Scenic Spot Recommendation Method Integrating Knowledge Graph and Distance Cost

Yue Shen and Xiaoxu Zhu$^{(\boxtimes)}$

School of Computer Science and Technology, Soochow University, Suzhou, China
20195427025@stu.suda.edu.cn, xiaoxzhu@suda.edu.cn

Abstract. Aiming at the problem that the traditional collaborative filtering algorithm only considers external ratings and cold start when recommending attractions, this paper proposes an attraction recommendation algorithm integrated with knowledge graph. Firstly, we construct a user rating matrix based on user ratings and the number of reviews, and calculate the similarity of attractions. Then, we use TransR model to train the semantic vector matrix of attractions, and use cosine similarity formula to calculate the semantic similarity of attractions. Finally, the two similarities are fused and applied to ALS matrix factorization. At the same time, in order to make the model pay attention to user preferences and take into account the distance elements in the scenic spots for recommendation, the distance cost is integrated in the loss function. Experimental results on the scenic spots dataset show that the proposed algorithm is better than the traditional method in scenic spots recommendation.

Keywords: Collaborative filtering algorithm · Knowledge graph · Distance cost · Scenic spot recommendation

1 Introduction

With the development of the Internet and the continuous emergence of massive data, it is difficult for people to choose personalized information. In order to solve the problem of information overload and users' lack of clear needs, recommender systems in various fields have emerged. For example, e-commerce platforms provide similar products and related products to users through their purchase history and search history. Websites such as movies and books provide users with potentially interesting content through users' browsing history. Social platforms such as Weibo recommend relevant users and content through the friends that users have followed or the content that they have liked.

Recommender systems have made breakthroughs in these vertical fields, but there are still many challenges when they are applied to tourism. Compared with traditional commodity recommendation, the cold start problem in the tourism field is more prominent, and it is difficult to obtain users 'historical travel records and travel preferences of most users. It is also more difficult to model user preferences, as in addition to considering functions and effects, the selection of travel destinations usually includes extrinsic factors such as distance and weather and intrinsic factors such as emotions and preferences.

To solve the above problems, this paper proposes a recommendation method combining knowledge graph and distance cost. The main contributions of this paper are as follows:

- We propose to integrate tourism knowledge graph to solve the cold start problem of collaborative filtering algorithm;
- We integrate user rating similarity and semantic similarity and combine ALS matrix factorization algorithm to improve recommendation performance;
- We add the overall distance cost in the recommendation of attractions to adjust the influence of the distance of attractions on the interest of users.

2   Related Work

2.1   Traditional Scenic Spot Recommendation Method

In recent years, personalized travel recommendation has received much attention. As the travel destination of tourists, tourist attractions are the most important factors that affect tourists' travel decisions, and they are also the hotspots of tourism recommendation research. Compared with the recommendation in the field of books and movies, attraction recommendation in the tourism field faces many challenges, such as attraction diversity, tourists' personalized preferences, attraction feature diversity, data sparsity, cold start problem and vulnerability to context factors. These problems affect the personalization and accuracy of attraction recommendation.

The traditional scenic spot recommendation method is Collaborative Filtering (CF) algorithm [1], which recommends scenic spots by measuring the similarity of tourists or scenic spots. Xu and Chen et al. used CF algorithm to provide suggestions for tourists with similar topic preferences [2]. CUI et al. used collaborative filtering technology based on GPS trajectories for personalized travel route recommendation [3]. Fu et al. proposed a personalized collaborative filtering recommendation method based on Bayesian network [4]. In order to alleviate the sparsity of the data, researchers add different background information to their thinking. For example, Huang et al. designed three kinds of CF with context-aware functions, which can recommend scenic spots in line with tourists' preferences and backgrounds [5]. All the above methods improve the user similarity calculation by performing a more fine-grained analysis of the attractions, considering various factors that affect the user similarity, strengthening the association between the attractions, and alleviating the impact of data sparsity on the results to a certain extent. However, it is not enough to describe how much a user likes an attraction by only rating the attraction.

In recent years, the model-based collaborative filtering algorithm Matrix Factorization (MF) [6, 7] has become the focus of research, which calculates the user's rating of the item through the prediction of the user feature matrix and the item feature matrix. The existing attraction recommendation methods based on matrix factorization use traditional implicit matrix to express the potential characteristics of items. For example, Yong et al. used the traditional matrix factorization model to recommend attractions, and at the same time, added time and travel cost features, so as to make better recommendations for users [8]. Based on the traditional matrix factorization, Li et al. combined scenic spot features such as travel season, travel mode and interest category to calculate user interest preferences, so as to use the hybrid recommendation method to recommend scenic spots for users [9]. All of the above methods add scenic spot features to the traditional matrix factorization model, but because they use the implicit matrix, they do not really mine the scenic spot features, resulting in the lack of interpretability of the recommendation results.

2.2 Recommendation Method Based on Knowledge Graph

Knowledge Graph (KG) is a structure that describes entities or concepts and connects them using different types of semantic relationships. As an emerging auxiliary data source, knowledge graph has attracted more and more attention. For example, Wang et al. [10] proposed RippleNet model, which obtains the user's preference for candidate items by superadding multiple ripples on the knowledge graph caused by the items that users have clounded in the history, realizes the extraction of user features, and effectively improves the accuracy of the recommendation algorithm. Wang et al. [11] proposed a Knowledge Graph Attention Network (KGAT) based on graph convolutional network, which defines convolution on graph data. The core idea is to use the attention mechanism to retain the attributes shared by weights when calculating the neighborhood set of the central node. Wang et al. [12] proposed the KGCN model, which used user and item attributes to propose a graph neural network recommendation model using knowledge graph as auxiliary information, effectively alleviating the sparsity and cold start problems and improving the recommendation effect.

The introduction of knowledge graph into recommendation algorithm has been relatively mature in the fields of books and movies. For example, Zhou et al. [13] proposed a book recommendation method that integrates knowledge graph and collaborative filtering, and fuses the two results by replacing the high ones with the low ones to form the final recommendation results. Yuan et al. [14] used knowledge graph reasoning to complete movie knowledge and improve the accuracy of the recommendation algorithm. But it has yet to develop in tourism.

In summary, in order to better recommend attractions, this paper proposes an attraction recommendation algorithm combining knowledge graph and collaborative filtering. The knowledge graph is used as supplementary information to overcome the problem of lack of attraction semantic information in collaborative filtering algorithm and improve the cold start problem of items in recommendation algorithm.

3   Methodology

3.1   Overview of Our Approach

By fusing the semantic similarity and collaborative filtering similarity between attractions, the effect of combining external scoring and intensive knowledge is realized. In this paper, we first construct the tourism knowledge graph, obtain the low-dimensional vector representation of the attractions through the TransR model, and then calculate the semantic similarity between the attractions to obtain the semantic neighbors of the attractions. Then, the similarity between attractions is calculated through the user rating matrix, and the fusion ratio is set to fuse the semantic similarity matrix with the similarity matrix obtained by external scoring to calculate the prediction score. Finally, the distance cost was integrated into the prediction score to obtain the final recommendation result. The flow of the TransR-ALS algorithm is shown in Fig. 1.

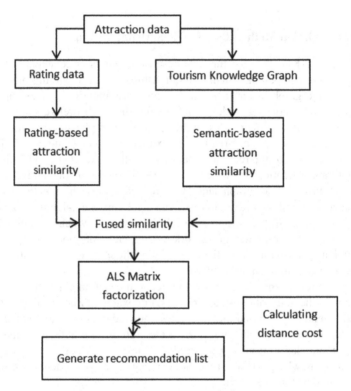

Fig. 1. Algorithm flow chart in this paper

3.2   Improved Collaborative Filtering Algorithm

Collaborative filtering recommendation algorithm is one of the most widely used recommendation algorithms. It discovers user preferences by mining user's historical behavior data, divides users into groups based on different preferences and recommends products with similar tastes. The improved collaborative algorithm in this paper can be mainly divided into three parts.

Construct the User-Attraction Scoring Matrix. Let $U = \{U_1, U_2, ..., U_m\}$ be the set of all users with m users. Let $I = \{I_1, I_2, ..., I_n\}$ be the set of all attractions with n attractions. Then the user-attraction rating matrix is:

$$R_{m \times n} = \begin{bmatrix} S_{11} & S_{12} & \cdots & S_{1n} \\ S_{21} & S_{22} & \ldots & S_{2n} \\ \vdots & \vdots & & \vdots \\ S_{m1} & S_{m2} & \cdots & S_{mn} \end{bmatrix} \tag{1}$$

where R_{ij} is the rating of the user U_i to the attraction I_j, and the level of the rating represents the liking degree of user U_i to attraction I_j. In view of the situation that the same user reviews the same scenic spot many times, this paper adopts the strategy of average score.

Calculate Attraction Similarity. When calculating the similarity of scenic spot vectors, cosine similarity is used as the evaluation criterion in this paper. Consider a user's rating of an attraction as an m-dimensional vector, for example, the rating vector of attraction i is $I_i = (S_{1i}, S_{2i}, \ldots, S_{mi})$, then the cosine similarity of attraction i and attraction j is:

$$Sim_{cf}(i, j) = \cos(I_i, I_j) = \frac{I_i \cdot I_j}{\|I_i\| \times \|I_j\|} = \frac{\sum_{u=1}^{m} S_{ui} \cdot S_{uj}}{\sqrt{\sum_{u=1}^{m} S_{ui}^2} \cdot \sqrt{\sum_{u=1}^{m} S_{uj}^2}} \tag{2}$$

where U_i and U_j denote the set of users who rate attractions I_i and I_j, the value of $Sim_{cf}(i, j)$ ranges from [0, 1], and the larger the value, the higher the similarity of two attractions.

Considering that in real life, users have different scoring habits, some users generally have higher scores, and some users generally have lower scores, which will affect the calculation of preference similarity. Therefore, if we subtract the average rating from the rating before calculating the cosine similarity, the formula becomes:

$$Sim_{cf}(i, j) = \frac{\sum_{u=1}^{m} (S_{ui} - \overline{S_u}) \cdot (S_{uj} - \overline{S_u})}{\sqrt{\sum_{u=1}^{m} (S_{ui}^2 - \overline{S_u})} \cdot \sqrt{\sum_{u=1}^{m} (S_{uj}^2 - \overline{S_u})}} \tag{3}$$

where $\overline{S_u}$ represents the average rating of the user. Subtract the average historical rating of the user from the user's rating of the scenic spot, which can avoid the problem of inconsistent standards when the user gives the rating.

Nearest Neighbor Selection. In the nearest neighbor selection, we first set the threshold, filter the attractions whose similarity is lower than the threshold, and then sort the similarity size of the remaining attractions, and finally take out the top k attractions.

3.3 Construct the Semantic Similarity Matrix

The knowledge graph consists of knowledge triple head entities, relation entities and tail entities. The study of mapping knowledge graph content (including entities and relations) to a continuous vector space is called knowledge graph embedding, also known as knowledge graph representation learning and knowledge representation learning. Knowledge representation learning models are mainly divided into translation models, distance models, neural network models and tensor models. Among them, the representative translation model is the TransE[15] model proposed by Bordes et al.

In TransE model, entities and relations are embedded into the same low-dimensional vector space, which makes up for the shortcomings of traditional methods that are complex to train and difficult to expand. However, it is only suitable for dealing with 1-1 typed relations, and has obvious defects when dealing with 1-N and N-N complex relations. However, there are one-to-many inclusion relationships and many-to-many orientation relationships in the attraction relationship, and the attributes of attractions are diverse. Therefore, this paper chooses the TransR model.

For each triple, the TransR model projects the entities in the entity space into the relationship space r through the matrix M_r, which are h_r and t_r respectively. Then the head and tail entities are mapped as $h_r + r \approx t_r$ in the TransR model. Thus the score function can be defined as:

$$f_r(h, t) = \|\mathbf{h_r} + \mathbf{r} - \mathbf{t_r}\|_2^2 \tag{4}$$

where $\| \cdot \|_2$ represents the 2-norm of the vector, i.e. the Euclidean distance.

The loss function at training time is shown in Eq. 5.

$$L = \sum_{(h,r,t)\in S} \sum_{(h',r,t')\in S'} \left[\gamma + f_r(h, t) - f_r(h', t') \right]_+ \tag{5}$$

where $[x]_+$ represents the maximum value between 0 and x, and γ is a marginal hyperparameter that can be used to control the distance between positive and negative triples in vector space and prevent weight collapse during model training. The main function of the objective function is to make the $f_r(h, t)$ value of the positive triple tend to 0 and the $f_r(h\prime, t\prime)$ value of the negative triple tend to infinity.

The semantic vector matrix and relational vector matrix of scenic spots were trained by the transR model, and then the semantic vector matrix of scenic spots was converted into the semantic similarity matrix of scenic spots by the similarity formula. Finally, the semantic nearest neighbor of each scenic spot could be obtained. When calculating semantic similarity, cosine similarity is selected in this paper, and the formula is as follows:

$$sim_{kg}(A, B) = \frac{\sum_{i=1}^{n} A_i \cdot B_i}{\sqrt{\sum_{i=1}^{n} (A_i)^2} \cdot \sqrt{\sum_{i=1}^{n} (B_i)^2}} \tag{6}$$

where A and B represent two attraction vectors. When the similarity of two attractions A and B is larger, the $sim_{kg}(A, B)$ is closer to 1, and the semantic similarity of two attractions in the knowledge graph is larger. Finally, the semantic similarity matrix of scenic spots to scenic spots was calculated.

3.4 Attraction Recommendation with Distance Cost

In this paper, the similarity obtained by collaborative filtering algorithm and the semantic similarity of scenic spots obtained by knowledge graph representation learning are fused in a linear weighted manner, and the fusion formula is as follows:

$$sim(I_i, I_j) = \alpha \cdot sim_{kg}(I_i, I_j) + (1 - \alpha) \cdot sim_{cf}(I_i, I_j) \tag{7}$$

where α is the weight coefficient and $0 < \alpha < 1$.

The similarity of attractions calculated by introducing the knowledge graph can more accurately estimate the predicted score of tourists for attractions, and form a recommendation list according to the predicted score. Let F_{ui} denote the predicted rating of user u for attraction i, which is calculated as follows:

$$F_{ui} = \frac{\sum_{j \in A(u) \cap X(i,k)} sim(i, j) \times S_{uj}}{\sum_{j \in A(u) \cap X(i,k)} sim(i, j)} \tag{8}$$

where $X(i, k)$ is the top k attractions that are similar to attraction i, $A(u)$ represents the attraction that has been rated by the user u, $A(u) \cap X(i, k)$ represents the intersection of two attraction sets, $sim(i, j)$ is the fusion similarity of attraction i and j, and $S_{u,j}$ is the rating of attraction j by user u.

Using matrix factorization algorithm to do collaborative filtering is a widely used method at present. By decomposing the co-occurrence matrix, the similarity of users and the similarity of items are expressed in the form of hidden vectors to achieve high-quality recommendation.

The most commonly used method is singular value decomposition (SVD), which requires that the matrix cannot have missing data and must be dense. However, the attraction user rating matrix is a typical sparse matrix, so this paper adopts alternating least squares matrix factorization (ALS). The knowledge graph is used to assist in calculating the similarity to predict the user rating and fill the user rating matrix, and the ALS decomposition is combined to form a recommendation list for users. The ALS decomposition formula is as follows:

$$R_{mn} \approx X_{m \times k} Y_{k \times n}^T \tag{9}$$

where $R_{m \times n}$ represents the user's rating matrix for the scenic spot, $X_{m \times k}$ represents the user preference feature matrix and $Y_{k \times n}$ represents the scenic spot feature matrix. Then the loss function of the matrix factorization model is as follows:

$$Loss(U, V) = \sum_{i,u}(r_{ui} - x_u y_i^T)^2 + \lambda(\sum_u \|x_u\|^2 + \sum_i \|y_i\|^2) \tag{10}$$

where r_{ui} is the actual rating, x_u is the user matrix, and y_i is the item matrix. The inner product of the user matrix and the item matrix, which represents the predicted rating of user u for attraction i. The λ is the regularization coefficient, in order to ensure the stability of the numerical calculation and prevent overfitting.

The predicted score of the attraction can be obtained by matrix multiplication of the decomposed user matrix and attraction matrix. The higher the rating value, the more likely the user likes the attraction. In order to make the model consider the distance element in the attraction sequence while paying attention to the user's preference, this paper proposes an attraction recommendation algorithm based on distance optimization. After calculating the prediction score, we add the distance cost calculation, which is calculated as follows:

$$r_{ui} = r_{ui} - \tau D(L_i) \tag{11}$$

$$D(L_i) = dist(pos(q_i) - pos(q_s)) = \arctan((J_i - J_s) * \cos(W_i)/(W_i/W_s)) \tag{12}$$

where r_{ui} is user u's predicted rating of attraction i. $D(L_i)$ is the distance cost, $pos(q_i)$ is the geographical location corresponding to the predicted value q_i, $pos(q_s)$ is the geographical location of the starting point, $dist(pos(q_j), pos(q_s))$ is the distance between q_j and q_s, J_i and J_s are the longitude of spots i and s, W_i and W_s are the latitude of spots i and s. τ is a hyper parameter to adjust the proportion of distance cost. Since the distance between scenic spots is at most 100 km, we set τ to 0.001.

4 Experiments

4.1 Datasets

STravel (Suzhou Travel Dataset), the dataset used in this paper, includes user travel behavior data and scenic spot knowledge graph data. Taking Suzhou as an example, we crawled user travel data from 'Ctrip' and 'Tong Cheng' websites, and finally collected 38,569 user reviews with a score range of [0, 5], part of the scoring data is shown in Table 1. We sorted the review set according to time, with the first 80% as the training set and the last 20% as the test set.

The entity relationship data of the tourism knowledge graph comes from the websites of "Ctrip" and "Baidu Baike". We construct the tourism knowledge graph through the graph database Neo4j, and finally obtain 200 scenic spot entities, including 10 attributes such as Chinese name, English name, address, contact phone number, and ticket and attraction relationships such as attraction level, attraction type, and distance.

Table 1. STravel dataset information

Dataset	STravel
#users	5921
#items	200
#interactions	38569
#KG triples	4269

4.2 Experimental Index

In order to compare with the baseline methods, we select three evaluation metrics, precision, Recall and AUC, to evaluate the performance of each model. The definition of recall is as follows (Table 2):

Table 2. Parameters

Real result	Need recommendation	No need
Practical recommendation	TP	FP
Not recommended	FN	TN

$$Precison = \frac{TP + TN}{TP + FN + FP + TN} \qquad (13)$$

$$Recall = \frac{TP}{TP + FN} \qquad (14)$$

The recall rate reflects the ratio of the attractions recommended to the user to the attractions that the user likes. The accuracy reflects whether the user preferences are correctly predicted. AUC is the surface area enclosed by the ROC curve and the abscissa. The closer the AUC is to 1, the better the recommendation.

4.3 Experimental Results and Analysis

Determination of the Fusion Factor. In this paper, we propose to fuse the similarity of collaborative filtering based on item ratings and the similarity of knowledge graph through the fusion factor, and the value range of is [0, 1]. In the experiment, it was increased from 0 to 1 by 0.1 each time, a total of 11 groups of experiments were carried out, and each experiment was repeated 10 times and the average value was taken. The experimental results are shown in Fig. 2.

As can be seen from the figure, we set the number of nearest neighbors k is 30, when the fusion factor is 0.6, the recommendation effect is the best, and when the fusion factor is greater than 0.6, the recommendation effect gradually decreases, so we set the fusion factor to 0.6.

Comparison of Algorithms. In order to verify the effectiveness of TranR-ALS algorithm, we conduct comparative experiments with benchmark algorithms CF, TransE-CF, RippleNet, DeepFM, and KGCN respectively. Among them, the embedding dimension of representation learning is set to 60, α is set to 0.6, and the number of nearest neighbors k is selected as 5, 10, 20, 30 and 50, respectively, and the experiment is performed 10 times and the average value is taken. The experimental results are shown in Fig. 3, Fig. 4 and Fig. 5.

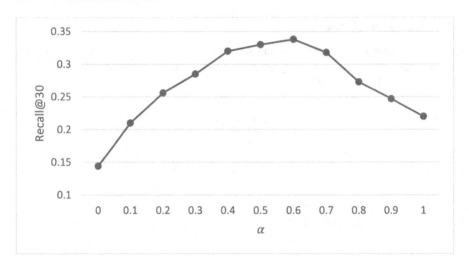

Fig. 2. Results for different fusion weights

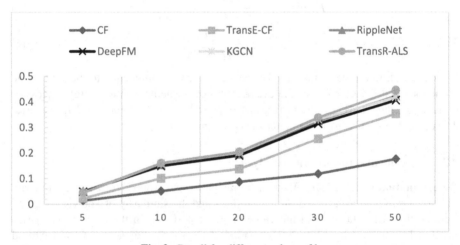

Fig. 3. Recall for different values of k

The experimental results show that as the number of nearest neighbors K gradually increases, the recall rate of each model also gradually increases. It can be seen from Fig. 3 that the proposed algorithm outperforms the baseline algorithm in both metrics of recall and precision, and the recall advantage is most obvious when the number of neighbors is 30. Although the accuracy decreases as the number of neighbors increases, the algorithms in this paper are all slightly higher than the other algorithms. It can be seen from Fig. 4 that the AUC of the proposed algorithm is significantly higher than that of the classical algorithm and slightly higher than that of the KGCN algorithm, indicating the rationality of the proposed algorithm for improving the quality of scenic spot recommendation.

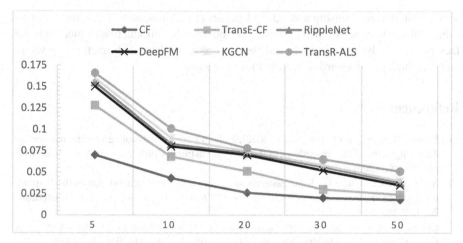

Fig. 4. Precision for different values of k

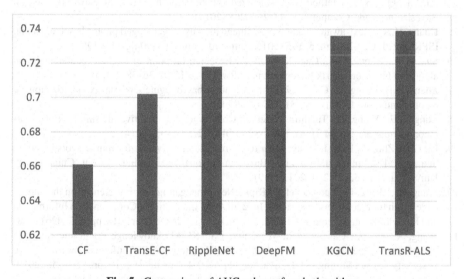

Fig. 5. Comparison of AUC values of each algorithm

5 Conclusion

This paper proposes an attraction recommendation method combining knowledge graph and collaborative filtering. Firstly, the knowledge graph is used to obtain the low-dimensional vector representation of the attraction and calculate the semantic similarity of the attraction. Then, the similarity of the attraction based on the rating is calculated by the user rating moment. Finally, the two similarities were fused and applied to the ALS matrix factorization technology for scenic spot recommendation. The distance cost calculation is added to the recommendation process to optimize the impact of distance on user travel. The algorithm takes into account not only the user's travel preference, but also the internal relationship and external factors of the attractions. However, the algorithm still needs to be optimized, such as considering the introduction of more external factors such as dynamic weather and the use of knowledge graph relationship vector matrix, which puts forward new ideas for future work.

References

1. Sarwar, B., Karypis, G., Konstan, J., Riedl, J.: Item-based collaborative filtering recommendation algorithms. In: Proceedings of the 10th International Conference on World Wide Web, pp. 285–295 (2001)
2. Xu, Z., Chen, L., Chen, G.: Topic based context-aware travel recommendation method exploiting geotagged photos. Neurocomputing 99–107 (2015). https://doi.org/10.1016/j.neucom.2014.12.043
3. Cui, G., Luo, J., Wang, X.: Personalized travel route recommendation using collaborative filtering based on GPS trajectories. Int. J. Digit. Earth **11**, 284–307 (2018). https://doi.org/10.1080/17538947.2017.1326535
4. Fu, Y.P., Qiu, Y.H.: Method of personalized collaboration filter recommendation based on Bayesian network. Comput. Sci. **43**, 266–268 (2016)
5. Huang, H.: Context-aware location recommendation using geotagged photos in social media. ISPRS Int. J. Geo-Inform. **5**, 195 (2016). https://doi.org/10.3390/ijgi5110195
6. Sun, H.W., Zhong, S.B., Cao, X.W., et al.: Research on point of interest recommendation algorithm based on matrix factorization. Softw. Guide **15**(9), 36–38 (2016)
7. Zhang, Q.B., Wang, B., Cui, N.N., et al.: Attention-based regularized matrix factorization for recommendation. J. Softw. **31**(3), 778–793 (2020)
8. Yong, G.E., Xiong, H., Tuzhilin, A., et al.: Cost-aware collaborative filtering for travel tour recommendations. ACM Trans. Inf. Syst. (TOIS) **32**(1), 1–31 (2014)
9. Li, G.L., Zhu, T., Hua, J., et al.: Hybrid recommendation system for tourist spots based on hierarchical sampling statistics and Bayesian personalized ranking. J. Cent. China Norm. Univ. (Nat. Sci.) **53**(2), 214–221 (2019)
10. Wang, H., Zhang, F., Wang, J., et al.: RippleNet: propagating user preferences on the knowledge graph for recommender systems. In: 27th ACM International Conference on Information and Knowledge Management (CIKM), Torino, Italy, 22–26 October 2018, pp. 417–426 (2018)
11. Wang, X., He, X., Cao, Y., Liu, M., Chua, T.S.: KGAT: knowledge graph attention network for recommendation. In: 25th ACM SIGKDD International Conference on Knowledge Discovery & Data Mining (KDD), Anchorage, AK, 04–08 August 2019, pp. 950–958 (2019)
12. Wang, H., Zhao, M., Xie, X., Li, W., Guo, M.: Knowledge graph convolutional networks for recommender systems. In: WWW 2019: The World Wide Web Conference, pp. 3307–3313 (2019)
13. Zhou, Q., Wang, S., Li, L., Huang, S., Wang, Y.: A book recommendation algorithm integrating knowledge map and collaborative filtering. Softw. Guide **008**, 021 (2022)
14. Yuan, Q., Cheng, Z.H., Jiang, Y.: Research on film recommendation algorithm based on knowledge graph and collaborative filtering. Comput. Eng. Sci. 714–721 (2020)
15. Bordes, A., Usunier, N., Garcia-Durán, A.: Translating embeddings for modeling multi-relational data. In: Nevada: Proceedings of the 26th International Conference on Neural Information Processing Systems, pp. 2787–2795 (2013)

A Unified Video Semantics Extraction and Noise Object Suppression Network for Video Saliency Detection

Zhenshan Tan[iD] and Xiaodong Gu[(✉)][iD]

Department of Electronic Engineering, Fudan University, Shanghai 200438, China
xdgu@fudan.edu.cn

Abstract. Video salient object detection (VSOD) aims to segment the most attractive objects from a video sequence. Exploring video semantics and suppressing noise objects are two challenges in the VSOD. In this paper, we propose a unified end-to-end network with video Semantics Extraction and Noise Object suppression (SENO). SENO has two modules, including a video semantics module (VSM) and a contrastive learning module (CLM). VSM extracts video semantics by calculating global pixel correspondences, locating the video salient objects. CLM pulls close video foregrounds and pushes away interference objects, which enhances effective video salient features and suppresses noise objects. CLM is only applied during training, avoiding extra overhead during inference. Besides, our SENO does not use the pre-processing temporal modeling techniques such as optical flow methods, which avoids high computational costs and accumulated inaccuracies caused by these complex models. Experimental results on five benchmark testing datasets show that our SENO outperforms state-of-the-art methods. In addition, the proposed SENO can detect results in real-time.

Keywords: Video salient object detection · Video semantics extraction · Noise object suppression

1 Introduction

Different from the saliency detection [20,21,23,26] that only detects objects from a single image and different from the co-saliency detection [22,24,25] that detects same semantic objects from multiple images, video salient object detection (VSOD) aims at exploring attractive and motion related objects from a given video sequence. Benefiting from this, VSOD has been widely used in various tasks such as video tracking, video retrieval, video person re-identification and video captioning.

Because of the special characteristic of video, the temporal information is very important. Nowadays, most of the VSOD methods [1,3–5,8,10,14,15,19,27] are based on deep neural networks and these methods can be roughly divided into two categories, including explicitly temporal extraction networks [3,5,14,15] and implicitly temporal extraction networks [4,8,10,19,27]. The explicit networks

L. Iliadis et al. (Eds.): ICANN 2023, LNCS 14260, pp. 337–348, 2023.
https://doi.org/10.1007/978-3-031-44195-0_28

usually adopt the pre-processing temporal modeling techniques such as Con-vLSTM and optical flow methods. They extract the moving information by the pre-training temporal methods first and then aggregate the spatiotemporal information. Although these methods achieve promising results, the pre-processing step consumes extra computational costs. Moreover, these temporal modeling techniques easily suffer from cumulative errors. Compared with the explicit-ness based methods, implicitly temporal extraction networks focus on directly extracting video salient objects without specifically calculating the temporal information. However, these methods still have two challenges: 1) video seman-tics extraction and 2) noise object suppression. For the first one, current methods usually extract video semantics by calculating the video representation at the image level, which may lose some necessary features. Gu et al. [10] utilize the constrained self-attention to extract video semantics. Nevertheless, the hand-crafted constrained operation may limit the global attentions. For the second one, due to the lack of explicitly temporal extraction, existing implicit methods are difficult to filter the noise objects such as non-same objects, non-moving objects, and non-salient objects.

Motivated by the above challenges, we propose a unified end-to-end network with video semantics extraction and noise object suppression (SENO). SENO is an implicitly temporal extraction network. To address these two challenges in implicit methods, we design two modules in SENO, including a video semantics module (VSM) and a contrastive learning module (CLM). To address the first challenge, VSM computes the video semantics at the pixel level among all frames in a video. Calculating the pixel-wise correspondences, VSM can maximize the inter-frame salient feature compactness and enable the network to concentrate on the video salient objects. To address the second challenge, CLM introduces the contrastive learning scheme into VSOD. CLM aims to pull the foreground pairs together and push the noise objects away [2,6]. Similarly, the contrastive learning scheme aims to pull positive samples close to the anchor and push negative samples away from the anchor. Obviously, the contrastive learning scheme can be naturally applied into the VSOD. Besides, we use two video sequences instead of the traditional single video sequence, because the added video sequence brings more information. If we regard these two video salient objects as opposing each other, the network will directly see non-same objects and therefore learn to suppress them. In addition, CLM suppresses non-moving objects and non-salient objects by pushing away foreground-background pairs. Consequently, CLM can filter out noise objects.

Generally, the main contributions of this paper can be summarized as:

- A video semantics module is designed to extract video semantics by calcu-lating the global correspondences at the pixel level, which maximizes the inter-frame compactness and make the network focus on the salient regions.
- We propose a contrastive learning module to enhance the effective informa-tion and suppress the noise objects, including non-same objects, non-moving objects, and non-salient objects. Besides, CLM is only used during training and avoids extra overhead during inference.

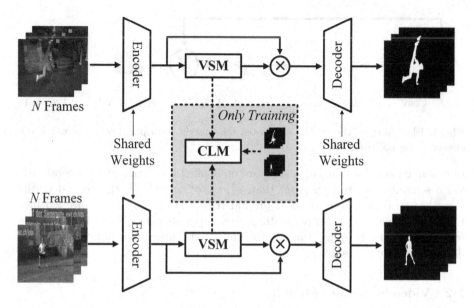

Fig. 1. Overall architecture. We use the shared-weights encoder and decoder as the baseline. Following previous methods, we adopt ResNet-101 as the encoder network. $\otimes$ denotes the element-wise multiplication. VSM: video semantics module. CLM: contrastive learning module. CLM is only used during training.

- Quantitative and qualitative experiments show that the proposed method outperforms other competitors. The ablation studies verify the effectiveness of each proposed module.

2   Proposed Method

2.1   Architecture Overview

Figure 1 illustrates the flowchart of the proposed method (SENO). Following previous methods, we adopt a commonly used encoder-decoder structure as the baseline. Besides, we design a video semantics module (VSM) to locate the video salient features. Then we propose a contrastive learning module (CLM) to pull the foregrounds together and push away the noise objects. These two modules and the adopted baseline are combined to a unified framework and supervised by a hybrid loss function.

Specifically, given two video sequences as inputs and each number of sequence frames is N, they are fed into a shared-weights ResNet-101 to generate the corresponding encoder features. We use the $5 - th$ encoder features e_5^1 and e_5^2 as the processed features, where $e_5 \in \mathbb{R}^{N \times C \times H \times W}$, C is the channel number, $H \times W$ is the dimensional size, and the superscripts 1 and 2 are the video sequence number. Then, e_5^1 and e_5^2 are transferred to the VSM to distill consensus

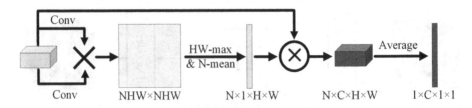

Fig. 2. Flowchart of the VSM. × denotes the matrix multiplication. ⊗ denotes the element-wise multiplication.

representations o^1 and o^2. e_5^1 and e_5^2 are multiplied by o^1 and o^2 to generate the video semantics s^1 and s^2. After that, e_5^1, e_5^2, o^1, o^2, s^1, s^2, the ground truths t^1 and t^2, and the reversed-phase ground truths $1 - t^1$ and $1 - t^2$ are fed into the CLM to enhance effective features and suppress noises. Note that CLM is only used during training. Finally, the enhanced features are inputted into the decoder to predict results m^1 and m^2.

2.2 Video Semantics Module

Video semantics locate the video salient features. Previous methods usually extract video semantics at the image level, which rely on the feature fusion manner. However, the widely used feature fusion manner applies the correlation operation and can be regarded as a local linear matching process, which easily loses vital details and lacks of global views. Although Gu et al. [10] use the constrained self-attention to address it, the limited attentions may fall into the local optimum. Considering these, we propose a VSM to model pixel-wise correspondences. Inspired by previous methods [7,9,18,24,25], VSM propagates inter-frame similar features and maximizes the inter-frame salient feature compactness. Benefiting from this, VSM can make the network focus on salient regions.

Figure 2 shows the flowchart of the proposed VSM. For a clear expression, we only take a single video sequence as an example to introduce the calculation processes because the processes of the two are the same. Firstly, the fifth encoder features e_5 are fed into the VSM and pass through two $1 \times 1 \times 1$ convolutional layers to generate the different representations. Here, we only use e_5 for saving GPU memory. Secondly, these two representations are matrix multiplied together to get the global attention matrix and the size is $NHW \times NHW$. Compared with previous image-level attentions such as spatial attention and channel attention, the global attention can calculate pixel-wise correspondences. Thirdly, we compute the maximal value at the spatial dimension (*i.e.*, $H \times W$ dimension) and the mean value at the batch dimension (*i.e.*, N dimension). Note that we only implement above operations on one of the two NHW. The first operation can predict the maximally spatial response maps, thereby extracts the salient regions in the feature maps. The second operation aims to calculate the assigned weights by each frame. Fourthly, the feature map with the size of $N \times 1 \times H \times W$ is element-wise multiplied by e_5 to determine the frame importance and spatial

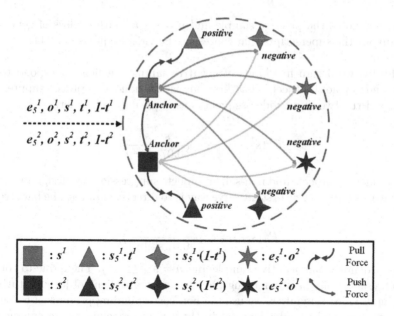

Fig. 3. Flowchart of the CLM.

importance. Finally, the feature maps are averaged to distill the consensus representation o. Such operation merges inter-frame information and intra-frame information, so as to achieve efficient information association.

2.3   Contrastive Learning Module

Though the VSM locates salient regions, there still needs the noise suppression. Due to the implicit network lacks the explicitly temporal extraction technique, the motion information is difficult to explore only by video semantics extraction. This weakness also exists in previous implicit methods. The motion information is usually used to suppress noises. Therefore, if we directly suppress noises, we will not explicitly extract the temporal features, avoiding the extra computational overhead. Motivated by this, we propose a CLM to suppress noise objects such as non-same objects, non-moving objects, and non-salient objects.

Figure 3 shows the flowchart of the proposed CLM. The inputs are the video semantics s^1 and s^2, the fifth encode features e_5^1 and e_5^2, the consensus representations o^1 and o^2, the ground truths t^1 and t^2, and the reversed-phase ground truths $1 - t^1$ and $1 - t^2$. Firstly, the video semantics s^1 and s^2 are used as the anchors. Secondly, the products of video semantics s^1 and s^2 and the corresponding ground truths t^1 and t^2 are used as the positive samples. This operation pulls the video semantics close to the effective information. This process can be modelled as follows.

$$F_+(s,p) = exp(\frac{s^T p}{0.07\,s||\,||p||}),\qquad(1)$$

where, p denotes the positive sample and $p = s \otimes t$. Without loss of generality, we drop out the superscripts that represent the video sequence number for clear expression.

Thirdly, we design five kinds of negative samples, which correspond to the three kinds of noise objects. The first one is the non-same object suppression. We regard the two input video sequences as opposing each other.

$$F_-^1(s^1, s^2) = exp(\frac{s^{1T} s^2}{0.07 \, s^1 \, s^2||}).\tag{2}$$

For non-moving objects and non-salient objects suppression, we design four kinds of negative samples. The first intuitive way is to directly suppress the background regions.

$$F^2(s, n) = exp(\frac{s^T n}{0.07 \, s|| \, ||n||}),\tag{3}$$

where, n denotes the negative sample and $n = s \otimes (1 - t)$. Then, due to consensus representations of non-moving objects and non-salient objects disturb the learning of video semantics, we use the non-corresponding product of consensus representation and encoder features in the two video sequences to enhance the discriminability of the network. The calculation process of negative relationship F_-^3 is similar to that of F^2, while the negative sample $n = e_5^1 \otimes o^2$ or $n = e_5^2 \otimes o^1$. In addition, we also push the processed video semantics away from the negative samples generated of the other video sequence, and build another two kinds of negative relationship F_-^4 and F_-^5. The detailed processes can be seen in Fig. 3. Based on these designed positive and negative samples, the noise objects can be effectively suppressed.

2.4 Loss Function

In this paper, the loss function can be divided into the saliency loss function and the contrastive loss function. Following previous methods [3,10,27], we supervise the saliency features from three levels, including the pixel-level supervision by the binary cross entropy loss function (BCE), the structure-level supervision by the structural similarity loss function (SSIM), and the map-level supervision by the Dice loss function. These loss functions use ground truths to supervise each decoder feature and the output during training, and can be denoted as follows.

$$\begin{aligned} \mathcal{L}_{bce} &= -(m \log t + (1 - m) \log(1 - t)), \\ \mathcal{L}_{ssim} &= 1 - \frac{(2\mu_m\mu_t + C_1)(2\kappa_{mt} + C_2)}{(\mu_m^2 + \mu_t^2 + C_1)(\kappa_m^2 + \kappa_t^2 + C_2)}, \\ \mathcal{L}_{dice} &= 1 - \frac{tm}{t + m}, \\ \mathcal{L}_{sal} &= \mathcal{L}_{bce} + \mathcal{L}_{ssim} + \mathcal{L}_{dice}. \end{aligned}\tag{4}$$

Then, the contrastive loss function pulls the anchor close to the positive samples and pushes the anchor away from the negative samples.

$$\mathcal{L}_{cl} = -\sum_{i=1}^{5} \log(\frac{F_+}{F_+ + F_-^i}). \tag{5}$$

Finally, the hybrid loss function can be denoted as follows.

$$\mathcal{L}_{total} = \alpha \mathcal{L}_{sal} + \beta \mathcal{L}_{cl}, \tag{6}$$

where, α and β are set to 1 because these two kinds of loss functions are equally important.

3 Experiments

3.1 Datasets and Evaluation Metrics

The performances of the proposed method SENO are evaluated on five prevailing datasets, including DAVIS2016 [17], DAVSOD [8], SegTrack-V2 [11], ViSal [12], and VOS [13].

Four evaluation metrics are used to evaluate our SENO and other state-of-the-art methods. The maximum F-measure (F_μ) is adopted in most of the VSOD methods. The mean absolute error (ϵ) and the average F-measure (F_γ) are used to measure the stability of the network and are also adopted in most of the VSOD methods. S-measure (S_α) focuses on measuring the structural performance of results, and is widely used in current VSOD methods.

3.2 Implementation Details

We implement the whole framework on the Pytorch platform with 2 NVIDIA 3090 GPUs. The basic pre-trained encoder network (*i.e.*, ResNet-101) is adopted in our framework as previous methods do. Note that, if we adopt a more powerful encoder such as the Transformer encoder [16], the resulting performance will be better. Besides, following previous methods [3,10,27], we adopt the same training technique. We first pre-train the baseline on a SOD dataset, and then we fine-tune the overall framework on the same dataset adopted by other methods [3,10,27]. During training, all inputs, including images and ground truths, are resized to 448×448. In addition, the ground truths and the reversed-phase ground truths used in CLM are resized to the size of the fifth encoder feature map. Similar to previous methods, we adopt the same data augmentation strategies, including random horizontal flipping and scaling. The batch size is 16, which means that the number of each video sequence is 16. The Adam optimizer with default hyper-parameters is used. The learning rates are set to 1e-6 and 1e-5 for the encoder and other modules, respectively.

Table 1. Comparison with state-of-the-art methods. LTIM$_{22}$ denotes the paper is publised in 2022. '-' denotes no result report; '↑' and '↓' represent the larger (lower) the value, the better the results; Values with bold and underline are the best and the suboptimal results.

Methods	DAVIS2016				DAVSOD				SegTrack-V2				ViSal				VOS			
	F_μ↑	ϵ↓	F_γ↑	S_α↑	F_μ↑	ϵ↓	F_γ↑	S_α↑	F_μ↑	ϵ↓	F_γ↑	S_α↑	F_μ↑	ϵ↓	F_γ↑	S_α↑	F_μ↑	ϵ↓	F_γ↑	S_α↑
SCOM [1]	0.819	0.045	0.688	0.841	0.483	0.222	0.379	0.571	0.810	0.029	0.747	0.824	0.864	0.119	0.654	0.767	0.698	0.148	0.564	0.692
FGRNE [14]	0.798	0.042	0.683	0.839	0.609	0.085	0.511	0.688	0.694	0.036	0.595	0.719	0.861	0.042	0.781	0.861	-	-	-	-
SSAV [8]	0.870	0.029	0.762	0.890	0.617	0.083	0.540	0.719	0.835	0.024	0.720	0.833	0.944	0.018	0.868	0.939	0.652	0.089	0.600	0.746
MGA [15]	0.892	0.023	-	0.910	0.640	0.084	-	0.738	0.821	0.030	-	0.865	0.933	0.017	-	0.936	-	-	-	-
PCSA [10]	0.888	0.022	0.794	0.900	0.643	0.077	0.556	0.724	0.872	0.019	0.789	0.884	0.943	0.016	0.887	0.940	0.714	0.072	0.647	0.785
STVS [4]	0.865	0.018	-	0.892	0.651	0.086	-	0.746	0.860	0.017	-	0.891	0.952	0.013	-	0.952	-	-	-	-
TENet [19]	0.889	0.017	0.821	0.904	0.673	0.067	0.595	0.756	-	-	-	-	0.948	0.012	0.906	0.942	-	-	-	-
MQP [5]	0.912	0.016	0.845	0.918	0.668	0.070	0.596	0.739	0.891	0.015	0.837	0.901	0.943	0.014	0.904	0.938	0.765	0.070	0.703	0.807
CAGDDE [3]	0.907	0.017	0.833	0.907	0.671	0.065	0.596	0.747	0.867	0.026	0.779	0.869	-	-	-	-	-	-	-	-
DCF [27]	0.905	0.016	0.864	0.914	0.653	0.065	0.599	0.729	0.885	0.013	0.863	0.902	0.952	0.010	0.921	0.946	0.802	0.058	0.755	0.839
SENO	0.913	0.015	0.866	0.919	0.677	0.063	0.605	0.753	0.895	0.012	0.867	0.905	0.957	0.010	0.926	0.950	0.807	0.057	0.760	0.843

3.3   Competing Methods

Quantitative Comparison. We compare the proposed SENO against 10 state-of-the-art VSOD methods, including SCOM [1], FGRNE [14], SSAV [8], MGA [15], STVS [4], PCSA [10], TENet [19], MQP [5], CAGDDE [3], and DCF [27]. SCOM [1] is a non-deep learning method, and other methods are deep learning methods.

Table 1 lists quantitative results between our SENO and other methods. It can be seen that our SENO outperforms other methods across most of the datasets under four metrics. Concretely, SENO achieves 18 best results and 2 suboptimal results under the all the 20 results (four metrics on five datasets). For the four evaluation criteria, SENO increases the ϵ most. We can observe that ϵ is hard to optimize because previous methods have optimized this metric well. Our SENO can further improve this metric, which verifies the effectiveness of the proposed network. Besides, compared with the best results, the two suboptimal results of our SENO only have slight gaps.

Visual Comparison. Figure 4 visualizes the comparison results between our SENO and other methods. For saving room, we select 6 typical compared methods. We can see that the results of our SENO achieve superior performances, which are visually closer the ground truth. Specifically, the first group shows several complex background. The video salient objects are easily interfered by the background such as the branches. We can observe that other methods cannot filter out the noise objects. Benefitting from the CLM that suppresses the noise objects, our SENO can detect the video salient objects accurately. The second group shows a slender object, which is hard to locate for other methods. With the aid of VSM, our SENO can locate the whole object and segment it with fine-grained edges. The third groups show a dark background, which usually appears in the real world. The low contrast scene makes other methods difficult to detect the objects. The proposed SENO can segment the video salient objects from complex background well.

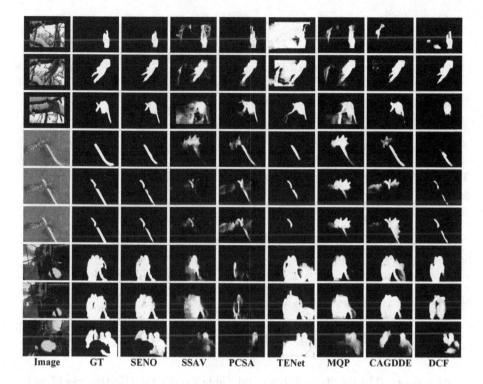

| Image | GT | SENO | SSAV | PCSA | TENet | MQP | CAGDDE | DCF |

Fig. 4. Visual comparison with state-of-the-art methods.

3.4 Ablation Studies

To validate the effectiveness of VSM and CLM, a series of detailed analyses are conducted. During the ablation studies, the training strategies and the hyper parameters keep unchanged. Table 2 reports the ablation studies on each proposed module, including VSM and CLM. The entry (a) of Table 2 denotes the baseline. Obviously, from the entry (a) to the entry (d), we can see that each proposed module promotes the performances. And the combination of VSM and CLM can collaboratively improve the results and achieve superior qualitative results. Besides, the VSM outperforms the CLM. The reason is that VSM merges inter-frame features and intra-frame features, locating the salient objects. The CLM without the location may weaken the ability of noise suppression.

Table 3 lists the ablation studies of the positive sample design and the negative sample design in CLM. The entry (a) and the entry (b) of Table 3 are the baseline and the VSM. From the entry (a) to the entry (e), we can see that these sample schemes are necessary. The single positive sample can be regarded as the enhancement of video semantics and the single negative sample can be regarded as the noise suppression. The combination of positive sample and negative sample can balance the relationship representations and increases the discriminability

Table 2. Ablation studies on each proposed module optimized by the hybrid loss.

	Module		Average Value			
	VSM	CLM	$F_\mu \uparrow$	$\epsilon \downarrow$	$F_\gamma \uparrow$	$S_\alpha \uparrow$
(a)			0.784	0.057	0.708	0.791
(b)	✓		0.821	0.042	0.733	0.832
(c)		✓	0.813	0.046	0.725	0.818
(d)	✓	✓	0.850	0.031	0.805	0.854

Table 3. Ablation studies on the sample design in the CLM optimized by the hybrid loss.

	CLM			Average Value			
	Anchor	Positive	Negative	$F_\mu \uparrow$	$\epsilon \downarrow$	$F_\gamma \uparrow$	$S_\alpha \uparrow$
(a)				0.784	0.057	0.708	0.791
(b)	✓			0.821	0.042	0.733	0.832
(c)	✓	✓		0.833	0.037	0.769	0.845
(d)	✓		✓	0.829	0.039	0.751	0.840
(e)	✓	✓	✓	0.850	0.031	0.805	0.854

of the network. The results in Table 2 and Table 3 verify the effectiveness of each proposed module and the designed noise suppression schemes.

4   Conclusion

In this paper, we propose a unified end-to-end network with video semantics extraction and noise object suppression for accurate and fast VSOD. Firstly, we introduce a video semantics module to extract video semantics by calculating the global correspondences at the pixel level. This module can maximize the inter-frame salient feature compactness and enable the network to concentrate on the video salient objects. Secondly, we propose a contrastive learning module to pull the foreground pairs together and push the noise objects away. With the aid of this module, non-same objects, non-moving objects, and non-salient objects are filtered out. These two modules are combined into a unified framework and supervised by a hybrid loss function. In addition, we do not use any pre-processing step such as optical flow model and ConvLSTM, which avoids high computational costs. Therefore, our method can detect video salient objects in real time. Experimental results on five testing datasets show that the proposed method outperforms the state-of-the-art methods. The Ablation studies verify the effectiveness of each proposed module. In addition, we also find that if we use a more powerful encoder or decoder, the resulting performance will be better. This is our current limitation, and we will address it in our future work.

Acknowledgements. This work was supported in part by National Natural Science Foundation of China under grant 62176062.

References

1. Chen, Y., Zou, W., Tang, Y., et al.: SCOM: spatiotemporal constrained optimization for salient object detection. IEEE Trans. Image Process. **27**(7), 3345–3357 (2018)
2. Chen, T., Kornblith, S., Norouzi, M., et al.: A simple framework for contrastive learning of visual representations. In: Proceedings of the International Conference on Machine Learning, pp. 1597–1607. ACM, Vienna (2020)
3. Chen, P., Lai, J., Wang, G., et al.: Confidence-guided adaptive gate and dual differential enhancement for video salient object detection. In: Proceedings of the IEEE International Conference on Multimedia and Expo. 2021, pp. 1–6. IEEE, Beijing (2021)
4. Chen, C., Wang, G., Peng, C., et al.: Exploring rich and efficient spatial temporal interactions for real-time video salient object detection. IEEE Trans. Image Process. **30**, 3995–4007 (2021)
5. Chen, C., Song, J., Peng, C., et al.: A novel video salient object detection method via semisupervised motion quality perception. IEEE Trans. Circ. Syst. Video Technol. **32**(5), 2732–2745 (2021)
6. Chen, C., Tan, Z., Cheng, Q., et al.: UTC: a unified transformer with inter-task contrastive learning for visual dialog. In: Proceedings of the IEEE/CVF Conference on Computer Vision and Pattern Recognition, pp. 18103–18112. IEEE, New Orleans (2022)
7. Cheng, Q., Tan, Z., Wen, K., et al.: Semantic pre-alignment and ranking learning with unified framework for cross-modal retrieval. IEEE Trans. Circ. Syst. Video Technol. 1 (2022). https://doi.org/10.1109/TCSVT.2022.3182549
8. Fan, D., Wang, W., Cheng, M., et al.: Shifting more attention to video salient object detection. In: Proceedings of the IEEE/CVF Conference on Computer Vision and Pattern Recognition, pp. 8554–8564. IEEE, Long Beach (2019)
9. Fan, Q., Fan, D., Fu, H., et al.: Group collaborative learning for co-salient object detection. In: Proceedings of the IEEE/CVF Conference on Computer Vision and Pattern Recognition, pp. 12288–12298. IEEE, Kuala Lumpur (2021)
10. Gu, Y., Wang, L., Wang, Z., et al.: Pyramid constrained self-attention network for fast video salient object detection. In: Proceedings of the AAAI conference on artificial intelligence, pp. 10869–10876. AAAI, New York (2020)
11. Li, F., Kim, T., Humayun, A., et al.: Video segmentation by tracking many figure-ground segments. In: Proceedings of the IEEE International Conference on Computer Vision, pp. 2192–2199. IEEE, Sydney (2013)
12. Wang, W., Shen, J., Shao, L.: Consistent video saliency using local gradient flow optimization and global refinement. IEEE Trans. Image Process. **24**(11), 4185–4196 (2015)
13. Li, J., Xia, C., Chen, X.: A benchmark dataset and saliency-guided stacked autoencoders for video-based salient object detection. IEEE Trans. Image Process. **27**(1), 349–364 (2017)
14. Li, G., Xie, Y., We, I.T., et al.: Flow guided recurrent neural encoder for video salient object detection. In: Proceedings of the IEEE Conference on Computer Vision and Pattern Recognition, pp. 3243–3252. IEEE, Salt Lake (2018)

15. Li, H., Chen, G., Li, G., et al.: Motion guided attention for video salient object detection. In: Proceedings of the IEEE/CVF International Conference on Computer Vision, pp. 7274–7283. IEEE, California (2019)
16. Liu Z, Lin Y, Cao Y, et al.: Swin transformer: hierarchical vision transformer using shifted windows. In: Proceedings of the IEEE/CVF International Conference on Computer Vision, pp. 10012–10022. IEEE, Kuala Lumpur (2021)
17. Perazzi, F., Pont-Tuset, J., McWilliams, B., et al.: A benchmark dataset and evaluation methodology for video object segmentation. In: Proceedings of the IEEE Conference on Computer Vision and Pattern Recognition, pp. 724–732. IEEE, Las Vegas (2016)
18. Qin, Y., Gu, X., Tan, Z.: Visual context learning based on textual knowledge for image-text retrieval. Neural Netw. **152**, 434–449 (2022)
19. Ren, S., Han, C., Yang, X., Han, G., He, S.: TENet: triple excitation network for video salient object detection. In: Vedaldi, A., Bischof, H., Brox, T., Frahm, J.-M. (eds.) ECCV 2020. LNCS. vol. 12350, pp. 212–228. Springer, Cham (2020). https://doi.org/10.1007/978-3-030-58558-7_13
20. Tan, Z., Hua, Y., Gu, X.: Salient object detection with edge recalibration. In: Farkaš, I., Masulli, P., Wermter, S. (eds.) ICANN 2020. LNCS. vol. 12396, pp. 724–735. Springer, Cham (2020). https://doi.org/10.1007/978-3-030-61609-0_57
21. Tan, Z., Gu, X.: Depth scale balance saliency detection with connective feature pyramid and edge guidance. Appl. Intell. **51**(8), 5775–5792 (2021). https://doi.org/10.1007/s10489-020-02150-z
22. Tan, Z., Gu, X.: Co-saliency detection with intra-group two-stage group semantics propagation and inter-group contrastive learning. Knowl. -Based Syst. **252**, 109356 (2022)
23. Tan, Z., Gu, X.: Feature recalibration network for salient object detection. In: Pimenidis, E., Angelov, P., Jayne, C., Papaleonidas, A., Aydin, M. (eds) Artificial Neural Networks and Machine Learning-ICANN 2022. ICANN 2022. Lecture Notes in Computer Science. vol. 13532. Springer, Cham (2022). https://doi.org/10.1007/978-3-031-15937-4_6
24. Tan, Z., Chen, C., Wen, K., et al.: A unified two-stage group semantics propagation and contrastive learning network for co-saliency detection. In: Proceedings of the IEEE International Conference on Multimedia and Expo, pp. 1–6. IEEE, Taipei (2022)
25. Tan, Z., Gu, X.: A unified multiple inducible co-attentions and edge guidance network for co-saliency detection. In: Pimenidis, E., Angelov, P., Jayne, C., Papaleonidas, A., Aydin, M. (eds.) Artificial Neural Networks and Machine Learning-ICANN 2022. ICANN 2022. Lecture Notes in Computer Science. vol. 13529. Springer, Cham (2022). https://doi.org/10.1007/978-3-031-15919-0_2
26. Tan, Z., Gu, X.: Bridging feature complementarity gap between encoder and decoder for salient object detection. Digital Sig. Process. **133**, 103841 (2023)
27. Zhang, M., Liu, J., Wang, Y., et al.: Dynamic context-sensitive filtering network for video salient object detection. In: Proceedings of the IEEE/CVF International Conference on Computer Vision, pp. 1553–1563. IEEE, Kuala Lumpur (2021)

Adaptive Token Excitation with Negative Selection for Video-Text Retrieval

Juntao Yu[1,2], Zhangkai Ni[1,2], Taiyi Su[1,2], and Hanli Wang[1,2(✉)]

[1] Department of Computer Science and Technology, Tongji University, Shanghai, People's Republic of China
hanliwang@tongji.edu.cn
[2] Key Laboratory of Embedded System and Service Computing, Ministry of Education, Tongji University, Shanghai, People's Republic of China

Abstract. Video-text retrieval aims to efficiently retrieve videos from large collections based on the given text, whereas methods based on the large-scale pretrained model have drawn sustained attention recently. However, existing methods neglect detailed information in video and text, thus failing to align cross-modal semantic features well and leading to performance bottlenecks. Meanwhile, the general training strategy often treats semantically similar pairs as negatives, which provides the model with incorrect supervision. To address these issues, an adaptive token excitation (ATE) model with negative selection is proposed to adaptively refine features encoded by a large-scale pre-trained model to obtain more informative features without introducing additional complexity. In detail, ATE is first advanced to adaptively aggregate and align different events described in text and video using multiple non-linear event blocks. Then a negative selection strategy is exploited to mitigate false negative effects, which stabilizes the training process. Extensive experiments on several datasets demonstrate the feasibility and superiority of the proposed ATE compared to other state-of-the-art methods. The source code of this work can be found in https://mic.tongji.edu.cn.

Keywords: Video-text retrieval · Adaptive token excitation · Negative selection

1 Introduction

Video-text retrieval is a vital research field that focuses on efficiently retrieving relevant videos from large collections. According to learning to measure the semantic similarity of video-text pairs, general video-text retrieval frameworks can rank videos based on their relevance to a given query. The increasing popularity of short video apps such as TikTok has led to a demand for efficient search algorithms. Based on video-text retrieval, users are able to instantly locate relevant videos to improve the overall experience. Additionally, video text retrieval methods can also be used by security professionals to effectively locate and review footage from surveillance cameras to gather information or evidence related to incidents.

This work was supported in part by National Natural Science Foundation of China under Grants 61976159 and 62062041, and Shanghai Innovation Action Project of Science and Technology under Grant 20511100700.

ⓒ The Author(s), under exclusive license to Springer Nature Switzerland AG 2023
L. Iliadis et al. (Eds.): ICANN 2023, LNCS 14260, pp. 349–361, 2023.
https://doi.org/10.1007/978-3-031-44195-0_29

Recently, the methods based on large-scale contrastive language-image pre-training have achieved promising results in video-text retrieval. For example, CLIP4Clip [13] directly uses CLIP [16] to extract frame and text representations separately, where the final video token is obtained by average pooling of all frame tokens. However, a single common high-dimensional semantic space is insufficient to represent abundant text and video information due to the inevitable loss of semantic information. To enhance the modeling of detailed information in text and video, a straightforward approach is to reserve all tokens given by the model. However, this solution also suffers from redundancy and alignment problems. Specifically, uniform sampling may cause the model to pay more attention to repeated scenes, while using all tokens may result in different numbers of unaligned video and text tokens. Furthermore, the false negative effect is another key issue plaguing video-text retrieval task. In the training stage, common methods adopt instance discrimination as a pretext task that treats corresponding video-text pairs as positives and all non-corresponding pairs as negatives [20]. Such settings may cause problems, as some video-text pairs that are semantically similar but considered negatives thus misleading the model.

To address the above problems, an adaptive token excitation (ATE) model with negative selection is proposed for the video-text retrieval task. First, an adaptive token excitation module is adopted to use multiple non-linear event blocks to capture and adaptively align different events described in text and video. Second, an accurate and effective negative selection strategy is designed based on a dynamic confidence threshold. Specifically, the proposed negative selection takes into account that sample pairs with relatively high similarity are actually false negatives. In this way, the proposed ATE model with negative selection reaches high-quality fine-grained feature alignment and alleviates the false negative problem. Extensive experiments have been conducted on several video-text retrieval benchmarks to evaluate the effectiveness and superiority of our model, including MSR-VTT [21], MSVD [3] and LSMDC [17].

2   Related Work

2.1   Video-Text Retrieval

Video-text retrieval is similar to commonly studied image-text retrieval but is more complex since the video has an additional temporal dimension. Existing video-text retrieval methods focus on learning a joint semantic embedding space. Gabeur *et al.* [6] introduce several expert models to enrich multi-modal features (RGB, motion, audio and etc.). Recently, with the help of the large-scale pre-training method CLIP, many works achieve promising results. Luo *et al.* [13] adopt CLIP and a temporal transformer to capture better video and text representation. Ji *et al.* [10] employ a novel loss to implicitly conduct dense sampling without introducing heavy computational cost. However, how to efficiently model abundant video information and adaptively align it with text remains to be studied.

2.2   Negative Selection in Contrastive Learning

A number of works based on contrastive learning employ instance discrimination as pretext tasks to guide the learned embeddings. Given a data sample, the objective is to discriminate its corresponding semantically similar samples from other samples with distinct semantics in the dataset. Although effective, this setting is sometimes incorrect. The negative samples are set too broadly and will lead to the false negative problem where the given negative samples are actually semantically similar to the anchor. As a solution, Huynh et al. [9] utilize support views to identify false negatives and transfer false negatives to positives for better supervision. Zolfaghari et al. [23] define influential samples as the samples with high connectivity within the dataset and removes them from the negatives set. Wu et al. [19] present a ring estimator that supports sampling negatives from a particular class of conditional distributions to reach a lower variance estimation. However, the above methods are designed for unsupervised contrastive learning and the false negative problem in the video-text retrieval task is not well resolved.

3   Adaptive Token Excitation with Negative Selection

3.1   Preliminary

Video-text retrieval aims to learn a function $sim(\cdot)$ to properly measure the similarity of given videos and texts. Based on the function $sim(\cdot)$, the videos can be sorted by the query text, or the text can be sorted by the query video according to the similarity between the video-text pairs. Typical video-text retrieval methods consist of two independent encoders for mapping video and text to a shared high-dimensional hypersphere. These methods are based on the assumption that a common embedding space is sufficient to represent video and text information. Therefore, the similarity score of a video-text pair (v_i, t_j) can be expressed as

$$sim(v_i, t_j) = h(v_i)^T g(t_j),\tag{1}$$

where $h(\cdot)$ and $g(\cdot)$ are the video and text encoders, respectively, and T is the transpose operation.

Video-text retrieval datasets usually consist of a large number of video-text corresponding pairs (v_i, t_i). The typical training strategy treats a corresponding video-text pair as the positive, however, all non-corresponding video-text pairs are assumed to be semantically distinct and treated as the negative. To optimize the model with a high similarity score for the positive and a low similarity score for the negative, a symmetric infoNCE loss [14] is employed as

$$\mathcal{L} = \frac{1}{2}\left(\mathcal{L}_{v2t} + \mathcal{L}_{t2v}\right),\tag{2}$$

$$\mathcal{L}_{v2t} = -\frac{1}{N}\sum_i^N \log \frac{\exp\left(h\left(v_i\right)^T g\left(t_i\right)/\tau\right)}{\sum_{j=1}^N \exp\left(h\left(v_i\right)^T g\left(t_j\right)/\tau\right)},\tag{3}$$

$$\mathcal{L}_{t2v} = -\frac{1}{N}\sum_i^N \log \frac{\exp\left(g\left(t_i\right)^T h\left(v_i\right)/\tau\right)}{\sum_{j=1}^N \exp\left(g\left(t_i\right)^T h\left(v_j\right)/\tau\right)},\tag{4}$$

where $\mathcal{L}_{v2t}$ is the video-to-text retrieval loss, $\mathcal{L}_{t2v}$ is the text-to-video retrieval loss, N is the batch size and τ is the temperature to control the sharpness of sample distribution in semantic space.

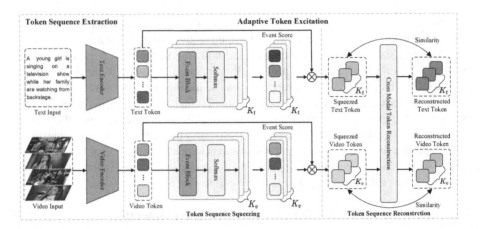

Fig. 1. Overview of the proposed ATE model for video-text retrieval, consisting of two components: token sequence extraction and adaptive token excitation.

3.2 Adaptive Token Excitation

As shown in Fig. 1, in order to efficiently obtain information-aligned video text features, the ATE model is designed, which consists of two components: token sequence extraction and adaptive token excitation. Specifically, the token sequence extraction module first encodes text and video by transformer and retains all text and video tokens, ensuring rich semantic information. Subsequently, the adaptive token excitation module refines the tokens by applying token sequence squeezing to reduce redundancy and token sequence reconstruction for adaptive alignment, which results in compact and semantically rich representations for text and video tokens.

Token Sequence Extraction. Based on large-scale pre-training models, video and text are first encoded by transformer. For the text, typical frameworks only use the output [EOS] token for text representation to avoid redundant information, but it also inevitably discards rich semantic information. Therefore, all N_t text tokens $T = \{t_1, \cdots, t_{N_t}\}$ are first reserved to avoid loss of semantic information. Similarly, for the video, we first uniformly sample video frames and convert the non-overlapped frame patches into visual sequences, where a [CLASS] token is padded at the beginning of the video sequence. Then, the output [CLS] tokens are used as compact representations of frame features and are subsequently input into a transformer to model the temporal relationships. Compared to typical methods that simply use average pooling for all frame tokens to obtain the final video representation, we keep all N_v video tokens $V = \{v_1, \cdots, v_{N_v}\}$. All obtained text and video tokens are respectively excited by the proposed ATE to achieve more compact and semantically rich representations.

Adaptive Token Excitation. The aforementioned token sequence contains abundant information describing the video and text, but there are repeated and redundant tokens. Specifically, for the text token sequence, there are many tokens corresponding to 'a', 'the', 'is' and so on that do not contain much semantic information. For the video token sequence, there are also many tokens corresponding to background frames. Moreover, the commonly used uniform sampling will also result in many frames describing the same scene, which may lead the model to pay more attention to repeated scenes and damage the ability of the model to characterize various scenarios.

To make more efficient use of abundant text and video token sequences, it is crucial to squeeze the token sequence and adaptively match video and text token pairs. Inspired by this, ATE is proposed to capture distinct and informative tokens in the text and video token sequences and adaptively align corresponding token pairs. Specifically, K_v video event blocks $\{E_1^v, \cdots E_{K_v}^v\}$ and K_t text event blocks $\{E_1^t, \cdots, E_{K_t}^t\}$ are learned, and each event block consists of multilayer perceptron with rectified linear units. The squeezed token for the i-th event block can be obtained as

$$s_i^t = \sum_j \alpha_{i,j}^t \cdot t_j, \tag{5}$$

$$s_i^v = \sum_j \alpha_{i,j}^v \cdot v_j. \tag{6}$$

Here $\alpha_{i,j}$ is the score between the i-th event block and j-th token, which is computed as

$$\alpha_{i,j}^t = \frac{\exp\left(E_i^t(t_j)/\kappa\right)}{\sum_{j=1}^{N_t} \exp\left(E_i^t(t_j)/\kappa\right)}, \tag{7}$$

$$\alpha_{i,j}^v = \frac{\exp\left(E_i^v(v_j)/\kappa\right)}{\sum_{j=1}^{N_t} \exp\left(E_i^v(v_j)/\kappa\right)}, \tag{8}$$

where κ is the temperature of softmax. As κ tends to be infinity, our token excitation module will degrade to commonly used average pooling. So, a relatively low κ is used in practice to capture diverse scenes.

A set of squeezed video tokens $S^v = \{s_1^v, \cdots, s_{K_v}^v\}$ and squeezed text tokens $S^t = \{s_1^t, \cdots, s_{K_t}^t\}$ are obtained after token sequence squeezing. Note that the number of video tokens is not equal to the number of text tokens. To adaptively align the video and text token sequences, both the video token sequence and the text token sequence are reshaped based on each other as

$$r_i^t = \sum_j \frac{\exp\left(s_i^{v^T} s_j^t/\tau\right)}{\sum_{j=1}^{K_t} \exp\left(s_i^{v^T} s_j^t/\tau\right)} \cdot s_j^t, \tag{9}$$

$$r_i^v = \sum_j \frac{\exp\left(s_i^{t^T} s_j^v/\tau\right)}{\sum_{j=1}^{K_v} \exp\left(s_i^{t^T} s_j^v/\tau\right)} \cdot s_j^v. \tag{10}$$

The reconstructed text tokens $R^t = \{r_1^t, \cdots, r_{K_t}^t\}$ and the squeezed text tokens $S^t = \{s_1^t, \cdots, s_{K_t}^t\}$ have the same number of tokens and are well aligned. Similarly, the reconstructed video tokens $R^v = \{r_1^v, \cdots, r_{K_v}^v\}$ and the squeezed video tokens $S^v =$

$\{s_1^v, \cdots, s_{K_v}^v\}$ are also aligned. The final video-text similarity can be calculated by the average distance between squeezed tokens and reconstructed tokens as

$$sim(T, V) = \frac{1}{K_t} \sum_i^{K_t} s_i^{v T} r_i^v + \frac{1}{K_v} \sum_j^{K_v} s_j^{t T} r_j^t. \tag{11}$$

3.3 Negative Selection

Common video-text retrieval datasets provide a set of video-text pairs which can naturally be regarded as positive. Negatives are then given based on the assumption that all non-corresponding pairs are semantically different. However, some text that is considered negative may partially or correctly describe a video. As discussed in [9], these negatives (*i.e.*, false negatives) will lead to slower convergence and loss of semantic information, resulting in degradation of model performance.

The process of identifying false negatives is fundamentally hard since there are no precise labels. However, with the help of large-scale pre-trained models, it is possible to compute video-text similarity with high confidence. Then, the video-text pairs with relatively high scores can be regarded as false negative pairs and thus removed from the negative set. Inspired by the above observations, a dynamic threshold-based negative selection strategy is designed in this work to select negatives. For a given query q, the negatives are selected as

$$\mathcal{N}_q = \{k | sim(q, k) < \lambda\} \cap \mathcal{N}, \tag{12}$$

where $sim(q, k)$ is the similarity between query and key, $\mathcal{N}$ is the original negative set, and λ is the proposed dynamic threshold given by

$$\lambda = \lambda_{\text{end}} - (\lambda_{\text{end}} - \lambda_{\text{start}}) \cdot \cos(1 + p\pi), \tag{13}$$

where λ_{start} and λ_{end} are the thresholds at the start and end of training respectively, and p indicates the percentage of the training process. The design of the cosine annealing threshold where $\lambda_{\text{start}} > \lambda_{\text{end}}$, is based on the intuition that the model has a higher confidence level in later training. In the early stages of training, the negatives with relatively high similarity scores can be reliably regarded as false negatives. Finally, the overall loss $\mathcal{L}^{ns}$ after negative selection can be obtained as

$$\mathcal{L}^{ns} = \frac{1}{2} \left(\mathcal{L}_{v2t}^{ns} + \mathcal{L}_{t2v}^{ns} \right), \tag{14}$$

where

$$\mathcal{L}_{v2t}^{ns} = -\frac{1}{N} \sum_i^N \log \frac{\exp(sim(V_i, T_i)/\tau)}{\sum_{T_{neg} \in \mathcal{N}_{V_i}} \exp(sim(V_i, T_{neg})/\tau)}, \tag{15}$$

$$\mathcal{L}_{t2v}^{ns} = -\frac{1}{N} \sum_i^N \log \frac{\exp(sim(T_i, V_i)/\tau)}{\sum_{V_{neg} \in \mathcal{N}_{T_i}} \exp(sim(T_i, V_{neg})/\tau)}. \tag{16}$$

4 Experiments

4.1 Experimental Details

Datasets. To comprehensively evaluate the performance of our proposed method on video text retrieval tasks, experiments are conducted on three benchmark datasets, including MSR-VTT [21], MSVD [3] and LSMDC [17]. The MSR-VTT dataset is composed of 10,000 videos ranging from 10 to 32 s and 200,000 captions collected from YouTube. Following the setting of JSfusion [22], we split the training and testing sets into 9,000 and 1,000 samples, respectively. The MSVD dataset contains 1,970 videos ranging from 1 to 62 s. The training set, validation set, and test set contain 1,200, 100, and 670 videos, respectively. The LSMDC dataset consists of 118,081 videos extracted from 202 movies, ranging in length from 2 to 30 s.

Metrics. Three widely-used metrics are used for quantitative comparison, *i.e.*, Rank K (R@K, higher is better), Median Rank (MdR, lower is better) and Mean Rank (MnR, lower is better).

Implementation Details. The text encoder and the video encoder are initialized with pre-trained CLIP (ViT-B/32) [16], while other modules are randomly initialized as in CLIP4Clip [13]. Both the dimensions of text and video tokens are 512. The number of video and text event blocks is set to 8 and 3, respectively. The temperature κ is 0.4 while τ is 0.01. λ_{start} and λ_{end} are set to 0.32 and 0.25, respectively. Using Adam as the optimizer, the initial learning rate is 1e-7 for text and video encoders, and 1e-4 for other modules. The length of the input text token and video token is 32 and 12, respectively. The batch size of the video-text pairs is set to 128 and the epoch is 5. All fine-tuning experiments are performed on 1 NVIDIA Tesla V100 GPU. To avoid memory overflow, the gradient accumulation strategy is utilized for contrastive learning [7].

4.2 Comparison to State-of-the-Arts

MSR-VTT. As presented in Table 1, the proposed ATE model with negative selection outperforms previous methods across different evaluation metrics. Specifically, ATE with negative selection achieves R@1 of 48.1, R@5 of 74.6, and R@10 of 83.8, which is significantly better than CLIP4Clip by 3.5%, 3.2%, and 2.2%, respectively. This is mainly attributed to the ability of our model to capture multi-event information.

MSVD. From Table 2, we can observe that the proposed ATE with negative selection achieves the best performance on all metrics compared to previous methods on MSVD. For instance, the proposed ATE model with negative selection achieves 11.7% improvement over CLIP4Clip, which demonstrates the effectiveness of our method on the small-scale dataset.

Table 1. Comparison with the state-of-the-art methods on MSR-VTT.

Method	Text-to-Video					Video-to-Text				
	R@1	R@5	R@10	MdR	MnR	R@1	R@5	R@10	MdR	MnR
JSFusion [22]	10.2	31.2	43.2	13.0	–	–	–	–	–	–
CE [11]	20.9	38.8	62.4	6.0	–	20.6	50.3	64.0	5.3	–
MMT [6]	24.6	54.0	67.1	4.0	–	24.4	56.0	67.8	4.0	–
T2VLAD [18]	29.5	59.0	70.1	4.0	–	31.8	60.0	71.1	3.0	–
Frozen [1]	31.0	59.5	70.5	3.0	–	–	–	–	–	–
CLIP4Clip [13]	44.5	71.4	81.6	2.0	15.3	42.7	70.9	80.6	2.0	11.6
CAMoE [4]	44.6	72.6	81.8	2.0	13.3	45.1	72.4	83.1	2.0	10.0
CLIP2Video [5]	45.6	72.6	81.7	2.0	14.6	43.5	72.3	82.1	2.0	10.2
X-Pool [8]	46.9	72.8	82.8	2.0	14.3	44.4	73.3	84.0	2.0	9.0
TS2-Net [12]	47.0	74.5	83.8	2.0	12.2	45.3	74.1	83.7	2.0	9.2
ATE (Ours)	**48.1**	**74.6**	**83.8**	**2.0**	**12.2**	**46.3**	**74.1**	**84.0**	**2.0**	**8.7**

Table 2. Comparison with the state-of-the-art methods on MSVD.

Method	Text-to-Video					Video-to-Text				
	R@1	R@5	R@10	MdR	MnR	R@1	R@5	R@10	MdR	MnR
CE [11]	19.8	49.0	63.8	6.0	–	–	–	–	–	–
SSB [15]	28.4	60.0	72.9	4.0	–	–	–	–	–	–
Frozen [1]	33.7	64.7	76.3	3.0	–	–	–	–	–	–
CLIP [16]	37.0	64.1	73.8	3.0	–	54.9	82.9	89.6	1.0	–
CLIP4Clip [13]	45.9	74.9	84.7	2.0	10.4	51.0	76.3	82.2	1.0	9.1
ATE (Ours)	**47.6**	**78.3**	**86.5**	**2.0**	**9.5**	**62.7**	**87.0**	**92.4**	**1.0**	**3.9**

LSMDC. As shown in Table 3, the proposed ATE model with negative selection consistently outperforms competitors on all benchmark metrics including R@1, R@5, R@10,

Table 3. Comparison with the state-of-the-art methods on LSMDC.

Method	Text-to-Video					Video-to-Text				
	R@1	R@5	R@10	MdR	MnR	R@1	R@5	R@10	MdR	MnR
JSFusion [22]	9.1	21.2	34.1	36.0	–	12.3	28.6	38.9	20	–
CE [11]	11.2	26.9	34.8	25.3	96.8	–	–	–	–	–
MMT [6]	12.9	29.9	40.1	19.3	75.0	12.3	28.6	38.9	20.0	76.0
Frozen [1]	15.0	30.8	39.8	20.0	–	–	–	–	–	–
CLIP [16]	15.1	28.3	35.8	31.0	132.0	7.5	18.4	25.1	58.0	151.0
CLIP4Clip [13]	22.6	41.0	49.1	11.0	61.0	20.8	39.0	48.6	12.0	54.2
ATE (Ours)	**24.1**	**46.0**	**54.8**	**8.0**	**52.4**	**23.6**	**43.3**	**53.1**	**9.0**	**47.1**

MdR, and MnR, which indicates that our method is able to deal with videos from diverse domains.

4.3 Ablation Study

In this section, extensive ablation studies are performed to further demonstrate the effectiveness of each component of the proposed method. The baseline model is set as CLIP4Clip which removes the token sequence squeezing module, token sequence reconstruction module and the negative selection strategy from ATE.

Effectiveness of Module. In Table 4, the importance of the token sequence squeezing (TS) module, the token sequence reconstruction (TR) module, and the negative selection (NS) strategy are evaluated respectively. It can be seen that each module yields considerable gains, while combining the three modules yields the best performance and significantly outperforms the baseline methods.

Table 4. Ablation studies on MSR-VTT to investigate the effectiveness of our proposed modules.

TS	TR	NS	Text-to-Video				Video-to-Text			
			R@1	R@5	R@10	MnR	R@1	R@5	R@10	MnR
			44.5	71.4	81.6	15.3	42.7	70.9	80.6	11.6
		✓	45.2	72.5	81.3	14.7	43.6	71.7	81.4	11.0
	✓		45.8	72.1	82.6	13.8	44.1	72.2	81.9	10.7
	✓	✓	46.7	72.2	82.1	13.0	44.7	72.9	82.5	10.0
✓	✓		47.4	73.1	83.2	12.9	45.4	73.3	83.6	9.6
✓	✓	✓	**48.1**	**74.6**	**83.8**	**12.2**	**46.3**	**74.1**	**84.0**	**8.7**

Effectiveness of Threshold. First, the impact of threshold λ to mitigate false negative effects as used in Eq. (12) is investigated, including constant threshold, linear threshold, and cosine threshold (currently employed in our method). As shown in Table 5, both the linear and cosine thresholds yield better results compared to the constant threshold. Furthermore, the cosine threshold achieves a more noticeable improvement over the linear threshold. The possible reason is discussed below. As stated in [2], negative samples can be categorized based on their similarity scores to three groups: the top 0.1% are considered false negatives, the top 5% are considered hard negatives, and the rest are considered easy negatives. Hard negatives are crucial for the convergence of the model. However, the boundary between hard negatives and false negatives is ambiguous. During the early stage of training, the model may struggle to differentiate between hard negatives and false negatives. Therefore, it is reasonable to set a more conservative threshold in the initial stages of training. The cosine function's slow decay characteristic serves this purpose well, while the linear function exhibits a faster decay rate than the cosine, resulting in marginally inferior performance.

Table 5. Ablation studies on MSR-VTT to investigate the impact of threshold.

Type	λ_{start}	λ_{end}	Text-to-Video				Video-to-Text			
			R@1	R@5	R@10	MnR	R@1	R@5	R@10	MnR
Const	0.32	0.32	47.2	73.5	82.8	12.7	45.1	73.3	83.4	9.4
Const	0.29	0.29	46.9	72.9	82.6	13.3	44.8	73.0	82.7	10.1
Const	0.25	0.25	44.9	70.7	81.1	14.5	43.0	71.1	81.2	11.4
Linear	0.32	0.25	47.7	74.0	83.5	12.4	45.9	73.5	83.8	9.0
Cosine	0.32	0.25	**48.1**	**74.6**	**83.8**	**12.2**	**46.3**	**74.1**	**84.0**	**8.7**

Moreover, experiments are conducted to select the optimal parameter values for the threshold λ. As shown in Fig. 2, the best results are achieved when setting λ_{start} to 0.32 and λ_{end} to 0.25. The model's performance is more sensitive to the changes in λ_{start}. For instance, when λ_{start} is set to 0.26, the R@1 performance for text-to-video retrieval degrades from 48.1 to 45.3, further substantiating the idea that the threshold should be set conservatively during the early stages of training. As depicted in Fig. 3, the similarity scores for the top 0.1% of negative samples and the mean similarity scores for positive samples are both approximately 0.3, corroborating the claim in [2] that the top 0.1% of negative samples indeed exhibit high similarity and should be considered as false negatives. Both empirical and theoretical evidence support that setting the threshold around 0.3 is a reasonable choice. By leveraging such an appropriate threshold, the model receives more accurate supervision signals, thereby achieving higher performances.

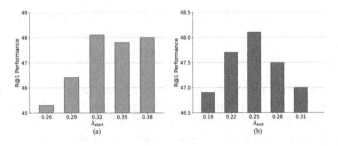

Fig. 2. Parameter selection on the MSR-VTT test set to investigate the effectiveness of different values of (a) λ_{start} and (b) λ_{end}.

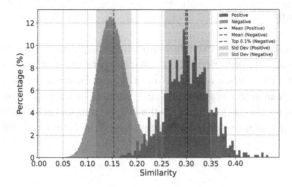

Fig. 3. Similarity distribution for positive sample pairs and negative sample pairs on the MSR-VTT test set.

4.4 Visualization

Figure 4 shows two examples of the videos retrieved by our model and CLIP4Clip, where the text queries consist of multiple events. In both of the two examples, ATE successfully retrieves the ground-truth videos, while the baseline model returns several videos that are relevant but imprecise to the text queries. Specifically, in the left example, ATE achieves better alignment between text and video with respect to "elderly man in a red hat", "man in a black jacket", and "playing field", while the baseline model only captures partial event information, such as "playing field" and "black jacket". In the right example, our model effectively captures the detailed elements of "man in a suit", "woman in a uniform", and "black fish", whereas the baseline model only focuses on a subset of the description, such as "woman" and "fish". The results demonstrate that our method is capable of effectively capturing and aligning multiple event cues.

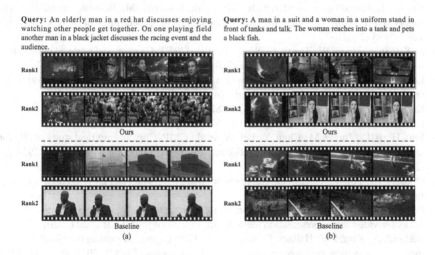

Fig. 4. Text-video retrieval results on MSR-VTT.

5   Conclusion

In this work, an adaptive token excitation model with negative selection is proposed for video-text retrieval. The proposed ATE is able to represent multiple scenario features without introducing too much redundant information. Besides, the proposed negative selection module can select negatives more accurately to train the model more stably. The experimental results demonstrate that the proposed model achieves the state-of-the-art performance on common video-text retrieval datasets, including MSR-VTT, MSVD, and LSMDC.

References

1. Bain, M., Nagrani, A., Varol, G., Zisserman, A.: Frozen in time: A joint video and image encoder for end-to-end retrieval. In: 2021 IEEE/CVF International Conference on Computer Vision (ICCV), pp. 1728–1738 (2021)
2. Cai, T.T., Frankle, J., Schwab, D.J., Morcos, A.S.: Are all negatives created equal in contrastive instance discrimination? In: arXiv:2010.06682 (2020)
3. Chen, D., Dolan, W.B.: Collecting highly parallel data for paraphrase evaluation. In: Proceedings of Annual Meeting of the Association for Computational Linguistics ACL 2011, pp. 190–200 (2011)
4. Cheng, X., Lin, H., Wu, X., Yang, F., Shen, D.: Improving video-text retrieval by multi-stream corpus alignment and dual softmax loss. In: arXiv:2109.04290 (2021)
5. Fang, H., Xiong, P., Xu, L., Chen, Y.: CLIP2Video: Mastering video-text retrieval via image clip. In: arXiv:2106.11097 (2021)
6. Gabeur, V., Sun, C., Alahari, K., Schmid, C.: Multi-modal transformer for video retrieval. In: Proceedings of ECCV 2020, pp. 214–229 (2020)
7. Gao, L., Zhang, Y., Han, J., Callan, J.: Scaling deep contrastive learning batch size under memory limited setup. In: Proceedings RepL4NLP 2021 (2021)
8. Gorti, S.K., et al.: X-Pool: Cross-modal language-video attention for text-video retrieval. In: Proceedings of CVPR 2022, pp. 5006–5015 (2022)
9. Huynh, T., Kornblith, S., Walter, M.R., Maire, M., Khademi, M.: Boosting contrastive self-supervised learning with false negative cancellation. In: Proceedings of WACV 2022, pp. 2785–2795 (2022)
10. Ji, K., Liu, J., Hong, W., Zhong, L., Wang, J., et al.: CRET: Cross-modal retrieval transformer for efficient text-video retrieval. In: Proceedings of SIGIR 2022, pp. 949–959 (2022)
11. Liu, Y., Albanie, S., Nagrani, A., Zisserman, A.: Use what you have: video retrieval using representations from collaborative experts. In: Proceedings of BMVC 2019 (2019)
12. Liu, Y., Xiong, P., Xu, L., Cao, S., Jin, Q.: TS2-Net: token shift and selection transformer for text-video retrieval. In: Proceedings of ECCV 2022, pp. 319–335 (2022)
13. Luo, H., Ji, L., Zhong, M., Chen, Y., Lei, W., et al.: CLIP4Clip: an empirical study of clip for end to end video clip retrieval and captioning. In: Neurocomputing. vol. 508, pp. 293–304 (2022)
14. Oord, A.V.D., Li, Y., Vinyals, O.: Representation learning with contrastive predictive coding. In: arXiv:1807.03748 (2018)
15. Patrick, M., Huang, P.Y., Asano, Y., Metze, F., Hauptmann, A.G., et al.: Support-set bottlenecks for video-text representation learning. In: Proceedings of ICLR 2020 (2020)
16. Radford, A., Kim, J.W., Hallacy, C., Ramesh, A., Goh, G., et al.: Learning transferable visual models from natural language supervision. In: Proceedings of ICML 2021, pp. 8748–8763 (2021)

17. Rohrbach, A., Rohrbach, M., Schiele, B.: The long-short story of movie description. In: Gall, J., Gehler, P., Leibe, B. (eds.) GCPR 2015. LNCS, vol. 9358, pp. 209–221. Springer, Cham (2015). https://doi.org/10.1007/978-3-319-24947-6_17

18. Wang, X., Zhu, L., Yang, Y.: T2VLAD: global-local sequence alignment for text-video retrieval. In: Proceedings of CVPR 2021, pp. 5079–5088 (2021)

19. Wu, M., Mosse, M., Zhuang, C., Yamins, D., Goodman, N.: Conditional negative sampling for contrastive learning of visual representations. In: Proceedings of ICLR 2020 (2020)

20. Wu, Z., Xiong, Y., Yu, S.X., Lin, D.: Unsupervised feature learning via non-parametric instance discrimination. In: Proceedings of CVPR 2018, pp. 3733–3742 (2018)

21. Xu, J., Mei, T., Yao, T., Rui, Y.: MSR-VTT: a large video description dataset for bridging video and language. In: Proceedings of CVPR 2016, pp. 5288–5296 (2016)

22. Yu, Y., Kim, J., Kim, G.: A joint sequence fusion model for video question answering and retrieval. In: Proceedings of ECCV 2018, pp. 471–487 (2018)

23. Zolfaghari, M., Zhu, Y., Gehler, P., Brox, T.: CrossCLR: cross-modal contrastive learning for multi-modal video representations. In: Proceedings of ICCV 2021, pp. 1450–1459 (2021)

Boosting Video Super Resolution with Patch-Based Temporal Redundancy Optimization

Yuhao Huang[1], Hang Dong[2(✉)], Jinshan Pan[3], Chao Zhu[1], Boyang Liang[1], Yu Guo[1], Ding Liu[2], Lean Fu[2], and Fei Wang[1]

[1] Xi'an Jiaotong University, Xi'an, China
[2] ByteDance Intelligent Creation Lab, Xi'an, China
dhunter1230@gmail.com
[3] Nanjing University of Science and Technology, Nanjing, China

Abstract. The success of existing video super-resolution (VSR) algorithms stems mainly exploiting the temporal information from the neighboring frames. However, none of these methods have discussed the influence of the temporal redundancy in the patches with stationary objects and background and usually use all the information in the adjacent frames without any discrimination. In this paper, we observe that the temporal redundancy will bring adverse effect to the information propagation, which limits the performance of the most existing VSR methods and causes the severe generalization problem. Motivated by this observation, we aim to improve existing VSR algorithms by handling the temporal redundancy patches in an optimized manner. We develop two simple yet effective plug-and-play methods to improve the performance and the generalization ability of existing local and non-local propagation-based VSR algorithms on widely-used public videos. For more comprehensive evaluating the robustness and performance of existing VSR algorithms, we also collect a new dataset which contains a variety of public videos as testing set. Extensive evaluations show that the proposed methods can significantly improve the performance and the generalization ability of existing VSR methods on the collected videos from wild scenarios while maintain their performance on existing commonly used datasets.

Keywords: video super-resolution · temporal redundancy · plug and play methods

---

Y. Huang and H. Dong—These authors contributed equally.

Supplementary Information The online version contains supplementary material available at https://doi.org/10.1007/978-3-031-44195-0_30.

1   Introduction

Video Super-Resolution (VSR) aims to reconstruct a high-resolution visual-pleasing video from a low-resolution one. Recent years have witnessed significant advances due to the use of deep convolutional neural networks (CNNs). The success of existing VSR stems mainly exploiting the temporal information from the neighboring frames through propagation.

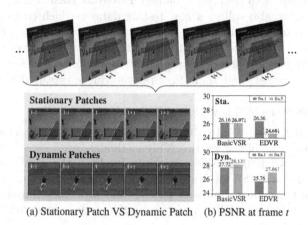

(a) Stationary Patch VS Dynamic Patch   (b) PSNR at frame t

Fig. 1. Effect of the temporal redundancy in stationary patches.

In this paper, we find that the temporal redundancy in stationary objects and background interfere with the high-resolution frame reconstruction if they are not specially handled. As shown in Fig. 1, we select one patch sequence with stationary objects and background $s_{[t-2:t+2]}$ and one patch sequence with dynamic scene $d_{[t-2:t+2]}$ from input frames $I_{[t-2:t+2]}$ and super-resolve them with two typical VSR networks in the local (EDVR [1]) and non-local (BasicVSR [2]) propagation-based methods. To evaluate the benefit of neighboring frames, we also super-resolve the reference patches (s_t and d_t) with two single frame counterparts of these two methods for comparisons. fra.N means method takes N frames as input. As expected, by exploiting the temporal information from the neighboring patches, both networks can achieve better results in the dynamic patch. In the meantime, the single frame counterparts outperform the VSR networks in the patch with stationary objects and background. The inconsistent performance demonstrates that the temporal redundancy may bring adverse effect on the VSR problem.

To overcome this problem, we try to handle the temporal redundancy patches and develop two simple yet effective plug-and-play methods to improve the performance and the generalization ability of existing VSR algorithms. Our work is motivated by an observations: the single frame super-resolution is more suitable for handling patches with temporal redundancy contents. This inspired us to propose a new VSR pipeline with temporal redundancy detection module for local propagation-based methods and deploy it to the original EDVR, namely **Boosted EDVR**. Moreover, we also optimize the non-local propagation-based VSR methods in a different way based on another observation: as for the non-local propagation-based VSR methods, one frame may strongly affect the next adjacent frame, but its influence is quickly lost after few time steps. To improve the effectiveness of the hidden states propagation in the presence of temporal redundancy contents, we propose a patch-based dynamic propagation (PDP) scheme and deploy it to BasicVSR, namely **Boosted BasicVSR**.

In addition, we also collect a new testing dataset which contains a variety of public videos to comprehensively evaluate the robustness and performance of VSR algorithms. More specifically, the collected testing dataset contains videos from live streaming, TV program, sports live, movie and television, surveillance camera, advertisement, and some first person videos captured with irregular trajectories.

The contributions of this work are summarized as follows:

- We find that the temporal redundancy is universal in public videos and will limit the potential of the existing VSR methods.
- We develop two plug-and-play methods for both the local and non-local propagation-based VSR methods, which can optimize the super-resolving process for the temporal redundancy patches and save computational cost.
- We collect a dataset with a variety of public videos to enrich the existing datasets.

2   Related Works

Most existing VSR algorithms focus on improving the motion compensation and frame aggregation modules to better exploit temporal information. SPMC [3] further improve the process by proposing a sub-pixel motion compensation strategy, which is validated by the physical imaging model. In DUF [4], a novel learned dynamic upsampling filter is proposed to exploiting the spatio-temporal of each pixel without explicit motion compensation. EDVR and TDAN [5] both adopt deformable convolutions [6] to align the features of the neighboring frames in a multi-scale architecture. However, these sliding-window frames can not discuss the effect of the temporal redundancy, which leads to sub-optimal results and causes unnecessary consumption.

Since the RNN architecture has been validated to be effective in processing the time sequence signals, it is also applied in the some video super-resolution tasks. FRVSR [7] first proposes a recurrent network to super-resolve the low resolution video by leveraging the HR output from last iteration. RRN [8] proposes a new recurrent residual block to solve the gradient vanish problem and preserve the texture information over long periods. Recently, BasicVSR and BasicVSR++ [9] achieves SotA performance on all the existing datasets by adopting a bidirectional propagation coupled with flow-guided deformable alignments. Despite the distinguished performance, the information in BasicVSR and BasicVSR++ are still sequentially propagated frame-by-frame which is not optimal when temporal redundancy patches exist.

3   Observations on Temporal Redundancy

3.1   The DTVIT Dataset

Currently, most VSR datasets are first-person videos, which contains only dynamic scenes due to consistent movement. However, there are a variety of videos with irregular movement in public videos. To better investigate temporal redundancy, We collected a Diverse Types Videos with Irregular Trajectories (DTVIT) Dataset. More specifically, we collect 96 videos with high-quality and high-resolution as ground-truth from the internet. To ensure the diversity of the datasets, the collected videos include live streaming, TV program, sports live, movie and television, surveillance camera, and advertisement. Then, we randomly select ten videos from DTVIT dataset as the validation set and try to investigate the influence of temporal redundancy based on it. Moreover, we also collect a new training dataset according to the categories of the DTVIT dataset, referred as to DTVIT-Train.

Table 1. Performance of EDVR-1f and two input types of EDVR-5f.

Models	stationary sequences	dynamic sequences
EDVR-1F	**39.20dB**	38.01dB
EDVR-5f(original)	37.81dB	**38.65dB**

Table 2. The performance of BasicVSR in the simulated stationary sequences.

Training dataset	DS	+10df	+20df	+30df	+40df	+50df
REDS	27.38 dB	27.31 dB	27.24 dB	27.12 dB	26.99 dB	26.84 dB
Vimeo	25.85 dB	25.78 dB	25.73 dB	25.69 dB	25.64 dB	25.58 dB

3.2   Temporal Redundancy in Videos

Observation 1: *Single frame super-resolution is more suitable for handling patches with temporal redundancy in stationary objects and background.*

Since the temporal redundancy contents is universal in widely-used public videos, we should also investigate whether it will interfere with existing local propagation-based VSR networks. Following the settings of the experiment in Sect. 1, we super-resolve all the stationary and dynamic sequences in the validation set with both the EDVR-1f and original EDVR (EDVR-5f). The EDVR-1F is modified upon the original EDVR for single frame input, which will be described in Sect. 4.1. As shown in Table 1, although the EDVR-5f achieves better results on the dynamic sequences, the single frame super-resolution method (EDVR-1f) can outperform EDVR-5f with lower computational cost on the stationary sequences. Therefore, the single frame super-resolution is more suitable for handling patches with temporal redundancy.

Observation 2: *Patches with temporal redundancy in the video sequence will hinder the propagation of non-local propagation-based VSR networks.*

According to the **Observation** 1, the existence of temporal redundancy will bring negative effect to local propagation-based VSR algorithms, where only local information can be exploited. On the other hand, non-local propagation-based VSR algorithms can exploit the long-term temporal information by taking all the inference frames as inputs. To investigate the influence of the temporal redundancy on such longer input sequences, we conduct an experiment based on the BasicVSR model. Specifically, we selected 4 downsampling videos with dynamic scenes from the REDS and super-resolve them with the BasicVSR trained on the REDS and the Vimeo respectively. Then, to simulate the stationary sequence and introduce the temporal redundancy, we randomly choose 10 frames from each video and replicated them several times (range from 1 to 5), progressively. For each time, we super-resolve all the extended videos with BasicVSR and record its performance. As shown in Table 2, the two BasicVSR models both suffer from the performance decline as the length of frames with temporal redundancy increases. Therefore, despite of long input sequences, the temporal redundancy will still bring negative effect to the RNN-based VSR network by hindering the information propagation.

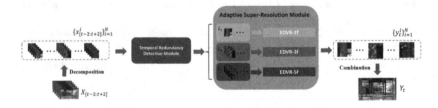

Fig. 2. Overview of the proposed Boosted EDVR.

4   Methodology

Since the temporal redundancy contents is universal in widely-used public videos, it's necessary to optimize the existing VSR algorithms to handle the patches with temporal redundancy. In this section, based on the **Observation** 1 and **Observation** 2, we introduce two effective plug-and-play methods for local and non-local propagation-based networks to optimize the super-resolving process for patches with temporal redundancy.

4.1   Boosting Local Propagation-Based Networks

Based on the **Observation** 1, the patches with temporal redundancy should be specially handled. To achieve this, we try to introduce a temporal redundancy detection module to the existing methods and super-resolve each patch adaptively. In the following parts, we will use the EDVR as example to show how the proposed method optimize the local propagation-based VSR methods.

Inspired by the recent work, Class-SR [10], we extend the original EDVR to a new pipeline, namely **Boosted EDVR**. As shown in Fig. 2, the proposed **Boosted EDVR** consists of two modules: Temporal Redundancy Detection Module (TRDM) and Adaptive Super-Resolution Module (ASRM). The input five LR neighboring frames $X_{[t-2:t+2]}$ are first decomposed into N overlapping patch sequences $\{x^i_{[t-2:t+2]}\}^N_{i=1}$. Then, each decomposed patch sequence $x^i_{[t-2:t+2]}$ is fed to the TRDM and assigned a movement label $(L^i_j, j \in \{1,3,5\})$ according to its motion state among neighboring patches. After that, all the patch sets with the same label will be concatenated in the batch-size dimension and super-resolved by the optimal EDVR model in ASRM. Finally, we combine all the super-resolved patches $\{y^i_t\}^N_{i=1}$ to get the final SR results Y_t.

Temporal Redundancy Detection Module. The goal of TRDM is to detect the temporal redundancy and assign a movement label to each patch sequence. Since the optical flow is a widely-used metric to describe the motion information, we use the mean values of the optical flow to represent the motion state, which can be formulated as:

$$m^i_{-1\to0} = mean(|f(x^i_{t-1}, x^i_t)|), \tag{1}$$

where f denotes the optical flow estimator, $|\cdot|$ denotes absolute value, *mean* is the mean value, and $m^i_{-1\to0}$ denotes the motion state between the reference patch (x^i_t) and its neighboring patch (x^i_{t-1}) in the patch sequence i. We choose the traditional DIS [11] algorithm as the optical flow estimator since it only slightly increase the computational cost.

For i-th patch sequence, we successively calculate the motion states of all the neighboring patches, which denote as $m^i_{-2\to-1}, m^i_{-1\to0}, m^i_{1\to0}$, and $m^i_{2\to1})$. Then, we assigned a movement label $(L_j(x^i_{[t-2:t+2]}), j \in \{1,3,5\})$ according to these motion states:

$$L^i_j = \begin{cases} L^i_1 & \text{if } m^i_{-1\to0} < \gamma \text{ and } m^i_{1\to0} < \gamma, \\ L^i_3 & \text{elif } m^i_{-2\to-1} < \gamma \text{ and } m^i_{2\to1} < \gamma, \\ L^i_5 & \text{otherwise,} \end{cases} \tag{2}$$

where γ is the threshold to discriminate the patch with stationary objects and background and L^i_j denotes j dynamic patches involved in i-th patch sequence. With TRDM, we can determine which model in the following ASRM should be used to obtain better super-resolved results.

Adaptive Super-Resolution Module. The ASRM, which consists of the original EDVR (EDVR-5f) and two of its variants (EDVR-3f and EDVR-1f), is designed to super-resolve each patch sequence with the optimal model. Specifically, we adopt the EDVR-1f model, which is modified for single frame input based on EDVR, to super-resolve all the patch sets with the movement label L_1, since there is no useful temporal information in the neighboring patches. Similarly, the EDVR-3f model and EDVR-5f model will process the patch sequences with the movement labels L_3 and L_5, respectively.

To acquire EDVR-1f and EDVR-3f with minimal modification, we only slightly changes the forward flow of the original EDVR (EDVR-5f) without any changes on the network architecture. For EDVR-1f and EDVR-3f, the PCD alignment module and the temporal attention layers in TSA module are only performed once and threes times, respectively, and the features will be replicated to the same shape as EDVR-5f before sending to the fusion convolutional layer in the TSA module. Since we remove the unnecessary calculation in the PCD alignment and TSA modules of the EDVR-1f and EDVR-3f, the proposed pipeline will be more efficient than the original EDVR. To ensure the EDVR-1f and EDVR-3f can achieve comparable super-resolving ability as EDVR, we also fine-tune them on the same training dataset (REDS) and with same hyperparameter as EDVR.

4.2   Boosting Non-local Propagation-Based Networks

Unlike local propagation-based methods, the non-local propagation-based methods can exploit long-term information by taking all the inference frames as inputs and sequentially propagation. However, based on the **Observation** 2, the patches with temporal redundancy in the video sequence will hinder the propagation, which inevitably limits the potential of the existing non-local propagation-based VSR methods. To better exploit the long-term information, we propose a new plug-and-play method by introducing a Patch-based Dynamic Propagation (PDP) branch to dynamically propagate the long-term information in a patch-wise way. As shown in Fig. 3(a), we deploy the proposed method to BasicVSR, namely **Boosted BasicVSR**, by replacing the original propagation branches with the proposed PDP branches. In the following parts, we will show how the PDP branch works in forward propagation (PDP_f), and the PDP branch in the backward propagation (PDP_b) can be derived accordingly.

The proposed forward PDP branch adopts dynamical propagation, where each patch of the current frame can receive information from different frames. To achieve this, the proposed forward PDP branch maintains a patch pool P_{rgb}^f and its corresponding hidden state pool P_ϕ^f to restore the useful information of patches from different frames. Then, the forward PDP branch takes the current LR frame X_t, P_{rgb}^f, and P_ϕ^f as inputs and generates the forward features h_t^f while updating P_{rgb}^f and P_ϕ^f based on the temporal redundancy detection. The detail of the PDP branch is shown in Fig. 3(b), which consists of two stages: features aggregation and patch pools update.

Features Aggregation. This stage is design to aggregate the information in the maintained pools (P_{rgb}^f and P_ϕ^f) with the current frame. The P_ϕ and P_{rgb}

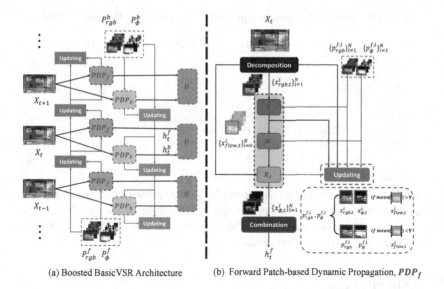

(a) Boosted BasicVSR Architecture   (b) Forward Patch-based Dynamic Propagation, PDP_f

Fig. 3. Overview of the proposed Boosted BasicVSR.

contains N overlapping patches $\{p_{rgb}^{f,i}\}_{i=1}^{N}$ and corresponding hidden state patches $\{p_{\phi}^{f,i}\}_{i=1}^{N}$ which are sorted by their positions in the frame.

To estimate the optical flow for spatial alignment of the hidden state pool P_{ϕ}^{f}, we first decompose current frame X_t into N overlapping patches $(\{x_{rgb,t}^{i}\}_{i=1}^{N})$. Then, the optical flows of all the patches $(\{x_{flow,t}^{i}\}_{i=1}^{N})$ are calculated by sending the correspond patches in the $\{x_{rgb,t}^{i}\}_{i=1}^{N}$ and $\{p_{rgb}^{f,i}\}_{i=1}^{N}$ to the optical estimator (S). After that, we perform warping (W) on the patches in the hidden state pool using the estimated flow for the further refinement in the residual blocks R_f. By feeding the warped hidden state pool and the overlapping patches of current frame into the residual blocks, the intermediate features patches of current frame $(\{x_{\phi,t}^{i}\}_{i=1}^{N})$ can be obtained. Finally, the forward features h_t^f can be obtained by combining the $\{x_{\phi,t}^{i}\}_{i=1}^{N}$.

Patch Pools Update. In this stage, we try to update the patch pool P_{rgb}^{f} and hidden state pool P_{ϕ}^{f} with the information of current frame. As shown in Fig. 3(b), we use a similar temporal redundancy detection method in **Boosted EDVR** to decide which patches in P_{rgb}^{f} and P_{ϕ}^{f} should be updated with current frame. Since we already obtain the optical flows $(\{x_{flow,t}^{i}\}_{i=1}^{N})$ in the features aggregation stage, we direct use Eq. (1) to obtain the motion states $\{m_t^i\}_{i=1}^{N}$ (**the box with red dashed line**) of all the corresponding patches between $\{p_{rgb}^{f,i}\}_{i=1}^{N}$ and $\{x_{rgb,t}^{i}\}_{i=1}^{N}$. Then, to ensure the useful information can be accumulated, each patch set ($p_{rgb}^{f,i}$ and $p_{\phi}^{f,i}$) in the two pools will be replaced by the information of corresponding patch of current frame ($x_{rgb,t}^{i}$ and $x_{\phi,t}^{i}$) when the motion state of

Table 3. Analysis on each component of the proposed Boosted EDVR.

Methods	EDVR	TR-EDVR	Boosted EDVR-(15)	Boosted EDVR-(135)
EDVR-5f	✓	✓	✓	✓
EDVR-3f				✓
EDVR-1f		✓	✓	✓
TR detection		✓	✓	✓
DIS flow			✓	✓
Flops	758M (100%)	661M (87%)	522M (69%)	**519M (68%)**
PSNR	33.42	34.30	34.50	**34.51**

this patch (m_t^i) is larger than the threshold γ. Otherwise, which means temporal redundancy exists in these two patch, the information of current frame will be discarded to avoid vanishing the useful information. Finally, the updated pools will be propagated to the next frame.

5   Experiments

5.1   Datasets and Settings

Since we aim to boost existing VSR algorithms with minimal modifications, we only fine-tune the EDVR-1f and EDVR-3f on the same datasets as EDVR-5f trained. Then, we use the REDS4, Vid4, Real-RawVSR dataset and DTVIT as the test set to compare the proposed models with existing VSR algorithms. For fair comparison, all the evaluated models are trained and tested on the dataset with 4× bicubic downsampling.

For the proposed two methods, each LR frame is decomposed into 64 × 64 patches with stride 56 (with 8 pixel overlaps), and the combination operation combines all the patches to an integrated frame by averaging overlapping areas. The threshold γ in **Boosted EDVR** and **Boosted BasicVSR** are set to 1 and 0.2, respectively. The DTVIT dataset and source code will be made available to the public.

5.2   Experiments on Network Configurations

To investigate the effect of different network configurations and find the optimal one for the proposed **Boosted EDVR** and **Boosted BasicVSR**, we evaluate several models with alternative configurations. When evaluating **Boosted EDVR**, we also calculate the average FLOPs to evaluate the efficiency. For quick verification during the design stage, we still select the validation set of the DTVIT dataset for the ablation study.

Study of the Boosted EDVR. Starting from the original EDVR, we first use the mean square errors (MSE) of pixel values to detect temporal redundancy and use the fine-tuned EDVR-1f models to super-resolve the patch sequences with movement label L_1. We denote these configuration as TR-EDVR. As shown in

Table 3, the TR-EDVR can achieve 0.88 dB performance gain over the original EDVR with less FLOPS. Since the optical flow is widely used to describe the motion information, we use the mean values of the DIS optical flow to represent the motion state and form the Boosted EDVR-(15). The Boosted EDVR-(15) outperforms TR-EDVR by a margin of 0.2 dB while the overall FLOPs drop from 661M to 522M. Futhermore, we also introduce a fine-tuned EDVR-3f model, namely Boosted EDVR-(135), to super-resolve the patch sets where the temporal redundancy only occurs at the border patches ($m^i_{-2 \to -1} < \gamma$ and $m^i_{2 \to 1} < \gamma$). Since both the performance and efficiency are slight improved by introducing EDVR-3f, we choose the Boosted EDVR-(135) as the final configurations of **Boosted EDVR**. Compared with the EDVR, the proposed **Boosted EDVR** can achieve 1.09 dB performance gain with only 68% computational cost.

Table 4. Analysis on each key factor of the proposed PDP branch.

Methods	BasicVSR	TR-BasicVSR	DP-BasicVSR	Boosted BasicVSR
Frame type classification		✓	✓	✓
Dynamic propagation			✓	✓
Patch-wise				✓
PSNR	27.96	32.57	33.22	**34.08**

Study of the Boosted BasicVSR. As shown in Table 4, the performance of BasicVSR trained on the REDS is much worse than the original EDVR (27.96 dB vs. 33.42 dB) on the validation set, which is contradictory to the results on the existing datasets. We owe this severe generalization problem of BasicVSR to the error accumulation of the optical flow. To overcome this problem, we propose a new pipeline, namely TR-BasicVSR, to super-resolve stationary and dynamic frames separately. Then, we combine all the dynamic sequences into one sequence and super-resolve it with BasicVSR. For stationary sequences, where all the frames are similar in one sequence, we super-resolve each frame independently to avoid the error accumulation of the optical flow. As shown in Table 4, the TR-BasicVSR obtain significant performance gain over the original BasicVSR.

Furthermore, we introduce the dynamic propagation scheme to TR-BasicVSR, namely DP-BasicVSR. Specifically, the DP-BasicVSR maintains an anchor frame and its corresponding hidden states to restore the long-term information from the closest dynamic frame and propagate it to current frame. Since the dynamic propagation scheme can directly propagate the information from the long-term frame to current frame without accumulating useless redundancy information of the stationary sequences, the DP-BasicVSR outperforms TR-BasicVSR by a margin of 0.65 dB.

Finally, by adopting the patch-wise strategy, the **Boosted BasicVSR** achieves 0.86 dB performance gain over DP-BasicVSR. Overall, the proposed **Boosted BasicVSR** can solve the generalization problem of the pre-trained BasicVSR and boost its performance without any training process, which demonstrates the effectiveness of the proposed PDP scheme.

Table 5. Quantitative comparison (PSNR/SSIM).

Methods	REDS4	Vid4	Real-RawVSR	DTVIT
	PSNR/SSIM	PSNR/SSIM	PSNR/SSIM	PSNR/SSIM
Bicubic	26.14/0.7292	23.78/0.6347	27.08/0.7666	29.46/0.8870
DUF [4]	28.63/0.8251	18.45/0.5117	21.30/0.5632	23.17/0.6517
RBPN [12]	30.09/0.8590	25.66/0.8029	30.10/0.7958	32.74/0.9208
MuCAN [13]	30.88/0.8750	25.33/0.7994	28.11/0.7841	30.58/0.9072
EDVR-L [1]	31.09/0.8800	25.40/0.8008	31.19/0.8795	32.39/0.9277
EDVR [1]	30.53/0.8699	25.34/0.7951	30.97/0.8733	32.00/0.9205
Boosted EDVR	30.53/0.8699	25.34/0.7950	**31.81/0.8799**	**32.91/0.9262**
BasicVSR [2]	**31.42/0.8909**	**25.75/0.8155**	30.69/0.8722	27.13/0.8165
Boosted BasicVSR	**31.42/0.8917**	**25.93/0.8202**	**31.30/0.8853**	**33.21/0.9340**

5.3   Comparisons with Existing VSR Algorithms

To further evaluate the proposed methods, we conduct comprehensive experiments by comparing **Boosted EDVR** and **Boosted BasicVSR** with several state-of-the-art VSR algorithms.

The first and second columns in Table 5 show the quantitative results on the REDS and Vid4, where all the testing videos are first-person videos with consistent movement. As expected, the proposed **Boosted EDVR** and **Boosted BasicVSR** only achieve comparable performance with EDVR and BasicVSR, since they are optimized for videos with temporal redundancy. However, the stable performance demonstrates that the proposed methods are robustness and will not bring any adverse influence to existing datasets.

To comprehensively evaluate the performance of VSR algorithms on different types of public videos, we also evaluate these algorithms on the Real-RawVSR dataset and the collected DTVIT dataset which contain more types of videos. As shown in the third column of Table 5, the proposed **Boosted EDVR** and **Boosted BasicVSR** can significant boost the EDVR and BasicVSR on the Real-RawVSR dataset respectively. The fourth column in Table 5 shows the quantitative results on the DTVIT dataset. Although the EDVR achieve favorable performance than other methods, the proposed **Boosted EDVR** can further improve the performance by up to 0.91 dB over EDVR with much lower computational cost. The BasicVSR trained on the REDS performs not well on the DTVIT dataset due to the generalization problem. However, the proposed **Boosted BasicVSR** can solve the generalization problem and significantly improve the performance by a large margin of 6.08 dB over BasicVSR. Overall, both **Boosted EDVR** and **Boosted BasicVSR** are able to achieve remarkable performance on the dataset containing stationary scenes while not to harm dynamic scenes, which demonstrates that the proposed plug-and-play methods can improve the performance and robustness of existing VSR algorithms.

To verify the proposed method can not only solve the generalization problem but also can enhance the effectiveness of the propagation branches. We make the train set and test set consistent on the Real-RawVSR dataset and DTVIT

Table 6. Quantitative comparison of different methods in consistent dataset.

Methods	Real-RawVSR	DTVIT
	PSNR/SSIM	PSNR/SSIM
EDVR	33.60/0.9139	32.64/0.9389
Boosted EDVR	**33.94/0.9122**	33.02/0.9393
BasicVSR	33.27/0.9113	**33.36/0.9406**
Boosted BasicVSR	33.27/0.9113	**33.73/0.9432**
Real-RawVSR	33.91/0.9182	\
Boosted Real-RawVSR	**34.18/0.9160**	\

respectively. Furthermore, We apply the proposed Adaptive Super-Resolution Module (ASRM) to the Real-RawVSR [14] similar to the **Boosted EDVR**, namely **Boosted Real-RawVSR**. We only evaluate Real-RawVSR on the Real-RawVSR dataset due to raw frames are required as input. As shown in the Table 6, Our proposed methods still achieve the better results compared to the original methods. It is noted that the proposed **Boosted Real-RawVSR** can also outperform the original Real-RawVSR and achieve SotA performance. This demonstrates the generality and effectiveness of our proposed method.

Unusually, the **Boosted BasicVSR** trained on the Real-RawVSR dataset can not be effective. We find that the flow estimation module of BasicVSR trained on the Real-RawVSR dataset is completely destroyed. This means temporal information can not be propagated and all inputs are processed as a single frame. This further proves that temporal redundancy harms the propagation of non-local networks.

Fig. 4. Qualitative comparison on the DTVIT dataset.

Qualitative comparisons are shown in Fig. 4. The **Boosted EDVR** and **Boosted BasicVSR** recover finer details and sharper texts.

6   Conclusion

In this paper, we focus on optimizing the existing VSR algorithms by taking the adverse effect of the temporal redundancy into consideration. Through introducing a temporal redundancy detection and adaptive super-resolution module to the original EDVR, we propose **Boosted EDVR**, a simple yet effective method can improve the performance and accelerate the inference time simultaneously. We also propose **Boosted BasicVSR** by adopting a Patch-based Dynamic Propagation (PDP) scheme to solve the generalization problem of the original BasicVSR and boost its performance without any training process. Extensive evaluations show that the proposed modifications can largely improve the performance on the Real-RawVSR dataset and the collected dataset without any adverse influence to existing datasets. We believe that these two plug-and-play methods can also be applied to others video restoration tasks since the temporal redundancy is universal in most public videos.

References

1. Wang, X., Chan, K.C., Yu, K., Dong, C., Change Loy, C.: EDVR: video restoration with enhanced deformable convolutional networks. In: Proceedings of the IEEE/CVF Conference on Computer Vision and Pattern Recognition Workshops (2019)
2. Chan, K.C., Wang, X., Yu, K., Dong, C., Loy, C.C.: BasicVSR: the search for essential components in video super-resolution and beyond. In: IEEE Conference on Computer Vision and Pattern Recognition, pp. 4947–4956 (2021)
3. Tao, X., Gao, H., Liao, R., Wang, J., Jia, J.: Detail-revealing deep video super-resolution. In: Proceedings of the IEEE International Conference on Computer Vision, pp. 4472–4480 (2017)
4. Jo, Y., Oh, S.W., Kang, J., Kim, S.J.: Deep video super-resolution network using dynamic upsampling filters without explicit motion compensation. In: The IEEE Conference on Computer Vision and Pattern Recognition (CVPR) (2018)
5. Tian, Y., Zhang, Y., Fu, Y., Xu, C.: TDAN: temporally deformable alignment network for video super-resolution. In: Proceedings of the IEEE/CVF Conference on Computer Vision and Pattern Recognition, pp. 3360–3369 (2020)
6. Dai, J., et al.: Deformable convolutional networks. In: Proceedings of the IEEE International Conference on Computer Vision, pp. 764–773 (2017)
7. Sajjadi, M.S., Vemulapalli, R., Brown, M.: Frame-recurrent video super-resolution. In: The IEEE Conference on Computer Vision and Pattern Recognition (CVPR), June 2018
8. Isobe, T., Zhu, F., Jia, X., Wang, S.: Revisiting temporal modeling for video super-resolution. arXiv preprint arXiv:2008.05765 (2020)
9. Chan, K.C., Zhou, S., Xu, X., Loy, C.C.: BasicVSR++: improving video super-resolution with enhanced propagation and alignment. arXiv, (2021)
10. Kong, X., Zhao, H., Qiao, Y., Dong, C.: ClassSR: a general framework to accelerate super-resolution networks by data characteristic. In: Proceedings of the IEEE/CVF Conference on Computer Vision and Pattern Recognition, pp. 12016–12025 (2021)

11. Kroeger, T., Timofte, R., Dai, D., Van Gool, L.: Fast optical flow using dense inverse search. In: Leibe, B., Matas, J., Sebe, N., Welling, M. (eds.) ECCV 2016. LNCS, vol. 9908, pp. 471–488. Springer, Cham (2016). https://doi.org/10.1007/978-3-319-46493-0_29

12. Haris, M., Shakhnarovich, G., Ukita, N.: Recurrent backprojection network for video super-resolution. In: IEEE Conference on Computer Vision and Pattern Recognition (CVPR) (2019)

13. Li, W., Tao, X., Guo, T., Qi, L., Lu, J., Jia, J.: MuCAN: multi-correspondence aggregation network for video super-resolution. In: Vedaldi, A., Bischof, H., Brox, T., Frahm, J.-M. (eds.) ECCV 2020. LNCS, vol. 12355, pp. 335–351. Springer, Cham (2020). https://doi.org/10.1007/978-3-030-58607-2_20

14. Yue, H., Zhang, Z., Yang, J.: Real-RawVSR: real-world raw video super-resolution with a benchmark dataset. arXiv preprint arXiv:2209.12475 (2022)

Bring the Noise: Introducing Noise Robustness to Pretrained Automatic Speech Recognition

Patrick Eickhoff[1(✉)], Matthias Möller[2], Theresa Pekarek Rosin[1],
Johannes Twiefel[1,3], and Stefan Wermter[1]

[1] Knowledge Technology, Department of Informatics, University of Hamburg,
Vogt-Koelln-Str. 30, 22527 Hamburg, Germany
{patrick.eickhoff,theresa.pekarek-rosin,
johannes.twiefel,stefan.wermter}@uni-hamburg.de
[2] Centre for Applied Autonomous Sensor Systems (AASS), Örebro University,
Örebro, Sweden
matthias.moeller@oru.se
[3] exXxa GmbH, Vogt-Koelln-Str. 30, 22527 Hamburg, Germany
https://www.knowledge-technology.info, https://exXxa.ai/

Abstract. In recent research, in the domain of speech processing, large End-to-End (E2E) systems for Automatic Speech Recognition (ASR) have reported state-of-the-art performance on various benchmarks. These systems intrinsically learn how to handle and remove noise conditions from speech. Previous research has shown, that it is possible to extract the denoising capabilities of these models into a preprocessor network, which can be used as a frontend for downstream ASR models. However, the proposed methods were limited to specific fully convolutional architectures. In this work, we propose a novel method to extract the denoising capabilities, that can be applied to any encoder-decoder architecture. We propose the Cleancoder preprocessor architecture that extracts hidden activations from the Conformer ASR model and feeds them to a decoder to predict denoised spectrograms. We train our preprocessor on the Noisy Speech Database (NSD) to reconstruct denoised spectrograms from noisy inputs. Then, we evaluate our model as a frontend to a pretrained Conformer ASR model as well as a frontend to train smaller Conformer ASR models from scratch. We show that the Cleancoder is able to filter noise from speech and that it improves the total Word Error Rate (WER) of the downstream model in noisy conditions for both applications.

Keywords: Conformer · Noise Robustness · Speech Recognition

1 Introduction

End-to-End (E2E) systems have been the state-of-the-art approach to Automatic Speech Recognition (ASR) for a few years now [1,4,17]. An E2E system usually takes audio as input, processes it into an internal representation, and

© The Author(s) 2023
L. Iliadis et al. (Eds.): ICANN 2023, LNCS 14260, pp. 376–388, 2023.
https://doi.org/10.1007/978-3-031-44195-0_31

produces a transcript of the speech. The big advantage of these systems is that all components are trained together, so they can learn a joint representation. However, the disadvantage is that they often require deep models with a large number of parameters to perform well. For example, the recent Whisper-large model [17] contains about 1550 M parameters. Training a model like this from scratch is computationally expensive and usually not possible for research institutions. However, most of these models can be successfully adapted to smaller domains through the use of transfer learning, which indicates the quality of speech representations learned [9,17]. Additionally, E2E systems usually do not have preprocessing applied to their input and the model itself has to learn how to separate speech from noise [17]. Usually, the earlier layers of recent ASR architectures are required to separate noise from speech implicitly. When a new ASR architecture is developed, the earlier noise-handling layers need to be trained again. This raises the question if it is possible to separate the processing capabilities of such a large and powerful pretrained ASR model and reuse them for another model.

Our work takes inspiration from the recent findings of Möller et al. [13]. They were able to utilize a pre-trained Jasper [12] ASR model to create a preprocessor, which increases the noise robustness of pretrained models and improves the performance of smaller ASR models trained from scratch. However, their approach has two disadvantages: 1) their approach is only applicable to a specific architecture of Jasper, and 2) Jasper is no longer state-of-the-art for English ASR. Instead, attention-based models derived from the Transformer [23] architecture have outperformed convolutional and recurrent ASR approaches [3,7,9,17]. Therefore, we propose a new extraction method (Parallel Weighted Sum), which is potentially applicable to any encoder-decoder ASR architecture. We apply this method to a Conformer [7] model, a state-of-the-art attention-based architecture, to create our preprocessor called Cleancoder. Our model can function either as an independent frontend for pre-trained ASR models or can be used in combination with architectures trained from scratch to improve their noise robustness. In our experiments, we measure the performance (Word Error Rate; WER) on different noise levels on the Noisy Speech Dataset (NSD) [20] to show that our methods improve the performance under noisy conditions and the performance does not decrease under clean conditions (LibriSpeech [16]) when using our preprocessor.

2   Related Work

To improve the noise robustness of a speech recognition model, training processes usually include adding both artificial and realistic noise to the training data. This leads to large-scale ASR models showcasing certain noise robustness without any further preprocessing steps. However, since smaller models might not be able to perform the same internal denoising steps, it is important to examine how the capabilities of larger models can be exploited by smaller models. When mentioning 'small', 'medium', and 'large' ASR models we refer to the number of parameters defined by Gulati et al. [7] for their Conformer configurations ($\sim$10M, $\sim$30M, $\sim$100M).

There are different approaches to creating external preprocessors, that denoise speech for further speech recognition. Many of these focus on filtering noise from speech using statistical methods in combination with deep learning methods [2,6,8]. A recent example of such a method is the Cleanformer model. Cleanformer [2] is a multichannel frontend architecture for speech enhancement based on the Conformer [7] architecture. The model combines raw noisy speech and enhanced input features, produced by a SpeechCleaner [10] noise cancellation algorithm, to create an Ideal Ratio Mask (IRM) [14]. This mask in the spectral space, estimates the ratio of speech in the noisy signal. These ratios are then applied to the input signal to filter out noise. The model works independently of the combined ASR model and can reduce WERs across multiple SNR values by approximately 50%.

Instead of applying a filtering method to the noisy signal, our approach reconstructs clean spectrograms completely from latent representations. Our work is based on the findings of Möller et al. [13], who created a frontend architecture for noise filtering based on the Jasper [12] architecture. Based on the findings of Li et al. [11] and their probing methods to extract and predict spectrograms from hidden representations, Möller et al. applied this method to gauge the denoising capabilities of a pre-trained Jasper model. The underlying assumption is that areas of speech that the model perceives as noise are filtered out very early by the system and are not represented in the model's latent space. Thereby, those filtering capabilities could be leveraged for other ASR models and increase their noise robustness.

Möller et al. demonstrate how the reconstructed representations of speech support other already pretrained ASR systems in noisy conditions. Additionally, they observe that those features support other ASR systems as input while training and that models with those representations generally perform better on noisy and clean data. However, their approach relies strongly on the architecture of Jasper [12] and its residual connections. They retrain the batch normalization layers in the model and are therefore limited to one specific architecture, which is not state-of-the-art anymore. Our work introduces a way that could potentially reconstruct speech from any ASR system while still retaining denoising capabilities.

3 Methodology

Our method of constructing a denoising preprocessor from a pretrained ASR model is inspired by the work of Möller et al. [13]. However, we propose an architecture that can extract latent representation from potentially any encoder-decoder ASR architectures and is not limited to the Jasper architecture. Our Cleancoder model extracts the latent representations of an ASR model's encoder and reconstructs denoised spectrograms.

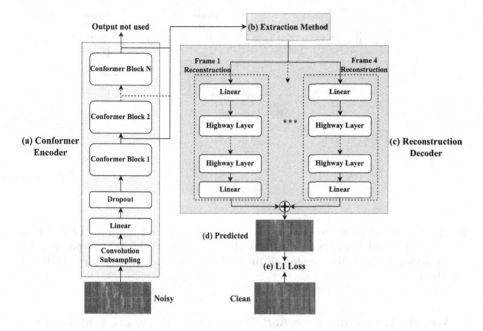

Fig. 1. This figure shows the architecture of our Cleancoder. On the left, we display the original Conformer encoder architecture (a). Then, the output of every Conformer block is fed into our extraction method (b). This method computes a weighted sum of the latent representation and feeds this vector to our reconstruction decoder (c). This decoder contains four different Highway Networks tasked with reconstructing one-fourth of the final output frame. The subsampling layer of the Conformer reduces the temporal dimension of the input by a factor of four. Thus we generate four outputs, which are appended along the temporal axis to reconstruct a complete spectrogram of a frame (d). Then we compute the L1 loss (e) between the reconstructed spectrogram and the clean ground truth.

The architecture follows an encoder-decoder structure, shown in Fig. 1. We choose pretrained Conformer models as a baseline to extract our preprocessor from it. These models are larger than the Jasper [12] used by Möller et al. [13] but still can be trained from scratch in a reasonable time. There are multiple pretrained Conformer models with Connectionist Temporal Classification (CTC) available from NVIDIA NeMo[1]. Jasper has been outperformed by many more recent ASR models, which are using attention-based architectures [4,5,7]. The Jasper model used by Möller et al. only reported a WER of 2.84%(test-clean)/7.84%(test-other) [12] on the LibriSpeech [16] test set, using an external language model. The large Conformer we base our model on reported 1.9%(test-clean)/3.9%(test-other) [7]. Thus, we assume that our Cleancoder will be able to yield better WER improvements for downstream models.

---

[1] https://catalog.ngc.nvidia.com/models.

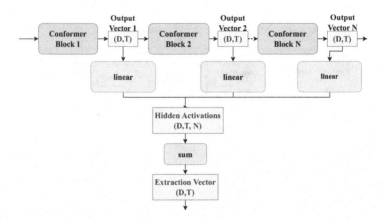

Fig. 2. This figure shows our Parallel Weighted Sum method. Each of the N latent vectors of the Conformer encoder has size (D, T) and is fed through a separate fully connected layer after which we sum all the projected vectors into one output vector of size (D, T).

We reuse the encoder of the ASR Conformer model (see Fig. 1, a). We disregard the decoder layers as we're only interested in the latent representations. To extract these hidden activations, we feed the output of each Conformer block into our extraction method. We create an approach that applies to potentially any encoder-decoder ASR architecture while remaining simple. We propose a Parallel Weighted Sum extraction method (see Fig. 1, b and Fig. 2), which extends the regular weighted sum. However, instead of choosing one weight vector to reduce all the hidden activations into one, our method feeds each layer through separate parallel projection layers and computes the sum across these layers. This way, we not only weigh the contribution of the different blocks to the denoised output but also weigh the information contained in each feature vector. We took inspiration from the work of Yang et al. [25], who compared different Self-Supervised Learned (SSL) representations.

For our decoder network, we choose to follow the example of Möller et al. [13] and use four-layer Highway Networks [18]. They have shown, that these networks can reconstruct spectrograms sufficiently for ASR from hidden representations. Since the Conformer preprocessing block reduces the temporal dimension by a factor of four, we train four different Highway Networks. The four outputs are appended along the temporal axis. Given the input x consists of t frames, the Conformer will reduce the temporal dimension by four yielding $t/4$ frames. We denote the latent representation constructed by our Parallel Weighted Sum as s_i for frame i and our four Highway Networks as $N_1, N_2, \ldots, N_4$. Since our decoder is almost identical to the one of Möller et al. [13], we obtain a similar equation for the output y of our model:

$$y = (N_1(s_0), N_2(s_0), N_3(s_0), N_4(s_0), \ldots, N_1(s_{t/4}), N_2(s_{t/4}), N_3(s_{t/4}), N_4(s_{t/4}))$$

4   Experimental Results

4.1   Datasets

Noisy Speech Database. The Noisy Speech Database (NSD) [20] was designed to test and train speech enhancement algorithms. It contains pairs of noisy and clean speech, sampled at 48 kHz, and is divided into a training and test set. For our experiments, we downsampled our input to 16 kHz. Each sample in the datasets provides noisy and clean audio, a transcript, information about the speaker, signal-to-noise ratio (SNR), and noise type. There are two sets of the NSD with 28 [22] and 56 speakers [21] taken from the Voice Bank Corpus [24]. The noisy samples were created by adding recorded noise from the DEMAND database [19] as well as generated babble and speech-shaped noise. These noise types were applied at different SNRs. We combine the 28 and 56-speaker sets to expose our model to a larger variety of speakers and noise conditions. Thus, we will ensure better generalization. We use the NSD to train our denoising preprocessor and to evaluate the performance of downstream ASR models on noisy data.

LibriSpeech. LibriSpeech [16] is a corpus of approximately 1000 h of clean English speech, sampled at 16 kHz. LibriSpeech is an established dataset for evaluating ASR models [7,12]. We use LibriSpeech in our experiments to train small ASR models from scratch.

4.2   Training the Cleancoder

To evaluate if the Cleancoder architecture filters the noise from speech we train two preprocessor models (medium, and large) on the NSD train set. This way, we can estimate the required size of the best preprocessor. Our preprocessors are trained to reconstruct spectrograms of the same form as the encoder's input. These are log-Mel spectrograms with 80 features, a window size of 0.025, and a windows stride of 0.01. We convert each clean and noisy audio signal of each sample in the NSD trainset into log-Mel spectrograms. While training, our models are fed the noisy spectrograms and predict denoised spectrograms.

Then, we can compute the L1 loss between the clean and denoised spectrograms. We train two different models with the medium and large-sized Conformer CTC models. The medium Conformer consists of ~30.7M parameters, while the large one consists of ~118.8M parameters [7]. For each encoder model, we train our preprocessor for 100 epochs on a batch size of 64 with L1 Loss. The learning rate is set to a magnitude of $1e^{-3}$, where the precise values are taken from a hyperparameter search, which we conduct before the actual training. The search was conducted on the NSD trainset. The Adam optimizer is configured with $\beta_1 = 0.9$, $\beta_2 = 0.98$ and a weight decay of $1e^{-4}$. The learning rates are set to the optimal values from our hyperparameter search. We choose to omit the learning rate scheduler since the initial learning rate is already very small. Our decoder is configured as four four-layer Highway Networks.

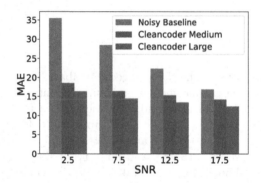

Fig. 3. This figure presents the mean absolute error (MAE) computed between the noisy and clean and respective denoised and clean spectrograms of the NSD test set grouped by the signal-to-noise ratio (SNR). We observe that the denoised spectrograms of both preprocessors show a lower MAE than the noisy baseline across all noise conditions. The large Cleancoder shows the lowest MAE.

After training the two models, we inspect the differences between the noisy, clean, and denoised spectrograms. We measure their deviation by computing the mean absolute error (MAE) between the clean and noisy as well as clean and denoised spectrograms. Our results on the MAE are shown in Fig. 3. For both preprocessors, we observe that they reduce the MAE compared to just the noisy input. The lower the SNR the larger the improvement, indicating that the Cleancoder models filter noise from speech. However, the MAE of the Cleancoders remains at similar values for all SNRs, which could suggest that the MAE reduction is already saturated at a low SNR.

4.3 Frontend for Pretrained Models

Next, we test how our Cleancoder affects the performance of existing pretrained ASR models. Therefore, we use our preprocessors as frontends to first denoise the input signal and generate spectrograms. These are fed into a pretrained downstream ASR model which predicts transcriptions. Finally, we measure the WER between the ground truth texts, the transcripts recognized from the unprocessed noisy spectrograms (noisy baseline), and the transcripts recognized from the preprocessed noisy spectrograms (our preprocessor).

For our experiments, we choose a medium-sized Conformer with CTC and a large Conformer Transducer as downstream ASR models, which are both publicly available through NVIDIA's model collection. We chose two different ASR models to ensure a degree of invariance to the downstream architecture. This experiment verifies if it is possible to combine our front end with other downstream architectures without the risk of degrading the performance.

Our results are shown in Fig. 4. We can see, that overall, while the WER increases with the medium preprocessor compared to the baseline, it decreases for almost all SNR configurations with the large Cleancoder. The large Cleancoder

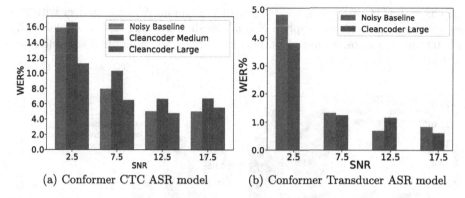

(a) Conformer CTC ASR model   (b) Conformer Transducer ASR model

Fig. 4. Figure (a) presents the WER on the NSD test set for evaluating our frontends using a Conformer CTC downstream model. Figure (b) presents the WER using a Conformer Transducer downstream model. The Transducer was only evaluated with the large Cleancoder, as the medium Cleancoder had already proven to be unable to improve ASR performance. Both plots show the WER grouped by SNR. Each bar denotes either the noisy spectrograms or respective denoised spectrograms. The WER improves the most on low SNR samples and slightly degrades WER on high SNR samples.

performs better on samples with low SNR, only for samples with the highest SNR of 17.5 the performance is slightly worse than the noisy baseline. We observe that the performance of the baseline Conformer Transducer got worse from SNR 12.5 to 17.5. When analyzing the errors we found minor anomalies in the predictions, however, since the WER is already very low we accredit this observation to general variance.

We further discuss the correlation between our MAE and WER results. Möller et al. [13] suggested, that the MAE and WER do not necessarily correlate. We found little research on the impact of the MAE between noisy and clean speech on the resulting WER. While we observe significant improvements of the MAE using our medium and large preprocessors, the WER shows significantly lower performance on the medium preprocessor. Only the large version yields positive results. There seems to be no strong correlation between the MAE and WER. We assume that a different loss function to train the preprocessor would be more appropriate, and we will examine this in our future work.

4.4   Training an ASR Model from Scratch

We evaluate how the Cleancoder impacts the training of a smaller downstream ASR model from scratch. The architecture of choice for the ASR model was a small Conformer using CTC without a language model. We train three different small Conformer models. All three are trained on LibriSpeech's training splits. The baseline model uses no front end, while the others are trained on the outputs of our medium and large preprocessor, respectively. All three are trained for 100 epochs with CTC loss using a batch size of 128 and an Adam optimizer with β_1 as 0.9 and β_2 as 0.98. We apply a NoamAnnealing learning rate scheduler with 10,000 warmup steps, an initial learning rate of 2.0, and a minimal learning rate of $1.0e^{-06}$.

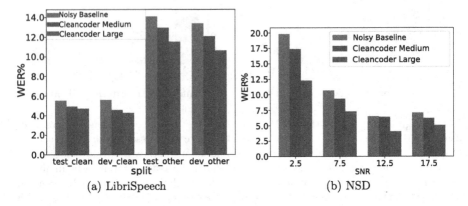

(a) LibriSpeech   (b) NSD

Fig. 5. Figure (a) shows the WER (%) of our three ASR models trained from scratch for the dev- and test-splits of LibriSpeech. Figure (b) shows the WER (%) for the NSD test set grouped by SNR. Each model used the same small Conformer architecture and was trained on either the raw input or the output of our medium and large preprocessors. We observe that the ASR model using the large preprocessor shows the lowest WER in both figures.

In the first plot of Fig. 5, we report the WER computed on the test-clean, test-other, dev-clean, and dev-other splits of LibriSpeech. We observe that both models using our preprocessors outperform the baseline ASR model. The large Cleancoder shows the lowest mean WER on all splits.

Furthermore, we show the WER of our ASR models on the NSD test set grouped by SNR in the second plot of Fig. 5. We observe that both models using our preprocessors outperform the baseline model. The large preprocessor shows the best performance with an almost 4% improvement overall. We also observe that using the Cleancoders yields the biggest improvements on samples with a low SNR. This shows the models are more robust to noise.

Finally, we investigate the impact of using our Cleancoders over the course of training. The evaluation CTC loss and evaluation WER are shown in Fig. 6. We observe that both models using our front end converge faster and reach a lower loss and WER than the baseline model. The loss curves and WER curves follow an almost identical course. We observe that the validation loss and WER are both lowest for the large Cleancoder. As previously discussed, this supports the assumption that the large Cleancoder generalizes better to different noise conditions.

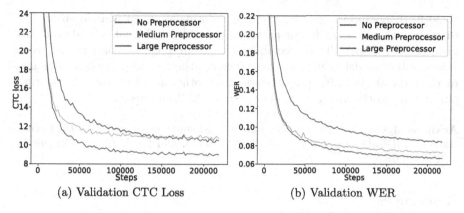

(a) Validation CTC Loss   (b) Validation WER

Fig. 6. Plot (a) shows the CTC loss over the number of training steps for the validation dataset. Plot (b) shows the WER, computed on the validation dataset, over the training steps. Each plot shows three curves for the baseline ASR model (blue), the medium preprocessor (orange), and the large preprocessor (green). Both preprocessors converge lower than the baseline ASR model, except for the CTC validation loss of the medium preprocessor. (Color figure online)

5 Conclusion

We created preprocessors from pretrained Conformer [7] ASR models by extracting the hidden activations and training a decoder to predict denoised spectrograms. In our experiments, we showed that our Cleancoder improves the performance (WER) under noisy conditions (SNR: 2.5 and 7.5) for two different downstream ASR models. Under clean audio conditions (SNR: 12.5 and 17.5) the performance stayed mostly stable (with one outlier). The results indicate that our preprocessor is capable of improving the performance of downstream ASR models under noisy conditions without the necessity of performing any training for the downstream ASR models. In the second experiment, we trained the downstream ASR model from scratch by first feeding the audio training data through the Cleancoder and then using the generated spectrograms as training data for our downstream ASR model. The performance substantially improved under both noisy and clean audio conditions. Comparing the results of the first and second experiments suggests, that reconstruction errors of our Cleancoder might disturb a pretrained ASR model, but can be compensated by training on these errors. Furthermore, we measured the training and validation loss while performing the training. These results show that the training time of an ASR model can be reduced due to an improved convergence, and the performance can be increased when using our preprocessor as input to a downstream ASR model.

In future work, we plan to research different loss functions aside from MAE to train the Cleancoder for denoising. One example could be the Ideal Ratio Mask (IRM) [15], which has recently been successfully utilized for a denoising frontend [2]. A loss function with better correlation to the downstream WER could further improve our Cleancoder's performance as an ASR frontend. Furthermore, we will evaluate our preprocessor using additional downstream ASR architectures. Especially the combination of our preprocessor and the recent Whisper [17] model would be worth investigating. Finally, applying our approach to create denoising preprocessors from other architectures will confirm if our method works with any encoder-decoder ASR architecture.

Acknowledgements. The authors gratefully acknowledge support from the German BMWK (SIDIMO), the DFG (CML, LeCAREbot), and the European Commission (TRAIL, TERAIS).

References

1. Baevski, A., Zhou, Y., Mohamed, A., Auli, M.: Wav2vec 2.0: a framework for self-supervised learning of speech representations. Adv. Neural Inf. Process. Syst. **33**, 12449–12460 (2020)
2. Caroselli, J., Naranayan, A., O'Malley, T.: Cleanformer: a microphone array configuration-invariant, streaming, multichannel neural enhancement frontend for ASR. ArXiv abs/2204.11933 (2022)
3. Chen, S., et al.: WavLM: large-scale self-supervised pre-training for full stack speech processing. IEEE J. Sel. Top. Signal Process. **16**(6), 1505–1518 (2022)
4. Chung, Y.A., et al.: w2v-BERT: combining contrastive learning and masked language modeling for self-supervised speech pre-training. In: IEEE Automatic Speech Recognition and Understanding Workshop (ASRU), pp. 244–250 (2021)
5. Chung, Y.A., et al.: W2v-BERT: combining contrastive learning and masked language modeling for self-supervised speech pre-training. In: 2021 IEEE Automatic Speech Recognition and Understanding Workshop (ASRU), pp. 244–250. IEEE (2021)
6. Fang, H., Wittmer, N., Twiefel, J., Wermter, S., Gerkmann, T.: Partially adaptive multichannel joint reduction of ego-noise and environmental noise. arXiv preprint arXiv:2303.15042 (2023)
7. Gulati, A., et al.: Conformer: convolution-augmented transformer for speech recognition. In: Proceedings of the Interspeech, pp. 5036–5040, October 2020
8. Heymann, J., Drude, L., Haeb-Umbach, R.: Neural network based spectral mask estimation for acoustic beamforming. In: IEEE International Conference on Acoustics, Speech and Signal Processing (ICASSP),. pp. 196–200 (2016)
9. Hsu, W.N., Bolte, B., Tsai, Y.H.H., Lakhotia, K., Salakhutdinov, R., Mohamed, A.: Hubert: self-supervised speech representation learning by masked prediction of hidden units. IEEE/ACM Trans. Audio Speech Lang. Process. **29**, 3451–3460 (2021)
10. Huang, Y.A., Shabestary, T.Z., Gruenstein, A.: Hotword cleaner: dual-microphone adaptive noise cancellation with deferred filter coefficients for robust keyword spotting. In: Proceedings of IEEE International Conference on Acoustics, Speech and Signal Processing (ICASSP), pp. 6346–6350 (2019)
11. Li, C., Yuan, P., Lee, H.: What does a network layer hear? Analyzing hidden representations of end-to-end ASR through speech synthesis. In: Proceedings of IEEE International Conference on Acoustics, Speech and Signal Processing (ICASSP), pp. 6434–6438. IEEE Press, May 2020

12. Li, J., et al.: Jasper: an end-to-end convolutional neural acoustic model. In: Proceedings of the Interspeech, pp. 71–75, September 2019
13. Möller, M., Twiefel, J., Weber, C., Wermter, S.: Controlling the noise robustness of end-to-end automatic speech recognition systems. In: Proceedings of the International Joint Conference on Neural Networks (IJCNN), July 2021
14. Narayanan, A., Wang, D.: Ideal ratio mask estimation using deep neural networks for robust speech recognition. In: IEEE International Conference on Acoustics, Speech and Signal Processing, pp. 7092–7096 (2013)
15. Narayanan, A., Wang, D.: Ideal ratio mask estimation using deep neural networks for robust speech recognition. In: Proceedings of IEEE International Conference on Acoustics, Speech and Signal Processing (ICASSP), pp. 7092–7096. IEEE Press (2013)
16. Panayotov, V., Chen, G., Povey, D., Khudanpur, S.: LibriSpeech: an ASR corpus based on public domain audio books. In: Proceedings of IEEE International Conference on Acoustics, Speech and Signal Processing (ICASSP), pp. 5206–5210. IEEE Press, April 2015
17. Radford, A., Kim, J.W., Xu, T., Brockman, G., McLeavey, C., Sutskever, I.: Robust speech recognition via large-scale weak supervision. arXiv preprint arXiv:2212.04356 (2022)
18. Srivastava, R.K., Greff, K., Schmidhuber, J.: Highway networks. arXiv preprint arXiv:1505.00387 (2015)
19. Thiemann, J., Ito, N., Vincent, E.: DEMAND: a collection of multi-channel recordings of acoustic noise in diverse environments (2013)
20. Valentini-Botinhao, C.: Noisy Speech Database for Training Speech Enhancement Algorithms and TTS Models (2017)
21. Valentini-Botinhao, C., Wang, X., Takaki, S., Yamagishi, J.: Investigating RNN-based speech enhancement methods for noise-robust Text-to-Speech. In: Speech Synthesis Workshop (SSW), pp. 146–152, September 2016
22. Valentini-Botinhao, C., Yamagishi, J.: Speech enhancement of noisy and reverberant speech for text-to-speech. IEEE/ACM Trans. Audio Speech Lang. Process. **26**(8), 1420–1433 (2018)
23. Vaswani, A., et al.: Attention is all you need. In: Guyon, I., et al. (eds.) Advances in Neural Information Processing Systems, vol. 30. Curran Associates, Inc., December 2017
24. Veaux, C., Yamagishi, J., King, S.: The voice bank corpus: design, collection and data analysis of a large regional accent speech database. In: Oriental COCOSDA held jointly with 2013 Conference on Asian Spoken Language Research and Evaluation (O-COCOSDA/CASLRE), International Conference. Institute of Electrical and Electronics Engineers (IEEE), United States, November 2013
25. Yang, S.W., et al.: SUPERB: speech processing universal performance benchmark. In: Proceedings of the Interspeech, pp. 1194–1198 (2021)

Correction while Recognition: Combining Pretrained Language Model for Taiwan-Accented Speech Recognition

Sheng Li[1] and Jiyi Li[2(✉)]

[1] National Institute of Information and Communications Technology, Kyoto, Japan
sheng.li@nict.go.jp
[2] University of Yamanashi, Kofu, Japan
jyli@yamanashi.ac.jp

Abstract. Taiwan-accented speech bears similarities to the Mandarin Min dialect, but with substantial differences in vocabulary, which significantly impacts spoken language recognition outcomes. This paper concentrates on integrating pre-trained language models (PLMs) with state-of-the-art self-supervised learning (SSL)-based speech recognition systems for Taiwan-accented speech recognition tasks. We propose a progressive error correction process in tandem with recognition to fully exploit the autoregressive nature of PLM models. Experimental results demonstrate that our method effectively addresses recognition errors stemming from misspelled vocabulary in accented speech. Our proposed progressive approach achieves roughly a 0.5% improvement compared to the conventional method. Furthermore, we demonstrate that fine-tuning PLMs solely with the text from the accented dataset can enhance recognition performance, despite the limitations of accented speech resources.

Keywords: speech recognition · pretrained language models (PLMs) · Taiwan-accented speech

1 Introduction

With the increasing number of East Asian tourists in Japan, particularly Taiwan tourists, the demand for general Taiwan-accented speech recognition systems is rising. This paper investigates an effective automatic speech recognition (ASR) method of Taiwan-accented speech to handle the vocabularies mismatch in applying a pre-trained language model (PLM) to low-resource language.

Accented speech recognition focuses on solving the accent, dialect, and non-standard speech's specific influence on the speech recognition system. With the development of deep learning, end-to-end (E2E) ASR models, especially transformers, have shown promising performance [1,6–8,10,14,18,39]. Current self-supervised learned (SSL) models [2], e.g., Wav2Vec series models [4], show state-of-the-art performance. However, the problem of accent speech still needs to be

© The Author(s), under exclusive license to Springer Nature Switzerland AG 2023
L. Iliadis et al. (Eds.): ICANN 2023, LNCS 14260, pp. 389–400, 2023.
https://doi.org/10.1007/978-3-031-44195-0_32

solved because the limit of accented speech resources remains a challenge in applying the PLM to low-resource language.

Since Taiwan's accent significantly differs from Mandarin spoken in the mainland vocabularies, one direct method is enhancing language models (LM). Incorporating language models, such as N-gram [15] and RNN-based LMs [23] into the ASR systems is an old practice. It can effectively improve recognition performance. More advanced PLMs [9,25] have been developed in recent years, independently trained on the large-scale corpus with self-supervised learning. Such LMs contain rich semantic information and capture contextual information from both directions. Benefiting from the development of the transformer framework, such LMs can capture contextual information free from direction and distance. Therefore, as an external resource, it has been a trend to integrate large language models into ASR systems in recent years.

Although many new applications of ASR with PLMs are booming in the industry [5,11,24,26,32,33,36,37], we only focus on two typical models from all these PLMs, i.e., decoder-based and encoder-based models. The first model is GPT-2, a transformer-decoder-based language model based on a casual transformer with masked self-attention specializing in text generation that could help correct the ASR prediction. Its integration is expected to do unidirectional corrections. The second model is BERT, proposing the masked language model to learn bi-directional semantics as a transformer encoder-based language model with self-attention. BERT and GPT-2 are also pretrained on the general corpus to learn universal semantics and perform well with the E2E models. However, the distribution should differ for a specific task, such as ASR in the Common Voice dataset. More tuning on a target-related domain is expected to bring more improvement, as investigated in [16,29].

This paper investigates the integration of pre-trained language models (PLMs) into the self-supervised learning (SSL)-based automatic speech recognition (ASR) system for Taiwan-accented speech recognition tasks. The conventional method for incorporating PLMs involves feeding the output of the SSL acoustic model into the PLMs, then using the PLMs' output as the word probability for the subsequent ASR prediction. Although this approach demonstrates improved results, several challenges may arise when integrating PLMs for accented speech recognition tasks. Differences in vocabulary between the accented and standard languages can lead to inaccuracies in pronunciation and word choice. Accented language recognition is often marred by errors in pronunciation and vocabulary. Considering the autoregressive nature of the word generation process in PLMs, we propose a progressive utilization of PLMs, incorporating the generated word probability into the successive word prediction process for speech recognition. Additionally, we fine-tune the PLM using task-specific text-only data to further enhance performance in the domain of Taiwan-accented speech recognition.

The contributions of this paper are addressed as follows.

- 1. We integrate of PLMs into the SSL-based ASR system for accented speech.

- 2. We propose a progressive utilization of PLMs instead of feeding PLMs whole sentences as input. We also fine-tune the PLM using task-specific text-only data.
- 3. The above work compares two typical encoder-based (BERT) and decoder-based PLMs (GPT-2).

The rest of this paper is structured as follows. Section 2 gives a brief overview of the related work. We then present the detail of our proposed method in Sect. 3. Section 4 describes the setup of the experiments and presents the result of all experimental models. We finally conclude the paper with final remarks in Sect. 5.

2   Related Work

2.1   ASR for Taiwan-Accented Speech

In current Mandarin large vocabulary continuous speech recognition (LVCSR) tasks (Mandarin), variations in the pronunciation of dialects greatly influence the accuracy. Traditionally, seven major groups of dialects have been recognized. Together with Mandarin, the other six are Wu, Hakka, Min, Xiang, Yue, and Gan. There are significant regional variations in pronunciation, vocabulary, and grammar among these dialects.

The regional accents of Mandarin speakers show significant differences. John Hopkins Summer Workshop[1] had a special report on this topic. The report of this summer workshop analyzed the nature of accent through temporal, frequential, and prosodic analysis. Table 1 shows vocabulary and pronunciation differences. Please note that the differences mentioned above are just a few examples and do not encompass the entire range of variations between Taiwanese and Mandarin. Furthermore, the writing system for Taiwan in this answer utilizes the Pe̍h-ōe-jī (POJ) Romanization system, which is one of the methods used to represent Taiwanese sounds in Latin script.

In this paper, we mainly focus on addressing these differences in language modeling/with LM-based approaches, especially for Taiwan-accented speech, similar to the Min dialect but with significant differences in vocabulary.

2.2   SSL Models for ASR Task

The current state-of-the-art model is the SSL model. The Wav2Vec2.0 [4] is a typical model of this category and a transformer-based architecture network. This model comprises a multi-layer convolutional network (CNN) as a feature extractor and inputs raw audio waveform. The outputting audio representations are fed into a transformer encoder to generate audio representations for downstream tasks. The training is based on self-supervised learning with unlabeled speech. Then the model is fine-tuned on labeled data with the Connectionist Temporal Classification (CTC) [13] algorithm for specific ASR tasks [22].

---

[1] http://old-site.clsp.jhu.edu/ws04/groups/ws04casr.

Table 1. Vocabulary and pronunciation differences.

Mandarin (Simplified, Pinyin)	Taiwan (Traditional, POJ Latin)	English
我(wǒ)	我(góa)	I, me
你(nǐ)	汝(lí)	You
好(hǎo)	好(hó)	Good
爸爸(bàba)	爸爸(pē-pē)	Father
不客气(bùkèqi)	無禮無(bô-kheh-ki)	You're welcome

2.3 PLMs for ASR

With the success of transformer-based language models, such as BERT and GPT-2, there have been attempts to incorporate them into speech tasks in recent years. They are mainly used for rescoring and error correction.

BERT [9], Bidirectional Encoder Representations from Transformers [30], is a bidirectional pretraining language model applying mask prediction and next sentence prediction. By pretraining in a large full-text corpus, BERT can learn rich linguistic knowledge and be applied in the fine-tuning downstream task such as text generation.

GPT series language models [25] are based on a transformer decoder. Similarly, it is also pretrained on a large-scale corpus with self-supervised learning. GPT has excellent capability to guess the next word in sentences. More precisely, inputs are sequences of continuous text, and the targets are the same sequence, shifted one token (word or word-piece) to the right.

Rescoring and Error Correction with PLMs: Zhang et al. [35] proposed a spelling corrector based on the transformer to reduce the substitution error in Mandarin speech recognition. [34] improved the BERT effectiveness in detecting spelling errors with the soft-masking technique as the bridge between error detector and corrector. Futami et al. [12] generated soft labels for ASR training with the BERT distilling knowledge. There are also some works [27,28] studying to improve ASR rescoring by BERT. Additionally, BERT has also been successfully applied in multi-modal study in vision-language pretraining [19–21,38] or voice-language pretraining [3,17,31].

3   Proposed Method

3.1   Baseline Introduction

As mentioned before, the PLMs could be directly used to enhance ASR results. Given the output sequence of the CTC model, it can be further fed into the PLMs.

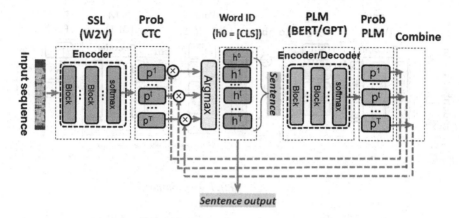

Fig. 1. The flowchart of the baseline method.

- In the GPT model, given that it predicts the next word in a sequence, the [CLS] token is positioned at the beginning of the predicted sequence. This alignment enables the GPT model's output to correspond with that of the CTC model. We exclude the final prediction of the GPT model, as predicting the next token for the last token is not necessary.

- The CTC model's output at each time step is a probability distribution over the vocabulary, derived from applying the softmax function to the model's logits. Similarly, the GPT model's output represents the probability distribution over the vocabulary for each subsequent token. By taking the product of the CTC and GPT outputs, we can achieve enhanced results in our language modeling tasks.

- BERT can be implemented similarly. Mask each token from CTC prediction and use BERT to obtain its prediction.

The baseline system compared in this study is only the vanilla CTC model. It can be extended to sophisticated acoustic models, e.g., LFMMI, CTC-Attention, and conformer. However, these strong models may eclipse the PLMs' error correction ability. Figure 1 shows the flowchart of the baseline method.

3.2 Our Proposed Method

The underlying principle of our proposed method is that for the input at step $t + 1$ in the PLM model, relying solely on the CTC prediction is insufficient; the PLM output at step t should also be taken into account. In other words, during each iteration, the combined prediction is obtained as the product of the CTC and PLM models, which is then fed into the PLM model to generate the prediction for the next step. The primary distinction between our approach and the baseline lies in progressively updating the combined prediction and using it

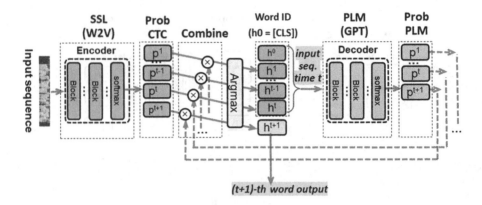

Fig. 2. The flowchart of the proposed method on GPT model.

as input for the PLM model, thereby improving input quality and, consequently, the final result. Figure 2 and Fig. 3 provide a detailed illustration of our proposed method.

In Fig. 2, the GPT model requires only the preceding results, which include the token of the current time step as illustrated in Eq. (2). We formulate the process as follows, where h^0 represents the [CLS] token.

$$h^r = \arg\max(p_{\text{CTC}}^r * p_{\text{PLM}}^r), \ r \in \{1, ..., t\} \tag{1}$$

$$H_{\text{PLM}}^t = [h^0; ...; h^t] \tag{2}$$

$$p_{\text{PLM}}^{t+1} = \Theta_{\text{PLM}}(H_{\text{PLM}}^t) \tag{3}$$

where $[\cdot; \cdot]$ denotes the concatenation function in Eq. (1), Θ_{PLM} represents the PLM model, while p^t, p_{CTC}^t, and p_{PLM}^t correspond to the combined prediction, CTC prediction, and PLM next word prediction probabilities at step t, respectively. The PLM prediction is initialized to one, with the same shape as the CTC prediction. The equation aims to obtain the tokens from the combined prediction at step t, where h^t is the predicted token ID with the maximum probability. H_{PLM}^t is the PLM's prompt input. It is important to note that PLMs necessitate long context input.

For the GPT model's prompt input H_{PLM}^t at step t, all the previous tokens $(h^0, ..., h^{t-1})$ and the current token h^t should be considered for more confident prediction, as shown in Eq. (2).

Similarly, in Fig. 3, the BERT model requires a complete sequence with only the token of the current step masked out as input to obtain bidirectional information, as demonstrated in Eq. (5). Equation (4) extracts the tokens at step t, in which h^t is the predicted token ID with the maximum probability. We feed the CTC output to the BERT model. We formulate the process, where h^0 represents the [CLS] token.

$$h^r = \arg\max(p_{\text{CTC}}^r * p_{\text{PLM}}^r), \ r \in \{1, ..., T\} - \{t\} \tag{4}$$

$$H_{\text{PLM}}^t = [h^0; ...; h^{t-1}; h^{t+1}; ...; h^T] \simeq [h^0; ...; h^{t-1}] \tag{5}$$

$$p_{\text{PLM}}^{t+1} = \Theta_{\text{PLM}}(H_{\text{PLM}}^t) \tag{6}$$

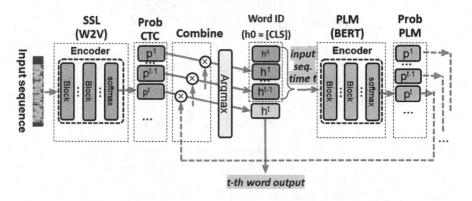

Fig. 3. The flowchart of the proposed method on BERT model.

For the BERT model's prompt input H_{PLM}^t at t step, only the token of the current step h^t is masked out, and the input is the whole sentence in Eq. (5). For the real-time decoding purpose, the future context of h^t can be ignored as an approximation. In this way, it works similarly to GPT-2 model as shown in Table 2.

4   Experiments

4.1   Experimental Settings

Dataset: The model is fine-tuned and evaluated on the Zh-Tw dataset of Common Voice[2]. The Common Voice dataset for fine-tuning is 3.3 h (3507 utterances), and the testing dataset is 2.9 h (2895 utterances). The vocabulary size is 21,128. The speech input is sampled at 16 kHz. Overall, the dataset used in this paper is small due to the data limit, so we focus on text-based PLMs.

Evaluation Criterion: We use character error rate (CER%) as the criterion for evaluation.

SSL Models: The wav2vec2-large-xlsr-53[3] is used as a pretrained SSL model and is fine-tuned on the Common Voice Taiwan dataset (Zh-Tw)[4]. The experiment is conducted on one A40 GPU.

PLM Models: The gpt2-base-chinese and BERT-base-chinese[5] are used as pretrained PLM models. They are also fine-tuned with text labels from the Common

---

[2] https://commonvoice.mozilla.org.

[3] https://huggingface.co/facebook/wav2vec2-large-xlsr-53.

[4] https://commonvoice.mozilla.org/zh-TW.

[5] https://github.com/ckiplab/ckip-transformers.

Table 2. The step-by-step process examples of our proposed method.

	example BERT	example GPT
Oracle	在我腦海之中	在我腦海之中
proposed	BERT-based	GPT-based
step 0	[M] _ _ _ _ _	在
Mask change	[0 1 1 1 1 1]	[1 0 0 0 0 0]
step 1	在[M] _ _ _ _	在我
Mask change	[1 0 1 1 1 1]	[1 1 0 0 0 0]
step 2	在我[M] _ _ _	在我腦
Mask change	[1 1 0 1 1 1]	[1 1 1 0 0 0]
step 3	在我腦[M] _ _	在我腦海
Mask change	[1 1 1 0 1 1]	[1 1 1 1 0 0]
step 4	在我腦海[M] _	在我腦海之
Mask change	[1 1 1 1 0 1]	[1 1 1 1 1 0]
step 5	在我腦海之[M]	在我腦海之中
Mask change	[1 1 1 1 1 0]	[1 1 1 1 1 1]
output	在我腦海之中	在我腦海之中

Table 3. Model Settings.

	Layers	Size (GB)	#Parameters
Wav2Vec2.0	24	1.35	337,094,920
BERT	12	0.40	102,290,312
GPT-2	12	0.41	102,068,736

Voice Taiwan dataset (Zh-Tw). The experiment is also conducted on one A40 GPU. Table 3 lists the model settings.

Fine-Tuning: The fine-tuning has four epochs (total_step/10). The learning rate is from 0 to $1*10^{-5}$, gradually decreasing to 0. Every training is this strategy without a development set. One thing that should be noticed is that the output of the SSL model (vocabulary) should be the same as the input of PLMs. Therefore we can multiply their prediction.

4.2   Experimental Results

Table 4 lists the experimental results. For the GPT-based method, our approach reduces the CER by 0.33% compared to the baseline. Considering that the GPT model is pre-trained on formal text (written style) different from the oral style, we further fine-tune the GPT model using the Common Voice training set. With fine-tuning, our model achieves a 25.09% CER.

For the BERT-base method, this result is expected, as BERT's embedding is based on bidirectional information, and both forward and backward embeddings should consider information from both directions. But the future context is ignored. Furthermore, fine-tuning the BERT model does not bring additional

Table 4. Comparison of baseline and our proposed method.

	CER (%)	Speed (RTF)
CTC	28.70	0.013
Baseline (CTC + GPT)	25.70	0.020
Our (CTC + GPT)	25.37	0.043
Our + fine-tuning GPT	**25.09**	0.043
Baseline (CTC + BERT)	25.57	0.042
Our (CTC + BERT)	25.54	0.042
Our + fine-tuning BERT	**25.93**	0.042

Table 5. Some examples showing the improvements by our proposed method.

	Example 1	Example 2
Oracle	北投就業服務站	透過網站公布優良廠商名單
CTC	北頭就業服誤展	透過網戰公布優良廠超明單
Baseline	北投就業服務展	透過網站公布優良廠商明單
Our	北投就業服務站	透過網站公布優良廠商名單

improvement. We suspect overfitting may be an issue with the Common Voice training dataset. Further research on the Zh-Tw oral dataset should be conducted. Table 5 presents examples of the improvements made by our proposed method and demonstrates its effectiveness.

We think another reason should be BERT model as typical encoder-based language models can sometimes face the low-rank problem. This issue arises when the continuous, fixed-size representations (embeddings) generated by the encoder fail to capture the entire spectrum of semantic and syntactic information present in the input text. In other words, the embeddings may not have enough dimensions to represent complex linguistic relationships accurately. The low-rank problem can lead to difficulties when it comes to distinguishing between similar words or phrases or understanding the nuances of meaning in the input text. Consequently, the model's performance on downstream tasks like text classification, sentiment analysis, or question-answering can be negatively impacted.

While decoder-based models have no such problem and will be widely used in tasks such as language generation, text summarization, and machine translation. Examples include GPT (like GPT-4) and OpenAI's Codex.

5 Conclusions

In this study, we propose a progressive error correction method that leverages PLMs to improve ASR recognition results for Taiwan-accented speech. Our proposed method surpasses the baseline performance. Additionally, we fine-tune PLMs for the accented spoken text dataset, yielding promising results for both

BERT and GPT-based models. Our approach also addresses the challenges posed by low-resource accented speech. In the future, we will continue to refine our proposed method and explore other state-of-the-art models for further enhancement.

Acknowledgements. This work was partially supported by JSPS KAKENHI Grant Number 23K11227 and 23H03402, and NICT tenure-track startup funding.

References

1. Amodei, D., et al.: Deep speech 2: end-to-end speech recognition in English and mandarin. In: Proceedings of The 33rd International Conference on Machine Learning (ICML). Proceedings of Machine Learning Research, vol. 48, pp. 173–182 (2016). https://proceedings.mlr.press/v48/amodei16.html
2. Baevski, A., Hsu, W.N., Conneau, A., Auli, M.: Unsupervised speech recognition. In: Advances in Neural Information Processing Systems (NeurIPS), vol. 34, pp. 27826–27839 (2021). https://proceedings.neurips.cc/paper_files/paper/2021/file/ea159dc9788ffac311592613b7f71fbb-Paper.pdf
3. Baevski, A., Mohamed, A.: Effectiveness of self-supervised pre-training for ASR. In: 2020 IEEE International Conference on Acoustics, Speech and Signal Processing (ICASSP), pp. 7694–7698 (2020). https://doi.org/10.1109/ICASSP40776.2020.9054224
4. Baevski, A., Zhou, Y., Mohamed, A., Auli, M.: wav2vec 2.0: a framework for self-supervised learning of speech representations. In: Advances in Neural Information Processing Systems (NeurIPS), vol. 33, pp. 12449–12460 (2020). https://proceedings.neurips.cc/paper_files/paper/2020/file/92d1e1eb1cd6f9fba3227870bb6d7f07-Paper.pdf
5. Bai, Y., Yi, J., Tao, J., Tian, Z., Wen, Z., Zhang, S.: Fast end-to-end speech recognition via non-autoregressive models and cross-modal knowledge transferring from BERT. IEEE/ACM Trans. Audio Speech Lang. Process. **29**, 1897–1911 (2021). https://doi.org/10.1109/TASLP.2021.3082299
6. Chiu, C.C., et al.: State-of-the-art speech recognition with sequence-to-sequence models. In: 2018 IEEE International Conference on Acoustics, Speech and Signal Processing (ICASSP), pp. 4774–4778. IEEE Press (2018). https://doi.org/10.1109/ICASSP.2018.8462105
7. Chorowski, J., Bahdanau, D., Cho, K., Bengio, Y.: End-to-end continuous speech recognition using attention-based recurrent nn: First results. arXiv preprint arXiv:1412.1602 (2014)
8. Chorowski, J., Bahdanau, D., Serdyuk, D., Cho, K., Bengio, Y.: Attention-based models for speech recognition. In: Proceedings of the 28th International Conference on Neural Information Processing Systems (NIPS), vol. 1, pp. 577–585 (2015)
9. Devlin, J., Chang, M.W., Lee, K., Toutanova, K.: BERT: pre-training of deep bidirectional transformers for language understanding. In: Proceedings of the 2019 Conference of the North American Chapter of the Association for Computational Linguistics: Human Language Technologies (NAACL), vol. 1 (Long and Short Papers), pp. 4171–4186 (2019). https://doi.org/10.18653/v1/N19-1423. https://aclanthology.org/N19-1423
10. Dong, L., Xu, B.: CIF: continuous integrate-and-fire for end-to-end speech recognition. In: 2020 IEEE International Conference on Acoustics, Speech and Signal Processing (ICASSP), pp. 6079–6083 (2020). https://doi.org/10.1109/ICASSP40776.2020.9054250

11. Futami, H., Inaguma, H., Ueno, S., Mimura, M., Sakai, S., Kawahara, T.: Distilling the knowledge of BERT for sequence-to-sequence ASR. In: Proceedings of Interspeech 2020, pp. 3635–3639 (2020). https://doi.org/10.21437/Interspeech.2020-1179

12. Futami, H., Inaguma, H., Ueno, S., Mimura, M., Sakai, S., Kawahara, T.: Distilling the knowledge of BERT for sequence-to-sequence ASR. CoRR abs/2008.03822 (2020). https://arxiv.org/abs/2008.03822

13. Graves, A., Fernandez, S., Gomez, F., Shmidhuber, J.: Connectionist temporal classification: labelling unsegmented sequence data with recurrent neural networks. In: Proceedings of ICML (2006)

14. Graves, A., Jaitly, N.: Towards end-to-end speech recognition with recurrent neural networks. In: Proceedings of ICML, pp. 1764–1772 (2014)

15. Heafield, K., Pouzyrevsky, I., Clark, J., Koehn, P.: Scalable modified kneser-ney language model estimation. In: Proceedings of ACL (2013)

16. Houlsby, N., et al.: Parameter-efficient transfer learning for NLP. In: Proceedings of ICML, pp. 2790–2799 (2019)

17. Hsu, W.N., Tsai, Y.H.H., Bolte, B., Salakhutdinov, R., Mohamed, A.: Hubert: how much can a bad teacher benefit ASR pre-training? In: Proceedings of IEEE-ICASSP, pp. 6533–6537 (2021)

18. Li, J., Wang, X., Li, Y., et al.: The speechtransformer for large-scale mandarin Chinese speech recognition. In: Proceedings of IEEE-ICASSP, pp. 7095–7099 (2019)

19. Li, L.H., Yatskar, M., Yin, D., Hsieh, C.J., Chang, K.W.: Visualbert: a simple and performant baseline for vision and language. arXiv preprint arXiv:1908.03557 (2019)

20. Li, X., et al.: Oscar: object-semantics aligned pre-training for vision-language tasks. In: Vedaldi, A., Bischof, H., Brox, T., Frahm, J.-M. (eds.) ECCV 2020. LNCS, vol. 12375, pp. 121–137. Springer, Cham (2020). https://doi.org/10.1007/978-3-030-58577-8_8

21. Lu, J., Batra, D., Parikh, D., Lee, S.: Vilbert: pretraining task-agnostic visiolinguistic representations for vision-and-language tasks. arXiv preprint arXiv:1908.02265 (2019)

22. Miao, Y., Gowayyed, M., Na, X., Ko, T., Metze, F., Waibel, A.: An emprical exploration of CTC acoustic models. In: Proceedings of IEEE-ICASSP (2016)

23. Mikolov, T., Karafiát, M., Burget, L., Cernockỳ, J., Khudanpur, S.: Recurrent neural network based language model. In: Proceedings of Interspeech, vol. 2, pp. 1045–1048 (2010)

24. Ogawa, A., Delcroix, M., Karita, S., Nakatani, T.: Rescoring n-best speech recognition list based on one-on-one hypothesis comparison using encoder-classifier model. In: Proceedings of IEEE-ICASSP (2018)

25. Radford, A., Wu, J., Child, R., Luan, D., Amodei, D., Sutskever, I., et al.: Language models are unsupervised multitask learners. OpenAI Blog 1(8), 9 (2019)

26. Salazar, J., et al.: Masked language model scoring. In: Proceedings of ACL (2020)

27. Salazar, J., Liang, D., Nguyen, T.Q., Kirchhoff, K.: Masked language model scoring. arXiv preprint arXiv:1910.14659 (2019)

28. Shin, J., Lee, Y., Jung, K.: Effective sentence scoring method using BERT for speech recognition. In: Proceedings of ACML, pp. 1081–1093 (2019)

29. Sun, C., Qiu, X., Xu, Y., Huang, X.: How to fine-tune BERT for text classification? In: Sun, M., Huang, X., Ji, H., Liu, Z., Liu, Y. (eds.) CCL 2019. LNCS (LNAI), vol. 11856, pp. 194–206. Springer, Cham (2019). https://doi.org/10.1007/978-3-030-32381-3_16

30. Vaswani, A., et al.: Attention is all you need. In: Proceedings of NeurIPS, vol. 30 (2017)
31. Wang, C., Wu, Y., Liu, S., Zhou, M., Yang, Z.: Curriculum pre-training for end-to-end speech translation. arXiv preprint arXiv:2004.10093 (2020)
32. Xu, L., et al.: Rescorebert: discriminative speech recognition rescoring with BERT. In: Proceedings of IEEE-ICASSP (2022)
33. Yu, F.H., Chen, K.Y., Lu, K.H.: Non-autoregressive ASR modeling using pre-trained language models for Chinese speech recognition. IEEE/ACM Trans. ASLP **30**, 1474–1482 (2022)
34. Zhang, S., Huang, H., Liu, J., Li, H.: Spelling error correction with soft-masked BERT. arXiv preprint arXiv:2005.07421 (2020)
35. Zhang, S., Lei, M., Yan, Z.: Investigation of transformer based spelling correction model for CTC-based end-to-end mandarin speech recognition. In: Proceedings of Interspeech, pp. 2180–2184 (2019)
36. Zhao, Y., et al.: Bart based semantic correction for mandarin automatic speech recognition system. In: Proceedings of Interspeech (2021)
37. Zheng, G., et al.: Wav-BERT: cooperative acoustic and linguistic representation learning for low-resource speech recognition. In: Proceedings of EMNLP findings (2021)
38. Zhou, L., Palangi, H., Zhang, L., Hu, H., Corso, J., Gao, J.: Unified vision-language pre-training for image captioning and VQA. In: Proceedings of AAAI, vol. 34, pp. 13041–13049 (2020)
39. Zhou, S., Xu, S., Xu, B.: Multilingual end-to-end speech recognition with a single transformer on low-resource languages. arXiv preprint arXiv:1806.05059 (2018)

Cross-Camera Prototype Learning for Intra-camera Supervised Person Re-identification

Bingyu Duan[1,2], Wanqian Zhang[1(✉)], Dayan Wu[1], Lin Wang[1,2], Bo Li[1,2], and Weiping Wang[1,2]

[1] Institute of Information Engineering, Chinese Academy of Sciences, Beijing, China
{duanbingyu,zhangwanqian,wudayan,wanglin5812,libo, wangweiping}@iie.ac.cn
[2] School of Cyber Security, University of Chinese Academy of Sciences, Beijing, China

Abstract. Person Re-Identification (ReID) aims at retrieving images of the specific pedestrian across disjoint cameras. However, the annotations are extremely costly as the number of cameras increases, which derives a new setting named Intra-Camera Supervision (ICS) ReID. ICS assumes that identity labels are independently annotated within each camera, while no cross-camera identity association is available. Previous ICS methods focus on connecting the inter-camera instances that are likely to be the same pedestrian, whereas fails to exploit the so far untapped yet informative supervision, i.e., 'the cross-camera prototype relations'. In this paper, we propose the novel Cross-Camera Prototype Learning (CCPL) method to tackle this issue. Firstly, we ensure identities to be discriminative and associated with corresponding intra-camera prototypes, which can be considered as the semantic representations for each local identity. Besides, we claim that the distance between the same inter-camera prototypes is inevitably large, due to the variances of different cameras in views, lights, backgrounds etc. To that end, we propose the Camera-invariant Prototype Alignment (CPA) module, which preserves the cross-camera prototype relations by explicitly pulling together the same inter-camera prototypes and pushing away the different ones. Last but not least, we also introduce the inter-camera prototype pulling loss to constrain the same prototypes as close as possible. Extensive experiments on three benchmarks show the superiority of our method.

Keywords: Person Re-Identification · Intra-Camera Supervision · Cross-Camera Prototype Learning

L. Iliadis et al. (Eds.): ICANN 2023, LNCS 14260, pp. 401–413, 2023.
https://doi.org/10.1007/978-3-031-44195-0_33

1   Introduction

Person Re-Identification (ReID) aims at retrieving images of the specific pedestrian across disjoint cameras. Due to its importance in surveillance and public safety, ReID has drawn significantly increasing research interests [8,18,25]. With a large amount of full annotations, fully supervised ReID [2,8,10,16,27] has achieved remarkable performance. However, in practical application scenarios, the global annotations across all the cameras are extremely costly as the number of cameras increases. Conversely, unsupervised ReID methods [9,20,23–25] conduct the model training without the supervision of annotations, which is efficient yet far from the performance requirements of real-world applications.

Recently, researchers introduce the Intra-Camera Supervised (ICS) setting [29,30], which represents a shift away from conventional ReID scenarios and towards a more practical setting, where identity labels are independently annotated within each camera, and no inter-camera identity association is provided during the whole training procedure. ICS greatly reduces the time-consuming annotation costs to improve the training efficiency, ensuring ReID models with both the availability and scalability in real-word applications.

Previous ICS methods [5,6,12,13,19,22,29,30] train the ReID model from two perspectives, i.e., the intra- and inter-camera learning. In the intra-camera learning, ICS tries to learn discriminative features for locally annotated identities in each camera. While in the inter-camera learning, they utilize the inter-camera instances through various schemes such as multi-label strategy [29,30], soft-labeling scheme [13], consistent discrepancy learning [12] etc. However, they focus only on connecting the inter-camera instances that are likely to be the same pedestrian, whereas neglecting the exploitation of 'inter-camera prototype relations'. As shown in Fig. 1, the distance between the same inter-camera prototypes, which represent the same pedestrian from different cameras, is usually large under the influence of the camera variances (such as backgrounds and angles), leading to the indiscriminative feature spaces. This will consequently lead to inevitable performance degradation, thus becomes the motivation of our work.

In this work, we propose the novel **Cross-Camera Prototype Learning** (CCPL) method to tackle the above issue. Specifically, we introduce the multitask framework along with instance triplet loss and intra-camera prototype loss, to facilitate identities with discriminative features within each camera. During the inter-camera learning, we excavate and preserve the cross-camera prototype relations by adopting the prototype pairwise matching mechanism, which identifies two prototypes as the same pedestrian only if they are mutually the closest in the other cameras. Then, we introduce the simple yet effective Camera-invariant Prototype Alignment (CPA) module, with the intuition that the same intercamera prototypes should be pulled together while the different ones should be pushed apart. This is also in consistent with the intrinsic semantic relations between different cross-camera prototypes. Finally, we argue that the distance between the same identity prototypes from different cameras is still large due to the camera variances. We thus further introduce the inter-camera prototype pulling loss to directly bridge them as close as possible.

In summary, our contributions are as follow: 1) We focus on the challenging Intra-Camera Supervised (ICS) ReID task and propose a novel Cross-Camera Prototype Learning (CCPL) method. To our best knowledge, we are the first to *unveil* the 'cross-camera prototype relations' which is neglected by previous ICS ReID methods. 2) We introduce the Camera-invariant Prototype Alignment (CPA) module to tackle this issue. In light of the prototype pairwise matching mechanism and the explicit inter-camera prototype pulling loss, CPA module ensures that the same inter-camera prototypes are pulled together while the different ones are pushed away. 3) Extensive experiments on Market-1501 [26], DukeMTMC-ReID [15] and MSMT17 [21] show the superiority of our method.

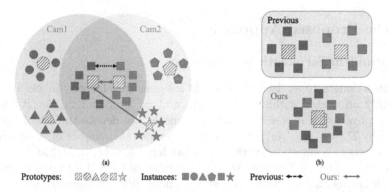

Fig. 1. (a): Previous ICS methods connect the inter-camera instances that are likely to be the same pedestrian, while neglecting the relationship between inter-camera prototypes. (b) Contrarily, ours directly minimizes the distance between the matched inter-camera prototypes of the same pedestrian. Different shapes denote different identities.

2   Related Work

Fully Supervised Person ReID formulates ReID as a classification task and trains the model with globally annotated labels [2,7,8,10,16,27]. To verify the availability of local features and data augmentation tricks, part-based methods [8,16] propose to align different parts of body by human pose estimation or roughly horizontal division. While GAN-based methods [2,27] improve the supervised feature representation learning with the generated person images. All of the above methods have achieved remarkable performance. Contrarily, **Unsupervised Person ReID** addresses this directly without the need of labeled training data [9,20,23–25], which also shows great progress in both efficiency and accuracy. Despite the success they have achieved, the overall performance of unsupervised ReID is still unsatisfactory for real-world implementations.

Intra-Camera Supervised Person ReID (ICS) is proposed in recent years [13,14,19,29,30], which consists of intra- and inter-camera learning. In the intra-camera learning, MTML [30] and MATE [29] propose a Multi-Camera Multi-Task framework while Precise-ICS [19] adopts a Hybrid Mining Quintuplet Loss with intra-camera images labels. Furthermore, PCSL [13] and ACAN [14] take the widely used triplet loss to obtain more discriminative features. In the inter-camera learning, it is necessary to construct inter-camera identity association. MTML [30] and MATE [29] adopt multi-label alignment to capture the underlying inter-camera identity correspondence relationships. Precise-ICS [19] designs a graph-based strategy for ID association and pseudo labeling. PCSL [13] utilizes a soft-labeling scheme and ACAN [14] develops a multi-camera adversarial learning approach. However, they all neglect the relationship between the inter-camera prototypes, making the learned features to be camera-agnostic.

3   The Proposed Approach

3.1   Problem Formulation

The intra-camera supervised (ICS) ReID assumes that identity labels are independently annotated within each camera and no inter-camera identity association is provided. Suppose there are C cameras, we denote the set of the c-th camera by $\mathcal{D}_c = \{(x_i, y_i, c_i)\}_{i=1}^{N_c}$, where N_c denotes the number of images in the c-th camera. x_i is annotated with an identity label $y_i \in \{1, ..., M_c\}$ and a camera label $c_i = c \in \{1, ..., C\}$, where M_c is the number of total IDs in c-th camera. It is worth noting that the same pedestrian under different cameras are assigned with different labels due to the lack of inter-camera identity association. Our purpose is to learn a ICS ReID model which can greatly discriminate both intra- and inter-camera pedestrian identities.

3.2   Intra-camera Learning

The overall framework is illustrated in Fig. 2. We design our backbone in the Exponential Moving Average (EMA) CNN (Convolutional Neural Network), which has the same structure as the regular CNN and updated by accumulated weights of the regular CNN with coefficient α. In intra-camera learning, we utilize the multi-task learning strategy to generate identity prototypes with the supervision of independently labelled identity information. Note that all tasks share the same weights of CNN. Each camera view task is treated separately and all tasks share a feature representation network for extracting the common knowledge in a multi-branch architecture design. The identity prototype is identified as a learnable feature vector, representing a pedestrian under one camera in the feature space. Thus, we can generate identity prototypes with implicit inter-camera discriminability, which facilitates the subsequent prototype pairwise matching mechanism. Specifically, given an image x_i, together with its annotated intra-camera identity label y_i and camera label c_i, the globe label j

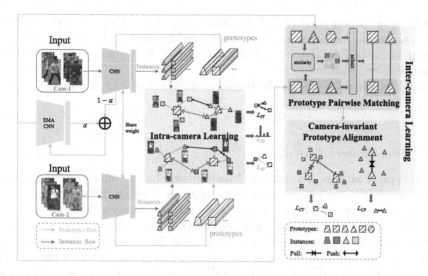

Fig. 2. Overview of the CCPL method. We introduce the multi-task framework along with intra-camera learning, to facilitate each identity with discriminative features. Then, we excavate the cross-camera prototype relations by adopting the Camera-invariant Prototype Alignment (CPA) module and the prototype pairwise matching mechanism, explicitly pulling the same prototypes while pushing the different ones.

of x_i is obtained by $j = B + y_i$, where $B = \sum_{k=1}^{c_i-1} M_k$. The objective function for intra-camera prototype learning is thus formulated as:

$$L_{intra\_ID} = -\sum_{i=1}^{N} log \frac{exp(g[j]^T f(x_i)/\tau_1)}{\sum_{k=B+1}^{B+M_{c_i}} exp(g[k]^T f(x_i)/\tau_1)}, \tag{1}$$

where $g[j]$ is the j-th prototype which is the learnable parameter of FC layer and τ_1 is temperature used to control the smoothness. In order to improve the intra-class compactness, we further introduce the instance triplet loss and intra-camera prototype loss to utilize both the hard positive and negative instance-instance pairs and instance-prototype pairs, respectively. Concretely, The instance triplet loss L_{IT} and intra-camera prototype loss L_{IP} are formulated as:

$$L_{IT} = \sum_{i=1}^{P} \sum_{a=1}^{K} [m_1 + \max_{p=1,...,K} dist(h(x_a^i), h(x_p^i)) \\ - \min_{n=1,...,K; j=1,...,P; j\neq i; c_a^i=c_n^j} dist(h(x_a^i), h(x_n^j))]_+, \tag{2}$$

$$L_{IP} = \sum_{i=1}^{P} \sum_{a=1}^{K} [m_1 + dist(f(x_a^i), g[B + y_a^i]) \\ - \min_{j=1,...,N_{c_a^i}; j\neq y_a^i} dist(f(x_a^i), g[B + j])]_+, \tag{3}$$

where m_1 is the margin, $h(x_a)$, $h(x_p)$ and $h(x_n)$ are the features of the anchor, the positive and negative instances respectively. $f(x_a)$ is the anchor's feature output from the BN (Batch Normalization) layer. $dist(,)$ represents the cosine distance of two features.

To date, the total loss for the intra-camera learning stage can be defined as:

$$L_{Intra} = L_{intra\_ID} + L_{IT} + L_{IP}. \tag{4}$$

3.3   Inter-camera Learning

Prototype Pairwise Matching Mechanism. In the inter-camera learning stage, we first delve into the semantic relations between different prototypes across various camera views. As for the prototypes between different cameras, the more similar two prototypes are, the more likely they are to be the same one. According to this intuition and inspired by Dual Alignment Consistency [3], we thus introduce the prototype pairwise matching mechanism. Given two sets of prototypes $G^i = \{g_k^i\}_{k=1}^{M_i}$ and $G^j = \{g_z^j\}_{z=1}^{M_j}$ from different cameras i and j, the pair (g_k^i, g_z^j) can be regarded as a matching pair if and only if g_k^i, g_z^j are mutually the most similar to each other, and the similarity should exceed the threshold, indicating a relatively high similarity.

Concretely, we calculate the similarities between g_k^i and $\{g_z^j\}_{z=1}^{M_j}$, which can be defined as:

$$S_{g_k^i}^{i \to j} = [S_{g_k^i g_1^j}, S_{g_k^i g_2^j}, ..., S_{g_k^i g_z^j}, ..., S_{g_k^i g_{M_j}^j}]. \tag{5}$$

Then, we nominate the selected prototype in camera j for g_k^i with the maximum similarity as the candidate matching prototype.

$$z^* = arg \max_{z \in \{1,2,...,M_j\}} S_{g_k^i g_z^j}, \tag{6}$$

where z^* is the index of the candidate matching prototype $g_{z^*}^j$.

Similarly, the candidate matching prototype $g_{z^*}^j$ is further calculated back to G^i, and the corresponding candidate matching prototype $g_{k^*}^i$ can be nominated according to $S_{g_z^j}^{j \to i}$. Thus, the matching operation between G^i and G^j is:

$$\begin{cases} \mathcal{I}(g_k^i, g_{z^*}^j) = & 1, if \quad g_k^i = g_{k^*}^i \ \wedge \ sim(g_k^i, g_{z^*}^j) > \theta, \\ \mathcal{I}(g_k^i, g_{z^*}^j) = & 0, otherwise, \end{cases} \tag{7}$$

where θ is the threshold and $sim(,)$ is the cosine similarity of two features. Note that this requires $g_k^i, g_{z^*}^j$ to be the reciprocal nearest neighbor of each other and the similarity of $g_k^i, g_{z^*}^j$ larger than the threshold.

Camera-Invariant Prototype Alignment. Previous ICS methods design various strategies, such as multi-label strategy, soft-labeling scheme and consistent discrepancy learning, to associate the inter-camera instances that are likely to be the same pedestrian. However, they neglect 'the cross-camera prototype relations' between different cameras. We thereby introduce the simple yet effective

Camera-invariant Prototype Alignment (CPA) module. This intuition behind is that the same inter-camera prototypes should be pulled together while the different ones should be pushed apart. This is also in consistent with the intrinsic semantic relations between different cross-camera prototypes. Specifically, the proposed inter-camera prototypes triplet loss L_{CT} is formulated as:

$$
L_{CT} = \sum_{i=1}^{C} \sum_{j=1}^{C} \sum_{k \in T_{i,j}} [m_2 + dist(g_k^i, F_{ij}(g_k^i))
$$
$$
- \min_{l=1,\ldots,M_j} dist(g_k^i, g_l^j)]_+,
$$

(8)

where m_2 is margin, g_k^i is the prototype in camera i, F_{ij} is the function mapping g_k^i to its matching counterpart in camera j, and $T_{i,j}$ is the set of prototypes in camera i who have matching counterpart in camera j.

Although L_{CT} ensures that the distance of same inter-camera prototypes is smaller than that of different ones, the distance of same pedestrian prototypes under different cameras is still large due to the variances of different cameras in views, lights, backgrounds etc. This leads to the failure of constructing a globally discriminative feature space. To further bridge up the same identity prototypes from different cameras, we also introduce the inter-camera prototype pulling loss L_{CP} to directly minimize the distance, which can be formulated as:

$$
L_{CP} = \sum_{i=1}^{C} \sum_{j=1}^{C} \sum_{k \in T_{i,j}} \|g_k^i, F_{ij}(g_k^i)\|_1,
$$

(9)

Combining all the above loss terms together, the total loss for the whole training procedure is defined as:

$$
L = L_{intra} + \lambda_1 L_{CT} + \lambda_2 L_{CP},
$$

(10)

where λ_1 and λ_2 are the trade-off parameters.

4   Experiments

4.1   Datasets and Evaluation Metrics

We use three large-scale ReID datasets, i.e., Market-1501 [26], DukeMTMC-ReID [15], and MSMT17 [21] to evaluate our method. The Market-1501 contains 32,668 person images of 1,501 identities from 6 camera views. MSMT17 has a total of 126,441 images of 4,101 persons captured from a 15-camera network. DukeMTMC-ReID contains 1,404 persons and 36,411 images from 8 cameras. We adopt the common Cumulative Matching Characteristic (CMC) and mean Average Precision (mAP) metrics for performance evaluation.

Table 1. Comparison with the state-of-the-arts on Market-1501, DukeMTMC-ReID and MSMT17.

Method	Market-1501				DukeMTMC-ReID				MSMT17			
	R1	R5	R10	mAP	R1	R5	R10	mAP	R1	R5	R10	mAP
Fully supervised												
PCB [16]	93.8	-	-	81.6	83.3	-	-	69.2	68.2	-	-	40.4
OSNet [28]	94.8	-	-	84.9	88.6	-	-	73.5	78.7	-	-	52.9
BOT [10]	94.5	-	-	85.9	86.4	-	-	76.4	-	-	-	-
DGNet [27]	94.8	-	-	86.0	86.6	-	-	74.8	77.2	87.4	90.5	52.3
Intra-camera supervised												
UTAL [6]	69.2	85.5	89.7	46.2	62.3	80.7	84.4	44.6	31.4	51.0	58.1	13.1
TAUDL [5]	63.7	-	-	41.2	61.7	-	-	43.5	-	-	-	-
UGA [22]	87.2	-	-	70.3	75.0	-	-	53.3	21.7	-	-	49.5
MTML [30]	85.3	-	96.2	65.2	71.7	-	86.9	50.7	44.1	-	63.9	18.6
PCSL [13]	87.0	94.8	96.6	69.4	71.7	84.7	88.2	53.5	48.3	62.8	68.6	20.7
ACAN [14]	73.3	87.6	91.8	50.6	67.6	81.2	85.2	45.1	33.0	48.0	54.7	12.6
MATE [29]	88.7	-	97.1	71.1	76.9	-	89.6	56.6	46.0	-	65.3	19.1
PIRID [17]	91.0	96.7	97.9	79.6	79.9	88.6	91.4	65.4	60.6	73.8	79.3	34.9
Precise-ICS [19]	93.1	97.8	98.6	**83.6**	83.6	92.6	94.7	72.0	57.7	71.1	76.3	31.3
CCPL	**93.3**	**98.0**	**98.7**	83.3	**85.7**	**93.5**	**95.4**	**72.1**	**75.2**	**85.6**	**88.7**	**46.4**

4.2   Implementation Details

We adopt the ImageNet [1] pre-trained ResNet-50 [4] (followed by a BN layer) as our backbone. The images are resized to 384×128. By default, the trade-off parameters $\lambda_1 = 5.0$ and $\lambda_2 = 1.0$. Threshold θ for prototype pairwise matching mechamism is set to 0.5 for Market-1501 and DukeMTMC-ReID and 0.6 for MSMT17. τ_1 in Eq. 1 is set to 0.04. m_1 for Eq. 2 and Eq. 3 is set to 0.3. m_2 for Eq. 8 is set to 0.5 for Market-1501 and DukeMTMC-ReID and 0.6 for MSMT17. There are total 120 epoch in both intra- and inter camera learning. The initial learning rate is 2.0×10^{-4} and is divided by 2 in 32, 64, 96 epoch. The optimizer is Adam. As for the training batch, we use the PK sampling strategy to randomly select 128 images of 32 identities. We evaluate our model using two GTX 2080Ti GPUs.

4.3   Comparison with the State-of-the-Arts

In this section, we compare our method with: (1) fully supervised methods PCB [16], BOT [10], OSNet [28] and DGNet [27]. (2) ICS methods UTAL [6], TAUDL [5], UGA [22], MTML [30], PCSL [13], ACAN [14], MATE [29] PIRID [17] and Precise-ICS [19]. Table 1 shows the overall performance results of our method and other SOTAs on Market1501 [26], DukeMTMC-ReID [15], and MSMT17 [21] datasets, respectively. Based on the results, we claim that our CCPL method achieves the best performance compared with other ICS methods. Especially, CCPL outperforms others by a significant margin on the most challenging ReID dataset MSMT17 [21], which contains more cross-view variations than Market1501 [26] and DukeMTMC-reID [15], e.g., 17.5%/15.1% higher than Precise-ICS [19] at Rank1/mAP. As for fully supervised methods, our method also achieves comparable performance, which is acceptable due to the challenging setting of ICS. Surprisingly, CCPL outperforms slightly the fully supervised baseline PCB [16], which is the pioneering work, indicating the efficacy of our method.

4.4 Ablation Study

Effectiveness of Different Components. We conduct the ablation study and show the results in Table 2. Clearly, compared with only conducting the intra-camera learning, i.e., w/ ID, IT and IP, we can observe a significant performance improvement when adding the CT loss of CPA, e.g., improves at Rank1/mAP by 6.2%/6.7% on MSMT17 and 4.4%/8.2% on Market-1501. Similarly, compared with only using the CT loss of CPA module, we can observe a significant performance improvement when using the full CPA module, e.g., improves by 6.5%/7.8% at Rank1/mAP on MSMT17 and 2.0%/5.1% at Rank1/mAP on Market. It is reasonable since the distance of same pedestrian prototypes across different cameras may be large, leading to the large difference between extracted features of same pedestrian. We argue that merely relying on the L_{CT} loss is not enough to alleviate this issue. The experimental results clearly show that our proposed L_{CP} loss can further optimize the cross-camera prototypes relationships to constrain the same prototype as close as possible.

Table 2. Ablation study on Market-1501 and MSMT17. ID: intra-camera ID loss, IT: instance triplet loss, IP: intra-camera prototype loss, CT: inter-camera prototype triplet loss and CP: inter-camera prototype pulling loss.

Model Component					Market-1501				MSMT17			
ID	IT	IP	CT	CP	R1	R5	R10	mAP	R1	R5	R10	mAP
✓					85.2	93.8	96.0	66.2	60.1	71.8	76.8	29.7
✓	✓	✓			86.9	94.7	96.5	70.0	62.5	74.5	79.0	31.9
✓	✓	✓	✓		91.3	96.6	97.9	78.2	68.7	80.2	84.0	38.6
✓	✓	✓	✓	✓	**93.3**	**98.0**	**98.7**	**83.3**	**75.2**	**85.6**	**88.7**	**46.4**

Prototype Pairwise Matching Mechanism. We study how the prototype pairwise matching mechanism affects the retrieval performance, and report the results of four strategies of prototype pairwise matching mechanisms as shown in Table 3. Given prototype g_k^i in camera i, we can find the most similar g_z^j in camera j according to Eq. 5 and Eq. 6. As in Fig. 3, two-way means g_k^i and g_k^i are mutually the most similar to each other, which is the original operation in our method. While one-way denotes that g_z^j is the most similar prototype to g_k^i in camera j, whereas g_k^i is the most similar prototype to g_z^j in camera i is

Table 3. Results of different prototype pairwise matching mechanism.

Strategy	Market-1501				DukeMTMC-ReID			
	R1	R5	R10	mAP	R1	R5	R10	mAP
one-way + w/o threshold	93.3	97.5	98.3	81.8	85.2	92.3	94.3	70.9
one-way + w/ threshold	**93.4**	97.6	98.3	83.1	85.0	92.4	94.7	71.0
two-way + w/o threshold	92.8	97.5	98.3	82.4	84.3	92.1	94.3	70.6
two-way + w/ threshold	93.3	**98.0**	**98.7**	**83.3**	**85.7**	**93.5**	**95.4**	**72.1**

not guaranteed. Obviously, we can conclude that our method is robust to the strategies of prototype pairwise matching mechanism, which can be verified by the average performance of all four variants. Besides, the threshold of similarity also plays an important role in the inter-camera learning stage, especially when combined with two-way matching. This demonstrates the efficacy of constraining the similarity of matching pairs to a relatively high level.

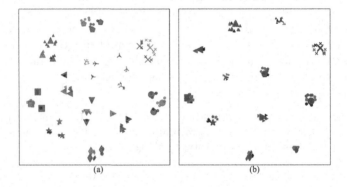

Fig. 3. T-SNE visualizations of prototypes and instances (a) before and (b) after CPA. Shapes denote the identities while colors denote the cameras.

Feature Visualizations. We utilize t-SNE [11] to visualize prototypes and instances learned by our proposed Camera-invariant Prototype Alignment (CPA) module. Figure 3 shows the features of instances and prototypes in 12 IDs under three cameras. We can find that before the CPA learning, the same pedestrian features of different cameras have distinctly larger distance between each other. While after the CPA learning, we can observe that the same pedestrian from different cameras become more compact, which is in consistency with the intuition behind our CPA module.

Compatibility with Other Baselines. We combine our CPA module to the recently proposed SOTA method CDL [12], which performs competitive results due to its complicated framework and computation complexity. As shown in

Fig. 4(a), we can see that our method can (1) integrate easily with other ICS methods without additionally modification and (2) further improve the retrieval performance of the existed CDL [12] method. This in turn verifies the efficiency and effectiveness of our CPA module.

Analysis of the Similarity Threshold. We evaluate our model with different threshold values, which controls the prototype pairwise matching mechanism of inter-camera prototypes. As can be seen in Fig. 4(b), a trend of accuracy gain is observed as the value of similarity threshold increases from 0 to 0.2, but when the value goes to a relatively large value, like 0.2 to 0.8, it tends to saturate and even goes down drastically from 0.8 to 0.9. Generally, our method shows great performance within a wide range of similarity threshold in [0.2,0.8].

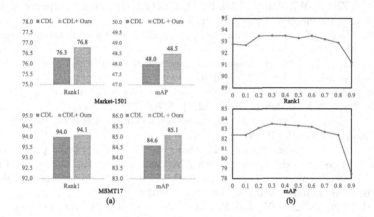

Fig. 4. (a). Compatibility with CDL method. (b). Robust analysis of threshold.

5 Conclusion

In this paper, we delve into the Intra-Camera Supervised (ICS) ReID task and, to the best of our knowledge, first unveil the 'cross-camera prototype relation' which is informative yet neglected by previous methods. Tackle this issue, we propose the novel Cross-Camera Prototype Learning (CCPL) method. By introducing the multi-task framework along with instance triplet loss and intra-camera prototype loss, we facilitate each identity with discriminative features within each camera. Besides, we further design the Camera-invariant Prototype Alignment (CPA) module to ensure that the same inter-camera prototypes are pulled together while the different ones are pushed away. Our full model outperforms SOTA ICS methods by a large margin, greatly reducing the gap to the fully supervised counterparts.

Acknowledgement. This work was supported by the National Key R&D Program of China under Grant 2022YFB3103500, the National Natural Science Foundation of China under Grants 62106258, 62006242 and 62202459, and the China Postdoctoral Science Foundation under Grant 2022M713348 and 2022TQ0363, and Young Elite Scientists Sponsorship Program by BAST (No. BYESS2023304).

References

1. Deng, J., Dong, W., Socher, R., Li, L.J., Li, K., Fei-Fei, L.: Imagenet: a large-scale hierarchical image database. In: CVPR (2009)
2. Ge, Y., Li, Z., Zhao, H., Yin, G., Yi, S., Wang, X., et al.: FD-GAN: pose-guided feature distilling GAN for robust person re-identification. In: Advances in Neural Information Processing Systems, vol. 31 (2018)
3. Hao, X., Zhang, W., Wu, D., Zhu, F., Li, B.: Dual alignment unsupervised domain adaptation for video-text retrieval. In: CVPR (2023)
4. He, K., Zhang, X., Ren, S., Sun, J.: Deep residual learning for image recognition. In: CVPR (2016)
5. Li, M., Zhu, X., Gong, S.: Unsupervised person re-identification by deep learning tracklet association. In: ECCV (2018)
6. Li, M., Zhu, X., Gong, S.: Unsupervised tracklet person re-identification. IEEE Trans. Pattern Anal. Mach. Intell. **42**(7), 1770–1782 (2019)
7. Li, W., Zhu, X., Gong, S.: Harmonious attention network for person re-identification. In: CVPR (2018)
8. Li, Y., He, J., Zhang, T., Liu, X., Zhang, Y., Wu, F.: Diverse part discovery: occluded person re-identification with part-aware transformer. In: CVPR (2021)
9. Lin, Y., Xie, L., Wu, Y., Yan, C., Tian, Q.: Unsupervised person re-identification via softened similarity learning. In: CVPR (2020)
10. Luo, H., Gu, Y., Liao, X., Lai, S., Jiang, W.: Bag of tricks and a strong baseline for deep person re-identification. In: CVPRws (2019)
11. Van der Maaten, L., Hinton, G.: Visualizing data using t-SNE. J. Mach. Learn. Res. **9**(11) (2008)
12. Peng, Y.X., Jiao, J., Feng, X., Zheng, W.S.: Consistent discrepancy learning for intra-camera supervised person re-identification. IEEE Trans. Multimedia (2022)
13. Qi, L., Wang, L., Huo, J., Shi, Y., Gao, Y.: Progressive cross-camera soft-label learning for semi-supervised person re-identification. IEEE Trans. Circuits Syst. Video Technol. **30**(9), 2815–2829 (2020)
14. Qi, L., Wang, L., Huo, J., Shi, Y., Geng, X., Gao, Y.: Adversarial camera alignment network for unsupervised cross-camera person re-identification. IEEE Trans. Circuits Syst. Video Technol. **32**(5), 2921–2936 (2021)
15. Ristani, E., Solera, F., Zou, R., Cucchiara, R., Tomasi, C.: Performance measures and a data set for multi-target, multi-camera tracking. In: ECCVws (2016)
16. Sun, Y., Zheng, L., Yang, Y., Tian, Q., Wang, S.: Beyond part models: person retrieval with refined part pooling (and a strong convolutional baseline). In: ECCV (2018)
17. Wang, L., Zhang, W., Wu, D., Hong, P., Li, B.: Prototype-based inter-camera learning for person re-identification. In: ICASSP (2022)
18. Wang, L., Zhang, W., Wu, D., Zhu, F., Li, B.: Attack is the best defense: towards preemptive-protection person re-identification. In: ACM MM (2022)
19. Wang, M., Lai, B., Chen, H., Huang, J., Gong, X., Hua, X.S.: Towards precise intra-camera supervised person re-identification. In: WACV (2021)

20. Wang, M., Lai, B., Huang, J., Gong, X., Hua, X.S.: Camera-aware proxies for unsupervised person re-identification. In: AAAI (2021)
21. Wei, L., Zhang, S., Gao, W., Tian, Q.: Person transfer GAN to bridge domain gap for person re-identification. In: CVPR (2018)
22. Wu, J., Yang, Y., Liu, H., Liao, S., Lei, Z., Li, S.Z.: Unsupervised graph association for person re-identification. In: ICCV (2019)
23. Xuan, S., Zhang, S.: Intra-inter camera similarity for unsupervised person re-identification. In: CVPR (2021)
24. Zeng, K., Ning, M., Wang, Y., Guo, Y.: Hierarchical clustering with hard-batch triplet loss for person re-identification. In: CVPR (2020)
25. Zhang, X., Ge, Y., Qiao, Y., Li, H.: Refining pseudo labels with clustering consensus over generations for unsupervised object re-identification. In: CVPR (2021)
26. Zheng, L., Shen, L., Tian, L., Wang, S., Wang, J., Tian, Q.: Scalable person re-identification: a benchmark. In: ICCV (2015)
27. Zheng, Z., Yang, X., Yu, Z., Zheng, L., Yang, Y., Kautz, J.: Joint discriminative and generative learning for person re-identification. In: CVPR (2019)
28. Zhou, K., Yang, Y., Cavallaro, A., Xiang, T.: Omni-scale feature learning for person re-identification. In: ICCV (2019)
29. Zhu, X., Zhu, X., Li, M., Morerio, P., Murino, V., Gong, S.: Intra-camera supervised person re-identification. Int. J. Comput. Vision **129**, 1580–1595 (2021)
30. Zhu, X., Zhu, X., Li, M., Murino, V., Gong, S.: Intra-camera supervised person re-identification: a new benchmark. In: ICCVws (2019)

ECDet: A Real-Time Vehicle Detection Network for CPU-Only Devices

Fei Gao[1]([✉])[iD], Zhiwen Wang[1][iD], Jianwen Shao[2][iD], Xinyang Dong[1][iD],
and Libo Weng[1][iD]

[1] Zhejiang University of Technology, Hangzhou 310023, China
{feig,zhiwen_wang,xinyang_dong,wenglibo}@zjut.edu.cn
[2] Zhejiang Institute of Metrology, Hangzhou 310018, China

Abstract. We study the problem of efficient vehicle detection for low-power devices in complex traffic environments and construct a lightweight real-time vehicle object detection model called Efficient Channel Detection (ECDet) to enhance the detection capability of vehicles at multiple scales. This work has three contributions: (1) the design of an efficient network backbone called Efficient Channel Network (ECNet); (2) the design of a lightweight real-time vehicle object detection model called ECDet; and (3) the design of a lightweight feature fusion structure called Lightweight Path Aggregation Network (LPAN). In addition, we quantitatively evaluated different methods on the UA-DETRAC dataset. The experiment shows that ECDet can quickly and accurately detect vehicles, and can be widely applied on embedded platforms such as intelligent transportation systems and unmanned driving systems.

Keywords: Vehicle detection · CPU-only devices

1 Introduction

In recent years, many researchers have proposed algorithms that can achieve real-time operation by utilizing the multi-threaded parallel transmission mechanism and high bandwidth of devices such as GPUs to process matrix multiplication and convolution calculations. However, many devices still cannot be equipped with GPUs to achieve accelerated convolution calculations. The limited computing power and storage space of devices in intelligent transportation systems and unmanned driving systems make it difficult to achieve real-time detection. Therefore, efficient vehicle detection on devices with low computing power and storage space is an urgent problem.

The latest trend in the design of deep neural networks is to explore portable and efficient network architectures that can be used on mobile devices, such as smartphones and autonomous vehicles. Efficient neural network designs have great potential for building efficient deep networks with fewer parameters and computations. With the need to deploy neural networks in embedded devices, a series of compact models have been proposed. MobileNets [1]

L. Iliadis et al. (Eds.): ICANN 2023, LNCS 14260, pp. 414–426, 2023.
https://doi.org/10.1007/978-3-031-44195-0_34

designed lightweight deep neural networks based on depth separable convolutions. MobileNetV2 [2] proposed a reverse residual structure. MobileNetV3 [3] further reduces the model parameter volume through AutoML technology. ShuffleNet [4] designed channel shuffle operations to enhance inter-group channel information transmission. ShuffleNetV2 [5] further considers the basic hardware of the target to carry out a compact design. However, these models still need more detailed optimization for the correlation and redundancy between feature maps. For low-power devices, the computational performance bottleneck needs to consider various factors such as CPU frequency, memory access, and inability to use Cuda acceleration.

To address these issues, we propose an efficient network backbone called ECNet, based on attention mechanism and depth separable convolution, to enhance the detection capability of multi-scale vehicles. In addition, we constructed a lightweight real-time vehicle detection model called ECDet based on ECNet.

2 Related Work

Deep Learning-Based Methods: Driven by the R-CNN [6] model, researchers have improved the performance of CNN-based detectors by optimizing candidate extraction methods, feature fusion methods, training strategies, and context inference. Based on R-CNN, two-stage networks with improved accuracy have increasingly complex network architectures and computational requirements.

With the emergence of YOLO [7], and SSD [8], researchers focused more on bridging the detection accuracy gap between two-stage and one-stage detectors. EfficientDet [9] builds on the concept of a scalable detector with higher accuracy and efficiency, using EfficientNet [10] as the backbone network.

Mobile Object Detection: Vehicle object detection for low-power devices requires not only high accuracy to ensure safety, but also real-time inference speed to ensure timely control of the vehicle. Additionally, the model size should be small and energy-efficient to enable deployment on embedded systems.

When coupled with a small backbone network, lightweight single-stage detectors can achieve inference at low frame rates on mobile devices, such as MobileNet SSD [1], and MobileNetV2 SSD [2]. YOLObile [11] proposed a network that improves the model's operating speed on mobile devices from the perspectives of compression and compilation. In the YOLObile optimization framework, a 14x compressed YOLOv4 [12] can achieve a running speed of 19 fps with high accuracy of 49 mAP. PP-YOLO-Tiny [13] designed an efficient object detection network by adopting MobileNetV3 [3] as the backbone and the Tiny FPN structure of PP-YOLO. Qiu et al. [14] designed an end-to-end method for recognizing, locating, and classifying vehicle images by fusing edge features. However, the model is limited by its feature extraction ability and cannot adapt to vehicle scale changes. Based on Tiny YOLO, Bharadhwaj et al. designed a Detect-Track-Count (DTC) framework [15], for efficiently counting vehicles on edge devices. Xu et al. reconstructed and pruned the YOLOv3 model and proposed YOLOv3-promote [16].

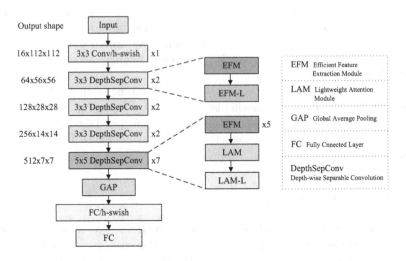

Fig. 1. The framework of ECNet. Its head adopts standard 3×3 convolution.

3   Efficient Channel Network

ECNet is obtained through lightweight structure design and loss function optimization based on the receptive field, attention, and loss function of the convolutional neural network. The framework diagram of ECNet is shown in Fig. 1. DepthSepConv is mainly composed of Efficient Feature Extraction Module (EFM) and Lightweight Attention Module (LAM).

3.1   EFM and LAM

To minimize the computational complexity while ensuring the feature expression capability, as shown in Fig. 2(A), the proposed EFM does not include any short-cut or other additional operations such as pixel-level addition, which can slow down the model's inference speed and have limited improvement on accuracy for lightweight networks. To improve the feature selection effectiveness of low-scale backbone networks, as shown in Fig. 2(B), the proposed LAM adds an attention mechanism to the bypass branch based on EFM to enhance feature selection.

The down-sampling module aims to eliminate redundant channels with attention mechanism and enhance the attention on effective channels. Unlike EFM and LAM, the input features of EFM-L and LAM-L are changed to two copies of features. The duplicated feature maps are convolved and merged, and the spatial scale is reduced to half of the original, while the feature channels are doubled, and then the channels are shuffled, as shown in Fig. 2(C) and Fig. 2(D).

3.2 Attention Mechanism

Adding complex attention structures in every layer is time-consuming, so LAM aims to learn effective channel attention in a more efficient way locally.

The attention module in LAM is a lightweight attention structure based on local channel correlation, as shown in Fig. 3. This module directly uses the depth of channels as the dimension of the vector, avoiding dimensionality reduction and effectively capturing cross-channel interaction information. After global average pooling without reducing dimensions, local cross-channel interaction information is obtained through each channel and its k neighboring channels.

The LAM module improves model accuracy through the attention mechanism between channels. However, blindly increasing the number of LAM modules can slow down model inference. To balance inference speed, ECNet only adds LAM modules in the last two levels.

3.3 Spatial and Channel Loss

The shape of the vehicle object is relatively stable and the details of the vehicle image are determined by multiple feature regions. To fully utilize the spatial multi-region properties of vehicles, we design the Spatial and Channel Loss (SAC loss). SAC loss is mainly composed of discrimination loss and diversity loss.

Discrimination Loss: Assuming the i-th feature channel after grouping is $F_i \in R^{\eta \times W \times H}$, where $i = 0, 1, ..., k\text{-}1$, k represents the number of groups of channels, and η represents the number of feature maps in each group of channels, W and H represent the width and height. Thus, $F = \{F_{i \times \eta+1}, F_{i \times \eta+2}, F_{i \times \eta+\eta}\}$, where $i = 0, 1, ..., k\text{-}1$. In vehicle images, vehicle samples are divided into several regions. Discrimination Loss is used to make different groups of feature channels focus on extracting features of different types of regions. Each group of feature channels should be representative of each category region. Discrimination Loss can be calculated using the following formulas.

$$f(x_i) = \frac{Exp(x_i)}{\sum_{i=0}^{C} Exp(x_i)}, i = 0, 1, 2, \dots C \quad (1)$$

$$L_{\text{dis}}(F) = L_{\text{ce}}(y, f(\frac{1}{WH}\sum_{k=1}^{WH} \max_{j=0,1,2,\dots,\eta}(F_{j,k}))) \quad (2)$$

where, L_{ce} denotes the cross-entropy loss function, y denotes the ground truth, and C denotes the number of categories.

Diversity Loss: It is difficult to achieve stable differentiation between channel groups during training of the feature maps clustered by channels. The average distance coefficient in the following formula represents the diversity in the feature group. The average distance coefficient is mainly determined by the proportion of the minimum distance of the highest response point to the average distance of all response points. The smaller the average distance coefficient of the response point, the larger the diversity loss.

$$L_{\text{div}} = Exp(-\frac{\min_{i,j=0,1,2,...,k} \{\text{dist}(p_i, p_j)\} \times k}{\sum_{i,j=0}^{k} \text{dist}(p_i, p_j)}) \tag{3}$$

where p represents the coordinate vector of the fused feature response center point, and dist represents the Euclidean distance between two points.

SAC loss can be directly connected to the backbone network in parallel with the cross-entropy losses to jointly constrain the network. The total loss formula of ECNet is as follows:

$$L_{\text{total}} = L_{\text{div}} + L_{\text{dis}} + L_{\text{ce}} \tag{4}$$

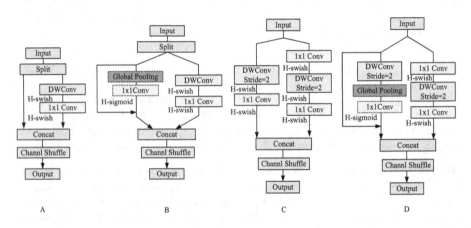

Fig. 2. EFM(A), LAM(B), EFM-L(C) and LAM-L(D). For down-sampling in ECNet, EFM-L and LAM-L with a stride of 2 are used as the basic modules.

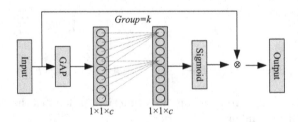

Fig. 3. Lightweight attention module in LAM.

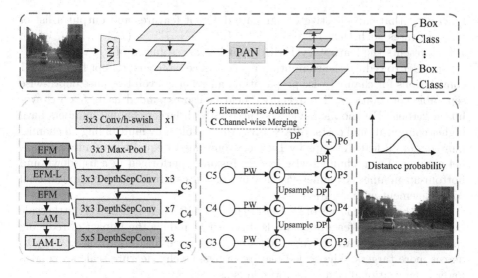

Fig. 4. Lightweight object detection framework ECDet.

4   Efficient Channel Detection

Our work is dedicated to optimizing key technologies and selecting architectures for vehicle object detection to improve its performance and efficiency.

We enhanced the ECNet and designed Lightweight Path Aggregation Network (LPAN) to improve the model's feature extraction ability. We improved the label assignment strategy. Through these optimizations, we constructed a lightweight vehicle detection model called ECDet, as shown in Fig. 4, and its backbone network is ECNet.

4.1   Improved ECNet

To adapt ECNet as the backbone network for ECDet, the following adjustments were made. As shown in Fig. 4(A), to extract the main features and reduce the parameters and computational cost, we adjust the 3×3 depth-wise separable convolution in the second step of ECNet to a 3×3 max pooling layer. Additionally, features from the third, fourth, and fifth layers are outputted for feature connection and fusion between adjacent feature maps in the subsequent path aggregation network layer.

4.2   Lightweight Path Aggregation Network

To solve the problem of multi-scale and minimize the computational cost of the feature fusion structure, we design LPAN, as shown in Fig. 5.

Assuming that the given multi-scale features are $P^{\text{in}} = (P_{l_1}^{\text{in}}, P_{l_2}^{\text{in}}, ...)$, where $P_{l_i}^{\text{in}}$ represents a feature at level l_i. The goal of LPAN is to find a transformation function f that can effectively aggregate different features and output a list of fused features such that $P^{out} = f(P^{in})$. In LPAN, $P^{in} = (P_3^{in}, ..., P_5^{in})$, where P_i^{in} represents the feature level with input image resolution of $1/2^i$.

In order to reduce the computational cost of convolution, except for the 1×1 convolutions for channel-wise propagation, all other convolutions use depth-wise separable convolutions. The receptive field is also expanded using 5×5 convolution kernels. For mobile devices, structures with larger channel numbers have higher computational costs. LPAN solves this problem by multiplying all channel numbers in all feature maps by 1×1 convolutions to equal the minimum channel number. Then, channel-wise feature fusion is performed in a top-down and bottom-up manner. Channel-wise feature fusion can reduce the computational cost of element-wise addition.

Since the feature levels of ECDet are from 3 to 5, there is relatively little scale information for the feature channels. In order to reduce the impact of reducing the input feature scale, LPAN adds a scaled feature fusion path at the top to detect more targets. The scaled feature brings a richer feature scale space at a lower computational cost. The formula is as follows:

$$P_6^{out} = \text{Concat}\left(\text{DP}\left(P_5^{in}\right), \text{DP}\left(P_5^{out}\right)\right) \tag{5}$$

where Concat represents channel-wise feature fusion and DP represents depth-wise separable convolution operation.

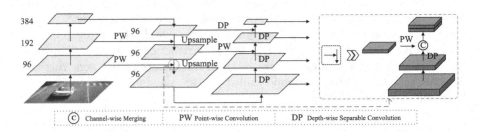

Fig. 5. LPAN structure. Channel-wise merging is used to achieve feature concatenation and fusion between adjacent feature maps, in order to obtain multi-level feature maps.

Table 1. Comparison of vehicle recognition results on Top-1 Acc(%) indicators.

Method	BaseModel	Stanford Cars	CompCars
B-CNN [21]	VGG16	91.3	93.5
KP [22]	VGG16	92.4	94.4
MA-CNN [20]	VGG19	92.8	95.8
DFL-CNN [23]	ResNet50	93.1	96.7
TASN [19]	ResNet50	93.8	97.6
ECNet	ECNet	93.9	97.8

4.3 Dynamic Label Allocation

In dynamic label allocation, the prediction confidence of each anchor point is a dynamic indicator for allocation. Anchor points with high confidence can be more easily learned by the network and assigned to relevant target objects. However, dynamic allocation strategies still suffer from ambiguous allocation problems because they cannot use global information. OTA [18] introduced optimal transport theory and obtained the optimal sample matching solution under global information. But OTA increases the additional training time by about 20–25%. The Sinkhorn-Iter operation in OTA also consumes a large amount of memory.

ECDet, based on the optimal solution, removed the time-consuming process of finding the optimal solution and optimized its dynamic allocation process. First, it determines the positive sample candidate region and selects the region of each center as the candidate region on spatial scale. Then, it calculates the classification loss and regression loss for each sample. For classification loss, Focal Loss combines classification prediction and quality prediction. For the regression loss, GIoU Loss and Distribution Focal Loss are used. The formula is as follows:

$$loss = loss_{vfl} + loss_{giou} + 0.25 loss_{dfl} \qquad (6)$$

where, $loss_{vfl}$ represents variation loss, $loss_{giou}$ represents GIoU loss, and $loss_{dfl}$ represents distribution focal Loss.

Using the predicted samples of each ground truth, determine the value of k that needs to be assigned to positive samples. The value of k is equal to the number of positive samples for the current ground truth with the top 10 IOUs. Sum up the IOUs of these top 10 samples and round it to get k, where the minimum number of positive samples is 1. Take the top k samples with the smallest loss for each ground truth as positive samples. Finally, remove the case where the same sample is assigned to multiple ground truths as positive samples.

Table 2. Experimental results of ECNet on ImageNet.

Model	Params(M)	FLOPs(M)	Top-1 Acc(%)	Top-5 Acc(%)	Latency(ms)
ShuffleNetV1-1.0x	1.9	139	67.80	88.70	5.12
ShuffleNetV2-0.5x	1.4	43	60.32	82.26	4.65
MobileNetV1	4.3	578	70.99	89.68	3.38
MobileNetV2	3.5	327	71.15	90.65	4.26
MobileNetV3-small	3.6	100	70.67	89.51	3.95
ECNet	3.0	161	**71.82**	90.03	**2.46**

5 Experiments

5.1 Experiments on ECNet

Comparative Experiments: Experiments were conducted on the performance of vehicle feature classification and comprehensive image classification performance of ECNet. During the training phase, training was conducted using 7 RTX3090 and stochastic gradient descent algorithm with a momentum of 0.9

and weight decay set to 4e-5. With an initial learning rate of 0.1, the batch size was set to 80, and a cosine decay learning rate scheduling strategy was used. During the training process, mainly random rotation, random scaling, and color jittering were used for data augmentation to reduce the probability of overfitting. To test the model's inference capability on mobile devices, the Qualcomm Snapdragon 865 processor was chosen for testing, with the main indicators being accuracy and inference time on the test set.

ECNet has evaluated on Stanford Cars and CompCars dataset. The results of the other methods are quoted from the original paper data. As shown in Table 1, ECNet's accuracy is comparable to TASN [19], which is based on the ResNet backbone network. But ECNet's model parameter is only 1/8 of TASN's. ECNet has an efficient and compact network structure, which reduces redundant parameters.

The ImageNet dataset was chosen to train and test the model's overall performance. To control the parameter and computational complexity of the compared models at a similar level, the model sizes of ShuffleNetV2 and MobileNetV3 were adjusted. As shown in Table 2, the highest Top-1 accuracy of ECNet is 71.82, representing a 42.2% increase in inference speed compared to MobileNetV2.

Ablation Study: The optimization strategies in ECNet were analyzed. As shown in Table 3, adding LAM can improve the accuracy by 1.69% and increase the inference time by 0.59 ms. SAC loss has the largest impact on accuracy improvement of 1.9%. Since SAC loss does not participate in the inference stage, the inference time is not affected.

To verify the effect of SAC loss, we visualized its feature maps through Grad-CAM. As shown in Fig. 6, after being constrained by discrimination loss and

Table 3. Ablation experiments of different ECNet components.

LAM	5*5 kernel	SAC loss	Top-1 Acc(%)	Latency(ms)
×	✓	✓	70.13	1.87
✓	×	✓	70.44	2.01
✓	✓	×	69.92	2.46
✓	✓	✓	71.82	2.46

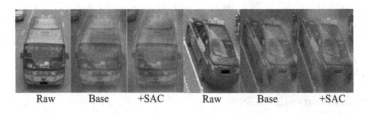

Raw   Base   +SAC   Raw   Base   +SAC

Fig. 6. Feature map visualization. The red taxi in the figure, after increasing the SAC loss, the characteristics of the left side also increase the distribution of hot spots. (Color figure online)

diversity loss, the areas that the network focuses on become more extensive and independent. The heat distribution of different representative regions has more differences, reducing the influence of local features on global attribute judgment.

5.2   Experiments on ECDet

We conducted experiments on the UA-DETRAC dataset and divided the training set into 39 sequences for training and 21 sequences for validation. We sample each training sequence once every 5 frames. We used the mean average precision (mAP) at an IoU threshold of 0.5 as the evaluation benchmark.

Comparative Experiments: Table 4 presents a comparison experiment between the proposed ECDet and other excellent detectors. To ensure fairness in the experiment, detectors with similar model parameters were selected for comparison. Additionally, all object detection networks were retrained using the same training strategy under the same experimental environment.

As shown in Table 4, YOLOv3-Tiny has the lowest mAP, but takes the longest inference time due to its Anchor-based detection head and the number of parameters in the backbone network. ECDet surpasses all current lightweight object detection models in terms of accuracy, with an mAP of 78.64 and an inference time of only 18.02 ms. In addition, ECDet also achieves the best detection results in various weather conditions such as cloudy, nighttime, and sunny.

Figure 7 displays the detection results of ECDet. The different types of vehicle detection results are represented by different colored bounding boxes. The

Table 4. Performance comparison experiment of different lightweight detectors.

Model	Latency (ms)	Params (M)	FLOPS (G)	mAP	Cloudy	Night	Rainy	Sunny
YOLOv3-Tiny [24]	28.62	8.86	5.62	68.38	83.66	73.97	56.11	72.15
YOLOv4-Tiny [12]	26.69	6.06	6.96	71.56	80.69	69.56	56.15	83.60
MobileNetv2-SSD [8]	20.12	3.38	1.36	71.75	80.45	70.56	57.23	83.50
PP-YOLO-Tiny [13]	18.48	1.08	1.02	72.72	80.65	78.00	65.38	83.53
YOLObile [11]	23.42	4.59	3.59	77.63	83.23	77.75	70.17	86.56
ECNet	**18.02**	2.50	2.62	**78.64**	**86.27**	**78.50**	67.97	**88.78**

Fig. 7. Detection results of ECDet.

Table 5. Ablation Experiment of ECDet.

Model	Params(M)	mAP
Base	0.96	72.8
+LPAN	1.12	76.2
+DLA	2.50	78.6

Table 6. Comparative Experiments of LPAN.

Model	mAP	Flops ratio
FPN [25]	76.29	1.0x
PANet [17]	78.08	1.21x
BiFPN [9]	77.94	0.72x
LPAN	78.64	0.68x

Original Image   **Without** LPAN   **With** LPAN

Fig. 8. Optimization comparison of LPAN for multi-scale vehicle detection. The network fused with LPAN has better detection effects on small vehicles in the distance.

test samples include vehicle images from different perspectives. ECDet performs excellently in dense vehicle scenes. Based on a compact and efficient vehicle detection backbone network, ECDet still performs well in nighttime scenes.

Ablation Study: As shown in Table 5, adding the LPAN and DLA can effectively improve the network detection accuracy with a small increase in parameter size. LPAN has a more significant impact on accuracy. To test the performance of LPAN, experiments were conducted to compare LPAN's performance with other excellent feature fusion structures, as shown in Table 6. The Flops ratio represents the current network's floating-point calculation volume compared to other networks' floating-point calculation volume. To ensure fairness in the experiments, ECDet with other structure as the neck was used as the baseline for comparison. As shown in Table 6, LPAN's performance is excellent at a similar scale, and the floating-point calculation volume accounts for only 68% of FPN's. Figure 8 shows the detection effect of vehicles of different sizes.

6   Conclusion

In this paper, we studied efficient vehicle target detection for low-power devices in complex traffic environments. To ensure efficient and accurate extraction of target feature information, we designed an efficient network backbone ECNet based on attention mechanisms and depth-wise separable convolution. To enhance the network's ability to detect multi-scale vehicles in complex traffic environments, we designed a lightweight real-time vehicle target detection model ECDet, including a lightweight feature fusion structure LPAN, which uses depth-wise separable convolution and channel-level feature fusion to improve the model's feature extraction ability. ECDet achieved better accuracy and speed on dataset.

Acknowledgements. This work is being supported by the National Key Research and Development Project of China under Grant No. 2020AAA0104001, the Zhejiang Provincial Science and Technology Planning Key Project of China under Grant No. 2021C01194 and the Eagle Plan of Zhejiang Provincial Administration for Market Regulation of China under Grant No. CY2022339.

References

1. Howard, A.G., Zhu, M., Chen, B., et al.: Mobilenets: efficient convolutional neural networks for mobile vision applications. arXiv preprint arXiv:1704.04861 (2017)
2. Sandler, M., Howard, A., Zhu, M., et al.: MobileNetV2: inverted residuals and linear bottlenecks. In: Proceedings of the IEEE/CVF Conference on Computer Vision and Pattern Recognition, pp. 4510–4520 (2018)
3. Howard, A., Sandler, M., Chu, G., et al.: Searching for mobilenetv3. In: Proceedings of the IEEE/CVF International Conference on Computer Vision, pp. 1314–1324 (2019)
4. Zhang, X., Zhou, X., Lin, M., et al.: Shufflenet: an extremely efficient convolutional neural network for mobile devices. In: Proceedings of the IEEE/CVF Conference on Computer Vision and Pattern Recognition, pp. 6848–6856 (2018)
5. Ma, N., Zhang, X., Zheng, H.T., et al.: Shufflenet v2: practical guidelines for efficient CNN architecture design. In: Proceedings of the European Conference on Computer Vision, pp. 116–131 (2018)
6. Girshick, R., Donahue, J., Darrell, T., et al.: Rich feature hierarchies for accurate object detection and semantic segmentation. In: Proceedings of the IEEE/CVF Conference on Computer Vision and Pattern Recognition, pp. 580–587 (2014)
7. Redmon, J., Divvala, S., Girshick, R., et al.: You only look once: unified, real-time object detection. In: Proceedings of the IEEE/CVF Conference on Computer Vision and Pattern Recognition, pp. 779–788 (2016)
8. Liu, W., et al.: SSD: single shot MultiBox detector. In: Leibe, B., Matas, J., Sebe, N., Welling, M. (eds.) ECCV 2016. LNCS, vol. 9905, pp. 21–37. Springer, Cham (2016). https://doi.org/10.1007/978-3-319-46448-0_2
9. Tan, M., Pang, R., Le, Q.V.: EfficientDet: scalable and efficient object detection. In: Proceedings of the IEEE/CVF Conference on Computer Vision and Pattern Recognition, pp. 10778–10787 (2020)
10. Tan, M., Le, Q.: Efficientnet: rethinking model scaling for convolutional neural networks. In: Proceedings of the IEEE/CVF Conference on Machine Learning, pp. 6105–6114 (2019)
11. Cai, Y., Li, H., Yuan, G., et al.: YOLObile: real-time object detection on mobile devices via compression-compilation co-design. In: Proceedings of the AAAI Conference on Artificial Intelligence, pp. 955–963(2021)
12. Bochkovskiy, A., Wang, C. Y., Liao, H. Y. M.: Yolov4: optimal speed and accuracy of object detection. arXiv preprint arXiv:2004.10934 (2020)

13. Ma, Y., Yu, D., Wu, T., et al.: PaddlePaddle: an open-source deep learning platform from industrial practice. Front. Data Domputing **1**(1), 105–115 (2019)
14. Qiu, L., Zhang, D., Tian, Y., et al.: Deep learning-based algorithm for vehicle detection in intelligent transportation systems. J. Supercomput. **77**(10), 11083–11098 (2021)
15. Bharadhwaj, M., Ramadurai, G., Ravindran, B.: Detecting vehicles on the edge: knowledge distillation to improve performance in heterogeneous road traffic. In: Proceedings of the IEEE/CVF Conference on Computer Vision and Pattern Recognition Workshop, pp. 3192–3198 (2022)
16. Xu, H., Guo, M., Nedjah, N., et al.: Vehicle and pedestrian detection algorithm based on lightweight YOLOv3-promote and semi-precision acceleration. IEEE Trans. Intell. Transp. Syst. **23**(10), 19760–19771 (2022)
17. Wang, K., Liew, J.H., Zou, Y., et al.: Panet: few-shot image semantic segmentation with prototype alignment. In: Proceedings of the IEEE/CVF International Conference on Computer Vision, pp. 9197–9206 (2019)
18. Ge, Z., Liu, S., Li, Z., et al.: OTA: optimal transport assignment for object detection. In: Proceedings of the IEEE/CVF Conference on Computer Vision and Pattern Recognition, pp. 303–312(2021)
19. Zheng, H., Fu, J., Zha, Z.J., et al.: Looking for the devil in the details: learning trilinear attention sampling network for fine-grained image recognition. In: Proceedings of the IEEE/CVF Conference on Computer Vision and Pattern Recognition, pp. 5012–5021 (2019)
20. Zheng, H., Fu, J., Mei, T., et al.: Learning multi-attention convolutional neural network for fine-grained image recognition. In: Proceedings of the IEEE/CVF International Conference on Computer Vision, pp. 5209–5217 (2017)
21. Lin, T.Y., RoyChowdhury, A., Maji, S.: Bilinear CNN models for fine-grained visual recognition. In: Proceedings of the IEEE/CVF International Conference on Computer Vision, pp. 1449–1457 (2015)
22. Cui, Y., Zhou, F., Wang, J., et al.: Kernel pooling for convolutional neural networks. In: Proceedings of the IEEE/CVF Conference on Computer Vision and Pattern Recognition, pp. 2921–2930 (2017)
23. Wang, Y., Morariu, V.I., Davis, L.S.: Learning a discriminative filter bank within a CNN for fine-grained recognition. In: Proceedings of the IEEE/CVF Conference on Computer Vision and Pattern Recognition, pp. 4148–4157 (2018)
24. Redmon, J., Farhadi, A.: Yolov3: an incremental improvement. arXiv preprint arXiv:1804.02767 (2018)
25. Lin, T.Y., Dollár, P., Girshick, R., et al.: Feature pyramid networks for object detection. In: Proceedings of the IEEE/CVF Conference on Computer Vision and Pattern Recognition, pp. 2117–2125 (2017)

Gated Multi-modal Fusion
with Cross-modal Contrastive Learning
for Video Question Answering

Chenyang Lyu[1], Wenxi Li[2], Tianbo Ji[3(✉)], Liting Zhou[1], and Cathal Gurrin[1]

[1] School of Computing, Dublin City University, Dublin, Ireland
chenyang.lyu2@mail.dcu.ie, {liting.zhou,cathal.gurrin}@dcu.ie
[2] Shanghai Jiao Tong University, Shanghai, China
wenxi.li@sjtu.edu.cn
[3] Nantong University, Nantong, China
jitianbo@ntu.edu.cn

Abstract. Video Question Answering (VideoQA) is a challenging task that requires the model to understand the complex nature of video data and the variety of questions that can be asked about them. Existing approaches often suffer from the problem of ambiguous answer candidates with low relevance to the visual and auditory part of the video, which limits the performance of VideoQA systems. In this paper, we introduce a novel approach that leverages multi-modal fusion and cross-modal contrastive learning to utilize multi-modal information and enhance the relevance of answer candidates in VideoQA. First, we introduce a gated multi-modal fusion network that learns to combine different modalities such as visual and speech based on their relevance to the question to enrich the representations of video and improve the accuracy of finding the correct answer. Second, we introduce cross-modal contrastive learning to increase the similarity between positive example pairs (i.e., correct answers and corresponding video clips) while decreasing the similarity between negative example pairs (i.e., incorrect answers and unpaired video clips). Specifically, we use three-way contrastive learning between answer and video frame, answer and audio, answer and cross-modal features. Our proposed approach is evaluated on two benchmark audio-aware VideoQA datasets, including AVQA and Music-AVQA, and compared to several state-of-the-art methods. The results show that our approach significantly improves the performance of VideoQA, achieving new state-of-the-art results on these benchmarks.

Keywords: Video Question Answering · Gated Multi-Modal Fusion · Cross-Modal Contrastive Learning

1 Introduction

Video Question Answering (VideoQA) is a challenging task that requires the model to understand the complex nature of video data and the variety of

---

C. Lyu and W. Li—Equal contribution.

L. Iliadis et al. (Eds.): ICANN 2023, LNCS 14260, pp. 427–438, 2023.
https://doi.org/10.1007/978-3-031-44195-0_35

questions that can be asked about them [29]. With the growing popularity of video content on various platforms, there is an increasing demand for automated systems that can analyze and understand the contents of videos and provide answers to questions asked about them. However, VideoQA is a challenging task due to the diversity and complexity of videos, the wide range of possible questions, and the need for the model to integrate information from multiple modalities, such as visual, audio, and textual information [30]. To address this challenging task, various approaches [13,32] have been proposed and achieved superior performance on benchmark VideoQA datasets. But they often suffer from limitations, such as the problem of ambiguous answer candidates with low relevance to the visual and acoustic part of the video. In many cases, the model may generate an answer that is technically correct but not semantically relevant to the video [9,35]. This is particularly true for VideoQA, when the model has to reason about the visual and auditory parts of the video and understand the context of the question to generate a relevant answer.

To overcome these limitations, in this paper, we introduce a novel approach that leverages multi-modal fusion and cross-modal contrastive learning to utilize multi-modal information and enhance the relevance of answer candidates in VideoQA. Our approach integrates multiple modalities, such as speech and visual information, to generate more accurate answers. Specifically, we use a multi-modal fusion network that learns to combine different modalities based on their relevance to the question. To control the degree of using visual or audio features depending on the question type, we introduce a visual-audio feature gating mechanism. We encode videos and audio into a multi-modal representation and train the model to find a more accurate answer by leveraging multiple modalities. We also propose a novel three-way cross-modal contrastive learning module, which aims to increase the similarity between positive example pairs (i.e., correct answers and corresponding video clips) while decreasing the similarity between negative example pairs (i.e., incorrect answers and unpaired video clips). We encode videos and answers into a shared embedding space and train the model to maximize the similarity between positive pairs and minimize the similarity between negative pairs. Specifically, the contrastive paris consist of answer and video frame, answer and audio, answer and cross-modal features. This encourages the model to focus on the most relevant video frames and audio segments when generating an answer.

Our proposed approach is evaluated on two benchmark audio-aware VideoQA datasets, including AVQA and Music-AVQA, and compared to several state-of-the-art methods. The results show that our approach significantly improves the performance of VideoQA, achieving new state-of-the-art results on these two benchmarks. The superior performance of our method highlights the benefits of integrating our proposed novel modules including Gated Multi-Modal Fusion and Cross-Modal Contrastive Learning for audio-visual understanding and reasoning, which can significantly improve the capabilities of existing question-answering systems in dealing with real-world audio-visual data.

2   Related Work

Video Question Answering (VideoQA) [11,24,28,29,34] is a complex and challenging task that requires a deep understanding of the spatio-temporal nature of videos and the ability to reason about objects, relations, and events across visual and linguistic domains [13,28,32]. To tackle this task, existing research has focused on cross-modal interaction with the aim of understanding videos under the guidance of questions. For example, Visual Relation Grounding in Videos (vRGV) [27], have addressed the challenges of spatio-temporal localization and the dynamic nature of visual relations in videos. Hierarchical Object-oriented Spatio-Temporal Reasoning (HOSTR) networks [4] focus on object-oriented reasoning, maintaining consistent object lifelines within a hierarchically nested spatio-temporal graph. Invariant Grounding for VideoQA [17] is another learning framework that focuses on grounding question-critical scenes and improving reasoning abilities by shielding the answering process from the negative influence of spurious correlations. There has also been a shift towards modeling video as a conditional graph hierarchy [28], which aligns with the multi-granular essence of linguistic concepts in language queries and improves performance and generalization across different types of questions. These methods have collectively contributed to advances in the field of VideoQA, enhancing accuracy, visual explainability, and generalization ability across various tasks and datasets.

However, existing approaches often have limitations, such as the problem of ambiguous answer candidates with low relevance to the visual and acoustic components of the video. Models may generate technically correct answers that are not semantically relevant to the video due to the need to reason about the visual and auditory parts of the video and understand the context of the question [9,35]. To address these limitations, we propose a gated multi-modal fusion network and cross-modal contrastive learning module in this paper to utilize multi-modal information and improve the relevance of answer candidates in VideoQA.

3   Methodology

In this section, we describe the methodology of our proposed approach for VideoQA, which consists of a Gated Multi-modal Fusion Network and a Cross-modal Contrastive Learning Module. An overview of our approach is shown in Fig. 1. First, we give the details of how to encode features such as video frames and audio in our system. Second, we introduce the gated multi-modal fusion network, which combines different modalities based on their relevance to the question. Furthermore, we describe the cross-modal contrastive learning module, which aims to improve the relevance between the paired answer candidates and the corresponding video. Finally, we integrate the cross-modal contrastive learning loss into the training objective of our VideoQA systems via learned weights.

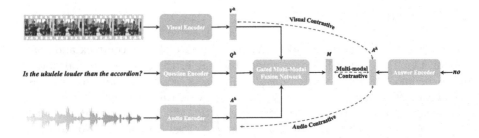

Fig. 1. Overview of our Gated Multi-modal Fusion Network and a Cross-modal Contrastive Learning Module. We fuse the visual and audio features to form multi-modal representations based on their relevance to the corresponding questions followed by a three-way contrastive learning module aiming to improve the similarity between these representations and answer representations.

3.1   Feature Encoder

The input to our model consists of video $\mathbf{V}$, audio $\mathbf{A}$, question $\mathbf{Q}$ and answer candidates $\{\mathbf{G}_1, ..., \mathbf{G}_K\}$, the aim is to find the most plausible answer from the candidate set based on the video according to the given question. We employ transformer-based [25] encoders for encoding video frames and audio associated with a video as well as the textual question and answer candidates.

Visual Encoder. For the visual encoder, we follow the architecture of Vision Transformer (ViT) [6] where each image is split into disjoint patches which are then flattened and fed into a transformer encoder. For a video with n frames: $\mathbf{V} = \{f_1, f_2, ..., f_n\}$, we encode V by encoding each frame f to $f^h \in R^{1 \times w}$ and then incorporate temporal information to obtain temporal-aware video-level representation [2,3,20], which is shown as follows:

$$\mathbf{V}^h = \mathcal{E}_{vis}(\mathbf{V}), \tag{1}$$

where $\mathcal{E}_{vis}$ is the transformer-based video encoder model where we inject temporal information following [2,20], $\mathbf{V}^h \in R^{n \times w}$ represents the temporal-aware video representation for all video frames, w is the dimension of features.

Audio Encoder. For the audio encoder, we firstly employ 1-D Convolutional Neural Networks to extract features from audio signals $\mathbf{A}$ and then use a transformer encoder to obtain the final audio features:

$$\mathbf{A}^h = \mathcal{E}_{aud}(\text{CNN}(\mathbf{A})) \tag{2}$$

where $\mathcal{E}_{aud}$ is the transformer-based audio encoder model [22], $\mathbf{A}^h \in R^{m \times w}$ represents the audio features.

Question and Answer Encoder. We use a transformer-based encoder following the architecture of BERT [5] to obtain the representations of *question* **Q** and *answers* **G**:

$$\mathbf{Q}^h = \mathcal{E}_{que}(\mathbf{Q}), \tag{3}$$

$$\mathbf{G}^h = \mathcal{E}_{ans}(\mathbf{G}), \tag{4}$$

where $\mathbf{Q}^h \in R^{1 \times w}$ and $\mathbf{G}^h \in R^{1 \times w}$ represent question features and answer features respectively.

3.2 Gated Multi-modal Fusion Network

The gated multi-modal fusion network is designed to integrate different modalities, such as visual and audio information, to generate a more accurate answer. Given a video **V**, we first extract visual features using a visual encoder $\mathcal{E}_{vis}(\cdot)$ and audio features using an audio encoder $\mathcal{E}_{aud}(\cdot)$. The visual and audio features are then concatenated and passed through a multi-modal fusion layer, which learns to combine the different modalities based on their relevance to the question. The output of the multi-modal fusion layer is a multi-modal representation **M**:

$$\mathbf{M} = \mathcal{F}_{fuse}(\mathbf{V}^h, \mathbf{A}^h), \tag{5}$$

where $\mathcal{F}_{fuse}(\cdot)$ is a linear layer for the multi-modal fusion and $M \in R^{1 \times w}$ represents the video-level multi-modal representation.

To control the degree of using visual or audio features depending on the question type, we introduce a visual-audio feature gating mechanism. Given the question representation $\mathbf{Q}^h$, we compute a relevance score $r_{vis} \in R^{1 \times w}$ and $r_{aud} \in R^{1 \times w}$ for the visual and audio features, respectively:

$$r_{vis} = \mathcal{F}_{gate}(\mathbf{Q}^h, \mathcal{E}_{vis}(\mathbf{V})) \tag{6}$$

$$r_{aud} = \mathcal{F}_{gate}(\mathbf{Q}^h, \mathcal{E}_{aud}(\mathbf{A})) \tag{7}$$

where $\mathcal{F}_{gate}(\cdot)$ is the gating function, which consists of a linear layer followed by a SIGMOID function so that each element in r_{vis} and r_{aud} is between 0 and 1. The relevance scores are then used to weight the visual and audio features before they are combined:

$$\mathbf{M}_{vis} = \mathcal{F}_{fuse}^{vis}(r_{vis} \cdot \mathcal{G}_{vis}(\mathbf{V}^h), (1 - r_{vis}) \cdot \mathcal{G}_{aud}(\mathbf{A}^h)) \tag{8}$$

$$\mathbf{M}_{aud} = \mathcal{F}_{fuse}^{aud}(r_{aud} \cdot \mathcal{G}_{vis}(\mathbf{V}^h), (1 - r_{aud}) \cdot \mathcal{G}_{aud}(\mathbf{A}^h)) \tag{9}$$

$$\mathbf{M} = \mathcal{F}_{fuse}(r_{vis} \cdot \mathbf{M}_{vis}, r_{aud} \cdot \mathbf{M}_{aud}) \tag{10}$$

where $(\cdot)$ is element-wise dot product, $\mathcal{G}_{aud}$ and $\mathcal{G}_{aud}$ are two linear layers used to transform visual and audio representations into a shared embedding space, the purpose of $(1 - r_{vis})$ and $(1 - r_{aud})$ is to balance the feature fusion. The multi-modal representation **M** is then fed into the cross-modal contrastive learning module.

3.3   Cross-modal Contrastive Learning

The cross-modal contrastive learning module is designed to increase the similarity between positive example pairs (i.e., correct answers and corresponding video clips) while decreasing the similarity between negative example pairs (i.e., incorrect answers and unpaired video clips). Specifically, we use three-way contrastive learning between answer and video frame, answer and audio, answer and cross-modal feature.

Given a question-answer pair $(\mathbf{Q}_h, \mathbf{G}_h)$, we encode $(\mathbf{Q}_h, \mathbf{G}_h)$ and the multi-modal representation $\mathbf{M}$ into a shared embedding space using two separate encoders $\mathcal{E}_{qa}(\cdot)$ and $\mathcal{E}_{mm}(\cdot)$, which consist of a linear layer followed by a ReLU. We then define a contrastive loss function that maximizes the similarity between positive pairs and minimizes the similarity between negative pairs:

$$\mathcal{L}_{contrast} = \frac{1}{N} \sum_{i=1}^{N} (\lambda d_{pos,i}^2 + (1 - \lambda) \max(0, \epsilon - d_{neg,i})^2) \tag{11}$$

where N is the number of examples, $d_{pos,i}$ is the distance between the answer representation and the corresponding multi-modal representation for the i-th positive example: $d_{pos,i} = \|\mathbf{X}^i - \mathbf{X}_{pos}^i\|_2$ and $d_{neg,i}$ is the distance between the answer representation and the multi-modal representation for the i-th negative example: $d_{neg} = \|\mathbf{X}^i - \mathbf{X}_{neg}^i\|_2$. The learned parameter λ controls the weight of the positive loss, and ϵ is the minimum offset between distances of unpaired answer and multi-modal representations.

We use three different types of contrastive learning to enforce the similarity between answer and visual features, answer and auditory features, answer and cross-modal features. Specifically, we define three different loss functions:

$$\mathcal{L}_{vc} = \mathcal{L}_{contrast}(\mathcal{E}_{qa}(\mathbf{Q}_h, \mathbf{G}_h), \mathcal{E}_{mm}(\mathbf{V}_{pos}^h), \mathcal{E}_{mm}(\mathbf{V}_{neg}^h)) \tag{12}$$

$$\mathcal{L}_{ac} = \mathcal{L}_{contrast}(\mathcal{E}_{qa}(\mathbf{Q}_h, \mathbf{G}_h), \mathcal{E}_{mm}(\mathbf{A}_{pos}^h), \mathcal{E}_{mm}(\mathbf{A}_{neg}^h)) \tag{13}$$

$$\mathcal{L}_{mc} = \mathcal{L}_{contrast}(\mathcal{E}_{qa}(\mathbf{Q}_h, \mathbf{G}_h), \mathcal{E}_{mm}(\mathbf{M}_{pos}), \mathcal{E}_{mm}(\mathbf{M}_{neg})) \tag{14}$$

where $\mathbf{V}^h$ and $\mathbf{A}^h$ are the representations of video frames and audio segments that correspond to the correct answer, respectively.

3.4   Training Objective

The overall loss function for our proposed approach is a combination of the cross-modal contrastive learning loss and a standard answer generation loss, which encourages the model to generate a correct answer:

$$\mathcal{L} = \alpha \mathcal{L}_{vc} + \beta \mathcal{L}_{ac} + (1 - \alpha - \beta) \mathcal{L}_{mc} + \mathcal{L}_{ans} \tag{15}$$

where α and β are two learned hyperparameters that controls the weight of the visual and auditory contrastive loss, and $\mathcal{L}_{ans}$ is the answer generation loss, which is standard cross-entropy loss and calculated by:

$$\mathcal{L}_{ans} = -\frac{1}{M} \sum_{i=1}^{M} \sum_{j=1}^{K} (\mathbf{G}_{i,j} log(p(\mathbf{G}_{i,j} | \mathbf{V}, \mathbf{A}, \mathbf{Q}))) \tag{16}$$

where M is the total number of training examples, K represents the number of answer candidates for each example, and $\mathbf{G}_{i,j}$ is the actual probability of the true answer for the i-th example is the j-th answer candidate, $\mathbf{G}_{i,j}$ is 1 only if the true answer for the i-th example is the j-th answer candidate, otherwise it's 0. $p(\mathbf{G}_{i,j} | \mathbf{V}, \mathbf{A}, \mathbf{Q})$ is the probability that the true answer for the i-th example is the j-th answer candidate predicted by our model, which is given by:

$$p(\mathbf{G}_{i,j} | \mathbf{V}, \mathbf{A}, \mathbf{Q}) = \frac{e^{\mathcal{E}_{sim}(G_{i,j}^h, M_i^h)}}{\sum_{K=1}^{N} e^{\mathcal{E}_{sim}(G_{i,K}^h, M_i^h)}} \tag{17}$$

where $\mathcal{E}_{sim}(\cdot)$ is used to measure the similarity between the representations of answer candidates and multi-modal video representations.

4   Experiments

4.1   Experimental Setup

Dataset. We evaluate the proposed approach on two popular benchmark saudio-aware VideoQA datasets, including: 1) AVQA [30] is a novel audio-visual question answering dataset focused on real-life scenario videos. It consists of 57,015 videos collected from daily audio-visual activities, alongside 57,335 specially-designed question-answer pairs that rely on clues from both modalities. The dataset contains over 158 h of content and is divided into three subsets: 34,401 samples for the training set, 5,734 samples for the validation set, and 17,200 samples for the test set. 2) Music-AVQA [14], which is designed to assess multimodal understanding and spatio-temporal reasoning in audio-visual scenes. It includes 45,867 question-answer pairs that span 9,288 videos, amounting to more than 150 h of content. The dataset is divided into training, validation, and testing sets containing 32,087, 4,595, and 9,185 QA pairs, respectively.

Training Setup. During training, we optimize the model parameters using AdamW [18], for which the ϵ is set to 1×10^{-8}. Our implementation is based on CLIP [21][1] from Huggingface [26]. CLIP is used to initialize our VISUAL-ENCODER and TEXT-ENCODER for encoding questions and answers. We train our system with a learning rate of 1×10^{-5} for 20 epochs, with a batch size of 4. We use a maximum gradient norm of 5. We perform early stopping when the performance on validation set degrades.

---

[1] https://openai.com/blog/clip/.

4.2 Results

We firstly evaluate our proposed approach on the test set of AVQA [30]. The results are presented in Table 1, where we compared the performance of our proposed method with several state-of-the-art approaches for audio-visual question answering including HME [7], PSAC [16], LADNet [15], ACRT [33], HGA [10], HCRN [12] and HAVF [30]. Each method's performance was evaluated based on various question types used in [30], including *Which, CF (Come From), Happening, Where, Why, BN (Before Next), When,* and *UF (Used For)* as described in [30]. The overall accuracy was also provided for a comprehensive assessment of each method.

Table 1. Experimental results on AVQA divided by question types.

Methods	Which	CF	Happening	Where	Why	BN	When	UF	Accuracy
HME [7]	82.2	85.9	79.3	76.6	57.0	80.0	57.1	76.5	81.8
HME+HAVF [30]	85.6	88.3	83.1	83.5	61.6	80.0	57.1	88.2	85.0
PSAC [16]	78.7	80.0	77.0	79.4	44.2	76.0	42.9	58.8	78.6
PSAC+HAVF [30]	89.0	91.1	83.2	81.7	61.6	82.0	52.4	76.5	87.4
LADNet [15]	81.1	87.1	76.6	81.8	67.4	78.0	47.6	76.5	81.9
LADNet+HAVF [30]	84.2	89.0	79.1	81.4	68.6	82.0	52.4	76.5	84.1
ACRT [33]	82.5	82.8	79.4	82.5	54.7	80.0	47.6	58.8	81.7
ACRT+HAVF [30]	88.5	91.7	83.9	84.9	50.0	82.0	57.1	64.7	87.8
HGA [10]	82.1	84.3	79.5	83.1	59.3	82.0	57.1	88.2	82.2
HGA+HAVF [30]	88.6	92.2	83.8	82.6	61.6	78.0	52.4	82.4	87.7
HCRN [12]	83.7	84.1	80.2	80.9	52.3	74.0	57.1	70.6	82.5
HCRN+HAVF [30]	89.8	92.8	86.0	84.4	57.0	80.0	52.4	82.4	89.0
Our method	**92.9**	**96.7**	**89.6**	**88.3**	**61.7**	**86.0**	**66.5**	**88.2**	**92.3**

Our method achieved the highest performance across all question types and overall accuracy. Specifically, our method attained an accuracy of 92.9% for *Which*, 96.7% for *Come From*, 89.6% for *Happening*, 88.3% for *Where*, 61.7% for *Why*, 86.0% for *Before Next*, 66.5% for *When*, and 88.2% for *Used For*. The overall accuracy of our method was 92.3%. The results indicate that our method outperforms the existing state-of-the-art approaches in terms of overall accuracy and performance across all question types with a large margin - our approach achieves 3.3% absolute improvements on overall accuracy and approximately 4% absolute improvement for question type *CF*. This suggests that our proposed method effectively captures the spatio-temporal information and audio-visual cues necessary for accurate question answering in complex real-life scenarios.

We further evaluate our approach on Music-AVQA [14]. The results are shown in Table 2 for audio and visual questions, and Table 3 for audio-visual questions. We compared our method with various state-of-the-art approaches for audio and visual question answering. The performance is evaluated based on question types

Table 2. Experimental results of Audio&Visual Questions on Music-AVQA testset.

Method	Audio Question			Visual Question		
	Counting	Comparative	Acc.	Counting	Location	Acc.
FCNLSTM [8]	70.45	66.22	68.88	63.89	46.74	55.21
CONVLSTM [8]	74.07	68.89	72.15	67.47	54.56	60.94
GRU [1]	72.21	66.89	70.24	67.72	70.11	68.93
BiLSTM Attn [36]	70.35	47.92	62.05	64.64	64.33	64.48
HCAttn [19]	70.25	54.91	64.57	64.05	66.37	65.22
MCAN [31]	77.50	55.24	69.25	71.56	70.93	71.24
PSAC [16]	75.64	66.06	72.09	68.64	69.79	69.22
HME [7]	74.76	63.56	70.61	67.97	69.46	68.76
HCRN [12]	68.59	50.92	62.05	64.39	61.81	63.08
AVSD [23]	72.41	61.90	68.52	67.39	74.19	70.83
Pano-AVQA [32]	74.36	64.56	70.73	69.39	75.65	72.56
Music-AVQA [14]	78.18	67.05	74.06	71.56	76.38	74.00
Our Method	**83.71**	**72.18**	**79.46**	**73.37**	**79.62**	**76.54**

under audio, visual and audio-visual questions such as *Counting, Comparative,* and *Location*, etc. Our method outperformed other state-of-the-art approaches in both audio and visual question answering tasks. Especially for audio questions, our method achieved an accuracy of 79.46%, with counting and comparative scores of 83.71% and 72.18%, respectively. These results are significantly higher than the second-best method with a large improvement of 5.4% on overall accuracy. Our approach also achieves an improvement on overall accuracy of 2.5% for visual questions. Furthermore, the results on audio-visual questions in Table 3 show that our proposed approach obtains 4.3% absolute improvement on overall accuracy. The results demonstrate the effectiveness of our method in handling both audio and visual question answering tasks. The significant improvement over existing methods suggests that our approach can better understand and integrate the information from different modalities to find accurate and reliable answers.

4.3   Ablation Results

We performed an ablation study to investigate the contributions of different components of our proposed method on the test set of Music-AVQA. Three approaches were considered: the vanilla approach (without the two proposed modules in this paper), the approach with Gated Multi-Modal Fusion network, and the approach with both Gated Multi-Modal Fusion network and Cross-Modal Contrastive learning module. The results are shown in Table 4. The vanilla approach achieved an accuracy of 72.07% for audio, 73.59% for visual, and 68.94% for audio-visual tasks. By incorporating the Gated Multi-Modal Fusion

Table 3. Experimental results of Audio-Visual Questions on Music-AVQA testset.

Method	Audio-Visual Question					Acc.
	Existential	Location	Counting	Comparative	Temporal	
FCNLSTM [8]	82.01	46.28	59.34	62.15	47.33	60.06
CONVLSTM [8]	82.91	50.81	63.03	60.27	51.58	62.24
GRU [1]	81.71	59.44	62.64	61.88	60.07	65.18
BiLSTM Attn [36]	78.39	45.85	56.91	53.09	49.76	57.10
HCAttn [19]	79.10	49.51	59.97	55.25	56.43	60.19
MCAN [31]	80.40	54.48	64.91	57.22	47.57	61.58
PSAC [16]	77.59	55.02	63.42	61.17	59.47	63.52
HME [7]	80.30	53.18	63.19	62.69	59.83	64.05
HCRN [12]	54.47	41.53	53.38	52.11	47.69	50.26
AVSD [23]	81.61	58.79	63.89	61.52	61.41	65.49
Pano-AVQA [32]	81.21	59.33	64.91	64.22	63.23	66.64
Music-AVQA [14]	81.81	64.51	70.80	66.01	63.23	69.54
Our Method	**83.57**	**68.49**	**75.31**	**71.16**	**69.63**	**73.86**

Table 4. Experimental results of ablation study Music-AVQA testset.

Approaches	Audio	Visual	Audio-Visual
Vanilla approach	72.07	73.59	68.94
+ Gated Multi-Modal Fusion	76.13	75.67	71.41
+ Cross-Modal Contrastive	79.46	76.54	73.86

technique, we observed an improvement in the performance, with accuracies of 76.13% for audio, 75.67% for visual, and 71.41% for audio-visual tasks. Further enhancement was observed when we added the Cross-Modal Contrastive learning component to the approach with Gated Multi-Modal Fusion. The resulting method yielded accuracies of 79.46% for audio, 76.54% for visual, and 73.86% for audio-visual tasks. These results highlight the importance of both Gated Multi-Modal Fusion network and Cross-Modal Contrastive learning module in improving the performance of our method for audio, visual, and audio-visual question answering tasks. The ablation study demonstrates that each of these components contributes to the overall effectiveness of our proposed approach.

5   Conclusion and Future Work

In this paper, we propose a novel approach that leverages multi-modal fusion and cross-modal contrastive learning. Our method uses a multi-modal fusion network along with a visual-audio feature gating mechanism to control the degree of using visual or audio features depending on the question type. Furthermore, we introduced a novel three-way Cross-Modal Contrastive Learning module, which increases the similarity between positive example pairs and decreases the similarity between negative example pairs. This encourages the model to focus on the most relevant video frames and audio segments when generating an answer. We evaluated our proposed approach on two benchmark audio-aware VideoQA datasets, AVQA and Music-AVQA, and compared it to several state-of-the-art methods. Our method achieved significant improvements in performance, setting new state-of-the-art results on both benchmarks. The superior performance of our approach demonstrates the benefits of integrating our proposed novel modules, Gated Multi-Modal Fusion, and Cross-Modal Contrastive Learning, for audio-visual understanding and reasoning. In conclusion, our method has the potential to significantly improve the capabilities of existing question-answering systems in dealing with real-world audio-visual data. The proposed approach can serve as a foundation for future research in VideoQA and related tasks, where multi-modal fusion and contrastive learning techniques can be further explored to enhance the interpretability and adaptability of these models to handle more complex and diverse video content and questions.

References

1. Antol, S., et al.: VQA: visual question answering. In: ICCV (2015)
2. Bain, M., Nagrani, A., Varol, G., Zisserman, A.: Frozen in time: a joint video and image encoder for end-to-end retrieval. In: ICCV (2021)
3. Bain, M., Nagrani, A., Varol, G., Zisserman, A.: A clip-hitchhiker's guide to long video retrieval. arXiv preprint arXiv:2205.08508 (2022)
4. Dang, L.H., Le, T.M., Le, V., Tran, T.: Hierarchical object-oriented spatio-temporal reasoning for video question answering. arXiv preprint arXiv:2106.13432 (2021)
5. Devlin, J., Chang, M.W., Lee, K., Toutanova, K.: BERT: pre-training of deep bidirectional transformers for language understanding. In: NAACL (2019)
6. Dosovitskiy, A., et al.: An image is worth 16x16 words: transformers for image recognition at scale. In: ICLR (2020)
7. Fan, C., Zhang, X., Zhang, S., Wang, W., Zhang, C., Huang, H.: Heterogeneous memory enhanced multimodal attention model for video question answering. In: CVPR (2019)
8. Fayek, H.M., Johnson, J.: Temporal reasoning via audio question answering. IEEE/ACM TASLP **28**, 2283–2294 (2020)
9. Gan, Z., et al.: Vision-language pre-training: basics, recent advances, and future trends. FTCGV **14**(3–4), 163–352 (2022)
10. Jiang, P., Han, Y.: Reasoning with heterogeneous graph alignment for video question answering. In: AAAI (2020)
11. Kim, J., Ma, M., Pham, T., Kim, K., Yoo, C.D.: Modality shifting attention network for multi-modal video question answering. In: CVPR, pp. 10106–10115 (2020)
12. Le, T.M., Le, V., Venkatesh, S., Tran, T.: Hierarchical conditional relation networks for video question answering. In: CVPR (2020)
13. Lei, J., Yu, L., Bansal, M., Berg, T.L.: TVQA: localized, compositional video question answering. arXiv preprint arXiv:1809.01696 (2018)

14. Li, G., Wei, Y., Tian, Y., Xu, C., Wen, J.R., Hu, D.: Learning to answer questions in dynamic audio-visual scenarios. In: CVPR (2022)
15. Li, X., et al.: Learnable aggregating net with diversity learning for video question answering. In: ACM MM (2019)
16. Li, X., et al.: Beyond RNNs: positional self-attention with co-attention for video question answering. In: AAAI (2019)
17. Li, Y., Wang, X., Xiao, J., Ji, W., Chua, T.S.: Invariant grounding for video question answering. In: CVPR (2022)
18. Loshchilov, I., Hutter, F.: Decoupled weight decay regularization. In: ICLR (2019)
19. Lu, J., Yang, J., Batra, D., Parikh, D.: Hierarchical question-image co-attention for visual question answering. arXiv preprint arXiv:1606.00061 (2016)
20. Lyu, C., Nguyen, M.D., Ninh, V.T., Zhou, L., Gurrin, C., Foster, J.: Dialogue-to-video retrieval. In: ECIR (2023)
21. Radford, A., et al.: Learning transferable visual models from natural language supervision. In: ICML (2021)
22. Radford, A., Kim, J.W., Xu, T., Brockman, G., McLeavey, C., Sutskever, I.: Robust speech recognition via large-scale weak supervision. CoRR abs/2212.04356 (2022)
23. Schwartz, I., Schwing, A.G., Hazan, T.: A simple baseline for audio-visual scene-aware dialog. In: CVPR (2019)
24. Tapaswi, M., Zhu, Y., Stiefelhagen, R., Torralba, A., Urtasun, R., Fidler, S.: Movieqa: understanding stories in movies through question-answering. In: CVPR, pp. 4631–4640 (2016)
25. Vaswani, A., et al.: Attention is all you need. In: NeurIPS (2017)
26. Wolf, T., et al.: Transformers: state-of-the-art natural language processing. In: EMNLP (2020)
27. Xiao, J., Shang, X., Yang, X., Tang, S., Chua, T.-S.: Visual relation grounding in videos. In: Vedaldi, A., Bischof, H., Brox, T., Frahm, J.-M. (eds.) ECCV 2020. LNCS, vol. 12351, pp. 447–464. Springer, Cham (2020). https://doi.org/10.1007/978-3-030-58539-6_27
28. Xiao, J., Yao, A., Liu, Z., Li, Y., Ji, W., Chua, T.S.: Video as conditional graph hierarchy for multi-granular question answering. In: AAAI, vol. 36, pp. 2804–2812 (2022)
29. Yang, H., Chaisorn, L., Zhao, Y., Neo, S.Y., Chua, T.S.: Videoqa: question answering on news video. In: ACM MM (2003)
30. Yang, P., et al.: AVQA: a dataset for audio-visual question answering on videos. In: ACM MM (2022)
31. Yu, Z., Yu, J., Cui, Y., Tao, D., Tian, Q.: Deep modular co-attention networks for visual question answering. In: CVPR (2019)
32. Yun, H., Yu, Y., Yang, W., Lee, K., Kim, G.: Pano-AVQA: grounded audio-visual question answering on 360° videos. In: ICCV (2021)
33. Zhang, J., Shao, J., Cao, R., Gao, L., Xu, X., Shen, H.T.: Action-centric relation transformer network for video question answering. IEEE TCSVT **32**(1), 63–74 (2020)
34. Zhao, Z., Yang, Q., Cai, D., He, X., Zhuang, Y.: Video question answering via hierarchical spatio-temporal attention networks. In: IJCAI (2017)
35. Zhong, Y., Ji, W., Xiao, J., Li, Y., Deng, W., Chua, T.S.: Video question answering: datasets, algorithms and challenges. arXiv preprint arXiv:2203.01225 (2022)
36. Zhou, P., et al.: Attention-based bidirectional long short-term memory networks for relation classification. In: ACL (2016)

Learning Video Localization on Segment-Level Video Copy Detection with Transformer

Chi Zhang[1,2], Jie Liu[2], Shuwu Zhang[3], Zhi Zeng[2,3], and Ying Huang[3(✉)]

[1] University of Chinese Academy of Sciences, Beijing, China
[2] Institute of Automation, Chinese Academy of Sciences, Beijing, China
[3] Beijing University of Posts and Telecommunications, Beijing, China
ying.huang@bupt.edu.cn

Abstract. At present, research on segment-level video copy detection algorithms mainly focuses on end-to-end optimization from key frame selection and feature extraction to similarity pattern detection, causing the deployment of such algorithms to be difficult and expensive, and ignoring specific research on optimizing detectors for similarity pattern detection. To address the above issues, we propose the segment-level Video Copy Detection Transformer (VCDT), a transformer-based detector designed for similarity pattern detection. Its main novelty can be summarized by two points: (1) An anchor training strategy that allows the model to use the positional prior information in the anchor boxes to make predictions more precisely, (2) A query adaptation module to fine-tune the anchor boxes dynamically. Our experiments show that, without bells and whistles, VCDT achieves state-of-the-art performance while showing an impressive convergence speed.

Keywords: Video Copy Localization · Content Based Video Retrieval · Temporal Alignment

1 Introduction

Segment-level video copy detection, also known as video copy localization, aims to locate the start and end times of the copied segments in a pair of potentially copied videos. As the phenomenon of copying emerges endlessly in many videos, segment-level video copy detection has turned into one of the most urgent technologies in copyright protection. An efficient and popular pipeline has been summarized in [11]. As shown in Fig. 1, first, the two videos get their respective key frames through key frame selection, and then the features of frames are obtained through feature extraction. After that, cosine similarities of the features are calculated to generate the frame-to-frame similarity matrix. Finally, by detecting similarity patterns of copied segments on the matrix, the video copy localization system can give predictions of the start and end timestamps of the copied segments. Traditional methods for similarity pattern detection include Temporal

L. Iliadis et al. (Eds.): ICANN 2023, LNCS 14260, pp. 439–450, 2023.
https://doi.org/10.1007/978-3-031-44195-0_36

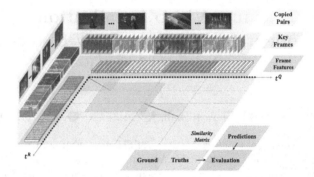

Fig. 1. A popular video copy localization pipeline nowadays. Elements marked in dark red on the similarity matrix indicate that they have a greater value than surrounding elements. (Color figure online)

Networks [13,18,19], Dynamic Programming [2], Temporal Hough Voting [4,13], etc. In recent years, due to the superior performance of deep object detectors, many works such as [8,11] have replaced these traditional methods with deep detection models to detect similarity patterns on the similarity matrix.

However, there are some omissions in the current research. First, as the performance improvement of object detection algorithms slows down [3], the focus of research has become to simultaneously optimize key frame extraction, feature extraction, and similarity pattern detection to seek the end-to-end optimum to improve performance [6,8,11,19]. But most of the video databases store the extracted key frame features, so this kind of algorithms are difficult to completely deploy, leading to performance limitations. Second, most video copy localization algorithms directly use existing deep object detectors for similarity pattern detection, but these detectors are usually designed for detecting natural objects in the real world. From the two points above, it is necessary to modify the general object detectors to make them more suitable for detecting similarity patterns.

To address the two issues mentioned above, we propose VCDT: the segment-level **V**ideo **C**opy **D**etection **T**ransformer, a transformer-based detector to detect similarity patterns of copied segments on similarity matrix. The VCDT is a DETR-like model, since it is improved from DINO [22], which is a variant of DETR [1]. There are 2 main contributions in VCDT:

- **Anchor training:** We propose a novel method to introduce anchor boxes into transformer detector for similarity pattern detection. In this way, the positional prior information in anchor boxes effectively improves the performance of the model. Besides, with this strategy, the Hungarian matcher can be removed to speed up the convergence of the model.
- **Query adaptation module:** We propose a query adaptation module to dynamically adjust anchor boxes. In this way, the anchor box can provide a more accurate initial position and size for the final prediction, which further improves the performance of the model.

Our experiment results show that, without bells and whistles, VCDT outperforms the previous state-of-the-art (SOTA) method without optimizing key frame selection and feature extraction. In addition, our method yields an impressive convergence speed.

2 Related Work

Video copy detection is one of the important tasks in multimedia retrieval. Datasets like FIVR [14] and SVD [12] are commonly used benchmarks of video-level copy detection algorithms. Since 2014, the most widely used segment-level video copy detection dataset is VCDB [13], which contains more than 9,000 copied segment pairs. VCSL [9] proposed by He et al. in 2022 is the largest dataset for segment-level video copy detection, including 280k copied segments.

As for video copy localization algorithms, common traditional methods are Temporal Networks [13,18], Dynamic Programming [2], and Temporal Hough Voting [4,13], etc. [10] formulated the similarity pattern detection as an object detection problem, [11] inherited this way, and proposed a novel frame extraction method, so that the model can be trained end-to-end. Besides, both [8] and [19] use attention layer to enhance frame features to improve performance.

For transformer [20] detectors, DETR [1] is the earliest transformer-based detector. There are also attempts on other structures of transformer-based detectors, and a typical work is ViTDet [15]. Anchor-DETR [21] uses anchor boxes to introduce prior information, which is close to our method. Besides, some vision transformers also perform well on detection tasks, such as Swin Transformer [16]. Deformable-DETR [23] proposed deformable attention, thus greatly boosting up the convergence speed. Based on Deformable-DETR, Zhang et al. proposed DINO [22], which is currently the most powerful DETR variant.

3 Method

3.1 Problem Formulation

Given a pair of potentially copied videos $(V^Q, V^R) = (\{f_n^Q\}_{n=1}^{N^Q}, \{f_n^R\}_{n=1}^{N^R})$, where Q and R denote query video and reference video, N is the number of video frames, and f is the frame feature. Usually, the videos are organized as matrices $V = \{f_n^Q\}_{n=1}^{N^Q} \in R^{N \times d}$, and each row is a normalized feature vector. The format of annotations is $[(i_{s1}^Q, i_{e1}^Q, i_{s1}^R, i_{e1}^R), (i_{s2}^Q, i_{e2}^Q, i_{s2}^R, i_{e2}^R), \ldots]$, where sn and en are the start and end frames of the n-th copied segment, and i represents the frame index. The frame to frame similarity matrix will be:

$$S = V^Q(V^R)^T = (s_{i,j}) \in R^{N^Q \times N^R} \tag{1}$$

Then, the similarity pattern detection is executed on the matrix, and the detector can give the prediction as one or several bounding box(s), whose four coordinate values are just the prediction of a copied segment.

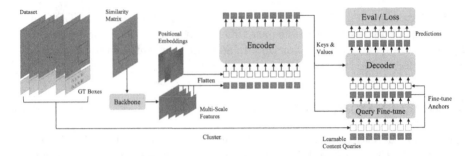

Fig. 2. Overview of our method. The solid and hollow squares represent content queries and positional queries respectively. The "Query Fine-tune" is our proposed query adaptation module, which is responsible for boosting the initial queries.

3.2 Model Overview

VCDT is mainly modified from DINO [22], and just like other DETR-like models, it contains a multi-layer transformer encoder, a multi-layer transformer decoder, and a MLP prediction head. Figure 2 shows the pipeline of our method. Given a similarity matrix, the backbone like ResNet [7] treats it as an image and yields multi-scale features. Then, features with corresponding positional embeddings are fed into the encoder to be enhanced. Instead of initializing reference boxes from encoder output as DINO, the anchor boxes clustered from the training data will serve as the initial reference boxes in our method. In addition, we add a query adaptation module before decoder, which initializes decoder queries and fine-tunes the anchor boxes. Finally, the decoder outputs the prediction bounding boxes by refining the initial reference boxes layer by layer, and each prediction has a confidence score.

3.3 Anchor Training

It has been proven in classic deep detection models like YOLO [5], that the anchor boxes can improve the performance of model by introducing positional prior information. As shown in Fig. 1, the similarity patterns basically follow the same two characteristics: **a.** Appearing as a path on, or near the main or auxiliary diagonal of the similarity matrix. **b.** The element values on the path are greater than the surrounding elements. Therefore, similarity pattern detection can be formulated as a single-class object detection problem.

The most representative work of introducing anchor boxes into the DETR architecture is Anchor-DETR [21]. However, since Anchor-DETR is a general detector, it is designed not to be sensitive to the number of classes, and its anchor boxes are manually set without obtaining prior information from data, because the positional prior information obtained from multiple classes will confuse each other and lose the ability to predict a certain category's target. As shown in Fig. 2, we take the cluster centers of training data as the anchor boxes:

$$A = Cluster(tgt) \qquad (2)$$

where $A \in R^{N^q \times 4}$ denotes anchor boxes. $tgt \in R^{N^t \times 4}$ denotes all the ground truth bounding boxes in training set. N^q is the number of decoder queries. Note that the anchor boxes are set as parameters of the model, so that the model can utilize the positional prior information in them during inference.

In a single input, namely a similarity matrix, there may be more than one target that corresponds to the same anchor box. In order to handle this, Anchor-DETR [21] sets N^p patterns for each decoder query, so that one query can predict N^p boxes. However, when the number of targets belonging to the same anchor is greater than N^p, there will be predictions refined by other anchors are selected by the Hungarian matcher to calculate the loss with the extra targets, thus misleading the learning process. Here, our solution is to merge the targets belonging to the same anchor:

$$t_k = Merge(\{t_{k,j}\}_{j=1}^{N^k}) \tag{3}$$

$$t_k^i = \begin{cases} min(\{t_{k,j}^i\}_{j=1}^{N^k}), & i \in \{0,1\} \\ max(\{t_{k,j}^i\}_{j=1}^{N^k}), & i \in \{2,3\} \end{cases} \tag{4}$$

where k denotes the k-th anchor box, t_k denotes the merged target, and N^k is the number of all targets belonging to this anchor box in the current training sample. $t_{k,j}$ means the j-th target belongs to the k-th anchor. Note that both in Eqs. 3 and 4, t_k and $t_{k,j}$ are of the form (x_0, y_0, x_1, y_1), which means the first two dimensions are normalized coordinates of left top, and the last two dimensions are right bottom. Considering it is important to recall all the copied segments in copyright protection, we design this $Merge$ function so that when there are multiple targets corresponding to one anchor, a prediction wrapping these target boxes will be output to recall them all.

Additionally, because each target has been bound to its cluster center, that is, the anchor box, in the clustering process, the Hungarian matcher is no longer needed to match predictions and targets, which makes the convergence of the model being greatly faster than the original DINO [22].

3.4 Query Adaptation Module

Just as DETR [1] and almost all its variants follow, the decoder query consists of two parts, which respectively contain the positional information of the initial reference box and the content information of current input:

$$Q = Q^c + Q^p \tag{5}$$

where $Q \in R^{N^q \times C}$ is the decoder queries, and C denotes the dimension of the query. Superscript c and p stand for content query and positional query. One thing that's very important is the initialization of queries Q. Usually Q^p is obtained by sine-cosine encoding the initial reference boxes, so the problem of initializing Q^p is how to initialize the reference boxes:

$$Q^{p,init} = Sine(Ref^{init}) \tag{6}$$

where $Ref^{init} \in R^{N^q \times 4}$ denotes initial reference boxes, and $Sine$ is the sine-cosine encoding. DINO [22] initializes Ref^{init} from the encoder output embeddings, and leaves the Q^c as model's parameters and learnable:

$$Q^c = Embedding(N^q, C) \tag{7}$$

Recall Sect. 3.3 and Fig. 2, in our model, Ref^{init} is the anchor boxes, namely A in Eq. 2, lacking the information of current input similarity matrix included in encoder output embeddings. Therefore, we add a query adaptation module before the decoder, which is composed of a cross-attention layer, a self-attention layer and a feed-forward network:

$$Q^f = FFN(MHA(MSDA(Q, K, V))) \tag{8}$$

where

$$Q = Q^c + Q^p = Embedding(N^q, C) + Sine(A) \tag{9}$$

$$K = V = encoder\_output \tag{10}$$

In Eq. 8, $MSDA$ is the multi-scale deformable attention layer that implements cross-attention, MHA is the multi-head attention layer to implement self-attention, and FFN is the feed-forward network. In Eq. 9, we set content queries Q^c the same as Eq. 7, and positional queries Q^p is the sine-cosine embedding of anchor boxes in Eq. 2. In Eq. 10, the $encoder\_output \in R^{H \times W \times C}$ serves as the keys and values in Eq. 8. At last, after $Q^f \in R^{N^q \times C}$ pools the information of current input similarity matrix from encoder output, it is used to fine-tune the anchor boxes, and serves as the content queries of decoder:

$$Q^d = Q^{d,c} + Q^{d,p} \tag{11}$$

where

$$Q^{d,c} = Q^f \tag{12}$$

$$Q^{d,p} = Sine(Encode(Q^f) + A) \tag{13}$$

Superscripts c and p denote content and positional query respectively, as always. A is the anchor boxes as in Eq. 2, and the function $Encode$ is an auxiliary prediction layer in the query adaptation module to predict the offset of A from Q^f. Finally, the queries that will be feed into decoder are the $Q^d \in R^{N^q \times C}$ in Eq. 11, which contain not only the content information of the current input similarity matrix, but also the positional prior information from the training set.

3.5   Learning Objective

We adopt the same configuration as DINO [22] to optimize the model: L1 loss and GIOU loss for box regression and focal loss for classification.

Table 1. Main results of the comparison on VCSL dataset. * indicates that the performance of these methods are published by the VCSL official team in [8]. † indicates that these methods follow the same hyperparameters, and the performance are taken from the convergence point.

Method	HV*	TN*	DP*	DTW*	SPD*	TransVCL*	DINO†	Deformable DETR†	VCDT (ours)†
Recall	86.94	75.25	49.98	45.10	56.49	65.59	64.78	64.89	65.70
Precision	36.82	51.80	60.61	56.67	68.60	67.46	67.83	67.19	70.34
F1-score	51.73	61.36	54.48	50.23	61.96	66.51	66.27	66.02	**67.94**

Table 2. Comparison of the video-level performance.

Method	FRR	FAR	F1-score
SPD	0.2974	0.0958	79.08
TransVCL	0.1666	0.0173	90.19
VCDT	0.1594	0.0157	**90.68**

Table 3. Comparison on VCDB. * indicates fixed anchors.

Method	Recall	Precision	F1-score
TransVCL	76.69	74.09	75.37
VCDT*	77.12	75.01	76.05
VCDT	77.37	75.34	**76.34**

4 Experiments

4.1 Datasets and Evaluation Metrics

We use the VCSL dataset [9] due to its remarkably large scale. Besides, we adopt VCDB [13] to verify the generalization ability of the anchor boxes.

For evaluation metrics, we use the novel method proposed in VCSL [9] to calculate recall and precision. Rather than metrics like Intersection over Union (IOU) that are used in object detection, this metric can better reflect the performance of video copy localization. Besides, we adopt F1-score to reflect the overall performance. Because there are many distractive samples in the testing set that do not have any copied segments, we also adopt False Rejection Rate (FRR) and False Alarm Rate (FAR) to evaluate the video-level retrieval performance.

4.2 Implementation Details

Experiments are performed on a single NVIDIA GeForce RTX 3090. The cluster method is K-Means, and the number of queries, namely the number of anchor boxes, 100. Backbone is ResNet50 [7], which extracts 4-scale features. The optimizer is AdamW, and the initial learning rate is 1×10^{-4}. Batch size of 8, and weight decay 1×10^{-4}. The confidence threshold of valid predictions is 0.32.

4.3 Main Results

Performance. We compare the performance of our method with several typical algorithms. There are four traditional methods, including Hough Voting (HV), Dynamic Programming (DP), Temporal Network (TN) and Dynamic Time Warping (DTW). Two CNN-based methods SPD [11] and TransVCL [8]

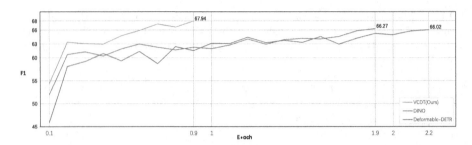

Fig. 3. Convergence curves on VCSL of the three transformer-based methods.

(SOTA). In addition, since our method is mainly improved from DINO [22], and DINO is derived from Deformable-DETR [23], we also add them in the comparison. The main results are shown in Table 1, where we can see that our method (VCDT) outperforms all other methods. Compared with the previous SOTA method TransVCL, our method (VCDT) has a significant improvement in the F1-score (+1.43%), reaching 67.94%. Especially in terms of precision, our method reaches 70.34%, having strong advantages over TransVCL (+2.88%) and SPD (+1.74%), both of which use CNN detectors. For the video-level performance reflected by FRR and FAR, our method exceeds the previous SOTA TransVCL by +0.49% F1 as shown in Table 2. As for the other two transformer-based detectors, our method improves +1.92% and +1.67% F1 respectively compared to Deformable-DETR [23] and DINO [22].

Convergence Speed. During the experiment, we found that the transformer-based models converge very fast on the dataset in 20-epoch setting experiment. Therefore, in order to verify the effect of our strategies on improving the convergence speed, we save the models every 0.1 epoch and verify their performance on the testing set. The convergence curves are plotted in Fig. 3. Our method provides an impressive convergence speed, and it reaches convergence in less than 1 epoch, which means 2.1× faster than the original DINO (1.9 epochs) and 2.4× than the Deformable-DETR (2.2 epochs). Moreover, compared with the method SPD [11], which also does not enhance the frame features and similarity matrices as we do, our method reaches 63.35% F1 at only 0.2 epoch, and leads SPD (61.96%) by +1.39% F1. This means that VCDT only needs 2442 iterations, or 19536 training samples to defeat the CNN-based method significantly.

Generalization. Since the anchor boxes are obtained from the training data, it is necessary to verify the generalization ability of them on different benchmark. We trained two versions of VCDT on VCDB [13], one of which fixes the anchor boxes obtained from VCSL [9], and the other one is trained from scratch. The results are shown in Table 3, and it is intuitive that the version trained from scratch performs better. However, the performance gap (0.29% F1) between the

Table 4. Ablation comparison of our proposed strategies. "AT" and "QAM" represent our anchor training and query adaptation module strategies. In the "Epoch" column are convergence points of the methods.

#. Method	Epoch	Recall	Precision	F1-score
1. DINO (baseline)	1.9	64.78	67.83	66.27
2. +AT	1.1	65.52	67.53	66.46
3. +AT+QAM (ours)	0.9	65.70	70.34	67.94

two versions is acceptable, indicating the generalization ability of anchor boxes. In addition, both versions are stronger than TransVCL (SOTA) [8].

4.4 Ablation

The results of our ablation study are shown in Table 4. DINO [22] is set as the baseline, since our method is mainly modified from it. Note that the query adaptation module cannot be separated from the anchor training to be an independent strategy. Compared with the baseline, the anchor training reduces the convergence point from 1.9 epochs to 1.1 epochs, which means a 73% increase in convergence speed. In addition, the recall is obviously increased (+0.74%), which shows the effect of the merge function in Eq. 4. However, compared to the reference boxes from the encoder output in DINO, the anchor boxes obtained from training data lack information about the current input, despite including prior information, so the precision decreases slightly. Still, anchor boxes brings performance improvement (+0.19% F1) to the model and obviously accelerates the convergence, illustrating the superiority of positional prior information.

After appending the query adaptation module before decoder, the anchor boxes can provide more accurate initial reference positions and sizes, so that the overall performance of model is further improved, and achieves state-of-the-art.

4.5 Visualization

We combine visualization to analyze the mechanism behind the performance growth. For DINO [22], since the training process is a single-class object detection task, in the initial stage of the learning, the model tends to use only a part of decoder queries to predict targets, and these queries therefore learn more information from the backpropagation. Then, the Hungarian matcher always matches targets with the predictions from these queries, because their predictions have higher confidence scores. Finally, there is an unbalanced learning between queries which result in a waste of parameters. In the PyTorch [17] implementation, the queries that dominate the initial learning stage are those in the front of the decoder, which have the smallest indexes. The above analysis can be easily verified in Fig. 4. In DINO, as the index increases, there is a very large gap between the number of predictions output by the subsequent queries and the previous

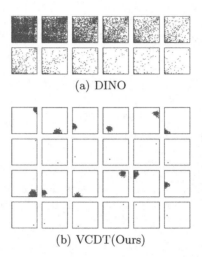

(a) DINO

(b) VCDT(Ours)

Fig. 4. Visualization of the predictions from the first 12 decoder queries of DINO and VCDT. The blue points represent the centers of prediction boxes, and the green points are centers of the anchor boxes corresponding to each query. (Color figure online)

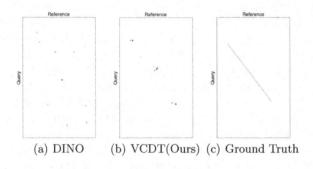

(a) DINO   (b) VCDT(Ours)   (c) Ground Truth

Fig. 5. Visualization of the cross-attention. The red points are reference points, and the blue points are sampling locations, where the darker points have greater attention. (Color figure online)

ones. With the anchor training strategy, the predictions are more concentrated and distributed near the corresponding anchor boxes, and the numbers of predictions between queries are also on the same level, which means VCDT can make full use of all decoder queries to predict the targets.

We also observed that our strategy makes the model more sensitive to the similarity patterns. Take the test sample in Fig. 5 as an example, where both DINO [22] and VCDT have a valid output with nearly identical confidence, and we visualize the cross-attention in the last decoder layer. The reference point marked in red is the center of the current reference box, and the sampling locations marked in blue are the positions on the input similarity matrix that the attention layer focuses on. It can be observed that the reference point of

VCDT is closer to the center of the ground truth than DINO. In Fig. 5(a), even at the last decoder layer, the cross-attention is still searching for the target in a lot of irregular positions. This is because DINO uses encoder output to initialize reference boxes, causing the initial reference box's center change frequently at different inputs, and this didn't happen in VCDT thanks to the anchor boxes. With a stable initial position provided by anchor boxes, cross-attention in VCDT learns a specific rule for finding similarity patterns. In Fig. 5(b), the sampling locations proposed by VCDT are mostly on the line from upper left to lower right, which just looks like the ground truth. Besides, points near the reference point, and the ones at top-left and right-bottom are given greater attention weights. Compared with DINO, the cross-attention of VCDT is obviously better at finding the centers and starting and ending points of similarity patterns.

5 Conclusion

In this paper, we propose VCDT, a transformer-based detector for video copy localization. Our method leads the previous SOTA by a large margin. In the future, we hope that other researchers will be interested in further exploring the potential of transformer architecture in segment-level video copy detection.

Acknowledgement. This work was supported by the National Key R&D Program of China under Grant 2021YFF0901604.

References

1. Carion, N., Massa, F., Synnaeve, G., Usunier, N., Kirillov, A., Zagoruyko, S.: End-to-end object detection with transformers. In: Vedaldi, A., Bischof, H., Brox, T., Frahm, J.-M. (eds.) ECCV 2020. LNCS, vol. 12346, pp. 213–229. Springer, Cham (2020). https://doi.org/10.1007/978-3-030-58452-8_13
2. Chou, C.L., Chen, H.T., Lee, S.Y.: Pattern-based near-duplicate video retrieval and localization on web-scale videos. IEEE Trans. Multimedia **17**(3), 382–395 (2015)
3. Code, P.W.: Object detection on coco test-dev (2018). https://paperswithcode.com/sota/object-detection-on-coco
4. Douze, M., Jégou, H., Schmid, C.: An image-based approach to video copy detection with spatio-temporal post-filtering. IEEE Trans. Multimedia **12**(4), 257–266 (2010)
5. Ge, Z., Liu, S., Wang, F., Li, Z., Sun, J.: YOLOX: exceeding yolo series in 2021. arXiv preprint arXiv:2107.08430 (2021)
6. Han, Z., He, X., Tang, M., Lv, Y.: Video similarity and alignment learning on partial video copy detection. In: Proceedings of the 29th ACM International Conference on Multimedia, pp. 4165–4173 (2021)
7. He, K., Zhang, X., Ren, S., Sun, J.: Deep residual learning for image recognition. In: Proceedings of the IEEE Conference on Computer Vision and Pattern Recognition, pp. 770–778 (2016)
8. He, S., et al.: TransVCL: attention-enhanced video copy localization network with flexible supervision. arXiv preprint arXiv:2211.13090 (2022)

9. He, S., et al.: A large-scale comprehensive dataset and copy-overlap aware evaluation protocol for segment-level video copy detection. In: Proceedings of the IEEE/CVF Conference on Computer Vision and Pattern Recognition, pp. 21086–21095 (2022)

10. Hu, Y., Mu, Z., Ai, X.: STRNN: end-to-end deep learning framework for video partial copy detection. In: Journal of Physics: Conference Series, vol. 1237, p. 022112. IOP Publishing (2019)

11. Jiang, C., et al.: Learning segment similarity and alignment in large-scale content based video retrieval. In: Proceedings of the 29th ACM International Conference on Multimedia, pp. 1618–1626 (2021)

12. Jiang, Q.Y., He, Y., Li, G., Lin, J., Li, L., Li, W.J.: SVD: a large-scale short video dataset for near-duplicate video retrieval. In: Proceedings of the IEEE/CVF International Conference on Computer Vision, pp. 5281–5289 (2019)

13. Jiang, Y.-G., Jiang, Y., Wang, J.: VCDB: a large-scale database for partial copy detection in videos. In: Fleet, D., Pajdla, T., Schiele, B., Tuytelaars, T. (eds.) ECCV 2014. LNCS, vol. 8692, pp. 357–371. Springer, Cham (2014). https://doi.org/10.1007/978-3-319-10593-2_24

14. Kordopatis-Zilos, G., Papadopoulos, S., Patras, I., Kompatsiaris, I.: FIVR: fine-grained incident video retrieval. IEEE Trans. Multimedia **21**(10), 2638–2652 (2019)

15. Li, Y., Mao, H., Girshick, R., He, K.: Exploring plain vision transformer backbones for object detection. arXiv preprint arXiv:2203.16527 (2022)

16. Liu, Z., et al.: Swin transformer: hierarchical vision transformer using shifted windows. In: Proceedings of the IEEE/CVF International Conference on Computer Vision, pp. 10012–10022 (2021)

17. Paszke, A., et al.: PyTorch: an imperative style, high-performance deep learning library. In: Advances in Neural Information Processing Systems, vol. 32 (2019)

18. Tan, H.K., Ngo, C.W., Hong, R., Chua, T.S.: Scalable detection of partial near-duplicate videos by visual-temporal consistency. In: Proceedings of the 17th ACM International Conference on Multimedia, pp. 145–154 (2009)

19. Tan, W., Guo, H., Liu, R.: A fast partial video copy detection using KNN and global feature database. In: Proceedings of the IEEE/CVF Winter Conference on Applications of Computer Vision, pp. 2191–2199 (2022)

20. Vaswani, A., et al.: Attention is all you need. In: Advances in Neural Information Processing Systems, vol. 30 (2017)

21. Wang, Y., Zhang, X., Yang, T., Sun, J.: Anchor DETR: query design for transformer-based detector. In: Proceedings of the AAAI Conference on Artificial Intelligence, vol. 36, pp. 2567–2575 (2022)

22. Zhang, H., et al.: DINO: DETR with improved denoising anchor boxes for end-to-end object detection. arXiv preprint arXiv:2203.03605 (2022)

23. Zhu, X., Su, W., Lu, L., Li, B., Wang, X., Dai, J.: Deformable DETR: deformable transformers for end-to-end object detection. arXiv preprint arXiv:2010.04159 (2020)

Linear Transformer-GAN: A Novel Architecture to Symbolic Music Generation

Dingxiaofei Tian^(✉), Jinyan Chen, Zheyan Gao, and Gang Pan

College of Intelligence and Computing, Tianjin University, Tianjin, China
tdxf1717@163.com

Abstract. Long-structured music generation that can be compared to human compositions remains an unresolved area of research. Since their introduction, the Transformer model and its variations, which rely on self-attention, have gained popularity in generating long-structured music. However, these models employ the teacher-forcing approach during training, which causes an exposure bias problem. Consequently, the generative model is incapable of producing music that consistently adheres to music theory. To address this issue, we propose a new Linear Transformer-GAN structure that generates high-quality music using a discriminator that has been trained to detect exposure bias. The Linear Transformer, a new and efficient variation of transformers, is creatively integrated with a generative adversarial network (GAN) to form our proposed model. In order to overcome the limitations of discrete domain data in GAN, we use the Policy Gradient and present a new discriminator structure that evaluates the current sequence reward based on several dimensions of music information. We use both the cross-entropy loss of different information dimensions and a music-theoretic mechanism to train the discriminator. Our experiments demonstrate that the proposed model generates music more consistent with music theory and is perceived as more pleasurable by listeners. This conclusion is supported by objective metrics and human evaluation. Overall, our approach offers a promising solution to the exposure bias problem in long-structured music generation and provides a more effective means of generating music that adheres to established music theory principles.

Keywords: Adversarial learning · Transformer · Music generation

1 Introduction

Music is aural imagery composed of musical elements such as notes and chords and is an art form that moves people. Throughout its formation, music has distinct cyclical patterns and programmatic characteristics. With the increasing popularity of AI, the advantages of AI as a cross-technology sector in the music industry are now becoming apparent. Google's Magenta Project, Open AI, and SONY have all researched deep learning approaches and achieved improved outcomes.

L. Iliadis et al. (Eds.): ICANN 2023, LNCS 14260, pp. 451–463, 2023.
https://doi.org/10.1007/978-3-031-44195-0_37

In recent years, attention mechanisms and transformer architectures have been extensively applied to symbolic music generation domains to advance the field. Several models, such as Transformer-XL [1] and Linear Transformer [2], have been proposed to generate high-quality music with long structures. However, these models follow the standard teacher-forcing strategy [3], which employs the corresponding preceding item of the ground truth during the training of the network. Although this strategy accelerates the convergence speed of the model, it results in inconsistent decoding behavior during training and prediction, leading to the exposure bias problem.

To address the exposure bias issue, some studies have explored the use of generative adversarial networks (GAN) as an alternative training approach. However, using GAN for sequence generation is challenging due to the discontinuous output of the generator and the inability to transmit back the gradient of the discriminator to the generator.

Thereby, we propose a music theory-based Linear Transformer-GAN model for the generation of piano music. We use human evaluation and some traditional music quality metrics to evaluate the model's performance. Our main contributions include:

(1) We extract the music information from the score and further extract the higher-order features of the music by chord extraction and velocity prediction to construct a music dataset in which the completeness of the musical information is better than the existing symbolic music dataset.
(2) Based on the use of the Compound Word Transformer as the generative model, the discriminator is added to increase the diversity of generated music. We use the lightweight Linear Transformer as a discriminator.
(3) A new discriminator structure is proposed to facilitate the use of the Policy Gradient to improve the limitations of GAN structure in discrete domains and to be able to discriminate music information from different dimensions while using music theory to complement the cross-entropy loss.

2   Related Work

2.1   Representation for Music

In the process of music generation, the selection and processing of data types and the choosing of algorithms play a crucial role. A music score and audio are used to store music. The score maintains entire information about the music's notes and rhythms but needs to recognize the velocity of the notes. PDFTO-Music Pro and PhotoScore & NotateMe are mature types of software for the recognition of musical scores. The audio of music enables us to hear the initial sound and has benefits for determining note velocity. There are still significant difficulties in identifying the primary melody and accompaniment. "Oneset and Frames" [4] is now used for the recognition of audio to estimate the pitch, onset, and offset time of the audio's notes. In the process of music creation, "good" and "bad" music is determined primarily by the choice of notes and the structure of the music. Likewise, the velocity is solely determined by the performer's emotional expression. Lastly, we extract music information through the recognition of music scores and provide a variety of music retrieval techniques to enhance the advanced characteristics of music.

Both language and music have the principle of representing data as discrete characters and organizing them into sequences. MIDI-like [5] and REMI [6] are text-like data representations. The only difference is in the representation of time. MIDI-like uses a time representation similar to that of a MIDI file, while REMI uses [position/bar] to indicate where in the whole music the note is in the bar, where in the bar the note is located. CP [7] follows the temporal representation of REMI and adds [type] to further classify music information, which is helpful for the model to identify different types of music information and grasp their laws. Comparatively, CP can tag all music information of the same type simultaneously, which greatly decreases the length of musical sequences.

2.2   Models for Music Generation

Music generative models need to generate long-structured musical sequences, and attention-based models are suitable for this task. For example, Pop Music Transformer [6] uses REMI encoding and Transformer-XL to generate longer and more complete music. And the further improved Compound Word Transformer [7] uses CP encoding and Linear Transformer. The proposed model converges 5–10 times faster during training, and can generate long-structured high-quality music. However, in the process of training the network, these two models use the corresponding previous item of the standard answer (ground truth) of the training data as the input of the next token (the teacher forcing strategy). As a result of this method, most of the music did not grasp the creation rules of music in the generation stage.

MuseGAN [8] attempts to overcome this issue by generating music through convolution-based processes using an image-like representation of music in continuous space. However, it fails to capture the temporal dependence between different musical occurrences.

To better learn the temporal dependence between different music information and solve the exposure bias problem, Zhang [9] proposes a model that combines Transformer and GAN. In this model, Transformer is used as a generator and discriminator, and the policy gradient is employed to solve the problem of the generator not being microscopic in the sampling process. The model is trained using maximum likelihood and adversarial training methods. However, the Transformer used by the model is slow to converge during training, which is not conducive to adversarial training. Furthermore, although a discriminator is constructed that can calculate the reward for each generation step of a long sequence, it does not use music theory to constrain the music generation. Our proposed model uses a Linear Transformer to speed up the convergence of the model. At the same time, the constructed discriminator can take into account the differences between different categories of music information. In music theory, the discriminator can also fully tune the generator.

3 Methodology

3.1 Data Pre-processing

We gathered 16,095 images of piano sheet music from the Internet. The scores were initially loaded into PDFTOMusic Pro for batch processing, and the scores that showed errors in identification were put into PhotoScore & NotateMe for time alignment processing. The final result is a corresponding MIDI file, which is a computer-readable technical standard representing the music.

Chord Extraction. In music, phrases are typically split by chords, with one or more notes matching each chord. We use the chord extraction algorithm proposed in [10] in two steps segmenting the music by HarmAn, a more efficient graph search algorithm, and labeling the optimal chords by template matching (Fig. 1).

Algorithm 1 HarmAn

Require all the split points of a piece of music where each note begins or ends p_{all}; a split point in p_{all} $p(i)$, $1 \leq i \leq n$; method to get the weight between two split points GetWeight( )

Note: $p(i)$ is implemented with a linked table; n is the number of split points in the whole music; $p(i)$. score indicates the weight between the current split point and the first split point; $p(i)$. prev indicates the previous split point of the current split point

1. Initialize $p(1)$, $p(2)$

2. For i in range(3, $|p_{all}| + 1$)

3.   If removing the (i-1)th split point makes $p(i)$. score larger

4. $p(i)$. prev $= p(i - 2)$

5. $p(i)$. score $= $ GetWeight$(i - 2, i) + p(i - 2)$. score

6.   If keeping the (i-1)th split point allows for a larger $p(i)$. score

7. $p(i)$. prev $= p(i - 1)$

8. $p(i)$. score $= $ GetWeight$(i - 1, i) + p(i - 1)$. score

Start from the last split point, traverse the previous node of the current split point to obtain the optimal split route

---

Fig. 1. The algorithm of chord extraction.

Velocity Prediction. Velocity is an important element in music, and the importance of sound and velocity in musical performance has been recognized since very early times. Musicians often adjust the velocity of notes to express emotion by pressing the keys with varying intensity. This is an essential feature of a musical piece. We predicted the velocity of a note based on its position in the bar, duration, and pitch using the MidiBERT-Piano model [11].

Eventually, we obtain a dataset with complete music information, from which the user can obtain the current music beat, tempo, whether the current note is a melody note or an accompaniment note, the velocity of the note, the start position of the note, and the duration. The dataset will be publicly available at the following website: https://drive.google.com/drive/folders/1BfHG5SMx1_ RCQTZK8ZTnAGVVFX7hH9bL?usp=share_link. Table 1 shows our music dataset (Piano MIDI 16095) as well as most of the existing datasets [12–14]. Although POP909 has the same complete information on music, it uses manual methods to predict tempo changes, which greatly reduces efficiency, and the dataset is substantially smaller and differs significantly from ours.

Table 1. Piano MIDI 16095 and most existing datasets.

Dataset	Size	Tempo	Time Signature	Chord	Melody and Accompaniment	Velocity
Piano MIDI 16095	16095	✓	✓	✓	✓	✓
Lakh MIDI	176581	✓	✓	×	×	✓
ADL Piano	11086	✓	✓	×	×	✓
POP909	909	✓	✓	✓	✓	✓

3.2 Linear Transformer-GAN Architecture

We use Compound Word Transformer as a generative model, which uses linear attention and is an efficient generative model suitable for adversarial training. It also uses different feedforward heads to model different types of tags in CP encoding, which facilitates learning various different types of features of music.

Usually, the discriminator in the GAN structure can only evaluate the score of the whole generated sequence and cannot refine it to evaluate the goodness of the currently generated token and its impact on the later generation. In SeqGAN [15], the Monte Carlo (MC) search is used to complete the current sequence and then put it into the discriminator for evaluating the goodness of the sequence, which is less efficient and not suitable for long sequence generation and convergence of adversarial training. Therefore, Li et al. [16] proposed a new idea to decompose the complete sequence into subsequences so that the training set includes both partial and complete sequences, and the discriminator obtained by training in this way has improved efficiency compared with the method of the MC search, but the accuracy of the discriminator will be reduced. In Zhang's paper, he proposed a discriminator structure in which the discriminator is able to judge the local harmony and global correctness of the token at each time step, where both parts of the data are calculated by cross-entropy loss. In the field of music, on the other hand, there are certain patterns between each note as well as a chord that can be expressed by specific mathematical formulas, so the calculation of local harmony should also be performed using formulas that are more in line with music theory. At the same time, music information is divided into many different types, and if different types of music information are mixed together for the calculation of global correctness, this will obviously bring some errors.

Thereby, we propose a new discriminator structure as shown in Fig. 2. It uses different embedding sizes, output settings, and cross-entropy losses for each dimension of information of the token at each time step. Define the current input sequence as $nt_{i,j}, i = 1, \cdots, L; j = 0, \cdots, 6$. We can set a different embedding size for each dimension of each input token, which is more conducive to the model for learning the features of different types of information. The specific calculation formula is as follows.

$$p_{i,j} = \text{Embedding } (nt_{i,j}) \tag{1}$$

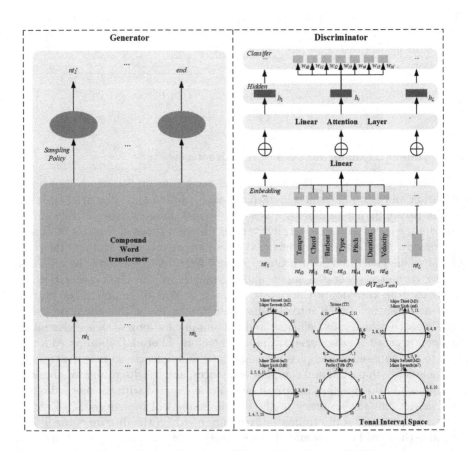

Fig. 2. The architecture of Linear Transformer-GAN.

Also, when getting the output results, we want to get the classification results for each dimension of each token. Therefore, we set up a linear network with different dimensions $\{W_j\}, j = 0, \cdots, 6$. We define the output after the linear attention layer as h_i. The specific formula of the output is as follows.

$$w_{i,j} = \text{softmax}(W_j h_i) \tag{2}$$

The calculation of the loss function will be described in detail later. Finally, we add a music-theoretic mechanism to assist the discriminator in the "true" or "false" determination. For each note, we calculate its distance from the current corresponding chord as its local harmony, as described in detail later.

3.3 Music-Theoretic Mechanisms

$nt_{p,j}, j = 0, 1, 2, 3, 4, 5, 6$ is the current note and $nt_{c,j}, j = 0, 1, 2, 3, 4, 5, 6$ is the chord corresponding to the current note. Both are 7-dimensional vectors after CP encoding. Each dimension corresponds to pitch, duration, velocity, bar position, tempo, chord, and type, respectively. We take out the pitch $nt_{p,1}$ corresponding to the current note, and the chord label $nt_{c,4}$ corresponding to the chord.

We represent all pitches and chords in the Tonal Interval Space, which is computed by the weighted discrete Fourier transform [17]. In this space, the angles and Euclidean distances between pitches and chords are in accordance with music theory.

First, the pitch $nt_{p,1}$ and chord $nt_{c,4}$ are represented as 12-dimensional 0, 1 vectors for p(n) and c(n), respectively. Then the 12-dimensional vectors are mapped into Tonal Interval Space, denoted as $T_p(k)$ and $T_c(k)$.

$$w(k) = \{2, 11, 17, 16, 19, 7\}, k \in \{1, 2, 3, 4, 5, 6\} \tag{3}$$

$$T_p(k) = w(k) \sum_{n=0}^{N-1} p(n) e^{-\frac{j2\pi kn}{N}}, k \in \{1, 2, 3, 4, 5, 6\}, N = 12 \tag{4}$$

$$T_c(k) = w(k) \sum_{n=0}^{N-1} \overline{c(n)} e^{-\frac{j2\pi kk}{N}}, \overline{c(n)} = \frac{c(n)}{\sum_{n=0}^{N-1} c(n)} \tag{5}$$

Finally, we take the distance between the pitch of the current note and the corresponding chord as the music-theoretic loss of the current note.

$$d\{T_p(k), T_c(k)\} = \sqrt{\|T_p(k) - T_c(k)\|} = \sqrt{\sum_{k=1}^{6} |T_p(k) - T_c(k)|^2} \tag{6}$$

4   Tricks of Adversarial Training

4.1   Policy Gradient

SeqGAN applies Policy Gradient from reinforcement learning to adversarial training in order to alleviate the restrictions posed by discrete data in GAN.

In reinforcement learning, every action has a reward. The whole algorithm is required to maximize the desired reward. When the generator generates a token, we are able to get a feedback reward, which is obtained through the discriminator. We no longer need to rely on the discriminator's backpropagation to update the parameters.

4.2   Generator

Before adversarial training, we pre-train the generator and discriminator, which allows our model to converge faster. For pre-training, we use Maximum Likelihood Estimation (MLE) to pre-train the generator. In the process of adversarial training, according to the Policy Gradient in reinforcement learning, our goal is to maximize the desired reward, hoping to obtain a set of generative model G parameters θ. The best choice can be made at s_0 to obtain the maximum reward R_L, and how to choose the action depends on the value of the action Q.

$$Q_{D_{\emptyset}}^{G_{\theta}}\left(s = NT_{1:i-1}, a = nt_i\right) = D_{\emptyset}\left(NT_{1:L}\right)(i), i \leq L \tag{7}$$

$$J_{\theta} = E\left(R_L \mid s_0, \theta\right) = \sum_{nt_1 \in NT} G_{\theta}\left(nt_1 \mid s_0\right) \cdot Q_{D_{\emptyset}}^{G_{\theta}}\left(s_0, nt_1\right) \tag{8}$$

The gradient of the generator's objective function is derived as follows.

$$\nabla_{\theta} J(\theta) = \sum_{i=1}^{L} E_{NT_{1:i-1} \sim G_{\theta}} \sum_{nt_i \in NT} \nabla_{\theta} G_{\theta}\left(nt_i \mid NT_{1:i-1}\right) \cdot Q_{D_{\emptyset}}^{G_{\theta}}\left(NT_{1:i-1}, nt_i\right) \tag{9}$$

$$\theta \leftarrow \theta + \nabla_{\theta} J_{\theta} \tag{10}$$

4.3   Discriminator

The same loss function is utilized for the pre-training and adversarial training of the discriminator, which consists of two parts: a binary classification using a cross-entropy loss and a music-theoretic mechanism that complements the results of the discriminator.

In calculating the cross-entropy loss, we make classification predictions for each dimension of each token and record each loss separately. Finally, the pre-training loss is defined as the mean of all dimensional feature losses. Where $y_{i,j}, i = 1, \cdots, L; j = 0, \cdots, 6$ consists of 0 or 1 and is the desired output.

$$\text{loss} = \left[\sum_{j=0}^{6} \text{CrossEntropyLoss}\left(w_{ij}, y_{ij}\right)\right] / 7 \tag{11}$$

Once we have generated a piece of music with the generator, we will retrain the discriminator with this music and real music composed by humans, as follows:

$$\text{music} = E_{Y \sim p_g}[d\{Y\}] \tag{12}$$

$$\min_{\emptyset} -E_{Y \sim p_r} \left[\log D_{\emptyset}(Y) \right] - E_{Y \sim p_g} \left[\log \left(1 - D_{\emptyset}(Y) \right) \right] + \text{music} \qquad (13)$$

where p_r is the real music clip and p_g is the music clip generated by the generator. By optimizing the first two terms of the formula, $D_{\emptyset}$ learns to judge the real music as "true" and the generated sequence as "false". *music* is used to guide $D_{\emptyset}$ to calculate the distance between the chord label of the generated music and the current note and to determine whether the current music fragment conforms to the music rules. The final training process is shown in Fig. 3.

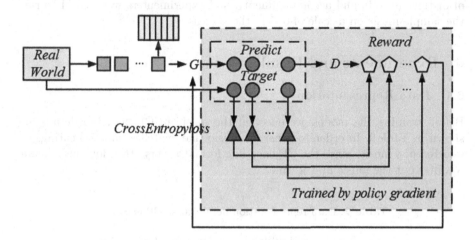

Fig. 3. The training process.

5 Metrics

5.1 Objective Metrics for Evaluation

For an objective evaluation of our model, we selected EB and QN [8], two objective metrics traditionally used for the evaluation and proposed MD, a new metric for the evaluation of the melody.

EB: percentage of blank time in a piece of music that is longer than one beat duration.

QN: the percentage of qualified notes. We consider a note with a duration of not less than 32nd notes as a qualified note. QN indicates whether the music is overly fragmented.

MD: the distance of adjacent notes in the melody. We represent the notes of the melody in Tonal Interval Space and calculate the mean value of the distance of adjacent notes as MD.

5.2 Human Evaluation

On the basis of the objective assessment described above, we also conducted a subjective assessment of the generated music. In this subjective test, we invited 50 subjects, including 25 music professionals and 25 non-music professionals. We randomly selected 5 songs from all the music generated by the experimental model, respectively, and edited about 10–15 s music clips from them as the sample music for this evaluation. Our questionnaire was set up with three sections, namely: melodic beauty, coherence, and clear musical structure (presence of distinct melody and accompaniment), and experimenters were asked to rate the sample music on a scale of 0–5 in these areas.

6 Experiments and Results

6.1 Data Representation

Before training the model, we encoded the music in CP, and the details are shown in Table 2. In order to generate music that matches human hearing, we selected pop music. Since the CP encoding format is very strict for music beats, we filter out the music in 4/4 time.

Table 2. Data representation details after CP encoding.

Encoding method	Token type	Voc.size	Embed.size
CP	tempo	66	128
	position/bar	18	64
	chord	129	256
	pitch	93	512
	duration	18	128
	velocity	55	128
	type	4	32

6.2 Evaluation

To validate our model, we selected Compound Word Transformer and Linear Transformer-Bert (a model with Linear Transformer as the generator and Bert as the discriminator) as the comparison models. We randomly selected 10 pieces of music from their generated music as sample music for the calculation of metrics and questionnaire. The results are shown in Table 3.

We found that Linear Transformer-GAN has the lowest values of EB, QN, and MD among all models. For Compound Word Transformer, we believe that it is due to the lack of discriminators, and the generative model in the GAN

Table 3. Result of objective metrics.

	EB ↓	QN ↓	MD ↓	Generator	Discriminator
Compound Word Transformer	5.53	1.22	0.48	Linear Transformer	–
Linear Transformer-Bert	2.60	0.32	0.44	Linear Transformer	Bert
Linear Transformer-GAN	0.78	0.26	0.43	Linear Transformer	Linear Transformer

structure can generate more realistic music. While Linear Transformer-Bert uses the discriminator Bert with higher operational complexity, Linear Transformer-GAN uses Linear Transformer as a discriminator to improve the convergence efficiency and generate music that is more consistent with human samples using music theory.

We gave a set of basic track clips from the three experimental models mentioned above to some music majors as well as non-music majors and asked them to evaluate each of them in terms of three aspects: melodic beauty, coherence, and clear musical structure. To make the music more realistic, we used FluidSynth to synthesize the MIDI music into MP3 format, and the full music can be found at https://musiccloud.cf/tdxf1717/songs. The results of the listening test are shown in Fig. 4.

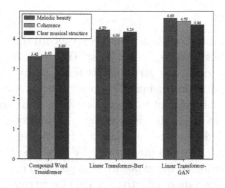

Fig. 4. Human Evaluations.

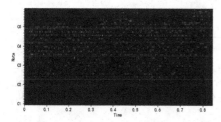
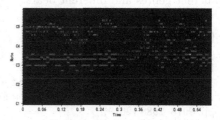

Fig. 5. Generated music from the Compound Word Transformer.

Fig. 6. Generated music with the discriminator.

In Fig. 5, Fig. 6, we found that the music generated by the adversarial model constructed using the generator and discriminator was more beautiful and coherent than the music generated by Compound Word Transformer and had a clearer musical structure. To visualize the structure of the music, we further visualized the generated music with the horizontal coordinates in time and the vertical coordinates in pitch.

The music generated by Linear Transformer-Bert and Linear Transformer-GAN has a more evident primary melody and accompaniment, which is similar to the structure of music composed by musicians. Therefore, our model has learned the laws of music well and can generate music people enjoy.

The main difference between Linear Transformer-Bert and Linear Transformer-GAN is that the former uses Bert as a discriminator, while the latter uses Linear Transformer as a discriminator. The former uses a traditional, highly complex discriminator, which puts some pressure on training and inference. At the same time, when computational resources are limited, we can only divide the music into shorter segments for training. The latter uses a lightweight discriminator, which is able to reduce the training burden, and it is able to generate long-structured music. Clearly, Linear Transformer-GAN is able to generate music with a longer structure that is more consistent with human hearing and more in line with music theory.

7 Conclusion

We propose a new Linear Transformer-GAN structure that uses a discriminator trained to detect exposure bias. The Linear Transformer is integrated with a GAN, and a new discriminator structure that evaluates the current sequence reward based on several dimensions of music information is presented. Both the cross-entropy loss of different information dimensions and a music-theoretic mechanism are used to train the discriminator. Our experiments demonstrate that the proposed model generates music that is more consistent with music theory and is perceived as more pleasurable by listeners. Overall, our approach offers a promising solution to the exposure bias problem in long-structured music generation and provides a more effective means of generating music that adheres to established music theory principles. In future work, we plan to generate music of different genres and different beats.

References

1. Dai, Z., Yang, Z., Yang, Y., Carbonell, J., Le, Q., Salakhutdinov, R.: Transformer-XL: attentive language models beyond a fixed-length context. In: Proceedings of the 57th Conference of the Association for Computational Linguistics, ACL 2019, pp. 2978–2988 (2019)
2. Katharopoulos, A., Vyas, A., Pappas, N., Fleuret, F.: Transformers are RNNs: fast autoregressive transformers with linear attention. In: Proceedings of the 37th International Conference on Machine Learning, ICML 2020, vol. 119, pp. 5156–5165 (2020)

3. Bengio, S., Vinyals, O., Jaitly, N., Shazeer, N.: Scheduled sampling for sequence prediction with recurrent neural networks. In: Advances in Neural Information Processing Systems 28: Annual Conference on Neural Information Processing Systems 2015, pp. 1171–1179 (2015)
4. Hawthorne, C., et al.: Onsets and frames: dual-objective piano transcription. In: Proceedings of the 19th International Society for Music Information Retrieval Conference, ISMIR 2018, pp. 50–57 (2018)
5. Oore, S., Simon, I., Dieleman, S., Eck, D., Simonyan, K.: *This time with feeling*: learning expressive musical performance. Neural Comput. Appl. **32**, 955–967 (2020). https://doi.org/10.1007/s00521-018-3758-9
6. Huang, Y., Yang, Y.: Pop music transformer: beat-based modeling and generation of expressive pop piano compositions. In: MM 2020: The 28th ACM International Conference On Multimedia, pp. 1180–1188 (2020)
7. Hsiao, W., Liu, J., Yeh, Y., Yang, Y.: Compound word transformer: learning to compose full-song music over dynamic directed hypergraphs. In: Thirty-Fifth AAAI Conference on Artificial Intelligence, AAAI 2021, pp. 178–186 (2021)
8. Dong, H., Hsiao, W., Yang, L., Yang, Y.: MuseGAN: multi-track sequential generative adversarial networks for symbolic music generation and accompaniment. In: Proceedings of the Thirty-Second AAAI Conference on Artificial Intelligence (AAAI-2018), pp. 34–41 (2018)
9. Zhang, N.: Learning adversarial transformer for symbolic music generation. IEEE Trans. Neural Netw. Learn. Syst. **34**(4), 1754–1763 (2023)
10. Pardo, B., Birmingham, W.: Algorithms for chordal analysis. Comput. Music. J. **26**, 27–49 (2002)
11. Chou, Y., Chen, I., Chang, C., Ching, J., Yang, Y.: MidiBERT-Piano: large-scale pre-training for symbolic music understanding. CoRR. abs/2107.05223 (2021)
12. Raffel, C.: Learning-Based Methods for Comparing Sequences, with Applications to Audio-to-MIDI Alignment and Matching. Columbia University, USA (2016)
13. Ferreira, L., Lelis, L., Whitehead, J.: Computer-generated music for tabletop role-playing games. In: Proceedings of the Sixteenth AAAI Conference on Artificial Intelligence and Interactive Digital Entertainment, pp. 59–65 (2020)
14. Wang, Z., et al.: POP909: a pop-song dataset for music arrangement generation. In: Proceedings of the 21th International Society for Music Information Retrieval Conference, ISMIR 2020, pp. 38–45 (2020)
15. Yu, L., Zhang, W., Wang, J., Yu, Y.: SeqGAN: sequence generative adversarial nets with policy gradient. In: Proceedings of the Thirty-First AAAI Conference on Artificial Intelligence, pp. 2852–2858 (2017)
16. Li, J., Monroe, W., Shi, T., Jean, S., Ritter, A., Jurafsky, D.: Adversarial learning for neural dialogue generation. In: Proceedings of the 2017 Conference on Empirical Methods in Natural Language Processing, EMNLP 2017, pp. 2157–2169 (2017)
17. Bernardes, G., Cocharro, D., Caetano, M., Guedes, C., Davies, M.: A multi-level tonal interval space for modelling pitch relatedness and musical consonance. J. New Music Res. **45**, 1–14 (2016)

MBMS-GAN: Multi-Band Multi-Scale Adversarial Learning for Enhancement of Coded Speech at Very Low Rate

Qianhui Xu[1], Weiping Tu[1(✉)], Yong Luo[1], Xin Zhou[2], Li Xiao[1], and Youqiang Zheng[1]

[1] School of Computer Science, National Engineering Research Center for Multimedia Software and Hubei Key Laboratory of Multimedia and Network Communication Engineering, Wuhan University, Wuhan, China
{xuqianhui,tuweiping,luoyong,xiaoli1996,youqiangzheng}@whu.edu.cn
[2] Jiangxi Science and Technology Normal University, Nanchang, China
zhouxin@jxstnu.edu.cn

Abstract. Speech coding is to effectively represent speech signals in the form of digital signals. Existing solutions usually have large quantization error when coding at very low rate. This would result in serious spectrum energy distortion of the reconstructed speech, and most of the current approaches do not consider that the distortion is often unevenly distributed across the spectrum. To address these issues, we propose a novel multi-band multi-scale generative adversarial network (MBMS-GAN) for speech coding. In particular, the speech coding is trained in an adversarial manner at different sub-bands and scales to consider both the global and local spectral energy distortion. Besides, a unified codebook matching strategy is designed by integrating the Euclidean distance and cosine similarity to consider both the absolute distance and directions of two vectors in the matching. We very effectiveness of our method on the popular CSTR-VCTK dataset, and the results demonstrate that our method can significantly improve the quality of reconstructed speech at 600 bps by 0.19 in terms of MOS score. Our study has high application value in the scenario of narrow communication channels such as satellite communication.

Keywords: speech coding · adversarial learning · multi-band · multi-scale · codebook matching

1 Introduction

Speech is an important way for efficient information exchange between people. As network and communication technologies advance, pervasive speech communication is now largely feasible, with the corresponding technical standards improving. However, typical devices such as mobile phones and walkie-talkies are limited in that they may have signal blind area or only appropriate for

L. Iliadis et al. (Eds.): ICANN 2023, LNCS 14260, pp. 464–475, 2023.
https://doi.org/10.1007/978-3-031-44195-0_38

short-range communication, which restrict the widespread application of traditional speech communication technology. Recently, satellite communication has attracted increasing attention due to its large capacity, wide coverage and flexible multi-access. However, the satellite communication channel is usually very narrow. In order to realize efficient speech communication, it is necessary to address the contradiction between small communication bandwidth and large communication data volume.

To achieve efficient transmission of speech signals, speech is often coded as digits and compressed to reduce the bit rate as much as possible while maintaining speech quality. The traditional codec of speech extracts the key feature parameters of speech. At very low rates, the number of bits that can be used to quantify these features is very small, resulting in large quantization errors. Therefore, there are usually mechanical and unnatural problems in reconstructing speech. With the developement of deep learning, some hybrid methods that utilize traditional approaches to extract speech features and then use deep learning to perform speech synthesis. This can often achieve better speech reconstruction results in a bit rate of more than 1.6 kbps, but the computational complexity is usually much high. Recently, end-to-end speech coders can achieve better reconstruction results at a minimum of 1.2 kbps, but their encoding of speech waveform has a higher feature dimension. When adopting the Euclidean distance for codebook matching, much larger quantization errors may be obtained [15]. Besides, the current speech coder mainly pays attention to the overall optimization of the spectrum energy of the reconstructed speech signal, while the energy distribution of the speech signal in the spectrum is often uneven, which will cause the local spectrum amplitude to be unable to maximally optimized, and the reconstructed speech still has a certain degree of distortion.

To remedy these drawbacks, we propose an end-to-end speech coding method to improve the quality of reconstructed speech at a very low bit rate. In particular, to address local distortion in the reconstructed speech spectrum at extremely low bit rates, we train the speech encoder and decoder/generator in an adversarial manner [24], where a novel multi-band multi-scale (MBMS) Short-Time Fourier Transform (STFT) discriminator is incorporated. That is, the speech signals are divided into multiple subbands, and a multi-scale STFT discriminator is applied on each subband to reduce the local spectral energy distortion in the reconstructed speech. Furthermore, for the high-dimensional latent variables obtained from the encoder output, we design a strategy that combines Euclidean distance and cosine similarity for codebook matching. Such strategy considers both the similarity in vector direction and magnitude during codebook matching, and thus reduces the quantization errors compared with using only Euclidean distance.

We conduct ViSQOL objective evaluation and MOS subjective evaluation on the well-known CSTR-VCTK [19] dataset. The results demonstrate that our proposed method at 600 bps can achieve reconstructed speech quality comparable to some recent or competitive counterparts at much higher rates, including

Lyra [12] (3 kbps), Opus [2] (6 kbps), AMR-WB [6] (4.75 kbps), and Encodec [18] (6 kbps). To sum up, the main contributions of this paper are:

- We propose a multi-band multi-scale STFT discriminator to reduce the local distortion of the reconstructed speech signal spectrum amplitude.
- We design a codebook matching strategy to improve the quantization accuracy of the codebook.

2   Related Work

The existing speech coding methods can be roughly grouped as traditional speech coding and deep learning based speech coding methods. Deep learning based speech coding can be further categorized as the hybrid ones, which is a combination of traditional and deep learning based speech coding methods, and the end-to-end speech coding approaches.

Codec2 [1], as a traditional speech encoder, applies harmonic sine speech coding to achieve effective speech compression. Codec2 inputs 16-bit 8kHz speech samples, and the samples complete high-quality speech coding at 1.4 kbps after gene estimation, gene quantization, Fourier transform, linear prediction, speechless judgment, energy quantization and other steps. J. M. Valin et al. introduced an Opus codec [2], which can simultaneously use linear prediction (LP) and improved discrete cosine transform (MDCT) to achieve speech compression, and can expand from 6 kbps low bit rate narrowband speech to 510 kbit/s high quality stereo speech. M. Dietz et al. proposed the EVS codec that supports the full frequency band [3]. It is an improved code-excited linear prediction (ACELP), and also uses a linear prediction model suitable for different speech categories. EVS can operate at a minimum of 5.9 kbps, with high robustness, and can obtain higher quality speech.

The hybrid speech coding method usually extracts the code stream parameters through the traditional encoder, and then feeds them into the neural network for synthesis. The synthetic neural network used here is usually a vocoder [4]. Using Codec2 [1] to replace the original text of WaveNet [5] with quantitative parameters such as frequency, speechless and speechless, and the text sequence used as conditional information in the speech (TTS) application can achieve better reconstruction effect at 2.4 kbps than AMR-WB [6]at 23.05 kbps [7]. The STFT feature of the original speech is extracted by the convolutional cyclic network, and the convolutional neural network is used to improve the coding quality of the traditional Codec2. This method can achieve better speech quality at 3.6 kbps than that of Opus [2] at 6 kbps [8]. A backward compatibility method is proposed to improve the quality of Opus [2] at low bit rate by synthesizing speech from decoding parameters again. This study compares two different neural generation models, WaveNet and LPCNet [9]. The method based on WaveNet has high complexity and poor compatibility. The model based on LPCNet can achieve better speech quality at 6kb/s, but it has a long distance from the extremely low bit rate [10]. A method of combining LPCNet [9] encoder with StyleMelGAN [11] generator and discriminator is proposed. This method can generate better speech quality at 1.6 kbps.

End-to-end codecs generate hidden variables at the encoding end and transmit them after quantization. The decoding end uses these hidden variables to synthesize speech. W.B. Kleijn et al. studied and proposed a generation model - Lyra [12]. It uses neural network encoder to encode and quantize speech, and uses autoregressive WaveGRU model to decode. It provides the most advanced coding performance of 3 kbps. Neil Zeghidour et al. proposed the SoundStream model [13], which introduced the multilevel vector quantization (MSVQ) method [14]. The training process combines the antagonism and reconstruction loss, allowing the generation of high-quality speech content from quantization embedding, and can achieve the operation from 3 kbps to 18 kbps bit rate.

3   The Proposed Method

Our end-to-end speech coding framework is illustrated in Fig. 1. Firstly, the original speech is encoded using a Convolutional Neural Network (CNN) encoder. The high-dimensional vectors output from the CNN encoder are matched to a codebook using a combination of Euclidean distance and cosine similarity, taking into account both the distance and direction relationships between the two vectors, thus reducing codebook matching errors. The quantized discrete features are decoded by a CNN generator, and the reconstructed speech output from the generator is compared to the original speech during training. The speech signals are divided into multiple subbands, and a multi-scale Short-Time Fourier Transform (STFT) discriminator is applied on each subband to reduce the local spectral energy distortion in the reconstructed speech. More details of each component are depicted as follows.

3.1   Encoder

The encoder adopts the classic convolutional neural network (CNN) structure of traditional VQ-VAE [16]. During model training, the input acoustic features are reduced to hidden layer variables through the encoder. The network model uses gradient descent method to minimize the loss function and adjust the weight parameters in the network layer by layer, and improves the accuracy of the network through frequent iterative training. The low hidden layer of convolution neural network is composed of convolution layer and maximum pool sampling layer alternately.

3.2   Vector Quantizer

Vector quantization converts high-dimensional data into low-dimensional data by partitioning the original data into multiple clusters and representing each cluster

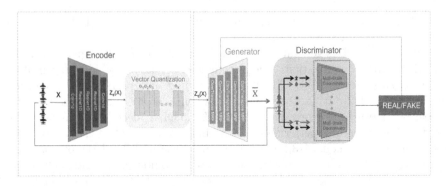

Fig. 1. The proposed multi-band multi-scale generative adversarial network for speech coding. The encoder is composed of conv1d and resnet1d convolutional blocks with relu activation function. In the vector quantization codebook matching, we utilize the combination of Euclidean distance and cosine similarity. For the generator, we employ the vocoder, and propose a multi-subband multi-scale STFT discriminator to improve the quality of reconstructed speech.

with a representative vector, thereby achieving data compression and simplification. In practical models, the quantizer receives latent variables from the encoder output and passes them through codebook matching to output indices fed into the decoder. Codebook matching is typically implemented using Euclidean distance, which measures the distance between two vectors to determine the cluster to which the vector belongs [25]. Specifically, in traditional vector quantization, the nearest neighbor method is used to calculate the Euclidean distance between the latent variable output of the encoder and several vectors in the codebook, using the vector with the smallest distance to represent the hidden vector's value, i.e.,

$$d(X,Y) = \sqrt{\sum_{i=1}^{n}(X_n - Y_n)^2}. \tag{1}$$

Thus, the vector quantization process using Euclidean distance requires selecting representative vectors, calculating distances, allocating vectors, and updating representative vectors to achieve a low-error representation of the high-dimensional vectors output by the encoder. However, for the feature vectors output by CNN encoders, the dimensions are often relatively high, and Euclidean distance, utilizing mean squared error for codebook matching, computes the difference between the dimensions of the two vectors, ultimately obtaining the vector with the smallest overall dimensional error as the quantized vector. When using Euclidean distance for codebook matching, local similarity between vector dimensions is not considered, often leading to significant errors in the local dimensions of the vector and, consequently, substantial quantization errors in codebook matching. Cosine similarity (Eq. 2) measures the similarity between two n-dimensional vectors by calculating the cosine value of the angle between them, with similarity determined by the relationship between the two vectors' directions, i.e.,

$$\cos(X, Y) = \frac{X \cdot Y}{|X||Y|} = \frac{\sum_{i=1}^{n} X_i Y_i}{\sqrt{\sum_{i=1}^{n} X_i^2} \sqrt{\sum_{i=1}^{n} Y_i^2}}. \tag{2}$$

During the codebook matching and training processes, we combined the advantages of Euclidean distance and cosine similarity by minimizing the weighted sum of the Euclidean distance and cosine similarity between the two vectors, enabling a more accurate codebook matching process. That is, the loss function for codebook matching is given by:

$$l = d(X, Y) + \alpha * (1 - \cos(X, Y)), \tag{3}$$

where α is an adjustable parameter. In our experiments, we determined the most suitable value of α through ablation studies to balance the importance of Euclidean distance and cosine similarity in the codebook matching process. The codebook selection process achieves global optimization of codebook matching by minimizing the loss l.

3.3   Generator

The decoder includes generator and discriminator. For the generator, we use the neural vocoder in HiFiGAN to decode the speech signal in the discrete representation. The generator first converts the quantized discrete representation into a continuous representation according to the lookup table (LUT) embedded in the discrete representation, and then uses the transposed convolution to upsample the representation to match the input sampling rate [17]. Each transposed convolution is followed by a residual block with an expansion layer to increase the receptive field and observe the patterns under different lengths in parallel. The lookup table (LUT) embedded with discrete representation and a series of blocks composed of transposed convolution and residual blocks with expansion layer. The transposed convolution upsamples the encoded representation to match the input sampling rate, while the expanded layer increases the receptive field.

3.4   Multi-Band Multi-Scale STFT Discriminator

In this paper, the multi-scale discriminator and multi-period discriminator in HiFiGAN [17] are used to realize the global high-quality discrimination of the reconstructed speech. At the same time, to address the problem of the local distortion of the spectrum amplitude of the reconstructed speech signal, a multi-subband multi-scale STFT discriminator that takes into account the global and local spectrum energy distortion is established. Multi-subband multi-scale STFT discriminator divides the speech waveform output by the generator into different sub-bands, and divides multi-scale [23] within the sub-band. In this paper, we use the PQMF (Pruned-Tree Quadrature Mirror Filter) technology [21] to divide the reconstructed speech and real speech into sub-bands. PQMF divides

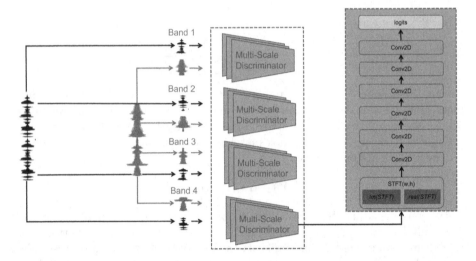

Fig. 2. Schematic diagram of multi-subband multi-scale STFT discriminator. We first divide the real speech sample and the reconstructed speech sample into sub-bands, and then conduct multi-scale STFT discrimination in the sub-band.

the signal into multiple sub-bands through filter banks, each with a certain frequency range, to achieve effective signal decomposition and reconstruction in the frequency domain. This facilitates subsequent processing, such as data compression, spectrum analysis, etc. The time-frequency mapping of sub-band encoding using PQMF technology is achieved through a filter bank containing multiple filters. After the speech signal of each sub-band passing through the convolution filter and the downsampling module, the modulated sub-band signal is obtained.

In the divided sub-band, we use multi-scale discriminator. Multi-scale STFT discriminator [18] is to fuse a group of discriminators with the same structure and different input speech sizes. Each discriminator consists of a network with the same structure. Multi-scale discriminator can capture more different structures in the speech signal, refine the speech synthesis frame, and improve the quality of speech synthesis. The input of each subnetwork is a complex STFT spliced by real and imaginary parts. The loss function of the discriminator is constructed as follows,

$$L_d(\boldsymbol{x}, \widehat{\boldsymbol{x}}) = \sum_{i=1}^{B} \left(\frac{1}{K} \sum_{k=1}^{K} \max\left(0, 1 - D_k(\boldsymbol{x})\right) + \max\left(0, 1 + D_k(\widehat{\boldsymbol{x}})\right) \right), \quad (4)$$

where B is the number of subbands and K is the number of discriminators in a single subband.

3.5   Training Objectives

Our training goal is to minimize the generation confrontation loss, Mel-spectrum loss, feature matching loss and quantization loss to obtain better reconstructed speech quality. The loss of reconstructed speech is defined as:

$$\mathcal{L}_{FM}(G; D) = \mathbb{E}_{(x,s)} \left[\sum_{i=1}^{T} \frac{1}{N_i} \left\| D^i(x) - D^i(G(s)) \right\|_1 \right]. \tag{5}$$

The Mel-spectrum loss is defined as:

$$\mathcal{L}_{Mel}(G) = \mathbb{E}_{(x,s)} \left[\|\phi(x) - \phi(G(s))\|_1 \right]. \tag{6}$$

The feature matching loss is defined as:

$$\mathcal{L}_{FM}(G; D) = \mathbb{E}_{(x,s)} \left[\sum_{i=1}^{T} \frac{1}{N_i} \left\| D^i(x) - D^i(G(s)) \right\|_1 \right], \tag{7}$$

which is used as the training loss of the generator to extract the intermediate features of the discriminator, and calculate the L1 distance between the real speech samples and the conditional generated samples in each feature space. The vector quantization loss is the distance between the quantized codebook and the pre-quantized codebook, which is defined as:

$$\mathcal{L}_{FM}(G; D) = \mathbb{E}_{(x,s)} \left[\sum_{i=1}^{T} \frac{1}{N_i} \left\| D^i(x) - D^i(G(s)) \right\|_1 \right]. \tag{8}$$

To sum up, the total loss function is defined as:

$$\mathcal{L}_G = \mathcal{L}_{Adv}(G; D) + \lambda_{fm}\mathcal{L}_{FM}(G; D) + \lambda_{mel}\mathcal{L}_{Mel}(G) + \lambda_w \mathcal{L}_w. \tag{9}$$

4   Experiment

4.1   Dataset and Evaluation Criteria

The dataset employed in our experiments is the classic CSTR-VCTK English speech dataset [19], which is created and maintained by the Centre for Speech Technology Research (CSTR) at the University of Edinburgh. The dataset comprises speech data from 109 native English speakers with various accents. The original sampling rate of the dataset is 44.1 kHz, and during the preprocessing stage, we downsampled it to 16 kHz. Additionally, in our experiments, we randomly selected audio samples from 12 speakers as the test set to eliminate the model's limitations in capturing speaker-specific timbres. For the remaining 97 speakers, we divided their speech data into training, validation, and test sets at a ratio of 7:1:2.

To compare the generated speech with the original speech quality, we employed subjective evaluation using the Mean Opinion Score (MOS) and objective evaluation using ViSQOL. In the subjective scoring process, we compared the subjective perception of the original speech corpus and the degraded speech corpus processed by different systems to obtain MOS scores and ultimately calculated the average value. The scoring range for both methods includes five levels: [1, 2, 3, 4, 5]. The quality of the reconstructed speech is directly proportional to the scores for both the subjective evaluation standard MOS and objective evaluation standard ViSQOL. Specifically, for the subjective evaluation method, a score of 1 represents severe pitch/timbre distortion accompanied by significant noise or buzz, a score of 2 indicates the presence of more serious distortions mentioned earlier, a score of 3 signifies average pitch/timbre distortion, a score of 4 denotes extremely slight distortion, and a score of 5 represents high-quality speech without any distortion.

4.2   Results

Improved VQ Results. In our experiment, according to the magnitude of cosine similarity and Euclidean distance, we initially set the weight of cosine similarity to 50, and then adjust it upward with a step rate of 25. The ViSQOL [20] objective score of the adjustment process is shown in the following table (Table 1):

Table 1. Results for different cosine similarity coefficients α.

parameter α	ViSQOL
50	2.28
75	2.29
100	2.33
125	2.31
150	2.29

It can be seen that when cosine similarity is used and the coefficient of cosine similarity is set to 100, higher reconstructed speech quality can be obtained (Table 2).

Multi-Band Multi-Scale STFT GAN. The experimental results using the multi-band multi-scale STFT discriminator are shown in the table below. For

Table 2. Comparison of ViSQOL scores after adding a multi-band multi-scale STFT discriminator to the baseline model.

Models	ViSQOL
VQ-VAE+HiFiGAN	2.24
VQVAE+HiFiGAN+MBMSD	2.40

Table 3. Results of ViSQOL and MOS comparison between our model and other models at 600 bps.

Models	ViSQOL	MOS
Opus [2]	2.18	2.43
Lyra [12]	2.24	3.47
AMR-WB [6]	2.21	2.88
Encodec [18]	2.71	3.35
VQ-VAE+HiFiGAN [22]	2.24	3.71
ours	2.41	3.90

the initial VQ-VAE combined with HiFiGAN model, the objective score ViSQOL value is 2.24. When the multi band multi-scale STFT discriminator is added, the objective score increases by 0.16.

Comparison with Other Models. In this work, we compared the reconstructed speech of our model with that of the state-of-the-art reference models: Lyra at a bitrate of 3.2 kbps, Opus at 6 kbps, AMR-WB at 4.75 kbps, Encodec at 6 kbps, and our baseline model VQVAE+HiFiGAN at 600 bps. Objective evaluation metrics ViSQOL and subjective evaluation metrics MOS were employed to assess the performance of these models. Specifically, we randomly selected reconstructed speech samples from eight untrained speakers and obtained 24 test speech samples for each of the seven models. Five listening test participants were invited to conduct subjective scoring tests, ultimately yielding our experimental results. The evaluation results are as follows (Table 3):

5 Conclusion

In this work, we propose an end-to-end speech coder that can achieve better reconstructed speech quality at extremely low bit rates. By combining Euclidean distance and cosine similarity for codebook matching, we can reduce the quantization error caused by Euclidean distance using mean square error for codebook matching. The proposed multi-band multi-scale generative adversarial network can take into account both the global and local distortion, and avoid the change of the frequency characteristics before and after the average speech and the loss of part of the spectrum characteristics when judging the whole spectrum. Compared with the most advanced Lyra, Opus, AMR-WB and Encodec, our work can achieve better reconstructed speech quality at very low rates. In the future, we will investigate approaches to reduce quantization errors and mitigate noise and timbre distortion issues at the current and even lower encoding bitrates. Simultaneously, we aim to decrease the number of parameters, enabling more efficient speech encoding at extremely low bitrates.

Acknowledgements. This work is supported by the Fundamental Research Funds for the Central Universities (No. 2042023kf1033), the National Natural Science Foundation of China (No. 62276195 and 62262026), and the project of Jiangxi Education Department (No. GJJ211111).

References

1. Rowe, D.: Codec 2-Open source speech coding at 2400 bits/s and below. In: TAPR and ARRL 30th Digital Communications Conference, pp. 80–84. Springer, Heidelberg (2011). https://doi.org/10.10007/1234567890

2. Moore, R.K., Skidmore, L.: On the use/misuse of the term "phoneme". In: Kubin , G., Kacic, Z., (eds.) Proc. INTERSPEECH 2019–20th Annual Conference of the International Speech Communication Association, Graz, Austria, Sep. 2019, LNCS, vol. 1234, pp. 2340–2344. Springer, Heidelberg (2019). https://doi.org/10.10007/1234567890

3. Dietz, M., et al.: Overview of the EVS codec architecture. In: 2015 IEEE International Conference on Acoustics, Speech and Signal Processing (ICASSP), pp. 5698–5702. IEEE, Heidelberg (2015). https://doi.org/10.10007/1234567890

4. Kleijn, W.B., et al.: Wavenet based low rate speech coding. In: 2018 IEEE International Conference on Acoustics, Speech and Signal Processing (ICASSP), pp. 676–680. IEEE, Heidelberg (2018). https://doi.org/10.10007/1234567890

5. van den Oord, A., et al.: WaveNet: a generative model for raw audio. arXiv preprint arXiv:1609.03499 (2016)

6. Bessette, B., et al.: The Adaptive Multirate Wideband Speech Codec (AMR-WB). IEEE Trans. Speech Audio Process. **10**(8), 620–636 (2002)

7. Lin, J., Kalgaonkar, K., He, Q., Lei, X.: Speech enhancement for low bit rate speech codec. In: ICASSP 2022–2022 IEEE International Conference on Acoustics, Speech and Signal Processing (ICASSP), pp. 7777–7781. IEEE (2022). https://doi.org/10.1109/ICASSP49725.2022.9414849

8. Skoglund, J., Valin, J.-M.: Improving Opus low bit rate quality with neural speech synthesis. arXiv preprint arXiv:1905.04628 (2019)

9. Valin, J.-M., Skoglund, J.: LPCNet: improving neural speech synthesis through linear prediction. In: ICASSP 2019–2019 IEEE International Conference on Acoustics, Speech and Signal Processing (ICASSP), pp. 5891–5895. IEEE (2019). https://doi.org/10.1109/ICASSP.2019.8682434

10. Mustafa, A., Büthe, J., Korse, S., Gupta, K., Fuchs, G., Pia, N.: A streamwise GAN vocoder for wideband speech coding at very low bit rate. In: 2021 IEEE Workshop on Applications of Signal Processing to Audio and Acoustics (WASPAA), pp. 66–70. IEEE (2021). https://doi.org/10.1109/WASPAA51851.2021.9583419

11. Mustafa, A., Pia, N., Fuchs, G.: StylemelGAN: an efficient high-fidelity adversarial vocoder with temporal adaptive normalization. In: ICASSP 2021–2021 IEEE International Conference on Acoustics, Speech and Signal Processing (ICASSP), pp. 6034–6038. IEEE (2021). https://doi.org/10.1109/ICASSP39728.2021.9413884

12. Kleijn, W.B., et al.: Generative speech coding with predictive variance regularization. In: ICASSP 2021–2021 IEEE International Conference on Acoustics, Speech and Signal Processing (ICASSP), pp. 6478–6482. IEEE (2021). https://doi.org/10.1109/ICASSP39728.2021.9413897

13. Zeghidour, N., Luebs, A., Omran, A., Skoglund, J., Tagliasacchi, M.: SoundStream: an end-to-end neural audio codec. IEEE/ACM Trans. Audio Speech Lang. Process. **30** 495–507 (2021)

14. LeBlanc, W.P., Bhattacharya, B., Mahmoud, S.A., Cuperman, V.: Efficient search and design procedures for robust multi-stage VQ of LPC parameters for 4 kb/s speech coding. IEEE Trans. Speech Audio Process. **1**(4), 373–385 (1993)

15. Giannella, C.R.: Instability results for Euclidean distance, nearest neighbor search on high dimensional Gaussian data. Inf. Process. Lett. **169**, 106115 (2021)

16. van den Oord, A., Vinyals, O., et al.: Neural discrete representation learning. In: Advances in Neural Information Processing Systems 30 (2017)

17. Kong, J., Kim, J., Bae, J.: HiFi-GAN: generative adversarial networks for efficient and high fidelity speech synthesis. Adv. Neural. Inf. Process. Syst. **33**, 17022–17033 (2020)

18. D'efossez, A., Copet, J., Synnaeve, G., Adi, Y.: High fidelity neural audio compression. arXiv preprint arXiv:2210.13438 (2022)

19. Veaux, C., Yamagishi, J., MacDonald, K., et al.: CSTR VCTK corpus: English multi-speaker corpus for CSTR voice cloning toolkit. University of Edinburgh, The Centre for Speech Technology Research (CSTR) (2017)

20. Hines, A., Skoglund, J., Kokaram, A.C., Harte, N.: ViSQOL: an objective speech quality model. EURASIP J. Audio Speech Music Process. **2015**(1), 1–18 (2015)

21. Princen, J., Bradley, A.: Analysis/synthesis filter bank design based on time domain aliasing cancellation. IEEE Trans. Acoust. Speech Signal Process. **34**(5), 1153–1161 (1986)

22. Polyak, A., et al.: Speech resynthesis from discrete disentangled self-supervised representations. arXiv preprint arXiv:2104.00355 (2021)

23. Zhang, J., Tao, D.: FAMED-Net: a fast and accurate multi-scale end-to-end dehazing network. IEEE Trans. Image Process. **29**, 72–84 (2019)

24. Yang, Q., Luo, Y., Hu, H., Zhou, X., Du, B., Tao, D.: Robust metric boosts transfer. In: 2022 IEEE 24th International Workshop on Multimedia Signal Processing (MMSP), pp. 1–6 (2022)

25. Zhan, Y., Yu, J., Yu, Z., Zhang, R., Tao, D., Tian, Q.: Comprehensive distance-preserving autoencoders for cross-modal retrieval. In: Proceedings of the 26th ACM International Conference on Multimedia, pp. 1137–1145 (2018)

OWS-Seg: Online Weakly Supervised Video Instance Segmentation via Contrastive Learning

Yuanxiang Ning[1], Fei Li[1], Mengping Dong[1], and Zhenbo Li[1,2,3,4(✉)]

[1] College of Information and Electrical Engineering,
China Agricultural University, Beijing 100083, China
{ningyuanxiang,leefly072,dongmengping,lizb}@cau.edu.cn
[2] National Innovation Center for Digital Fishery,
Ministry of Agriculture and Rural Affairs, Beijing 100083, China
[3] Key Laboratory of Smart Farming Technologies for Aquatic Animal and Livestock,
Ministry of Agriculture and Rural Affairs, Beijing 100083, China
[4] Key Laboratory of Agricultural Information Acquisition Technology,
Ministry of Agriculture and Rural Affairs, Beijing 100083, China

Abstract. Video Instance Segmentation (VIS) aims to detect, segment, and track instances appearing in a video. To reduce annotation costs, some existing VIS methods use the Weakly Supervised Scheme (WSVIS). However, those WSVIS methods usually run in an offline manner, which fails in handling ongoing and long videos due to the limited computational resources. It would be considerable benefits if online models could match or surpass the performance of offline models. In this paper, we propose OWS-Seg, an end-to-end, simple, and efficient online WSVIS network with box annotations. Concretely, OWS-Seg consists of two novel contrastive learning branches: the Instance Contrastive Learning (ICL) branch learns instance level discriminative features to distinguish different instances in each frame, and the Mask Contrastive Learning (MCL) branch with Boxccam learns pixel level discriminative features to differentiate foreground and background. Experimental results show that OWS-Seg achieves promising performance, e.g., 43.5% AP on YouTube-VIS 2019, 36.6% AP on YouTube-VIS 2021, and 21.9% AP on OVIS. Besides, OWS-Seg achieves comparable performance to offline WSVIS and surpasses recent fully supervised methods, demonstrating its wide range of practical applications.

Keywords: Weakly supervised · Video instance segmentation · Contrastive learning

1 Introduction

Video Instance Segmentation (VIS) has drawn substantial interest in the computer vision community and is widely used in many areas such as augmented

L. Iliadis et al. (Eds.): ICANN 2023, LNCS 14260, pp. 476–488, 2023.
https://doi.org/10.1007/978-3-031-44195-0_39

reality, autonomous driving, and video editing [10,25,26]. However, constructing datasets for VIS, need video mask annotations. According to BBam [8], it takes approximately 4 min to label a pixel-level mask for an image with an average of 2.8 objects. Annotation for VIS renders the task exceedingly labor-intensive. In contrast, labeling class labels take around 20 s, and box annotations take about 38.1 s [8]. Since class and box annotations are much faster to obtain compared to mask annotations [17], Weakly Supervised VIS (WSVIS) methods utilized class or box annotations instead of mask annotations to obtain pixel-wise mask sequences of instances. Although WSVIS methods have shown great potential for VIS, they typically focus on offline methods that generate the entire video masks in a single step by taking the whole video as input. It needs huge computer resources and fails to handle real-time tasks, which impedes extending them to other application scenarios. In contrast, the online method avoids the aforementioned issues by processing the input video frame by frame.

A crucial observation is that two pixels exhibiting similar color characteristics are also probable to pertain to the same instance [17]. The experiment, following [17], denotes a simple color feature that can directly distinguish foreground and background with 96% correct rate, shown in Fig. 1. It is reasonable to assume that more discriminative features enable better segmentation and distinguishing between different instances. Therefore, discrim-

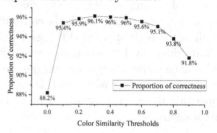

Fig. 1. Enlightening experiments on Youtube-VIS 2019 training sets.

inative features can directly locate the same instance in different frames. An intuition question arises: *could we design an online WSVIS method with discriminative features?*

To answer the above question, we propose a novel WSVIS method that uses box annotations via contrastive learning. Specifically, a novel contrastive learning scheme to obtain discriminative features, which consists of Instance Contrastive Learning (ICL) and Mask Contrastive Learning (MCL). The ICL utilizes instance level discriminative features to ensure that instances are similar across frames when they are the same, and distinct from other instances in all frames, even those exhibiting similar appearances and belonging to the same classification. And MCL learns pixel level discriminative features to widen the gap between foreground and background. The OWS-Seg is evaluated on the YouTube-VIS 2019, YouTube-VIS 2021, and OVIS benchmarks to verify its effectiveness. The main contributions of our study can be summarized in the following points:

- We propose an Online WSVIS model with box annotations, dubbed OWS-Seg, that can train end-to-end without complex model design.
- A novel ICL forms contrastive learning between different instances to learn instance level discriminative features for association instances across frames.

- The MCL utilizes a novel Boxccam to form contrastive learning between foreground and background, learning pixel level discriminative features for segmenting.
- OWS-Seg sets a SOTA Online WSVIS method, achieving 43.5 AP on the validation sets of YouTube-VIS 2019, 36.6 AP on YouTube-VIS 2021, and 21.9 AP on OVIS. We achieve comparable performance to offline WSVIS even surpassing some recent fully supervised methods.

2   Related Works

Fully Supervised Video Instance Segmentation (FVIS). Currently, FVIS can be divided into online and offline methods. Online methods process each frame considering only previous frames. CrossVIS [26] used cross-learning to obtain instance features to improve segmentation. IDOL [21] employed contrastive learning to obtain the mask of discriminative features to associate instances. And offline methods can enrich contextual information by referring to all adjacent frames. VisTR [18] is the first method that uses Transformer to obtain video-level masks and tracks with full video input. VITA [5] associates video with frame processing and designs a new offline paradigm. However, FVIS requires annotating with mask labels, which needs a lot of labeling effort. To solve this issue, we proposed a novel box supervision method instead of mask annotations.

Weakly Supervised Video Instance Segmentation (WSVIS). Getting mask annotations is very expensive. Compared to images [8,17], WSVIS has developed more slowly. MaskConsist [13] is only supervised by class labels and trains an optical flow model to associate instances, which needs input whole video or clip. Although the cost of labeling is reduced, accuracy is difficult to meet expectations. STC-seg [24] is designed for box supervision to improve accuracy by acquiring pseudo-labels with an unsupervised depth estimation module and an optical flow module. However, both MaskConsist and STC-seg suffer from high complexity and are hard to train as a whole. SOLOTrack [2] trains on image instance segmentation with mask annotations and then only tests on the videos whose categories overlap with COCO to reduce video annotation, which limits its application. MaskFree [7] utilizes box annotations to reduce the cost of labeling in an offline way, it brings forth the Temporal KNN-patch Loss (TK-Loss), utilizing the abundant temporal mask consistency constraints found within videos. In contrast, Our OWS-Seg explores contrastive learning [9] to design an *end-to-end* and *online* method with box annotations for WSVIS.

3   Methodology

3.1   Overview

The comprehensive network structure of OWS-Seg is depicted in Fig. 2. The inputs are a key frame and a reference frame selected from the key frame's temporal vicinity. The shared-weight encoder of Deformable DETR [28] maps key

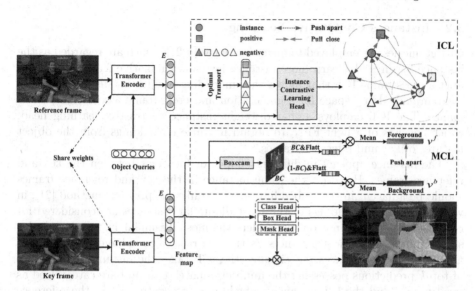

Fig. 2. The training network structure of the OWS-Seg. Instances embeddings sharing the same color belong to the same instance. In ICL, the instance embeddings of Reference frame are processed to get the positive and negative embedding. C: the channel of features; BC: the output of Boxccam, denotes the foreground activative map; Flatt: matrix flattening; Mean: average in channel dimension; $\otimes$:matrix multiplication; w: the parameter of mask head.

and reference frames and object queries to feature map and instance embedding, respectively. After that, the instances embeddings of the key frame are decoded into class labels, box coordinates, and parameters ω of the mask head, separately. And mask head employed the parameters ω utilizes feature map F_{mask} that is 1/8 resolution of input to produce the output mask m:

$$m = \text{MaskHead}(F_{mask}, \omega). \tag{1}$$

For each ground truth instance, ICL constructs embedding of different instances pairs to form contrastive learning loss $\mathcal{L}_{embed_i}$. Moreover, Boxccam and F_{mask} are used in MCL to get the features of foreground and background from the feature map. Then MCL utilizes those features to construct $\mathcal{L}_{embed\_fb}$ to learn pixel level discriminative features. Finally, the entire model is optimized with the following loss function:

$$\mathcal{L} = \mathcal{L}_{cls} + \lambda_1 \mathcal{L}_{box} + \lambda_2 \mathcal{L}_{embed\_i} + \lambda_3 \mathcal{L}_{embed\_fb}, \tag{2}$$

where λ_1, λ_2, and λ_3 are weight of loss. The $\mathcal{L}_{cls}$ denotes a Focal loss [12]. The $\mathcal{L}_{box}$ is is an amalgamation of $\mathcal{L}_1$ loss and the generalized IoU loss [16]. The $\mathcal{L}_{embed\_i}$ and $\mathcal{L}_{embed\_fb}$ are the contrastive losses that are shown in the following section.

3.2   Instances Contrastive Learning

Object queries are employed to query instances [6,21], which are regarded as the instance features. To learn more instance level discriminative features, we conduct a cross-frame ICL that moves the embedding of different instances further away in embedding space for segmentation and cross-frame association performance. The ICL employs a shared-weight instance contrastive learning head, which consists of a light FFN, to obtain instance embeddings from the object features of key and reference frames.

The instance appears in different shapes or locations between the key and reference frames. However, the same instance in the key and reference frames should be adjacent in the embedding space. Unlike the previous method [21], in which only the embeddings of the most dissimilar instances are considered for contrastive. Our ICL not only considers the most dissimilar instances but also similar but not identical instances as the contrastive to enlarge the difference among different instances. Specifically, the ICL takes the instance embeddings of top k predictions possessing the minimum match cost and are categorized as positive k^+, and the left instance embeddings as negative k^- in the reference frame. This match cost is obtained by matching the predicted categories and boxes with the ground truth. And the value of k is dynamically determined using the optimal transport method [3]. Finally, the ICL introduces a loss function $\mathcal{L}_{embed\_i}$ for positive pairs, which is defined as follows:

$$
\begin{aligned}
\mathcal{L}_{embed\_i} &= -\log \frac{\exp(\mathbf{n} \cdot \mathbf{k}^+)}{\exp(\mathbf{n} \cdot \mathbf{k}^+) + \sum_{\mathbf{k}^-} \exp(\mathbf{n} \cdot \mathbf{k}^-)} \\
&= \log[1 + \sum_{\mathbf{k}^-} \exp(\mathbf{n} \cdot \mathbf{k}^- - \mathbf{n} \cdot \mathbf{k}^+)]
\end{aligned}
\tag{3}
$$

We augment Eq. 3 to accommodate multiple positive scenarios:

$$
\mathcal{L}_{embed\_i} = \log[1 + \sum_{\mathbf{k}^+} \sum_{\mathbf{k}^-} \exp(\mathbf{n} \cdot \mathbf{k}^- - \mathbf{n} \cdot \mathbf{k}^+)].
\tag{4}
$$

where $\mathbf{n}$ is the instance embeddings from the key frame. $\mathbf{k}^+$ and $\mathbf{k}^-$ represent the embeddings of positive and negative instances from the reference frame, respectively.

3.3   Mask Contrastive Learning

The MCL aims to learn the difference at the pixel level between foreground and background to get pixel level discriminative features. It conducts the contrast between pixel features of foreground and background from the feature map. However, differentiating the foreground from the background becomes arduous when there is an absence of pixel-level labels during the training phase. Previous methods typically depend on a Class-agnostiC Activate Map (CCAM) [22] to derive the region of the foreground objects, and the remaining part is the background. However, the predicted foreground region contains some non-foreground

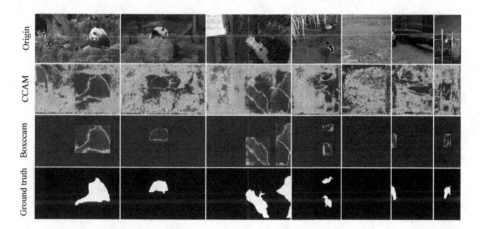

Fig. 3. Visualization of Boxccam. For each image, the first row is the original image, the second row is the output of CCAM [22], the third row is the output of Boxccam, and the final row is the ground truth mask annotations. Boxccam can provide more precise localization. Best viewed in color. (Color figure online)

region, as shown in Fig. 3. This leads to bad performance as shown in Table 6. In contrast, our MCL proposes Boxccam to limit the predicted foreground regions in the ground truth box area. Our *Boxccam* consists of a 3×3 convolution with a batch normalization layer, which aims to activate the foreground regions with guidance from ground truth boxes. We fed feature maps and ground truth boxes into Boxccam. The feature map is subjected to Boxccam to obtain the activated map of the foreground, and the area outside the ground truth boxes becomes the background, as illustrated in Fig. 3. The Boxccam output is defined as BC, and the feature map F_{mask}. The MCL takes the feature of $BC \times F_{mask}$ as foreground features v^f and the feature of $(1 - BC) \times F_{mask}$ as background features v^b. Then, the MCL introduces a loss function $\mathcal{L}_{embed\_fb}$:

$$\mathcal{L}_{embed\_fb} = -\log(1 - \text{sim}(v^f, v^b)), \tag{5}$$

where $\text{sim}(v^f, v^b)$ is the cosine similarity between v^f and v^b. In this way, MCL can learn discriminative features to segment instances.

4   Experiments

4.1   Datasets and Evaluation Metrics

We conduct experiments on YouTube-VIS 2019 [25] and YouTube-VIS 2021 [23], and OVIS [15] with only box annotations. YouTube-VIS 2019 is the first benchmark dataset for video instance segmentation. It contains 2,238 training videos, 302 validation videos, and 343 high-resolution test videos. YouTube-VIS 2021 contains a total of 3,859 videos, including 2,985 for training, 421 for validation,

Fig. 4. Visualization of OWS-Seg on the YouTube-VIS 2019. Each row represents different frames within the same video. For each video, instances are indicated by masks of the same color. Best viewed in color. (Color figure online)

and 453 for testing. The category label sets of both datasets are slightly different, although both have 40 categories. OVIS is another challenging VIS dataset that focuses on scenarios of objects with heavy occlusions that are belonging to 25 categories. Meanwhile, the longest video of OVIS is around 50 s which is much longer than that of YouTube-VIS. And the instances with the same categories have almost similar appearances, thus previous approaches show relatively low accuracy. We report standard metrics for Average Precision (AP) and Average Recall (AR), with the video Intersection over Union (IoU) of the mask sequences as the threshold, such as $AP, AP_{50}, AP_{75}, AR_1$, and AR_{10}.

4.2   Implementation Details

Model Settings. Our OWS-Seg builds upon IDOL [21] implemented with PyTorch. The loss weights λ_1, λ_2, and λ_3 are set to 1.0, 2.0, and 1.0. We employ ResNet-50 [4] as the backbone unless otherwise specified. The OWS-Seg utilizes the same setting for the dynamic mask head, and only uses the instance embeddings to associate instance cross-frames [21].

Training. The model is trained with AdamW [14] optimizer of base learning rate being 1×10^{-4}. The OWS-Seg is initialized with IDOL weights pre-trained on COCO. Then the OWS-Seg is trained for 18000 iterations on the respective training set, with the learning rate decaying by a factor of 10 after 10000 iterations. For YouTube-VIS 2019 and YouTube-VIS 2021 datasets, the input frames are downsampled and randomly cropped to ensure that the longest side is no more than 768 pixels. The model is trained on two V100 GPUs with 32G RAM each, using a batch size of 8. For the OVIS dataset, we resize the input images such that the shortest side is between 480 and 800 pixels, while the longest side

Table 1. The comparison of results on Youtube-VIS2019 validation sets. supr. means the manner of supervision. The IDOL+BoxInst denotes IDOL uses the loss function of BoxInst [17] to train without mask annotations.

Methods	Type	supr.	AP	AP_{50}	AP_{75}	AR_1	AR_{10}
Fully supervised							
IFC [6]	offline	mask	42.8	65.8	46.8	43.8	51.2
Seqformer [20]	offline	mask	47.4	69.8	51.8	45.5	54.8
SipMask [1]	online	mask	32.5	53.0	33.3	35.4	40.1
CrossVIS [26]	online	mask	36.3	56.8	38.9	35.6	40.7
EfficientVIS [19]	online	mask	37.9	59.7	43.0	40.3	46.6
Hybrid [11]	online	mask	41.3	61.5	43.5	42.7	47.8
Weakly supervised							
MaskConsist [13]	offline	class	10.5	27.2	6.2	12.3	13.6
STC-seg [24]	offline	box	31.0	52.4	33.2	32.9	36.2
MaskFree [7]	offline	box	43.8	70.7	46.9	41.5	52.3
IDOL+BoxInst(ours)	online	box	8.7	33.7	2.9	10.6	13.9
SoloTrack [2]	online	-	30.6	50.7	33.5	31.6	37.1
OWS-Seg(ours)	online	box	**43.5**	**71.0**	**46.9**	**41.4**	**50.3**

is at most 1,333 pixels. The model is trained with each GPU processes 2 pairs of frames simultaneously.

Inference. During the inference phase, for YouTube-VIS 2019, YouTube-VIS 2021, and OVIS datasets, the input frames are downscaled according to the method used in previous work. OWS-Seg utilizes a memory bank to store embeddings of appeared instances. When OWS-Seg processes the current frame, it calculates embedding similarity, from [21], with those in the memory bank to associate instances. For predictions with high classification scores but low similarity, a new instance embedding is stored in the memory bank. Notably, ICL and MCL are not used for generating results.

4.3 Main Results

We evaluate the performance of OWS-Seg against current state-of-the-art weakly supervised and fully supervised VIS methods on the validation sets of YouTube-VIS 2019, YouTube-VIS 2021, and OVIS datasets, while the test sets cannot be obtained. The results are presented in Tables 1, 2, and 3, respectively. Notably, the OWS-Seg demonstrates a remarkable improvement over all previous online weakly supervised methods, achieving a minimum of 12.5% higher AP. Additionally, the OWS-Seg also outperforms most mainstream fully supervised methods, which proves our effectiveness on WSVIS. In general, our method represents

Table 2. Comparison on YouTube-VIS 2021 validation sets.

Methods	Type	supr.	AP	AP_{50}	AP_{75}	AR_1	AR_{10}
Fully supervised							
IFC [6]	offline	mask	36.6	57.9	39.3	–	–
Seqformer [20]	offline	mask	40.5	62.4	43.7	36.1	48.1
SipMask [1]	online	mask	31.7	52.5	34.0	30.8	37.8
CrossVIS [26]	online	mask	34.2	54.4	37.9	30.4	38.2
Hybrid [11]	online	mask	35.8	56.3	39.1	33.6	40.3
Weakly supervised							
MaskFree [7]	offline	box	37.2	61.9	40.3	35.3	46.1
IDOL+BoxInst(ours)	online	box	7.3	25.8	1.8	8.3	11.7
OWS-Seg(ours)	online	box	**36.6**	**64.2**	**37.1**	**33.3**	**45.2**

Table 3. Comparison on OVIS validation sets.

Methods	Type	supr.	AP	AP_{50}	AP_{75}	AR_1	AR_{10}
Fully supervised							
IFC [6]	offline	mask	13.1	27.8	11.6	9.4	23.9
VITA [5]	offline	mask	19.6	41.2	17.4	11.7	26.0
SipMask [1]	online	mask	10.2	24.7	7.8	7.9	15.8
CrossVIS [26]	online	mask	14.9	32.7	12.1	10.3	19.8
TeViT [27]	online	mask	17.4	34.9	15.0	11.2	21.8
Weakly supervised							
MaskFree [7]	offline	box	15.7	35.1	13.1	10.1	20.4
IDOL+BoxInst(ours)	online	box	2.5	11.1	0.4	2.3	6.6
OWS-Seg(ours)	online	box	**21.9**	**43.4**	**21.2**	**12.1**	**30.4**

a straightforward yet powerful WSVIS method. Figure 4 showcases qualitative results on sample videos from the YouTube-VIS dataset, illustrating the efficacy of our method. Here is a detailed analysis of the performance:

YouTube-VIS 2019. OWS-Seg achieves a significant improvement with at least 12.9% AP over online weakly supervised methods. Moreover, it surpasses the SOTA offline WSVIS method over 0.3% AP_{50} and even outperforms most recent fully supervised methods. That experiment demonstrates the effectiveness of OWS-Seg, shown in Table 1.

YouTube-VIS 2021. Table 2 demonstrates OWS-Seg achieves 36.6% AP, which is SOTA online WSVIS and competitive performance with offline WSVIS and fully supervised methods. Moreover, OWS-Seg outperforms the offline

Table 4. The ablation experiment on ICL and MCL.

ICL	MCL	AP	AP$_{50}$	AP$_{75}$	AR$_1$	AR$_{10}$
		14.7	32.9	11.1	17.7	22.3
✓		41.5	69.5	43.3	40.4	49.4
✓	✓	**43.5**	**71.0**	**46.9**	**41.4**	**50.3**

Table 5. The extended experiment on ICL. The CS indicates the strategy of contrastive learning.

CS	AP	AP$_{50}$	AP$_{75}$	AR$_1$	AR$_{10}$
IDOL	37.6	62.6	39.1	38.8	46.4
ICL	**41.5**	**69.5**	**43.3**	**40.4**	**49.4**

Table 6. The ablation experiment on Boxccam in MCL.

MCL	AP	AP$_{50}$	AP$_{75}$	AR$_1$	AR$_{10}$
CCAM	22.1	58.3	11.4	22.7	29.1
Boxccam	**43.5**	**71.0**	**46.9**	**41.4**	**50.3**

Table 7. Impact of the number k in ICL. Experiments show that k being 10 is the best setting.

k	AP	AP$_{50}$	AP$_{75}$	AR$_1$	AR$_{10}$
5	35.1	63.4	33.7	36.3	44.5
6	37.1	67.8	37.5	38.2	45.8
7	41.4	68.7	42.9	39.7	48.8
8	38.4	66.8	39.1	39.1	48.0
9	38.6	64.0	38.7	38.8	47.0
10	**41.5**	**69.5**	**43.3**	**40.4**	**49.4**
11	39.4	68.4	39.4	38.3	47.3
12	36.0	62.8	36.1	36.8	45.0
15	33.4	63.0	31.4	34.6	42.1

WSVIS method by 2.3% AP$_{50}$, which shows well segmentation ability. The experiments indicate the capability of OWS-Seg to handle the challenge of weakly supervised.

OVIS. We validate the competitiveness of OWS-Seg on the OVIS validation set as shown in Table 3. The OWS-Seg achieves 21.9% AP with box annotations, surpassing recent online and offline WSIVS over at least 6.2% AP, and even fully supervised methods. This shows that instance level and pixel level discriminative features still have good performance in complex scenes. This is likely due to the fact that these features capture detailed and precise information about the object instances, enabling better discrimination between different instances and improving object tracking and segmentation accuracy.

4.4 Ablation Studies

To understand the contributions of the proposed components, we conduct extensive ablation experiments on YouTube-VIS 2019.

Instance Contrastive Learning. To evaluate the importance of ICL, we compare not use of ICL. The ICL greatly improves by 26.8% on AP, which can prove the discriminative feature is helpful, shown in Table 4. Furthermore, we compare the similar contrastive strategy from the previous SOTA FVIS method IDOL [21], shown in Table 5. The ICL outperforms the IDOL by 3.9% AP which can prove the effectiveness of our ICL. To explore the numbers of positive instance embedding that affect the performance of ICL, we conduct the ablation experiment of the different k, as shown in Table 7. According to the result, we found that when k is small, the negative instance embeddings include similar ground truth instances. When k is large, the positive instance embeddings have the wrong instance embedding. In conclusion, ICL can learn instance level discriminative features for WSVIS.

Mask Contrastive Learning. The MCL further performs better on the AP by 2.0% in Table 4, which demonstrates MCL enables the model to differentiate between foreground and background on a pixel level, thereby improving segmentation. Furthermore, to confirm the efficiency of Boxccam, we perform a comparative analysis to CCAM [22] which is a popular module for segmentation foreground without mask-label, shown in Table 6. The results show that Boxccam can better segment than CCAM by 21.4% AP. This indicates that Boxccam can provide more guidance information from box annotations than CCAM during the training process.

5   Conclusion

In this paper, we reconsider the approach to weak supervision in VIS tasks and proposed a novel online weakly supervised video instance segmentation with a box supervision scheme (OWS-Seg). More specifically, a new ICL is proposed to learn the instance level discriminative features, the novel MCL with Boxccam can accurately locate the foreground and utilize the features of foreground and background to learn pixel level discriminative features. Through the experiment, we showcase that OWS-Seg considerably improves the performance in VIS without utilizing the pixel label annotations. Even in difficult datasets OVIS, OWS-Seg surpasses all online and offline WSVIS methods by 6.2% AP and outperforms most fully supervised work. Due to the accumulation of frame level labeling errors in the video, there are still some gaps between our model and the SOTA fully supervised VIS methods, which is the direction of our further research. We believe that the idea of our model can inspire future work.

Acknowledgements. The authors gratefully acknowledge the financial support from the National Key R&D Program of China (No.2021ZD0113805, No.2020YFD0900204), and the Key Research and Development Plan Project of Guangdong Province(No.2020B0202010009). We appreciate the seminar participants' comments at the Center for Deep Learning of Computer Vision Research at China Agricultural University, making the manuscript improve significantly.

References

1. Cao, J., Anwer, R.M., Cholakkal, H., Khan, F.S., Pang, Y., Shao, L.: SipMask: spatial information preservation for fast image and video instance segmentation. In: Vedaldi, A., Bischof, H., Brox, T., Frahm, J.-M. (eds.) ECCV 2020. LNCS, vol. 12359, pp. 1–18. Springer, Cham (2020). https://doi.org/10.1007/978-3-030-58568-6_1

2. Fu, Y., Liu, S., Iqbal, U., De Mello, S., Shi, H., Kautz, J.: Learning to track instances without video annotations. In: Proceedings of the IEEE/CVF Conference on Computer Vision and Pattern Recognition, pp. 8680–8689 (2021)

3. Ge, Z., Liu, S., Li, Z., Yoshie, O., Sun, J.: OTA: optimal transport assignment for object detection. In: Proceedings of the IEEE/CVF Conference on Computer Vision and Pattern Recognition, pp. 303–312 (2021)

4. He, K., Zhang, X., Ren, S., Sun, J.: Deep residual learning for image recognition. In: Proceedings of the IEEE conference on Computer Vision and Pattern Recognition, pp. 770–778 (2016)

5. Heo, M., Hwang, S., Oh, S.W., Lee, J.Y., Kim, S.J.: VITA: video instance segmentation via object token association. In: Advances in Neural Information Processing Systems (2022)

6. Hwang, S., Heo, M., Oh, S.W., Kim, S.J.: Video instance segmentation using interframe communication transformers. Adv. Neural. Inf. Process. Syst. **34**, 13352–13363 (2021)

7. Ke, L., Danelljan, M., Ding, H., Tai, Y.W., Tang, C.K., Yu, F.: Mask-free video instance segmentation. In: Proceedings of the IEEE/CVF Conference on Computer Vision and Pattern Recognition (2023)

8. Lee, J., Yi, J., Shin, C., Yoon, S.: BBAM: bounding box attribution map for weakly supervised semantic and instance segmentation. In: Proceedings of the IEEE/CVF conference on Computer Vision and Pattern Recognition, pp. 2643–2652 (2021)

9. Li, F., Shen, L., Mi, Y., Li, Z.: DRCNet: dynamic image restoration contrastive network. In: Avidan, S., Brostow, G., Cisse, M., Farinella, G.M., Hassner, T. (eds.) Computer Vision – ECCV 2022. ECCV 2022. LNCS, vol. 13679. Springer, Cham (2022). https://doi.org/10.1007/978-3-031-19800-7_30

10. Li, F., Zhang, L., Lei, J., Liu, Z., Li, Z.: Multi-frequency representation enhancement with privilege information for video super-resolution. In: Proceedings of the IEEE/CVF International Conference on Computer Vision (2023)

11. Li, X., Wang, J., Li, X., Lu, Y.: Hybrid instance-aware temporal fusion for online video instance segmentation. In: Proceedings of the AAAI Conference on Artificial Intelligence, vol. 36, pp. 1429–1437 (2022)

12. Lin, T.Y., Goyal, P., Girshick, R., He, K., Dollár, P.: Focal loss for dense object detection. In: Proceedings of the IEEE International Conference on Computer Vision, pp. 2980–2988 (2017)

13. Liu, Q., Ramanathan, V., Mahajan, D., Yuille, A., Yang, Z.: Weakly supervised instance segmentation for videos with temporal mask consistency. In: Proceedings of the IEEE/CVF Conference on Computer Vision and Pattern Recognition, pp. 13968–13978 (2021)

14. Loshchilov, I., Hutter, F.: Decoupled weight decay regularization. arXiv preprint arXiv:1711.05101 (2017)

15. Qi, J., et al.: Occluded video instance segmentation: a benchmark. In: IJCV (2022)

16. Rezatofighi, H., Tsoi, N., Gwak, J., Sadeghian, A., Reid, I., Savarese, S.: Generalized intersection over union: a metric and a loss for bounding box regression. In: Proceedings of the IEEE/CVF Conference on Computer Vision and Pattern Recognition (2019)

17. Tian, Z., Shen, C., Wang, X., Chen, H.: BoxInst: high-performance instance segmentation with box annotations. In: Proceedings of the IEEE/CVF Conference on Computer Vision and Pattern Recognition, pp. 5443–5452 (2021)

18. Wang, Y., et al.: End-to-end video instance segmentation with transformers. In: Proceedings of the IEEE/CVF Conference on Computer Vision and Pattern Recognition, pp. 8741–8750 (2021)

19. Wu, J., Yarram, S., Liang, H., Lan, T., Medioni, G.: Efficient video instance segmentation via tracklet query and proposal. In: Proceedings of the IEEE/CVF Conference on Computer Vision and Pattern Recognition, pp. 959–968 (2022)

20. Wu, J., Jiang, Y., Bai, S., Zhang, W., Bai, X.: SeqFormer: sequential transformer for video instance segmentation. In: Avidan, S., Brostow, G., Cissé, M., Farinella, G.M., Hassner, T. (eds.) Computer Vision – ECCV 2022. ECCV 2022. LNCS, vol. 13688. Springer, Cham (2022). https://doi.org/10.1007/978-3-031-19815-1_32

21. Wu, J., Liu, Q., Jiang, Y., Bai, S., Yuille, A., Bai, X.: In defense of online models for video instance segmentation. In: Avidan, S., Brostow, G., Cissé, M., Farinella, G.M., Hassner, T. (eds.) Computer Vision – ECCV 2022. ECCV 2022. LNCS, vol. 13688. Springer, Cham (2022). https://doi.org/10.1007/978-3-031-19815-1_34

22. Xie, J., Xiang, J., Chen, J., Hou, X., Zhao, X., Shen, L.: C2AM: contrastive learning of class-agnostic activation map for weakly supervised object localization and semantic segmentation. In: Proceedings of the IEEE/CVF Conference on Computer Vision and Pattern Recognition, pp. 989–998 (2022)

23. Xu, N., et al.: Youtubevis dataset 2021 version (2022)

24. Yan, L., Wang, Q., Ma, S., Wang, J., Yu, C.: Solve the puzzle of instance segmentation in videos: a weakly supervised framework with spatio-temporal collaboration. IEEE Trans. Circuits Syst. Video Technol. **32**, 393–406 (2022)

25. Yang, L., Fan, Y., Xu, N.: Video instance segmentation. In: Proceedings of the IEEE/CVF International Conference on Computer Vision, pp. 5188–5197 (2019)

26. Yang, S., et al.: Crossover learning for fast online video instance segmentation. In: Proceedings of the IEEE/CVF International Conference on Computer Vision, pp. 8043–8052 (2021)

27. Yang, S., et al.: Temporally efficient vision transformer for video instance segmentation. In: Proceedings of the IEEE/CVF Conference on Computer Vision and Pattern Recognition, pp. 2885–2895 (2022)

28. Zhu, X., Su, W., Lu, L., Li, B., Wang, X., Dai, J.: Deformable DETR: deformable transformers for end-to-end object detection. In: International Conference on Learning Representations (2020)

Replay to Remember: Continual Layer-Specific Fine-Tuning for German Speech Recognition

Theresa Pekarek Rosin[(✉)] and Stefan Wermter

Knowledge Technology, Department of Informatics, University of Hamburg,
Vogt-Koelln-Str. 30, 22527 Hamburg, Germany
{theresa.pekarek-rosin,stefan.wermter}@uni-hamburg.de
http://www.knowledge-technology.info

Abstract. While Automatic Speech Recognition (ASR) models have shown significant advances with the introduction of unsupervised or self-supervised training techniques, these improvements are still only limited to a subsection of languages and speakers. Transfer learning enables the adaptation of large-scale multilingual models to not only low-resource languages but also to more specific speaker groups. However, fine-tuning on data from new domains is usually accompanied by a decrease in performance on the original domain. Therefore, in our experiments, we examine how well the performance of large-scale ASR models can be approximated for smaller domains, with our own dataset of German Senior Voice Commands (SVC-de), and how much of the general speech recognition performance can be preserved by selectively freezing parts of the model during training. To further increase the robustness of the ASR model to vocabulary and speakers outside of the fine-tuned domain, we apply Experience Replay [20] for continual learning. By adding only a fraction of data from the original domain, we are able to reach Word-Error-Rates (WERs) below 5% on the new domain, while stabilizing performance for general speech recognition at acceptable WERs.

Keywords: Automatic Speech Recognition · Transfer Learning · Continual Learning · Domain Adaptation

1 Introduction

Automatic Speech Recognition (ASR) models have previously reached unseen state-of-the-art performance after the introduction of unsupervised and self-supervised pre-training methods from raw audio data, which allowed models to utilize a larger amount of speech data for training [3,5]. However, this has been accompanied by state-of-the-art models increasing in size and requiring thousands of hours of speech data to be trained properly. A recent example is Whisper [19] which, in its largest release, contains 1550 M parameters and is trained on 680,000 h of multilingual speech.

Fortunately, it is not necessary to train such a model from scratch for different languages and domains. Multilingual models like Whisper, or XLSR-53 [5] and

L. Iliadis et al. (Eds.): ICANN 2023, LNCS 14260, pp. 489–500, 2023.
https://doi.org/10.1007/978-3-031-44195-0_40

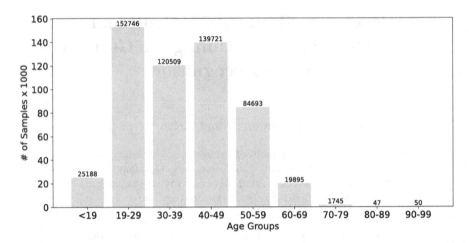

Fig. 1. The age distribution for Common Voice DE 10.0 [1]. As can be seen, of the labeled samples (ca. 70%), the majority are between 19 and 59 years old. Older adults only constitute a fraction of the available samples.

its successor XLS-R [2], generally perform better on low-resource languages than monolingual models trained from scratch, since similarities between languages can be leveraged. However, there is still improvement to be gained by fine-tuning for a specific language. For example, we observe a Word-Error-Rate (WER) of 15.2% for Whisper-small [19] on Common Voice German 10.0 (CV-de) [1] without any adaptation, still, through fine-tuning on additional hours of German speech this can be improved to 11.2% [10].

However, often a more specific adaptation for sub-groups or speakers is necessary due to the fact that performance usually is much lower for speech that differs from the norm, e.g. due to accents, age, or speech disorders [16,17]. This is due to the demographic distribution in most available datasets, where the majority of speakers are male, white, and middle-aged [17]. As can be seen in Fig. 1, this issue transcends languages, as older age groups are similarly underrepresented in CV-de [1], the most commonly used resource to train German speech recognition models. The same problem exists for the distribution of gender: of the subset labeled with additional demographic information in CV-de (ca. 70%), female and diverse speakers only constitute 14%.

To address this problem and thereby create more reliable ASR models, we can facilitate the knowledge contained in large-scale models, similar to how multilingual models can be utilized to improve ASR for low-resource languages. However, End-to-End ASR models also suffer from catastrophic forgetting [18], even for within-language adaptation, which usually destroys the performance of general speech recognition [23]. Therefore, a careful combination of transfer learning, i.e. leveraging the information contained in pre-trained models to facilitate learning on new domains, and continual learning, i.e. preventing the deterioration of performance on previously learned domains, is required.

We collect a dataset of German Senior Voice Commands (SVC-de) and compare the performance of Whisper [19], XLSR-53 [5], and XLS-R [2], three state-of-the-art multilingual speech recognition models. We follow research for layer-specific fine-tuning [12,21] and examine how unfreezing different layer configurations influences the performance of the ASR model. Since domain adaptation usually leads to a decrease in performance on the original domain, we utilize Experience Replay (ER) [20] for continual learning to lessen the drop in performance for general speech recognition, and thereby increase the ASR model's robustness to out-of-domain vocabulary and speakers.

2   Related Work

2.1   Multilingual Speech Recognition

The availability of pre-trained multilingual models in ASR has enabled transfer learning approaches for domains with limited data. This has been especially beneficial for improving speech recognition for non-standard speech and low-resource languages.

XLSR-53 [5] and its successor XLS-R [2] are based on the wav2vec 2.0 [3] architecture and offer large-scale cross-lingual speech recognition. Pre-training in multiple languages, 53 for XLSR-53 and 128 for XLS-R, improves speech recognition across different languages since similarities between them are exploited during training. Whisper [19] is a recent large-scale multilingual model, trained in an unsupervised manner for zero-shot cross-lingual speech recognition, speech translation, and language identification across 97 different languages with 680 000 h of speech data. The underlying architecture is a simple encoder-decoder transformer [24].

The results presented alongside these models show that multilingual ASR models usually perform better than monolingual models on low-resource languages. However, for languages where a large number of transcribed speech data is available, these models are outperformed by models utilizing supervised training [2,19]. This shows that it is beneficial to combine unsupervised pre-training with language- or domain-specific supervised fine-tuning.

2.2   Layer-Specific Fine-Tuning

While the transfer learning capabilities of large-scale speech recognition models have been demonstrated for multilingual [2,5,19] as well as monolingual adaptations [14,16], the question remains if it is necessary to adapt the entire model during the fine-tuning process, especially for very specific or smaller domains.

Shor et al. [21] fine-tune different layer combinations in Listen, Attend, and Spell (LAS) models [4] and RNN-T models [6] to find the subset of layers encoding the most information. For the LAS model, the best results are achieved through fine-tuning the entire model, but for the RNN-T model, 91% of relative WER improvement is achieved by only fine-tuning the joint layer and the first layer of the encoder.

Similarly, Huang et al. [12] look at the influence of different layer configurations on the performance of a Conformer-Transducer [11] model in the context of efficient speaker adaptation. They observe that adaptation of the mid and bottom layers of the Conformer [9] encoder offers a slight decrease in WER over adaptation of the top layers.

Shrivasta et al. [22] examine how much model performance depends on trained weights in the encoder and decoder of RNN-T [6] and Conformer models [9]. They randomly initialize different parts of the model and confirm that, while randomly initializing the encoder immediately hurts model performance, there is no significant difference in results for randomly initializing the decoder.

While research on layer-specific fine-tuning has been mainly focused on performance approximations for new domains, the loss of performance for general speech recognition in monolingual layer-specific adaptations has not been examined in detail. The occurrence of catastrophic forgetting might be greatly dependent on the number of updated parameters, while the performance of attention-based models on the fine-tuned domain might not be. Therefore, we examine layer-specific fine-tuning for both domains, to see how much knowledge is gained for the new domain and lost for out-of-domain speech recognition in each configuration.

2.3 Experience Replay

Experience Replay (ER) [20] is a rehearsal-based continual learning (CL) method that aims to counteract catastrophic forgetting [18] by including a small fraction of data from the original domain in the training data for the new domain. While CL for speech recognition is still relatively unexplored, ER has been utilized successfully for monolingual Dutch accent adaptation before [23]. One advantage of rehearsal-based CL methods is that as long as data from the original domain is available or can be generated, the approaches can be used in a model-agnostic fashion.

3 Experiments

3.1 Data

We fine-tune the models on the German Senior Voice Commands (SVC-de) dataset, a dataset we collected for the development of an ASR system for German senior citizens in the context of a home assistant system. The data has been collected with the approval of the Ethics Commission at the University of Hamburg.

SVC-de consists of short speech commands recorded by German speakers between the ages of 50 and 99. Overall 30 people (21 female, 9 male) recorded 52

Table 1. An overview of the WER (%) of our baseline models (*-de* indicates fine-tuning on CV-de), evaluated on the test-split of Common Voice DE 10.0 [1] and our own German Senior Voice Commands (SVC-de) dataset.

Model	CV-de 10.0 test	SVC-de	# of Params
XLSR-53-large-de [7]	12.8	18.4	315 M
XLS-R-1B-de [8]	11.6	20.0	962 M
XLS-R-300m-de [15]	22.8	31.3	315 M
Whisper-base-de	20.4	25.7	74 M
Whisper-small-de [10]	11.2	18.4	244 M

sentences each with two microphones, for a total of 3 h 9 m, with approximately 6–7 min of audio data per speaker. The recorded sentences were manually cut and transcribed afterward to give a realistic estimation of the examined ASR models' performance. We use 70% of the dataset for training, 10% for validation, and the remaining 20% for testing.

Common Voice DE (CV-de) [1] is one of the largest and most utilized German speech datasets, and features a large variety of recording conditions and speakers due to the crowd-sourced nature of the collection. We utilize CV-de 10.0, which has 1136 validated hours of audio from 16,944 different speakers and contains additional demographic data (e.g. age group, gender, accent) for about 70% of the samples. We use the predefined dataset splits for training and testing.

3.2 Base Models

As can be seen in Table 1, the performance for German speech varies even for large-scale ASR models. While fine-tuning on data like CV-de improves the average performance for German speech, the improvement does not immediately translate to elderly speech. Additionally, a higher number of parameters does not seem to automatically lead to a better performance. The performance of XLS-R-1B-de [2], a model with approximately 1 B parameters is comparable to its predecessor XLSR-53-large [5] and to Whisper-small [19], with only 244 M parameters, after fine-tuning on CV-de.

In our experiments, we utilize a selection of pre-trained models from the publicly available checkpoints in Huggingface's[1] model repository. All models are approximately the same size and have been adapted to German speech with CV-de. We include a pre-trained version of XLS-R, with 300 M parameters [15], a pre-trained XLSR-53-large model [7], and a pre-trained Whisper-small model [10]. XLSR-53-large and XLS-R-300M both consist of 24 encoder layers and use character-based tokenization. Whisper-small consists of 12 encoder- and 12 decoder-layers and utilizes a byte-level BPE text tokenizer for an output vocabulary size of 51,865. All models include punctuation to some degree, but

---

[1] https://huggingface.co/.

to enable a fair comparison, we normalize the generated transcripts before the evaluation.

3.3   Experiments

In all our experiments, unless specifically stated otherwise, we train our models for five epochs with a batch size of 128 and AdamW [13] optimizer. The learning rate is set to 3e-4 for XLS-R and XLSR-53, and to 3e-5 for Whisper. It decays linearly after a warm-up of 50 steps. We set the dropout for XLSR-53 and XLS-R to 0.1, and use mean CTC loss reduction. All hyperparameters were determined empirically by comparing the behavior of the models during the layer-specific fine-tuning experiments. We train our models on an NVIDIA A100 80G graphics card.

Transfer Learning. The transfer learning capabilities of large pre-trained speech recognition models have been proven for adaptation to non-standard speech before [14,21]. Therefore, we establish a baseline by fine-tuning the entirety of our selected models on the SVC-de dataset. For XLSR-53 and XLS-R, we keep the feature extractor frozen.

Then, following similar approaches [12,21,22], we fine-tune different layer combinations to determine the most efficient subset for the adaptation of the model. Table 2 shows the layer configurations for our baseline models. Since XLSR-53-large [5] and XLS-R-300m [2] share a network structure of 24 encoder layers, we can apply the same configurations to both models. While Whisper contains the same number of layers, the network structure is split into 12 encoder and 12 decoder layers. Therefore, we examine the layer configurations for the encoder and decoder in separate experiments and then apply them to both parts of the model simultaneously. For example, in the encoder-decoder fine-tuning scenario, we would apply the 'first 6' configuration to both the encoder and the decoder, leading to a total of 12 adaptable layers.

We examine how much the performance differs between layer configurations for SVC-de and how much the performance for CV-de degrades due to domain adaptation. This should serve as an indicator as to which parts of the model are essential for the creation of general speech representations and therefore more sensitive to change, and which parts can be adapted for another domain without affecting the performance of the original dataset too drastically.

Continual Learning. To reduce the loss of knowledge regarding general speech recognition, we implement Experience Replay (ER) [20] for continual learning. However, instead of including a fixed number of samples from the original domain in each batch, we include either 10% or 20% of the original domain in the SVC-de training data spread out over all batches. We examine these data splits for the models with the best layer configurations, regarding their WER reduction on CV-de and their WER and convergence on SVC-de. We compare the performance between our best models with and without ER for both datasets.

Table 2. The fine-tuning layer configurations for our baseline models. XLSR-53-large [5] and XLS-R-300m [2] share the same number of encoder layers and therefore we can apply the layer configurations to both models. Due to the encoder-decoder architecture of Whisper [19], we apply these configurations first to the 12 layers of the encoder and the 12 layers of the decoder separately, and then to both simultaneously.

XLS-R & XLSR-53		Whisper	
Name	Layer Configuration	Name	Layer Configuration
first 12	[0, 1, ..., 10, 11]	first 6	[0, 1, 2, 3, 4, 5]
last 12	[12, 13, ..., 22, 23]	last 6	[6, 7, 8, 9, 10, 11]
f4-i4-l4	[0, ..., 3, 10, ..., 13, 20, ..., 23]	f1-i2-l1	[0, 5, 6, 11]
f2-i2-l2	[0, 1, 11, 12, 22, 23]	f2-i2-l2	[0, 1, 5, 6, 10, 11]
last 6	[18, 19, 20, 21, 22, 23]	last 3	[9, 10, 11]

4   Results and Discussion

4.1   Layer-Specific Fine-Tuning

As can be seen in Fig. 2, fine-tuning the entire model generally leads to the best performance for all examined models. This aligns with the observations by Shor et al. [21] in their experiments with LAS. However, Whisper shows a clear difference in performance between layer configurations that adapt only the layers of the encoder or the decoder. Fine-tuning only the encoder layers leads to a final average WER of 15.5%, which is an average increase of 13.3% compared to the final WER obtained by fine-tuning the entire model (2.2%). The encoder-decoder layer configurations reach an average WER of 4.8% and the decoder configurations follow close behind with a final average WER of 6.2% after five epochs.

The closest approximation of fine-tuning the entire Whisper model is obtained by fine-tuning the last six layers of the encoder and the decoder at the same time (WER: 3.1%), followed closely by fine-tuning only the decoder (WER: 3.5%). For XLSR-53, adapting only the first 12 layers (WER: 6.6%) or configuration 'f4-i4-l4' (WER: 7.1%) offers a close approximation of the best model performance (WER: 5.5%). Meanwhile, XLS-R shows the largest gap in WER between fine-tuning the entire model (WER: 7.4%) and the next best 'f4-i4-l4' configuration (WER: 12.2%), but also the largest improvement on SVC-de compared to its performance before the adaptation (Table 1). However, Whisper outperforms both XLS-R and XLSR-53 on average after five epochs of training, despite an initial spike in WER on SVC-de.

As expected, the performance of CV-de deteriorates as a result of the fine-tuning process. Figure 3 shows a drastic increase in WER for all layer configurations and all examined models. However, the most forgetting occurs when the entire model is trained, and fine-tuning only a reduced number of layers generally leads to a lower WER for CV-de. This is especially interesting for cases, where adapting a smaller selection of layers is a close approximation of the original

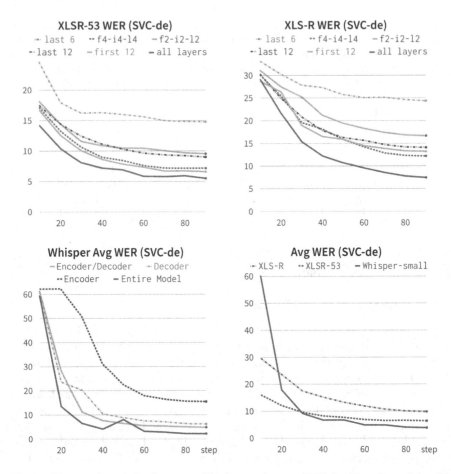

Fig. 2. The results of the layer-specific fine-tuning on SVC-de. For all models, the largest increase in performance can be observed after fine-tuning the entire model. However, for Whisper-small this performance can be approximated by layer configurations that only adapt the decoder or both model parts in unison. While XLSR-53 also offers a close approximation for some layer configurations, this is not the case with XLS-R. On average, Whisper's best layer configurations outperform both XLSR-53 and XLS-R after five epochs of training.

model performance. For example, fine-tuning only the last 6 layers of Whisper's encoder and decoder achieves a similar WER on SVC-de as adapting the entire model, with a difference of only 0.9%. The WER on CV-de, however, is approximately 5% lower for the smaller selection (24.5%) compared to the entire model (29.1%), which indicates that adapting only a smaller layer configuration is beneficial for preserving the performance of the original domain.

For XLS-R and XLSR-53 the behavior is similar, as most forgetting occurs when the entire model is fine-tuned. But, compared to Whisper, the WER on CV-de does not show any major changes after the first 10 optimization steps and is

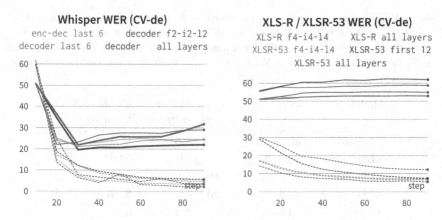

Fig. 3. The performance decay of CV-de during fine-tuning on SVC-de, measured in WER (lower is better, dashed lines indicate corresponding results on SVC-de). The most forgetting occurs for Whisper if the entire model is fine-tuned or all decoder layers are fine-tuned. For XLS-R and XLSR-53 the largest decay of performance happens (1) within the first 10 optimization steps and (2) when the entire model is fine-tuned on SVC-de.

generally much higher. This is due to the selected learning rate. While a learning rate of 3e-3 leads to a better performance on SVC-de, the decay on CV-de is even more drastic and the learning process is overall more unstable. In comparison, a learning rate of 3e-4 offered the best trade-off between performance on the new and the old domain.

4.2   Experience Replay

After applying ER during the fine-tuning process, we observe that ER with as little as 10% of original data not only helps to stabilize Whisper's training on SVC-de but also diminishes the performance decrease on CV-de. As can be seen in Table 3, fine-tuning only the last 6 layers of the encoder and the decoder leads to our best performance, with a final WER of 18.1% on CV-de and 3.0% on SVC-de, after five epochs of training. This is closely followed by adapting only the last 6 layers of the decoder with ER on 20% of CV-de. XLS-R and XLSR-53 also experience a WER reduction from ER, even though they do not reach the same level of performance as Whisper.

Table 3. A comparison of our best models with and without Experience Replay (ER). While all models benefit from ER, a trade-off can be observed if we increase the percentage of samples from CV-de. Of all examined models, Whisper is the only one that can be stabilized at an acceptable WER for CV-de, while showing vast improvements for SVC-de.

Model	Layer Config	ER (%)	SVC-de WER (%)	CV-de 10.0 WER (%)
XLSR-53	all layers	–	**5.5**	55.0
XLSR-53	first 12	–	6.6	52.9
XLSR-53	all layers	10	**5.6**	42.7
XLSR-53	all layers	20	5.9	**31.6**
XLS-R	all layers	–	**7.4**	62.0
XLS-R	all layers	10	8.1	53.5
XLS-R	all layers	20	8.1	**47.3**
Whisper-small	all layers	–	**2.2**	29.1
Whisper-small	enc/dec last 6	–	3.2	24.5
Whisper-small	enc/dec last 6	10	**3.0**	18.1
Whisper-small	dec last 6	10	5.0	17.6
Whisper-small	dec last 6	20	4.9	**16.8**

5   Conclusion and Future Work

In this work, we demonstrate the effectiveness of combining layer-specific fine-tuning and continual learning to improve performance for under-represented speaker groups, while keeping the performance for general speech recognition from deteriorating in the process. Adapting smaller layer sub-groups for specific domains can, depending on the choice of model and configuration, approximate the performance of a model that has been fine-tuned in its entirety. Additionally, since fewer parameters are adapted during training, the performance decay on the original domain is decreased. We show that utilizing Experience Replay (ER) [20] with only a small fraction of data from the original domain can lead to vast improvements in WER for the original, as well as minor improvements for the new domain.

Our best model is a pre-trained German Whisper-small architecture [10,19], fine-tuned on SVC-de with 10% ER, which reduces the WER for SVC-de from 18.4% to 3.0%. By adapting only the last six layers of the encoder and the decoder, we are able to stabilize the performance of CV-de at 18.1% WER. By adding more data from the original domain, the WER on the original domain can be lowered further. However, we observe that at 20% ER a trade-off starts to happen, where the performance on CV-de can only be improved with detriment to the performance of the new domain.

While we utilize our own novel dataset of elderly German speech (SVC-de) in our experiments, the methods we use are model- and dataset-independent, which indicates that our approach could be applied to other domains (e.g. dialects) as well. Additionally, since the vocabulary in SVC-de is limited, our approach promises more robustness for out-of-domain words and a larger variety of speakers than traditional fine-tuning approaches.

Acknowledgements. The authors gratefully acknowledge support from the German BMWK (SIDIMO), the DFG (CML, LeCAREbot), and the European Commission (TRAIL, TERAIS). We would also like to thank Henri-Leon Kordt for helping with the post-processing of our German Senior Voice Commands dataset.

References

1. Ardila, R., et al.: Common voice: a massively-multilingual speech corpus. In: Proceedings of the 12th Language Resources and Evaluation Conference. European Language Resources Association, Marseille, France (2020)
2. Babu, A., et al.: XLS-R: self-supervised Cross-lingual Speech Representation Learning at Scale. In: Proceedings of INTERSPEECH 2022, pp. 2278–2282. ISCA, Incheon, Korea (2022)
3. Baevski, A., Zhou, H., Mohamed, A., Auli, M.: Wav2vec 2.0: a framework for self-supervised learning of speech representations. In: Proceedings of the 34th International Conference on Neural Information Processing Systems (NeurIPS). Curran Associates Inc., Vancouver, BC, Canada (2020)
4. Chan, W., Jaitly, N., Le, Q., Vinyals, O.: LIsten, attend and spell: a neural network for large vocabulary conversational speech recognition. In: Proceedings of 2016 IEEE International Conference on Acoustics, Speech and Signal Processing (ICASSP), pp. 4960–4964. IEEE Press, Shanghai, China (2016)
5. Conneau, A., Baevski, A., Collobert, R., Mohamed, A., Auli, M.: Unsupervised cross-lingual representation learning for speech recognition. In: Proceedings of INTERSPEECH 2021, pp. 2426–2430. ISCA, Brno, Czechia (2021)
6. Graves, A.: Sequence transduction with recurrent neural networks. In: ICML 2012 Workshop on Representation Learning (2012)
7. Grosman, J.: Fine-tuned XLSR-53 Large model for speech recognition in German. https://huggingface.co/jonatasgrosman/wav2vec2-large-xlsr-53-german (2021)
8. Grosman, J.: Fine-tuned XLS-R 1B model for speech recognition in German. https://huggingface.co/jonatasgrosman/wav2vec2-xls-r-1b-german (2022)
9. Gulati, A., et al.: Conformer: convolution-augmented transformer for speech recognition. In: Proceedings of INTERSPEECH 2020, pp. 5036–5040. ISCA, Shanghai, China (2020)
10. Huang, B.: Fine-tuned whisper model for speech recognition in German. https://huggingface.co/bofenghuang/whisper-small-cv11-german (2022)
11. Huang, W., Hu, W., Yeung, Y.T., Chen, X.: Conv-transformer transducer: low latency, low frame rate, streamable end-to-end speech recognition. In: Proceedings of INTERSPEECH 2020, pp. 5001–5005. ISCA, Shanghai, China (2020)
12. Huang, Y., Ye, G., Li, J., Gong, Y.: Rapid speaker adaptation for conformer transducer: attention and Bias are all you need. In: Proceedings of INTERSPEECH 2021, pp. 1309–1313. ISCA, Brno, Czechia (2021)
13. Loshchilov, I., Hutter, F.: Decoupled weight decay regularization. In: Proceedings of 7th International Conference on Learning Representations (ICLR). New Orleans, LA, USA (2019)

14. MacDonald, R.L., et al.: Disordered speech data collection: lessons learned at 1 million utterances from project Euphonia. In: Proceedings of INTERSPEECH 2021, pp. 3066–3070. ISCA, Brno, Czech Republic (2021)

15. McDowell, A.: Fine-tuned XLS-R 300M model for speech recognition in German. https://huggingface.co/AndrewMcDowell/wav2vec2-xls-r-300m-german-de (2022)

16. Moro-Velazquez, L., et al.: Study of the performance of automatic speech recognition systems in speakers with Parkinson's Disease. In: Proceedings of INTERSPEECH 2019, pp. 3875–3879. ISCA, Graz, Austria (2019)

17. Ngueajio, M.K., Washington, G.: Hey ASR system! Why aren't you more inclusive? In: Chen, J.Y.C., Fragomeni, G., Degen, H., Ntoa, S. (eds.) HCI International 2022 – Late Breaking Papers: Interacting with eXtended Reality and Artificial Intelligence. HCII 2022. LNCS, vol. 13518. Springer, Cham (2022). https://doi.org/10.1007/978-3-031-21707-4_30

18. Parisi, G.I., Kemker, R., Part, J.L., Kanan, C., Wermter, S.: Continual lifelong learning with neural networks: a review. Neural Netw. **113**, 54–71 (2019)

19. Radford, A., Kim, J.W., Xu, T., Brockman, G., McLeavey, C., Sutskever, I.: Robust speech recognition via large-scale weak supervision. arXiv:2212.04356 (2022)

20. Rolnick, D., Ahuja, A., Schwarz, J., Lillicrap, T., Wayne, G.: Experience replay for continual learning. In: Proceedings of the 33rd International Conference on Neural Information Processing Systems (NeurIPS), pp. 348–358. Curran Associates Inc, Vancouver, BC, Canada (2019)

21. Shor, J., et al.: Personalizing ASR for Dysarthric and accented speech with limited data. In: Proceedings of INTERSPEECH 2019, pp. 784–788. ISCA, Graz, Austria (2019)

22. Shrivastava, H., Garg, A., Cao, Y., Zhang, Y., Sainath, T.N.: Echo state speech recognition. In: Proceedings of 2021 IEEE International Conference on Acoustics, Speech and Signal Processing (ICASSP), pp. 5669–5673. IEEE Press, Toronto, ON, Canada (2021)

23. Vander Eeckt, S., Van Hamme, H.: Continual learning for monolingual end-to-end automatic speech recognition. In: Proceedings of 30th European Signal Processing Conference (EUSIPCO), pp. 459–463. IEEE Press, Belgrade, Serbia (2022)

24. Vaswani, A., et al.: attention is all you need. In: Proceedings of the 31st International Conference on Neural Information Processing Systems (NeurIPS), pp. 5998–6008. Curran Associates Inc, Long Beach, CA, USA (2017)

Self-supervised Video Object Segmentation Using Motion Feature Compensation

Tianqi Zhang and Bo Li$^{(\boxtimes)}$ ⓘD

School of Electronic and Information Engineering, South China University
of Technology, Guangzhou 510640, China
eetqzhang@mail.scut.edu.cn, leebo@scut.edu.cn

Abstract. Video object segmentation is a popular area of research in computer vision. Traditional models are trained using annotated data, which is both time-consuming and expensive. Training models in unsupervised manner has been proposed as a solution to this issue. However, previous works have focused only on spatial features extracted by self-supervised learning method, without considering the temporal information between frames. In this paper, we propose a new video object segmentation model that utilizes self-supervised learning to extract spatial features, and incorporates a motion feature, extracted from optical flow, as compensation of temporal information for the model, namely motion feature compensation (MFC) model. Additionally, we introduce an attention-based fusion method to merge features from both modalities. Notably, for each video used to train models, we only select two consecutive frames at random to train our model. The dataset Youtube-VOS and DAVIS-2017 are adopted as the training dataset and the validation dataset. The experimental results demonstrate that our approach outperforms previous methods, validating our proposed design. The source code is available at: https://github.com/CVisionProcessing/MFC.

Keywords: Video object segmentation · Self-supervised learning · Attention fusion

1 Introduction

Video object segmentation (VOS) is an appealing research topic in computer vision. The task of VOS is fulfilled by segmenting the foreground objects from a given video sequence. The model of VOS can empower machines to perceive the motion mode, position, and boundaries of the object of interest in the video, then, such models have been widely applied in autonomous driving [22], video surveillance [3], action detection [13], *etc.*. Depending on whether the specific segmented objects are provided in the first frame, VOS can be categorized into semi-supervised VOS and unsupervised VOS. Our model presented in this paper is implemented for semi-supervised VOS. Conventionally, semi-supervised VOS

L. Iliadis et al. (Eds.): ICANN 2023, LNCS 14260, pp. 501–513, 2023.
https://doi.org/10.1007/978-3-031-44195-0_41

models are trained in a supervised manner that heavily relies on large amounts of annotated data. This results in significant manual effort required to annotate each frame of videos at the pixel level (as shown in Fig. 1(a)).

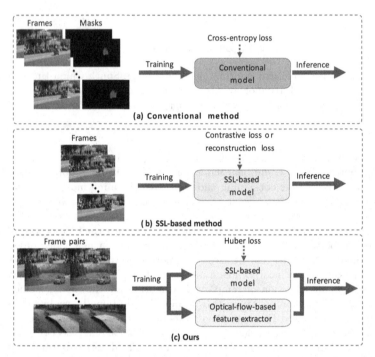

Fig. 1. The training mode of semi-supervised VOS: (a) Conventional method. Training such models require the annotated data, *i.e.*, original videos and masks of segmented objects. Usually, the cross-entropy loss is used. (b) The model built upon SSL. The training data is original video only, and the loss function can either be a contrastive loss or a reconstruction loss, while training. (c) Our proposed method. For each video in training dataset, only two consecutive frames selected randomly are employed as training data. The data is also not annotated. Note that we incorporate temporal information of videos, represented as a motion cue. The loss function is the Huber loss.

Self-supervised learning (SSL) model as an alternative method can be used to addressed the issue, since such models do not need to be trained by using the annotated data (as shown in Fig. 1(b)). Objects presented in an video could be variant in scales, shapes, position, *etc.*, from frame to frame, hence, each frame of the video can be regarded as an alternative way of data augmentation which is the way of obtaining training data to train SSL models. Therefore, it is legitimate to apply SSL into VOS, making VOS models to subtly learn features of the segmented objects. Previous works, *e.g.*, [4,5,23], used SSL model to strengthen the representation learning ability of the network through the inter-frame reconstruction. The features are extracted from color space (RGB space), namely spatial features for simplicity. However, the correlation in time perspective is ignored in previous works. The objects presented in the video are variant from frame to frame, meaning that the motion behaved by the objects is closely coherent.

In this paper, we build a dual-stream network upon SSL model to address the mentioned issues (See Fig. 1(c) and Fig. 2). In our method, apart from spatial features, we introduce the temporal coherence of frames into our model. Specifically, we construct a affinity matrix, generated by comparing the feature maps extracted from two consecutive frames, to determine and mark semantically the regions containing similar objects for the two frames. Moreover, aiming to improve the capability of our model to discriminate foreground and background, we intend to extract the motion cue of objects from optical flow by using a optical-flow network. The cue demonstrate the motion trend of the foreground and background, respectively, and the temporal coherence of objects between frames. Then, we fuse the features of the two modalities, i.e., the spatial information and the motion cue, together to predict and segment the target objects provided in the first frame. Rather than directly fusing the features by concatenating or addition, we devise an attention-based fusion network to effectively integrate the features. Finally, the relevant experimental results demonstrate the effectiveness of our method.

Our contributions are summarized as follows:

- We propose a SSL-based model, namely Motion Feature Compensation model (MFC), to accomplish the task of VOS. The model can achieve promising results on the validation dataset.
- We extract the motion cue from optical flow to solve the issue of mismatching between auxiliary tasks and downstream tasks in previous SSL-based models.
- A fusion module is designed based on the attention mechanism to merge the spatial features and the motion cue.
- The experiments conducted for performance evaluation and ablation study demonstrate that our model is batter than previous works, trained with unannotated data, and the effectiveness of each component of the proposed model.

2   Related Work

Training with annotated data is a conventional mindset for semi-supervised VOS. Based on the full convolutional neural network [14], VOS models can be implemented. OSVOS [1] transfers generic semantic information learned from an image dataset to the task of foreground segmentation in videos, and finally learns the appearance of a single annotated object in the test sequence. TMVOS [8] built a triple matching model upon triple loss. The model extracts the nearest positive embedding, and expand the distance between embeddings of objects of different classes, thereby generating accurate matching maps. STM [11] builds a memory bank to store the features of all previous frames, and combines the information to accomplish segmentation, achieving appealing results. Although, such models achieve a prevailing results, they rely on large numbers annotated data to train the model.

The intrinsic characteristic of SSL model provide possibility to address issues of conventional method. The model can learn subtle features, and can be trained with unlabeled data. TWIAA [23] introduces the feature space enhancement modules and the dual stream channel modules to integrate the feature of spatial and channel dimensions, enabling the network to focus on segmented objects. LDR [4] decomposes inter-frame reconstruction relationships into a representation strategy of paired and unary terms, learning to capture salient object information of inter-frame spatiotemporal and intra-frame through the terms. MAST [5] reconsiders the traditional selection of self-supervised training and reconstruction losses, and uses a memory component to enhance the architecture, achieving satisfying results. These methods mainly cover the learning of spatial characteristics, but the motion information of foreground are ignored.

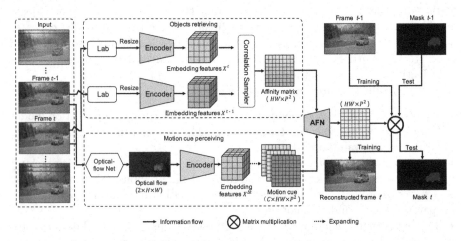

Fig. 2. Framework of our method. Based on the embedding features, *objects retrieving* module engages in comparing and retrieving objects which could be variance in the two frames, and outputs a affinity matrix. *Motion cue perceiving* module employs an encoder to extract the motion cue after optical flow is obtained. Then, the module *attention-based fusion network (AFN)* merges the affinity matrix and the motion cue into a feature map including reconstruction information.

3 Method

3.1 Overview

Figure 2 shows the architecture of our method, including three modules: frame-to-frame objects retrieving module (FOR), motion cue perceiving module (MCP), and attention-based fusion network (AFN).

The module FOR captures discrepancies between two consecutive frames in an video, and generates an affinity matrix based on the discrepancy. The discrepancy is obtained by correlation computation performed on feature maps extracted from the two frames, and presented in the affinity matrix. The module focuses on capture the subtle information of objects to contribute accurately segment objects given in the first frame. MCP module uses an encoder to extracts the motion cue from optical flow between the two consecutive frames. The cue offers guidance for building foreground from temporal perspective while the affinity matrix provides morph of objects from spatial perspective. AFN module fuses the motion cue and the affinity matrix together. During training phase, for each training video, only two consecutive frames are randomly sampled as the training data, making our training method much more efficient compared to the way of using entire video to train model. Moreover, we engage in promoting the model's reconstructing capability by using original frame at the inference stage to generate the predicted frame $t^{'}$, as shown in Fig. 2. In testing phase, the original frame is substituted with the mask of the last frame, and then, the output is the predicted mask of the current frame.

3.2 Frame-to-Frame Objects Retrieving

The affinity matrix is used to represent the difference of visual characteristics between two consecutive frames. Considering that the characteristics of the two frames from the same video do not change greatly, we select adjacent frames for orderly reconstruction and feature representation learning, which helps to reduce the distance of feature points between different views of the same object. This way, the invariance of the same object in the video sequence can be learned. Since that Lab color space can perform better in representation learning compared with RGB color space [5], a channel-wise dropout in Lab colour space is applied to the RGB images. Dropout can reduce the visual information directly obtained by the model, so it can force the model to learn more robust representation.

Specifically, take two consecutive frames, represented with $I_{t-1}, I_t \in \mathbb{R}^{H \times W \times 3}$, respectively, from an video as inputs, where H and W denote the height hand the width of the frame, the subscript t is the index of the frame in the video, and 3 means the 3 channels (Red, Green, and Blue, respectively). An encoder $\Phi(I; \theta)$ is employed to extract the features, denoted as $X_{t-1}, X_t \in \mathbb{R}^{h \times w \times c}$, from I_{t-1} and I_t, respectively, where c means the number of channels.

Intuitively, the discrepancy of the pairwise between X_{t-1} and X_t can be used to form the affinity matrix. Considering objects in I_{t-1} could move to a new position in I_t, we define a tiny area around the pixel i in X_t as the *responding area* (denoted as Z) of the pixel at the same position i in X_{t-1}. The size of Z is controlled by a hyperparameter P, and, conveniently, Z is a square area centered on i. Then, we define the relation between the pixel at i in X_{t-1}

and pixels in Z of $\boldsymbol{X}_t$:

$$A_Z^{i,j} = \frac{\exp(\langle \boldsymbol{X}_{t-1}^i, \boldsymbol{X}_t^j \rangle / \sqrt{c})}{\sum_{j \in Z} \exp(\langle \boldsymbol{X}_{t-1}^i, \boldsymbol{X}_t^j \rangle / \sqrt{c})}. \tag{1}$$

where i and j indicate the pixel in $\boldsymbol{X}_{t-1}$ and pixel in Z of $\boldsymbol{X}_t$, respectively. The operation $\langle \cdot, \cdot \rangle$ is the dot product between two vectors. Then, all pixels of $\boldsymbol{X}_{t-1}$ and $\boldsymbol{X}_t$ can be imported into Eq. 1 to generate the affinity matrix $\boldsymbol{A}$. Each $A_Z^{i,j}$ in $\boldsymbol{A}$ is arranged as a vector, that is, $A_Z^{i,j} \in \mathbb{R}^{P^2 \times 1}$. Then, the size of $\boldsymbol{A}$ is $HW \times P^2$.

3.3   Motion Cue Perceiving

To improve our model's ability to differentiate the segmented objects from backgrounds, we use temporal coherence implicitly included in an video as guidance to rebuild and segment the foreground. Optical flow of the video carries the temporal consistency of the video and presents the motion trend of objects. Therefore, after obtaining optical flow using an optical-flow network, we extract the motion cue from it. The cue offers more information about the segmented objects that is independent from the feature extracted in FOR. The module implemented to perceive the motion cue is named motion cue perceiving module (MCP).

Specifically, we adopt RAFT [16] as the optical-flow network, which is a lightweight model. After optical flow is obtained, we fed it into an encoder to capture the motion cue. We use ResNet-18 as the backbone of the encoder. The number of input channels of the first layer is set to 2, matching the channels of optical flow. The perceived motion cue is denoted as $\boldsymbol{M}_o \in \mathbb{R}^{C \times HW \times P^2}$.

3.4   Attention-Based Fusion Network

Instead of using a simple operation, *e.g.*, concatenation, addition, *etc.*, to merge the affinity matrix and the motion cue, we intentionally design a fusion module based on the attention mechanism (as shown in Fig. 3), namely the attention-based fusion network, to merge the output of FOR and MCP, and produce more effective feature maps for the final frame reconstruction in training phase, and mask prediction in testing phase.

Fusing the affinity matrix $\boldsymbol{A}$ and the motion cue $\boldsymbol{M}_o$, we can get the inter-frame reconstruction features. Before fulfilling the fusion process, $\boldsymbol{M}_o$ is needed to be reshaped with regard to decreasing the computational complexity of the fusion module. Inspired by [2], we use the space reduction and the space recovery operations to reshape the motion cue into $\boldsymbol{M}_o \in \mathbb{R}^{C \times H \times W}$, and then downsample k times, by which the complexity of the fusion can be reduced drastically. Each entry in $\boldsymbol{A}$ and each pixel in $\boldsymbol{M}_o$ are used as query, key, and value of the cross-attention. $\boldsymbol{R}$ is more applicable to reconstruct the t-th frame, or to predict the mask of the t-th frame. In order to prevent negative effects of motion cue,

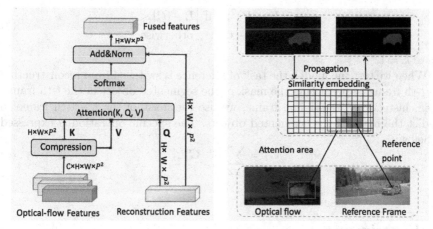

Fig. 3. The proposed attention-based fusion network (AFN). The structure of AFN built upon the attention mechanism is presented on the left. The right part demonstrates that the optical flow as a query can strengthen the area including foreground. Then, the final prediction can be optimised when we test the model.

we add the fused features to the affinity matrix A to obtain the final result. The fusion process can be expressed as below:

$$R = \text{softmax}\left(\frac{AW^q\left(M_oW^k\right)^T}{\sqrt{d_{\text{head}}}}\right)(M_oW^v) + A. \tag{2}$$

where W^q, W^k, and W^v are learnable weights used for linear transformation; d is the dimension of queries and keys. The function softmax is used for normalization.

3.5   Frame Reconstruction

The fused feature R serves as the basis for frame reconstruction. R contains motion information and visual representation of objects in the frame. During training phase, we attempt to reconstruct the t-th frame by using its previous frame of the same video. Due to the area Z centered on the pixel i in I_{t-1} have a great impact on constructing the pixel i in I_t, then the reconstruction for each pixel of I_t is fulfilled as:

$$\widehat{I}_t^i = \sum_{j \in Z} R^{i,j} I_{t-1}^j. \tag{3}$$

And we use Huber Loss [15] as the loss function to train our model. That is, the original frames in the video are served as the ground truth for training the model. The loss is expressed as following:

$$\mathcal{L} = \frac{1}{n}\sum_{i=1}^{N} l_i \tag{4}$$

$$l_i = \begin{cases} 0.5(\widehat{I_t^i} - I_t^i)^2, & \text{if } |\widehat{I_t^i} - I_t^i| < 1 \\ k|\widehat{I_t^i} - I_t^i| - 0.5k^2, & \text{otherwise.} \end{cases} \tag{5}$$

where $k = 1$.

When we test the model, the task of inference is switched from reconstructing the t-th frame to predicting the mask of the segmented object in the t-th frame. Then, instead of the original frame, we use the mask of the $t - 1$-th frame to predict the mask of the segmented objects. The specific operation is expressed as below:

$$G_t = \sum_{j \in Z} R^{i,j} G_{t-1}. \tag{6}$$

where G_t is mask of each frame.

4   Experiments

4.1   Implementation Details

Training. The encoders of extracting respective features from frames and optical flow are built upon ResNet-18. They have identical architectures, but parameters. Their parameters are randomly initialized. The two consecutive frames fed into encoders are randomly selected from the training dataset. For the module FOR, the scale of inputs are resized into 256×256. The model is trained in end-to-end manner on Youtube-VOS [19] dataset with a batch size of 12 and 20 epochs.We utilize the Adam optimizer with a base learning rate of 1e−3. The training process takes approximately 40 h on a single NVIDIA TiTan GPU with 12 GB RAM.

Testing. During testing the model, optical flow is computed between the current frame and each frame in the memory, and then fed into the same network as in the training stage for similarity computation. The mask of the previous frame is used as the initial reconstruction term to propagate to the following frames. For consistency with the benchmark, our model is evaluated on YouTube VOS validation set and full resolution DAVIS-2017 validation set. The results on DAVIS-2017 are obtained using the official evaluation code. The testing process takes approximately 0.56 h on a single NVIDIA TiTan GPU with 12 GB memory.

4.2   Datasets

DAVIS-2017 [12] is a popular dataset for VOS with *short* video clips and complex scenes. It contains 150 videos over 200 objects. The validation set of DAVIS-2017 contains 30 videos.

YouTube-VOS [19] is the largest dataset for VOS with *long* video clips. It contains over 4000 high-resolution videos with more than 7000 objects. The validation set of YouTube-VOS 2018 contains 474 videos. Unlike previous methods,

Table 1. Performance evaluation on DAVIS-2017 validation set. The best results is presented with bold font. The upper 8 methods are trained with un-annotated data, while the rear 7 methods are trained with annotated data at pexel-level. 'T. Data' means training datasets, including: C = COCO, D = DAVIS, E = ECSSD, H = HKU-IS, I = ImageNet, K = Kinetics, M = Mapillary, O = OxUvA, P = PASCAL-VOC, S = MSRA10K, Y = YouTube-VOS.

Method	Backbone	Param	T. Data	$\mathcal{J}$ & $\mathcal{F}$	$\mathcal{J}$ (Mean)	$\mathcal{F}$ (Mean)
Vid. Color. [17]	ResNet-18	5M	K	34.0	34.6	32.7
CorrFlow [6]	ResNet-18	5M	O	50.3	48.4	52.2
UVC [7]	ResNet-18	3M	K	59.5	57.7	61.3
MuG [9]	ResNet-50	9M	O	54.4	52.6	56.1
TWIAA [23]	ResNet-50	9M	O	57.5	58.2	56.7
LDR [4]	ResNet-18	5M	Y	61.7	60.2	63.2
MAST [5]	ResNet-18	5M	O	63.7	61.2	66.3
Ours	ResNet-18	5M	Y	**65.4**	**63.4**	**67.4**
OSVOS [1]	VGG-16	15M	ID	60.3	56.6	63.9
OSMN [20]	VGG-16	15M	ICD	54.8	52.5	57.1
RGMP [10]	ResNet-101	43M	IDY	66.7	64.8	68.6
TMVOS [8]	ResNet-34	22M	IDY	71.6	69.6	73.5
STM [11]	ResNet-50	9M	ICPSEDY	81.8	79.2	84.3
CFBI [21]	ResNet-101	43M	ICDY	81.9	79.1	84.6
RMNet [18]	ResNet-50	9M	ICPSEDY	**83.5**	**81.0**	**86.0**

e.g., [11,18], we train our model on YouTube-VOS only. Unless specified otherwise, the YouTube-VOS dataset in this paper refers to the version released in 2018, which is consistent with previous benchmarks.

4.3 Evaluation Metrics

We use the region similarity $\mathcal{J}$ and the countour accuracy $\mathcal{F}$ to evaluate models. $\mathcal{J}$ is defined as the average intersection-over-union (IoU) between the reconstructed prediction and the ground truth. $\mathcal{F}$ is defined as an average boundary similarity measure of the boundary of the reconstructed prediction and the ground truth.

4.4 Performance Evaluation

We compare the proposed model with 14 methods on dataset DAVIS-2017. The 14 methods include 7 models trained in unsupervised manner, and 7 models trained in supervised manner. For fair comparison, their experimental results are quote from original papers, or obtained by running the official code released by the original author. The experimental results are presented in Table 1.

Table 2. Comparison of the attributes-based performance w.r.t the motion speed of objects between LDR [4] and our model.

Video	Num	Motion	LDR			Ours		
			$\mathcal{J}$ & $\mathcal{F}$	$\mathcal{J}$	$\mathcal{F}$	$\mathcal{J}$ & $\mathcal{F}$	$\mathcal{J}$	$\mathcal{F}$
breakdance	1	Fast	55.86	54.8	57.0	**65.78**	**66.6**	**65.0**
soapbox	2	Fast	62.44	58.5	66.4	**70.87**	**66.8**	**75.0**
horsejump	2	Fast	77.87	70.2	85.6	**81.45**	**73.7**	**89.2**
bike-packing	2	Slow	**67.14**	**72.9**	**61.4**	63.2	57.7	68.7
gold-fish	5	Slow	79.7	79.3	80.1	**81.4**	**80.8**	**82.0**
judo	2	Slow	75.13	75.6	74.7	**77.38**	**75.6**	**79.2**

From Table 1, among the unsupervised methods, our model achieves promising results. Specifically, compared to MAST [5] which performs best among previous unsupervised-trained methods, the performance of our model on the metric $\mathcal{J}$ & $\mathcal{F}$ leads a margin of 1.7%. Because our model is not trained with annotated data, the performance is left behind some methods trained in supervised manner.

Regarding to impact on classifying foreground and backgrounds caused by the motion of objects in the video, we categorized the videos in the DAVIS-2017 test set into two groups: fast motion and slow motion. Then we conduct an experiment to evaluation the performance. Table 2 presents the performance of our method and the model LDR [4] on 6 typical videos. In videos labeled 'Fast', our model can achieve better results than LDR. For the videos marked 'Slow', except the video 'bike-packing', our model performs better than LDR on the metric $\mathcal{J}$ & $\mathcal{F}$.

4.5   Ablation Studies

In this subsection, we identify the effectiveness of each component of our model, including the motion cue, the fusion module, and the training efficiency. The baseline in the experiment is FOR module only.

Effectiveness of the Motion Cue. Figure 4 demonstrate that the motion cue extracted form optical flow can enable the model discriminate the segmented objects from backgrounds. In this instance, the scene is clutter, and it is hard to segment the target object from backgrounds by using the spatial feature extracted by the module FOR. The motion cue contains information of the motion difference between the foreground and backgrounds, independently offering information for the model to identify the foreground. As it turns out, the accuracy of segmentation is improved distinctly (as shown in the third row of Fig. 4).

Effectiveness of Attention-Based Fusion Module. We do not just incorporate the features of the two modality together in a simple way. We intend to use the motion cue to strengthen the area of the segmented objects. Then, we conduct the experiments to compare our fusion method with two simple and popular way including concatenation and addition. The results are shown in Table 3. It can be observed that AFN is more effective than the two fusion method.

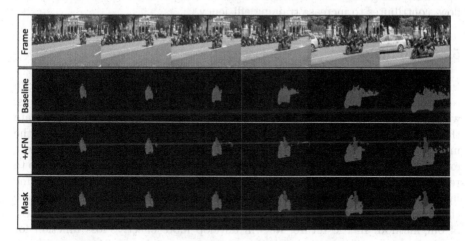

Fig. 4. Under a clutter scene, the model working with the feature extracted from RGB frame is hard to discriminate the foreground from backgrounds (as shown in the second row). The motion cue extracted from optical flow can improve the performance (the third row).

Training Efficiency. We intend to show that the motion cue can significantly increase the efficiency of the model training. The training procedure is conducted on the YouTube-VOS dataset, and the results are shown in Fig. 5. W In the figure, the ratio treated as the evaluation index is calculated by using the results obtained from the experiment over the current epoch to the best one. The blue polyline shows that our model can reach 97.66% of the best result after training

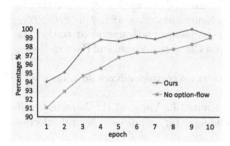

Fig. 5. The effect of the two methods after each epoch of training.

Table 3. Comparison between three fusion methods.

Components	DAVIS-2017		
	$\mathcal{J}$ & $\mathcal{F}$	$\mathcal{J}$	$\mathcal{F}$
Baseline (pairwise)	60.75	59.0	62.5
Concat. (+0.95)	61.7	59.6	63.7
Add (+1.45)	62.2	60.6	63.8
AFN (+4.65)	**65.4**	**63.4**	**67.4**

over 3 epochs, and the model almost converges to a steady state after training over 4 epochs. Comparatively, the model without the motion cue need to be trained over 10 epochs before reaching convergence (as shown by the orange poly-line in Fig. 5). The experimental results indicate that, for the model built upon SSL, using the feature extracted from the temporal perspective, *i.e.*, optical flow, contributes to increase training efficiency.

5   Conclusion

In this paper, we propose MFC model to tackle issues of VOS task. Regarding to requiring lots of manual effort to label data, used to train conventional methods, we built a SSL-based model to release the restriction. Meanwhile, we incorporate the motion cue extracted from optical flow as the temporal information into the model. Then, we design an attention-based fusion network to fuse the feature extracted by SSL encoder and the motion cue together as the final feature map to reconstruct frames in training phase, or to predict the mask for the current frame in testing phase. The experiments conducted on dataset DAVIS-2017 indicate that our model can achieve a promising results, and validate the effectiveness of our method. In the future, we will develop more effective loss function for auxiliary tasks to further improve the performance of the model.

Acknowledgments. This work was supported by the National Natural Science Foundation of China (No. 11627802, 51678249, 61871188).

References

1. Caelles, S., Maninis, K.K., Pont-Tuset, J., Leal-Taixé, L., Cremers, D., Van Gool, L.: One-shot video object segmentation. In: CVPR, pp. 221–230 (2017)
2. Fan, H., et al.: Multiscale vision transformers. In: 2021 IEEE/CVF International Conference on Computer Vision (ICCV), pp. 6804–6815 (2021)
3. Girisha, R., Murali, S.: Object segmentation from surveillance video sequences. In: 2010 First International Conference on Integrated Intelligent Computing, pp. 146–153 (2010). https://doi.org/10.1109/ICIIC.2010.52
4. Hou, W., Qin, Z., Xi, X., Lu, X., Yin, Y.: Learning disentangled representation for self-supervised video object segmentation. Neurocomputing **481**, 270–280 (2022)
5. Lai, Z., Lu, E., Xie, W.: Mast: a memory-augmented self-supervised tracker. In: Proceedings of the IEEE/CVF Conference on Computer Vision and Pattern Recognition (CVPR) (2020)
6. Lai, Z., Xie, W.: Self-supervised learning for video correspondence flow. In: BMVC (2019)
7. Li, X., Liu, S., De Mello, S., Wang, X., Kautz, J., Yang, M.H.: Joint-task self-supervised learning for temporal correspondence. In: Advances in Neural Information Processing Systems, vol. 32 (2019)
8. Liu, J., Dai, H.N., Zhao, G., Li, B., Zhang, T.: TMVOS: triplet matching for efficient video object segmentation. Signal Process. Image Commun. **107**, 116779 (2022)

9. Lu, X., Wang, W., Shen, J., Tai, Y.W., Crandall, D.J., Hoi, S.C.H.: Learning video object segmentation from unlabeled videos. In: Proceedings of the IEEE/CVF Conference on Computer Vision and Pattern Recognition (CVPR) (2020)

10. Oh, S.W., Lee, J.Y., Sunkavalli, K., Kim, S.J.: Fast video object segmentation by reference-guided mask propagation. In: CVPR, pp. 7376–7385 (2018)

11. Oh, S.W., Lee, J.Y., Xu, N., Kim, S.J.: Video object segmentation using space-time memory networks. In: ICCV, pp. 9226–9235 (2019)

12. Pont-Tuset, J., Perazzi, F., Caelles, S., Arbeláez, P., Sorkine-Hornung, A., Van Gool, L.: The 2017 Davis challenge on video object segmentation. arXiv:1704.00675 (2017)

13. Rui, H., Chen, C., Shah, M.: An end-to-end 3D convolutional neural network for action detection and segmentation in videos (2017)

14. Shelhamer, E., Long, J., Darrell, T.: Fully convolutional networks for semantic segmentation. In: 2015 IEEE Conference on Computer Vision and Pattern Recognition (CVPR), pp. 3431–3440 (2015)

15. Taggart, R.J.: Point forecasting and forecast evaluation with generalized Huber loss (2021)

16. Teed, Z., Deng, J.: RAFT: recurrent all-pairs field transforms for optical flow. In: Vedaldi, A., Bischof, H., Brox, T., Frahm, J.-M. (eds.) ECCV 2020. LNCS, vol. 12347, pp. 402–419. Springer, Cham (2020). https://doi.org/10.1007/978-3-030-58536-5_24

17. Vondrick, C., Shrivastava, A., Fathi, A., Guadarrama, S., Murphy, K.: Tracking emerges by colorizing videos. In: Proceedings of the European Conference on Computer Vision (ECCV), pp. 391–408 (2018)

18. Xie, H., Yao, H., Zhou, S., Zhang, S., Sun, W.: Efficient regional memory network for video object segmentation. In: CVPR, pp. 1286–1295 (2021)

19. Xu, N., et al.: Youtube-vos: a large-scale video object segmentation benchmark. arXiv preprint arXiv:1809.03327 (2018)

20. Yang, L., Wang, Y., Xiong, X., Yang, J., Katsaggelos, A.K.: Efficient video object segmentation via network modulation. In: Proceedings of the IEEE Conference on Computer Vision and Pattern Recognition, pp. 6499–6507 (2018)

21. Yang, Z., Wei, Y., Yang, Y.: Collaborative video object segmentation by foreground-background integration. In: Vedaldi, A., Bischof, H., Brox, T., Frahm, J.-M. (eds.) ECCV 2020. LNCS, vol. 12350, pp. 332–348. Springer, Cham (2020). https://doi.org/10.1007/978-3-030-58558-7_20

22. Zhang, Z., Fidler, S., Urtasun, R.: Instance-level segmentation for autonomous driving with deep densely connected MRFs. Comput. Sci. (2015)

23. Zhu, W., Meng, J., Xu, L.: Self-supervised video object segmentation using integration-augmented attention. Neurocomputing **455**, 325–339 (2021)

Space-Time Video Super-Resolution Based on Long-Term Time Dependence

Xinyi Huang[1], Tong Xue[2], Yiwen Hu[3], Hui Lan[1(✉)], and Jinshan Sun[2]

[1] School of Artificial Intelligence, Jianghan University, Wuhan 430056, China
hlanblue@foxmail.com
[2] State Key Laboratory of Precision Plasting, Jianghan University, Wuhan 430056, China
sunjinshan@jhun.edu.cn
[3] School of Foreign Languages, Jianghan University, Wuhan 430056, China

Abstract. Space-Time Video Super Resolution (STVSR) is designed to recover low resolution (LR), low frame rate (LFR) video into video with higher resolution (HR) and high frame rate (HFR). Recently, good STVSR performance has been achieved by deformation convolution-based methods. However, all current STVSR models synthesize the embedding of missing frame features by the short-term temporal information of two adjacent frame features, ignoring the role of long-term temporal information of other consecutive input frames for missing frame synthesis. In addition, it is difficult for the existing STVSR to explicitly utilize space-time correlation features to assist in high-resolution frame reconstruction. To alleviate these problems. In this paper, we propose a long-term time-dependent space-time video super-resolution network (LTTDN) based for STVSR. The network design as a bidirectional deformable convolutional gated cyclic interpolation (BDCGCI) module for STVSR. the BDCGCI module is able to extract long-term temporal information from more input frames and effectively use the long-term temporal information of video frames for interpolation. In addition, we propose a spatial-temporal attention fusion module. This module adaptively aggregates the spatial-temporal features in video frames. In this way, it helps high-resolution frame reconstruction. Extensive experiments on several benchmark datasets show that our method outperforms the state-of-the-art STVSR method.

Keywords: Space-Time video super resolution · Bidirectional deformable convolutional gated cyclic interpolation · Spatial-temporal attention fusion module

1 Introduction

Space-Time Video Super Resolution (STVSR) aims to generate high resolution (HR) and high frame rate (HFR) video sequences from a given low resolution (LR) and low frame rate (LFR) video. STVSR has attracted a lot of attention due to its multi-disciplinary applications. It includes movie production, video

© The Author(s), under exclusive license to Springer Nature Switzerland AG 2023
L. Iliadis et al. (Eds.): ICANN 2023, LNCS 14260, pp. 514–526, 2023.
https://doi.org/10.1007/978-3-031-44195-0_42

conferencing, HR slow motion generation. Because high frame rate and high resolution videos provide more visually appealing content. Many STVSR [3,14, 17,18] models have been proposed successively.

In recent years, deep convolutional neural networks have been widely used in video recovery tasks such as video super-resolution (VSR) [15,16], video frame interpolation (VFI) [9,12], and the more challenging STVSR. A straightforward approach to STVSR is to perform VFI and VSR sequentially for low-resolution and low-frame-rate videos, in to improve the spatial resolution and frame rate of the video. However, such a two-stage approach ignores the intrinsic correlation between the temporal and spatial dimensions, and the two-stage STVSR approach usually has a large model size that cannot be deployed in practical applications.

To further explore the intrinsic correlation between the temporal and spatial dimensions of STVSR, several single-stage STVSR methods were proposed [17,18]. The single-stage STVSR models perform temporal interpolation and spatial super-resolution on the video. However, current single-stage STVSR models only use the short temporal context of the corresponding two neighboring frames to interpolate the generated missing frame features. In fact, the long-term temporal information of the video sequence is utilized during the interpolation process to better optimize the details of the missing frame features. Moreover, the existing single-stage STVSR network has limitations in fully utilizing the spatial-temporal context information between multiple frames for SR reconstruction

To solve these problems, in this paper, our proposed bidirectional deformable convolutional gated cyclic interpolation module (BDCGCI) uses a bidirectional RNN structure to generate the missing intermediate frames. The bidirectional deformable convolutional gated recurrent interpolation module contains multiple recurrent gated interpolation units, which mainly consists of deformable convolutional feature interpolation unit (DFI) [17] and convolutional gated recurrent unit (ConvGRU) [2]. Specifically, we sample two neighboring frames using a before-and-after spatial deformation alignment to generate preliminary intermediate frame features. Then, the generated preliminary intermediate features are blended with the hidden states generated by the previous cyclic gating interpolation unit to obtain the final interpolated features. The final interpolated features fuse the temporal information of other neighboring frames as well as the long-term temporal information provided by the hidden state. The hidden states aggregate useful long-term temporal information from other input video frames to help temporal interpolation deal with complex visual motion. To further improve the quality of video reconstruction. We also apply an attention-based blending module to further enhance the temporally and spatially useful features. Finally, the HR framework is reconstructed using fused features. Experimental results on several widely used benchmark datasets show that our proposed STVSR model outperforms existing methods in terms of PSNR/SSIM values and visual quality.

In summary, we made the following contributions:1) We designed a long-term spatial-temporal dependence network (LTTDN) to handle STVSR.Our model has fewer parameters and achieves state-of-the-art performance on multiple datasets; 2) Proposed a bidirectional deformable convolutional gated cyclic interpolation module to interpolate missing frame features using temporal information from more neighboring frames; 3) We developed a Spatial-Temporal Attention Fusion module. to further enhance the features in both spatial and temporal dimensions of video sequences for HR reconstruction.

2   Related Work

2.1   Video Frame Interpolation

The goal of video frame interpolation (VFI) is to generate nonexistent intermediate frames between two consecutive video frames as a way to improve the frame rate of the video. [12] introduced a phase-based frame interpolation method to generate intermediate frames by pixel-by-pixel phase modification. [13] estimated the pixels of intermediate video frames using a convolution kernel by implicitly aligning the input frames by learning a dynamic convolution kernel. [5] introduced a stream-based method to achieve VFI by estimating the optical flow between frames and distorting the input frames by the estimated stream to synthesize the missing frames. However, this approach relies heavily on the quality of the estimated optical flow. [9] introduced flexible spatial sampling using deformable convolution, combining the stream-based approach with a kernel-based approach. The VFI based on the deformable convolution method is adapted to larger motions and scenes with complex textures.

2.2   Video Super Resolution

The task of video super resolution (VSR) recovers low-resolution video into high-resolution video sequences with improved resolution in the spatial dimension. Most current CNN-based VSR methods use a strategy of fusing spatial features from multiple aligned frames, but this depends heavily on the quality of the alignment. [6] use an optical flow method to align reference frames with adjacent frames. However, the effects of fast motion and occlusion result in the estimated optical flow is not always accurate. The reconstruction network is less effective. [15] introduced deformable convolution for implicit temporal alignment in the feature space and achieved impressive performance. Meanwhile [16] applied deformable convolution to a multiscale module to further enhance feature alignment.

2.3   Space-Time Video Super-Resolution

Unlike Video super resolution, STVSR enhances both video spatial and temporal resolution. Recently, the success of cnn has driven the development of STVSR methods. [17] proposed a single-stage STVSR method that employs a Bidirectional deformable convolutional LSTM (BDConvLSTM) to align and aggregate temporal contexts. [18] received inspiration from Zooming slow-mo and added the temporal modulation module to their network framework named TMNet,

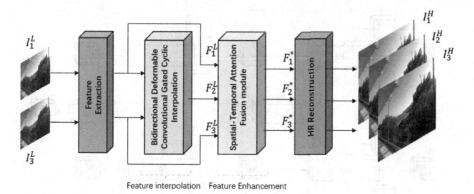

Fig. 1. Our proposed LTTDN architecture. bidirectional deformable convolutional gated cyclic interpolation aggregates more temporal information of adjacent LR frames and synthesizes intermediate frames at the feature level by aggregating long-term time. spatial-temporal attention fusion module enhances the HR frame reconstruction by capturing the spatial-temporal correlation features of the video frames. This figure only shows the case when the input video frames are two frames.

which is capable of frame interpolation at any intermediate moment, allowing for better temporal resolution. However, the above method only uses the local time information of two adjacent frame features to interpolate the missing frame features when synthesizing the missing frame features. The role of global temporal information for missing frame synthesis is ignored. To solve these problems, we designed a space-time video super-resolution network based on long-term temporal dependence using long-term temporal information for feature interpolation. And the spatial-temporal attention fusion module aggregates the spatial-temporal correlation features between video frames for HR frame reconstruction.

3   Our Approach

The network structure proposed in this paper is shown in Fig. 1 it consists of four parts: feature extraction module, bidirectional deformable convolutional gated cyclic interpolation (BDCGCI) module, Spatial-temporal attention fusion module, and frame feature reconstruction module. Given a LR, LFR video sequence $\{I_{2t-1}^L\}_{t=1}^{n+1}$, our goal is to generate the corresponding high resolution, high resolution video sequence: $\{I_t^H\}_{t=1}^{2n+1}$. We first use a feature extractor with 3×3 convolutional layers and 5 residual blocks to extract feature mappings from the input video frames: $\{F_{2t-1}^L\}_{t=1}^{n+1}$. The feature mapping of the missing frames is synthesized using the proposed BDCGCI module $\{F_{2t}^L\}_{t=1}^{2n}$. In addition, the interpolated feature sequence $\{F_t^L\}_{t=1}^{2n+1}$ is are fed into our proposed spatial-temporal attention fusion module, in which attention is applied to both time and space to enhance the spatial-temporal information in the video features.

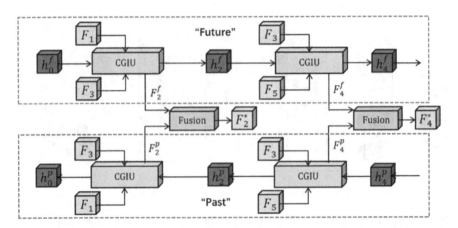

Fig. 2. The framework of our BDCGCI module. The framework of our BDCGCI module. A bidirectional RNN structure is used for interpolation. Note that h_0^f and h_4^p represent the initialized hidden states for the recursive propagation of the "future" and "past" time branches, respectively.

for subsequent reconstruction of video frames. Finally, we reconstruct the high-resolution, high-frame rate video sequence $\{I_t^H\}_{t=1}^{2n+1}$ based on the spatial-temporal fused feature maps. The main modules of our model are described below.

3.1 Bidirectional Deformable Convolutional Gated Cyclic Interpolation Module

As shown in Fig. 2, the BDCGCI module is mainly composed of two time branches, "past" and "future". The two time branches contain several cyclic gated interpolation units (CGIU). Here the "future" time branch is used as an example. In order to fully exploit the long-term temporal information of other input frames, we fuse the "past" and "future" time branches. "The structure of CGIU is shown in Fig. 3, which consists of DFI module [17] and ConvGRU [2]. Given the adjacent frame features F_1 and F_3, we use deformable convolution to capture the forward and backward motion information of the adjacent frame features. Take forward motion as an example. The two frames are stitched by channel dimension, and the offset of the forward motion is predicted by an offset generation network containing 1×1 convolutional layers. And deformable convolution is used to obtain motion compensation.

$$\theta_{1\to3} = M(F_1, F_3) \tag{1}$$

$$F_{1\to3} = DConv(F_1, \theta_{1\to3}) \tag{2}$$

where M() denotes the offset generation network, [,] denotes the channel splicing, and DConv denotes the deformable convolution operation. In order to mix

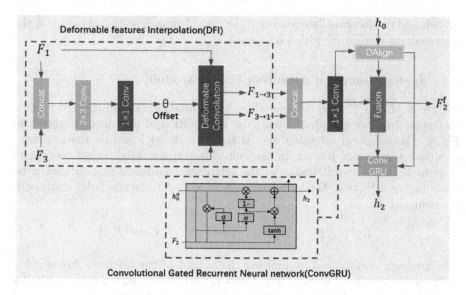

Fig. 3. Cyclic gated interpolation unit structure, mainly composed of deformable feature interpolation and convolutional GRU.

the front and back motion-compensated features $F_{1 \to 3}$ and $F_{3 \to 1}$, we use a 1 × 1 convolutional layer with linear weighting to obtain a preliminary intermediate feature mapping F_2. Here F_2 is generated using the short-term temporal information of the adjacent frames. In order to combine the hidden state h_0^f with long-term temporal information generated by the previous CGIU, we first align h_0^f with the current feature F_2 to obtain h_0^a. Then F_2 and the aligned hidden state h_0^a are fused to become the intermediate feature F_2^f with "future" long-term temporal information. h_0^a and F_2^f are fed to the ConvGRU unit and updated to h_2^f and passed to the next CGIU to refine the intermediate frame features $\{F_{2t}^L\}_{t=1}^{2n}$ in the "future" branch.

$$F_2 = H_{1 \times 1}(F_{1 \to 3}, F_{3 \to 1}) \tag{3}$$

$$h_0^a = DAlign(h_0, F_2) \tag{4}$$

$$F_2^f = S_{fusion}(F_2, h_0^a) \tag{5}$$

$$h_2 = f_{ConvGRU}(F_2^f, h_0^a) \tag{6}$$

where $H_{1 \times 1}$ denotes the linear mixing function and DAlign(.) denotes the operation of alignment. where S_{fusion} is the fusion function. The intermediate frame feature F_2^f passes through the convolutional GRU layer to provide the hidden state h_2^f for the next CGIU.

In order to fully explore the long-term temporal information of both "past" and "future" branches in the video, the intermediate feature F_2^f of "future" branch and the intermediate feature F_2^p of "past" branch are fused to obtain the intermediate feature F_2^* with long-term temporal dependence.

3.2   Spatial-Temporal Attention Fusion Module

We input $\{F_t^L\}_{t=1}^{2n+1}$ into the spatial-temporal attention fusion (STAF) module to further enhance the Spatial-temporal information of the video, as shown in Fig. 4. The temporal attention map is first calculated based on the similarity of adjacent reference frames. In the embedding space, neighboring coordinate systems that are more similar to the reference coordinate system should be given higher attention. For each frame $i \in [-N : +N]$, the similarity distance L is calculated as :

$$L\left(F_{t-i}, F_t\right) = sigmoid\left(\mathrm{Conv}\left(F_{t-i}\right)^{\mathrm{T}} \mathrm{Conv}\left(F_t\right)\right) \qquad (7)$$

The gradient is stabilized by limiting the output of the reference frame using a sigmoid activation function. The temporal attention maps are computed by multiplying them pixel by pixel with their associated feature maps. A fused convolutional layer is used to aggregate these attention modulated features. The spatial attention map is then computed using the fused $F_{temporal}$ features.

$$F'_{t-i} = F_{t-i} \odot L\left(F_{t-i}, F_t\right) \qquad (8)$$

$$F_{\text{temporal}} = \mathrm{Conv}\left(\left[F'_{t-N}, \cdots, F'_t, \cdots, F'_{t+N}\right]\right) \qquad (9)$$

where $\odot$ and $[...]$ denote the element-wise multiplication and concatenation, respectively. As shown in Fig. 4. The pyramid structure is used to increase the spatial attention perception domain. We use the maximum pooling layer to reduce the scale. Feature maps of the same size are added together. Subsequent multi-scale features are fused into spatial attention maps, and the final fused spatial-temporal feature $F_{temporal-spatial}$ is obtained by modulating the feature $F_{temporal}$ by multiplication and addition between elements. the fused temporal-spatial feature $F_{temporal-spatial}$ is used for HR frame reconstruction.

3.3   HR Reconstruction

To reconstruct the HR frames from the enhanced features $\{F_t^L\}_{t=1}^{2n+1}$, the HR frames are reconstructed using subpixel layers. It is added to the superscript feature map in the form of a global residual join by bi-triple interpolation. In addition we use Unet network with 3 deconvolution layers and 4 residual blocks to improve the final output to achieve the final super-resolution output $\{I_t^H\}_{t=1}^{2n+1}$.

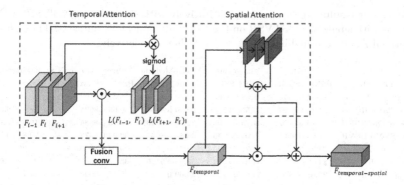

Fig. 4. Spatial-Temporal Attention Fusion module containing temporal and spatial attention respectively. The final output $F_{temporal-spatial}$ is used for HR reconstruction.

4 Experiments and Results

4.1 Setting

For training, we use the Vimeo90K [19] dataset to train our proposed LTTDN, which consists of more than 60,000 seven-frame video sequences. This dataset is widely used in previous VFI and VSR models. Here, the input LFR and LR frames are set to be 3 frames with a size of 112×64, and the output HFR and HR frames are 5 frames with a size of 448×256 (downsampling factor of 4). We used Vid4 [11] and Vimeo90K [19] testset as evaluation datasets. To measure the performance of different methods under different motion conditions, we divided the Vimeo90K testset into fast motion, medium motion, and slow motion sets. They consist of 1225, 4975 and 1610 video clips, respectively. Our model is trained by the Adam [7] optimizer with settings $\beta_1 = 0.9$ and $\beta_2 = 0.999$. we use cosine annealing to gradually decay the initial learning rate from 2e−4 to 1e−7. the batch size is set to 12, and we implement LTTDN using PyTorch and train our model on 3 NVIDIA GTX 3080Ti gpu to train our model. To optimize our network, we use a Charbonnier function [8] as the loss: $G\left(\hat{I}^H, I^H\right) = \sqrt{\left\|\hat{I}^H - I^H\right\|^2 + \epsilon^2}$, $\hat{I}^H$ denotes the ground truth after reconstruction, ϵ^2 is empirically set to 1×10^{-3}. With the loss function, our LTTDN can be trained end-to-end to generate HR, HFR videos from the corresponding LR, LFR videos. To quantitatively compare different STVSR networks, our experiments use peak signal-to-noise ratio (PSNR) and structural similarity (SSIM) as evaluation metrics. the higher the PSNR and SSIM, the better the super-resolution and interpolation performance. In addition, we compare the parameters and inference speed of various STVSR.

4.2 Quantitative Analysis

We compared LTTDN with the state-of-the-art two-stage and single-stage ST-VSR methods. In the two-stage STVSR based approach, the two-stage

Table 1. Our results are compared quantitatively with the two-stage STVSR method as well as with single-stage STVSR on the Vid4 and Vimeo90K datasets. The best and suboptimal results are highlighted in red and blue, respectively.

Method VFI+VSR	Vid4 PSNR↑ SSIM↑	Vimeo-Fast PSNR↑ SSIM↑	Vimeo-Medium PSNR↑ SSIM↑	Vimeo-Slow PSNR↑ SSIM↑	FPS ↑	Parameters (Millions)↓
SuperSloMo Bicubic	22.84 0.5772	31.88 0.8793	29.94 0.8477	28.37 0.8102	-	19.8
SuperSloMo RCAN	23.80 0.6397	34.52 0.9076	32.50 0.8884	30.69 0.8624	-	19.8+16.0
SuperSloMo RBPN	23.76 0.6362	34.73 0.9108	32.79 0.8930	30.48 0.8584	-	19.8+12.7
SuperSloMo EDVR	24.40 0.6706	35.05 0.9136	33.85 0.8967	30.99 0.8673	-	19.8+20.7
SepConv Bicubic	23.51 0.6273	32.27 0.8890	30.61 0.8633	29.04 0.8290	-	21.7
SepConv RCAN	24.92 0.7236	34.97 0.9195	33.59 0.9125	32.13 0.8967	-	21.7+16.0
SepConv RBPN	26.08 0.7751	35.07 0.9238	34.09 0.9229	32.77 0.9090	-	21.7+12.7
SepConv EDVR	25.93 0.7792	35.23 0.9252	34.22 0.9240	32.96 0.9112	-	21.7+20.7
DAIN Bicubic	23.55 0.6268	32.41 0.8910	30.67 0.8636	29.06 0.8289	-	24.0
DAIN RCAN	25.03 0.7261	35.27 0.9242	33.82 0.9146	32.26 0.8974	-	24.0+16.0
DAIN RBPN	25.96 0.7784	35.55 0.9300	34.45 0.9262	32.92 0.9097	-	24.0+12.7
DAIN EDVR	26.12 0.7836	35.81 0.9323	34.66 0.9281	33.11 0.9119	-	24.0+20.7
STARnet	26.06 0.7816	36.19 0.9368	34.86 0.9356	33.10 0.9164	14.08	111.61
Zooming Slow-Mo	26.31 0.7976	36.81 0.9415	35.41 0.9361	33.36 0.9138	16.50	11.10
TMNet	26.43 0.8016	37.04 0.9435	35.60 0.9380	33.51 0.9159	14.69	12.26
LTTDN(Ours)	26.65 0.8053	37.28 0.9473	35.83 0.9412	33.73 0.9184	16.77	9.81

STVSR method consists of VFI and VSR algorithms. the VFI task uses Sep-Conv [13], SuperSloMo [5] and DAIN [1], and the VSR uses Bicubic Interpolation, RBPN [4], RCAN [20] and EDRR [16]. For single-stage STVSR-based methods, we compared LTTDN with Zooming-SlowMo [17], STARnet [3], and TMNet [18]. The quantitative results of various STVSR methods are shown in Table 1. From the table, we can see that: We obtained state-of-the-art (SOTA) performance on both Vid4 [10] and Vimeo90K [19] using LTTDN with fewer parameters. On the Vimeo90K-Fast dataset, our proposed LTTDN model outperforms the current best single-stage model TMNet by 0.24 dB in PSNR value. and is 2.08 fps faster in computational speed and only about 82% computational cost. In addition, LTTDN also achieves competitive accuracy with fewer parameters and computational cost. These results verify the effectiveness of the STVSR method proposed in this paper.

4.3   Qualitative Comparisons

Figure 5 shows the qualitative results of different methods on the Vid4 dataset [10]. As can be seen in the zoomed image patch, even if the texture structure of the image is complex, the LTTDN proposed in this paper can obtain finer texture details, such as the texture of the numbers in the calendar and the edge part behind the car in Fig. 5. Both quantitative and qualitative results are shown to illustrate the importance of long-term temporal information in the STVSR interpolation process. And our proposed LTTDN method obtains better STVSR reconstruction results than existing methods.

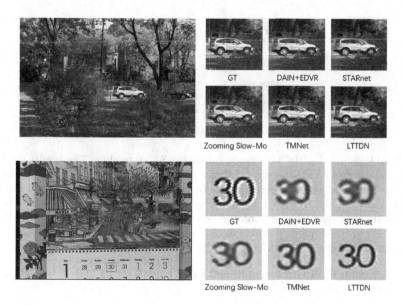

Fig. 5. Visualizations on the Vid4 dataset [10] were compared. LTTDN achieves state-of-the-art performance in terms of visual quality for a variety of scenes.

4.4 Ablation Study

To investigate the effect of the modules proposed in our LTTDN, we perform a full-scale ablation study in this section. We are divided into three sets of experiments here: the first set of experiments is set up to interpolate using only the DFI module with short-term information and then reconstruct the HR video frames directly through the frame feature reconstruction module without going through the STAF module. The second set of experiments is set to use the BDCGCI module with long-term time information for interpolation. Then, the HR video frames are reconstructed directly by the frame feature reconstruction module. without going through the STAF module. The third set of experiments is set up as our proposed original model while going through our proposed two modules. Finally, the HR video frames are reconstructed by reconstruction. The experimental data are shown in Table 2. From the data in Table 2. The BDCGCI module combining long-term information improves the PSNR value by 0.5 dB compared to the DFI module using only short-term temporal information, and with the STAF module there is a 0.29 dB improvement in the PSNR value. From the visualization results in Fig. 6, it is clear that our proposed module is able to recover more accurate texture details of the image.

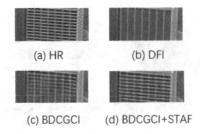

Fig. 6. Ablation of the BDCGCI module with the STAF module. The results obtained on the dataset from Vid4. Figure (a) shows the real high-resolution image. Figure (b) shows the image after HR reconstruction by the DFI module. Compared to the DFI module, our proposed BDCGCI is able to recover the texture part of the image better by using the long-term temporal information of the input video frames. Figure (d) also shows that our STAF module is able to reconstruct more accurate visual content using the temporal features of the video.

Table 2. Results of BDCGCI module and STAF module for LTTDN network ablation experiments in Vid4 datasets.

Number of modules	1	1	2
Modules name	DFI	BDCGCI	BDCGCI+STAF
PSNR	25.82	**26.32**	**26.61**
Parameter [M]	6.56	7.32	9.81

5   Conclusion

In this paper, we propose a deformable attention network LTTDN for STVSR. our LTTDN can utilize more input video frame temporal information for interpolation, forming a long-term temporal dependency. In addition, the network enhances SR reconstruction by aggregating the spatial-temporal context between frames through fusion with temporal and spatial attention. Thanks to the BDCGCI and STAF modules, our model outperforms recent STVSR methods on the public datasets Vid4 and Vimeo90K.

Acknowledgement. This work is supported by the Project of Hubei Provincial Science and Technology Department 2020BCA084, 2021BAD004, T2022045 and the Provincial Teaching Research of Higher Education Institutions in Hubei Province (2021286); the projects of Jianghan University 06650001.

References

1. Bao, W., Lai, W.S., Ma, C., Zhang, X., Gao, Z., Yang, M.H.: Depth-aware video frame interpolation. In: Proceedings of the IEEE/CVF Conference on Computer Vision and Pattern Recognition, pp. 3703–3712 (2019)

2. Chung, J., Gulcehre, C., Cho, K., Bengio, Y.: Empirical evaluation of gated recurrent neural networks on sequence modeling. arXiv preprint arXiv:1412.3555 (2014)
3. Haris, M., Shakhnarovich, G., Ukita, N.: Space-time-aware multi-resolution video enhancement. In: Proceedings of the IEEE/CVF Conference on Computer Vision and Pattern Recognition, pp. 2859–2868 (2020)
4. Haris, M., Shakhnarovich, G., Ukita, N.: Recurrent back-projection network for video super-resolution. In: Proceedings of the IEEE/CVF Conference on Computer Vision and Pattern Recognition, pp. 3897–3906 (2019)
5. Jiang, H., Sun, D., Jampani, V., Yang, M.H., Learned-Miller, E., Kautz, J.: Super slomo: high quality estimation of multiple intermediate frames for video interpolation. In: Proceedings of the IEEE Conference on Computer Vision and Pattern Recognition, pp. 9000–9008 (2018)
6. Jo, Y., Oh, S.W., Kang, J., Kim, S.J.: Deep video super-resolution network using dynamic upsampling filters without explicit motion compensation. In: Proceedings of the IEEE Conference on Computer Vision and Pattern Recognition, pp. 3224–3232 (2018)
7. Kingma, D.P., Ba, J.: Adam: a method for stochastic optimization. arXiv preprint arXiv:1412.6980 (2014)
8. Lai, W.S., Huang, J.B., Ahuja, N., Yang, M.H.: Deep Laplacian pyramid networks for fast and accurate super-resolution. In: Proceedings of the IEEE Conference on Computer Vision and Pattern Recognition, pp. 624–632 (2017)
9. Lee, H., Kim, T., Chung, T.Y., Pak, D., Ban, Y., Lee, S.: Adacof: adaptive collaboration of flows for video frame interpolation. In: Proceedings of the IEEE/CVF Conference on Computer Vision and Pattern Recognition, pp. 5316–5325 (2020)
10. Liu, C., Sun, D.: A Bayesian approach to adaptive video super resolution. In: CVPR 2011, pp. 209–216. IEEE (2011)
11. Liu, C., Sun, D.: On Bayesian adaptive video super resolution. IEEE Trans. Pattern Anal. Mach. Intell. **36**(2), 346–360 (2013)
12. Meyer, S., Wang, O., Zimmer, H., Grosse, M., Sorkine-Hornung, A.: Phase-based frame interpolation for video. In: Proceedings of the IEEE Conference on Computer Vision and Pattern Recognition, pp. 1410–1418 (2015)
13. Niklaus, S., Mai, L., Liu, F.: Video frame interpolation via adaptive separable convolution. In: Proceedings of the IEEE International Conference on Computer Vision, pp. 261–270 (2017)
14. Shechtman, E., Caspi, Y., Irani, M.: Space-time super-resolution. IEEE Trans. Pattern Anal. Mach. Intell. **27**(4), 531–545 (2005)
15. Tian, Y., Zhang, Y., Fu, Y., Xu, C.: TDAN: temporally-deformable alignment network for video super-resolution. In: Proceedings of the IEEE/CVF Conference on Computer Vision and Pattern Recognition, pp. 3360–3369 (2020)
16. Wang, X., Chan, K.C., Yu, K., Dong, C., Change Loy, C.: EDVR: video restoration with enhanced deformable convolutional networks. In: Proceedings of the IEEE/CVF Conference on Computer Vision and Pattern Recognition Workshops (2019)
17. Xiang, X., Tian, Y., Zhang, Y., Fu, Y., Allebach, J.P., Xu, C.: Zooming slowmo: fast and accurate one-stage space-time video super-resolution. In: Proceedings of the IEEE/CVF Conference on Computer Vision and Pattern Recognition, pp. 3370–3379 (2020)
18. Xu, G., Xu, J., Li, Z., Wang, L., Sun, X., Cheng, M.M.: Temporal modulation network for controllable space-time video super-resolution. In: Proceedings of the IEEE/CVF Conference on Computer Vision and Pattern Recognition, pp. 6388–6397 (2021)

19. Xue, T., Chen, B., Wu, J., Wei, D., Freeman, W.T.: Video enhancement with task-oriented flow. Int. J. Comput. Vision **127**, 1106–1125 (2019)
20. Zhang, Y., Li, K., Li, K., Wang, L., Zhong, B., Fu, Y.: Image super-resolution using very deep residual channel attention networks. In: Proceedings of the European Conference on Computer Vision (ECCV), pp. 286–301 (2018)

Author Index

L. Iliadis et al. (Eds.): ICANN 2023, LNCS 14260, pp. 527–529, 2023.
https://doi.org/10.1007/978-3-031-44195-0

Printed in the United States
by Baker & Taylor Publisher Services

Printed in the United States
by Baker & Taylor Publisher Services